lonely planet

Borneo

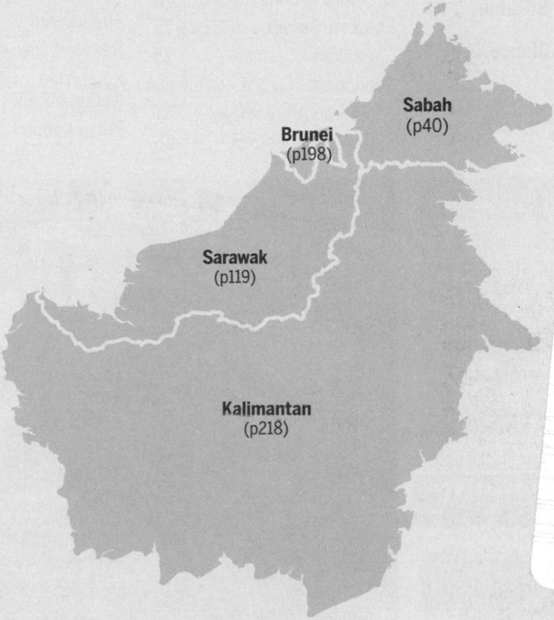

THIS EDITION WRITTEN AND RESEARCHED BY
Isabel Albiston, Loren Bell, Richard Waters

PLAN YOUR TRIP

ON THE ROAD

ANDERS BLOMQVIST / GETTY IMAGES ©

SARAWAK STATE ASSEMBLY P128

ALEXGCS / GETTY IMAGES ©

SEMPORNA ARCHIPELAGO P98

KEREN SU / GETTY IMAGES ©

FLOATING MARKET P241, KALIMANTAN

Contents

Welcome to Borneo

It's a jungle out there! Borneo has some of the world's most species-rich equatorial rainforests with prime patches that are easily accessible from modern, multi-ethnic cities.

Ancient Rainforests

If you've always longed to experience the humid fecundity of a real equatorial rainforest, Borneo will fulfil your wildest dreams. The island's jungles conjure up remoteness and adventure, bringing to mind impenetrable foliage and river trips into the 'heart of darkness'. But look a little closer and nuances emerge: the pitcher plants, lianas and orchids of the lowland forest give way to conifers and rhododendrons as you ascend the flanks of Mt Kinabalu. Deforestation makes for depressing headlines, but significant parts of the Bornean rainforest remain intact, protected by conservation projects whose viability depends in part on income from tourists.

Jungle Wildlife

For many visitors to Borneo, their most memorable moment is glimpsing a wild orangutan swinging through the jungle canopy, spotting an Irrawaddy dolphin in the shimmering waters of the South China Sea, or locking eyes with the reptilian gaze of a saltwater croc. Jungle animals are shy by nature, but a good guide can help you tell the difference between a vine and vine snake, between a twig and a stick insect, and between the call of a gibbon and the cry of a hornbill.

Cultural Riches

Borneo brings together an astonishing array of cultures, religions and languages, and age-old traditions of hospitality mean visitors are welcomed. Most cities have significant Chinese communities, while the picturesque coastal *kampung* (villages) of Sabah and Sarawak are populated mainly by Malays, but head inland and the dominant culture is indigenous. Borneo's Dayak groups stopped headhunting long ago, but many other ancient customs and ceremonies live on in longhouse communities. There's no better way to experience the indigenous way of life than to drop by for a visit – easy to arrange with a local guide.

Culinary Melting Pot

The varied ethnic and cultural backgrounds of Borneo's people means the island's cuisines are as wide-ranging as they are delicious. Seafood from the South China Sea is served fresh at Chinese restaurants, smoky chicken satay stalls beckon at Malay night markets and Indonesian eateries offer spicy sambal. Even tiny Brunei has its own culinary traditions, not to mention Borneo's numerous indigenous groups. From the sublime cooking of the Kelabit people – including Bario rice and pineapple curry – to dishes such as bamboo chicken and *midin* jungle fern, Dayak cuisine is unlike anything you've ever tasted.

Why I Love Borneo

By Isabel Albiston, Writer

I've often found that it's in places of true wildness and potential peril that human warmth and kindness is most immediate, and nowhere is that more true than in Borneo. There is a sense of magic in this land where the forest itself is believed to be inhabited by spirits who may or may not wish you well, and trekking from longhouse to longhouse means shimmying across rickety bamboo bridges, collecting wild mushrooms and fiddlehead ferns for dinner and keeping an eye out for wildlife – possibly even shaggy orangutans – moving through the canopy above.

For more about our writers, see page 336

Above: Summit of Mt Kinabalu (p59)

Borneo

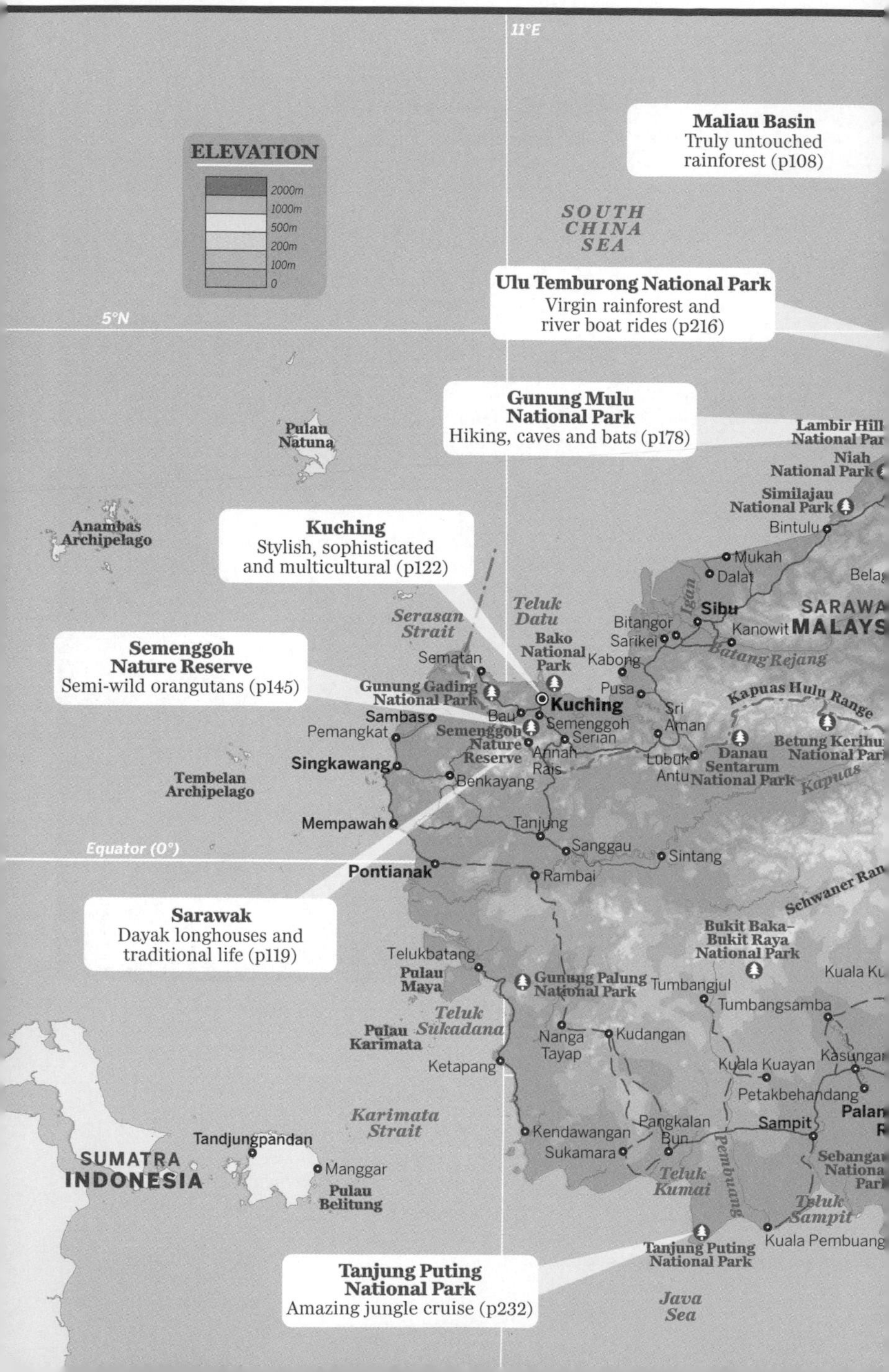

11°E
Maliau Basin
Truly untouched rainforest (p108)
ELEVATION
2000m
1000m
500m
200m
100m
0
SOUTH CHINA SEA
Ulu Temburong National Park
Virgin rainforest and river boat rides (p216)
5°N
Gunung Mulu National Park
Hiking, caves and bats (p178)
Pulau Natuna
Anambas Archipelago
Kuching
Stylish, sophisticated and multicultural (p122)
Niah National Park
Similajau National Park
Bintulu
Mukah
Dalat
Igan
Sibu
Teluk Datu
Serasan Strait
Bitangor
Sarikei
Kanowit
SARAWAK
MALAYSIA
Batang Rejang
Semenggoh Nature Reserve
Semi-wild orangutans (p145)
Sematan
Bako National Park
Kabong
Gunung Gading National Park
Pusa
Kapuas Hulu Range
Kuching
Sambas
Bau
Semenggoh
Sri Aman
Pemangkat
Semenggoh Nature Reserve
Serian
Betung Kerihun National Park
Singkawang
Annah Rais
Lubuk Antu
Danau Sentarum National Park
Kapuas
Tembelan Archipelago
Benkayang
Mempawah
Tanjung
Sanggau
Equator (0°)
Sintang
Pontianak
Rambai
Sarawak
Dayak longhouses and traditional life (p119)
Bukit Baka–Bukit Raya National Park
Telukbatang
Pulau Maya
Gunung Palung National Park
Tumbangjul
Tumbangsamba
Teluk Sukadana
Pulau Karimata
Nanga Tayap
Kudangan
Ketapang
Kuala Kuayan
Petakbehandang
Karimata Strait
Pangkalan Bun
Sampit
Kendawangan
Tandjungpandan
Sukamara
SUMATRA
INDONESIA
Manggar
Pulau Belitung
Teluk Kumai
Pembuang
Teluk Sampit
Kuala Pembuang
Tanjung Puting National Park
Tanjung Puting National Park
Amazing jungle cruise (p232)
Java Sea

0
400 km
0
200 miles
Mt Kinabalu
By far Borneo's highest peak (p59)
Sepilok Orangutan Rehabilitation Centre
Orangutans up close (p81)
Sungai Kinabatangan
River banks teeming with animals (p86)
Danum Valley
Primeval jungle, pygmy elephants, orangutans (p92)
Kelabit Highlands
Cool air, smiles, great trekking (p184)
Derawan Archipelago
Unspoilt tropical islands (p265)
Loksado
Mountain retreat (p245)
Balabac Strait
Pulau Balambangan
Pulau Banggi
Kudat
Pulau Malawali
Cagayan Sulu Island
Sulu Sea
Pulau Jambongan
11°30'E
12°E
Kota Belud
Kpg Datong
Tunku Abdul Rahman National Park
Mt Kinabalu (4095m)
Turtle Islands National Park
Kota Kinabalu
Ranau
Beluran
Sandakan
Papar
Tambunan
Sepilok
Parang
Jolo Island
Siasi
Tawitawi Island
Crocker Range National Park
Mt Trus Madi (2642m)
Sungai Kinabatangan
SABAH
ANDAR SERI GAWAN
Keningau
Lahad Datu
Tungku
Teluk Brunei
Tenom
MALAYSIA
Maliau Basin Conservation Area
Sipitang
5°N
PHILIPPINES
Kuala Tomani
Danum Valley Conservation Area
Teluk Lahad Datu
Lawas
Limbang
Sapulot
Semporna
BRUNEI
Ulu Temburong National Park
Kalabakan
Gunung Mulu (2337m)
Sebuku Sembakung National Park
Nunukan Timur Island
Tawau
Pulau Sipadan
Gunung Mulu National Park
Teluk Sebuko
Baram
Pulau Bunyu
Celebes Sea
Kelabit Highlands
Tarakan
Teluk Sekatak
Kayan Mentarang National Park
Iran Range
Kayan
Tanjung Batu
Berau
Derawan Archipelago
Tidung Estuary
Semerut
Sambaliung Mountains
KALIMANTAN
INDONESIA
Sangkulirang
Muara Wahau
Kutai National Park
Bontang
Equator (0°)
Longiram
Lake Semayang
Lake Melintang
Tenggarong
Lake Jempang
Samarinda
Muara Teweh
Makassar Strait
Palu
Barito
Teluk Adang
SULAWESI
INDONESIA
Tanahgrogot
Teluk Apar
Amuntai
Loksado
Kandangan
Rantau
Palopo
Pegunungan Meratus
Kotabaru
Pulau Sebuku
Martapura
Pagatan
Pelaihari
Pulau Laut
Batakam

Borneo's Top 15

1

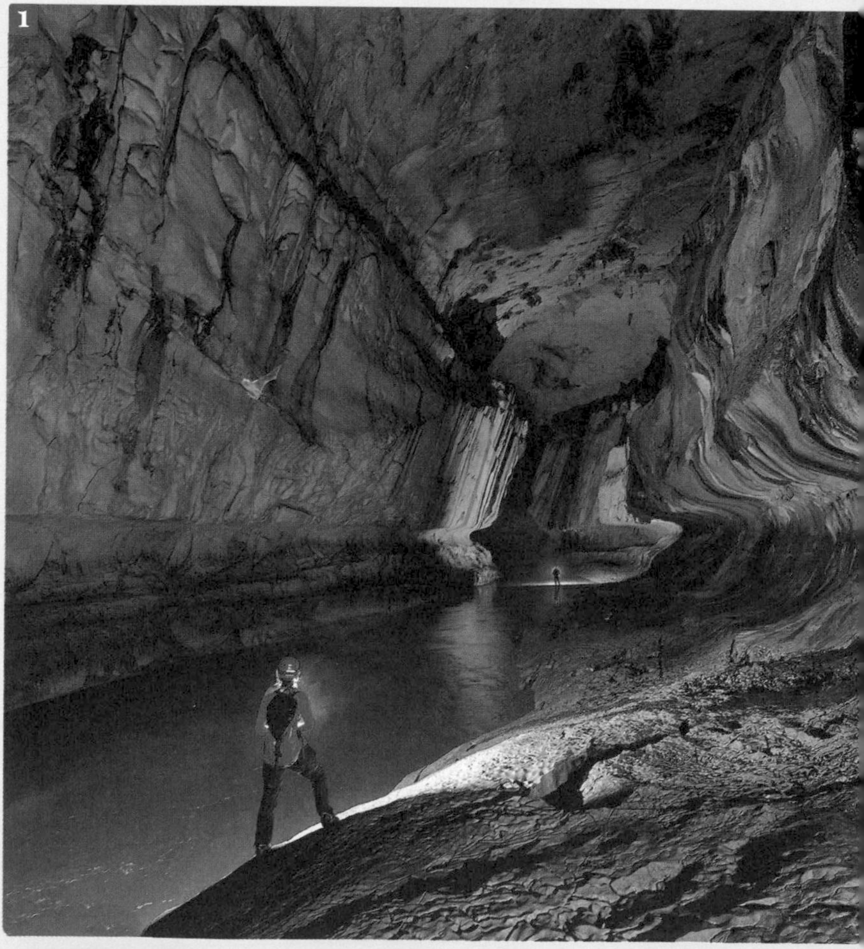

Gunung Mulu National Park

1 If the only marvel at Sarawak's Gunung Mulu National Park (p178) were some of the biggest caverns on earth, and the only fauna were the twirling, spiralling clouds of bats that emerge from the Deer Cave at dusk, it would still deserve Unesco World Heritage status. And if the only activity was spotting 20cm-long stick insects on a night walk, the flight from Miri would still be worth it. But add in Gunung Mulu and the Pinnacles and you have one of Southeast Asia's true wonders.

Maliau Basin

2 You came to Borneo looking for something wild, right? The Maliau (p108) in Sabah is as wild as it gets. The basin is a rock-rimmed depression filled with primary rainforest – that's untouched, uncut jungle, as old as the hills. We asked a local ranger what he thought of the Maliau, and his Malay response was *'Adan da Hawa'* – Adam and Eve. That's how fresh and perfect this forest feels, and while it may look expensive to enter, with a bit of initiative you too can experience the world as it once was. Maliau Falls (p108)

ROBBIE SHONE / GETTY IMAGES ©

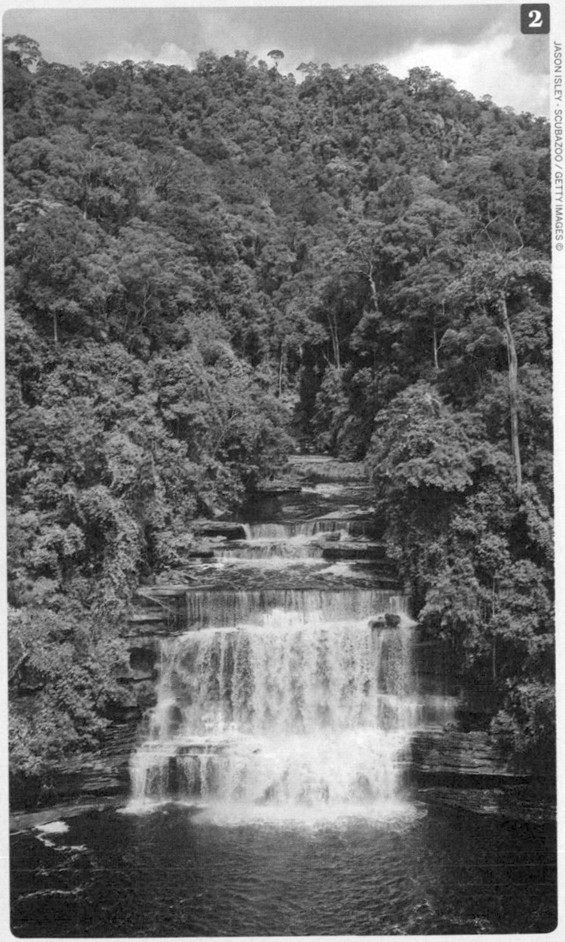

JASON ISLEY - SCUBAZOO / GETTY IMAGES ©

3

4

Tanjung Puting National Park

3 Arguably one of the best places in the world to experience close-up encounters with semi-wild orangutans, Kalimantan's Tanjung Puting (p232) offers an unforgettable upriver journey on a chugging *klotok*: a boat that's both your home and your lookout tower. Sleep with fireflies under the stars on the top deck, wake to the call of gibbons in the morning, and watch Borneo's critically endangered, charismatic orangutans as they swing ponderously through the open jungle to the feeding platforms.

Mt Kinabalu

4 Sabah's Mt Kinabalu (p59) is so many things we don't know where to start. Highest mountain in Borneo and Malaysia? Check. Climbable even by novices, but great fun for veteran trekkers? Check. Abode of the spirits of local indigenous tribes? Check. Home to several unique-to-Borneo ecosystems and some 6000 plant species, many of them endemic? Check. Even on an island bursting with astonishing natural beauty, the sight of Mt Kinabalu's peak early in the morning causes most folks to lose their breath.

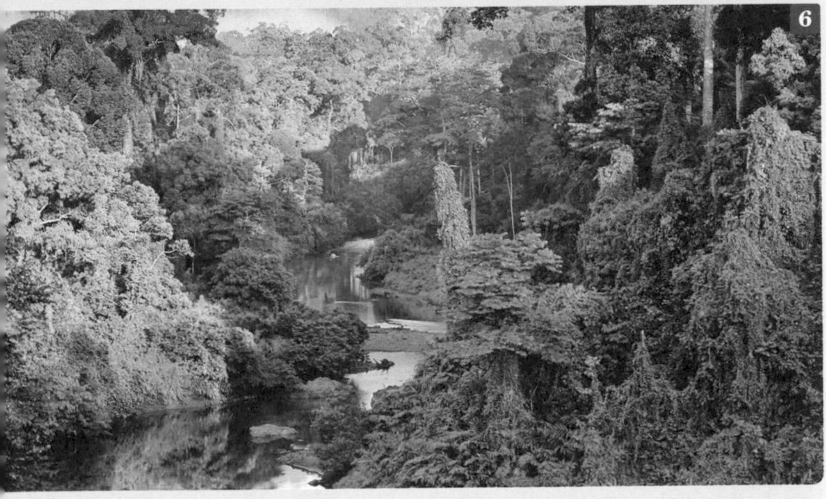

Kelabit Highlands

5 The air is clean and cool, the rice fields impossibly green, the local cuisine scrumptious, and the hiking – from longhouse to longhouse – some of the best in Borneo, but the star attraction in the Kelabit Highlands (p184) is the people, justifiably famous for their ready smiles and easy way with visitors. Getting to this remote corner of northeastern Sarawak is half the fun – you can either bust your butt on logging roads for 12 hours or take an exhilarating flight in a 19-seat Twin Otter turboprop. Bario Asal Longhouse (p185)

Danum Valley

6 If the primeval jungle of Sabah's Danum Valley (p92) makes you think of dinosaurs, we'll understand – the area really does look like Jurassic Park. Confirmed sightings of a *T. rex* eating a lawyer? Not that we know of, but visitors often spot pygmy elephants, wild orangutans and clouds of bird life. Some, though, don't actually *see* any animals at all, as the jungle is so thick it can cloak fauna mere metres from where you're standing. But that's part of Danum's enchanting and timeless appeal.

Kuching

7 Borneo's most sophisticated city (p122) is a charming combination of atmospheric old town, romantic waterfront, fine cuisine for all budgets and buzzing nightlife. But the city's biggest draw is what's nearby: some of Sarawak's finest natural sites, easy to visit on day trips. You can spot semi-wild orangutans or search out a giant rafflesia flower in the morning, look for proboscis monkeys and wild crocs on a sundown cruise in the South China Sea, and then dine on super-fresh seafood or crunchy *midin* fern tips.

Loksado

8 Nestled by a rushing stream in the foothills of the Meratus in Kalimantan scenic Loksado (p245) feels more like a mountain retreat than part of Borneo. There are waterfalls, swimming holes, endless hiking opportunities, hot springs, bamboo rafting, and lots of friendly locals. Accommodation options are sparse, but you'll find everything you need for an extended stay, including a great riverside budget lodge and a new private resort. Backpackers take note: if you need to re-energise, this is the place.

7

8

MATT MUNRO / LONELY PLANET ©

ANDERS BLOMQVIST / GETTY IMAGES ©

Semenggoh Nature Reserve

9 With free-roam of the reserve's rainforest and fruit trees, the semi-wild orangutans at Semenggoh Nature Reserve (p145) near Kuching in Sarawak are not guaranteed to show up at the twice-daily feeding sessions, but there's a pretty good chance of catching the endlessly entertaining sight of our shaggy jungle cousins stuffing half a dozen bananas into their mouths, grabbing a coconut and then scrambling back up into the jungle canopy – swinging from tree to tree, dangling nonchalantly from vines and taking care of their adorable infants. Male Bornean orangutan

Sarawak's Longhouses

10 There's no better way to experience Sarawak's diverse indigenous tribal culture than to visit a longhouse (p280). Essentially a whole village under a single roof, these dwellings can be longer than two football pitches and contain dozens of family units, each of which opens onto a covered common verandah used for economic activities, socialising and celebrations. Although these days all longhouses enjoy some modern amenities, many still have a few skulls on display from the bygone time when headhunting was practised. Longhouse in the Batang Ai region (p155)

Kinabatangan River Safaris

11 Indiana Jones would love the Sungai Kinabatangan (Kinabatangan River). Like a muddy brown python, Sabah's longest river wends its way through the epic jungles south of Sandakan, bracketed by riverine forest teeming with civet cats, orangutans, proboscis monkeys, saltwater crocodiles, monitor lizards, hornbills, kingfishers and hawks. Book yourself into one of several jungle camps in the villages of Sukau (pictured above; p88) and Bilit, or stay with locals in a homestay, and set out on a river cruise (p87) for an excellent shot at spotting some of Borneo's most iconic animals.

12

13

Sepilok Orangutan Rehabilitation Centre

12 One of the better dedicated research and rehabilitation facilities in Borneo, Sepilok (p81), in eastern Sabah, is also one of the easiest places to see rescued orangutans. View them up close at feeding platforms and at the brilliant orphanage nursery, where, from the comfort of an air-conditioned room, you can sit and watch the youngsters as they learn to climb. Also new at Sepilok is the Borneo Sun Bear Conservation Centre, where these adorable creatures are rehabilitated for eventual release.

Ulu Temburong National Park

13 From the sky, Brunei's Temburong District looks like all of Borneo once did: an unbroken carpet of primary rainforest unblemished by roads, buildings or logging gashes. On the ground, most of the sultanate's eastern sliver is off-limits except to researchers, but you can get a taste of the primeval jungle at Ulu Temburong National Park (p216). The only way in is an exciting longboat ride, and once there you can climb into the jungle canopy and have wild fish nibble your feet in a cool stream.

Derawan Archipelago

14 Choose your own adventure in this diverse island chain (p265) on the northeastern fringe of Kalimantan. The sandy streets and waterfront losmen (budget guesthouses) of Pulau Derawan are a first-rate backpacker destination, while the postcard-pretty twin resort isles of Nabucco and Nunukan offer some truly extraordinary diving, along with high-end bungalow accommodation. And for those intent on finding an authentic tropical paradise, the massive Maratua atoll and the virtually untouristed islands beyond offer a shot at bliss that is increasingly hard to find. Starfish on coral reef

Cross-Borneo Trek

15 Welcome to the triathlon of adventure travel (p223)! Starting on Borneo's east coast, you travel hundreds of kilometres upriver, deep into the heart of one of the world's most fabled jungles, trek through back-of-beyond hills like the explorers of old, and then head down to the west coast on a thrilling white-water canoe ride. Along the way you'll sample everything Kalimantan has to offer, from wildlife to Dayak culture to pure adrenalin. If you can't do it all, the journey up the Mahakam River is great by itself.

RSM IMAGES / ALAMY STOCK PHOTO ©

Need to Know

For more information, see Survival Guide (p299)

Currency

Malaysian ringgit (RM), Brunei dollar (B$), Indonesian rupiah (Rp).

Language

Bahasa Malaysia, Bahasa Indonesia, Chinese dialects and indigenous languages.

Visas

Visas generally issued on arrival for Malaysia and Brunei, and to visitors entering Indonesia at Balikpapan, Pontianak or Tebedu–Entikong. Indonesian visas must be obtained in advance for other Kalimantan entry points.

Money

ATMs widely available in cities and larger towns. Credit cards usually accepted at top-end establishments.

Mobile Phones

Local SIM cards can be used in an unlocked 900/1800MHz phone.

Time

GMT/UTC plus eight hours in Sabah, Sarawak, Brunei, and West and Central Kalimantan. UTC plus seven hours in East, North and South Kalimantan.

When to Go

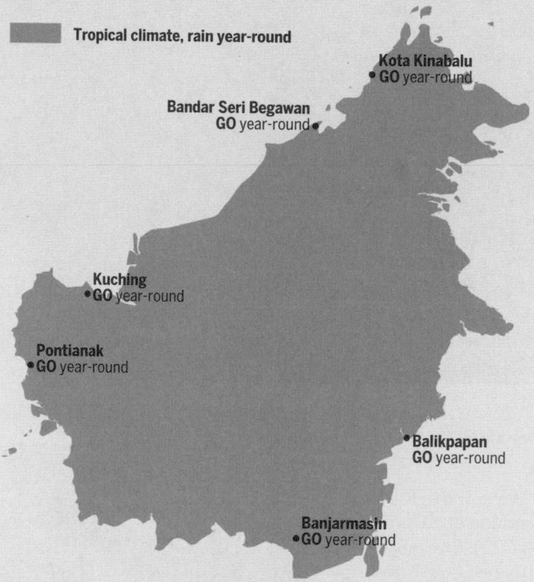

Year-round

- ➡ No especially good or bad season to visit.
- ➡ Lowland areas always hot and humid.
- ➡ Rain a real possibility every day, all year.

'Wet' Season
(Oct–Feb)

- ➡ Indistinct wet season October to February; can affect boat links to offshore islands and visibility for divers.
- ➡ Rains can render Kalimantan's dirt roads impassable, especially from October to April.

High Season
(Jul–Sep)

- ➡ Accommodation and trekking guides may be booked out in some areas in July, August and perhaps September.

Useful Websites

Brunei Tourism (www.bruneitourism.travel) Lots of great info.

Sabah Parks (www.sabahparks.org.my) Sabah's national parks.

Sabah Tourism (www.sabahtourism.com) Official site.

Sarawak Forestry (www.sarawakforestry.com) Sarawak's national parks.

Sarawak Tourism (www.sarawaktourism.com) Official site.

Lonely Planet (www.lonelyplanet.com) Information, bookings, forums and more.

Important Numbers

Country codes for Borneo:

Brunei	☎673
Indonesia	☎62
Malaysia	☎60

Exchange Rates

	RM	B$	Rp
Australia A$1	3.05	1.03	9868
Canada C$1	3.19	1.07	10,307
Euro €1	4.72	1.59	15,238
Japan ¥100	3.46	1.17	11,173
New Zealand NZ$1	2.79	0.94	9008
Singapore S$1	2.97	1.00	9588
UK UK£1	6.37	2.15	20,570
USA US$1	4.15	1.34	13,407

For current exchange rates see www.xe.com.

Daily Costs

Budget: Less than US$30

- Dorm bed: US$5–10
- Meals at food stalls, self-catering at fruit and veg markets: US$1–2
- National park admission: US$5 (Malaysia), US$11 (Indonesia)
- Museums: Almost all are free

Midrange: US$30–80

- Air-con double room with bathroom: from US$20
- Meals at all but the priciest restaurants: US$5–12
- Taxis, chartered motorboats or tours to nature sites: US$10–50

Top end: More than US$80

- Luxury double room: US$100
- Seafood dinner: US$8–20 per kilo

Opening Hours

All businesses in Brunei close from noon until 2pm on Fridays. In all of Borneo business hours may be shorter during Ramadan.

Banks 10am to 3pm or 4pm on weekdays and 9.30am to 11.30am on Saturday

Cafes 6am or 7am until early or late afternoon

Restaurants 11.30am to 10pm

Shops 9.30am to 7pm (10am to 10pm for shopping malls)

Arriving in Borneo

Sabah and Sarawak Major airports, such as Kuching, Kota Kinabalu and Miri, have ATMs, car rental desks, kiosks selling SIM cards, and orderly taxi queues with fixed prices and vouchers for trips into town.

Brunei Brunei International Airport has ATMs, car rental and bus connections with the centre of Bandar Seri Begawan. City tours are available for transit passengers. Singapore dollars are universally accepted, with a conversion rate of one to one.

Kalimantan Taxis and other conveyances meet all incoming flights.

Getting Around

Boats and planes are often the best or only option to reach the places that asphalt roads don't.

Bus Frequent buses link major cities in Sarawak, Brunei and Sabah.

Plane Short-haul flights connect towns and outlying villages across Sarawak and Sabah and major towns in Kalimantan.

Express ferries and speedboats Boat services link coastal and river towns in Sarawak, Sabah, Brunei and Kalimantan.

Motorised longboat Often the only form of transport to remote villages, longhouses and national parks.

For much more on **getting around**, see p312.

If You Like...

Jungle Trekking

Kinabalu National Park Much more than just the famous summit climb. (p59)

Gunung Mulu National Park Options include the Pinnacles hike and climbing Gunung Mulu itself. (p178)

Maliau Basin Conservation Area Remote hikes through old-growth forest. (p108)

Bario to Ba Kelalan A classic three- to four-day trek through the Kelabit Highlands. (p189)

Pegunungan Meratus (Meratus Mountains) Trails from Loksado criss-cross forested valleys. (p245)

Muller Mountains Borneo's remotest mountain range. (p261)

Orangutans

Semenggoh Wildlife Centre One of the easiest places to see semi-wild orangutans. (p145)

Sepilok Orangutan Rehabilitation Centre Rescued orangutans, living free in the forest, drop by for fruit. (p81)

Sungai Kinabatangan (Kinabatangan River) Home to some truly wild orangutans. (p86)

Tanjung Puting National Park Combine semi-wild orangutan spotting with an unforgettable boat trip. (p232)

Batang Ai National Park Catch a glimpse of wild orangutans on a trek through the park and beyond. (p155)

Kutai National Park The best place to go in Kalimantan for the chance of seeing wild orangutans. (p262)

Indigenous Culture

Kelabit Highlands One of the best places in Borneo to hike from longhouse to longhouse. (p184)

Batang Ai Region Old-time Iban longhouses, many accessible only by boat. (p155)

Upper Sungai Mahakam Dayak culture in the heart of Borneo. (p255)

Kapuas Hulu Some of Kalimantan's oldest and most welcoming longhouse communities are around Putussibau. (p229)

Pegunungan Meratus Animist beliefs are strong in these remote mountain communities. (p245)

Western Sarawak Bidayuh longhouses and the Sarawak Cultural Village. (p139)

River Trips

Rivers were once the only transport arteries into Borneo's interior, and in some areas – especially in Kalimantan – ferries, longboats and canoes are still the only way to get around.

Tanjung Puting National Park The shores of Sungai Sekonyer teem with macaques, orangutans and crocs up towards Camp Leakey. (p232)

Sungai Mahakam (Mahakam River) The further upriver you go, the wilder the wildlife. (p255)

Sungai Bungan (Bungan River) Borneo's most thrilling canoe trip. (p230)

Sungai Kinabatangan Spot an ark's worth of animals, including pygmy elephants. (p86)

Batang Rejang (Rejang River) Take a 'flying coffin' river express to Belaga. (p160)

Bandar Seri Begawan to Bangar Slap through palm-lined waterways and weave among mangroves on an exhilarating ride. (p214)

Multicultural Cities

Kuching Fantastic for strolling and aimless exploration, with 19th-century forts, two Chinatowns, and excellent cuisine for every budget. (p122)

Bandar Seri Begawan Picturesque water villages, two stunning mosques, and some outstanding food stalls. (p200)

Top: Dayak festival, Kalimantan
Bottom: Central Market, Kota Kinabalu (p42)

Sibu The mostly Chinese 'Swan City' has a thriving food scene and Malaysia's largest indoor market. (p156)

Singkawang Kalimantan's most Chinese city sometimes feels like Shanghai c 1930. (p226)

Kota Kinabalu A burgeoning arts scene and bustling street markets are two highlights of this cosmopolitan city. (p42)

Exploring Caves

Borneo has an incredible variety of underground wonders. While some of the caves must be visited with a professional guide, others are easily accessible on plankwalks.

Gunung Mulu National Park Some of the world's most spectacular caves, dripping with stalactites, are home to millions of bats. (p178)

Gomantong Caves The cathedral-like grand chamber is speckled with rays of sunlight. (p86)

Niah National Park Niah's enormous caverns, once home to prehistoric humans, are easy to explore on boardwalks. (p168)

Wind Cave and Fairy Cave Stairs and paths make it possible to visit these caves unaccompanied. (p150)

Kuching Caving This small spelunking outfit offers adventurous day expeditions to Kuching-area caves. (p150)

Goa Beloyot A tiny cave containing ancient handprints. (p264)

Month by Month

TOP EVENTS

Rainforest World Music Festival, August

Gawai Dayak, June

Harvest Festival, May

Chinese New Year, February

Hari Raya Puasa, June

February

The weather is hot and humid, with rain always likely. February is one of the wettest months of the year in Kuching (Sarawak) and Banjarmasin (South Kalimantan). The seas off Sarawak and around Kalimantan's Derawan Archipelago can be rough.

Chinese New Year

Borneo's Chinese communities, especially large in Kuching and Sibu in Sarawak and Singkawang in Kalimantan, welcome the New Year with bright red lanterns, lion and dragon dances, drums, night markets and fireworks.

April

Even in Sandakan (Sabah), where months don't get any drier, there is a good chance of rain.

Regatta Lepa

The Bajau sea gypsies of Semporna (Sabah) deck out their *lepa* (boats) with streamers, bunting, flags, ceremonial umbrellas and gorgeously decorated sails. The mid-April weekend festivities are further animated with violin, cymbal and drum music, duck-catching competitions, and tug-of-war contests with boats.

May

This quiet month, before the school holidays kick in, is a good time to visit.

Borneo Jazz Festival

An eclectic assemblage of artists from Europe, North America and Southeast Asia makes the Borneo Jazz Festival (www.jazzborneo.com) – held in Miri in Sarawak on a weekend in mid-May – Borneo's premier jazz event.

Ramadan

During the month of Ramadan, Muslims abstain from eating and drinking during daylight hours. Ramadan food markets pop up in cities and celebratory meals to break the fast are held after sundown.

Harvest Festival

Rice is the key staple for Sabah's indigenous groups. To mark the annual harvest, people gather in their home villages on 30 and 31 May for a colourful thanksgiving festival that's also known as Pesta Kaamatan.

June

June is the wettest month of the year in Balikpapan (West Kalimantan). As it's the northern hemisphere summer, tourist numbers rise.

Gawai Dayak

An official holiday in Sarawak (it's also celebrated in West Kalimantan and by the Iban in Brunei), this Dayak festival marks the end of the rice harvest. City-dwelling folk return to their longhouses to make music, eat and drink *tuak* (rice wine). Held from the evening of 31 May to 2 June.

Hari Raya Puasa

This festive three-day Muslim holiday marks the end of the fasting month of Ramadan. Many people travel to their home towns, creating traffic jams and a shortage of air, boat and bus tickets.

July

The driest month in Kuching, but expect rain nonetheless. Northern hemisphere tourist numbers are high so consider booking guides for treks and tours in advance.

Bario Food Festival

Visitors flock to the Kelabit Highlands in Sarawak for this three-day culinary festival usually held in July. Delicacies include wild spinach, asparagus and ginger, and plenty of Bario pineapples.

Borneo Cultural Festival

A week-long festival in Sibu (Sarawak) of food, music and dance representing Central Sarawak's Chinese, Iban, Bidayuh, Orang Ulu and Malay-Melanau cultures and traditions.

Sultan of Brunei's Birthday

Colourful official ceremonies are held on 15 July to mark the birthday of Sultan Hassanal Bolkiah. In Bandar Seri Begawan, events include an elaborate military ceremony and cannon-firing presided over by the sultan himself.

August

While August is the driest month in Banjarmasin (South Kalimantan), rain is always likely. Northern hemisphere tourist numbers remain high.

Rainforest World Music Festival

This three-day musical extravaganza (www.rwmf.net), held in the Sarawak Cultural Village near Kuching in July or August, brings together local bands and international artists. Accommodation fills up long in advance.

Erau Festival

The Erau Festival sees thousands of Dayaks from all over Kalimantan converging in Tenggarong in a whirl of tribal costumes, ceremony and dance – an international celebration of traditional cultures.

Hungry Ghost Festival

On the 15th day of the seventh Chinese lunar month, when ghosts are free to roam the earth, offerings of food, prayer, incense and (fake) paper money are made to appease the spirits of the deceased.

September

Haze from forest and field-clearance fires in Indonesia create urban smog across the region, particularly in western Sarawak.

Belaga Rainforest Challenge

Orang Ulu longhouses along the Batang Rejang share their music, dance, traditional costumes and cuisines with each other and with visitors. Competitions include boat races and a 20km jungle run. Held in even-numbered years, it lasts for five days.

Borneo International Kite Festival

Held on the runway of the old airport in Bintulu (Sarawak), this festival (www.borneokite.com) brings a marvellous array of kites to Borneo's natural-gas capital. Takes place over four or five days in September or October.

LUNAR CALENDAR

Muslim and Chinese festivals follow a lunar calendar, so the dates for many religious festivals vary each year. Muslim holidays typically move forward 11 days each year, while Chinese festivals change dates, but fall roughly within the same months. Contact local tourist offices for exact festival dates, as many are variable.

Itineraries

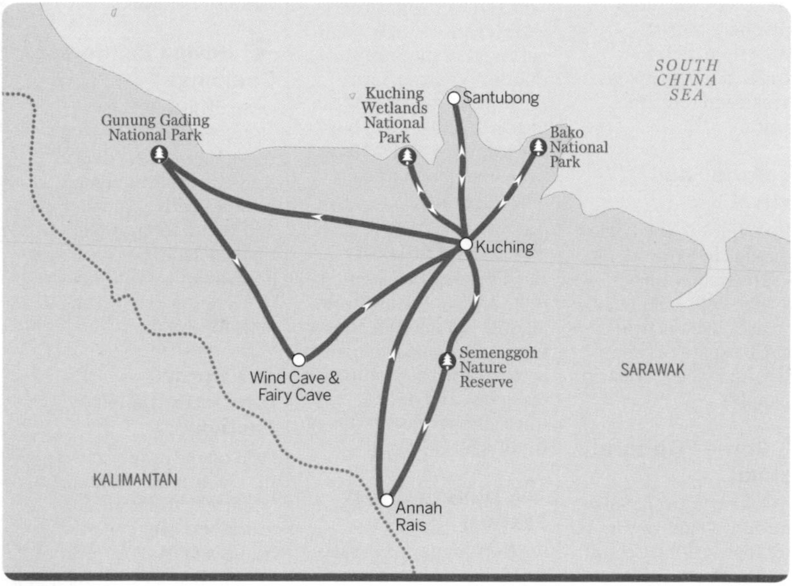

1 WEEK Kuching Excursions

Borneo's most sophisticated city is surrounded by first-rate nature sites that can easily keep you occupied for a week or more.

Spend your first day in **Kuching**, tuning into the vibe of the city's kaleidoscopic mix of cultures and cuisines. Explore the narrow streets of Old Chinatown, ride a tiny passenger ferry to the English Renaissance–style Fort Margherita, and take a sunset stroll along the Waterfront Promenade. If a giant Rafflesia flower happens to be in bloom in **Gunung Gading National Park**, drop everything and rush over before it starts to spoil. On the way back explore the **Wind Cave** and **Fairy Cave**.

Allow half a day to spot orangutans at **Semenggoh Nature Reserve**, then drive further inland to the longhouse of **Annah Rais**, where you can stay overnight before returning to Kuching. From here, take a bus then a boat to **Bako National Park**, keeping an eye out for proboscis monkeys, macaques and pitcher plants as you spend a day or two hiking around the peninsula before heading back to enjoy Kuching's fine eateries and buzzing nightlife. On your final day, relax on the beach in **Santubong**, then spend the sunset hour on a cruise around **Kuching Wetlands National Park**, alert for fireflies and crocs.

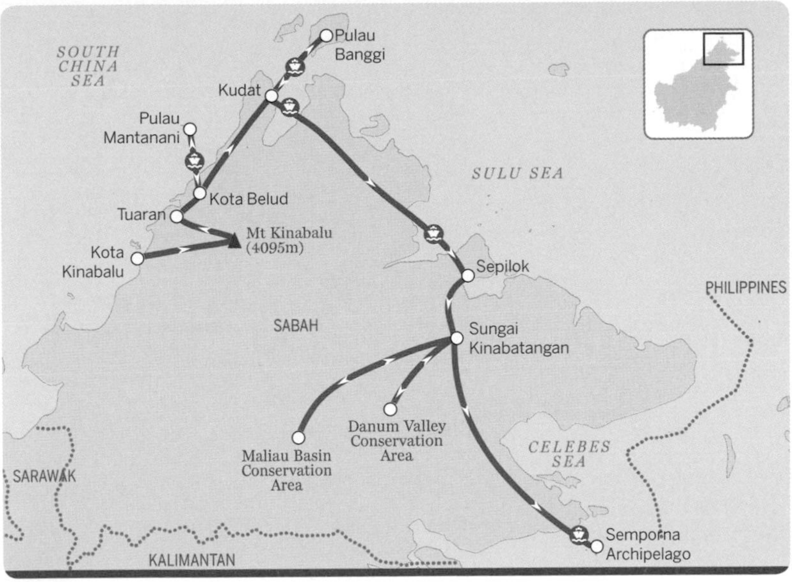

3 WEEKS Around Sabah

Strolling city streets, climbing into the heavens, relaxing on a beach, hiking through the rainforest and diving deep into the ocean – most of the highlights of this beautiful state can be covered in a three-week trip.

Arrive in **Kota Kinabalu** (KK) and give yourself two days to pre-book accommodation in places such as Sungai Kinabatangan (Kinabatangan River), the Semporna Archipelago (if you plan on diving) and Mt Kinabalu – accommodation at the latter should ideally be booked before you arrive in Borneo. While in KK, make sure to eat at the Night Market and take a trip to the Mari Mari Cultural Village and Sabah Museum, where you can get a taste of the cultures, landscapes and animal life you're about to encounter firsthand. Party on the KK waterfront your first night in town, but try to keep your head clear the morning you leave Sabah's capital.

If you decide to climb **Mt Kinabalu**, it's easiest to leave from KK. You'll need to allow two or three days for the mountain – there's the climb itself, and the day of rest you'll need afterwards! Whether or not you climb Mt Kinabalu, give yourself a few days to explore northwest Sabah. In the vicinity of **Tuaran** you can visit a lovely water village, while Mañana guesthouse near **Kota Belud** is a great place to relax; if you time things right you can also see Kota Belud's famous Sunday *tamu* (market). Further north lie the hidden beaches of **Kudat**, while offshore lie the isolated, off-the-tourist-trail islands of **Pulau Mantanani** (reached from Kota Belud) and **Pulau Banggi**. This area is great for homestays.

Now a little over a week into your trip, head east to **Sepilok** and its famous orangutan sanctuary. After watching our arboreal cousins being fed in a wildlife reserve, try to spot them in the wild during a river cruise down the **Sungai Kinabatangan**. There are great lodges and homestays out this way. Allow three days for Kinabatangan and another three to four days for trekking in the **Danum Valley** or **Maliau Basin**, leaving just enough time for three unforgettable days of diving at Sipadan in the **Semporna Archipelago**.

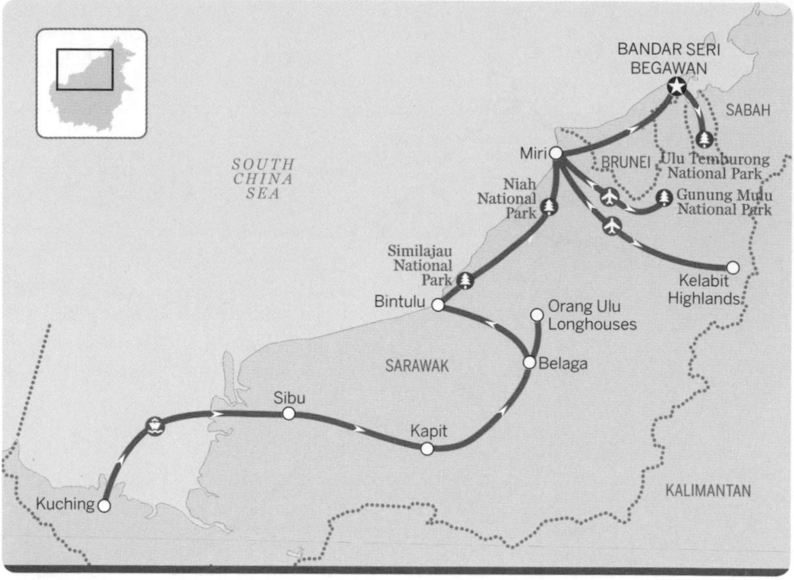

3 WEEKS Kuching to Brunei

With stops at some of the world's best caves and traditional longhouses, this trip across Sarawak and Brunei by road, river and air passes through remote rainforests and modern urban centres.

Fly into **Kuching** and spend a few days exploring this multicultural city, delving into its scrumptious cuisine scene for breakfast (Sarawak laksa), lunch and dinner. Take day trips to nearby national parks in search of orangutans, proboscis monkeys and exotic flora. Then hop on the daily express ferry to the river port of **Sibu**, where you can continue to eat well – don't miss the Foochow specialities on offer in the vast Central Market.

Sibu serves as the gateway to the mighty Batang Rejang (Rejang River). Board an early-morning express boat and head upriver to **Kapit**, a bustling trading centre founded in the days of the White Rajahs. If the river level is high enough, continue on to back-of-beyond **Belaga**, jumping-off point for hikes to a number of **Orang Ulu longhouses**.

A jarring 4WD ride will get you down to the coastal city of **Bintulu**, Borneo's natural-gas capital. Avoid the city centre and head straight to the beaches, rainforest trails and bungalows of **Similajau National Park**, which stretches along the coast for 30km.

Hop on a bus heading northeast to Batu Niah Junction, situated just a few kilometres from the vast caves, chirping bat colonies and prehistoric archaeological sites of **Niah National Park**. Next stop is the shiny petroleum city of **Miri**, home to some excellent dining options. Chilling here amid mod cons is a great way to spend a day or two before flying into Borneo's interior for a few days – travellers speak glowingly of both **Gunung Mulu National Park** and the gorgeously green **Kelabit Highlands**.

After flying back to Miri, take a bus to **Bandar Seri Begawan**, the surprisingly laid-back capital of the tiny, oil-rich sultanate of Brunei. Several museums showcase Bruneian culture, and culinary creations can be enjoyed at BSB's superb hawker centres. End your Bornean odyssey back in the primeval rainforest by taking a speedboat, a car and finally a longboat to the pristine jungles of **Ulu Temburong National Park**.

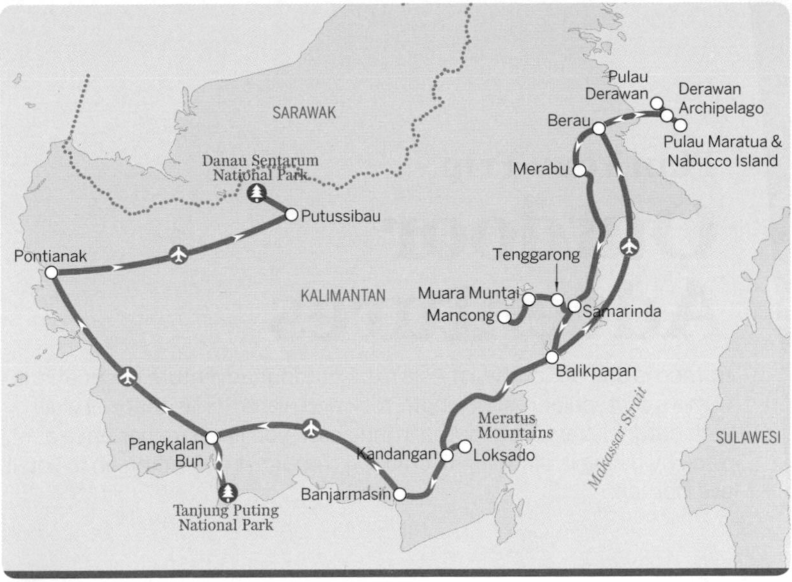

4 WEEKS Around Kalimantan

Kalimantan is big and cloaked in jungle, with many places accessible only by boat. With a bit of planning, however, it's possible to pack a great deal into a four-week journey.

Start at **Balikpapan** (where you can get your visa on arrival) before flying to **Berau**. From there, explore the nearby **Derawan Archipelago**, home to some world-class diving. You can spend the night swapping stories with travellers on **Pulau Derawan**, or head to the little-touristed outer islands, such as **Pulau Maratua** (backpacker heaven) or tiny **Nabucco Island**, home to a high-end dive resort.

Once back in Berau, head south via karst mountains and the village of **Merabu** to exotic **Samarinda**, gateway to the Sungai Mahakam (Mahakam River) and home to an eye-popping mosque. Head upriver via **Tenggarong**, with its resplendent *keraton* (palace), to **Muara Muntai** at the centre of the lake country, where you can hire a gaily-coloured *ces* (longtail canoe) for an unforgettable backwater journey to **Mancong**. Continue up or down river as far as you like aboard the *kapal biasa* (a river ferry that acts as a floating hostel) before returning to Balikpapan.

Take a bus south to the pleasant market village of **Kandangan** where you can hop on a pick-up truck bound for **Loksado**, a quiet hamlet in the foothills of the Meratus Mountains. There you can equally enjoy hiking, bamboo rafting or simply relaxing. Continue on to **Banjarmasin** and visit the floating market in the early hours before flying to **Pangkalan Bun** and travelling to **Tanjung Puting National Park**, where you can cruise the Sungai Sekonyer (Sekonyer River) in search of wildlife and watch orangutans feed at one of Indonesia's most popular destinations.

With your final week, fly north via **Pontianak** to **Putussibau** to visit Kalimantan's oldest longhouses and least-explored forests in the wild Kapuas Hulu, before capping off your tour of Indonesian Borneo by floating through the stunning seasonal wetlands of **Danau Sentarum National Park**.

Plan Your Trip

Outdoor Adventures

Borneo is one of Southeast Asia's top outdoor adventure destinations, with a spectacular mix of jungle, rock and water thrills that will wow both nature lovers and adrenalin junkies. If you like to experience a place by hiking it, climbing it, crawling through it or floating on it, you'll love Borneo.

Best Areas For...

Wildlife Spotting

Tanjung Puting National Park; Mancong, Sungai Mahakam (Mahakam River); Bako National Park; Wildlife River Safaris, Sungai Kinabatangan (Kinabatangan River); Kuching Wetlands National Park; Gunung Mulu National Park

Mountain Climbing

Mt Kinabalu; Gunung Mulu; Mt Besar

Jungle Day Hikes

Rafflesia Loop Trail, Gunung Gading National Park; Lubuk Baji, Gunung Palung National Park; Danum Valley Conservation Area; Bako National Park; Similajau National Park

Rainforest Canopy Walks

Gunung Mulu National Park; Ulu Temburong National Park; Poring Hot Springs; Danum Valley; Sepilok Rainforest Discovery Centre

Jungle Trekking

When to Go

Borneo has some of the best jungle hikes anywhere in the world. While the island's forests are disappearing at an alarming rate, vast swaths of old-growth (primary) tropical rainforest still cover the middle of the island and much of Brunei, and pristine patches remain in parts of Sabah and Sarawak.
If you've never walked through genuine tropical jungle, the experience – even if you don't see many mammals, which tend to be nocturnal, very shy or both – is likely to be a revelation: you simply won't believe the teeming fecundity.

Borneo has wet months and less-wet months – the timing depends on where you are – but precipitation varies so widely from year to year that a month that's usually dry can be very rainy, and vice versa. In short, no matter when you go you are likely to get wet.

What *is* seasonal, however, is the number of other travellers you'll be competing with for experienced guides and lodgings. For obvious reasons, northern hemisphere residents often come to Borneo (especially Sabah and Sarawak) during summer holidays in their home countries, so if you'd like to trek – particularly in popular national parks such as Gunung Mulu, Kinabalu and

Tanjung Puting – in July, August or September, it's a good idea to book a guide or tour in advance.

Guides

Many national parks have well-marked day trails that can be hiked unaccompanied. But for almost all overnight trails, only a fool would set out without a local guide. Remember, trail maps of any sort are completely unavailable and signage along remote trails nonexistent.

Especially in Sabah, Brunei and Sarawak, the national parks are very strict about allowing only licensed guides to show visitors around. We've heard stories of groups being turned back when they arrived with an uncertified leader. Before you fork over any cash, compare notes with other travellers and ask to see the guide's national park certification.

Guides for day walks can sometimes be hired at national park headquarters, but for overnight trekking you'll generally need to contact either a freelance guide or a tour agency before you arrive.

Physical Demands

Hiking in the tropics is much more strenuous than in temperate zones – one kilometre of slogging through Borneo is roughly equivalent to two in Europe or North America. Thanks to the combination of high temperatures and high humidity, you will sweat enough to discover what eyebrows are for, so be sure to drink plenty of water. In *kerangas* (heath forests) and on high mountains, prepare for intense sun by wearing a hat and sunscreen. Make sure your guide is aware of the pace you can handle.

Borneo is hardly the Himalayas, but in places like the Kelabit Highlands (1500m) you may feel the altitude, at least for a few days.

Pre-Trip Preparation

To the uninitiated, jungle trekking can be something of a shock – like marching all day in a sauna with a floor as slippery as ice. To make the experience as safe and painless as possible, it's necessary to prepare ahead:

➡ On overnight trips, bring two sets of clothing: one for hiking and one to wear at the end of the day (keep your night kit dry in a plastic bag). Within minutes of starting, your hiking kit will be drenched and will stay that way throughout your trip. Never blur the distinction between your day and night kits, or you'll find that you have two sets of wet clothes.

➡ If you'll be hiking through dense vegetation, wear long trousers and a long-sleeved shirt. Otherwise, shorts and a T-shirt will suffice. Whatever you wear, make sure it's loose fitting.

TRAVEL LITERATURE: STORIES OF ADVENTURE

Borneo has fired the world's imagination for centuries. Perhaps the best recent title is *Stranger in the Forest* by Eric Hansen, in which the author recounts his 1976 journey across the island in the company of Penan guides. It is not just the difficulty of the feat, but the author's brilliant and sensitive storytelling that make the book a classic. One cannot read it without a sense of sadness, for the world and the people described are now almost completely gone.

The most popular book about Borneo is Redmond O'Hanlon's *Into the Heart of Borneo*, a humorous account of the author's 1983 journey up a river in Sarawak. While O'Hanlon makes a bit much of what was a fairly unremarkable journey, one cannot help but enjoy his colourful narrative.

Espresso with the Headhunters: A Journey Through the Jungles of Borneo by John Wassner tells of a more extensive trip by an Australian traveller (and inveterate caffeine and nicotine addict). Not nearly as famous as O'Hanlon's book, this gives a more realistic account of what life is like in Sarawak.

If you climb Mt Kinabalu, you'll notice the gaping chasm of Low's Gully to your right as you ascend the final summit pyramid. *Kinabalu Escape: The Soldiers' Story* by Rich Mayfield tells of the British Army's ill-fated 1994 attempt to descend the gully. The expedition, a textbook case in how not to run an expedition, led to an expensive rescue operation and the near deaths of several team members.

➡ Bring fast-drying synthetic clothes. Once cotton gets wet, it won't dry until you bring it back to town.

➡ Evenings can be cool in the mountains, so if you'll be spending time in higher altitudes, bring a fleece top to keep warm.

➡ If you're going to be trekking on well-used trails and don't need a lot of ankle support, consider hiking in running shoes with good traction. Many locals opt for rubber shoes, sometimes known as 'jungle Reeboks', with rubber cleats that offer good grip on the slippery trails. The other big advantage is that they are quick drying, and only cost around US$2 a pair.

➡ To keep the leeches at bay, buy spandex pants or a pair of light-coloured leech socks. It's not always possible to find these in Borneo (guesthouses in Miri may carry them), so buy them online before your trip.

➡ Drink plenty of water. If you're going long distances, you'll have to bring either a water filter or a water-purification agent like iodine (most people opt for the latter to keep weight down).

LEECHES SUCK (BLOOD)

There's just no getting around it: if you want to experience Borneo's magnificent tropical rainforests, at some point you're going to find yourself getting up close and intimate with a leech – or, more likely, with lots of them. If you can't stand the sight of blood, wear dark-coloured socks.

Common Leech Varieties

There are two main varieties of leech in Borneo: the ground-dwelling brown leech and the striped yellow-reddish tiger leech, which often lives higher up on foliage. Leeches, which are attracted by the vibrations and carbon dioxide you produce, are probably the jungle's quietest creatures. Since you can't feel the bite of the brown leech, you'll only realise what's going on when you actually spot it, or when you notice blood seeping through your clothing. But you can feel the bite of a tiger leech – it's similar to an ant sting – which means that if you're quick, you can take action before making an involuntary blood donation.

Leeches are pretty horrible, but almost completely harmless; in Borneo they don't generally carry parasites, bacteria or viruses that can infect humans. However, a bite may itch and bleed profusely for a few hours due to the anticoagulant the leech injects. The spot may itch for another week, and then it will scab over and resolve into a small dark spot that completely disappears after several weeks. The only danger is that the bite may get infected, which is why it's important to disinfect the bite and keep it dry.

Self-Defence Against Leeches

Like hangover cures, everyone has a favourite method of protecting themselves from leeches. The problem is, most don't work. There is only one really effective method of keeping leeches at bay: wearing an impenetrable fabric barrier. Knee-length leech socks, made from tightly knit calico, work, as does Spandex. The best leech socks are light coloured so you can see the leeches ascending your legs and pick them off. You can find these online; guesthouses in Miri may also sell them.

If you do discover a leech making a pass at you, don't panic. Yanking off a leech can leave part of its jaws in the wound, and burning it or dousing it with vinegar, lemon juice or alcohol can increase the likelihood of infection. Instead, slide your fingernail along your skin at the point where the leech is attached to break the suction. The leech will try to grab your finger with its other end so roll it around to prevent it from getting a grip and flick it away. Don't squirt DEET directly on sucking leeches as the chemical may get in your wound.

Remember: salt is to leeches what kryptonite is to Superman. Some people put a teaspoon of salt inside some thin cloth and tie it to the top of a stick – touch a leech with something salty and it will recoil.

- Get in shape before coming to Borneo and start slowly. Try day hikes before longer treks.
- Always go with a guide unless you're on a well-marked, commonly travelled trail, for example in a national park. Navigating in the jungle is extremely difficult because most of the time – even when you're on top of a hill – all you can see is trees.
- Bring talcum powder to cope with the chafing caused by wet undergarments. Wearing loose underwear will also help prevent chafing.
- If you wear glasses, you might want to treat them with an antifog solution (ask your optician). Otherwise, you may find yourself in a foggy white-out within minutes of setting out.
- Your sweat will soak through the back of your backpack. Consider putting something waterproof over the back padding to keep the sweat out; otherwise, consider a waterproof sack for your stuff or line your back with a heavy-duty garbage bag.
- Keep your camera gear, including extra batteries, in an airtight plastic container, with a pouch of silica gel or other desiccant.

Guides & Agencies

Tour agencies and guides can help you head for the hills.

Sabah

- **Adventure Alternative Borneo** (p46)
- **Borneo Adventure** (p47)
- **Equator Adventure Tours** (p47)
- **Fieldskills Adventures** (p47)
- **Sticky Rice Travel** (p46)
- **Tampat Do Aman** (p73)

Sarawak

Guides can be found at Gunung Mulu National Park and in the Kelabit Highlands. Other options:

- **Adventure Alternative Borneo** (p129)
- **Borneo à la Carte** (p129)
- **Borneo Adventure** (p129)
- **Borneo Experiences** (p129)
- **Borneo Touch Ecotour** (p192)
- **Borneo Tropical Adventure** (p174)

Brunei

- **Borneo Guide** (p206)
- **Sunshine Borneo Tours** (p206)

Kalimantan

For day trips, many of the agencies specialising in river trips also offer guided hikes. Serious trekking in remote areas can be dangerous, so for a multiday expedition we recommend two outfits:

- **De'Gigant Tours** (p252)
- **Kompakh** (p230)

Mountain Climbing

Towering above the forests of Borneo are some brilliant mountains. Even non-climbers know about 4095m Mt Kinabalu (www.mountkinabalu.com), the highest peak between the Himalayas and the island of New Guinea. This craggy monster simply begs to be climbed, and there is something magical about starting the ascent in humid, tropical jungle and emerging into a bare, rocky alpine zone so cold that snow has been known to fall. But beyond the transition from hot to cold, it's the weird world of the summit plateau that makes Mt Kinabalu among the world's most interesting peaks. It's got a dash of Yosemite and a pinch of Torres del Paine, but at the end of the day, it's pure Borneo. Following the June 2015 earthquake, in which 18 climbers died, most trails have now been repaired and reopened.

Gunung Mulu (2377m) isn't quite as high, but it's almost as famous, thanks in part to it being a Unesco World Heritage site. If you're a glutton for punishment, you'll probably find the five-day return trek to the summit of this peak to your liking. Those who make the journey experience a variety of pristine natural environments, starting with lowland dipterocarp forest and ending with rhododendron and montane forest.

Pre-Trip Preparation

Climbing one of Borneo's iconic mountains is like a jungle trek except more so – more exhausting, more psychologically challenging and, naturally, more vertical. Be prepared for ascents that turn your legs to rubber and for much colder weather. Book guides, permits and accommodation well ahead.

Guides & Agencies

Many of the agencies that handle trekking also offer mountain ascents. Some of the more experienced guides in Sarawak's Kelabit Highlands can take you to two rarely climbed peaks, Batu Lawi and Gunung Murud.

Caving

Slice one of Borneo's limestone hills in half and chances are you'll find that inside it looks like Swiss cheese. Borneans have been living, harvesting birds' nests, planning insurgencies and burying their dead in these caves for tens of thousands of years. These days, the island's subterranean spaces – including some of the largest caverns anywhere on earth – are quiet, except for the flow of underground streams, the drip of stalactites, the whoosh of bat and swiftlet wings, and the awed murmurs of travellers.

Sarawak's Gunung Mulu National Park is a place of spelunking superlatives. It's got the world's second-largest cave passage (the Deer Cave, 2km in length and 174m in height), the world's largest cave chamber (the Sarawak Chamber, 700m long, 400m wide and 70m high) and Asia's longest cave (the Clearwater Cave, with 225km of passages). Several of the park's finest caves are – like their counterparts in Niah National Park and Sabah's Gomantong Caves – accessible to non-spelunkers on raised walkways.

A pitch-black passageway deep in the bowels of the earth is not the ideal place to discover that you can't deal with narrow, confined spaces. Before heading underground, seriously consider your susceptibility to claustrophobia and fear of heights (some caves require scaling underground cliffs). If you have any concerns about a specific route, talk with your guide beforehand.

Be prepared to crawl through muck, including bat guano, and bring clothes you won't mind getting filthy (some guides and agencies supply these).

When to Go

Rain can flood the interior of some caves at any time of the year.

Gunung Mulu National Park has a shortage of trained spelunking guides, so unless you'll be hiring a private guide or going with a tour agency, make reservations in advance. Some (but not all) dates in July, August and September can be booked out several months ahead.

Guides & Agencies

- **Gunung Mulu National Park** (p178)
- **Kuching Caving** (p150)

Jungle River Trips

The mountains and jungles of Borneo are drained by some of Southeast Asia's longest rivers. Whether it's tearing up a mainline *batang* (Iban for 'large river') in a speedboat, rafting down a *sungai* (Bahasa Malaysia and Bahasa Indonesia for 'river') or kayaking on a narrow *ai* (Iban for 'small river') in an *ulu* (upriver) part of the interior, you'll find that these watery highways are one of the best ways to experience Borneo.

Many parts of Borneo's interior can be reached only by river, so hopping on a boat is a necessity. There's something magical about heading to a human settlement connected by road to absolutely nowhere, especially if you're in the safe hands of an experienced boatman and accompanied by locals.

On larger rivers, transport is often by 'flying coffin' – passenger boats so-named for their long, narrow shape, with about 70 seats, not including the people sitting on the roof. Thanks to their mighty engines, these vessels can power upriver against very strong currents. Note that ferry safety is a major issue in Kalimantan.

In a smaller upriver craft, such as a *temuai* (shallow-draft Iban longboat), be prepared for you and your (hopefully waterproofed) kit to get dunked – and to get out and push if it hasn't rained for a while. Whatever the size of the vessel, be aware that rivers can suddenly rise by 2m or more after a downpour. If a boat looks unseaworthy or lacks basic safety equipment (especially life vests), don't be shy about speaking up.

Top: Western tarsier, Sabah

Bottom: Mulu Canopy Skywalk (p180), Gunung Mulu National Park

JUNGLE KIT LIST

General Kit

- ☐ backpack
- ☐ waterproof backpack liner
- ☐ day pack
- ☐ water bottles
- ☐ personal medical kit
- ☐ water purifier
- ☐ insect repellent (DEET)
- ☐ pocket knife
- ☐ head torch (flashlight)
- ☐ spare mini-torch
- ☐ small binoculars

Clothing

- ☐ jungle boots
- ☐ breathable waterproof socks or boot liners
- ☐ socks
- ☐ leech socks
- ☐ sandals
- ☐ underwear
- ☐ Lycra bras
- ☐ long trousers (2)
- ☐ shorts
- ☐ long-sleeve shirts (2)
- ☐ lightweight waterproof jacket or poncho
- ☐ swimwear
- ☐ warm top
- ☐ sunhat
- ☐ sarong
- ☐ sweat rag/chamois towel

Sleeping

- ☐ basha (tarpaulin) sheet
- ☐ hammock
- ☐ mosquito net
- ☐ sleeping mat
- ☐ sleeping bag
- ☐ sleeping-bag liner

Cooking & Eating

- ☐ mess tin
- ☐ spoon
- ☐ mug

Miscellaneous

- ☐ wash kit
- ☐ sunscreen
- ☐ towel
- ☐ toilet paper
- ☐ sewing kit
- ☐ waterproof freezer bags

Sea-going craft travelling along the coast and out to offshore islands have to deal with rougher waters than their inland counterparts. In Sarawak and parts of Kalimantan, this is especially true from November to March, when the northeast monsoon can bring choppy conditions.

Costs

Travel by boat does not come cheap, mainly because marine engines and outboards, which must shove aside prodigious quantities of water, really slurp up the petrol. For a small motorboat with a capacity of four to six people, count on paying about RM500 per day. While the boat is moored somewhere – at an island or a remote beach, for instance – you'll have to remunerate the driver but, obviously, there are no fuel costs when the motor is off.

Guides & Agencies

The following agencies can organise longboat trips, rafting, kayaking and other water-borne adventures (and in many cases day hikes, too).

Sabah

- **Borneo Authentic** (p47)
- **Borneo Eco Tours** (p48)
- **Borneo Nature Tours** (p48)
- **Only in Borneo** (p114)
- **River Junkie** (p47)
- **Riverbug/Traverse Tours** (p47)
- **SI Tours** (p78)
- **Uncle Tan** (p84)

Sarawak

- **Gunung Mulu National Park** (p178)
- **Rainforest Kayaking** (p129)
- **Stu Roach** (p186) Kayaking in the Kelabit Highlands.

Kalimantan

Guides can be found in Banjarmasin, Loksado, Tanjung Puting National Park and the Samarinda. Other options:

- **Canopy Indonesia** (p223)
- **Wow Borneo** (p237)

Plan Your Trip

Diving Pulau Sipadan

With fewer and fewer sites remaining around the world that can really deliver the thrill of a once-in-a-lifetime dive, Pulau Sipadan is definitely one of them. Regularly topping best lists compiled by serious divers and travel magazines alike, there is no doubt that the waters off the island of Sipadan contain some of the world's best dive sites.

Visiting Pulau Sipadan

Every year thousands of divers come to the Semporna Archipelago to explore Sipadan's plunging sea wall – home and transit point for a staggering array of marine life, including green and hawksbill turtles, hammerhead sharks, parrotfish, manta rays and schools of fish so massive they resemble silver tornadoes or shimmering walls of armour.

But those same divers make it hard for Sipadan to remain what Jacques Cousteau once described as 'untouched art'. Sipadan is many things, including one of Borneo's most popular tourism destinations, but untouched it is not. The Malaysian government has seen the need to preserve the integrity of Sipadan and as a result visiting the island is a tightly regulated process (although visitors never have to deal with the paperwork themselves). No tourists are allowed to stay overnight on the island of Sipadan itself; rather, it is the surrounding waters that attract mobs of divers, many of whom have travelled great distances to embark on a marine trek they will never forget.

Best Times for Diving

April to September

This is turtle time, when hawksbill and green turtles come to the archipelago to lay their eggs in the soft sand. You're unlikely to actually see turtles laying eggs, but you may spot them dancing their slow ballet beneath the waves. That said, turtles are always present in these waters – they're just more highly concentrated during this period.

July to August

Visibility is often stunning at this time of year, and clear views to 25m are common. You'll likely have to deal with more crowds as well, as this is prime holiday time in the northern hemisphere. Book well in advance if you want to visit during this period.

December to February

This is the local wet season. The rain doesn't impact visibility too badly, but monsoon winds may keep boats from accessing Sipadan and the other Semporna islands. On the other hand, by January crowds have thinned out a bit. The rains sometimes continue into March.

Planning

When to Go

The good news: there isn't a bad time to dive Sipadan, at least as far as visibility and marine life go. But consider how much you want to balance factors like weather (ie rain or no rain), crowds and abundance of marine life. The general rule of thumb: the better the conditions, the larger the crowds. However, wildlife spotting is almost always good and, thanks to the strict permit process, crowds rarely feel too overwhelming.

Getting to Sipadan

Sipadan is an island in the Semporna Archipelago, situated just off Sabah's eastern tip. Eight islands within the archipelago form the Semporna Marine Park, the largest marine park in Malaysia. The closest town is also named Semporna; a nearby naval station has the area's only decompression chamber. The closest airport is at Tawau, 72km west of Semporna town; a taxi from the airport to Semporna will cost around RM150. Otherwise, there are numerous bus connections between Semporna and the rest of Sabah. Note that unless you arrive in Semporna town early in the day, you will probably have to stay there overnight.

ARE YOU EXPERIENCED?

Sipadan rewards advanced-certified (and beyond) divers, but you don't have to be a scuba veteran to enjoy the island, and nearby places such as Mabul are easy for beginners. Even if you've never dived, every tour company we list can get you open-water certified, for very reasonable prices compared to most of the rest of the world.

If your travelling companion is a diver and you are not, consider snorkelling. The underwater world that can be viewed from the water's surface may not quite match the world-class dive sites, but the waters here are so clear and teeming with life that you may see stingrays and turtles, as well as other kinds of macro-marine wildlife.

SEMPORNA TRAVEL WARNING

Depending on the current situation, you may read warnings from European and Australian governments advising against travel to the Semporna Archipelago because of the threat of kidnapping by militant groups from the Philippines. Yet at the time of writing, for more than a year 120 divers a day had been enjoying one of the world's best dive sites without incident.

Be sure to check the latest security situation before travelling.

Permits & Dive Operators

Access to Sipadan is regulated by a tightly controlled permitting process. You can't get out there on your own; you must book with a tour operator, who will determine the day(s) you are allowed to dive Sipadan (note: you can dive other sites in the Semporna Archipelago without a permit).

The dive operators also run places to stay. Most accommodation, and all budget options, are on the small island of Mabul. Other possibilities include ritzier choices on the islands of Mataking, Kapalai and Pom Pom. Note that diving is the main event here – while the islands mentioned are pretty, they're too small to be enjoyed as island retreats in and of themselves.

Best Diving Sites

Pulau Sipadan

There are roughly a dozen delineated dive sites orbiting Sipadan island:

The Sea Wall The water here drops into a blue abyss some 2000m deep. Arising from this cleft are clouds of marine life – the abundance of which almost defies hyperbole. It's the most famous marine destination in the Semporna Archipelago.

Mid Reef The central, eastern-facing portion of the Sea Wall, which often contains one of the finest concentrations of marine life in the entire archipelago.

Barracuda Point Schools of undulating barracuda form seemingly impenetrable walls of scales and fins.

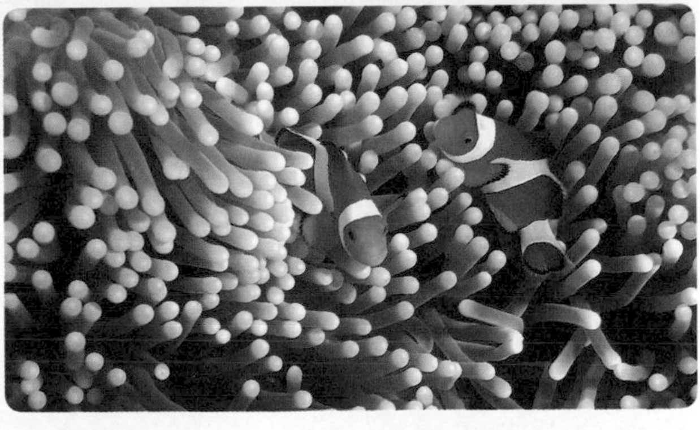

Top: Diving, Sipadan (p98)

Bottom: Clown anemonefish (clownfish)

Coral Garden A sloped wall inhabited by macro sea life. White tip reef sharks sometimes roll by, pecking the coral clean – but don't worry, they'll leave you alone.

Hanging Garden Sea fans peek out among the many overhangs that give this area its name.

South Point Excellent spot for larger marine life such as manta rays.

Turtle Tombs/Caves You can't fit into these coral caverns, which may be for the best, as they shelter the bones and shells of countless sea turtles who got lost inside and drowned.

Around Semporna

Other diving locations around Semporna:

Mabul Rich in all types of marine life, and particularly good for muck diving (searching out smaller life forms in the sea mud), although you're also likely to spot rays and sea turtles.

Mataking Vertical wall dives here lead you past grey reef sharks and manta rays, among other outstanding forms of marine life.

Kapalai Relatively easy, but offers exceedingly rewarding diving in conditions that are often shallow and sandy. Also one of the best places in the world for macro diving, with an excellent chance of seeing blue-ring octopus, bobtail squid, cardinal fish and orangutan crabs.

WATERY WAYPOINT

Travellers know Sipadan as a diving destination. But if you're a marine biologist (or a fish), you'll know Sipadan as, essentially, the grand highway interchange for the Indo-Pacific basin, one of the world's seminal marine habitats. Any tropical fish worth its fins ends up swimming by here at some point. OK, that's a bit of an exaggeration, but the Semporna Archipelago does sit atop a pretty incredible watery confluence, and Sipadan is the crossroads of that confluence. Part of the reason is the excellent condition of local reefs; sadly, much of the nearby coral, especially in the Philippines and Indonesia, has been seriously degraded by pollution and dynamite fishing.

Elsewhere in Borneo

Derawan Archipelago Has some brilliant pier, cave and wall dives.

Layang Layang A remote island renowned for wall dives, pristine coral and real adventure.

Pulau Mantanani Two little flecks of land ringed by a halo of colourful coral.

Brunei Burgeoning dive scene, pristine reefs and accessible wrecks.

Miri Visibility is variable, but the area has some interesting wrecks.

Responsible Diving

Here's how you can do your part to keep the Semporna Archipelago healthy for future generations of fish and divers:

- Don't touch or stand on coral. Even a strong flipper kick can irreparably damage a reef.
- Practise neutral buoyancy. It makes for a more pleasant dive, and keeps you off the coral.
- Keep your gear tight. Don't let gauges, fins and other accessories scrape the sea floor or coral.
- Observe the sea life, but don't try and handle any living creatures, especially turtles; trying to touch them causes them stress and can be especially detrimental to egg-bearing females.
- Don't feed sea creatures. When you feed wildlife, it stops being wild.
- Make sure your operators don't anchor on coral (this isn't much of an issue in Semporna, where operators are quite conscientious, but it's always a good idea to be vigilant).
- Put all rubbish into a bag and take it out. Don't toss anything overboard.
- Participate in local conservation efforts. Every now and then accommodation owners in Mabul try and clean up rubbish in the local villages – give a helping hand.
- Avoid eating the local marine life – especially shark fin soup (sold at local Chinese restaurants).

Regions at a Glance

Sabah, in Borneo's far north, brings together lush rainforests – prime orangutan habitat – with some of the world's most phenomenal scuba diving. More excellent diving awaits south of the Indonesian border on Kalimantan's east coast, and there's plenty of jungle adventures to be had inland, along and between Kalimantan's major rivers. On Borneo's northwest coast, Sarawak is home to the island's most accessible national parks – based in the sophisticated but laid-back city of Kuching, you can take day trips to see orangutans and (if you're lucky) a 75cm-wide rafflesia flower, hike in the jungle and visit longhouse communities. Tiny Brunei, with a tempo and culinary customs all its own, offers visitors pristine rainforest and grand architecture – from opulent mosques to the world's largest water village.

Sabah

Hiking & Trekking
Diving
Jungle Wildlife

Climbing Kinabalu

The highest mountain in Borneo is an endurance test awaiting the fit and willing – with the right preparation even novice climbers can make it to the summit of Mt Kinabalu.

Spectacular Semporna

With clouds of marine life including hammerhead sharks, parrotfish, and green and hawksbill turtles, the diving at Sipadan in the Semporna Archipelago is some of the finest in the world.

Orangutan Encounters

Slowly swinging through the canopy comes the shaggy ginger mass of an orangutan – to glimpse one of these primates is to be reduced to grinning awe. Sepilok Orangutan Rehabilitation Centre is one of the best places in the world to see semi-wild orangutans up close.

p40

Sarawak

Hiking & Trekking
Cave Exploration
Jungle Wildlife

Highland Treks

There is no shortage of places to take a stroll through Sarawak's equatorial rainforest, but the cooler air of the remote Kelabit Highlands is perfect for an exhilarating trek through the jungle from Bario to Ba Kelalan.

Caving at Mulu

Sarawak is home to a number of impressive caverns with stalactites and bats, but for sheer size and spectacle you can't beat the caves of Gunung Mulu National Park, renowned for the gigantic Deer Cave and the 700m-long Sarawak Chamber.

Bako's Wildlife

Wild jungle animals including proboscis monkeys, bearded pigs and families of long-tailed macaques are easy to spot on the rocky peninsula of Bako National Park, where hiking trails lead through rare lowland ecosystems with pitcher plants and orchids.

p119

Brunei

Culture
Food
Primary Jungle

Extraordinary Architecture

Bandar Seri Begawan's two opulent 20th-century mosques feature eye-popping architecture and sumptuous interior decor, but many visitors find the traditional lifestyle and architecture of Kampong Ayer, a Malay stilt village, more engaging.

Night Market Magic

Bruneian cuisine may not be well known, but we can guarantee you've never eaten anything like *ambuyat* (made from sago starch), and that the delicious *kuih* (baked sweets) at Gadong Night Market will perfectly complement a quick chicken satay or curry meal.

Ulu Temburong

The sultanate has done a fine job of preserving its tracts of primary jungle, especially at Ulu Temburong. It's protected within a tightly controlled national park, providing breathing space for Borneo's beasts.

p198

Kalimantan

Hiking & Trekking
Jungle Wildlife
Diving

Meratus Mountains

The easiest area for jungle exploration – with a wide range of guides available – is the stunning Pegunungan Meratus (Meratus Mountains), using Loksado as base camp.

Kutai's Orangutans

If you're an amateur naturalist, Kalimantan's rainforests will exceed even your wildest dreams. A good guide can help you identify gibbons, macaques, flying squirrels, monitor lizards, crocodiles and giant butterflies; Kutai National Park is your best bet for spotting truly wild orangutans.

Diving Derawan

In the Derawan Archipelago, surrounded by the Celebes Sea, you can swim in coral-blue water with giant green turtles, manta rays, myriad reef fish, sharks and whales. Borneo's best-kept secret!

p218

On the Road

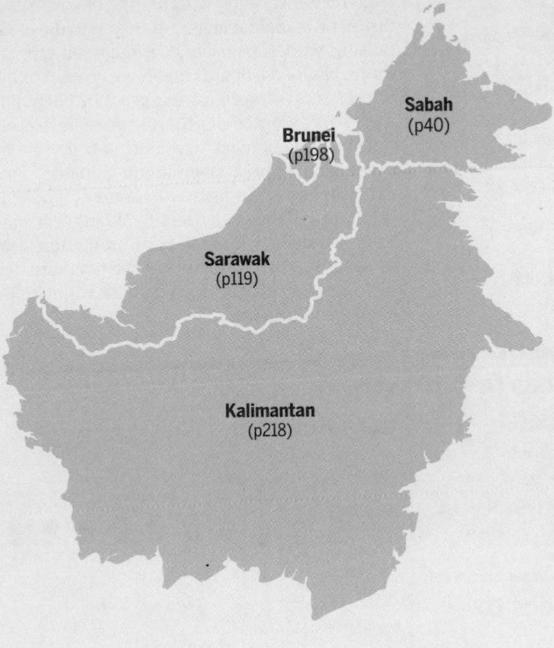

Sabah

POP 3.12 MILLION / AREA 76,115 SQ KM

Includes ➡

Best Places to Eat

- ➡ Kohinoor (p52)
- ➡ Sim Sim Seafood Restaurant (p79)
- ➡ Alu-Alu Cafe (p51)
- ➡ KK Night Market (p52)

Best Places to Stay

- ➡ Shangri-La's Tanjung Aru Resort & Spa (p50)
- ➡ Mañana (p71)
- ➡ Lupa Masa (p68)
- ➡ Tampat Do Aman (p73)
- ➡ Orou Sapulot (p112)

Why Go?

Pint-sized Sabah occupies a relatively small chunk of the world's third largest island, yet what a colourful punch it packs: the treasure of turquoise-fringed desert islands with coral reefs swarming with marine biodiversity; trekkers' paradise Mt Kinabalu reaching 4095m into the clouds; and jungles pulsing with a menagerie of bug-eyed tarsiers, gibbons, pythons, clouded leopards and huge crocs. Around 55% of Sabah is forest, and protected areas like the Maliau Basin and the Danum Valley Conservation Area are more accessible than ever.

Given its compact size, getting from one of Sabah's highlights to the next is eminently doable, plus as a former British colony, English is commonly spoken here, making it extremely traveller friendly. Whether it's pearl hunting in Kota Kinabalu, watching baby orangutans learning to climb at Sepilok, beach flopping on the northern Tip of Borneo, or diving or trekking, your time here will feel like five holidays condensed into one.

When to Go

Kota Kinabalu

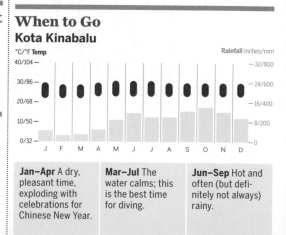

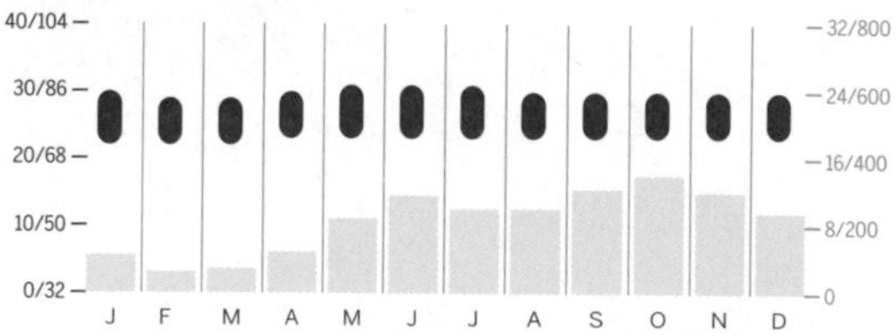

Jan–Apr A dry, pleasant time, exploding with celebrations for Chinese New Year.

Mar–Jul The water calms; this is the best time for diving.

Jun–Sep Hot and often (but definitely not always) rainy.

Sabah Highlights

1. Diving among wild sea turtles and sharks on the multicoloured reefs of the **Semporna Archipelago** (p98).
2. Exploring the misty wilderness of the **Danum Valley Conservation Area** (p92), between scoping for tarsiers, clouded leopards and orangutans.
3. Hoofing it over granite moonscapes for the ultimate Bornean sunrise atop **Mt Kinabalu** (p59).
4. Breathing in the air of an actual virgin rainforest in the **Maliau Basin Conservation Area** (p108).
5. Watching rescued orangutans and sun bears in **Sepilok** (p81).
6. Floating down a river through primary jungle to the Batu Punggul rock formation in **Sapulot** (p112).
7. Enjoying the thriving art scene of **Kota Kinabalu** (p42).
8. Facing off with very large crocs while cruising in a little tin boat down the **Sungai Kinabatangan** (p86).

KOTA KINABALU

088 / POP 457,325

Kota Kinabalu (KK) won't immediately overwhelm you with its beauty, but you'll soon notice its friendly locals, breathtaking fiery sunsets, blossoming arts and music scene, and rich culinary spectrum spanning Malay to Japanese, Western to Cantonese, street food to high end. Alongside swanky new malls springing up at every turn, and a wave of expensive condos accommodating a rush of expats, old KK, with its markets stocked to the gills with leviathans, pearls, and busy fishers shuttling about the waterfront, happily endures. This may be a city on the move with the 21st century, but its old-world charm and history are very much alive.

While on any given day it's much too humid to walk from one end of the city to the other – you'll be hopping in and out of cabs – the city is conveniently compact when it comes to booking your wildlife and diving adventures, and treks to Mt Kinabalu. Believe us, KK will soon grow on you once you get to know it.

Sights & Activities

City Centre & Waterfront

Night Market MARKET

(Jln Tun Fuad Stephens; late afternoon-11pm) Huddled beneath Le Méridien hotel, the northeast end of the market is a huge hawker centre where you can eat your way through the entire Malay range of food, while the fish-and-food market behind extends to the waterfront. Think row upon row of bug-eyed bream, tuna, tiger prawns and red snapper and everything in between…a rainbow of silver and pink scales; the oddly intoxicating scent of saltwater, death, blood and spices intensifying the closer you get to the water.

Signal Hill Observatory Platform LANDMARK

(Jln Bukit Bendera; 8am midnight) Up on Signal Hill, among the art deco mansions at the eastern edge of the city centre, there's an unmissable UFO-like observation pavilion. Come here to make sense of the city layout below. The view is best as the sun sets over the islands. To reach it, catch a cab (RM15), as there's no bus.

Atkinson Clock Tower LANDMARK

The modest timepiece at the foot of Signal hill is one of the only structures to survive the Allied bombing of Jesselton in 1945. It's a square, 15.7m-high wooden structure that was completed in 1905 and named after the first district officer of the town, FG Atkinson, who died of malaria aged 28.

Central Market MARKET

(Jln Tun Fuad Stephens; 5.30am-5.30pm) The Central Market is a nice spot for people watching as locals go about their daily business. Nearby, the **Handicraft Market** (Filipino Market; Jln Tun Fuad Stephens; 8am-9pm) is a good place to shop for inexpensive souvenirs. Offerings include pearls (most are farmed), textiles, seashell crafts, jewellery and bamboo goods, some from the Philippines, some from Malaysia and some from other parts of Asia. Bargaining a must.

Sunday Market MARKET

(Jln Gaya; 6am-about noon Sun) On Sundays, a lively Chinese street fair takes over the entire length of Jln Gaya. It's vividly chaotic, with stalls cheek by jowl hawking batik sarongs, umbrellas, fruit and antiques.

KK Heritage Walk WALKING TOUR

(012-802 8823; www.kkheritagewalk.com; walk incl tea break, batik bandana & booklet RM200; 2½hr walk departs 9am daily) This 2½-hour tour, which can be booked through any of KK's many tour operators (just ask at your hotel front desk), explores colonial KK and its hidden delights. Stops include Chinese herbal shops, bulk produce stalls, a *kopitiam* (coffee shop) and Jln Gaya (known as Bond St when the British were in charge). Guides speak English, Chinese and Bahasa Malaysia.

There's also a quirky treasure hunt at the end leading tourists to the Jesselton Hotel.

Beyond the City Centre

Some of KK's best attractions are located beyond the city centre, and it's well worth putting in the effort to check them out.

Sabah Museum MUSEUM

(Kompleks Muzium Sabah; 088-253 199; www.museum.sabah.gov.my; Jln Muzium; admission

SUNDAY MARKET WARNING

During KK's big Sunday Market, animals lovers may prefer to avoid the market area where Jln Gaya intersects Beach St; overheating, thick-furred Persian kittens and gasping puppies in mesh cages are likely to distress.

KK'S ART SCENE

KK is buzzing with festivals and gigs, you just need to keep an eye out for them. While the free and widely available monthly glossy magazine *Sabah* lists upcoming events, it's also worth checking out **SPArKS** (Society of Performing Arts Kota Kinabalu; www.sparks.org.my). SPArKS works with the US Embassy to bring world-famous acts over here to play gigs in intimate venues, as well as organising the hugely popular **Jazz Festival** in June or July (check out http://kkjazzfest.com), and the **KK Arts Festival**, which also runs through June and July.

Look out too for the new and quirky street market, **Tamutamu**, which is part arts and crafts, part eclectic gathering, with artists, musos and tarot readers. Happening on the third Sunday of every month from 10am to 5pm, it also features the work of the brilliant Cracko Art Gallery (p53). Enquire at Biru Biru restaurant (p50).

RM15; ⏰9am-5pm Sat-Thu; P) About 2km south of the city centre, this refurbished museum is the best place to go in KK for an introduction to Sabah's ethnicities and environments, with new signage and clear explanations. Expect tribal and historical artefacts, including ceramics and a centrepiece whale skeleton, and replica limestone cave. The **Heritage Village** has traditional tribal dwellings, including Kadazan bamboo houses and a Chinese farmhouse, all nicely set on a lily-pad lake.

The adjoining **Science & Education Centre** has an informative exhibition on the petroleum industry, from drilling to refining and processing. The **Sabah Art Gallery** features regular shows and exhibitions by local artists. Hold on to your ticket: it also includes entry to the Museum of Islamic Civilisation, and Agnes Keith House in Sandakan.

Mari Mari Cultural Village MUSEUM
(☎088-260 501; www.traversetours.com/sabah/marimari-cultural-village; Jln Kiansom; adult/child RM160/130; ⏰tours at 10am, 2pm & 6pm; P) With three-hour tours, Mari Mari showcases various traditional homes of Sabahan ethnic communities – the Bajau, Lundayeh, Murut, Rungus and Dusun – all of which are built by descendants of the tribes they represent. Along the way you'll get the chance to see blowpipe making, tattooing, fire-starting, and an insight into the mystical belief systems of each of these groups, as well as a notable culinary nibble from each tribe! It's touristy, sure, but good fun – especially for families.

A short dance recital is also included in the visit. The village is a 20- to 30-minute drive north of central KK. There is also a small waterfall – **Kiansom Waterfall** – about 400m beyond the cultural village, which is easily accessible by private transport or on foot. The area around the cascade lends itself well to swimming and it's a great place to cool off after a visit to Mari Mari.

Monsopiad Cultural Village MUSEUM
(☎088-774 337; www.monsopiad.com; Kg Kuai/Kandazon, Penampang; adult/child RM75/free; ⏰9am-5pm; P) Monsopiad is named after a legendary warrior and head-hunter. The highlight is the House of Skulls, which supposedly contains the ancient crania of Monsopiad's unfortunate enemies, as well as artefacts illustrating native rituals from the time when the *bobolian* (priest) was the most important figure in the community. The village is 16km from KK; to get here independently, take bus 13 from central KK to Donggongon (RM1.50), where you can catch a minivan to the cultural village (RM1). Taxis from KK cost RM40.

Kota Kinabalu Wetland Centre BIRD SANCTUARY
(☎088-246 955; www.sabahwetlands.org; Jln Bukit Bendera Upper, Likas District; admission RM15; ⏰8.30am-6pm Tue-Sun; P) Featuring 1.4km of wooden walkways passing through a 24-hectare mangrove swamp, expect to see scuttling fiddler and mangrove crabs, mud lobsters, mudskippers, skinks, turtles, water monitors and mangrove slugs (sadly, there are also plastic bottles.). For many, the big attraction is a stunning variety of migratory birds. To get here, take the bus towards Likas from the bus stations in front of City Hall or Wawasan Plaza in the city, to Likas Sq. A taxi from KK costs around RM15.

Museum of Islamic Civilisation MUSEUM
(☎088-538 234; admission RM15; ⏰9am-5pm Sat-Thu; P) This museum consists of six galleries devoted to Muslim culture and

Kota Kinabalu

Malaysian history. The five domes represent the holy Five Pillars of Islam. It's in need of a facelift and an update, but can fill up an hour or two of a slow afternoon.

To get to the museum, 2km south of the city, catch a bus (RM1) along Jln Tunku Abdul Rahman and alight just before the mosque. It's a short but steep walk uphill to the museum. A taxi will cost around RM10 to RM15.

Bus 13 also goes right round past the Queen Elizabeth Hospital and stops near Jln Muzium (look for the Sacred Heart Church).

Kota Kinabalu

Sights

1 Atkinson Clock Tower A3
2 Central Market C3
3 Night Market B3
4 Signal Hill Observatory Platform D2
5 Sunday Market A2

Activities, Courses & Tours

6 Adventure Alternative Borneo A2
7 Borneo Adventure A6
8 Borneo Divers B1
9 Borneo Nature Tours B6
10 Downbelow Marine & Wildlife Adventures A6
11 GogoSabah A1
12 River Junkie A1
Riverbug/Traverse Tours .... (see 14)
Scuba Junkie .... (see 11)
13 Sticky Rice Travel A3
14 Sutera Harbour A1

Sleeping

15 Borneo Backpackers B2
16 Borneo Gaya Lodge B2
17 Bunibon B2
Celyn City Hotel .... (see 26)
18 Grandis Hotel D1
19 Hotel Eden 54 .... B1
20 Hotel Sixty3 .... B1
21 Hyatt Regency Kota Kinabalu C2
22 Imperial Boutec Hotel B4
23 Jesselton Hotel B2
24 Kinabalu Backpackers B2
25 Kinabalu Daya A2
26 Klagan Hotel B4
Le Hotel .... (see 26)
27 Le Méridien Kota Kinabalu B3
28 Lucy's Homestay B2
29 Pod's Backpackers B4
30 Rainforest Lodge A2
31 Seasons Street Lodge A3
32 Sky Hotel B6
33 Summer Lodge A3

Eating

7-Eleven .... (see 36)
34 Alu-Alu Cafe D1
Biru Biru .... (see 15)
35 Centre Point Food Court B4
36 Chili Vanilla A2
37 El Centro A2
38 Grazie D1
39 Kedai Kopi Fatt Kee A2
40 Kohinoor B4
41 Milimewa Superstore A2
Nagisa .... (see 21)
42 Night Market B3
43 October Cafe B2
44 Print Cafe B2
45 Tong Hing Supermarket B1
46 Wisma Merdeka Food Court A1
47 Ya Kee Bah Kut Teh B2

Drinking & Nightlife

48 Bed B4
49 Black World A2
El Centro .... (see 37)
Hunter's .... (see 25)
Shamrock .... (see 40)
Shenanigan's .... (see 40)
50 Upperstar C2

Entertainment

Suria Sabah .... (see 38)

Shopping

51 Borneo Shop A1
52 Borneo Trading Post B3
53 Cracko Art Gallery B2
54 Handicraft Market B3
55 Natural History Publications A1
56 Oceanus Waterfront Mall B4
57 Suria Sabah Shopping Mall D1

Information

Australian Consulate .... (see 20)
58 British Honorary Consul B2
59 HSBC B1
60 Indonesian Consulate B6
61 Maybank A1
62 Standard Chartered Bank B1

Puh Toh Tze Buddhist Temple BUDDHIST TEMPLE

(Mile/Batu 5.5, 20min north of KK; 8am-5pm) FREE This impressive temple features a stone staircase-pavilion flanked by 10 Chinese deities leading up to a main temple complex dominated by Kwan Yin, Goddess of Mercy. A Chinese-style reclining Buddha rests inside. The temple is on a small hill west of the main highway junction north; you can get here by taking the Jln Tuaran bus or, more easily, by hiring a taxi; a round-trip shouldn't be more than RM36.

Che Sui Khor Moral Uplifting Society RELIGIOUS SITE

(Jln Tuaran) FREE About four minutes north-east of KK, this complex has an 11-storey pagoda that shimmers in orange and green. The Society espouses believing in the best Islam, Taoism, Buddhism and Christianity have to offer. Get here via the bus terminal at Wawasan Plaza going north on the Jln Tuaran route (RM3). To get home, just stand outside the temple on the main road and a minibus or regular bus will pick you up. A return taxi should cost around RM30.

City Mosque MOSQUE
(off Jln Tun Fuad Stephens) Built in classical style, this mosque is far more attractive than the State Mosque in both setting and design. Completed in 2000, it can hold up to 12,000 worshippers. It can be entered by non-Muslims outside regular prayer times, but there's not much worth seeing inside. It's about 5km north of the centre. To get here, take bus 5A from Wawasan Plaza going towards UMS (RM1.50). Ask the conductor to drop you off outside the City Mosque after the Tanjung Lipat roundabout.

Entry is free but robe hire will set you back a few ringgit.

State Mosque MOSQUE
(Jln Tunku Abdul Rahman) Sabah's State Mosque is a perfect example of contemporary Malay Muslim architecture: all modernist facade and geometric angles. The building is south of the city centre past the Kampung Air stilt village, not far from the Sabah Museum; you'll see the striped minaret and chevronned dome on your way to or from the airport. Non-Muslim visitors are allowed inside, but should dress appropriately.

Tanjung Aru BEACH
This pretty sweep of sand begins around the Shangri-La's Tanjung Aru Resort and stretches south to the airport. Tanjung Aru is a locals' beach, full of picnic spots and swoony-eyed couples. Food stalls are plentiful, most closing up come dark. We would advise against swimming here; the water may look pretty, and some locals may tell you it's fine, but others claim it's tainted by run-off from KK and nearby water villages.

Orchid De Villa FARM
(☎088-380 611; www.orchid-de-villa.com.my; Jln Kiansom; ⏲8am-5pm; P) If you're crazy about flora, head to this farm, located about 20km from central KK, along the road to Penampang. The farm specialises in rare Bornean orchids, hybrid orchids, cacti and herbal plants, and provides all of the five-star hotels in the region with flower arrangements. At the last count there were 300 different kinds of orchids.

Lok Kawi Wildlife Park ZOO
(☎088-765 710, 088-765 793; Jln Penampang; adult/child RM25/10; ⏲9.30am-5.30pm, last entry at 4.30pm; P) About an hour from KK (20km), a visit to this zoo offers a chance to see Sabah's creatures if you are unable to spot them in their natural environment. We warn you, however, that the tiger and sun bear enclosures are lamentably bare and small, and the orangutans are made to peel coconuts for tourists. Other animals include tarsiers, proboscis monkeys, pygmy elephants and rhinoceros hornbills, and there's a train which carts you around the park (RM2).

Bring plenty of water, hats and snacks (there's no shop in the park but there is a store outside), and order a cab from your hotel. It should cost around RM130 there and back, plus waiting time. The 20A minibus goes to Lok Kawi (RM2). Visitors with a private vehicle can access the park via the Papar–Penampang road or the Putatan–Papar road.

Tours

KK has a huge number of tour companies, enough to suit every taste and budget. Head to Wisma Sabah – this office building on Jln Haji Saman is full of agents and operators.

★Sticky Rice Travel ADVENTURE TOUR
(☎088-251 654; www.stickyricetravel.com; 3rd fl, 58 Jln Pantai; ⏲9am-6pm) *National Geographic* prefers this outfit for a reason: they're organised, original in their choice of tours and have excellent knowledgeable guides. Responsible community-based tourism; expect adventure, culture and something very different. Sticky Rice will sit down with you and tailor your experience around your interests, fitness and budget; your trip may last four days or a few weeks.

★Adventure Alternative Borneo ADVENTURE TOUR
(☎019-802 0549; www.aaborneo.com; 1st fl, 97 Jln Gaya; ⏲9am-6pm) Sustainable and ethical travel are key to this British-owned company, which works closely with Sabah Tourist Board, and run tours to Lupa Masa rainforest camp, close to Mt Kinabalu. If you're looking for remote natural immersion, they also operates trips to Sapulot.

★Borneo Divers DIVING
(☎088-222 226; www.borneodivers.net; 9th fl, Menara Jubili, 53 Jln Gaya; ⏲9am-6pm) Top-notch dive outfit with a strong pedigree as the longest operator in Sabah, and excellent authoritative dive instructors who are especially good at teaching Professional Association of Diving Instructors (PADI) courses. Also based on Mabul island, it can take you diving all over Sabah. Good kit, great safety record, nice people.

★Scuba Junkie DIVING
(☎088-255 816; www.scuba-junkie.com; Ground fl, lot G7, Wisma Sabah, Jln Haji Saman; ⏰9am-6pm) Also based on Mabul island, Scuba Junkie is the most ecologically progressive dive outfit, ploughing part of their profits into their turtle hatchery and turtle rehab centre, as well as employing a shark conservationist and an environmentalist. SJ tends to attract a younger, Western crowd. Great vibe, friendly instructors. Along with Borneo Divers, these are your go-to-guys on Mabul.

River Junkie RAFTING
(☎088-255 816 017-601 2145; www.river-junkie.com; Ground fl, lot G7, Wisma Sabah, Jln Haji Saman) Diving operator Scuba Junkie's affiliated river-rafting outfit, River Junkie, comes highly recommended by travellers. Day trips out of KK (costing from RM200 to RM400 per person with transfers) include leisurely boat tours and proboscis-monkey spotting through to more expensive white-water rafting expeditions and side trips to sites like the Mari Mari Cultural Village. Bookings normally require 24 hours' advance notice.

Equator Adventure Tours CULTURAL TOUR
(☎013-889 9535, 088-766 351; www.facebook.com/equator.tours; ⏰9am-6pm) Equator runs the Hajah Halimah Traditional cooking course (RM175), giving you the chance to get savvy with Malaysian cuisine in an authentic environment. You'll be picked up at 9am from your hotel and spirited to the wet market for ingredients, then learn how to make two memorable dishes. Runs until 12.30pm, transfers included.

GogoSabah TOUR
(☎012-838 5566; www.gogosabah.com; Lot G4, ground fl, Wisma Sabah, Jln Haji Saman; ⏰9am-6pm Mon-Sat) Gogo is useful for car and motorbike rentals and has a range of 150cc enduro bikes for tackling dirt roads (RM80 per day), as well as small cars (RM120 per day).

Bike Borneo BICYCLE TOUR
(☎088-484 734; www.bikeborneo.com; City Mall, Jln Lintas, Kota Kinabalu; 1-day tours from RM245; ⏰9am-6pm) Fieldskills Adventures, who operate Bike Borneo, run their mountain-biking activities largely out of Tuaran; packages include a one-day ride in the vicinity of town that crosses three swinging bridges, and a four-day cycling adventure across the foothills of Mt Kinabalu. Groups are small with a maximum of six persons. Bikes are well maintained, guides experienced. City Mall is about 6km east of central KK.

FIND YOUR WAY IN KK

Downtown KK is a dense grid of concrete buildings nestled between the waterfront and a range of low, forested hills to the east. It's compact, walkable (when not too humid) and easy to navigate – most of the restaurants, markets, accommodation, tourist offices and tour operators are located here. Transport terminals bookend the city on either side.

Riverbug/Traverse Tours ADVENTURE TOUR
(☎088-260 511, 088-260 501; www.riverbug.asia/sabah; Lot 227, 2nd fl, Wisma Sabah, Jln Tun Fuad Stephens; ⏰9am-6pm) An excellent and forward-thinking operator that makes admirable efforts to engage in sustainable travel practices. Runs a wide variety of tours across Sabah, including white-water rafting trips down the Sungai Padas from Beaufort.

The rafting day trip starts in KK at 5.20am, involves a three-hour train journey to Beaufort, then riding seven separate grade 3 & 4 rapids over 9km of the muddy-brown Padas river. Riverbug deliver you back to KK for 6pm, dog-tired but fully exhilarated!

Fieldskills Adventures ADVENTURE TOUR
(☎088-484 734; http://fieldskills.com.my; City Mall, Jln Lintas; ⏰9am-6pm) If you're into outdoor activities and adventure, get in touch with this outfit, which leads well-regarded cycling, rock climbing, trekking and diving trips across Sabah. City Mall is about 6km east of central KK.

Borneo Adventure ADVENTURE TOUR
(☎088-486 800; www.borneoadventure.com; block E-27-3A, Signature Office, KK Times Sq; ⏰9am 6pm) Award-winning Sarawak-based company with very professional staff, imaginative sightseeing and activity itineraries and a genuine interest in local people and the environment. Get in touch if you're heading to the Maliau Basin.

Borneo Authentic BOAT TOUR
(☎088-773 066; www.borneo-authentic.com; Lot 3, 1st fl, Putatan Point, Jln JKR) A friendly operation offering a variety of package tours including day-trip cruises on the Sungai Klias, as well as diving and cycling options. Located in Putatan, about 11km south of central KK.

Downbelow Marine & Wildlife Adventures DIVING
(☎012-866 1935; www.divedownbelow.com; Lot 67 & 68, 5th fl, KK Times Sq Block; ⏰9am-6pm) A well-respected dive outfit, with an office in KK and a PADI Centre on Pulau Gaya, that can arrange all kinds of travel packages across Borneo.

Borneo Eco Tours TOUR
(☎088-438 300; www.borneoecotours.com; Pusat Perindustrian Kolombong Jaya, Mile 5.5 Jln Kolombong; ⏰9am-6pm) Arranges tours throughout Malaysian Borneo to Danum Valley, Mt Kinabalu, the Crocker Range and Maliau Basin, as well as a new community-based program at Camp Lemaing (near Mt Kinabalu). Its office is about 6km northeast of the city centre.

Borneo Nature Tours NATURE TOUR
(☎088-267 637; www.borneonaturetours.com; Block D, lot 10, Kompleks Sadong Jaya, Ikan Juara 4; ⏰9am-6pm) Borneo Nature Tours runs Danum Valley's luxurious Borneo Rainforest Lodge, as well as operating tours to the Maliau Basin. Its office building is on the corner near a canal.

Sutera Harbour TREKKING
(Sutera Sanctuary Lodges; ☎088-308 914/5; www.suteraharbour.com; Ground fl, lot G15, Wisma Sabah, Jln Haji Saman; ⏰9am-6pm) Sutera runs a lot of the tourism activities in Sabah, and has a monopoly on accommodation in Mt Kinabalu National Park (p59). Make this your first stop in KK if you're planning to climb Kinabalu and didn't book your bed in advance.

Borneo Dream DIVING
(☎088-244 064; www.borneodream.com; F-G-1 Plaza Tanjung Aru, Jln Mat Salleh) Operating out of Kota Kinabalu and at the Gaya Island Resort (p58), on Pulau Gaya, this outfit has a good name and can take you diving on a try dive excursion or take you through your PADI paces to become an open-water diver. Near terminal 2 of the airport, southeast of town.

THE SABAH LOOP

A decent sealed road makes a frowning arc from KK to Tawau, passing Mt Kinabalu, Sepilok, Sandakan, Lahad Datu and Semporna (the gateway to Sipadan) along the way. So, getting from KK to Tawau via the northern half of the island, via a big frown, is simple. And now, thanks to the recent completion of the road between Sapulot and Tawau, the same can be said of the south side of the loop (going back to KK from Tawau). Sealed in 2015, it passes right by the formerly elusive Maliau Basin, dropping explorers right by the park entrance, and will save you bags of time.

Sleeping

Check out the Sabah Backpacker Operators Association (www.sabahbackpackers.com), which was set up in an effort to help shoestring travellers in the region. KK's midrange options proliferate less than the many high-end and backpacker choices, but there are deals to be found off-peak.

★ **Pod's Backpackers** HOSTEL $
(☎088-287 113; admin-kk@podsbackpacker.com; 1st fl, Api-Api Centre, Jln Centre Point; dm/s/d RM35/60/80; ❄📶) Everyone's rightly talking about Pod's. This uber-friendly hostel is clean, helps you with forward travel and organising trips, and has six fresh avocado-green rooms with a zen-like simplicity (three doubles, three dorms), free wi-fi and free safety lockers. But most of all, we love the easy vibe they've created here; they want you to feel like you're at home.

★ **Borneo Backpackers** HOSTEL $
(☎088-234 009; www.borneobackpackers.com; 24 Lg Dewan; dm/s/d incl breakfast from RM37/60/80; ❄📶) Turquoise and chic with Hoi An lanterns, choice art, wood floors and an excellent cafe down below firing up Asian fusion cuisine, this is one of KK's best backpacker haunts. Dorms and rooms are immaculate, with art-stencilled walls, a balcony and reading room to chill in, and constantly whirring fans. Better still, it's the HQ of Sticky Rice Travel (p46).

Borneo Gaya Lodge HOSTEL $
(☎088-242 477; www.borneogayalodge.com; 1st fl, 78 Jln Gaya; dm incl breakfast from RM25, d/q with bathroom RM85/119; ❄@📶) This friendly hostel pipes air-con through its entirety – phew! With a cosy communal lounge, the place is quiet and clean, while the friendly staff are happy to help you book tours and give you general advice.

Lucy's Homestay HOSTEL $
(Backpacker's Lodge; ☎088-261 495; http://borneohostel.wix.com/lucyshomestay; Lot 25, Lg Dewan, Australia Pl; dm/s/d incl breakfast RM28/58/68; 📶) Lucy's welcomes with brightly muralled walls, a book exchange (lots of travel tomes) and a plant-filled balcony

to flop on. There's a house-proud kitchen and basic wood floor, and fan-only rooms and dorms, all with shared bathroom. It's calm, quiet and without a hint of laddish noise. Check out the 100-year-old banyan tree towering above you out the back.

Seasons Street Lodge HOSTEL **$**
(☎088-253 867; seasonsstreet123@gmail.com; 123 Jln Gaya; dm/s/d/f incl breakfast RM40/50/75/130; ❄@📶) This popular new digs has a busy, happening vibe and thumping soundtrack in reception. There's a TV room, plenty of places to sit in the breezy lobby, fresh basic dorms and rooms with stencilled artwork, colourful walls, free lockers, and clean bathrooms.

Bunibon HOSTEL **$**
(☎088-210 801; www.bunibonlodge.com; Lot 21, Lg Dewan; dm RM30, r without/with bathroom 70/85; ❄📶) This friendly hostel has large double rooms, uncramped dorms, a great kitchen area and chilling/TV lounge with loads of DVDs. The staff can help you book trips around Sabah. While the decor is unimaginative, there is, however, air-con throughout.

Kinabalu Backpackers HOSTEL **$**
(☎088-253 385; www.kinabalubackpackers.com; Lot 4, Lg Dewan; dm/s/d from RM25/55/68; ❄📶) Despite lacking any vibe whatsoever, this bland hostel is clean, icy-cool and OK to kip for the night while trying to get in to a more atmospheric option. They can organise onward travel and tours.

Summer Lodge HOSTEL **$**
(☎088-244 499; www.summerlodge.com.my; Lot 120, Jln Gaya; dm/d RM35/65; ❄📶) Summer Lodge, compared to the new backpacker haunts, feels unloved and decrepit. That said, it's cheap, central and just above the booming Beach St bar complex.

★ **Hotel Sixty3** HOTEL **$$**
(☎088-212 663; www.hotelsixty3.com; Jln Gaya 63; r/f from RM276/452; ❄@📶) This fabulous hotel has an international feel in its 100 rooms, with glossy floors, evocative black-and-white photos on the walls, dark-wood fittings, subtle down-lighting, olive colour schemes, flat screens and safety deposit boxes. Stylish.

Klagan Hotel HOTEL **$$**
(☎088-488 908; www.theklagan.com; Block D, Warisan Sq, Jln Tun Fuad Stephens; r/f RM313/470; ❄📶) Superfresh rooms with thick carpets, rain showers, tangerine-hued walls, large beds and attractive furniture. Rooms also boast comfy work chair, desk, flat screen and downlighting. There's a nice cafe/bakery in the lobby, but the real ace card is the restaurant on the 11th floor with widescreen views of the sea and nearby islands. The buffet breakfast is superb; for nonresidents it costs RM30.

Hotel Eden 54 BOUTIQUE HOTEL **$$**
(☎088-266 054; www.eden54.com; 54 Jln Gaya; d/f RM139/239; ❄📶) In the shadow of Signal Hill, this dinky hotel boasts plenty of boutique flair, with stylish rooms decked in chocolate drapes, glass-topped desks, contemporary bedheads and burgundy or peacock-green walls. Eden is fragrant, like walking into a perfume factory, and there's a communal kitchen area behind the lounge. A fine choice for flashpackers, couples, even families. Avoid windowless rooms.

Jesselton Hotel HOTEL **$$**
(☎088-223 333; www.jesseltonhotel.com; 69 Jln Gaya; r RM215-239; ❄📶) The time-worn stucco facade may suggest faded grandeur, but within, all is sumptuous; think thick carpets, Rungus bed runners, marble-heavy bathrooms and sleek two-tone walls. The lobby is deliciously welcoming, the restaurant bright and airy. The oldest hotel in KK doesn't need to manufacture character – it fairly drips with it.

Sky Hotel HOTEL **$$**
(☎154-876 1941; www.skyhotelkk.com; Lg Kemajuan Karamunsing; r/f from RM208/418; P⊖❄@📶≋) In the business district close to the city centre, this skyscraping, modern hotel is great value if there's more than one of you. With cool, spacious suites enjoying modern fittings, amazing city views, self-catering facilities, flat screens, huge beds and, even better, a rooftop swimming pool and an excellent vegetarian breakfast buffet crammed with fresh fruits, yoghurt, cereal and eggs.

Le Hotel HOTEL **$$**
(☎088-319 696; www.lehotel.com.my; Block B, 3rd fl, Warisan Sq, Jln Tun Fuad Stephens; r RM120-158, f RM195; ❄📶) Up on the 3rd floor you'll find this colourful, pint-sized hotel with friendly staff. The rooms, while decidedly spacious for hobbits, are not so for anyone else. That said, they're nicely finished with upscale touches. Ask for one with a view of the water.

Kinabalu Daya HOTEL **$$**
(☎088-240 000; www.kkdayahotel.com; Lot 3-4, block 9, Jln Pantai; r/ste incl breakfast from RM146/320; ❄📶) While it won't win any design awards, this basic midtier hotel is solid,

with tastefully finished, comfy, clean rooms with fridges, flat screens, desks and contemporary bathrooms. Doubles are cramped.

Rainforest Lodge HOTEL $$
(☎088-258 228; www.rainforestlodgekk.com; Jln Pantai; dm/s/d/ste from RM40/115/135/165; ❄@🛜) Located in the swinging centre of the 'Beach Street' complex, the Rainforest is all of a stairward stumble from some of KK's best nightlife. Rooms are refreshingly chic, a nice mix of modern and Sabah-tribal style, and many have cool balconies that look onto the Beach St parade below. Just be warned: it gets loud at night.

Imperial Boutec Hotel HOTEL $$
(☎088-525 969; 7th fl, Warisan Sq; r RM175-220; 🚭❄🛜) This hotel has almost 100 rooms of varying sizes with laminate floors, flatscreens, contemporary fittings and modern bathrooms. Everywhere you look there's an overpowering theme of orange. Up on the 7th floor of Warisan Sq, it feels a little cut off and bland, but the rooms are nonetheless adequate.

Celyn City Hotel HOTEL $$
(☎088-448 787; www.celyns.com; Lot 21, Warisan Sq; r from RM150-180; ❄🛜) Located in a mall, this 72-room hotel has decent rooms with contemporary furniture, safety deposit box and flat-screen TVs. The walls and carpets feel fresh. Though perhaps lacking in overall character, the hotel has a handy, central location.

★**Shangri-La's Tanjung Aru Resort & Spa** RESORT $$$
(STAR; ☎088-327 888; www.shangri-la.com/kotakinabalu/tanjungaruresort; Tanjung Aru; r from RM550; P❄🛜🏊) Located in the Tanjung Aru area about 3km south of the city centre, this may be the finest hotel in Sabah; think beautifully stylish rooms with huge baths, comfy-as-cloud beds, sea-view balconies looking out over manicured, flower-filled gardens, spa treatments, a chic breakfast bar, plus lashings of water sports available. Pure, unblemished bliss; this is the place to relax.

★**Grandis Hotel** HOTEL $$$
(☎088-522 888; www.hotelgrandis.com; Grandis Hotels & Resorts, Suria Sabah Shopping Mall 1, Jln Tun Fuad Stephens; r from RM368-498; 🚭❄@🛜🏊) Attached to the Suriah Sabah Shopping mall, this four-star hotel is unfailingly clean and stylish. Standard rooms are huge, while family suites are large enough to tenpin bowl in. The last word in style, rooms have soaring views of the waterfront, baths, plush modern fittings, downlighting and flat-screen TVs. Another ace is the Sky Bar on the rooftop with unblemished views and a swimming pool.

Hyatt Regency Kota Kinabalu HOTEL $$$
(☎088-221 234; www.kinabalu.regency.hyatt.com; Jln Datuk Salleh Sulong; r from RM560; P❄🛜🏊) Built in '67, from the outside the Hyatt looks decidedly dated; however inside it's a marble oasis of soaring ceilings, dark-wood chic and an inviting open-plan restaurant and lounge in the lobby. Lowlit rooms are huge, stylish affairs with all the mod cons: flat screen, rainshower, fine linen. Be sure to ask for discounts outside of peak season.

Le Méridien Kota Kinabalu HOTEL $$$
(☎088-322 222; www.lemeridienkotakinabalu.com; Jln Tun Fuad Stephens; r from RM450-500; P❄🛜🏊) Five-star comfort with a freshly refurbished lobby contrasting sober dark woods with soothing lighting seguing blue to pink. Rooms are less inventive with international, somewhat anonymous decor, and minibar, flat screens and cable TV. That said, at the time of research rooms were due a date with the makeover wizard, so watch this space. Prices come down in low season.

Eating

KK is one of the few cities in Borneo with an eating scene diverse enough to refresh the noodle-jaded palate. Besides the ubiquitous Chinese *kedai kopi* (coffee shops) and Malay halal restaurants, you'll find plenty of interesting options around the city centre.

City Centre

★**Print Cafe** CAFE $
(☎013-880 2486; 12 Lg Dewan; mains RM12; ⏲8.30am-10.30pm) In the backpacker street of Lg Dewan, this brilliant cafe is a cool (in both senses of the word) place to catch your breath, read a book or play Jenga at one of its tables. Excellent coffee, papaya and orange shakes, a selection of cakes and waffles, pizza and lovely service. Keep an eye out for ingeniously foamed cappuccinos.

Biru Biru FUSION $
(24 Lg Dewan; mains RM9-13; ⏲9am-late) Based at Borneo Backpackers, this blue joint is Asian fusion galore, with dishes like fish cooked in lime and ginger, huge tacos and an ever-evolving menu. Try the Lihing rice wine (aka rocket fuel). With its parasols and bikes on the wall, and lovely manager Jules, it's easy to fall in love with this place.

October Cafe CAFE $

(☎016-810 1274; Lg Dewan; bagels RM5; ⏰11am-10pm) Adding more appeal to backpacker street Lg Dewan, October is fresh with a wood-accented interior and upstairs balcony; great coffee, herbal teas, French toast, juices, cakes and bagels.

Ya Kee Bah Kut Teh CHINESE $

(☎088-221 192; 74 Jln Gaya; mains from RM8; ⏰4-11pm) Expect brisk service at this rammed plastic-chair joint spilling noisily onto the pavement in the centre of the old town. The buffet counter bubbles with noodles and glistens with sauce-laden pork. That's right, Cantonese-style pork, in herbal soup, fatty pork ribs…every which way you can. It's hot, crowded and delicious.

El Centro INTERNATIONAL $

(☎019-893 5499; www.elcentro.my; 32 Jln Haji Saman; mains RM15; ⏰11am-midnight Tue-Sun; 📶) Turquoise-and-orange-walled El Centro is superfriendly and cool, with a menu spanning Malysian and Mexican fare: tacos, pizza, chorizo wraps, chicken and beef burgers. They even do bangers and mash. Occasional live music.

Kedai Kopi Fatt Kee CHINESE $

(28 Jln Bakau; mains from RM8; ⏰noon-10pm Mon-Sat) The woks are always sizzlin' at this popular Cantonese joint next to Ang's Hotel. Look out for sweet-and-sour shrimp and oyster-sauce chicken wings.

Wisma Merdeka Food Court FOOD COURT $

(Wisma Merdeka, Jln Haji Saman; mains from RM5; ⏰9am-5pm) For cheap, excellent eats, head to the top floor of the Wisma Merdeka mall and get stuck into stalls serving mainly Asian street food; the Chinese dumpling stand is particularly delicious. In general this is a breakfast and lunch food court.

★ **Alu-Alu Cafe** SEAFOOD $$

(Jessleton Point; mains from RM15-30; ⏰10.30am-2.30pm & 6.30-10pm; ❄) 🍃 Drab on the outside, perhaps, but this restaurant wears its stripes in the tastiness of its food, and the fact it gets its seafood from sustainable sources – no shark-fin soup here. Alu-Alu

MAKAN: KK-STYLE

Kota Kinabalu's (KK's) melting pot of cultures has fostered a lively dining scene that differentiates itself from the rest of Malaysia. KK's four essential eats:

Sayur Manis Also known as 'Sabah veggie', this bright-green jungle fern can be found at any Chinese restaurant worth its salt. It's best served fried with garlic, or mixed with fermented shrimp paste. The *sayur manis* plant is a perennial and can grow about 3m high. It is harvested year-round, so it tends to be very fresh. Adventurous eaters might want to try other local produce like *tarap*, a fleshy fruit encased in a bristly skin, or *sukun*, a sweet-tasting tuber used to make fritters.

Filipino Barbecue Located at the north end of the KK Night Market (p52), the Filipino Barbecue Market is the best place in town for grilled seafood at unbeatable prices. Hunker down at one of the crowded tables and point to your prey. Once one of the waitstaff has sent your order off to the grill, they'll hand you a cup (for drinking), a basin (to wash your hands) and a small plate to prepare your dipping sauce (mix up the chilli sauce, soy sauce, salt and fresh lime for your own special concoction). No cutlery here! Just dig in with your bare hands and enjoy steaming piles of fresher-than-fresh seafood. Figure around RM15 for a gut-busting meal.

Hinava Perhaps the most popular indigenous appetiser, colourful *hinava* is raw fish pickled with fresh lime juice, *chilli padi*, sliced shallots and grated ginger. The melange of tangy tastes masks the fishy smell quite well. The best place to try *hinava* is Grace Point, a posh local food court near Tanjung Aru. You'll find it at the 'Local Counter' for around RM2 per plate (the portions are small – the perfect size for a little nibble).

Roti Canai The ubiquitous *roti canai*, a flaky flat bread fried on a skillet, is served from dawn till dusk at any Indian Muslim *kedai kopi* (coffee shop) around town. Although the dish may appear simple, there's actually a lot of skill that goes into preparing the perfect platter. The cook must carefully and continuously flip the dough (à la pizza chef) to create its signature flakiness. *Roti canai* is almost always served with sauce, usually dhal (lentil curry) or another curry made from either chicken or fish.

DON'T MISS

KK'S HAWKER CENTRES & FOOD COURTS

As in any Southeast Asian city, the best food in KK is the street food and hawker stalls. If you're worried about sanitation, you really shouldn't be, but assuage your fears by looking for popular stalls, especially those frequented by families.

Night Market (Jln Tun Fuad Stephens; satay RM1, fish/prawn per 100g from RM4/15; ⊙5-11pm) The night market is the best, cheapest and most interesting place in KK for barbecued squid, ray and a vast selection of delicious seafood cooked up right before your eyes.

Centre Point Basement Food Court (Basement, Centre Point Shopping Mall, Jln Raya Pantai Baru; mains from RM3; ⊙9am-9.30pm; ☑) Your ringgit will go a long way at this popular and varied basement food court in the Centre Point mall. There are Malay, Chinese and Indian options, as well as drink and dessert specialists.

Grace Point (Jln Pantai Sembulan; mains RM2-8; ⊙11am-3pm) Take bus 15 out near Tanjung Aru for some local grub at this KK mainstay. The development is actually quite chic compared to the smoke-swathed food courts in the city centre – KKers joke that the public bathrooms here are Borneo's nicest (and it's true!). Go for the Sabahan food stall (located in the far right corner when facing the row of counters) and try *hinava* (raw fish pickled with fresh lime juice, *chilli padi*, sliced shallots and grated ginger).

excels in taking the Chinese seafood concept to new levels, with dishes such as lightly breaded fish chunks doused in a mouthwatering buttermilk sauce, or simmered amid diced chillies.

★**Kohinoor** INDIAN $$
(☑088-235 160; Lot 4, Waterfront Esplanade; mains RM17-30; ⊙11.30am-2.30pm & 5.30-11pm; ❄☑) Come to this silk-festooned waterfront restaurant for northern Indian cuisine and classic dishes ranging from chicken tikka masala to prawn biryani and lamb rogan josh. The aromas from its tandoori oven are mouth watering, the naan bread pillowy-soft, and the service pure old-world charm. You'll be back more than once.

Grazie ITALIAN $$
(☑019-821 6936; 3-36, 3rd Fl, Suria Sabah Shopping Mall; mains from RM20; ⊙noon-10pm Mon-Sun; ❄) Delightful Italian cuisine in a stylish restaurant with exposed-brick walls and mozaic floors. Dishes span from ravioli with spinach to spaghetti bolognaise, seafood risotto, heavenly thin-crust pizza and melt-in-the-mouth panna cotta.

Chili Vanilla FUSION $$
(35 Jln Haji Saman; mains RM20-30; ⊙10am-10.30pm Mon-Sat, 5-10.30pm Sun; ❄🌐) This cosy bijoux cafe is run by a Hungarian chef and is a real fave with travellers thanks to its central location. The menu makes an eclectic voyage through goulash, spicy duck tortillas, Moroccan lamb stew and gourmet burgers. Inside it's dinky, tasteful and peaceful.

Nagisa JAPANESE $$$
(☑088-221 234; Hyatt Regency, Jln Datuk Salleh Sulong; mains RM40-220; ⊙noon-10pm; ❄☑) Superswanky Nagisa exudes class and executes Japanese cuisine with élan, with a wealth of sushi dishes from California *temaki* (crabstick, avocado and prawn roe) and *ebi tempura maki* (crispy prawn rolled with rice) to *agemeon* (deep-fried dishes) and noodles. Located in the Hyatt Regency.

Self-Catering

There is a variety of places to stock up on picnic items and hiking snacks, including the centrally located **Milimewa Superstore** (Jln Haji Saman; ⊙9.30am-9.30pm) and **Tong Hing Supermarket** (Jln Gaya); **7-Eleven** (Jln Haji Saman; ⊙24hr) is conveniently open throughout the evening.

🍴 Tanjung Aru

In the early evening, head to Tanjung Aru, at the south end of town near the airport, for sunset cocktails and light snacks along the ocean. The area has three beaches: First Beach offers up a few restaurants, Second Beach has steamy local stalls, and Third Beach is a great place to bring a picnic as there are no establishments along the sand. A taxi to Tanjung Aru costs RM20, or you can take bus 16, 16A or city bus 2 from Wawasan Plaza (RM2).

🍷 Drinking & Nightlife

Get ready for loads of karaoke bars and big, booming nightclubs, clustered around the

Waterfront Esplanade, KK Times Sq, where the newest hot spots are congregating, and Beach St, in the centre of town, a semipedestrian street cluttered with bars and eateries.

★El Centro BAR

(32 Jln Haji Saman; ⏲5pm-midnight, closed Mon) El Centro is understandably popular with local expats and travellers alike; it's friendly, the food is good and it makes for a nice spot to meet other travellers. With cool tunes, and a laid-back vibe, nonsmokey El Centro also hosts impromptu quiz nights, costume parties and live-music shows.

Bed CLUB

(☎088-251 901; Waterfront Esplanade; admission Fri & Sat incl drink RM20, beer from RM21; ⏲8pm-2am, to 3am Fri & Sat) KK's largest club thunders with pop, gyrating Filipino musicians, shrill teenagers and boasts guest DJs nightly. It's overcrowded and cheesy, but if you're looking for a party, this is it. Bands play from 9pm.

Shenanigan's BAR

(☎088-221 234; Hyatt Regency Hotel, Jln Datuk Salleh Sulong; ⏲5pm-1am Mon-Fri, to 2am Sat) Shani's, as it's affectionately known, enjoys a loyal crowd who are happy to pay the high prices. Below the Hyatt at street level, it has a beer garden and pool table, plus live bands from the Philippines. Head here for happy hour (daily 5pm to 9pm) to avoid being fleeced.

Shamrock BAR

(☎088-249 829; 6 Anjung Samudra, Waterfront Esplanade; ⏲noon-1am Sun-Thu, to 2am Fri & Sat) About as Irish as a Made-in-China leprechaun, this is, however, a good spot for a bit of rock music in its wood-panelled interior. Cool Guinness on tap, but best of all is the alfresco, sea-fronting terrace when the sunset douses the sky with bloody fire.

Hunter's BAR

(☎016-825 7085; Kinabalu Daya Hotel, Jln Pantai; ⏲11am-2am) A favourite for local guides and expats, Hunter's offers up karaoke, sport on the plasma TV and balmy outdoor seating in the heart of the city.

Upperstar BAR

(Jln Datuk Salleh Sulong; mains RM10-25; ⏲noon-11pm) Festooned with eclectica from Bruce Lee pics to musical instruments, Upperstar has a fine balcony that's a breezy place for a sundowner come evening, plus if you're feeling peckish, there's a Western-leaning menu featuring grilled meats and fish and chips.

Black World BAR, KARAOKE

(Jln Pantai; ⏲24hr) We know. This is the only spot that stays open past 2am in central KK. But here's what to expect: cheap beer served in iced buckets, ear-shredding karaoke and dance music, sleazy male clientele, ladies of negotiable affection and bathrooms from the deepest pits of hell.

☆ Entertainment

Suria Sabah CINEMA

(Suria Sabah Shopping Mall, Jln Haji Saman) The Suria Sabah mall houses a huge multiplex that shows all the Hollywood hits, usually in the original English with subtitles.

Shopping

KK is fast becoming a shopaholic's heaven, with leading brands in uber smart malls across the city. The latest is the Oceanus Waterfront Mall, chock-full of designer brands, and Western coffee and food outlets.

★Cracko Art Gallery ARTS

(www.facebook.com/crackoart; cnr Jln Bakau & Jln Gaya; ⏲noon-8pm) Made up of a group of brilliantly talented KK artists, high up on the 3rd floor (look for the Cracko sign outside on the street), you'll find a vivid working studio of abstract and figurative art, stunning jewellery, and sculpture from Manga-style figurines to mannequin-art. Affordable and original work, a visit here makes for a great hour.

In the same space, keep an eye out for Lost At Sea, a boutique tattoo parlour with amazing designs by Taco Joe and his ink men.

Oceanus Waterfront Mall SHOPPING CENTRE

(Jln Tun Fuad Stephens; ⏲10am-10pm; 📶👪) The city centre's newest mall, this gleaming palace of consumerism has all the top Western brands, from sunglasses shops to coffee-house chains, beauty products to fashion.

Natural History Publications BOOKS

(☎088-240 781; www.nhpborneo.com; 9th fl, Wisma Merdeka Mall, Jln Haji Saman; ⏲9am-8pm Mon-Sat) Easily the best resource in the country for pictorial and textual books on Sabah's culture, ethnicity, traditions, and wildlife and flora, at a fraction of the price you'll pay elsewhere.

Borneo Trading Post CRAFTS
(☎088-232 655; Lot 16, Waterfront Esplanade, Jln Tun Fuad Stephens) Upmarket tribal art and souvenirs.

Borneo Shop BOOKS
(☎088-241 050; Shop 26, ground fl, Wisma Merdeka Phase 2, Jln Haji Saman; ⊙10am-8pm Mon-Sun) Books, gifts, prints and postcards. There's a wealth of wildlife and flora books all focused on Borneo.

Information

Free maps of central KK and Sabah are available at almost every hostel or hotel.

EMERGENCY

Ambulance (☎088-218 166, 999)

Fire (☎994)

Police (☎088-253 555, 999; Jln Dewan, near Australia Pl)

INTERNET ACCESS

The majority of accommodation options have some form of wi-fi internet connection.

Borneo Net (Jln Haji Saman; per hour RM4; ⊙9am-midnight) Twenty terminals, fast connections and loud head-banger music wafting through the air.

Net Access (Lot 44, Jln Pantai; per hour RM5; ⊙9am-midnight) Plenty of connections and less noise than other net places in KK. LAN connections are available for using your own laptop.

IMMIGRATION OFFICES

Immigration office (☎088-488 700; Kompleks Persekutuan Pentadbiran Kerajaan, Jln UMS; ⊙7am-1pm & 2-5:30pm Mon-Fri) In an office complex near the Universiti Malaysia Sabah (UMS), 9km north of town. Open on weekends, but only for Malaysian passport processing.

MEDICAL SERVICES

Permai Polyclinics (☎088-232 100; www.permaipolyclinics.com; 4 Jln Pantai; consultation weekday RM60, Sat & Sun RM80; ⊙doctors on duty 8am-6pm, emergency 24hr) Excellent private outpatient clinic.

Sabah Medical Centre (☎088-211 333; www.sabahmedicalcentre.com; Lg Bersatu, off Jln Damai) Good private hospital care, located about 6km southeast of the city centre.

MONEY

Central KK is chock-a-block with 24-hour ATMs.

HSBC (☎088-212 622; 56 Jln Gaya; ⊙9am-4.30pm Mon-Thu, to 4pm Fri)

Standard Chartered Bank (☎088-298 111; 20 Jln Haji Saman; ⊙9.15am-3.45pm Mon-Fri)

POST

Main Post Office (Jln Tun Razak; ⊙8am-5pm Mon-Sat) Western Union cheques and money orders can be cashed here.

MAIN DESTINATIONS & FARES FROM KOTA KINABALU

The following bus and minivan transport information was provided to us by the Sabah Tourism Board and should be used as an estimate only: transport times can fluctuate due to weather, prices may change and the transport authority has been known to alter departure points.

DESTINATION	DURATION	PRICE	TERMINAL	FREQUENCY
Beaufort	2hr	RM15	Padang Merdeka	7am-5pm (frequent)
Keningau	2½hr	RM25	Padang Merdeka	7am-5pm (8 daily)
Kota Belud	1hr	RM10	Padang Merdeka	7am-5pm (frequent)
Kuala Penyu	2hr	RM20	Segama Bridge	8-11am (hourly)
Kudat	3hr	RM22	Padang Merdeka	7am-4pm (frequent)
Lahad Datu	8hr	RM55	Inanam	7am, 8.30am, 9am, 8pm
Lawas (Sarawak)	4hr	RM25	Padang Merdeka	8am
Mt Kinabalu National Park	2hr	RM15-20	Inanam & Padang Merdeka	7am-8pm (very frequent)
Ranau	2hr	RM20	Padang Merdeka	7am-5pm
Sandakan	6hr	RM45	Inanam	7am-2pm (frequent) & 8pm
Semporna	9hr	RM75	Inanam	7.30am, 8.30am, 2pm & 7.30pm
Tawau	9hr	RM80	Inanam	7.30am, 8am, 10am, 12.30pm, 4pm & 8pm
Tenom	3½hr	RM25	Padang Merdeka	8am, noon, 2pm & 4pm

DON'T MISS

RIDING THE BORNEO RAILS

Back in the late 19th century, colonials used to swan around the western Sabah coast on the **North Borneo Railway**, which eventually fell into disuse and disrepair. Recently, the old iron horse has been restored, with natural wood interiors and the original exterior colour scheme of green and cream, set off with the railway's old brass emblem of a crown surmounting a tiger holding a rail wheel.

While it's not an unmissable great train journey of the world, and yes it's a bit twee, it's still great family fun. The train leaves KK at 9.30am and arrives in Papar at 11.45am, taking in mountains and rice paddies, with stops for a look at a Chinese temple and the Papar wet market. On the trip back to KK (12.20pm to 1.40pm), a smashing colonially inspired tiffin lunch of cucumber sandwiches and satay is served.

The railway is operated by Sutera Harbour (p48); adult/child tickets cost RM318/159. The train leaves the station in Tanjung Aru twice a week, on Wednesday and Saturday. It's worth mentioning, however, that the old train occasionally runs out of steam (literally), forcing passengers to taxi back to KK from wherever the train retires. For more information or to book tickets, contact Sutera Harbour (www.suteraharbour.com/north-borneo-railway).

TOURIST INFORMATION

Sabah Parks (☎088-486 430, 088-523 500; www.sabahparks.org.my; 1st-5th fl, lot 45 & 46, block H, Signature Office KK Times Sq; ⏰8am-1pm & 2-4.30pm Mon-Thu, 8-11.30am & 2-4.30pm Fri, 8am-12.50pm Sat) Source of information on the state's parks.

Sabah Tourism Board (☎088-212 121; www.sabahtourism.com; 51 Jln Gaya; ⏰8am-5pm Mon-Fri, 9am-4pm Sat, Sun & holidays) Housed in the historic post-office building, KK's tourist office has plenty of brochures, maps and knowledgeable staff keen to help you with advice tailored around your needs – they won't just try and sell you a package tour! Their website, packed with helpful information from accommodation to sights, is equally worth a visit. Organised.

Tourism Malaysia (☎088-248 698; www.tourism.gov.my; Ground fl, Api-Api Centre, Jln Pasar Baru; ⏰8am-4.30pm Mon-Thu, 8am-noon & 1.30-4.30pm Fri) This office is of limited use for travellers, but does offer a few interesting brochures on sights in Peninsular Malaysia.

ℹ Getting There & Away

AIR

KK is well served by **Malaysia Airlines** (☎1300-883 000; www.malaysiaairlines.com) and **AirAsia** (www.airasia.com; ground fl, Wisma Sabah, Jln Haji Saman; ⏰8.30am-5.30pm Mon-Fri, to 3pm Sat), which offer the following international flights to/from KK: Brunei, Shenzhen, Jakarta, Manila, Singapore and Taipei. Within Malaysia, flights go to/from Johor Bahru, Kuala Lumpur and Penang in Peninsular Malaysia, and Kuching, Labuan, Lawas, Miri, Kudat, Sandakan, Lahad Datu and Tawau in Borneo. **Jetstar** (www.jetstar.com) and **Tiger Airways** (www.tigerairways.com) both offer flights to Singapore.

BOAT

All passengers must pay an adult/child RM3.80/1.90 terminal fee for ferries departing from KK. Passenger boats connect KK to Pulau Labuan twice daily at 8am and 1.30pm (adult 1st/economy class RM41/36, child 1st/economy class RM28/23), with onward service to Brunei and to Tunku Abdul Rahman National Park. Ferries depart from Jesselton Point, located a little way north of the **Suria Sabah shopping mall** (Jln Haji Saman).

BUS & MINIVAN

Several different stations around KK serve a variety of out-of-town destinations. There is a bus to Brunei.

In general, land transport heading east departs from Inanam (Utara Terminal; 9km north of the city), while those heading north and south on the west coast leave from Padang Merdeka (Merdeka Field) Bus Station (also called Wawasan or 'old bus station'; at the south end of town). Local buses (RM1.80) from Wawasan can take tourists to Inanam if you don't want to splurge on the RM20 taxi. Have your hotel call ahead to the bus station to book your seat in advance. Same-day bookings are usually fine, although weekends are busier than weekdays. It's always good to ring ahead because sometimes transport will be halted due to flooding caused by heavy rains.

TAXI

Share taxis operate from the Padang Merdeka Bus Station. Several share taxis do a daily run between KK and Ranau, passing the entrance road to the Kinabalu National Park office. The fare to Ranau or Kinabalu National Park is RM30 or you can charter a taxi for RM120 per car (note that a normal city taxi will charge around RM250 for a charter).

Getting Around

TO/FROM THE AIRPORT

The international airport is in Tanjung Aru, 7km south of central KK and takes around 25 to 40 minutes to reach by taxi. Note that the two terminals of Kota Kinabalu International Airport (KKIA) are not connected, and at rush hour it can take a while to get from one to the other in the event you go to the wrong one. Most airlines operate out of Terminal 1, but an increasing number of carriers, including Air Asia, depart from Terminal 2.

Airport shuttle buses (adult/child RM5/3) leave Padang Merdeka station hourly between 7.30am and 8.15pm daily, arriving first at Terminal 2 then Terminal 1. Public transport runs from 6am to 7pm daily.

Taxis heading from terminals into town operate on a voucher system (RM30) sold at a taxi desk on the terminal's ground floor. Taxis heading to the airport should not charge over RM40, if you catch one in the city centre.

CAR

Major car-rental agencies have counters on the first floor at KKIA and branch offices elsewhere in town. Manual cars start at around RM120 to RM140 per day and most agencies can arrange chauffeured vehicles as well.

Borneo Express (☎016-886 0793, in Sandakan 016-886 0789; http://borneocar.com/; Lot 1-L01 C4, Kota Kinabalu Airport)

Extra Rent A Car (☎088-218 160, 088-251 529; www.e-erac-online.com; 2nd fl, Beverly Hotel, Jln Kemajuan)

Kinabalu Heritage Tours & Car Rental (☎088-318 311; www.travelborneotours.com; Block F, Tanjung Aru Plaza)

MINIVANS

Minivans operate from several stops, including Padang Merdeka Bus Station, Wawasan Plaza, and the car park outside Milimewa Superstore (near the intersection of Jln Haji Saman and Beach St). They circulate the town looking for passengers. Since most destinations in the city are within walking distance, it's unlikely that you'll need to catch a minivan, although they're handy for getting to the airport or to KK Times Square. Most destinations within the city cost RM4 to RM6.

TAXI

Expect to pay a minimum of RM15 for a ride in the city centre (even a short trip!). Taxis can be found throughout the city and at all bus stations and shopping centres. There's a stand by Milimewa Supermarket (near the intersection of Jln Haji Saman and Beach St) and another 200m southwest of City Park.

AROUND KOTA KINABALU

Tunku Abdul Rahman National Park

Whenever one enjoys a sunset off KK, the view tends to be improved by the five jungly humps of Manukan, Gaya, Sapi, Mamutik and Sulug islands. These swaths of sand, plus the reefs and cerulean waters in between them, make up **Tunku Abdul Rahman National Park** (adult/child RM10/6), covering a total area of just over 49 sq km (two-thirds of which is water). Only a short boat ride from KK, the islands are individually quite pretty, but in an effort to accommodate the ever-increasing tourist flow (especially large numbers of Chinese), barbecue stalls and restaurants now crowd the beaches. On weekends the islands can get *very* crowded, but on weekdays you can easily find some serenity. Accommodation tends to be expensive, but most travellers come here for day trips anyway, and there are camping options.

Diving in the park (especially around Gaya and Sapi) – with a dizzying 364 species of fish found here – may bring you into contact with blue-ringed octopus, black-tip reef shark and shape-shifting cuttlefish. And, if you're here between November to February, it's possible you might sight a whale shark. Borneo Dream (p48) and Downbelow (p48) both run PADI Open Water diving programs on Pulau Gaya.

Getting There & Away

Boats to the park leave from 8.30am to 4.15pm when full from KK's Jesselton Point Ferry Terminal (commonly known as 'The Jetty' by locals and taxi drivers); the last boats leave the islands for KK around 5pm. Service is every 30 minutes, but on slower days this can be every hour. Enquire at the counter for the next available boat, sign up for your chosen destination and take a seat until there are enough passengers to depart. Boats also run from Sutera Harbour – more convenient for those staying near Tanjung Aru (or for those wanting to reach Pulau Gaya).

Return fares to Mamutik, Manukan and Sapi hover around RM23. You can also buy two-/three-island passes for RM33/43.

The set fee for charter to one island is RM250, but this can be negotiated. Try to deal directly with a boat person if you do this – don't talk to the touts who prowl the area. And don't consider paying until you return to the dock.

A terminal fee of RM7.20 is added to all boat journeys, and a RM10 entrance fee to the marine park, paid when you purchase your ticket (if you are chartering a boat this should be included).

Pulau Manukan

Though this dugong-shaped island may not lay claim to as beautiful a beach as Sapi, beneath its waters you'll find far richer coral, and therefore more marine life, attracting snorkellers and divers. It is the second-largest island in the group, its 20 hectares largely covered in dense vegetation. There's a good beach with coral reefs off the southern and eastern shores, a walking trail around the perimeter and a network of nature trails; if you want to thoroughly explore all of the above it shouldn't take more than two hours, and you don't need to be particularly fit. There are little clouds of tropical fish swimming around. When you depart the boat, you'll likely be pointed towards a kiosk that hires equipment masks and snorkels (RM15), beach mats (RM5) and bodyboards (RM10).

Manukan Island Resort (☎017-833 5022; www.suterasanctuarylodges.com; r from RM800; ❄🏊), managed by Sutera Sanctuary Lodges, has the only accommodation on the island. It comprises a restaurant, swimming pool and tennis courts, and 20 dark-wood villas, all overlooking the South China Sea and decked out in tasteful Bali-chic style.

Pulau Mamutik

Mamutik is the smallest island out here, a mere 300m end to end. A sandy 200m beach runs up and down the east coast, although beware of razor-sharp coral beneath the water that can cut your feet. Visibility can often be poor due to strong waves but on a still day the snorkeling is great. Better still, Pulau Mamutik picks up a small portion of the day-tripper footfall, so if you're here during the week, it will be mercifully quiet.

There's no resort here, but camping (RM40 per tent) is available – bring your own mozzie repellent. You'll also find a small store-restaurant-snorkel-rental place, barbecue stalls, resting pavilions, gift shop and public toilets. The last boat to Kota Kinabalu leaves at 5pm.

Pulau Sapi

The tiny sibling to Pulau Gaya, separated by a 200m channel, enjoys huge loads of day trippers to its lovely beach and can get a little overwhelmed on weekends. There are now lifeguards keeping vigil on the beach, and clearly defined areas for swimming. Disgorged from your ferry, expect to see busy clouds of fish swirling around the turquoise dock. There are multiple things to do, including bar flopping on the fine sand and hunting for monitor lizards (coralled behind a fenced area next to the main entrance; don't feed them).

Just back from the beach, you'll find **Borneo Sea Walking** (☎016-801 1161; www.borneoseawalking.com; Sapi dock; 30min sea-walk adult/child RM300/190; ⏲8.30am-3pm), giving nondivers the chance to go 5m deep among clownfish, breathing through a space-age helmet connected by a tube fed with air from

WATER MONITORING

If you look around the edge of the barbecue pits on Sapi, you may spot a fence cordoning off some of the jungle, and at said fence you'll usually find a hissing band of great, grey-green dragons: water monitor lizards, known locally as *biawak*. They're some of the largest reptiles in the world, with males averaging a length of 1.5m to 2m, sometimes growing as large as 3m, weighing anywhere from 19kg to 50kg. Within the lizard family they are only outstripped by Komodo dragons.

These mini-Godzillas are found all over Malaysia, but on Pulau Sapi they are the king of the jungle – and the waves. It's amazing watching these lumbering beasts take to the water, where they instantly transform into graceful sea monsters reminiscent of aquatic dinosaurs (which, indeed, are believed to be the ancestors of monitor lizards).

Warning: don't try and feed them or take a selfie next to one; their bite is poisonous (which can cause swelling and excessive bleeding) and their claws are very sharp.

the boat above. It's perfectly safe and kids love it. You'll also find **Seasport** (Sapi dock; fins, mask & snorkel per day RM15; ☺ 8am-4pm) nearby, where you can hire snorkelling equipment. Snorkelling off the main beach is popular, though drifts of plastic in the water can make the experience less idyllic.

Finally, a zip line connects Pulau Sapi with Pulau Gaya. The **Coral Flyer** (☑ 011-2984 2023; www.coralflyer.com; Sapi Dock; adult/child RM64/30; ☺ 10am-3.30pm) is 250m long, and gathers speeds up to 60km/h. Better still, there are two lines, so you can race a friend. Intrepid kids can go in tandem with a parent. The zip line starts in Gaya and ends in Sapi, so if on Sapi, catch the free transfer boat over the water.

Alternatively, you can explore the trails through Sapi's forest; it takes about 45 minutes to walk around the island. There are changing rooms, toilets, barbecue pits and a small snack kiosk, plus an outfitted campsite (RM40 per tent), but you'll need to bring most supplies from the mainland.

Pulau Gaya

With an area of about 15 sq km, Pulau Gaya is the Goliath of KK's offshore islands, rising to an elevation of 300m. It's also the closest to KK and covered in virtually undisturbed tropical forest. The bays on the east end are filled with bustling water villages, inhabited by Filipino immigrants (legal and otherwise) who live in cramped houses built on stilts in the shallow water, with mosques, schools and simple shops, also built on stilts. Residents of KK warn against exploring these water villages, saying that incidences of theft and other crimes have occurred. Recently, thanks to Sabah Police establishing an office here, crime has reduced considerably.

Three high-end resorts make up the accommodation options on Gaya.

🛌 Sleeping

Bunga Raya Island Resort RESORT $$$
(☑ 088-380 390; http://bungarayaresort.com; villas from RM1200; ✳ 🛜 🏊) Well-spaced villas boasting mod-cons such as satellite TVs, safe-deposit boxes, iPod docks and Bose sound systems, are spread around this tasty resort. The Plunge Pool has its own deep body of water that overlooks the beach, while the romantic Treehouse, reached by a private walkway, perches over a jacuzzi, lounge and its own natural jungle pool. Operated by the owners of Gayana Eco Resort.

Gaya Island Resort RESORT $$$
(☑ in KL 03-2783 1000; www.gayaislandresort.com; villas from RM800; ✳ 🛜 🏊) Around 100-odd beautifully finished villas set in either lush jungle foliage, atmospheric mangrove, or looking out on the greens and blues of the nearby sea. This is a beautiful spot to fish, snorkel and dive, kayak, practise yoga, go on a sunset cruise or take a relaxing spa at the treatment centre. Or, alternatively, swim in its 40m-long pool.

Gayana Eco Resort RESORT $$$
(☑ 088-380 390; www.gayana-eco-resort.com; villas from RM800; ✳ 🛜 🏊) 🍴 Fifty-two stunning villas stuffed with modern amenities and 'island-chic' touches make up posh Gayana. The Bakau (mangrove) Villa overlooks a series of tangled flooded forests, while the Palm Villa's deceptive simplicity masks steps that lead into the warm heart of Tunku Rahman's protected waters.

While here check out their inspiring on-site Marine Ecology Research Centre (MERC), which restores and rehabilitates different forms of marine wildlife; it has had great success in propagating giant clams. Also don't miss the excellent new Alu Alu Seafood restaurant, the sibling of the famous haunt in KK, with fish fresh from its organic farm.

Pulau Sulug

Shaped like a cartoon speech bubble, Sulug has an area of 8.1 hectares and is the least visited of the group, probably because it's the furthest away from KK. It only has one beach, on a spit of land extending from its eastern shore. Unfortunately, the snorkelling is pretty poor and rubbish often washes up on the beach and is not removed. If you want a quiet getaway, Sulug is a decent choice, but you'll have to charter a boat to get here as the normal ferries don't stop here. If you want a secluded beach and don't want to lay out for a charter (at least RM300), you'll do better by heading to Manukan and walking down the beach to escape the crowds.

NORTHWESTERN SABAH

The northern edge of Sabah manages to compact, into a relatively small space, much of the geographic and cultural minutiae that makes Borneo so special. The ocean? Lapping at miles of sandy beach, sky blue to stormy grey, and concealing superlative dive sites. The people? Kadazan-Dusun, Rungus, rice farmers, mountain hunters, ship builders and deep-sea fishers. And then, of course, 'the' mountain: Gunung Kinabalu, or Mt Kinabalu, the focal point of the island's altitude, trekkers, folklore and spiritual energy. For generations, the people of Sabah have been drawn to the mountain; don't be surprised when you fall under its spell too.

Mt Kinabalu & Kinabalu National Park

Gunung Kinabalu, as it is known in Malay, is more than the highest thing on the world's third-largest island. And it is more than scenery. Mt Kinabalu is ubiquitous in Sabah to the point of being inextricable. It graces the state's flag and is a constant presence at the edge of your eyes, catching the clouds and shading the valleys. It is only when you give the mountain your full attention that you realise how special this peak, the region's biggest tourist attraction, truly is.

The 4095m peak of Mt Kinabalu may not be a Himalayan sky-poker, but Malaysia's first Unesco World Heritage Site is by no means an easy jaunt. The main trail up is essentially a very long walk up a very steep hill, past alpine jungle and sunlit moonscapes, with a little scrabbling thrown in for good measure. If you don't feel up to reaching the mountain top, its base has some worthy attractions, including a large network of nature trails.

That said, the main detriment to climbing is not the physical challenge, but the cost. Things are expensive within Mt Kinabalu National Park. Bottled water costs four or five times what it goes for in KK, and Sutera Sanctuary Lodges has a monopoly on accommodation. You'll have to decide if you want to accept these fees, because they are basically the cost of climbing the mountain.

Amazingly, the mountain is still growing: researchers have found it increases in height by about 5mm a year. On a clear day you can see the Philippines from the summit; usually, though, the mountain is thoroughly wreathed in fog by midmorning.

History

Although it is commonly believed that local tribesmen climbed Kinabalu many years earlier, it was Sir Hugh Low, the British colonial secretary on Pulau Labuan, who recorded the first official ascent of Mt Kinabalu in 1851. Today Kinabalu's tallest peak is named after him, thus Borneo's highest point is ironically known as Low's Peak.

In those days the difficulty of climbing Mt Kinabalu lay not in the ascent, but in getting through the jungle to the mountain's base. Finding willing local porters was another tricky matter – the tribesmen who accompanied Low believed the spirits of the dead inhabited the mountain. Low was therefore obliged to protect the party by supplying a large basket of quartz crystals and teeth, as was the custom back then. During the subsequent years, the spirit-appeasement ceremonies became more and more elaborate, so that by the 1920s they had come to include loud prayers, gunshots, and the sacrifice of seven eggs and seven white chickens. You have to wonder at what point explorers started thinking the locals might be taking the mickey... These days, the elaborate chicken dances are no more, although climbing the mountain can still feel like a rite of passage.

On June 5 2015 an earthquake struck the mountain (p62), savagely taking the lives of 18 people.

Geology

Many visitors to Borneo assume Mt Kinabalu is a volcano, but the mountain is actually a huge granite dome that rose from the depths below some nine million years ago. In geological terms, Mt Kinabalu is still young. Little erosion has occurred on the exposed granite rock faces around the summit, though the effects of glaciers that used to cover much of the mountain can be detected by striations on the rock. There's no longer a snowline and the glaciers have disappeared, but at times ice forms in the rock pools near the summit.

Orientation & Information

Kinabalu National Park HQ is 88km by road northeast of KK and set in gardens with a magnificent view of the mountain. At 1588m the climate is refreshingly cool compared to the coast; the average temperatures are 20°C in the day and 13°C at night. The hike to the summit is difficult.

On the morning of your arrival, pay your park entry fee, present your lodging reservation slip to the Sutera Sanctuary Lodges office to receive your official room assignment, and check in with the Sabah Parks office to pay your registration and guide fees. Advance accommodation bookings are *essential* if you plan on climbing the mountain.

Mt Kinabalu Summit Trail

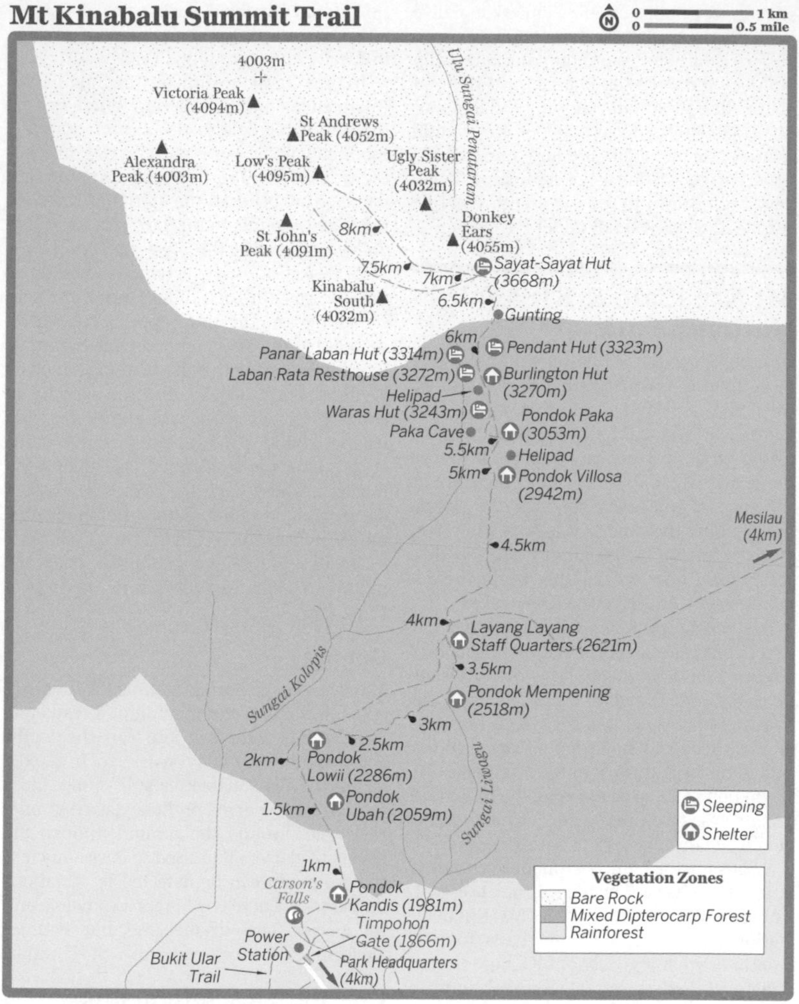

Permits, Fees & Guides

A park fee, climbing permit, insurance and a guide fee are *mandatory* if you intend to climb Mt Kinabalu. All permits and guides must be arranged at the **Sabah Parks office** (⏲7am-7pm), which is directly next door to the Sutera Sanctuary Lodges office, immediately on your right after you pass through the main gate of the park. Pay all fees at park HQ before you climb and don't ponder an 'unofficial' climb as permits (laminated cards worn on a string necklace) are scrupulously checked at two points you cannot avoid passing on the way up the mountain. Virtually every tour operator in KK can hook you up with a trip to the mountain; solo travellers are often charged around RM1400. It's possible, and a little cheaper, to do it on your own – but plan ahead. Packages are obviously easier.

All visitors entering the park are required to pay a park entrance fee: RM15 for adults and RM10 for children under 18 (Malaysians pay RM3 and RM1 respectively). A climbing permit costs RM106/RM42 for adults/children, while Malaysian nationals pay RM31.80/RM12.70. Climbing insurance costs a flat rate of RM7 per person. Guide fees for the summit trek cost RM203 for a group of one to five people. Climbers ascending Kinabalu along the Mesilau trail (when it reopens) will pay an extra RM18 (small group) or RM28 (large group) for their guide.

Your guide will be assigned to you on the morning you begin your hike. If you ask, the park staff will try to attach individual travellers to a group so that guide fees can be shared. Couples can expect to be given their own guide. Guides are mostly Kadazan from a village nearby and many of them have travelled to the summit several hundred times. Try to ask for a guide who speaks English – he or she (usually he) might point out a few interesting specimens of plant life. The path up the mountain is pretty straightforward, and the guides walk behind the slowest member of the group, so think of them as safety supervisors rather than trailblazers.

All this does not include at least RM669 for dorm-and-board or RM1349 for private room and board on the mountain at Laban Rata. With said lodging, plus buses or taxis to the park, you're looking at spending around RM900 for the common two-day, one-night trip to the mountain. It's no longer possible to do a one-day hike to the summit.

Optional extra fees include the shuttle bus (RM33, one way) or taxi (RM18, per person, group of four) from the park office to the Timpohon Gate, a climbing certificate (RM10) and a porter (RM80 per trip to the summit or RM65 to Laban Rata), who can be hired to carry a maximum load of 10kg.

If you need a helicopter lift off the mountain for emergency reasons, the going rate is RM6000.

Equipment & Clothing

No special equipment is required to successfully summit the mountain, however a headlamp is strongly advised for the predawn jaunt to the top – you'll need your hands free to climb the ropes on the summit massif. Expect freezing temperatures near the summit, not to mention strong winds and the occasional rainstorm. Don't forget a water bottle, which can be refilled at unfiltered (but potable) tanks en route. The average temperature range at Kinabalu Park is 15°C to 24°C. Along the Timpohon (the Summit trail), it's about 6°C to 14°C, and can sometimes drop to as low as 2°C.

The Climb to the Summit

This schedule assumes you're doing a two-day/one-night ascent of the mountain. You'll want to check in at park headquarters at around 9am – 8.45am at the latest for *via ferrata* (p63) participants – to pay your park fees, grab your guide and start the ascent (four to six hours) to Laban Rata (3272m), where you'll spend the night before finishing the climb. On the following day you'll start scrambling to the top at about 2.30am in order to reach the summit for a breathtaking sunrise over Borneo.

A climb up Kinabalu is only advised for those in adequate physical condition. The trek is tough, and *every step you take* will be uphill. You will negotiate several obstacles along the way, including slippery stones, blinding humidity, frigid winds and slow-paced trekkers. Mountain Torq (p63) compares the experience to squeezing five days of hiking into a 38-hour trek.

There are two trail options leading up the mountain – the Timpohon Trail and the Mesilau Trail. If this is your first time climbing Kinabalu, we advise taking the Timpohon Trail – it's shorter, easier (but by no means easy!), and more convenient from the park headquarters (an hour's walk or short park shuttle ride to the Timpohon Trail start. If

KINABALU PACKING LIST

- ☐ Headlamp (with spare batteries)
- ☐ Comfortable running or hiking shoes
- ☐ Whistle
- ☐ Energy food (Dextrasol tablets, sweets, chocolate, energy bars)
- ☐ Wool socks and athletic socks
- ☐ Hiking shorts or breathable pants
- ☐ Three T-shirts (one made of lightweight synthetic material)
- ☐ Fleece jacket
- ☐ Lightweight shell jacket, poncho or rain jacket
- ☐ Fleece or wool hat and fleece gloves
- ☐ Hand towel
- ☐ Water bottle
- ☐ Sunscreen and sunglasses
- ☐ Insect repellent
- ☐ Light, high-energy snacks
- ☐ Camera
- ☐ Money
- ☐ Earplugs for dorms

you are participating in Mountain Torq's *via ferrata,* you are required to take the Timpohon Trail in order to reach Laban Rata in time for your safety briefing at 4pm. The Mesilau Trail offers second-time climbers (or fit hikers) the opportunity to really enjoy some of the park's natural wonders. This 8km trail is less trodden so the chances of seeing unique flora and fauna are higher.

As you journey up to the summit, you'll happen upon signboards showing your progress – there's a marker every 500m. There are also *pondok* (rest shelters) at regular intervals, with basic toilets and tanks of unfiltered (but potable) drinking water. The walking times that follow are conservative estimates: don't be surprised if you move at a slightly speedier pace, and certainly don't be discouraged if you take longer – everyone's quest for the summit is different.

Timpohon Gate to Layang Layang

'Why am I sweating this much *already?*'

The trip to the summit officially starts at the Timpohon Gate (1866m) and from there it's an 8.72km march to the summit. There is a small bathroom outhouse located 700m before the Timpohon Gate, and there's a convenience shop at the gate itself for impulse snack and beverage purchases.

After a short, deceptive descent, the trail leads up steep stairs through the dense forest and continues winding up and up for the rest of the trip. There's a charming waterfall, **Carson's Falls**, beside the track shortly after the start, and the forest can be alive with birds and squirrels in the morning. Five *pondok* are spaced at intervals of 15 to 35 minutes between Timpohon Gate and Layang Layang and it's about three hours to the Layang Layang (2621m) rest stop. Near **Pondok Lowii** (2286m), the trail follows an open ridge giving great views over the valleys and up to the peaks.

Layang Layang to Pondok Paka

This part of the climb can be the most difficult for some – especially around the 4.5km marker. You've definitely made some headway but there's still a long trek to go – no light at the end of the jungly tunnel quite yet. It takes about 1¾ hours to reach Pondok Paka (3053m), the seventh shelter on the trail, 5.5km from the start.

Pondok Paka to Laban Rata

Also known as the 'can't I pay someone to finish this for me?' phase, this part of the climb is where beleaguered hikers get a second wind as the treeline ends and the summit starts to feel closer. At the end of this leg you'll reach Laban Rata (3272m), your 'home sweet home' on the mountain. Take a good look at the slender signpost announcing your arrival – it's the propeller of the helicopter once used to hoist the construction materials to build the elaborate rest station. This leg takes around 45 minutes.

Laban Rata to Sayat-Sayat Hut

It's 2am and your alarm just went off. Is this a dream? Nope. You're about to climb the

THE DAY THE MOUNTAIN SHOOK

On 5 June 2015 at 7.15am, an earthquake measuring 6.0 on the Richter scale struck Mt Kinabalu. It was until then a glorious morning, the sky a rich blue, the mountain teeming with trekkers. Massive landslides and huge rockfalls followed, even one of the famous 'Donkey's Ears' rock formations snapped off. The strongest to affect Malaysia since 1976, the quake lasted 30 seconds and tragically took the lives of 18 people, many of them students from Singapore. There were 137 people stranded on the mountain but later saved. That first evening alone three massive aftershocks were felt, and by 23 June, 90 had been felt as far away as Kota Kinabalu.

The 15-million-year-old mountain's name is derived from the Kadazan-Dusun tribe's phrase 'Aki Nabalu', meaning 'the resting place of the souls of the departed'. The Kadazan Dusun consider it a sacred temple and believe the earthquake was caused by 'Aki' (the mountain's protectors), who were enraged at the loutish behaviour of 10 Westerners (who allegedly stripped and urinated, insulted their guide, and two of their cohort even managed to have sex on their ascent of the mountain) on 30 May.

The trail from Timpohon to Laban Rata reopened to climbers in September 2015, with business as usual, and the trail from Laban Rata to the summit reopened on 1 December. At the time of research, the Mesilau Trail was closed until further notice. The number of climbers per day allowed on the mountain has also been reduced from 193 to 135.

VIA FERRATA

Mountain Torq (☎088-268126; www.mountaintorq.com; Low's Peak Circuit RM870, Walk the Torq RM650) has dramatically changed the Kinabalu climbing experience by creating an intricate system of rungs and rails crowning the mountain's summit. Known as *via ferrata* (literally 'iron road' in Italian), this alternative style of mountaineering has been a big hit in Europe for the last century and is just starting to take Asia by storm. In fact, Mountain Torq is Asia's first *via ferrata* system, and, according to the *Guinness Book of World Records*, it's the highest 'iron road' in the world.

After ascending Kinabalu in the traditional fashion, participants use the network of rungs, pallets and cables to return to the Laban Rata rest camp area along the mountain's dramatic granite walls. Mountain Torq's star attraction, the **Low's Peak Circuit** (minimum age 17), is a four- to five-hour scramble down metres upon metres of sheer rock face. This route starts at 3766m, passing a variety of obstacles before linking up to the Walk the Torq path for the last part of the journey. The route's threadlike tightrope walks and swinging planks will have you convinced that the course designers are sadistic, but that's what makes it such fun – testing your limits without putting your safety in jeopardy. Those who don't want to see their heart leaping out of their chest should try the **Walk the Torq** (minimum age 10) route. This two- to three-hour escapade is an exciting initiation into the world of *via ferrata*, offering dramatic mountain vistas with a few less knee-shaking moments. No matter which course you tackle, you'll undoubtedly think that the dramatic vertical drops are nothing short of exhilarating.

At the time of research a new *via ferrata* route was being established to replace Walk the Torq, due to the summit trail being rerouted after the earthquake. For more information, check out www.mountaintorq.com.

last part of the mountain in order to reach the summit before sunrise.

Most people set off at around 2.45am, and it's worth heading out at this time even if you're in great shape (don't forget your torch). The one-hour climb to Sayat-Sayat hut (3668m) involves a lot of hiker traffic and the crossing of the sheer Panar Laban rock face. There is little vegetation, except where overhangs provide some respite from the wind. It is one of the toughest parts of the climb, especially in the cold and dark of the predawn hours. Note that on some particularly steep sections, you have to haul yourself up specially strung ropes (gloves essential).

Sayat-Sayat Hut to Summit

After checking in at Sayat-Sayat, the crowd of hikers begins to thin as stronger walkers forge ahead and slower adventurers pause for sips from their water bottle. Despite the stunning surroundings, the last stretch of the summit ascent is, of course, the steepest and hardest part of the climb.

From just beyond Sayat-Sayat, the summit looks deceptively close and, though it's just over 1km, the last burst will take between one and three hours depending on your stamina. You might even see shattered climbers crawling on hands and knees as they reach out for the top of Borneo.

The Summit

This is it – the million-dollar moment. Don't forget the sunrise can be glimpsed from anywhere on the mountain. The summit warms up quickly as the sun starts its own ascent between 5.45am and 6.20am, and the weary suddenly smile; the climb up a distant memory, the trek down an afterthought.

Consider signing up with Mountain Torq to climb back to Laban Rata along the world's highest *via ferrata*.

The Journey Back to the Bottom

You'll probably leave the summit at around 7.30am and you should aim to leave Laban Rata no later than 12.30pm. The gruelling descent back down to Timpohon Gate from Laban Rata takes between three and four hours (if you're returning to the bottom along the Mesilau Trail it will take more time than descending to the Timpohon Gate). The weather can close in very quickly and the granite is slippery even when dry. During rainstorms the downward trek feels like walking through a river. Slower walkers often find that their legs hurt more the day after – quicker paces lighten the constant pounding as legs negotiate each descending step. If you participated in the *via ferrata* you will be absolutely knackered during your descent and will stumble into

FLORA & FAUNA OF MT KINABALU

Mt Kinabalu is a botanical paradise, designated a Centre of Plant Diversity as well as a Unesco-listed World Heritage Site. The wide range of habitats supports an even wider range of natural history, and over half the species growing above 900m are unique to the area.

Among the more spectacular flowers are orchids, rhododendrons and the *Insectivorous nepenthes* (pitcher plant). Around park HQ, there's dipterocarp forest (rainforest); creepers, ferns and orchids festoon the canopy, while fungi grow on the forest floor. Between 900m and 1800m, there are oaks, laurels and chestnuts, while higher up there's dense rhododendron forest. On the windswept slopes above Laban Rata vegetation is stunted, with *sayat-sayat* a common shrub. The mountain's uppermost slopes are bare of plant life.

Deer and monkeys are no longer common around park HQ, but you can see squirrels, including the handsome Prevost's squirrel and the mountain ground squirrel. Tree shrews can sometimes be seen raiding rubbish bins. Common birds are Bornean treepies, fantails, bulbuls, sunbirds and laughing thrushes, while birds seen only at higher altitudes are the Kinabalu friendly warbler, the mountain blackeye and the mountain blackbird. Other wildlife includes colourful butterflies and the huge green moon moth.

Timpohon Gate just before sunset (around 6pm to 6.30pm).

A 1st-class certificate can be purchased for RM10 by those who complete the climb; 2nd-class certificates are issued for making it to Laban Rata. These can be collected at the park office.

Walks Around the Base

It's well worth spending a day exploring the marked trails around park headquarters; if you have time, it may be better to do it before you climb the mountain, as chances are you won't really feel like it afterwards. There are various trails and lookouts.

The base trails interconnect with one another, so you can spend the day, or indeed days, walking at a leisurely pace through the beautiful forest. Some interesting plants, plenty of birds and, if you're lucky, the occasional mammal can be seen along the **Liwagu Trail** (6km), which follows the river of the same name. When it rains, watch out for slippery paths and legions of leeches.

At 11am each day a **guided walk** (per person RM5) starts from the Sabah Parks office and lasts for one to two hours. The knowledgeable guide points out flowers, plants, birds and insects along the way. If you set out from KK early enough, it's possible to arrive at the park in time for the guided walk.

Many of the plants found on the mountain are cultivated in the **Mountain Garden** (admission RM5; ⌚9am-1pm & 2.30-4pm) behind the visitors centre. Guided tours of the garden depart at 9am, noon and 3pm and cost RM5.

Sleeping

Laban Rata (On the Mountain)

Camping is not allowed on the mountain, and thus access to the summit is limited by access to the huts on the mountain at Laban Rata (3272m). This *must* be booked in advance, the earlier the better. In order to have any hope of clear weather when you reach the summit you must arrive around dawn, and the only way to do this is by spending a night at Laban Rata.

Sutera Sanctuary Lodges (☎088-287 887; http://suterasanctuarylodges.com.my; Lot G15, ground fl, Wisma Sabah; dm/tw incl 3 meals & bedding RM669/1349, nonheated dm incl 3 meals RM587) in Kota Kinabalu operates almost all of the accommodation here, but space is limited. Be mindful that travellers often report frustration with booking huts on the mountain – claiming the booking system is disorganised and inefficient, the huts are often full, or aren't full when they're told they are. Bookings can be made online (but only if you book at least two nights), in person or over the phone – our experience was that it was best to book at Sutera's offices in KK if you haven't done so in advance.

The most common sleeping option is the heated dormitory (bedding included) in the Laban Rata Resthouse, which sells for RM669 per person. If you need privacy, twin shares are available for RM1349. Three meals are included in the price. Nonheated facilities surrounding the Laban Rata

Kinabalu National Park Headquarters & Trails

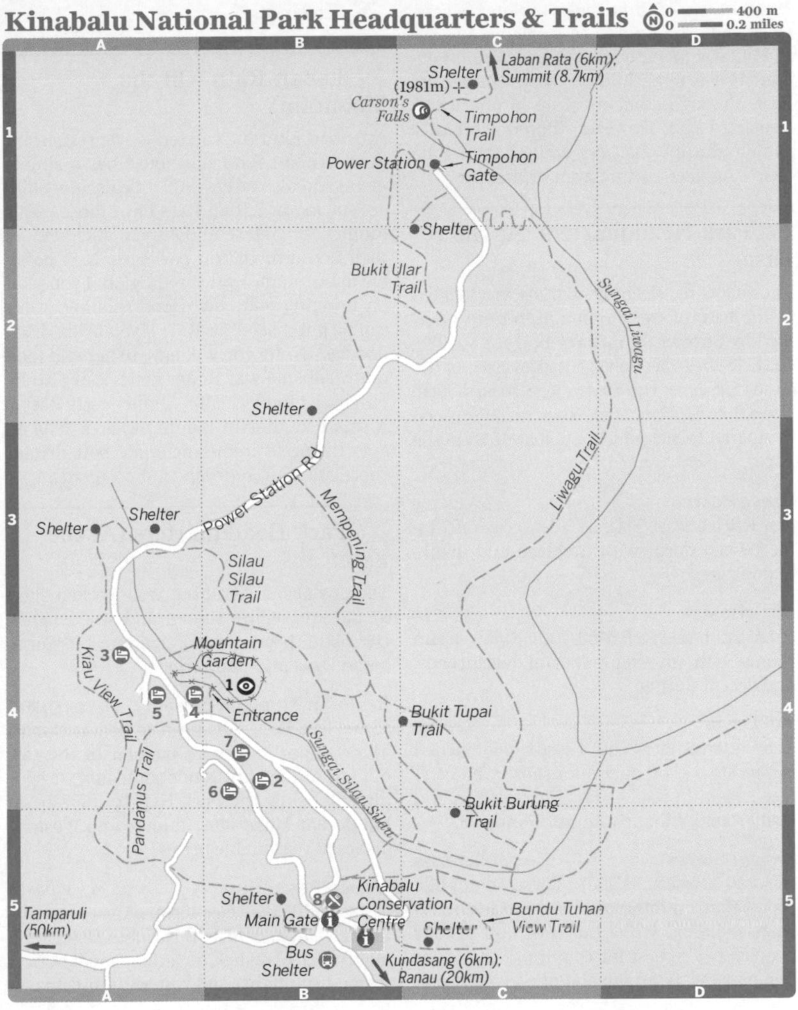

Kinabalu National Park Headquarters & Trails

Sights

1 Mountain Garden B4

Sleeping

2 Grace Hostel B4
3 Hill Lodge A4
4 Liwagu Suites A4
5 Nepenthes Villa A4
6 Peak Lodge B4
7 Rock Hostel B4

Eating

Liwagu Restaurant .... (see 4)
8 Restoran Kinabalu Balsam B5

building are also available for RM587 per person (meals included).

The other option at Laban Rata is to stay at Pendant Hut, which is owned and operated by **Mountain Torq** (☎088-268 126; www.mountaintorq.com; suite 1-3/4, Level 2 Menara MAA, 6 Lg Api Api 1, Kota Kinabalu; r incl via ferrata RM850-4000). All guests sleeping at Pendant

Hut take two of three meals at Sutera's cafeteria, and are required to participate in (or at least pay for) the *via ferrata* circuit. Pendant Hut is slightly more basic (there's no heat, although climbers sleep in uberwarm sleeping bags). However, there's a bit of a summer-camp vibe here while Laban Rata feels more like a Himalayan orphanage.

Park Headquarters (At the Base)

The following sleeping options are located at the base of the mountain and are operated by **Sutera Sanctuary Lodges** (☎088-243 629; www.suterasanctuarylodges.com; lot G15 Wisma Sabah, Jln Haji Saman; ⏰8.30am-4.30pm Mon-Sat, to 12.30pm Sun). They're overpriced compared to sleeping spots just outside the park.

Grace Hostel HOSTEL $
(dm incl breakfast RM250) Clean, comfortable 20-bed dorm with fireplace and drink-making area.

Rock Hostel HOSTEL $$
(dm/d incl breakfast RM250/700) Small clean rooms with inviting colourful bedspreads, and decent dorms.

Hill Lodge CABIN $$$
(cabin incl breakfast RM650) These semidetached cabins are a good option for those who can't face a night in the hostels. They're clean and comfortable, with private bathrooms.

Liwagu Suites HOTEL $$$
(ste incl breakfast RM700) These hotel-like rooms (four in total) can be found in the Liwagu Building. While they sleep up to four people, they're best for couples as they contain only one bedroom and one living room.

Nepenthes Villa HOTEL $$$
(lodge incl breakfast RM1100) These attached two-storey units fall somewhere between hotel rooms and private lodges. They have two bedrooms (one with a twin bed, one with a queen) and verandahs offering limited mountain views.

Peak Lodge UNIT $$$
(lodge incl breakfast RM980) These semidetached units have two bedrooms (one with a bunk bed and one with two twin beds), pleasant sitting rooms, fireplaces and nice views from their verandahs.

Eating

Laban Rata (On the Mountain)

At Laban Rata the cafeteria-style restaurant in the Laban Rata Resthouse has a simple menu and also offers buffet meals. Most hikers staying at Laban Rata have three meals (dinner, breakfast and lunch) included in their accommodation packages. It is possible to negotiate a price reduction if you plan on bringing your own food (boiling water can be purchased for RM1 if you bring dried noodles). Note: you will have to lug said food up to Laban Rata. Buffet meals can also be purchased individually – dinner costs RM45. A small counter in the dining area sells an assortment of items including soft drinks, chocolate, pain relievers and postcards.

Park Headquarters (At the Base)

There is also a small but well-stocked shop in Balsam selling tinned and dried foods, chocolate, beer, spirits, cigarettes, T-shirts, bread, eggs and margarine.

Restoran Kinabalu Balsam CAFETERIA $
(dishes RM5-15; ⏰6am-10pm, to 11pm weekends) The cheaper and more popular of the two options in the park is this canteen-style spot directly below the park HQ. It offers basic but decent Malaysian, Chinese and Western dishes at reasonable prices.

Liwagu Restaurant CAFETERIA $$
(dishes RM10-30; ⏰6am-10pm, to 11pm weekends) In the visitors centre, this cafeteria serves a huge range of dishes, including noodles, rice, seafood standards and 'American breakfast'.

Getting There & Away

It is highly advised that summit-seekers check in at the park headquarters by 9am, which means if you're coming from KK, you should plan to leave by 7am, or consider spending the night somewhere near the base of the mountain.

BUS

Express buses (RM30) leave KK from the Utara Terminal bus station every hour on the hour from 7am to 10am and at 12.30pm, 2pm and 3pm and leave at the same times in the reverse direction; alternatively take a Ranau-bound minivan (RM25) from central KK at Padang Merdeka bus terminal, asking the driver to drop you outside the gate at Kinabalu National Park. Minivans leave when full and run from early morning till around 2pm. We recommend leaving by 7am for the two-hour trip.

Express buses and minivans travelling between KK and Ranau (and Sandakan) pass the park turn-off, 100m uphill from the park entrance. You can go to Sandakan (RM40) if the bus has room.

JEEP

Share jeeps park just outside of the park gates and leave when full for KK (RM200) and Sandakan (RM500); each jeep can hold around five passengers, but they can be chartered by individuals.

TAXI

Share taxis leave KK from Inanam and Padang Merdeka Bus Stations (RM200).

Around Mt Kinabalu

Kinabalu National Park is home to Borneo's highest mountain and some of the island's best-preserved forest. Most travellers make a beeline for the mountain and the main park headquarters area, but there are some surrounding spots also worth exploring.

Sights & Activities

Kundasang War Memorial MEMORIAL
(Kota Kinabalu–Ranau Hwy; admission RM10; 8.30am-5pm) The junction for the Mesilau Nature Resort on the KK–Ranau Hwy is the site of the Kundasang War Memorial, which commemorates the Australian and British prisoners who died on the infamous Sandakan Death Marches (p78). While other memorials in Sabah often seem neglected and forgotten, the Kundasang gardens are remarkably touching. Four gardens, manicured in that bucolic yet tame fashion that is so very English, are separated by a series of marbled pavilions.

In the Anzac Garden you can see a full list of the deceased and at the back of the gardens is a stunning viewpoint of Mt Kinabalu.

The memorial is in Kundasang, 10km east of Kinabalu National Park headquarters. You'll know you're in Kundasang when you see the market stalls on either side of the road. Take the turn on the left for Mesilau Nature Resort. The memorial is on the right 150m after the turn-off. Look for the flags and the stone fort-like structure above the road.

Ranau Night Market MARKET
(central Ranau; Sat) Packed with aromas and produce from all over the region, this is where locals come to haggle and barter every Saturday evening; especially photogenic come dusk.

Sabah Tea Garden TEA PLANTATION
(088-440 882; www.facebook.com/sabahtea; KM17, Jln Ranau–Sandakan; admission free, guided tour RM12, with set lunch RM34, 2-day, 1-night package from RM190; 8am-4pm) A pretty tea plantation huddles in the mountains near Ranau. Contact the tea garden to arrange tours of both the plantation and surrounding rainforests and river valleys. Overnight packages are available in a cosy bungalow, a traditional longhouse or campsite. Also offers tours of the facilities coupled with a trip for a fish foot massage (RM110).

Mesilau Nature Resort TREKKING
(088-871 519; Kudasang, Ranau; adult/child RM15/10, guided nature walk RM10; 9am-4pm) Just 30 minutes' drive from Kinabalu Park, this peaceful resort, nestled amid lush jungle, sits at 6172m and is the highest point you can reach by car. The resort is terrific for walking trails, and is also an alternative starting point for ascending Mt Kinabalu, often favoured by trekkers as it's more challenging than the main route and much less crowded than park headquarters.

Tagal Sungai Moroli MASSAGE
(088-878 044; Kampung Luanti, Ranau; full body 'massage' RM25; 9am-5pm) After your epic Kinabalu climb, head to Tagal Sungai Moroli for a relaxing massage, courtesy of thousands of nibbling fish. The term 'tagal' means 'no fishing' in the local Kadazan-Dusun language, as the fish in the river (a species known locally as *ikan pelian*) are not to be captured – they are special massage fish.

The townsfolk claim that they've trained the little swimmers to gently nibble at weary feet (and more, if you're up for it). Kampung Luanti is half an hour's drive east of Ranau (24.5km).

Poring Hot Springs HOT SPRINGS
(Poring, Ranau; adult/child incl Kinabalu National Park RM15/10; entrance gate 7am-5pm, park until 8pm, Butterfly Garden & Canopy Walk closed Mon) One of the few positive contributions the Japanese made to Borneo during WWII, Poring Hot Springs has become a popular weekend retreat for locals. Located in a well-maintained forest park with nature paths that the elderly and children can enjoy, the springs steam with hot sulphurous

water channelled into pools and tubs, some of which feel a little rundown. Remember your towel and swimming trunks.

For our ringgit, the highlight of the place is actually way above the springs: a **Canopy Walkway** (admission RM15; 9am-4pm) that consists of a series of walkways suspended from trees, up to 40m above the jungle floor, providing unique views of the surrounding forest. Get there early if you want to see birds or other wildlife. A **tropical garden** (9am-4pm), **butterfly farm** (adult/child RM4/2; 9am-4pm Tue-Sun) and **orchid garden** (adult/child RM10/5; 9am-4pm) are also part of the Poring complex. Rafflesia sometimes bloom in the area; look out for signs in the visitors centre and along the road.

Part of Kinabalu National Park, the complex is 43km from park headquarters, east of Ranau.

Sleeping & Eating

It's worth spending a night around the base of Kinabalu before your ascent, and there are plenty of accommodation options suiting everyone's budget, which all come with attached restaurants.

The accommodation at Mesilau and Poring is run by Sutera Sanctuary Lodges with a notable exception. There are privately owned sleeping options looping around Kinabalu's base. Most of these are located along the road between the park headquarters and Kundasang (east of the park's entrance). Two homestays in Kundasang, **Walai Tokou** (019-860 2270, 088-888 166; koch_homestay@yahoo.com; Ranau; packages from RM240) and **Mesilou Atamis** (013-886 2474, 019-580 2474; www.facebook.com/Mesilou-Atamis-Homestay; 2-day/1-night package from RM350; P), are another option.

Mountain Guest House GUESTHOUSE $
(016-837 4040, 088-888632; KM53, Jln Tinompok, off Kinabalu Park, Ranau; dm/s/d/q incl breakfast from RM30/60/70/80) This friendly but clean guesthouse is endearingly ramshackle and sits (or hangs?) on different levels up the side of the mountain. About five minute's walk from the park entrance, houseproud basic rooms have a few sticks of furniture and spotless bathrooms. Breakfast included and vegetarian dinners (RM8) available. Run by lovely Anna.

★**Lupa Masa** ECO-CAMP $$
(016-806 8194, 012-845 1987; http://lupamasa.com; Poring; per person incl meals tent/chalet RM90/250) This incredible eco-camp is surrounded by forest and has two gin-clear rivers to bathe in, with waterfalls and natural jacuzzis. Lupa Masa isn't for everyone though…no electricity or wi-fi, but bugs and leeches at no extra cost. Accommodation is on mattresses in tents on raised platforms, or the delightful new chalets with striking river views.

Seasonally it even has its own flowering rafflesias. Meals, mostly vegetarian, are included. The camp can also help with booking onward travel and offers mountain biking and day and overnight trips to the jungle, river tubing and hidden caves. Lupa Masa contribute generously to local communities. About a 45-minute walk/10-minute drive from Poring.

Wind Paradise YURT $$
(088-714 563, 012-820 3360; http://windparadise2011.blogspot.com/; Jln Mesilau, Cinta Mata, Kundasang; d/tr RM170/200, 4-person yurt RM300; P) With staggeringly pretty views of the valley and town of Kundasang far below, these Mongolian yurts, and rooms in a central lodge – both set in pleasant lawns – are delightful. There's self-catering and a great lounge, and barbecue facilities to lap up the mountain view. Yurts have comfy beds and make for a great sleep with natural ventilation.

D'Villa Rina Ria Lodge LODGE $$
(088-889 282, 011-601 6936; www.dvillalodge.com.my; KM53, Jln Tinompok, off Kinabalu Park, Ranau; dm/d/q RM30/120/220; @ wifi) Close to the Kinabalu National Park entrance, with 'traveller magnet' tattooed across its open restaurant and balconied rooms with jaw-dropping valley views. This is a great one-stop shop – literally – stock up on everything from batteries to chocolate, and socks to ponchos here. Rooms are basic with yellow walls, cosy quilts and piping-hot showers.

Poring Hot Springs Resort RESORT $$
(Poring Hot Springs, Ranau; dm/r US$35/42) At the base of Mt Kinabalu, this hotel boasts a range of accommodation from clean dorms to fine rooms with lacquered wood floors, separate living room, big beds, stylish bathroom, private balcony, and satellite TV. Close to the forest pools, and the rest of the park.

Mesilau Nature Resort RESORT $$
(088-871 519; Pekan Ranau, Ranau; 3-bed chalet RM1285) Sitting at over 6000m and nestled in thick lush jungle makes for an atmospheric

DON'T MISS

THE ORANGUTANS OF SHANGRI-LA

The **Sanctuary** at Shangri-La's Rasa Ria Resort (p70), located near Tuaran, is a make-shift wildlife reserve owned and managed by the resort. There are all kinds of daily activities, from birdwatching trips to night walks (there are civets and loris on the reserve) to viewing the Sanctuary's orangutans from a canopy walkway. The red apes here are just as cute as the ones at Sepilok (p81), and it's way less crowded as well. Plus, your money is still going towards a preservation organisation. There's different rates for all of the above activities depending on whether or not you're a guest at the hotel.

For more information, visit: www.shangri-la.com/kotakinabalu/rasariaresort/sports-recreation/nature/nature-reserve-activities or call ☎088-797 888.

The two-hour orangutan viewing occurs daily at 10am. Kids between 5 and 12 years can help out the rangers responsible for feeding the orangutans.

spot to stay. The lodging is in functional dorms and doubles, with attractive though basic rooms with desks and colourful quilts (which you'll be glad of – it gets chilly), plus three-bedroom chalets. There's also a pleasant restaurant terrace where buffet-style dinner and breakfast is served.

J Residence BUNGALOW $$$
(☎012-869 6969; www.jresidence.com; r/tr RM88/99, villa RM480) Just 300m from Mt Kinabalu Park's entrance, this tasteful accommodation clinging to the mountainside is redolent with the scent of surrounding pine trees, fresh and peaceful. There are eight rooms with wood floors, balcony and bathroom, plus tasteful linen and soaring views. Note the prices listed are weekday prices; add an additional 40% at the weekend.

Nikgold Garden BUNGALOW $$$
(☎088-888 112; www.facebook.com/NikgoldGarden; Jln Tinompok, off Kinabalu Park, Ranau; r/f RM98/400; P Wi-Fi) Set on the side of Mt Kinabalu opposite a vegetable farm, this new dark-wood building has a flavour of Swiss chalet to it. Its 10 sunrise-facing rooms are minimalist chic, while the chalets are huge affairs with two bedrooms, lounge, flat screen, DVD player, and balcony. It's on the road to Kundasang, five minutes' drive after the park entrance.

Getting There & Around

KK round-trip buses stop in front of park headquarters and in Ranau (RM15 to RM20, two hours) from 7am to 8pm. Minivans operate from a blue-roofed shelter in Ranau servicing the nearby attractions (park HQ, Poring etc) for RM5. The national park operates a van service between the headquarters and Poring for RM25 – it leaves the park HQ at noon.

Northwest Coast

The northwest coast of Sabah is criminally underexplored. The A1 runs north from KK to Kudat and the Tip of Borneo past wide headlands, rice paddies and hidden beaches. This is a good area for renting a car or motorbike – the roads are pretty level, and public transport links aren't reliable for getting off the main road.

Tuaran

Tuaran, 33km from KK, is a bustling little town with tree-lined boulevard-style streets and the distinctive nine-storey **Ling Sang Pagoda**, the approaches of which are dominated by vividly painted guardian deities. There's little point stopping in the town itself unless you happen to pass through on a market day (Tuaran is likely named for the Malay word *tawaran*, meaning 'sale', reflecting its history as a trading post), but the surrounding area conceals a few cool sights. You'll see signs for **Mengkabong Water Village**, a Bajau stilt village built over an estuary, but development and pollution has diminished this spot's charms.

Sights

Rumah Terbalik & the 3D Wonders Museum HOUSE
(The Upside Down House; ☎088-260 263; www.upsidedownhouse.com.my; Kg Telibong, Batu 21, Jln Telibong Tamparuli; Upside Down House adult/child RM19/5, 3D Wonders Museum RM35/15, Combo ticket RM48/19; ⏲8am-10pm; P family) Sabah has few 'quirky' sights... Enter 'Rumah Terbalik': the Upside Down House; a modern, tastefully decorated house, but...upside down! Even the furniture and the car parked in the

garage *sticks to the ceiling*. In the same compound is the equally odd 3D Wonders Museum, which allows you to poke your heads in aperture on painted scenes of turtles and swinging orangutans and join the fun.

Sleeping & Eating

Given the town's proximity to KK (with its many accommodation options), you probably won't need to stay in town. However, if for some reason you need a room, try **Orchid Hotel** (☎088-793 789, 012-820 8894; 4 Jln Teo Teck Ong; r from RM40-100; ❄). It's somewhat overpriced but it'll do the trick for a night. Just a few doors away is **Tai Fatt** (Jln Teo Teck Ong; meals RM4; ⏰7am-10pm), the best *kedai kopi* in Tuaran. It excels at *char mien/mee goreng*, the local, mouth-watering take on Chinese fried noodles, overflowing with vegetables, pork, oil, pork, egg, pork, wheat noodles and, yes, pork.

Shangri La Rasa Ria Resort RESORT **$$$**
(☎088-792888; www.shangri-la.com; Pantai Dalit; r incl breakfast from RM730; P ❄ @ ☎ ≋) Occupying a fine stretch of peach-hued dunes about 45 minutes north of KK's airport, this beautiful resort boasts its own 18-hole golf course, several fine restaurants, a lovely pool (plus a great kids pool with a twirly slide) and a relaxing spa. While the resort may be more comfy than heaven, its best feature is the small nature sanctuary (p69).

Getting There & Away

All buses north pass through Tuaran, and minivans shuttle regularly to and from KK (RM5 to RM10, 30 minutes). Minivans to Mengkabong are less frequent and cost RM2. Regular minivans go from Tuaran to Kota Belud (around RM15, 30 minutes).

Kota Belud

You could be forgiven for missing Kota Belud off your 'must see' list, but this bustling town makes for a useful stopover if you're en route to Mañana beach, Mantanani or Kudat. Other than the gold mosque on the hill, and the presence of cows blithely wandering the streets, the town's Sunday *tamu* (market) – a congested, colourful melee of vendors, hagglers and hawkers – is definitely worth your camera's time.

Once a year in October, Kota Belud hosts the famous **Tamu Besar** – the biggest *tamu* organised in Sabah. The highlight is a procession of fully caparisoned Bajau horsemen from the nearby villages, decked out, along with their steeds, in vivid, multicoloured satin 'armour' and embroidered barding.

Visitors looking for tribal handicrafts and traditional clothing may find a prize here, but it's cheaply made stuff for tourists. Ironically, the best way to experience this commercial event is to come not expecting to buy anything – soak up the convivial, occasionally manic atmosphere, enjoy a good meal at the lovely food stalls and just potter about like Grandma at a Sunday flea market.

Activities

Big Fin Divers DIVING
(☎014-679 3679; www.bigfindivers.com; Mañana Borneo Resort, Kota Belud; 2 dives RM250, PADI 4-day Open Water Course RM990) This new outfit offers PADI courses and diving on a near-

THE BEACH

Travellers are currently whispering about a beach of silky sand backdropped by thick jungle, fiery sunsets and turquoise green waters home to whale sharks and manta rays. Intrepid types regularly tramp across rising tides, through jellyfish, rocks and vines to reach it, knowing full well its only accommodation is booked up. OK, enough of the prelude, **Mañana Beach** is its name, and for once, here's a place that's all it's cracked up to be, and more.

Reached by boat from tiny **Pituru Laut village** (rather than walking through the jungle cliffs and rising tide!), the journey takes all of 10 minutes. However, on arrival you feel as if it's taken you back in time to a place of simplicity: kids playing happily on the sand, glassy waves and bobbing surfers, the sound of music piping from the nearby guesthouse, divers returning from the deep with smiles on their faces.

Currently there's only Mañana you can stay at; simple it may be but the easy vibe it's created combined with the nearby unchartered reef, surfable waves and paradisial setting, have got travellers saying things like: 'Thailand twenty years ago…', plus a few names from Hollywood thinking of buying plots of land here.

by reef within the 'coral triangle'; a reef so large it's not yet been charted. Mayne Point has huge granite boulders, while Ella's Garden is coral-rich and bursting with squid, cuttlefish, nurse and leopard sharks, stingrays, barracuda, and – if you're here around April till June – whale sharks.

Dive sites are close by, one of which is a downed WWII Japanese tanker, so you waste little time getting there, and on a clear day as you ascend from the depths you can clearly see Mt Kinabalu in the distance. Based at Mañana.

Sleeping & Eating

Most people visit Kota Belud as a day trip from KK, since you can make it there and back with plenty of time for the market. There are no great places to stay, nor is it much of a gastronome's delight, but tasty snacks can be picked up at the Sunday market.

TD Lodge HOTEL $

(013-880 3833; block D, lot D20-D24, Kompleks Alapbana; r RM82-92, f RM106) This Soviet-style flat-top building is fine for a night with its pleasant rooms with bright walls, TV, bathroom, laminate floors, coffee-making facilities, desk and fresh linen. Certainly the cleanest central option in town.

★ **Mañana** GUESTHOUSE $$

(014-679 3679, 014-679 2679; www.mananaborneo.com; chalet/villa/family villa from RM120/180/350) Imagine a hidden beach and chilled vibe where young and old swap stories late into the night. Run by lovely Yan and Nani, Mañana's cabanas boast soulful views over an aquamarine bay. You can also learn yoga, paddle-board, surf, or dive with Big Fin Divers. The restaurant serves hot and cold food, and there's also a new bar. It's a special place.

Mañana feels as if it's on an island, given that you have to catch a boat from Kampung Pituru Laut to reach it. *Always* book ahead. It's possible to arrange a cab from KK with a trusted driver recommended by Mañana. If it is fully booked (which is highly likely), it's possible to rent a tent until a chalet becomes free.

Getting There & Away

Minivans and share taxis gather in front of Pasar Besar, the old market. Most of these serve the Kota Belud–KK route (RM10, two hours) or Kudat (RM20, two hours), departing from 7am to 5pm. To get to Kinabalu National Park, take any minibus going to KK and get off at Tamparuli, about halfway (RM10, 30 minutes). There are several minivans from Tamparuli to Ranau every day until about 2pm; all pass the park entrance (RM10, one hour). To go all the way to Ranau costs RM20 (the trip takes just over an hour).

Kudat

With its sunburnt stilted buildings, fishing boats out in the bay and slow tropical pace, there's a dreamy, end-of-the-world feeling in Kudat that will soon grow on you. Believe it or not, sleepy Kudat used to be an important trading post and capital of Borneo back in the late 19th century. You may notice some of the streets have Chinese names, harking back to the British adminstration's request to the Chinese to come and run their coconut plantations. Many of their descendants are still here today, along with a warm Bajau, Rungus and Filipino cast.

Kudat town's impressive **Chinese temple** FREE by the main square is worth a look, or you might visit **Tamu Kudat** (6am-2pm Tue & Wed) market with its tropical fruits, dried fish and edible seaweed. But it's the country that leads up to the Tip of Borneo that you really want to explore; think blood and vermilion sunsets, mile upon mile of powder-fine sand and cobalt blue water deserted but for the occasional fishing boat or local walking beneath her umbrella in the midday heat.

Swing by **New Way Car Rental & Souvenir Centre** (088-625 868; 40 Jln Lo Thien Chok) if you want to explore the area under your own steam. Staff can also book your accommodation on Pulau Banggi (p74).

Sleeping & Eating

Ria Hotel HOTEL $$

(088-622 794; http://riahotel.blogspot.com; 3 Jln Marudu; r RM135-146, f RM315;) Ria is central, has pleasant rooms with desk, comfy beds, fresh linen, TV and bathroom. The real boon though is the funky cafe downstairs which sells lovely pastries, sandwiches, cakes and decent coffee.

Kudat Golf Marina Resort HOTEL $$

(088-611 211; www.kudatgolfmarinaresort.com; off Jln Urus Setia; r RM166-186; P) Opposite a little marina, this faded dame has a huge banana-hued lobby complete with massage chairs and helpful staff, and large bedrooms with bathroom, decent fittings and TV. Breakfast is a buffet and egg station affair. Best of all is the huge alfresco swimming pool.

Getting There & Away

The bus station is in Kudat Plaza in the western part of town, very close to the Ria Hotel. Bus destinations include KK (RM25, three hours, twice daily), Kota Belud (RM15, 1½ hours, twice daily) and Sandakan (RM60, one daily). Minivans and jeeps also operate from here; a ride to KK in a full van will cost around RM50.

Around Kudat

The area around Kudat includes many hidden **coves**, **beaches** and **hill trails** that are almost all tucked away down hidden or unmarked roads. You'll want to get in touch with the folks at Tampat Do Aman or Tip of Borneo Resort to find the best spots. The Rungus **longhouses** (Bavanggazo Rungus Longhouses/Maranjak Longhouse; ☎088-612 846, 088-621 673; per person per night from RM70) of Kampung Bavanggazo, 44km south of Kudat, are highly touted by Sabah Tourism, but were in a bit of a neglected state when we visited them.

Tip of Borneo

Sabah's northernmost headland, at the end of a wide bay some 40km from Kudat, is known as Tanjung Simpang Mengayu, or the Tip of Borneo. Magellan reputedly landed here for 42 days during his famous 16th-century round-the-world voyage. Once a wild promontory, this windswept stretch where the cliffs meet the sea has been co-opted as a tourist attraction – there's a large, truncated globe monument dominating the viewpoint. A sign warns visitors not to climb down onto the rocks that form the mainland's actual tip due to lethal currents.

There's no public transport, so you'll need to negotiate a taxi from Kudat (around RM90, including waiting time upon arrival) or drive yourself. The area surounding the tip is also known as the Tip of Borneo, and it's here you'll find the best accommodation, diving and surfing. Of eight beaches, there are three of note: the northernmost Tip of Borneo Beach, otherwise known as Kosuhui Beach, where there are restaurants, dive shops and surfboards to hire; next up, the inaccessible private beach by dreamy Hibiscus Beach Resort; and finally, beautiful Bavang Jamal Beach, where you'll find a couple of excellent spots for refreshments.

Sights & Activities

Kudat Turtle Conservation Society WILDLIFE RESERVE

(☎013-839 7860; www.ktcs-borneo.org; Lupa Masa Bavang Jamal Homestay, Kampung Bavang Jamal; conservation fee RM15) Run by Roland, the Kudat Turtle Conservation Society is based at the Lupa Masa Bavang Jamal Homestay. An education centre has just been built here and it's possible to assist the society on night vigils of local beaches to protect the eggs of green and hawksbill turtles. Check the website for a list of long-term voluntary positions.

To get here from Kudat, call Driver Peter on ☎019-802 0084. It should cost around RM50.

Borneo Dive Centre WATER SPORTS

(☎016-830 0454; www.tipofborneoresort.com; Tip of Borneo Resort; fishing per boat RM400, snorkelling RM40, 2 dives RM300, surfboard hire RM80; ⏲9am-7pm) Based at the Tip of Borneo Resort, this funky-muralled dive hut is a tardis of surfboards, windsurfing and fishing equipment and diving paraphernalia. Also rents kayaks and bikes.

CATCHING THE MORNING TUBE

Surfing is beginning to take off on the west coast of Sabah, thanks to swells produced by the southwest and northeast monsoons – November to January being the best time to catch a glassy wave. The top spot is the northern Tip of Borneo, and its beautiful white-sand beaches and turquoise water are not the only pull; when the conditions are right, there's some very clean surf with glassy lefts and rights, perfect peels, and faces varying in size from 2ft to 9ft. Also there's no bad-tempered, overcrowded line-up; but for the odd local, the waves are yours and board hire is easy.

For surf lessons, get in touch with **Deep Borneo Adventures** (☎088-231 233; www.deepborneo.com; Lot 3.2, 2nd fl, Grace Sq, Lg Grace Square 1, Jln Pantai, Sembulan, Kota Kinabalu; private surf lessons RM180), which uses the smaller waves at Tanjung Aru or Kudat, depending on swells. Boards can be hired at Tip of Borneo Resort.

Sleeping

★Lupa Masa Bavang Jamal Homestay HOMESTAY $
(☎019-802 0549; http://lupamasa.com; Kampung Bavang Jamal; r incl breakfast RM45; P) This stunning Rungus-inspired longhouse has ventilated sleeping areas, and simple private rooms within its high-beamed expanse – no mod cons, just mozzie net, mattress and shared bathroom. Nearby is La Playa Beachfront Bar on Bavang Jamal Beach. Kudat Turtle Conservation Society is based here. It's also possible to visit Banggi Island from here on an overnight snorkelling trip (RM280).

★Tampat Do Aman HOMESTAY $$
(☎013-880 8395; http://tampatdoaman.com; r from RM43, chalet/family chalet RM160/220;) With its vernal maze of walkways, atmospheric Rungus longhouse rooms and powder-blue villas overlooking hibiscus-rich gardens, this is a fine place to stay. Owner Howard and his Rungus wife pour the profits into local initiatives like school building and nature conservation. There's an on-site museum, willdlife reserve, and the food is terrific. A new longhouse is currently being built. Recommended.

Take a hike, go snorkelling or hire a bike; Howard can hook you up with loads of activities.

Tip of Borneo Resort RESORT $$
(Tommy's Place; ☎088-493 468, 013-811 2315; http://tipofborneoresort.com/; r RM180-230, villa RM280;) With its welcoming cafe, dive and windsurf centre, as well as Tommy's wildlife conservation efforts, this is a cool place to stay. There's a new row of lovely mint-green triple rooms with balconies and bathroom, and the villas on the hill have widescreen views, huge beds, flat screen and cable. A new restaurant is in the making.

★Hibiscus Beach Retreat BUNGALOW $$$
(☎019-895 0704; www.hibiscusbeachretreat.com; 2-person bungalow RM525-625) Perched on a hill overlooking a beautiful 1.5km swath of sand lapped by teal-green sea, this bijou one-bedroom cabana has a high thatch roof, fan-only rooms, self-catering facilities, sundeck and loungers, contemporary art and choice furniture. Order a fresh fruit breakfast, snorkel, then kick back and witness the purple and amber sunset. Exquisite!

Hibiscus Villa Borneo VILLA $$$
(☎019-895 0704; www.hibiscusvillaborneo.com; per night US$900-1100 ;) With its infinity pool, dark-wood floors, moody subdued lighting, and exquisitely chosen furniture, this fine 3-bedroomed villa is on a private beach and leaps straight from the pages of a glossy interiors magazine. There's daily maid service but otherwise you'll feel like you have died and gone to heaven. Perfect for families in search of privacy and escape.

Eating & Drinking

The Secret Place Cafe MALAYSIAN $
(Bavang Jamal Beach; mains RM9; ⊙10am-9pm) This family-run joint on Bavang Jamal Beach is popular for its *nasi goreng* (fried rice), fresh fish, chicken wings and barbecued food. Whatever's been caught finds its way to the grill. There are hammocks to lounge on and drink up the sea view. You can even rent a tent (RM25). Look for the wood sign on the main road.

Tip Top Restaurant INTERNATIONAL $$
(☎013-880 8395; www.tampatdoaman.com/tip top-menu; Kosuhui Beach; mains RM17; ⊙8am-8pm) Just metres from the beach, here you can expect terrific food ranging from burgers to swordfish steak, curries, sweet-and-sour chicken, breakfasts, carrot cake and fresh juices. The restaurant has a shaded section and an outdoor decked area to chill. Run by the excellent Tampat Do Aman.

★La Playa Beachfront Bar BAR
(southern end of Bavang Jamal Beach; mains RM10) Next to the Kudat Turtle Conservation Society, this lantern-lit open-decked bar is one of the most peaceful, best located watering-holes in Sabah. Tibetan prayer flags flutter as you recline on loungers, scatter cushions and hammocks, sipping fresh coconut juice and cocktails, gobbling pizza cooked in the wood-fired oven and gazing at the equatorial fiery sunset. Perfection.

On Saturday mornings, locals sell handmade beaded jewellery and fresh fruit here.

Offshore Islands

The real highlights of northwestern Sabah lie offshore. The first gem is Pulau Mantanani, which is actually two perfect tropical islands lying about 40km northwest of Kota Belud. The second is Layang Layang, a diving mecca about 300km northwest of KK, basically an airstrip built on a reef way out in the middle of the South China Sea. Famous for great visibility, seemingly endless wall dives and the occasional school of hammerheads, it's second only to Sipadan on Malaysia's list of top dive spots.

Pulau Mantanani

The 3km-long **Pulau Mantanani Besar** (Big Mantanani Island) and **Pulau Mantanani Kecil** (Little Mantanani Island) are two little flecks of land fringed by bleach-blond sand and ringed by a halo of colourful coral, about 25km off the coast of northwest Sabah (about 40km northwest of Kota Belud). Dugongs are spotted here from time to time, as is the rare Scops owl. The 1000-odd islanders are Bajau sea gypsies, who have been in the news recently because of their opposition to resorts buying up land for development and the imminent possibility they might be forcibly relocated by the government.

Overnight options include the excellent **Mari Mari Backpackers Lodge** (☎088-260 501; www.riverbug.asia; dm RM442, tw per person RM552), operated by Riverbug. Guests are placed in raised stilt chalets around a white-sand beach. There are also dorms with shared bathrooms. Diving and snorkelling activities feature high on the itinerary list, but this is also a lovely tropical escape if you just want to chill. It's possible to be picked up from KK and taken to Kota Belud from where you catch a speedboat (included) to the island for one night before being returned to Kota Belud for 6.30pm the next day. Rates start at RM442 for a dorm and RM552 per person for a twin room. Mari Mari also has its own dive centre offering PADI courses.

For more luxury, head to **Bembaran Dive Lodge** (☎088-728 702; www.bembarandivelodge.com; 2-day, 1-night package incl 3 dives RM575; ❄) with larger, more comfortable cabanas and a private beach and cafe. They too have a decent dive school and offer refresher courses, open-water courses and snorkelling.

Wi-fi is very iffy on the island and there are just a few shops, but this is a chance to cut free of the outside world for a few days. You can kayak and night-dive at night here, birdwatch or take a sunset cruise.

Pulau Banggi

If you want to fall off the map, head to Pulau Banggi, some 40km northeast of Kudat where the Sulu and South China Seas meet. The Banggi people, known locally for their unusual tribal tree houses, are Sabah's smallest indigenous group, and speak a unique non-Bornean dialect. The island is a postcard-esque slice of sand, tropical trees and clear water, and is actually the largest offshore island in all Malaysia.

Firmly in the 'Coral Triangle', one of the most biodiverse submarine habitats on earth, the diving here is superb, but be warned, due to its proximity to the Balabic Straight Corridor, the currents are a challenge and only experienced drift divers should dive here. You'll possibly see whale sharks, turtles, dolphins and a colourful mix of coral such as gorgonian fan, staghorn and bubble. Amidst this are batfish, clownfish, squid and moray eels. Keep an eye out too here for dugong, thanks to the presence of the island's mangrove and seagrass.

Accommodation is available at the modest **Bonggi Resort** (☎088-671 572, 019-587 8078; Waterfront, Karakit; r fan/air-con RM65/80, huts RM85; ❄), which can arrange boat trips and other activities. The small huts have kitchens and twin beds – make sure you request the charming tree-house hut. This place can get fully booked on weekends, so reserve in advance. Ask staff about the trails that lead into the small jungle interior of the island.

Kudat Express (☎088-328118; 1-way 1st class/economy RM18/15) runs a ferry between Kudat and the main settlement on Pulau Banggi. It departs the pier (near the Shell station) at 1pm daily. In the reverse direction, it leaves Pulau Banggi daily at around 7.15am.

Layang Layang

This turquoise-haloed coral atoll, some 300km northwest of KK, is actually artificial, constructed for the Malaysian Navy, and debated between scubaholics as one of the top 10 dive sites in the world. However, what lies beneath what is now an exclusive diving resort could only have been created by nature: think Technicolor reefs teeming with gorgonian fans, excellent visibility, and impossibly steep walls down to 2000km. Beyond the macro fish found in its 20m deep lagoon (seahorses, pipefish, cuttlefish and batfish) large pelagics to the outer walls include hammerhead, grey reef, leopard, thresher, silvertip and whale sharks; as well as orcas, dolphins, manta and devil rays.

Keep in mind that there is no decompression chamber at Layang Layang, so don't press your luck while underwater. The resort only provides air – no nitrox.

The island's location offers absolute isolation; luckily there is an airstrip with regular flights from Kota Kinabalu, which is the only mode of transport for guests visiting Layang Layang. Isolation doesn't come cheap, especially when mixed with high luxury.

Avillion Layang Layang Resort (☎ in KL 03-2170 2185; www.avillionlayanglayang.com; 5-day, 4-night all-incl package, twin-share per person from US$985; ❄ 🏊) is the only digs and it's all about scuba, with five daily meals scheduled around dives. The standard rooms are very comfortable, with air-con, TV, private verandahs and hot-water showers. The all-inclusive packages include accommodation, food, 12 boat dives and tank usage. Be warned, nondivers: besides a little snorkelling, there's nothing for you to do here but sunbathe.

The resort operates its own Antonov 26 aircraft, which flies every Tuesday, Thursday, Friday and Sunday between KK and Layang Layang. The flight over from KK in this barebones Russian prop plane is a big part of the adventure. The return flight costs US$408, which is not included in the accommodation-food-dive package.

EASTERN SABAH

Eastern Sabah takes nearly everything that is wonderful about the rest of Borneo and condenses it into a richly packed microcosm of the island consisting of equal parts adventure, wildlife, undersea exploration and flat-out fun. Let's tick off some of the natural wonders of this relatively tiny corner of the island: the great ginger men – ie the orangutans – of Sepilok; pot-bellied, flop-nosed proboscis monkeys in Labuk Bay; the looming vine tunnels and muddy crocodile highway of the Sungai Kinabatangan; pygmy elephants and treetop canopies that scratch the sky in the Danum Valley and Tabin; plunging sea walls rainbow-spattered with tropical marine life in the Semporna Archipelago; a forest as old as human civilisation in the Maliau Basin.

Did we just pique your travel appetite? Thanks to decent flight connections, travel up and down the eastern seaboard is a cinch, plus a newly sealed road between Tawau on the southeast coast and KK on the west, finally makes it possible to access the interior of the Maliau Basin without a headache.

Sandakan

☎ 089 / POP 392,288

Looking out across the teal-blue bay of Sandakan dotted with Chinese trawlers and distant isles, it's hard to believe its population was once composed of such an exotic cast of foreign interests: German traders, Dutch and Chinese planters, Arab and Indian traders, and pearl divers. Sadly it was razed to the ground during WWII by the British in an attempt to shake off the grip of the invading Japanese. After the war, a roaring timber trade blossomed here with wood from Borneo imported all over the world, so much so that for a time, there were more millionaires per head here than anywhere in the world. Today this little city is buzzing again with the success of the palm-oil industry, its drab, hastily erected postwar buildings enjoying a much needed 21st-century makeover – particularly the waterfront area and Four Points hotel.

Curiously, a completely new city centre is currently being built 2.5km west of the city, set to be completed within a few years.

As well as being a gateway to the Sungai Kinabatangan and Sepilok, Sabah's second city is dotted with religious relics, haunting cemeteries and stunning colonial mansions. You'll find loads of things to see here, most of them a short cab ride away.

Sights

Central Sandakan is light on 'must-see' attractions, although history buffs will appreciate the *Sandakan Heritage Trail* brochure available at the tourist office. The centre, where you'll find most hotels, banks and local transport, consists of a few blocks squashed between the waterfront and a steep escarpment from where you can look out over the bay, Teluk Sandakan.

We're glad to report that the Sandakan Crocodile Park is currently closed until it improves the conditions for its 3000 scaled and feathered occupants, following a plethora of complaints.

Chinese Cemetery CEMETERY

Sandakan's Chinese Cemetery is huge. As you wander further along the cemetery, you'll notice the graves become older and more decrepit – many have been claimed by the jungle. You will also see some charnel houses that accommodate the important members of Sandakan's major Chinese

Sandakan

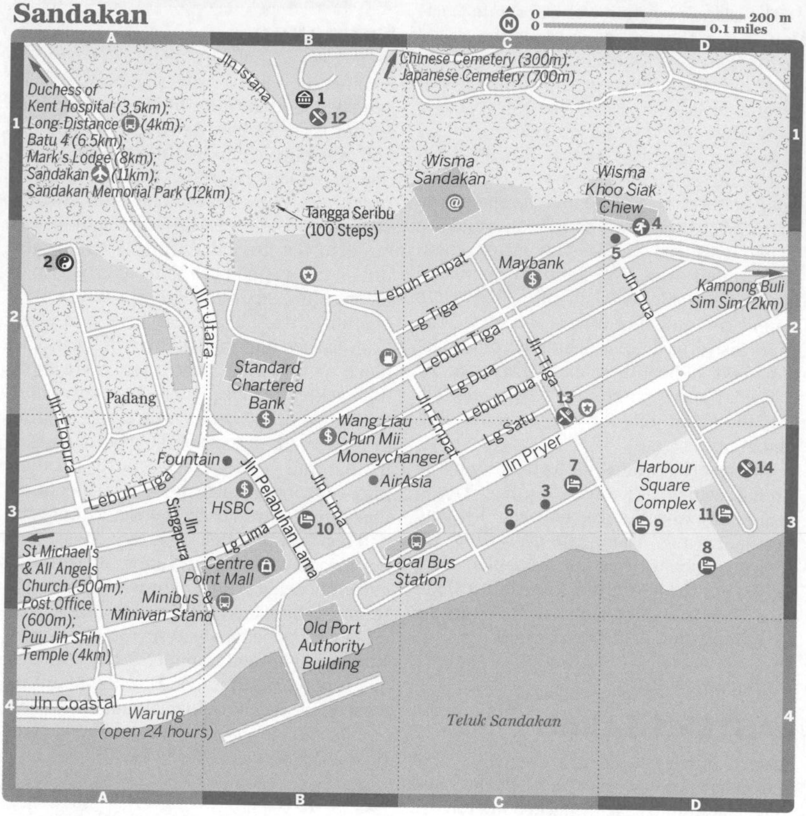

Sandakan

Sights

1 Agnes Keith House B1
2 Sam Sing Kung A2

Activities, Courses & Tours

3 Myne Travel C3
4 Ocean Quest D1
5 Sepilok Tropical Wildlife Adventure D2
6 SI Tours C3

Sleeping

7 Borneo Sandakan Backpackers C3
8 Four Points by Sheraton Sandakan D3
9 Ibis Styles Sandakan Waterfont D3
10 Nak Hotel B3
11 Sea View Sandakan D3

Eating

12 English Tea House & Restaurant B1
13 Habeeb Restaurant C2
14 Sandakan Central Market D3

Drinking & Nightlife

Balin Roof Garden .... (see 10)

clans. Across the road from the cemetery is a cremation ground for Hindus and Sikhs.

Japanese Cemetery CEMETERY

(Jln Istana) A poignant piece of Sandakan's ethnic puzzle, the cemetry was founded in the 1890s by Kinoshita Kuni, known as the successful madam-manager of Sandakan's lucrative 'Brothel 8'. Today's cemetery is small, but at one time there were hundreds of prostitutes buried here. A monument to the fallen Japanese soldiers of WWII was erected in the cemetery in 1989. To get here, climb the Tangga Seribu (100 Steps) to Jln

Residensi Dr and turn right, following signs to the cemetery.

Agnes Keith House MUSEUM
(089-221 140; www.museum.sabah.gov.my; Jln Istana; admission RM15; 9am-5pm) This atmospheric two-storey wooden villa, and former British colonial quarters, is now renovated as a museum. Living in Sandakan in the 1930s, Amercian Agnes Keith wrote several books about her experiences here, including the famous *Land Below the Wind*. The villa documents Sandakan in all its colonial splendour.

To reach the museum, head up the Tangga Seribu to Jln Istana and turn left. Also on the grounds is the English Tea House & Restaurant (p79).

Sandakan Memorial Park HISTORIC SITE
(9am-5pm) A beautiful forest orchard and series of gardens mark the unlikely site of a Japanese POW camp and starting point for the infamous WWII 'death marches' (p78) to Ranau. Of the 1800 Australian and 600 British troops imprisoned here, the only survivors by July 1945 were six Australian escapees. Rusting machines testify to the camp's forced-labour program, and a pavilion includes accounts from survivors and photographs from personnel, inmates and liberators. See www.sandakan-deathmarch.com for more details of the death-march route.

To reach the park, take any Batu 8 (or higher-numbered) bus from the local bus station on the waterfront in the city centre (RM1.50); get off at the 'Taman Rimba' signpost and walk down Jln Rimba. A taxi from downtown costs about RM30 one way.

Puu Jih Shih Temple CHINESE TEMPLE
(off Jln Leila) FREE Wrapped in the usual firework display of reds, golds and twining dragons, festooned with lanterns illuminating the grounds like a swarm of fireflies, this is one of the finest Chinese temples in Sabah. The temple is about 4km west of the centre. Take a bus to Tanah Merah and ask for directions. A taxi shouldn't cost more than RM10 one way, but don't be surprised if cabbies try to charge RM25 for a round trip plus waiting at the temple.

St Michael's & All Angels Church CHURCH
(off Jln Puncak; admission RM10) FREE As if airlifted from England's home counties, this pretty stone church sits like a relic of colonial times and monument to Christian worship, on a hillside high above Sandakan. Its construction reportedly involved prisoner labourers dragging huge stones across the Bornean jungle. The church avoided major damage during WWII. Notice its stunning stained-glass windows donated by Australians to commemorate the 60th anniversary of the end of this conflict.

Although the church is officially off Jln Puncak, many people call the street 'Church Rd'.

Sam Sing Kung TAOIST TEMPLE
(Jln Padang) FREE The Sam Sing Kung temple (also pronounced 'Sam Sing Gong') dates from 1887, making it the oldest building in Sandakan. The temple itself is a smallish, if attractive affair – a lovely example of a house of worship dedicated to the traditional Chinese Taoist pantheon.

Kampong Buli Sim Sim VILLAGE
This traditional stilt village, located about 3km east of the town centre, is the original settlement Sandakan grew from. You'll likely be grinned at as you wander around the wooden boards built over the water, as much an oddity to locals as their water village is to you, but please don't take pictures of people without asking permission. You can take a taxi here for no more than RM20.

Tours

It is possible to visit many of the attractions around Sandakan independently, but if you want to stay at the river lodges on the Kinabatangan, you'll need to prebook accommodation. It's advisable to do so in Sandakan or in KK. Sandakan also has plenty of general tour operators offering packages to Sepilok and the Gomantong Caves. Hotels in Sandakan and Sepilok are all capable of booking tours as well, as are many of the tour companies listed in KK.

Sabah Holidays NATURE TOUR
(089-225 718; www.sabahholidays.com; Ground fl, Sandakan Airport; 9am-6pm) Rents cars and minivans, and can arrange tours and accommodation in Kota Belud, the Danum Valley, Maliau Basin and Sepilok.

Sepilok Tropical Wildlife Adventure NATURE TOUR
(089 271 077; www.stwadventure.com; 13 Jln Tiga; 9am-6pm) This midpriced tour specialist is connected to Sepilok Jungle Resort and Bilit Adventure Lodge on the Sungai Kinabatangan.

SI Tours NATURE TOUR
(089-213 502; www.sitoursborneo.com; lot 59, block HS-5, Sandakan Harbour Sq Phase 2; 9am-6pm) This full-service agency operates Abai Jungle Lodge and Kinabatangan River Lodge and runs overnight turtle-spotting trips to the Sandakan Archipelago.

Myne Travel NATURE TOUR
(089-216 093; www.myne.com.my; 57 Harbour Sq; 8am-5pm, closed Sun) Myne sells river trips on the Kinabatangan, and excursions to Turtle Island (RM880 including guide, boat, meals and one night's accommodation), as well as a 'fireflies and mangrove' local cruise in Tanjung Arung.

Sleeping

If you're only passing through Sandakan to see the orangutans, it's better to stay at Sepilok itself. Sandakan has a few upscale options; on the opposite end of the luxe spectrum, it also has some friendly hostels.

★Borneo Sandakan Backpackers HOSTEL $
(089-215 754; www.borneosandakan.com; 1st fl, 54 Harbour Sq; dm/s/d RM30/55/70) These brilliant new digs are superclean with warm orange walls, a welcoming lobby, air-con in every room and – get this – flat screen and Xbox! Also, fresh sheets, safety lockers and a decent breakfast. There are six rooms and two well-sized dorms. There's a great vibe and helpful staff who are also qualified guides and run a number of tours.

Sea View Sandakan HOSTEL $
(089-221 221; 1st fl, lot 126, Jln Dua, Harbour Sq 14; dm RM25, d with fan & shared bathroom/d with bathroom & air-con RM66/84, breakfast incl) You won't get any sea views and the rooms are a bit airless and need painting. That said, it's a nice vibe here, and the Lemongrass cafe on the 3rd floor has a cool mural and misted glass, and dishes up pumpkin curry.

★Four Points by Sheraton Sandakan HOTEL $$
(089-244 888; www.fourpointssandakan.com; Harbour Sq, Jln Pryer; r incl breakfast from RM240) This new luxury option exudes international chic with a palatial lobby commanding great bay views, and even lovelier rooms with sleep-inducing ambient lighting, down pillows, uber-thick mattress, flat screen, desk and minibar. The Eatery Restaurant has arguably the best buffet breakfast in Sabah, while the Best Brew Bar serves great cocktails in sumptuous surroundings. Plus...a giant alfresco pool!

THE SANDAKAN DEATH MARCHES

Sandakan was the site of a Japanese prisoner-of-war camp during WWII, and in September 1944, 1800 Australian and 600 British troops were interned here. What is not widely known is that more Australians died here than during the building of the infamous Burma Railway.

Early in the war, food and conditions were bearable and the death rate stood at around three per month. However, as the Allies closed in, it became clear to the officers in command that they didn't have enough staff to guard against a rebellion in the camps. They decided to cut the prisoners' rations to weaken them, causing disease to spread and the death rate to rise.

It was also decided to move the prisoners inland – 250km through the jungle to Ranau, on a route originally cut by locals to hamper the Japanese invaders, passing mainly through uninhabited, inhospitable terrain. On 28 January 1945, 470 prisoners set off; 313 made it to Ranau. On the second march, 570 started from Sandakan; just 118 reached Ranau. The 537 prisoners on the third march were the last men in the camp.

Conditions on the marches were deplorable: most men had no boots, rations were less than minimal and many men fell by the wayside. The Japanese brutally disposed of any prisoners who couldn't walk. Once in Ranau, the surviving prisoners were put to work carrying 20kg sacks of rice over hilly country to Paginatan, 40km away. Disease, starvation and executions took a horrendous toll, and by the end of July 1945 there were no prisoners left in Ranau. The only survivors from the 2400 at Sandakan were six Australians who escaped, either from Ranau or during the marches.

As a final bitter irony, it emerged postwar that a rescue attempt had been planned for early 1945, but intelligence at the time had suggested there were no prisoners left at the camp.

Nak Hotel HOTEL $$
(☎089-272 988; www.nakhotel.com; Jln Pelabuhan Lama; s/d/f incl breakfast from RM88/138/218; ❄📶) We like Nak for its quirky lobby of ox-blood walls, Chinese lanterns, giant birdcages and oriental vases. Rooms are dinky but stylish; gunmetal-grey walls, retro elements and tasteful en suites. Best of all is the city's coolest cafe, the irresistible rooftop oasis Balin – a must even if you aren't staying here. Breakfast is pancakes and eggs. Look for the black Soviet facade.

Mark's Lodge HOTEL $$
(☎089-210 055; www.markslodge.com; Lot 1-7, block 36, Bandar Indah; r incl breakfast RM146-178; ❄📶) Peaceful and cool, just 8km from the centre, Mark's has some boutique elements and art-deco-style desks, as well as flat screens and a few movie channels, subtle lighting and sparkling bathrooms. The wood-panelled restaurant-bar is also inviting. It's a RM20 taxi ride into town.

Ibis Styles Sandakan Waterfont HOTEL $$
(☎089-240 888; www.ibisstyles.com; Harbour Sq; r RM158-173, f RM208; ❄📶) Contemporary, ice-cool and immaculate is a fair description of this popular French hotel chain's new acquisition on the waterfront. Tangerine-hued rooms are large and fresh with international-standard bathrooms, snow-white linen, flat screens and modern fittings. With widescreen views of the Sulu Sea and breakfast on the verandah, this place makes for a great stay.

Eating

For an authentic Malay meal, head to the waterfront Harbour Square Complex, where the restaurants surrounding it are cheap and flavourful. Most are standard Malay *kedai kopi*, with prices that rarely top RM6 per mains; all are open from roughly 9am to 9pm. **Habeeb Restaurant** (Jln Tiga; ⏲7am-3pm) is good for a cheap curry; it's actually part of a chain that serves good Indian Muslim food, so if you see other branches around town, consider them a solid bet.

Sandakan Central Market HAWKER $
(Jln Dua; mains RM1-8; ⏲7am-3pm) Despite being located in what looks like a multistorey car park, this is the best spot in town for cheap eats and food stalls. Upstairs you'll find strictly halal food stalls, with a mix of Chinese, Malay, Indonesian and Filipino stalls. Hours given for the food stalls are a bit flexible, but by 3pm most are empty.

Sim Sim Seafood Restaurant SEAFOOD $
(Sim Sim 8; dishes RM5; ⏲8am-2pm) Located in the heart of the stilt village of Kampong Buli Sim Sim, 3km east of the centre, this 'restaurant' is more of a dockside fishery, where the daily catch is unloaded and prepared for immediate consumption. Grab a red plastic seat and point to your prey! Ask a cab to drop you off at 'Sim Sim Bridge 8' (they'll very likely know where you're going).

English Tea House & Restaurant BRITISH $$
(☎089-222 544; www.englishteahouse.org; Jln Istana; mains RM15.50-55, cocktails RM16.80-20; ⏲10am-11pm) More English than a Graham Greene novel, this beautiful stucco-pillared villa, with its manicured croquet lawn, wood-blade fans and wicker chairs parked under a giant mango tree, is great for lunch. The menu spans fish 'n' chips to Oxford stew, enjoyed with a serene view of the bay below and a pot of tea.

Imagine staff dressed like Harrogate tea ladies and scones on triple-tiered cake trays. Sadly the dilatory service would induce paroxysms of purple rage in a Victorian gentleman, as the place is often saturated with overbearing package types and understaffed.

Drinking & Nightlife

Bandar Indah, commonly known as Mile 4 or Batu 4, is a buzzing grid of two-storey shophouses and the playground of choice for locals and expats alike, packed with restaurants, bars, karaoke lounges and nightclubs. It comes alive at night in a way that makes central Sandakan seem deader than the morgue in a ghost town. Bars generally close around 1am or 2am, music venues slightly later. A taxi to Bandar Indah should cost around RM20.

★**Balin Roof Garden** BAR
(Balin; ☎089-272 988; www.nakhotel.com; 18th fl, Nak Hotel, Jln Pelabuhan Lama; mains RM20, cocktails RM20-25; ⏲7.30am-1am, happy hour 2-8pm; 📶) A hidden treat at the top of the Nak Hotel, this stylish restaurant/bar has retro bubble lights, a '70s wicker swing-chair, and swallow-you-up couches. Eat inside or out; on the shaded verandah or up on the rooftop. Pizza, marinated New Zealand lamb, grass-fed burger and a wealth of juices and classy cocktails that any boutique 'mixologist' bar would be justifiably jealous of. Cool.

Information

INTERNET

Cyber Café (3rd fl, Wisma Sandakan, Lebuh Empat; per hour RM3; ⌚9am-9pm)

MEDICAL SERVICES

Duchess of Kent Hospital (☎089-248 600; http://hdok.moh.gov.my; Batu 2/Mile 2, Jln Utara; ⌚8am-10pm) Best private care in the area.

MONEY

Maybank (Lebuh Tiga) In addition to a full-service bank and ATM, a pavement currency-exchange window is open 9am to 5pm daily for changing cash and travellers cheques.

Wang Liau Chun Mii Moneychanger (23 Lebuh Tiga; ⌚8.30am-4.30pm) Cash only.

POST

Main Post Office (☎089-210 594; Jln Leila; ⌚8.30am-6pm Mon-Fri, to 12:30pm Sat)

Getting There & Away

AIR

Malaysia Airlines (www.malaysiaairlines.com)/**MASwings** (☎1300-883 000; www.maswings.com) has seven flights per day to/from KK and KL (RM248); two per day to/from Tawau (RM192) and two per week to Kudat (RM117). **AirAsia** (☎089-222 737; www.airasia.com; 1st & 2nd fl, Sandakan Airport) operates direct daily flights to/from KL and KK.

BUS

Buses and minibuses to KK, Lahad Datu, Semporna and Tawau leave from the long-distance bus station in a large car park at Batu 2.5, 4km north of town. Most express buses to KK (RM43, six hours) leave between 7am and 2pm, plus one evening departure around 8pm. All pass the turn-off to Kinabalu National Park headquarters.

Buses depart regularly for Lahad Datu (RM22, 2½ hours) and Tawau (RM43, 5½ hours) between 7am and 8am. There's also a bus to Semporna (RM40, 5½ hours) at 8am. If you miss it, head to Lahad Datu, then catch a frequent minivan to Semporna.

Minivans depart throughout the morning from Batu 2.5 for Ranau (RM30, four hours) and Lahad Datu (some of those continuing to Tawau). Minivans for Sukau (RM15) leave from a lot behind Centre Point Mall in town.

Getting Around

TO/FROM THE AIRPORT

The airport is 11km from the city centre. Batu 7 Airport bus (RM1.80) stops on the main road about 500m from the terminal. A coupon taxi to the town centre costs RM35; going the other way, around RM35.

BUS & MINIVAN

Buses run from 6am to 6pm on the main road to the north, Jln Utara, designated by how far from town they go, ie Batu 8. Fares range from RM2 to RM5.

Local minivans wait behind Centre Point Mall; fares cost from RM2. Use for the harbour area, about 7km west of town.

To reach the long-distance bus station, catch a local bus (RM1.50) from the stand at the waterfront; it takes about 20 minutes. The same bus leaves when full from the bus station for the city centre.

CAR

Borneo Express (☎016-886 0789; http://borneocar.com/; Lot GL 08 (A), ground fl, Terminal Building, Sandakan Airport), in KK, has an office at Sandakan airport, as does **Sandakan Car Rental** (☎019-823 7050, 016-815 0029; http://sandakancarrental.com; Bandar Maju Batu 1, Jln Utara).

TAXI

Short journeys around town should cost RM15; it's about RM20 to Bandar Indah and RM50

GETTING TO THE PHILIPPINES: SANDAKAN TO ZAMBOANGA

Getting to the border **Standard Marine** (☎089-216 996) links Sandakan with Zamboanga (economy/cabin RM280/320) on the Philippine island of Mindanao. Ferries depart Sandakan harbour at 10pm every Monday, arriving at 8pm the next day (22 hours). There are now no ferries to Jolo because of insurgency problems.

At the border Because of lawlessness, including kidnappings of foreign nationals, and Islamist insurgency, Western embassies warn against travel to or through Zamboanga, so check local conditions before you sail. Travellers we spoke to said you don't need an onward ticket to enter the Philippines; however, the Filipino government says otherwise, so it may be wise to have one.

Alternative route A ferry passenger service from Kudat to Palawan Island in the Philippines is expected to start operating by late 2016.

to Sepilok. A taxi from the long-distance bus station to town (or vice versa) will probably run RM20.

Sepilok

A visit to the world's most famous place to see orangutans in their natural habitat just became even more compelling thanks to the addition of an outdoor nursery for youngsters in the same complex, and the nearby, excellent Sun Bear Conservation Centre. On top of this, there's a stylish new restaurant and cafe that's recently opened.

What makes Sepilok work so well is its organisation, special-needs-friendly paths, and the fact that, with the exception of the nearby Labuk Bay Proboscis Monkey Sanctuary, it is all within walking distance. There are also some beautiful places to stay here in the clasp of the jungle.

Sights & Activities

Sepilok Orangutan Rehabilitation Centre ANIMAL SANCTUARY

(SORC; 089-531 189, emergency 089-531 180; sorc64@gmail.com; Jln Sepilok; adult/child RM30/15, camera fee RM10; ticket counter 9am-noon & 2-4pm Sat-Thu, 9-11am & 2-4pm Fri) Around 25km north of Sandakan, and covering some 40 sq km of the Kabili-Sepilok Forest Reserve, this inspiring world-famous centre welcomes orphaned and injured orangutans for rehabilitation before returning them to forest life. There are currently between 60 and 80 living here. The new showstopper is the recently opened **outdoor nursery**, just two minutes' walk from the feeding platforms, where abandoned toddlers are taught the building blocks they'll need to keep them alive back in the wild.

The youngsters you'll be charmed by are between six and nine years, and in the refrigerated cool of the nursery viewing area, you can sit and watch them focusing on their swinging skills; it's a laugh a minute as they tumble comically into one another and do their best to irritate the trainers by walking on the ground instead of climbing. Try and get here early in the morning before they're fed and become sleepy.

➡ Platform Feeding

Feedings at the platforms are at 10am and 3pm and last 30 to 50 minutes. Schedules are posted at the visitor reception centre. Tickets are valid for one day, although you can see two feedings in the same day. Watching the trees begin to shake, the cat's cradle of ropes vibrating, the first swatch of orange shifting through the branches, is a moment you'll never forget.

Also worth noting is that only around two to four of the population will feed at any one time. The larger males almost never congregate here. In order to get a good spot for your camera or kids, get here 20 minutes early. Finally, the morning feeding tends to be more tour-group heavy, so if you want a quieter experience, try the afternoon. It's

Sepilok

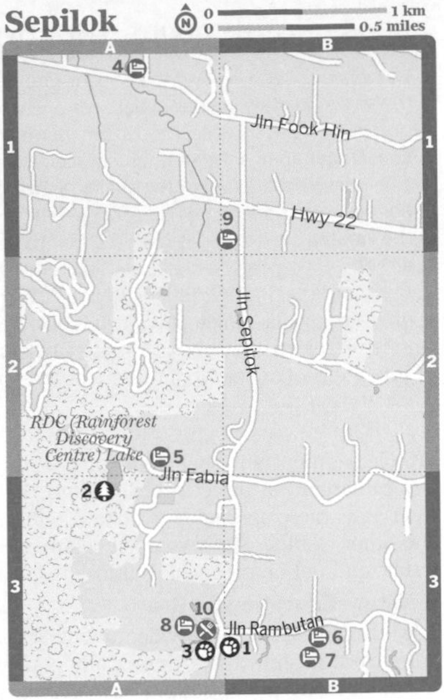

Sepilok

Sights

1 Borneo Sun Bear Conservation Centre B3
2 Rainforest Discovery Centre A3
3 Sepilok Orangutan Rehabilitation Centre A3

Sleeping

4 Paganakan Dii Tropical Retreat A1
5 Sepilok B&B A2
6 Sepilok Forest Edge Resort B3
7 Sepilok Jungle Resort B3
8 Sepilok Nature Resort A3
9 Uncle Tan Guesthouse B1

Eating

10 Lindung Gallery Cafe A3

CROSSING THE DIVIDE: THE COLLECTORS!

Be warned, when visiting the Sepilok Orangutan Rehabilitation Centre (SORC), it's better to leave valuables in your coach, car or locker (available on request) before entering the orangutan feeding area, for certain members of their population are renowned for their collecting habits; they're not fussy, Leica cameras and Ray Ban sunglasses will suffice. One ape in particular (with a distinguished black face) usually singles out a female member of the audience and makes a beeline, only to cross the divide between the arboreal to the viewing area. He may get attached to you, literally, and has been known to occasionally bite. If he gets too close, alert a member of staff.

If you're very lucky, you might spot C.I.D, a fully flanged large male and resident king of this particular jungle, though he's only seen once or twice a year. To learn more about these orangutans so you can spot them by name, check out the following link: www.orangutan-appeal.org.uk/about-us/meet-the-orangutans.

especially important that you don't bring any containers of insect repellent into the reserve, as these are highly toxic to the apes and other wildlife. Spray yourself before entering, and put on plenty of sunblock.

➡ **Nature Education Centre**

A worthwhile 20-minute video about Sepilok's work is shown five times daily (9am, 10.30am, 11am, noon, 2.10pm and 3.30pm) opposite reception in the auditorium here.

➡ **Walking Trails**

If you want to explore the sanctuary further, several walking trails lead into the forest; register at the visitor reception centre to use them. Trails range in length from 250m to 4km, and different paths are open at different times of year. Guided night walks can be arranged through the centre or at the various lodges. There's also a 10km trail through mangrove forest to Sepilok Bay; this is quite a rewarding walk, and if you're especially fit you may be able to complete it between feeding times. A permit from the **Forestry Department** (☎089-213 966, 089-660 811; Jln Leila) is required in advance for this route. The department can also arrange basic overnight accommodation at the bay (RM100) or a boat back to Sandakan. Some travel or tour agencies can assist with the permit and other arrangements.

Borneo Sun Bear Conservation Centre ANIMAL SANCTUARY

(BSBCC; ☎089-534 491; www.bsbcc.org.my; Jln Sepilok; adults/child under 12yrs RM30/free; ⏲9am-4pm) These rescued loveable pint-sized bears recently found a home here at Sepilok with the fantastic new Borneo Sun Bear Conservation Centre (BSBCC), which opened in 2014. The centre has full access for the disabled, and it's possible to see the bears from an elevated glassed viewing area as they climb up trees close by you. There are also telescopes set up for micro examination. There's also a gift shop that sells T-shirts, toys, and has an educational video-lounge.

So called because of the golden bracelet of fur around their necks, the bears' Rorschach-like pattern is never duplicated, varying as they do in colour from cream to orange. At a maximum of 150cm and 60kg in weight, they are are little larger than 'Paddington' and are the smallest of the world's bears. Sun bears are found throughout Southeast Asia in eastern India, southern China, Myanmar, Laos, Vietnam and Borneo, usually at an altitude of around 2700m. An average male sun bear needs at least 39 sq km of forest to find sufficient food. They're excellent climbers, equipped with long claws to scale high trees in search of beehives. As they rip a cavity in the trunk to get to their honey, they create a safe place for hornbills and other birds to nest at a later date. They also control the forest's destructive population of termites, as they are a critical part of the bears' diet.

Across Asia the sun bear is caught and slaughtered for meat and Chinese medicine. In countries like China and Vietnam, the poor beasts are strapped in tiny cages and hooked to IVs that pump bile from their gall bladders. Thankfully this does not happen in Sabah, although the bears are still under enormous threat from habitat loss. Animals donated to the centre are first checked for diseases they may have caught as humans' pets, before being transferred to the training pen. A new arrival will learn to climb, build nests and forage before its eventual release into the wild. Sadly while we were researching, a female was struck by lightning and fell from high in a tree and died on impact.

For RM100, it's possible to adopt a bear, and there are around 30 to choose from. If you wish to volunteer here as a keeper, it costs RM7060 for a month or RM4150 for two weeks, including accommodation and meals. Contact Mr Wong Siew Te, BSBCC's founder, for more info on ☎016-555 1256.

Rainforest Discovery Centre NATURE RESERVE
(RDC; ☎089-533 780; www.forest.sabah.gov.my/rdc; adult/child RM15/7; ⏲ticket counter 8am-5pm, park until 8pm) The RDC, about 1.5km from SORC, offers an engaging graduate-level education in tropical flora and fauna. Outside the exhibit hall filled with child-friendly displays, a botanical garden presents samples of tropical plants. There's a gentle 1km lakeside walking trail, and a series of eight canopy towers connected by walkways to give you a bird's-eye view of the tops of the trees; by far the most rewarding element of a trip here.

Paddle boats (RM5) are available to ride around the inviting lake near the centre's entrance. You can also book night walks, which afford the chance to spot nocturnal animals like tarsiers and wild cats.

It's best to get here either at 8am or 4pm, as wildlife tends to hibernate during the sweltering hours in the middle of the day. A proper visit along the trails and towers takes around 1½ hours. This is a good spot to while away time between feedings at the SORC.

Labuk Bay Proboscis Monkey Sanctuary ANIMAL SANCTUARY
(☎089-672 133; www.proboscis.cc; admission adult/child RM60/30, camera/video RM10/20; ⏲8am-6pm) A local palm-plantation owner has created a private proboscis monkey sanctuary, attracting the floppy-conked locals with sugar-free pancakes at 9.30am and 2.30pm feedings at Platform A, and 11.30am and 4.30pm at Platform B, a kilometre away. An estimated 300 wild monkeys live in the 6-sq-km reserve. The proboscis monkeys are enticed onto the main viewing platform so tourists can get better pictures, which may put you off if you're looking for a more ecologically minded experience. Also keep an eye out for the delicately featured silver leaf monkeys.

Proboscis monkeys *(Nasalis larvatus)* are found only on Borneo, although if you take a close look at them, you'd swear you've spotted one in the corner of a dodgy bar. Named for their long bulbous noses, proboscis monkeys are pot-bellied and red-faced, and males are constantly, unmistakably... aroused. With the arrival of Europeans, Malays nicknamed the proboscis *monyet belanda* (Dutch monkey).

Food and accommodation are provided at the Nipah Lodge, on the edge of the oil-palm plantations that surround the sanctuary; the lodge is quite comfortable, a collection of bungalows that are simply adorned, airy and inviting in a tropical-chic way. Guests can also venture out on mangrove

THE WILD MAN OF BORNEO & HOW TO HELP HIM

The term 'orangutan' literally means 'man of the wild', or 'jungle man' – a testament to the local reverence for these great ginger apes. Traditionally, orangutans were never hunted like other creatures in the rainforest; in fact, Borneo's indigenous people used to worship their skulls in the same fashion as they did the heads taken from enemy tribesmen. Orangutans are the only species of great ape found outside Africa. A mature male is an impressive creature with an arm span of 2.25m, and can weigh up to 144kg. Dominant males also have distinctive wide cheek pads to reinforce their alpha status. It was once said that an orangutan could swing from tree to tree from one side of Borneo to the other without touching the ground. Sadly this is no longer the case, and hunting and habitat destruction continue to take their toll; it's estimated 50,000 to 60,000 specimens exist in the wild.

If you'd like to get involved with the work of the Sepilok Orangutan Rehabilitation Centre, contact Sepilok Orangutan Appeal UK (www.orangutan-appeal.org.uk), a UK-based charity. The Appeal's orangutan adoption scheme is a particular hit with visitors: for UK£30 a year, you can sponsor a ginger bundle of fun and receive updates on its progress; see the Appeal's website for details. If you're really taken with the place, Sepilok has one of the most popular overseas volunteer programs in Malaysia. Apply through Travellers Worldwide (www.travellersworldwide.com); as of recently, the cost of an eight-week volunteer package, including accommodation, meals and a number of excursions, was UK£3345.

treks into the surrounding jungle, night treks with guides, and are often invited to give basic English lessons at a nearby village schoolhouse.

Independent travel here is difficult unless you have your own vehicle, as Teluk Labuk (Labuk Bay) sits 15km down a rough dirt track off the main highway. If you're staying here, Nipah Lodge will handle all transfers; otherwise your lodging in Sepilok will be able to arrange transport for around RM120. You can also look for minivans and taxis in the car park of SORC; travellers who want to go to Teluk Labuk should be able to negotiate shared taxis and vans to the proboscis feeding for around RM150 (round trip from Teluk Labuk back to your Sepilok lodging).

Sleeping & Eating

If you came to Sandakan for the orangutans of Sepilok, do yourself a favour and stay near the apes. The lodging here tends to have more character than Sandakan. Most accommodation options are scattered along Jln Sepilok, the 2.5km-long access road to the rehabilitation centre.

Sepilok B&B HOSTEL $
(☎089-534 050, 019-833 0901; www.sepilokbednbreakfast.com.my; Jln Fabia; dm with fan/air-con RM35/45, d fan only RM68, d with air-con RM108-188) Located opposite the Rainforest Discovery Centre, this place has an authentic hostel vibe with a cosmo cast of backpackers. Dorms are spartan but clean. Rooms are nice with white walls, colourful curtains and fresh linen. Pitta Lodge has self-catering facilities for families and fan-only rooms. Camping here is better in March and April when there's less rain.

★Paganakan Dii Tropical Retreat BOUTIQUE HOTEL $$
(☎089-532 005; www.paganakandii.com; dm/s/d RM35/60/155, 2-/4-person bunaglow RM175/236; ❄📶) Popular with families wanting a taste of nature, this place has hammocks at every turn, and brick-and-wood bungalows with balcony and nicely crafted furniture, wood floors and step-in showers. Make sure you ask for one with a view of the lake and mountains. There are also eight new box-standard rooms with shared bathroom. Transfers to Sepilok are included. Perfect.

Sepilok Nature Resort RESORT $$
(☎089-674 999, 089-673 999; http://sepilok.com; r from RM265; ❄@) Beside an ornamental pond, this beautiful wood-accented hotel is a study in comfort: think mature rubber plants shading its two-tiered central lodge, carriage lamps casting their glow on its welcoming lounge. Chalets are roomy with sumptuous bathrooms, huge beds and private balconies. The Pan-Asian menu is superb with dinner on the candlelit terrace. Romantic.

Uncle Tan Guesthouse GUESTHOUSE $$
(☎016-824 4749; www.uncletan.com; Jln Batu 14; dm RM51, d without/with bathroom RM106/116; ❄@📶) The Uncle Tan empire is one of the oldest backpacker/adventure travel outfits in Sabah. Dorms are boxy, rooms have lino floors and bare walls, though both are clean. It's a summer camp vibe here, and the owners can hook you up with trips to places like the Sungai Kinabatangan (RM265).

Sepilok Forest Edge Resort RESORT $$
(☎089-533 190, 013-869 5069; www.sepilokforestedgeresort.com; Jln Rambutan; dm/d RM48/100, chalets RM265; ❄📶🏊) Set within manicured lawns, this stunning accommodation is

PROBOSCIS MONKEY: PROFILE OF A BIG NOSE

Proboscis monkeys are a curiosity, and not just because of those Cyrano de Bergerac hooters. Dominant males have a harem of wives while the other males form a lacklustre bachelor group trying to impress the ladies with their erections and gymnastic displays; often dejectedly resorting to one another as a source of pleasure. The more wobbly and huge the nose, the more attractive a male is to the comparatively smurf-nosed female. Sworn enemy of the aggressive domineering macaque monkey, the proboscis is also a favourite meal of crocodiles. Pursued by the former, they vault as far as they can across forest tributaries, land with an audible splash and swim like hell to the other side before they become lunch. Nature has kindly improved the probability factor of survival by endowing them with webbed fingers. Because of their diets, proboscis monkeys tend to have severe flatulence, another attractive element of this already most graceful of species. In the wild a group of these monkeys can number as many as 80 individuals.

choking on plants and flowers and has chalets fit for a colonial explorer, with polished-wood floors, choice art, and private balcony with wrought-iron chairs. There's also a dorm and double rooms located in a pretty longhouse, plus a relaxing tropical pool/jacuzzi. Around 15-minutes' walk from the Orangutan Rehabilitation Centre.

Sepilok Jungle Resort RESORT **$$**
(☎089-533 031; www.sepilokjungleresort.com; Jln Rambutan; dm RM37, r RM120-190; P ❄ @ ≈) Recently refurbished rooms with more colour on the walls and quilts than a bird of paradise. Rooms are tile-floored with desk, bathroom, TV and fan or air-con. There's a boardwalk over an ornamental pond and plenty of birdlife here. Pleasant staff.

Lindung Gallery Cafe INTERNATIONAL **$$**
(Jln Sepilok; mains RM16-24; ⏲10am-10pm) Sitting on a hill close to the Borneo Sun Bear Conservation Centre, this new spaceship-shaped restaurant leaps from a design magazine, with its steel-raftered ceiling, buffed-cement floor, tin chairs and exposed brick interior. Thankfully the food easily lives up to the decor, with a menu featuring eggs Benedict, gourmet burgers, stone-baked pizza and fish 'n' chips, as well as cocktails and fresh juices.

Information

Sepilok is located at 'Batu 14', 14 miles (23km) from Sandakan. The street connecting the highway to the centre is lined with various accommodation options.

It's best to get money in Sandakan, but an ATM has been installed in a Petronas Station on the road between Sandakan and Sepilok. The next-closest ATM is in Sandakan Airport. Money can be changed at upmarket sleeping spots for a hefty change fee.

Getting There & Away

BUS

Bus 14 from Sandakan (RM3) departs hourly from the city centre. If coming from KK, board a Sandakan-bound bus and ask the driver to let you off at 'Batu 14'. You will pay the full fare, even though Sandakan is 23km away.

TAXI

If you are coming directly from Sandakan, a taxi should cost no more than RM45 (either from the airport or the city centre). If you want one to wait and return you to Sandakan, you're looking at RM100. Taxi 'pirates', as they're known, wait at Batu 14 to give tourists a ride into Sepilok. It's RM3 per person for a lift. Travellers spending the night can arrange a lift with their accommodation if they book ahead of time. Walking to the SORC is also an option – it's only 2.5km down the road.

VAN

You can usually organise a pick-up (in a shared minivan from the Kinabatangan operators) from Sepilok after the morning feeding if you are planning to head to Sungai Kinabatangan in the afternoon.

Sandakan Archipelago

While everyone knows about the Semporna Archipelago, it seems hardly anyone wants to visit the Sandakan Archipelago, off the coast of its namesake port. Don't they like fluffy specks of emerald sprouting like orchids out of the Sulu Sea, or tales of POW derring-do?

The archipelago is made up of a number of large islands like Libaran and Berhala, while islands Selingan, Bakungan Kecil and Gulisan comprise the national park. All three have turtle hatcheries, however the only one you can visit is Selingaan.

Recent reports of Turtle Island Park suggest that the former circus of gawping visitors watching a mother hawksbill or green turtle shuffling up the beach and laying her eggs, has become much more considerate of the reptiles' needs, with smaller numbers and stricter regulation on how close you get. For your part, please don't shine lights in the hatching mother's eyes in pursuit of a photo, nor allow any of your party to touch hatchlings – however cute they are – as they are released from their 50-day incubation. You may have to wait a while for the mothers to come, but come they will, often late in the night. Your ticket includes simple air-con accommodation on **Pulau Selingan**, boat transfer and meals. You leave Sandakan Jetty at 9.30am for Selingan (an hour away), and return the next morning.

To organise a trip here, book through **Ocean Quest** (☎089-212 711; cquest1996@gmail.com; Jln Buli Sim-Sim; boat transfer from Sandakan, accommodation & dinner on Selingaan Island RM800, camera fee RM10, entrance fee RM60), or SI Tours (p78), based in Sandakan.

Pulau Lankayan

Pulau Lankayan isn't just photogenic, it's screen-saver material. Water isn't supposed to get this clear, nor sand this squeaky

WORTH A TRIP

PULAU BERHALA

Part of the Sandakan Archipelago, Pulau Berhala is supremely serene, an exemplar of a rare genre: a lovely tropical island hardly touched by tourists. Sandstone cliffs rise above the Sulu Sea, hemming in quiet patches of dusty, sandy prettiness. The vibe is so sleepy it's narcoleptic, an atmosphere accentuated by a quiet water village inhabited by fishing families, loads of migrating birds (their presence is heaviest in October and November) and...well, OK. There's not a lot else, except some very big rocks.

But, oh, what rocks. Rock climbers grade the formations here F5a – F6b, which is jargon for a mix of slow sloping walls and vertical cliff faces. Fieldskills Adventures (p47) in Kota Kinabalu runs two-day/one-night rock-climbing trips out here for RM500 per person.

Berhala was a leper colony during the colonial period, and the Japanese used the island as a civilian internment centre and POW camp during WWII. American writer Agnes Newton Keith was kept here awhile, as was a group of Australian POWs who managed to escape the island by boat and sail to Tawi Tawi in the Philippines.

clean. A spattering of jungle, a few swaying palms...sigh. No wonder so many lovers come here for their honeymoons, which are often (but not necessarily) accompanied by dive expeditions at **Lankayan Island Resort** (☎088-238 113, 089-673 999; http://lankayan-island.com/; Batu 6; r diver/nondiver RM3350/RM2728), the one accommodation option on Lankayan. There are a few dozen cabins dotted along the sand where the jungle meets the sea, decked out in flowing light linens and deep tropical hardwood accents. Transfers from Sandakan are included in your accommodation.

Sungai Kinabatangan

The Kinabatangan River is Sabah's longest: 560km of chocolatey-brown water, coiling like the serpents that swim its length far into the Bornean interior. Riverine forest creeps alongside the water, swarming with wildlife that flee ever-encroaching palm-oil plantations. Lodges are tastefully scattered along the banks, while homestay programs pop up with the frequency of local monkeys.

Dozens of tin boats putter along the shores offering tourists the opportunity to have a close encounter with a wild friend. This is the only place in Sabah where you can find a concentration of 10 primates including: orangutan, Bornean gibbon, long-tailed and short-tailed macaque, three kinds of leaf monkey, western tarsier, slow loris and proboscis monkey. Add to this eight different kinds of hornbill, herds of pygmy elephants, crocs, wild boar and perhaps – if you're superlucky – a clouded leopard.

Sights

Gomantong Caves CAVE

(☎089-230 189; www.sabah.gov.my/jhl; Gomantong Hill, Lower Kinabatangan; adult/child RM30/15, camera/video RM30/50; ⏲8am-noon & 2-4.30pm, closing periods apply) Imagine a massive crack in a mountain, a cathedral-like inner chamber shot with splinters of sunlight and swarming with cockroaches and scorpions, and you have the Gomantong Caves. Yes, the smell is disgusting thanks to the ubiquity of bat shit, but these caves are magnificent. The forested area around the caves conceals plenty of wildlife – we spotted, and met many other travellers, who saw orangutans here. The most accessible cave is **Simud Hitam** (Black Cave). Rotate counterclockwise on the raised platform over a steaming soup of guano and roaches.

A 45-minute uphill trek beyond the park office leads to **Simud Putih** (White Cave), containing a great abundance of prized white swiftlets' nests. Both trails are steep and require some sweaty rock climbing.

The majority of visitors to Gomantong come as part of an add-on to their Kinabatangan tour package. It is possible to visit the caves under one's own steam though, usually by private vehicle. The turn-off is located along the road connecting Sukau to the main highway and is quite well signposted. Minivans plying the route between Sandakan and Sukau (RM20) can drop you off at the junction, but you'll have to walk the additional 5km to the park office.

Due to dwindling swiftlet bird populations, the caves are closed over certain periods, so check before planning your visit.

Bukit Belanda HILL

Bukit Belanda – Dutch Hill – is a 420m hill located behind the village of Bilit. The land is owned by the citizens of Bilit, who, despite pressures from logging companies, have not opened the hill to the timber industry, preferring to maintain it as a haven for wildlife. Hike to the top early in the morning – before it gets hot – where you'll be rewarded by lovely views of Sungai Kinabatangan and, if you're lucky, glimpses of local wildlife.

There's no official infrastructure when it comes to visiting the hill; just ask someone in your lodge or Bilit itself to guide you to the beginning of the ascent path. So only attempt it if you're physically fit.

Batu Tulug CAVES

(089-565 145; http://museum.sabah.gov.my; above Batu Putih village; adult/child RM5/3; 9am-5pm, closed Fri) This hill is studded with caves housing the ancestors of local Chinese and Orang Sungai (People of the River). Because the Kinabatangan has a habit of frequently flooding, the final resting place of the dead has traditionally been located in cave complexes. Heavy wooden coffins are interred in the Batu Tulug caves with spears, knives, gongs, bells and Chinese curios, making the hill one of the most important archaeological sites in Sabah. An interpretive information centre is also located on-site.

Wooden staircases snake up the 40m hill. There are two main caves to explore, but if you climb the stairs to the top, you'll be rewarded with a nice view of the surrounding jungle and the Kinabatangan River.

The easiest way to get here is to include the caves in your package tour of the Kinabatangan. If you've got your own vehicle, look for signs indicating the turn-off to Batuh Putih or Muzium Batu Tulug on the Sandakan–Lahad Datu road. The village is south of Sukau Junction, about 1½ hours from Sandakan and 45 minutes from Lahad Datu. GPS coordinates are N 5024.935° E 117056.548°.

Kinabatangan the Orangutan Conservation Project (KOCP) RESEARCH CENTRE

(088-413 293; www.hutan.org.my; Sukau) Inside Sukau village, this conservation camp, run in partnership with a French NGO, is dedicated to studying and protecting the orangutan. They also establish environmental-education programs, reforestation initiatives and an elephant-conservation project in the Sukau-Bilit area. It's not open to casual visitors, but staff may be willing to hire out guides for tracking wild orangutans. Ask for Dr Isabel.

Activities

Wildlife River Cruises

A wildlife cruise down the Kinabatangan is unforgettable. In the late afternoon and early morning, binocular-toting enthusiasts have a chance of spotting nest-building orangutans, nosy proboscis monkeys, basking monitor lizards and hyper long-tailed macaques. The reason so many animals are here though is depressing: the expansion of oil palm plantations has driven local wildlife to the riverbank. They simply have nowhere else to live. Add to this that the Green Belt rule, established to ensure a safe corridor of cover next to the river for animals to pass by new plantations, is being regularly broken by greedy farmers who want to maximise every centimetre of their land, and it's even more concerning.

THE BUSINESS OF BIRD NESTS

The Gomantong Caves are Sabah's most famous source of swiftlet nests, used for one of the most revered dishes of the traditional Chinese culinary oeuvre: the eponymous bird's-nest soup, made from dried swiftlet spit, which when added to the broth dissolves and becomes gelatinous.

There are two types of soupworthy bird nests: black and white. The white nests are more valuable and Gomantong has a lot of them. A kilogram of white swiftlet spit can bring in over US$4000, making nest-grabbing a popular profession, despite the perilous task of shimmying up bamboo poles.

In the last few years visiting has been restricted due to dwindling bird populations (cash-hungry locals were taking the nests before the newborn birds had enough time to mature). Today, the caves operate on a four-month cycle, with closings at the beginning of the term to discourage nest hunters. It's worth asking around before planning your visit – often the caves are empty or off limits to visitors. The four-month cycles are strictly enforced to encourage a more sustainable practice of harvesting.

Mammals can be seen all year, moving around in small groups. Colourful birds are a huge draw: all eight varieties of Borneo's hornbills, plus brightly coloured pittas, kingfishers and, if you're lucky, a Storm's stork or the bizarre Oriental darter all nest in the forests hugging the Kinabatangan. Avian wildlife is more numerous and varied during rainier months (usually October to late March), which coincides with northern-hemisphere migrations. Though friendly for birds, the rainy season isn't accommodating for humans. Flooding has been a problem of late and a couple of lodges will sometimes shut their doors when conditions are severe.

The success rate of animal-spotting largely depends on luck and the local knowledge of your guide. In the late afternoon you'll be looking for proboscis monkeys and crocs. River cruises by night are even more dramatic, the sky a silent theatre of electric-yellow lightning, or jeweller's cloth of glittering gems, as you sign a waiver of rights at your lodge (in the event you get eaten by a croc… just kidding!), then set out into the black mass of the Kinabatangan River. Your life and the success of the cruise is in the hands of your multitasking driver who scopes the trees with his torch whilst driving. You'll possibly see sleeping Stork kingfishers with their eyes open, pygmy elephants in the river, pythons coiled in trees, civet cats, egrets hanging like phantom pods from branches, buffy fish owls, flat-headed cats, and the red eyes of crocodiles emerging like periscopes as they slyly chart your progress.

River tours should always be included in lodge package rates. If you prefer to explore independently, contact local homestay programs, which will be able to hook you up with a boat operator. Or ask about renting a boat in Sukau – everyone in the village is connected to the tourism industry either directly or through family and friends, and someone will be able to find you a captain. Another option: just before the entrance to Sukau village is a yellow sign that says 'Di sini ada boat servis' (Boat service here); different river pilots hang out here throughout the day. Whatever way you choose to find a boat and a guide, expect to pay at least RM100 for a two-hour river cruise on a boat that can hold up to six people (ie you can split the cost with friends).

Hiking

Depending on the location of your lodge, some companies offer short hikes (one to three hours) through the jungle. Night hikes are some of the best fun to be had on the Kinabatangan – there's something magical about being plunged into the intense, cavernlike darkness of the jungle at night. Headlamps should be carried in your hand rather than on your head – wasps and bats tend to be attracted to light sources.

Sleeping & Eating

You'll need to book at the river lodges in advance. In Kinabatangan lingo, a 'three-day, two-night' stint usually involves the following: arrive in the afternoon on day one for a cruise at dusk, two boat rides (or a boat-hike combo) on day two, and an early morning departure on day three after breakfast and a sunrise cruise. When booking a trip, ask about pick-up and drop-off prices – this is usually extra.

Sukau

Tiny Sukau sits on the river across from massive stone cliffs seemingly lifted from a Chinese silk-scroll painting.

Sukau Greenview B&B B&B **$**

(☎089-565 266, 013-869 6922; www.sukaugreenview.net; dm/r RM45/60, 3-day, 2-night package incl breakfast & 3 x 2hr river trips per person RM499) Run by locals, this lime-green wooden affair had OK dorms and basic rooms. There's also a pleasant cafe looking out on the river. Greenview runs special elephant-sighting trips, and also crocodile trips in the early morning and at night (both priced at RM250).

★ **Sukau Rainforest Lodge** LODGE **$$$**

(☎088-438 300; www.sukau.com; 3-day, 2-night package RM1688;) One of *National Geographic's* 'Top 30 Lodges in the World', this is the most upscale digs on the river. Think beautifully appointed split-level rooms with wood and terrazzo floors, rain shower, lounge area and mozzie nets. There's a fine restaurant, an onsite naturalist who gives wildlife talks and night walks, plus a welcome plunge pool to cool off in. Romantic.

The Rainforest Lodge participates in tree-planting projects aimed at reviving degraded portions of riverine forest and is pioneering the use of quiet electric motors on its river cruises. Don't miss the 440m boardwalk in the back that winds through the canopy.

Kinabatangan Riverside Lodge LODGE **$$$**

(☎089-213 502; www.sitours.com; 2-day, 1-night packages incl visit to Sepilok's Sun Bear Conservation Centre & Orangutan Nursery from US$510; ❄📶) Come here to fall gently asleep in a series of luxury chalets, adrift in simple white sheets and polished wood floors, all connected by a series of shady raised walkways through the jungle. A looping nature trail is out the back and an adorable dining area abounds with stuffed monkeys, faux foliage and traditional instruments. It's managed by SI Tours, which charges in US$.

Bilit

Bilit is a friendly village with a number of homestays. River lodges are located on both the Bilit side of the Kinabatangan River and the opposite bank. There's a jetty from which boats depart to lodges on the other side of the river, and across the street is a small yard where you can park a car if you drove here; the family that owns the house charges RM20 a day for the privilege. A small banana orchard acts as a magnet for pygmy elephants.

★Myne Resort RESORT **$$**
(☎089-216 093; www.myne.com.my; longhouse/chalet RM250/280; ❄📶) Situated on the bend of the river, Myne has an open, breezy reception, games room and restaurant festooned with lifeguard rings, and is vaguely reminiscent of an old wooden ship. Chalets are beautiful with peach drapes, river-facing balcony, glossed wood floors, comfy beds, dresser, flat screen and cable TV. Night cruises cost RM75, transfers RM100.

Nature Lodge Kinabatangan LODGE **$$**
(☎088-230 534, 013-863 6263; www.naturelodgekinabatangan.com; 3-day, 2-night package dm/chalet RM402/583) Located close to Bilit, this backpacker jungle retreat has two sections: the Civet Wing with dorm-style huts, and the Agamid Wing with twin-bed chalets with high ceilings and wood floors. The activity schedule is fantastic: the three-day, two-night packages include four boat tours, one guided hike *and* all meals, which is as good value as you'll find in these parts.

Proboscis Lodge Bukit Melapi LODGE **$$**
(☎088-240 584; www.sdclodges.com; 2-day, 1-night package tw share per person RM350, river cruises RM95; ❄) Based on a promontory that saw a battle between local *Orang Sungai* (People of the River) and the Japanese in WWII, this lodge's fruit-luxuriant grounds are popular with sweet-toothed elephants. There's a games room and pleasant lounge here, while rooms are huge with river-facing balcony, cable TV, bathroom, desk and comfy beds. Watch out for the hornbills. Staff are superfriendly.

The two-day, one-night packages include three meals, one river cruise and a pick-up from the Lapit jetty.

Kinabatangan Jungle Camp LODGE **$$**
(☎013-540 5333, 019-843 5017, 089-533 190; www.kinabatanganjunglecamp.com; 2-day, 1-night package RM550) This earth-friendly retreat caters to birders and serious nature junkies; facilities are functional, with the focus on quality wildlife-spotting over soft, comfortable digs, with fan-only rather than air-con rooms. Packages include three meals, two boat rides, guiding and transfers. The owners also run the Labuk B&B in Sepilok, and four out of five travellers opt for a Kinabatangan–Sepilok combo tour.

Borneo Nature Lodge LODGE **$$$**
(☎088-230 534; www.naturelodgekinabatangan.com; Kampung Bilit, Kinabatangan District; 3-day, 2-night stay incl 3 boat rides RM1057) 🍃 Welcoming staff and deliciously cool, cosy rooms await in this fine eco-conscious lodge. The food is particularly tasty and there's an open lounge to read or watch DVDs (don't you dare!). The guides here are top-notch and know every centimetre of the river. Watch out for nosy macaques – keep your windows shut!

Last Frontier Resort RESORT **$$$**
(☎016-676 5922; www.thelastfrontierresort.com; 3-day, 2-night package RM600; ❄@📶) Maybe they should rename this place the Last Breath Resort after the torturously steep hill you have to ascend via an infinity of steps to reach the place. Only the fit should attempt it, however your reward is a serene view of the flood plains and a sense of absolute escape with boutique-style rooms with chocolate-brown walls, dark-wood beds and red linen. There's also the dinky Monkey Cup Cafe which serves pasta bolognese, chicken curry and pancakes.

The price includes two river cruises and one trek. The transfer here costs RM40 extra. You'll also be glad to hear there's a store room at the bottom of the 538 steps, to leave your heavy bag while you carry up the bare essentials.

Bilit Rainforest Lodge LODGE **$$$**
(☎088-448 409; http://bilitrainforestlodge.com; 2-day, 1-night package incl meals & 1 night river cruise RM420; ❄📶) Rainforest has 24 rooms

DON'T MISS

HOMESTAYS ON THE KINABATANGAN

Homestay programs are popping up with increasing frequency in Sukau, Bilit and other villages, giving tourists a chance to stay with local *Orang Sungai* and inject money almost directly into local economies. Please note the contacts we provide are for local homestay program coordinators who will place you with individual families.

The villagers of **Abai** love hosting guests and chatting with you – you can expect to be asked to participate in the local village volleyball matches! A homestay is best arranged through Adventure Alternative Borneo (p46) in Kota Kinabalu, which maintains direct contact with the villagers. It should cost RM870 for a two-night package that includes meals, guided village walk and jungle walk, one day and night river cruise, plus boat from Sandakan and room and meals.

In **Sukau**, **Bali Kito Homestay** (☎013-869 9026, 089-568 472; http://sukauhomestay.com; 3-day, 2-night package for 4 persons RM650, 1 night incl 2 meals RM50) can connect you with several different families and, for additional fees, hook you up with cultural programs, fishing trips, opportunities to work on traditional farms, treks, wildlife cruises and other fun. A special walk-in rate of RM30 is also available if you just rock up at the village (meals are RM10 each). A four-person three-day, two-night package that includes meals, four river cruises, transport to and from Sandakan and a visit to the Gomantong Caves costs RM650 per person, but different packages can be arranged for smaller groups.

Homestays in **Bilit** are on a rotation system of nine households so they all get a fair crack of the whip. The houses we visited were all fiercely houseproud with mattresses on clean floors (expect squat loos). You can just turn up here or look for the official 'Homestay Malaysia' sign. Alternatively, call **Mr Janggai** (☎013-891 2078; www.bilithomestay.wordpress.com; Bilit) the **Bilit Homestay Coordinator**. Three-day, two-night rates, which include river cruises and trekking, costs RM840 per person.

Near **Batu Puti** (the village adjacent to the Batu Tulug caves), **Miso Walai Homestay** (☎089-551070, 019-582 5214, 012-889 5379; www.mescot.org; r RM70) is one of the oldest, best-run community ecotourism initiatives in the area and works with the excellent KOPEL, a village co-operative managed and run by the local people themselves. We've had really glowing reports from travellers who have stayed and worked here on the volunteer program planting trees. You'll be encouraged to learn to cook, take part in village sports and farming as part of the experience. By dint of its location, this homestay also happens to be outside the tourist crush in Sukau and Bilit, so your chances of spotting wildlife are much better.

When staying in a homestay, it is important to act as a guest in someone's home. Privacy will be reduced, and you may be expected to help with chores, cooking, cleaning etc (this depends on the family you stay with). Men and women should dress modestly and couples will want to avoid overt displays of affection, which locals tend to frown on. English may not be widely spoken. The experience is a different one, one which many visitors absolutely love, but it's certainly not everyone's cup of tea. That said, we strongly encourage giving homestays a shot if you haven't done so before.

with stained-wood floors, balcony complete with hammock, armoire and bathroom. Comparatively bland compared with some of the competition, the service is warm, the grounds large. There's also a handsome central building with a nice bar come evening. An additional cruises cost RM120 per person.

Bilit Adventure Lodge LODGE $$$
(☎089-271 077; www.stwadventure.com; 2-day, 1-night package from RM665, with air-con RM740; ❄) Built 10 years ago, this cosy lodge has 16 air-con and eight fan rooms. It feels authentic with its river-bar cafe and bamboo-accented rooms with colourful quilts. The fan-only rooms are less impressive. Set in 10 acres of untamed wilderness, the lodge's lights are kept low at night to encourage the presence of visitors.

For RM30 you can take a cooking class with a local person.

Upriver

★**Tungog Rainforest Eco Camp** CABIN $
(☎089-551 070, 019-582 5214; www.mescot.org; per night incl 3 meals RM95, river cruises RM45)

This eco camp faces a pretty oxbow lake by the Kinabatangan River. Luxurious it isn't – expect wooden shelters with mattress, fragrant sheets and pillows, plus a mozzie net and shared bathrooms; however, the immersion in nature and chance to put something back by planting trees is magical. Given there are no other camps for kilometres, you have the wildlife to yourself.

On the road between Sandakan and Lahad Datu, ask the bus to drop you at the Kinabatangan bridge, from where you catch a boat to the camp. The office of KOPEL Ltd, which manages the camp, is located under the Kinabatangan River bridge. Book ahead.

Uncle Tan's Jungle Camp LODGE **$$**
(☎089-535 784, 016-824 4749; www.uncletan.com; 2-day, 1-night packages from RM350, 3-day, 2-night packages from RM450) Uncle Tan was one of the earliest environmentalists working along the Kinabatangan. His legacy lives on in his lodges. As the website clearly explains, it is *not* the Hilton. Expect very basic digs but bags of enthusiasm from the great staff, knowledgeable guides and a warm atmosphere. Due to its isolated location, animal sightings are high.

Abai Jungle Lodge LODGE **$$$**
(☎089-213 502, 013-883 5841; www.sitoursborneo.com; 2-day, 1-night packages incl visit to Sepilok's Sun Bear Conservation Centre & Orangutan Nursery from US$510) Managed by SI Tours (p78), ecofriendly Abai Jungle Lodge sits 37km upstream from Sukau as the river emerges from secondary forest. While it's basic, rooms are comfortable fan-only affairs, and the food is nothing to get excited about either, the wildife here is terrific, and reports of Abai's guides tend to be that they go all out to find what you're looking for.

Getting There & Away

Transfers are usually arranged with your lodging as part of your package, but you can save by arriving independently. Arrange transport from any of the drop-off points with your tour operator or with a local minivan. Don't get on Birantihanti buses – they stop any time someone wants to get on or off, which could quadruple travelling time.

BUS & MINIVAN

From KK, board a Tawau- or Lahad Datu–bound bus and ask the driver to let you off at 'Sukau Junction', also known as 'Meeting Point' – the turn-off road to reach Sukau. If you are on a Sandakan-bound bus, make sure your driver remembers to stop at the Tawau-Sandakan junction, it's called 'Batu 32' or 'Checkpoint' (sometimes it's known as Sandakan Mile 32).

From Sepilok or Sandakan, expect to pay around RM20 to reach 'Batu 32', and around RM35 if you're on a Sandakan–Tawau bus and want to alight at 'Meeting Point'.

Arrange in advance with your Sepilok accommodation to be picked up from these drop-off points. The alternative is vastly overcharging taxis.

A minivan ride to 'Meeting Point' from Lahad Datu costs RM25. When buying your bus tickets, remember to tell the vendor where you want to get off so you don't get overcharged.

CAR

If you are driving, note that the Shell petrol station on the highway at Sukau Junction (at the turn-off to Sukau) is the last place to fill up before arriving at the river. The road to Sukau is pretty smooth, but as you get closer to Bilit you'll start running into some dirt patches. It is possible to get to Bilit via 2WD – just drive carefully, especially if it's been raining.

Lahad Datu

POP 105,620

This little coastal town has a fish market, dry goods market, wilting sun-scorched buildings and very little else to keep you here. Travellers wishing to visit Tabin Wildlife Park and the Danum Valley – if they haven't already booked – arrive in town, head to the respective offices and stay a night before leaving for the jungle the next morning. If you *have* booked, you'll likely arrive on an early flight and be spirited away by your guide from either **Borneo Nature Tours** (☎089-880 207; www.borneonaturetours.com; Lot 20, block 3, Fajar Centre), which runs the Borneo Rainforest Lodge (BRL), or the **Danum Valley Field Centre** (☎089-881 092, 088-326 300; rmilzah@gmail.com; Block 3, Fajar Centre). Both of these outfits have offices next to each other in the upper part of town – known as Taman Fajar, or Fajar Centre.

There's a major difference between the two Danum Valley sleeping options, and that's price and luxury. The Borneo Rainforest Lodge is upscale and very comfortable, the Field Centre, rough, ready and very authentic. The Field Centre's office can be slow about responding to emails or phone calls asking for lodging. They offer ample rooms and dorm space these days for non scientific types, but it's always best to book ahead by a few days. For groups you may have to book much earlier. You can just show up in person, and politely request to speak with someone about sleeping arrangements.

At the airport terminal building you'll find the efficient and friendly booking office of Tabin Wildlife Holidays (p95), a secondary forest sanctuary on the other side of Lahad Datu.

Sleeping

Full Wah HOTEL $

(089-884 100; Jln Anggerik; s/d from RM45/65;) If you're on a tight budget, Full Wah will do. Rooms are exceedingly mediocre, but clean and mould free.

★**Bike & Tours B&B** GUESTHOUSE $$

(017-864 2016, 017-293 6376; www.bikeandtours.com; Lot 62, Taman Hap Heng, Batu 1 1/4, Jln Segama; s/d with shared bathroom RM160/184 incl breakfast, d with bathroom RM230;) Winning applause for their cycling excursions in the area, and the quality of their digs, B&T is run by a friendly Swiss/Malay couple and their five rooms are cool affairs with laminate floors and fresh linen. There's a pool in the garden, great breakfast and a complimentary pick-up from the bus station/airport.

B&T are all about mindfulness in nature; taking your time on two wheels to get to know the locals and the environment around you. Recommended.

Bay Hotel HOTEL $$

(089-882 801; Block O, lot 1 & 2, 7b Jln Panji; s RM95, d RM105-118) Fresh rooms with flat screen, swish decor, bathroom and air-con – plus a pleasant cafe downstairs serving Western food – make this a nice addition to the currently limited sleeping options in town.

Hotel De Leon HOTEL $$

(089-881 222; www.hoteldeleon.com.my; Darvel Bay Commercial Centre; s/d from RM148/178;) Lahud Datu's plushest option, seaward Leon is cool, with a chic baroque-accented lobby and restaurant, and fresh, air-conditioned rooms. Perfect for those needing a night of comfort after the bush. Free wi-fi is available in all the rooms.

Eating

It's worth stopping by one of the convenience stores in Fajar Centre on Lorong Fajar to stock up on a couple of snacks before your trip into the Danum Valley.

Kak Tini Restaurant MALAYSIAN $

(cnr Jln Bunga Raya & Jln Teratai; mains RM3.50; 24hr) This 24-hour mint-green restaurant close to the bus station is popular for its buffet of fried chicken, soups, fresh fish and noodle dishes.

MultiBake BAKERY $

(Fajar Centre; cakes from RM1.80; 8am-10pm;) Malaysia's franchised patisserie is located in Fajar Centre (it has free wi-fi too).

Dovist CHINESE $

(mains from RM5; 9am-10pm) Around the corner from the Danum booking offices; a respectable spot for a more substantial meal of Chinese-style seafood dishes.

Getting There & Away

AIR

MASwings (1800-883 000, outside Malaysia 03-7843 3000; www.maswings.com) currently operates five daily flights to Lahad Datu from KK. The airport is in the upper part of town near Fajar Centre. You must take the first flight of the day (departing KK at 7.25am) if you don't want a one-day layover in town before heading to the Danum Valley.

BUS

Express buses on the KK–Tawau route stop at the Shell station (Fajar Centre) behind the Danum Valley office in the upper part of town. Other buses and minivans leave from a vacant lot near Tabin Lodge in the lower part of town. There are frequent departures for Sandakan (RM25, 2½ hours), Sukau (RM25, two hours), Semporna (RM22 to RM25, two hours) and Tawau (RM20, 2½ hours). Charter vehicles and 4WDs wait in an adjacent lot; these guys are difficult to hire after sunset.

Danum Valley Conservation Area

Flowing like a series of dark, mossy ripples over 440 sq km of central Sabah, the Danum Valley Conservation Area is like something out a children's story book: the sheer spectrum of furry and scaled friends you find within its dipterocarp forest is mind-blowing: orangutans, tarsiers, sambar deer, bearded pigs, flying squirrels, king cobras, proboscis monkeys, red-leaf monkeys, gibbons and pygmy elephants (to name a few). The area is also known for its medium-sized cats, with the beautifully marked clouded leopard spotted on night drives, as well as the flat-headed cat, marbled cat, leopard cat and cartoon-like bay cat. This almost impenetrable arboreal fortress is watered by Sungai Segama and shaded by 70m-high old-growth canopy and 1093m-high Mt Danum. Recognised as one of the world's most complex ecosystems, and astonishingly, a new species of plant is found by scientists here every week. Your alarm clock is the melodic ray gun 'zap' of dawn gibbons and the chainsaw drone of cicadas, your bedtime cue the shrill of crickets and your aching calves (which will have done so much trekking, they'll be marching you to sleep).

This pristine rainforest is currently under the protection of **Yayasan Sabah** (Sabah Foundation; www.ysnet.org.my), a semigovernmental organisation tasked with both protecting and utilising the forest resources of Sabah. They say that at any given time, there are over a hundred scientists doing research in the Danum Valley. Accommodation has been expanded so more travellers can experience its rare delights with a capacity of up to 135 people. See the website of the South East Asia Rainforest Research (www.searrp.org) for more information on research occurring in the valley.

There are two lodging options in the Danum Valley: the Borneo Rainforest Lodge (p94) (BRL), and the Danum Valley Field Centre (p94). You absolutely must have accommodation arranged with one of them before you visit – no dropping in. Danum is a jungle, and while one person's night drive/day walk might yield multiple sightings, another's can be sparse; it really is the luck of the draw.

Sights & Activities

Both the Borneo Rainforest Lodge and the Danum Valley Field Centre offer a variety of jungle-related activities. Only the BRL has official nature guides, whereas the Field Centre offers park rangers. If you're booked with a tour company however, you will be attached to a trained English-speaking guide.

Watching the World Wake Up

Getting out of bed while it's still dark and your clock reads 5.30am is no fun; the jungle quiet as a cemetery, the air shivery cold. But driving through the forest to a vertiginously high wooden watchtower, climbing to its top and waiting for the sun to appear over the rim of the earth below make it all worthwhile. As the first cicadas wake, the melodic call of the gibbon reaching out of the mist-veiled jungle, you feel like a privileged voyeur witnessing a sacred, primal moment. Then slowly the fireworks begin as a sliver of sun appears over the distant forest ridge, the sky seguing through ruby to salmon, orange to vermilion. Priceless. Tip: it's cold, so bring a jumper!

> **DANUM SURVIVAL KIT**
>
> We strongly recommend leech socks (especially if there's been rain), a stash of energy sweets, insect repellent, plasters for blisters, a strong torch and, if you're looking for that front-cover shot of a rhinoceros hornbill in flight, a powerful zoom lens. Sneakers are fine in dry weather; hiking boots, though heavier, provide better support in slippery conditions.

Trekking in the Valley

The main activities at the BRL and the Danum Valley Field Centre are walking on more than 50km of marked, meandering trails. Your average group is about six to eight persons and fitness will vary considerably; if you're in a troupe of superheroes and get left behind, don't be afraid to ask the guide to slow down. Depending on the zeal of your group, you might walk as much as 16km or more in one day over a series of short treks or one long and short one (excluding night walks); remember you're in the jungle and clambering over roots and fallen trees is hard work, so don't push yourself unnecessarily.

At the BRL, take advantage of the well-trained guides who can point out things you would have never seen on your own. The **Coffincliff Trail** is a good way to start your exploration and get your bearings. It climbs 3km to a cliff where the remains of some Kadazan-Dusun coffins can be seen (although the provenance of the coffins is unclear). After reaching a fairly eye-popping panoramic viewpoint 100m further up the way, you can either return the way you've come or detour around the back of the peak to descend via scenic **Fairy Falls** and **Serpent Falls**, a pair of 15m falls that are good for a quick dip.

The **Danum Trail**, **Elephant Trail** and **Segama Trails** all follow various sections of the Danum Valley and are mostly flat trails offering good chances for wildlife spotting. All can be done in an hour or two. The **Hornbill Trail** and **East Trail** have a few hills, but are still relatively easy, with similarly good chances for wildlife sightings. Finally, if you just need a quick breath of fresh air after a meal, the **Nature Trail** is a short plankwalk near the lodge that allows you to walk into the forest unmolested by leeches.

There are heaps of fantastic trails weaving around the Field Centre – you must bring a ranger along if you aren't a scientist (note that a guide is better than a ranger though, as rangers are not trained to work with tourists). About a two-hour hike away are the **Tembaling Falls**, a cool slice of tropical Edenic beauty. A more strenuous, four-hour trek gets you to the immensely rewarding **Sungai Purut** falls, a series of seven-tiered pools that are fed by waters that drop down 20m from the nearby mountains. The likelihood is you'll climb the 40m-high observation tower just behind the Field Centre at dawn, the mist like a veil over the canopy. The summit platform is reached via a rickety ladder with an ineffective cage around it. Hold on tight and don't look down; if you make it to the top, the view of the jungle is like a sea of green velvet, and is utterly stupendous.

At the Centre you'll also take **night walks**; these tend to be shorter, but give you the chance to see chameleons flopping on branches like drunken 'Rangos', bug-eyed tarsiers, various snakes and curious sambar deer.

Birdwatching

Birdwatchers from around the world come to see a whole variety of rainforest species including the great argus pheasant, crested fireback pheasant, blue-headed pitta, Bornean bristlehead and several species of hornbill, among many others. If you're serious about birding, it may be best to stay at the Borneo Rainforest Lodge. The canopy walkway here is ideal for birdwatching, and some of the guides are particularly knowledgeable about birds. The access road to BRL is also a good spot for birding, as is, frankly, your porch.

Canopy Walkway

As you'll probably know, most of the action in a tropical rainforest happens up in the forest canopy, which can be frustrating for earthbound humans. The BRL's 107m-long, 27m-high canopy walkway gives mere mortals a means of transcending the surly bonds of earth. The swinging bridges traverse a nice section of forest, with several fine *mengaris* and *majau* trees on either side. Birdwatchers often come here at dawn in hope of checking a few species off their master list. Even if you're not a keen birder, it's worth rolling out of bed early to see the sun come up over the forest from the canopy walkway – when there's a bit of mist around, the effect is quite magical. It's located on the access road, a 10-minute walk from the lodge. You need to be a guest at the BRL to access the walkway.

Night Drives

This is one of the surest ways to see some of the valley's 'night shift'. Expect to see one or two species of giant flying squirrels, sambar deer, civets, porcupines and possibly even leopard cats; lucky sightings could include elephants and slow loris.

Night drives leave the BRL and Field Centre most evenings; the best trips are the extended night drives, which depart at about 8.30pm and return at 1am or 2am. Things you'll be glad you brought: light waterproof jacket, binoculars and a powerful torch. It can be cold, too, so bring another layer.

Sleeping & Eating

Danum Valley Field Centre LODGE **$$**
(DVFC; ☎088-326 300, 088-881 688; rmilzah@gmail.com; resthouse r & board from RM180, camping RM30; ❄) An outpost for scientists and researchers, the field centre also welcomes wildlife enthusiasts. Accommodation is organised into four categories: hostel, resthouse, VIP and camping. We recommend the resthouse – with basic clean rooms, ceiling fans and twin beds – located by the canteen. Treks start from here, so if you're staying in the dorms you'll constantly be walking between the two.

Towels are provided for the cold-water showers. The simple hostel is about a seven-minute walk from the canteen, and the barracks-style rooms are separated by gender. If you want to camp, you can lay your sleeping kit (no tent needed) out on the walkways – bug spray recommended!

There are no professionally trained guides at the centre – only rangers who can show you the trails if you just turn up – but book with a tour company and they will provide you with one. We recommend Sticky Rice Travel (p46). Tourists take their meals in the cafeteria-style canteen (veggie friendly). Near the camp is a clear stretch of shallow river to cool off in.

Borneo Rainforest Lodge RESORT **$$$**
(BRL; ☎089-880 207, 088-267 637; www.borneonaturetours.com; d standard/deluxe 3-day & 2-night package per person RM3296/3190) Set beside the Danum River, Borneo Rainforest Lodge

is for Indiana Jones types with healthy wallets – adventure combined with luxury, if you will. If you can afford to splash out on one of their lovely 31 en suite chalets – the deluxe numbers have private balcony with hot tub overlooking the jungle – you won't be disappointed.

Crackling with classy atmosphere and having had a recent facelift, there are talks on wildlife and conservation, slide shows, and raised wooden walkways and a romantic outside terrace.

Getting There & Away

The Danum Valley is only accessible by authorised private vehicle. Borneo Rainforest Lodge guests depart from the lodge office in Lahad Datu at 9am, arriving by lunchtime. If you do not want to spend the night in Lahad Datu, take the 7.25am MASwings flight from KK.

Tourists staying at the Danum Valley Field Centre must board one of two jungle-bound vans that leave the booking office in Lahad Datu at 3.30pm on Mondays, Wednesdays and Fridays. Transport is around RM100 per person each way. Vans return to Lahad Datu from the Field Centre at 8.30am.

Tabin Wildlife Reserve

About an hour's drive from Lahad Datu, this 1205-sq-km reserve consists mainly of lowland dipterocarp forest with mangrove areas – most of it is technically secondary forest, but that doesn't seem to trouble the wildlife or visitors. The stars here are the elephants and primates: gibbons, red-leaf monkeys and macaques, plus a lot of orangutans. Rescued orangutans from Sepilok are actually released here, so you've got a pretty good chance of spotting some. Birdlife is particularly abundant with a staggering 260 species recorded here, including all eight of the hornbill family, from rhino through to helmeted.

Tabin has a number of mud volcanoes and salt licks where animals and birds gather for their precious minerals, and you can watch them, cameras poised, from viewing towers. Sadly you're unlikely to see the Sumatran rhino, which is now believed to be extinct in Borneo. The park is managed by **Tabin Wildlife Holidays** (☎088-267 266; www.tabinwildlife.com.my; Lahud Datu airport terminal; 2-day, 1-night package incl meals from RM1450), which runs the on-site Tabin Wildlife Resort, a pretty retreat with a clutch of upscale chalets. Fair warning: the chalets are attractive, but they're overpriced for what you get. Five trails snake out into the jungle from in front of the resort. Try the Elephant Trail (800m) if you're interested in seeing belching mud pits and improving your complexion by wiping it on your skin. The Gibbon Trail (2.8km) leads to the pretty Lipa Waterfall.

Tabin can be accessed with a rental vehicle (4WD is a must), but most people arrange transport with Tabin Wildlife, the office of which is now conveniently located at the airport terminal at Lahad Datu, which is around 2½ hours' drive from Tabin. There are several entrances to the reserve; the easiest one to navigate to is near the junction of Ladan Tungju and Ladang Premai.

Semporna

POP 62,640

You won't be using your camera's memory card up in the town of Semporna, which, but for its mosque, is not immediately captivating. There's a wet market and some pretty stilted water-hotels, but little reason to extend a stay beyond dumping your bags and going for a chat with one of the many dive companies – all conveniently located in the same street. They'll soon have you salivating over what lies waiting for you in the Semporna Archipelago, a short boat journey away. Many of these companies have a dive centre at the resorts on Mabul island. If you've booked your dive and stay from KK already, you'll be picked up from the airport by your respective tour company and spirited straight to Semporna's port to take you to your end destination, so no need to stay a night.

There are a couple of OK sleeping options, one or two restaurants worth a look, shops to stock up on supplies, and a few decent bars come happy hour, so it's not all bad if you do have to stay.

Sights & Activities

Scuba is the town's lifeline, and there's no shortage of places to sign up for it. Due to the high volume of interest, it is best to do your homework and book ahead – diving at Sipadan is limited to 120 persons per day. This means that if you're in a large group, it's impossible you'll be able to dive together at Sipadan the next day; however, if you're a couple or travelling solo, you're in with a better chance.

Semporna

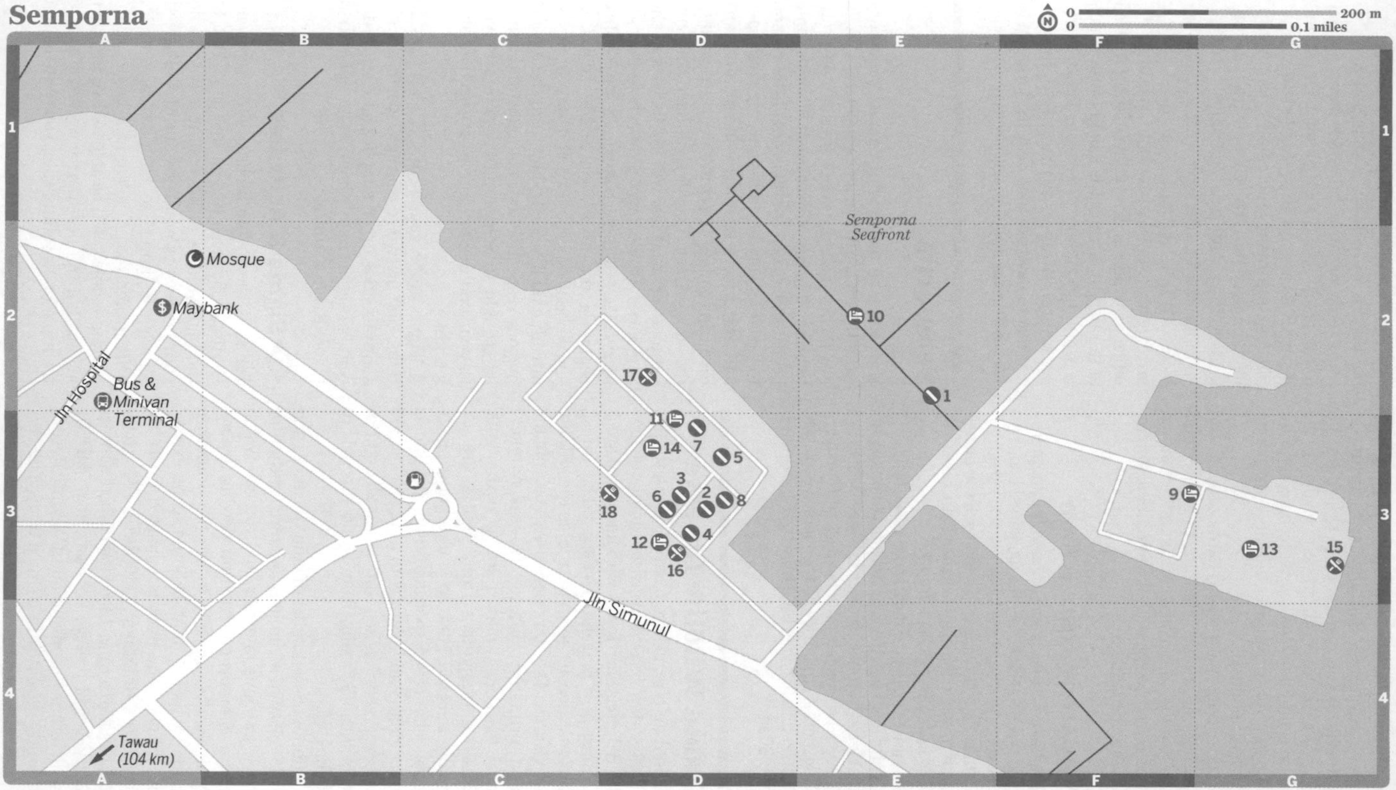
0 200 m
0 0.1 miles
N
A
B
C
D
E
F
G
1
2
3
4
Semporna Seafront
Mosque
Maybank
Jln Hospital
Bus & Minivan Terminal
Jln Simunul
Tawau (104 km)
1
2
3
4
5
6
7
8
9
10
11
12
13
14
15
16
17
18

Sleeping

★Scuba Junkie Dive Lodge HOSTEL $
(☎089-785 372; www.scuba-junkie.com/accommodations; Block B 36, 458 Semporna seafront; dm diver/nondiver RM25/50, r without bathroom diver/nondiver RM75/150, r with bathroom diver/nondiver RM95/190; ❄📶) Fresh yellow walls peppered with underwater shots of marine life, clean bathrooms and a variety of air-con rooms to choose from, make this a sure bet. Also it's directly opposite Scuba Junkie's office, and next to the Diver's Bar, a good spot for breakfast before you head of to the Semporna Archipelago.

Borneo Global Sipadan BackPackers HOSTEL $
(☎089-785 088; www.bgbsipadan.com; Jln Causeway; dm/tr/f incl breakfast RM27/99/130; ❄@📶) There are nine rooms comprising dorm, triples and family options with bathroom. The walls are fresh, the air is cool and there's a friendly lobby area to chill in. They also run three-day PADI Open Water courses for RM920. Run by energetic Max.

Sipadan Inn HOTEL $$
(☎089-781 766; www.sipadaninn-hotel.com; Block D, lot 19-24, Semporna seafront; d/f from RM110/170; ❄@📶) A slice of refrigerated comfort, the Inn has simple but tidy rooms with wood walls, fresh linen, bed runners, coffee-making facilities, spotless bathrooms and very friendly staff.

Holiday Dive Inn HOTEL $$
(☎089-919 128; www.holidaydiveinn.com; Lot A5-A7, Semporna seafront; r RM86-96, f RM168; ❄📶) This recent addition has spotless rooms with cheerful colours, fresh bathrooms, TVs and some rooms with balcony. Good value, it's affiliated with Sipadan Scuba nearby. There's also a nice sundowner roof lounge.

Seafest Hotel HOTEL $$
(☎089-782 333; www.seafesthotel.com; Jln Kastam; r/f RM135/250; ❄) Palatial in proportions, this white monolith at the far end of the 'Semporna seafront' neighbourhood is good value if there's two of you, with well-appointed rooms with desk, bathroom and an international feel. Plus there's a shop, adjacent fish restaurant by the water, and an outdoor pool. Atmosphere? We've been to more effervescent funerals.

Dragon Inn HOTEL $$
(Rumah Rehat Naga; ☎089-781 088; www.dragoninnfloating.com.my; 1 Jln Kastam, Semporna Ocean Tourism Centre; dm RM45, r incl breakfast from RM122, f RM170-190; ❄@📶) Arriving at Dragon Inn, built on stilts and connected by an infinity of a boardwalk over bottle-green water, the first thing you see is a taxidermied giant grouper outside its lobby. Rooms are simple but appealing with wood floors, TV and bathroom. There's also a peaceful shaded cafe to watch the harbour life buzzing by.

Semporna

Activities, Courses & Tours

1	Big John Scuba	E2
2	Billabong Scuba	D3
3	Blue Sea Divers	D3
4	Scuba Junkie	D3
5	Seahorse Sipadan	D3
6	Seaventures	D3
7	Sipadan Scuba	D3
8	Uncle Chang's	D3

Sleeping

9	Borneo Global Sipadan BackPackers	F3
10	Dragon Inn	E2
11	Holiday Dive Inn	D3
12	Scuba Junkie Dive Lodge	D3
13	Seafest Hotel	G3
14	Sipadan Inn	D3

Eating

15	Anjung Lepa	G3
16	Diver's Bar	D3
17	Fat Mother	D2
18	Mabul Steak House	D3

Eating

Various *kedai kopi* (coffee shops) line the 'Semporna seafront', while restaurants at the Seafest Hotel complex offer Chinese seafood. If you wanna go native, sample the *nasi lemak* or *korchung* (rice dumplings) – Semporna is well known for these two dishes.

★Fat Mother CHINESE $
(Semporna seafront; mains RM15; ⏲5-10pm) Mother's has terrific reviews for its warm service and wide-ranging seafood menu – your dinner will be glowering at you from the glass tanks. They'll even prepare your own fish if you've caught it. There's grouper and mango sauce, fish porridge, salted egg and squid, Malay curries and noodle dishes, plus free Chinese tea and melon dessert.

Anjung Lepa SEAFOOD $
(Jln Kastam; mains RM15; ⏲5-10pm) Parked beside the Seafest hotel, this is a lovely little spot to tuck into fresh fish and Malay dishes

come early evening. Squid, prawns, crab... all the treasures of the deep.

Diver's Bar INTERNATIONAL **$$**
(Semporna seafront; mains RM18-32; ⏲7-9am & 1pm-midnight) Beside Scuba Junkie Dive Lodge and opposite the Scuba Junkie office, this terracotta-interiored, partially open-air joint is popular with divers and has a very underwhelming breakfast of fruit and cold eggs (RM10), but come lunch and dinner, it gets better with New Zealand beef and fries, Greek salad and various pasta dishes.

Mabul Steak House STEAK **$$**
(☎089-781 785; Semporna seafront; mains from RM15-20; ⏲noon-11pm) This breezy balcony with an easy vibe and phonebook-thick menu is heavy not just on steak but seafood, serving everything from grouper to parrot fish, mullet, lobster and squid, steak and lamb cutlets, as well as omelettes and glacial 'ice-blended juices'.

ℹ Information

If you're arriving in Semporna under your own steam, leave the bus and minivan drop-off area and head towards the mosque's minaret. This is the way to the waterfront. Follow the grid of concrete streets to the right until you reach 'Semporna seafront' – home to the diving outfitters, each stacked one next to the other in a competitive clump.

Decompression Chamber (☎089-783 100, 012-483 9572; www.navy.mil.my; Pangkalan TLDM, Semporna) There is a decompression chamber at the naval base 14km southwest of Semporna.

Maybank (☎089-784 852; Jln Jakarullah; ⏲9.15am-4.30pm) Expect small lines and the occasional beggar, especially in the evening.

ℹ Getting There & Away

AIR

Flights to Tawau from KK and KL land at Tawau Airport, roughly 28km from town. A private taxi from Tawau Airport to Semporna costs RM100, while Tawau–Semporna buses (RM20) will stop at the airport if you ask the driver nicely. Buses that do not stop at the airport will let you off at Mile 28, where you will have to walk a few (unshaded) kilometres to the terminal. Remember that flying less than 24 hours after diving can cause serious health issues, even death.

BUS

The 'terminal' hovers around the Milimewa supermarket not too far from the mosque's looming minaret. All buses run from early morning until 4pm (except Kota Kinabalu) and leave when full.

Kota Kinabalu (RM75, nine hours) leaves at around 7am or 7pm.

Lahad Datu (RM30, 2½ hours)

Sandakan (RM45 to RM40, 5½ hours)

Tawau (RM25, 1½ hours)

Semporna Archipelago

The stunning sapphires and emeralds of the Semporna Archipelago, home to copper-skinned Bajau sea gypsies in crayon-coloured boats and lush desert islands plucked from your deepest fantasies, are a sight for cynical souls. But no one comes this way for the islands, such as it were – rather, it is the ocean and everything beneath it, that appeals, because this is first and foremost a diving destination, consistently voted one of the best in the world.

Activities

In local speak Semporna means 'perfect', but there is only one island in the glittering Semporna Archipelago that takes this title. Miniature-sized **Sipadan**, moored 36km off the southeast coast, is perfection: turquoise water lapping sugar-fine sand, backdropped by a lush forest of palm trees and strangler fig trees. The island sits atop a pinnacle of rock and prompted world-famous diver Jacques Cousteau to describe it as 'An untouched piece of art'. With a virtual motorway of marine life passing on its way around you on any given day, locals include: parrotfish, batfish, octopuses and cuttlefish changing colour like underwater disco lights; reef sharks, lionfish and clownfish. Pelagic visitors include hammerhead and whale sharks and regular visits from majestic manta and eagle rays. And we haven't even gotten to the reef itself – think staghorn, black and sea-whip corals, barrel sponges and filigree coral fans all looking as if they've been dipped in funhouse paint.

Roughly a dozen delineated dive sites orbit the island, the most famous being **Barracuda Point**, where chevron and blacktail barracuda collide to form impenetrable walls of undulating fish. Reef sharks seem attracted to the strong current here and almost always swing by to say hello. **South Point** hosts the large pelagics like hammerhead and thresher sharks and manta, as well as bumphead parrotfish. Expect the current to be strong here too. The west side of the island features walls that tumble down to an impossibly deep 2000m – words can't do the sight of this justice. The walls are best appreciated from out in the blue on a clear afternoon.

Although Sipadan outshines the neighbouring sites, there are other reefs in the marine park that are well worth exploring. The macro-diving around **Mabul** (or 'Pulau Mabul') is world-famous, and on any given day you can expect to see blue-ringed octopuses, bobtail squid, boxer and orangutan crabs and cardinal fish. In fact, the term 'muck diving' was invented here. The submerged sites around **Kapalai**, **Mataking** and **Sibuan** are also of note.

It's unlikely you can rock up in Semporna and chance upon an operator willing to take you to Sipadan the following day, because you'll have to do an orientation dive on Mabul first. And if you're here in the peak months of July and August or the Christmas period and haven't booked in advance, you're likely to have a wait. Groups need to book many weeks in advance to get a shot at Sipadan.

The government issues 120 passes (RM40) to Sipadan each day (this number includes divers, snorkellers and day trippers). Bizarre rules and red tape, like having certain gender ratios, make the permit process even more frustrating. Each dive company is issued a predetermined number of passes per day depending on the size of its operation and the general demand for permits. Each operator has a unique way of 'awarding' tickets – some companies place their divers in a permit lottery, others promise a day at Sipadan after a day (or two) of diving at Mabul and Kapalai. No matter which operator you choose, you will be required to do a non-Sipadan intro dive unless you are a Divemaster who has logged a dive in the last six months. Permits to Sipadan are issued by day (and not by dive), so make sure you are getting at least three dives in your package.

A three-dive day trip costs between RM250 and RM500 (some operators include park fees, other do not – be sure to ask), and equipment rental (full gear) comes to about RM50 or RM60 per day. Cameras (around RM100 per day) and dive computers (around RM80 per day) are also available for rent at most dive centres. Top-end resorts on Mabul and Kapalai offer all-inclusive package holidays (plus a fee for equipment rental).

Although most of the diving in the area is 'fun diving', Open Water certifications are available, and advanced coursework is popular for those wanting to take things to the next level. Diving at Sipadan is geared towards divers with an Advanced Open Water certificate (currents and thermoclines can be strong), but Open Water divers should not have any problems (they just can't go as deep as advanced divers). A three-day Open Water course will set you back at least RM975. Advanced Open Water courses (two days) cost the same, and Divemaster certification costs around RM2800 and takes four weeks.

Several dive operators are based at their respective resorts, while others have shopfronts and offices in Semporna and/or KK. Please note we have listed the following dive operators alphabetically, not in order of preference.

Big John Scuba DIVING
(BJ Scuba; ☎089-785 399; www.bigjohnscuba.com; Jln Kastam; 3-dive day trip RM280, snorkelling day trip RM150-180) 'Big John' specialises in macro photography and muck diving. Has an office by the Dragon Inn (p97).

Billabong Scuba DIVING
(☎089-781 866; www.billabongscuba.com; Lot 28, block E, Semporna seafront) Accommodation can be arranged at a rickety 'homestay' on Mabul. And we mean rickety.

SNORKELLING IN SEMPORNA

Many nondivers wonder if they should visit Semporna. Of course you should! If you're travelling in a group or as a couple where some dive and some don't, the Semporna islands are a lot of fun; dive and snorkelling trips are timed so groups leave and come back at similar times, so you won't feel isolated from each other. If you're on your own and only want to snorkel, it's still great, but not as world class as the diving experience, and a bit pricey relative to the rest of Malaysia – snorkel trips cost around RM150, and you also have to factor in the relatively high cost of accommodation here and the price of getting out to the islands. Then again, you still have a good chance of seeing stingrays, sea turtles and all sorts of other macro-marine wildlife while in the midst of a tropical archipelago, so really, who's complaining?

DON'T MISS

REGATTA LEPA

The big annual festival of local Bajau sea gypsies is the Regatta Lepa, held in mid-April. Traditionally, the Bajau only set foot on mainland Borneo once a year; for the rest of the time they live on small islets or their boats. Today the Bajau go to Semporna and other towns more frequently for supplies, but the old cycle of annual return is still celebrated and marked by the regatta *lepa* (a traditional single mast sailing boat). For visitors, the highlight of the festival is the *lepa*-decorating contest held between Bajau families. Their already rainbow-coloured boats are further decked out in streamers, flags (known as *tapi*), bunting, ceremonial umbrellas (which symbolise protection from the omnipresent sun and rain that beats down on the ocean) and *sambulayang*, gorgeously decorated sails passed down within Bajau clans. Violin, cymbal and drum music, plus 'sea sports' competitions like duck catching and boat tug of war, punctuate the entire affair. The regatta occurs in mid-April; check www.sabahtourism.com/events/regatta-lepa-semporna-0 for details.

Blue Sea Divers DIVING
(☎089-781 322; www.blueseadivers-sabah.com; Semporna seafront) Budget day-trip operator in Semporna.

★**Borneo Divers** DIVING
(☎088-222 226; www.borneodivers.net; 9th fl, Menara Jubili, 53 Jln Gaya, Kota Kinabalu) The original and still one of the best dive outfits thanks to their high safety standards, quality equipment, excellent PADI teachers and divemasters. The office is located in Kota Kinabalu, plus a lovely resort on Mabul. Recommended.

★**Scuba Junkie** DIVING
(☎089-785 372; www.scuba-junkie.com; Lot 36, block B, Semporna seafront; 4 days & 3 nights on Mabul incl 3 dives per day at Kapilai, Mabul & 4 dives at Sipadan per person RM2385, snorkelling day trips incl lunch RM120; ⊙9am-6pm) The most proactive conservationists on Mabul, Scuba Junkie employ two full-time environmentalists and recycle much of their profits into their turtle hatchery and rehab centre and 'shark week' initiative. They're also a favourite with Westerners thanks to their excellent divemasters and comfortable, nonpackage type digs at Mabul Beach Resort (p102).

Scuba Jeff DIVING
(☎017-869 0218, 019-585 5125; www.scubajeffsipadan.com; Mabul Island) Jeff, a friendly local bloke, runs his adventures out of the local fishing village in Mabul. Accommodation is very basic.

Seahorse Sipadan DIVING
(☎089-782 289, 012-279 7657; www.seahorse-sipadanscuba.org; 1st fl, lot 1, Semporna seafront; 3-day, 2-night package incl 3 dives per day, accommodation, equipment & boat transfer RM690) Backpacker-oriented outfit with a new 1st-floor office on Semporna seafront, and accommodation on Mabul. Seahorse has been around for five years now.

Seaventures DIVING
(☎017-811 6023, 088-251 669; www.seaventuresdive.com; Lot 28, block E, Semporna seafront; 4-day, 3-night package incl 10 dives in total, with 3 dives on Sipadan, incl meals & transfers to island & airport RM2730) Based out of their funky blue/orange ocean platform close to Mabul island, this is a well-regarded outfit. Offices in Semporna and in KK's Wisma Sabah building.

Sipadan Scuba DIVING
(☎089-784 788, 089-781 788, 012-813 1688, 089-919 128; www.sipadanscuba.com; Lot 28, block E, Semporna seafront; 3-day & 2-night package incl dives, accommodation, transfer & equipment RM919) Twenty years' experience and an international staff make Sipadan Scuba a reliable, recommended choice. You can take your PADI Open Water course here for RM760.

Sipadan Water Village DIVING
(☎089-751 777, 089-950 023, 010-932 5783, 089-784 227; www.swvresort.com) A private operator based at the Mabul resort of the same name.

SMART DIVING
(☎088-486 389; www.sipadan-mabul.com.my) The dive centre operating at Sipadan-Mabul Resort and Mabul Water Bungalow; both are located on Mabul. Also has offices in KK.

Uncle Chang's DIVING
(Borneo Jungle River Island Tours; ☎089-781 002, 017-897 0002; www.ucsipadan.com; 36 Semporna seafront) Offers snorkelling day trips to Mataking (RM170), plus diving at Sipadan and digs at its basic lodge on Mabul.

Sleeping & Eating

From opulent bungalows to ragtag sea shanties, the marine park offers a wide variety of accommodation catering to all budgets, with most clustered on Mabul (Sipadan's closest neighbour), which is now threatening to become overcrowded. No one is allowed to stay on Sipadan. Note that prices rise in August and September. Nondivers are charged at different rates than divers.

At almost all of the places listed below, you're tied to a set schedule of three to five meals broken up by roughly three diving (or snorkelling) trips per day. Meals are included, drinks extra, although tea and coffee are often gratis. High-end resorts have their own bars and restaurants; you may be able to eat and drink there if you're staying in a budget spot and the person at the gate is in a good mood, but you'll pay for it. Remember there is still a 6pm curfew to be off the beach.

Divers and snorkellers can also opt to stay in the town of Semporna. That means slightly better bang for your buck, but no fiery equatorial sunsets. Perhaps more pertinently, it takes at least 30 minutes, and usually a bit longer, to get to dive sites from Semporna town.

Every one of the accommodation options listed below can arrange diving trips, including certification courses and trips to Sipadan.

Singamata

Not an island at all, but rather a floating village built onto a sandbar about 30 minutes from Semporna, **Singamata Reef Resort** (☎089-784 828; www.singamata.com; 3-day & 2-night incl diving & transfers RM1000-1200; ❄) is a pretty assemblage of stilt bungalows and decks with its own pool full of giant fish (which you can snorkel amid). If you feel like dipping into the water, you can literally just step out of your room (annoyingly, rubbish from Semporna sometimes still floats into the vicinity). Rooms are basic but pretty and breezy. You may feel isolated out here, but if you need an escape, this is a lovely option.

Mabul

Home to Bajau sea gypsies and a Malaysian village (where the budget accommodation is found), Mabul boasts a long sandy beach and is fairly crammed with resorts, a number of which are built out to sea on stilted water villages. With its excellent 'muck diving', fiery sunsets, desert island good looks and comfy resorts, the island makes for a nice play to chill, but really Mabul is your springboard for the neighbouring diving sites. For a little atmosphere, head to Scuba Junkie's bar at Mabul Beach Resort (p102).

It's worth having a walk around the island, passing a Bajau graveyard with its salt-worn wood-carved tombstones, and sidestepping giant monitor lizards. Behind the resorts are generators and barracks-style housing for resort staff. There are little shops in the villages that sell confectionery, crisps, cigarettes and other incidentals. Try to be sensitive if taking pictures of local people, we sensed that long zoom lenses and 'human zoo' behaviour from certain package-trip tourists was beginning to wear on the patience of islanders.

Sipadan Dive Centre (SDC) HOMESTAY $
(☎088-240 584, 012-821 8288; www.sdclodges.com; dm/r RM150/190, 3 dives RM280; ❄) Simple rainbow-coloured huts with attached bathroom, air-con, Caribbean-blue walls, fresh linen, wood floors, and a dive outfit – and less cramped quarters compared to other budget digs thanks to its spacious compound – make this a winner. Friendly management too; they cook up barbecue feasts by night.

Uncle Chang's GUESTHOUSE $
(☎089-781 002, 089-786 988, 017-895 002; www.ucsipadan.com; dm RM75, d with/without air-con & bathroom RM150/110; ❄) Shipwrecked amid the stilted weaveworld of the Malay village, if Chang's was an avuncular connection, he'd be a rough old seadog; think banana-yellow basic rattan-walled rooms in small chalets, a lively threadbare communal deck with occasional jam sessions and a happy, sociable vibe. There's also a well-known dive school here with seven daily dive permits to Sipadan.

Seahorse Sipadan Scuba Lodge GUESTHOUSE $
(☎Semporna 089-782 289; www.seahorse-sipadanscuba.com; dm/d from RM70/100) Seahorse has a few rooms showing their age with patchy lino floors, yellow walls and an open deck to catch the breeze. With nice little touches like conch shells on tables, there's also a dependable dive outfit here.

Scuba Jeff LODGE $
(☎017-869 0218, 019-585 5125; www.scubajeffsipadan.com; r with shared bathroom RM80; 📶) Crimson-walled Jeff is a fan-only, wood

affair with corridors darker than the Minotaur's labyrinth. There's a breezy open deck offering unblemished sea views, and budget dive centre. Basic accommodation with forgettable wooden box rooms – and don't think of getting steamy as there's a passion-killing gap at the top of the walls! – but indie travellers love this place.

Summer Friends Homestay HOMESTAY $

(☎013-557 1668; www.summerfriendshomestay.com; Malayan village; r RM50) This cheap as chips and not overly homely custard-yellow, wood affair is OK for a night if the island is full and you're waiting to get in elsewhere. There's a hammock out back, a shared bathroom and about as much atmosphere as the dark side of the moon. Fan only.

★Scuba Junkie Mabul Beach Resort RESORT $$

(☎089-785 372; www.scuba-junkie.com; dm RM175, d with fan RM245-310, d with air-con RM320-380; ❄📶) 🍃 Run by a lovely American couple, this place attracts a younger international crowd with a little cash to splash on semiluxe digs. Superfresh rooms come with porches and bathrooms, polished-wood floors and choice decor. Dorms are airy and of a good size, plus there's a welcoming central gazebo which houses the lively restaurant/bar. Prices include generous buffet meals.

There's also an exhibition of the many eco-marine causes Scuba Junkie is pioneering in the Semporna Archipelago. Divers (but not snorkellers) who book with Scuba Junkie get a 25% discount.

Billabong Scuba Backpackers GUESTHOUSE $$

(☎089-781 866; www.billabongscuba.com; Mabul; r with fan/air-con RM90/120, chalets with fan/air-con RM140-240, 3 dives at Sipadan RM700) Select from a choice of forgettable old rooms and dorm, faded chalets and brand new chalets

MEN IN BLACK: THE ONGOING SECURITY SITUATION

If staying in Mabul, you'll inevitably notice the presence of black-clad armed police patrolling the beach and the fact there's a 6pm curfew to be back in your resort. No doubt arriving at Sipadan after your first dive you'll also double-take at the dozen or so members of the Malaysian military stationed in a little hut with machine guns while you're diving. Try not to be alarmed, they're here for your safety and as a powerful deterrent. And so far it's working.

Here's a brief chronology of why their presence is so vital.

2000 The notorious Abu Sayyaf group abducted 21 people in Sipadan in April 2000.

2013 The Lahad Datu stand-off was a military conflict that arose after 235 Filipino armed militants arrived by boats in Lahad Datu claiming their objective was to assert the unresolved territorial claim of the Philippines over eastern Sabah.

2013 Two Taiwanese tourists were attacked in their room at the Sipadan Pom Pom Resort, off the coast of eastern Sabah; a male tourist was killed and his wife kidnapped.

2014 A Chinese tourist, and a Filipino hotel employee from Singamata Reef Resort, were taken in Semporna; a Malaysian fish breeder and his Filipino employee were seized by gunmen from their farm in Sabah.

2014 Armed men arrived by speedboat in Mabul with rocket launchers. In the ensuing crossfire with police, one officer was killed before the armed men, thought to be from Jolo island in the Phillipines, fled, taking another policeman hostage.

Esscom (Eastern Sabah Security Command; set up in 2013 and covering 1400km of the east coast of Sabah from Kudat to Tawau) claims there are 14 kidnap-for-ransom groups from southern Philippines, four of which have carried out kidnappings in Sabah's east coast.

So quite a litany of dramas. But is it now safe in the archipelago? Many international embassies recommend reconsidering your need to travel here, yet for the last year 120 divers per day have been enjoying one of the best dive sites in the world without incident. With the proactively beefed-up police numbers on the islands, the kidnappers are having to look elsewhere for their ransoms. Furthermore, a recent international assessment of the security situation in the Semporna Archipelago was judged to be positive. For now the curfew remains, but should you choose to come here you will be more than handsomely rewarded by its underwater treasures for any risks you may have taken.

with ox-blood-coloured walls and wood floors, which are built right out to sea (with great views). There's a communal decked area too. Billabong's diving outfit is only allocated seven diving permits per day for Sipadan, so try and book ahead.

★**Borneo Divers Mabul Resort** RESORT $$$ (☎088-222 226; www.borneodivers.net; 3-days, 2-nights incl transfer, food & dives per diver/non-diver RM1800/1400; ❄@📶) With flower-filled lawns, this charming accommodation has a pool, lovely chalets with wood floors and boutique accents, and a resident monitor lizard. The restaurant is terrific, the lounge open and comfy, their staff ever-friendly. Slow wi-fi is available in the dining room. Attracts a slightly older family-geared crowd.

Runs the archipleago's best dive centre; Borneo Divers introduced Cousteau to Sipadan back in '89.

Mabul Water Bungalow RESORT $$$ (☎088-486 389; www.mabulwaterbungalows.com; 3-day, 2-night dive package per diver/nondiver from RM3838/2339; ❄📶) Idyllically lapped by turquoise water, these Balinese-style stilted bungalows with their peaked roofs, fine interiors and palm-fronted porches are exquisite. When we say built out to sea we mean it – thoughtfully the hotel has a fleet of gleaming golf buggies to spirit your tired feet down the wooden walkway to your watery paradise. There's also a decent restaurant here.

Seaventures Dive Resort RESORT $$$ (☎088-261 669; www.seaventuresdive.com; 4-day, 3-night dive package per person twin share from RM2730; ❄) Moored beside nearby Mabul, this orange and polar-blue former oil rig accommodation platform, was made in Panama. The dive centre is terrific, as are the comfortable rooms and restaurant. Memorable digs and perfect for divers wanting to focus on their passion, eschewing noisy family joints. It sits on its own house reef, which is also ideal for beginners.

Sipadan-Mabul Resort RESORT $$$ (SMART; ☎088-486 389; www.sipadan-mabul.com.my; 7-day, 6-night dive package per diver/nondiver from RM4819/3643; ❄📶🏊) Winking with fairy lights and choking on palms, there's a welcoming restaurant here with belle epoque lights, glossed wood floors and a well-stocked shop. Bungalows are tastefully finished with art, private balcony and fresh linen. The stand-alone bungalows cost an extra RM112 per night, but are larger with fridge, private alfresco shower and settee.

Sipadan Water Village Resort RESORT $$$ (☎089-751 777; www.swvresort.com; 4-day, 3-night package diver/nondiver US$1215/835; ❄@) Set in a horseshoe design with a decent restaurant at the centre, these 42 stilted chalets perched on the turquoise water are connected by wooden walkways. Expect fresh, inviting rooms with bathroom and unblemished views of the Celebes Sea. Be prepared to be lulled to sleep by the lap of the waves.

Kapalai

Set on stilts on the shallow sandbanks of the Ligitan Reefs, this is one of the best macro dive sites in the world; on any given day you'll see blue-ringed octopuses, bobtail squid, cardinal fish and orangutan crabs. Although commonly referred to as an island, Kapalai is more like a large sandbar sitting slightly under the ocean surface. Upon it is based **Kapalai Resort** (☎088-316 011/3; http://sipadan-kapalai.com/; 4-day, 3-night package from RM2790; ❄@), a sumptuous water village with beautiful, upscale wood-accented rooms. Unlike busy Mabul, there's a sense of escape here with a long, thin powdery sandbar you can sunbathe on and snorkel from between dives.

Mataking

Mataking is also essentially a sandbar, two little patches of green bookending a dusty tadpole tail of white sand. **Mataking Island Resort** (☎089-786 045, 089-770 022; www.mataking.com; 2-day, 1-night package for divers/nondivers from RM1415/1235; ❄@) is the only accommodation here. This is an impeccably luxurious escape full of dark-wood chalets and gossamer sheets. This sandy escape has some beautiful diving – an artificial reef and sunken boats provide havens for plenty of sea life – and has a novel 'underwater post office' at a local shipwreck site. Mataking's eastern shore is a sloping reef and drops to 100m, making it great for sighting macro treasures as well as pelagics. Among the regular visitors large and small, expect to see trevally, eagle rays and barracuda, and pygmy seahorses and mandarin fish.

Pom Pom

About an hour from Semporna, and deep within the Tun Sakaran Marine Park, this pear-shaped idyll with its perfect azure water and white sand backed by pompom trees is a more attractive option than Mabul for those who want to dive *and* beach flop. With only two hotels on the island, it's far less crowded here; in fact, many come to get married and explore the underwater treasures as a secondary pursuit. That said, the diving is amazing.

There are two spots to stay: **Sipadan Pom Pom Island Resort** (089-781 918; www.pompomisland.com; 3-day, 2-night package RM1500-1800;) has a range of tasteful rooms, from garden chalets to dreamy stilted water cabanas, and resident turtles looking for a swimming date. There's also a solid dive school here. And just opened up is the splendid **Celebes Beach Resort** (089-782 828, 017-867 2232; www.celebescuba.com; 2-days, 1-night diver/nondiver RM730/610), with its deluxe seaview chalets exuding a zen minimalist decor. There's a great dive school here too offering PADI courses, and a fleet of three boats taking you to the best dive sites in the archipelago.

Roach Reefs

Roach Reefs Resort (089-779 332; www.roachreefsresort.com; 2-day, 1-night package for divers/nondivers per person US$185/148;) is built upon two sunken steel barges and an artificial reef at the edge of the Borneo shelf. Romantic water chalets with fresh, mint-white rooms with laquered wood floors, private bathroom and sea-view balconies are tempting, yes, but then there's the cosy bamboo bar, tasty Asian-fusion restaurant and excellent diving school. The waters are particularly fertile, with schools of bumphead parrotfish passing by at dawn and whale sharks visiting four months of the year. There's a cleaning station here too. Keep in mind boat transfers here come from Tawau, as opposed to Semporna.

Information

The Semporna Islands are loosely divided into two geographical sections: the northern islands (protected as Tun Sakaran Marine Park, gazetteered in 2004) and the southern islands. Both areas have desirable diving: Sipadan is located in the southern region, as is Mabul and Kapalai. Mataking and Sibuan belong to the northern area. If you are based in Semporna, you'll have a greater chance of diving both areas, although most people are happy to stick with Sipadan and its neighbours.

Consider stocking up on supplies (sunscreen, mozzie repellent etc) before making your way into the archipelago. Top-end resorts have small convenience stores with inflated prices. ATMs are nonexistent, but high-end resorts accept credit cards (Visa and MasterCard). Mabul has a small police station near the village mosque, as well as shack shops selling basic foodstuffs and a small pharmacy. Internet is of the wi-fi variety; most resorts now offer it, but service is spotty.

The closest decompression chamber (p98) is at the Semporna Naval Base.

Getting There & Around

With the exception of Roach Reefs, all transport to the marine park goes through Semporna. Your accommodation will arrange any transport needs from Semporna or Tawau airport (sometimes included, sometimes for an extra fee – ask!), which will most likely depart in the morning. That means if you arrive in Semporna in the afternoon, you will be required to spend the night in town.

Tawau

089 / POP 306,460

Sabah's third city, Tawau is not the most picturesque of places, despite its position beside the Celebes Sea and proximity to the Semporna Archipelago, but let's give it a break; poor Tawau has seen more conflict than a hard-bitten mercenary. Bombed by the British in 1944 to force out the invading Japanese army, today many of its hastily erected buildings don't merit much of a glance, but don't give up on it yet, for what the town lacks in photogenic charm, it more than makes up for with friendly locals and vibrant markets oozing pungent aromas and old-world atmosphere.

Tawau is Sabah's border crossing with Kalimantan and the only place where foreigners can get a visa to enter Indonesia.

Sights

Bukit Gemok Forest Reserve NATURE RESERVE
(adult/child RM5/1; 8am-5pm) About 10km from Tawau's centre, this reserve is great for a day visit, the jungle filled with chattering monkeys and popular with trekkers and tour groups. About an hour's hiking will bring you to the **Titian Selara canopy walkway**, which, at 231m long, offers terrific views of Tawau and the countryside. There are seven huts along the way for walkers to rest and relax. Be on the lookout for enormous flying seeds of the gourd *Alsomitra*

Tawau

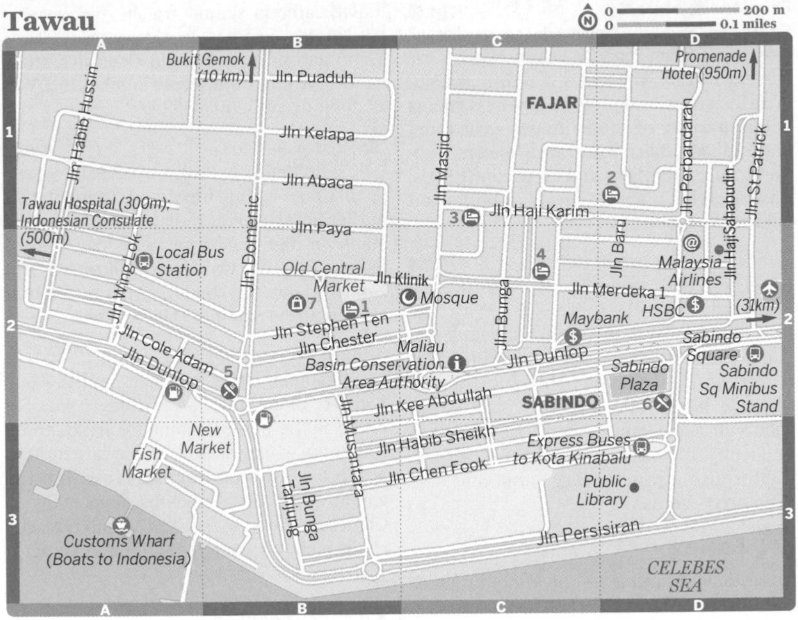

macrocarpa, gliding hundreds of metres through the forest.

A taxi to the park costs RM35; make sure your driver either sticks around to wait for you or is willing to come back and pick you up, as there's little public transport out this way.

Sleeping

Splurge for a midrange option in Tawau. Jalan Bunga and Jalan Haji Karim are packed with good-value accommodation. Budget accommodation tends to be pretty dire.

Kingston Executive Hotel HOTEL $

(☎089-702 288; 4581-4590 Jln Haji Karim; d RM80; ❄ @) Kingston's smoked-glass doors hide an arty lobby and gawping fish watching you check in. Rooms are clean with glass-topped desk, TV, coffee-making facilities and capacious bathroom. But can someone explain what those fake fireplace fixtures in the corridor are all about?

Monaco Hotel HOTEL $

(☎089-769 911/2/3; Jln Haji Karim; r from RM63; ❄ 📶) With its crappy lobby, Monaco is not exactly evoking Camparis and film stars, but its en suite rooms are OKish wood-accented affairs with slightly thirsty walls but enough room for a barn dance. Expect a sofa, desk, TV and reading lamp. And plump for one away from the noisy road. The shuttle service to the airport costs RM40.

Hotel Soon Yee HOTEL $

(☎089-772 447; 1362 Jln Stephen Tan; r RM35-40; ❄) On an atmospheric old street in the Central Market that's reminiscent of a Tintin cartoon, follow the steps up the bright turquoise stairway to the 1st floor and these distinctly budget but palatable rooms (air-con or fan) with colourful bedspreads and faintly Soviet bathrooms. The owner is a nice fella and the place is something of a magnet for indie travellers.

Tawau

Sleeping

1 Hotel Soon Yee B2
2 Kingston Executive Hotel D1
3 Monaco Hotel C1
4 Shervinton Executive Hotel C2

Eating

Restoran Azura .... (see 6)
5 Restoran Azura B2
6 Sabindo Hawker Centre D2

Shopping

7 Servay Department Store B2

Promenade Hotel HOTEL $$
(☎089-982 888; www.promenade.com.my/tawau/index.php; Eastern Plaza, Jln Kuhara, Mile 1; r incl breakfast RM233; ❄📶) This is rightly considered the superior option in town. Its rooms within a towering monolith are welcoming dark-walled affairs with rain showers, subtle lighting, city views and large comfy beds. There's cable TV, a great breakfast buffet and bakery. Wi-fi in lobby.

Shervinton Executive Hotel HOTEL $$
(☎089-770 000; www.shervintonhotel.com; Jln Bunga; r/f from RM188/428; ❄📶) With the kind of lobby that would get Liberace excited (think kitsch mirrored front desk festooned with fairy lights) this is a friendly place to hang your wig. Heavily fragrant rooms boast copper sinks, rainshowers, ambiently lit headboards and flat screen. There's also a gym, bakery, salon and spa. Who needs Vegas?

Eating

Locals love splurging on the buffet lunch at the Belmont Marco Polo hotel, opposite the Old Central Market on Jln Klinik, which, for RM18 (RM33 on weekends), is a steal considering the variety of tasty bites. There are cheap Chinese *kedai kopi* along Jln Bunga; most open around 7am and close around 10pm.

Self-caterers should try the **Servay Department Store** (Jln Musantara; ⏰10am-10pm) across from the Old Central Market, for everything from picnic lunches to DVDs of dubious authenticity.

★**Restoran Azura** INDIAN $
(☎012-863 9934; Jln Dunlop; mains RM7; ⏰8am-9pm) Cool, white, fresh and friendly, this authentic southern Indian restaurant is a staple in many a Tawau local's day. Choose from a host of curries and pillow-soft *roti canai* (flaky, flat bread). There's another branch at the Sabindo Hawker Centre.

Sabindo Hawker Centre HAWKER $
(Jln Waterfront; dishes from RM5; ⏰11am-10pm) Located along the Tawau waterfront, Sabindo is the place to come for fresh street-stall food, which, as is often the case in Asia, is the tastiest stuff around. Prices run the gamut from cheap-as-chips soup stalls to Chinese seafood emporiums. Grab a plastic chair, pick out your leviathan and watch it grilled before your eyes.

Information

BANKS

HSBC (Jln Perbandaran)

Maybank (☎089-762 333; Jln Dunlop)

TAWAU TREATS

Thanks to Tawau's proximity to Indonesia and large population of Indonesians, Filipinos, Bajau and Hakka Chinese, the town has developed some worthwhile culinary specialities. All of the following can be found in almost any of Tawau's *kedai kopi* and in the Sabindo Hawker Centre:

Mee jawa Javanese-style noodles, the Javanese take on Asia's ubiquitous noodle soup. This version comes with a yellowish broth swimming with bean sprouts, groundnuts, bean curd, fish balls, the occasional prawn and sometimes (interestingly) sweet potato, plus the usual garlic, shallots, chillies and shrimp paste.

Gado gado A deliciously simple Indonesian speciality: vegetable salad with prawn crackers and peanut sauce. The glory of *gado* is the variations of the standard recipe – every cook and hawker puts a different spin on it.

Nasi kuning Rice cooked with coconut milk and turmeric, hence the English translation of the name: 'yellow rice'. In Tawau, it is often wrapped and served in a banana leaf with deep-fried fish and eaten on special occasions.

Soto makassar Oh yes! *Soto* (also spelled *'coto'* and pronounced 'cho-to') *makassar* is buffalo/beef soup from southern Sulawesi, Indonesia. The dark broth is made incredibly rich by the addition of buffalo/cow blood, and enriched by a plethora of some 40 spices, plus beef heart, liver, tripe and brain. If you have a weak stomach, ignore those ingredients and trust us: this stuff is *delicious*, like liquid essence of beef spiced with all the wonderful herbs and spices of Southeast Asia.

GETTING TO INDONESIA: TAWAU TO TARAKAN

Getting to the border Tawau is the only crossing point with Kalimantan where foreigners can get a visa to enter Indonesia. The local **Indonesian consulate** (089-772 052, 089-752 969; Jln Sinn Onn, Wisma Fuji; 8am-noon & 1pm or 2-4pm Mon-Fri, closed Indonesian and Malaysian public holidays) is known for being fast and efficient – many travellers are in and out in an hour. The consulate is in Wisma Fuji, on Jln Sinn Onn. Flag down a taxi (RM15) and ask the driver to drop you off in front of the consulate.

Visa applications are processed between 9.30am and 2pm Monday to Friday. You technically need to either provide proof of onward travel or a credit card, which consulate staff will make a copy of. A 60-day tourist visa will cost RM170 and require two passport photos. Bank on spending at least one night in town before shipping off to Indonesia, given the ferry departure schedule, and bring extra cash to the consulate, as there are no ATMs nearby.

Ferry companies Tawindo Express and Indomaya Express make the three- to four-hour trip to Tarakan (RM140; 11.30am Monday, Wednesday and Friday, 10.30am Tuesday, Thursday and Saturday) and the one-hour trip to Nunukan (RM65; 10am and 3pm daily except Sunday). We recommend showing up at least 60 minutes before departure to get a ticket; less than that is cutting it fine. A taxi ride to the ferry terminal costs RM10. MASWings flies from Tawau to Tarakan (RM135) five times per week.

At the border Blue minivans in Tarakan can get you around the city for Rp3000; expect to pay around Rp20,000 to get to the airport.

Moving On Ferry company Pelni (www.pelni.co.id) has boats to Balikpapan and the Sulawesi ports of Toli-Toli, Pare-Pare and Makassar.

INTERNET ACCESS

City Internet Zone (089-760 016; 37 Kompleks Fajar, Jln Perbandaran; per hour RM2-3; 9am-midnight)

MEDICAL SERVICES

Tawau Hospital (089-773 533; Peti Surat 80; 24hr)

TOURIST INFORMATION

Maliau Basin Conservation Area Authority (089-759 214; maliaubasin@gmail.com; 2nd fl, UMNO Bldg, Jln Dunlop) Can provide information on and help arrange visits to the Maliau Basin.

Getting There & Away

AIR

Malaysia Airlines (089-761 293; www.malaysiaairlines.com.my; Jln Haji Sahabudin; 9am-6pm) and **AirAsia** (089-761 946; www.airasia.com; 1st fl, Tawau Airport Building, Jln Apas-Balung; 9am-6pm) have daily direct flights to KK and KL. **MASwings** (1300-883 000; www.maswings.com.my) flies to Sandakan twice daily, the afternoon flight continuing to KK.

BUS

Kota Kinabalu Daily express buses for KK (RM60, nine hours) leave from behind the Sabindo area in a large dusty lot at 8am and 8pm (not in between).

Sandakan Departs hourly from Sabindo Sq (RM43, five hours, 7am to 2pm), one block on a diagonal from the KK terminus, behind the purple Yassin Curry House sign. That's also the spot for frequent minivans to Semporna (RM25, two hours) and Lahad Datu (RM20, three hours).

Getting Around

The airport is 28km from town along the main highway to Semporna and Sandakan. A shuttle bus (RM10) from the airport to the local bus station in Tawau's centre leaves six times daily. A taxi costs RM45.

Tawau Hills Park

Hemmed in by agriculture and human habitation, this small reserve has forested hills rising dramatically from the surrounding plain. The **park** (admission RM10) was gazetteered in 1979 to protect the water catchment for settlements in the area, but not before most of the accessible rainforest had been logged. Much of the remaining forest clings to steep-sided ridges that rise to 1310m Gunung Magdalena.

If getting into the Maliau Basin or Danum Valley feels like too much of an effort, consider Tawau Hills a user-friendly alternative. The forest here may not be as primevally awesome, but it's still impressively thick jungle, and the trails are quite easy on your feet. On a clear day the Tawau Hills Park's peaks make a fine sight.

The first trail leads along the Sungai Tawau (chattering with birds like a Disney movie when we attempted it) for 2.5km to **Bukit Gelas Falls**, which when not swarmed with school groups and tourists, is perfectly picturesque. Another track leads 3.2km to a group of 11 **hot springs** that are frankly as impressive as anything you'll see in Poring; locals believe the *ubat kulit* (skin medication) water has medicinal properties. If the above doesn't appeal, you can always take a quick 30-minute walk to **Bombalai Hill** (530m) to the south – the views from here are also quite rewarding. Another reason for coming here is to see the **world's tallest tropical tree** (88m). From the main entrance take the 900m trail. As well as macaques, red and white leaf monkeys, giant tree squirrels, civet cats and several kinds of hornbill you'll most likely come across leeches first. If it's been raining you absolutely must wear leech socks!

There's accommodation at **Tawau Hills Park** (Taman Bukit Tawau; ☎089-918 827, 089-768 719, 019-800 9607; camping/dm/chalet RM5/20/200). Rates are lower on weekdays. Both dorms and chalets are utilitarian, and there's not much reason to stay here unless you can't stomach a night somewhere else. If you want to camp, you'll need to bring all of your own equipment.

Tawau Hills is 28km northwest of Tawau. A taxi will cost around RM40.

Maliau Basin Conservation Area

This pocket of primeval wilderness tells the same untouched story it did millenniums ago. Hemmed in by mountains, separated by distance and altitude and expanse, the Maliau Basin Conservation Area (MBCA), known very appropriately as 'Sabah's Lost World', is something special. Beneath the canopy of its soaring dipterocarp trees, it's easy to imagine the emergent form of a brachiosaurus.

The basin, a 25km-wide bowl-shaped depression of rainforest, was unnoticed by the world until a pilot almost crashed into the walls that hem it off in 1947. Run by the Sabah Foundation, this is the single best place in Borneo to experience old-growth tropical rainforest. More than that, it is one of the world's great reserves of biodiversity, a dense knot of almost unbelievable genetic richness. A visit to the basin is always a poignant affair, as you'll share the road with a parade of logging trucks hauling trees out of the forest at an astonishing rate.

Unbelievably, there is no known record of human beings entering the basin until the early 1980s (although it is possible that indigenous peoples entered the basin before that time). It is only recently that the area has been opened up to a limited number of adventurous travellers.

Getting here became much more straightforward in 2014, with the sealing of the road that runs from KK to Tawau (five hours by car), passing by the entrance to the Maliau Basin. Within the reserve the roads are gradually improving, but a 4WD is still necessary.

Activities

Trekking

The trek through the Maliau Basin will likely be the most memorable hike of your Borneo experience. And possibly the hardest! The density of the old-growth forest is striking, and as it is more remote than the Danum Valley, the preserved wildlife is *even* better. Eighty species of mammal and counting have been recorded here, including the clouded leopard, Sumatran rhino, Malayan sun bear, pygmy elephant, Bornean gibbon, red- and grey-leaf monkeys and banteng. That said, you are in the jungle, and wildlife is not easy to spot. You may walk away without seeing anything (unlikely) but for some of Borneo's most ancient trees, which isn't so bad really, given the sheer outlandishness of the place.

Several treks are possible in the basin, ranging from short nature walks around **Agathis Camp** to the multiday slog to the rim of the basin via **Strike Ridge Camp**. The vast majority of visitors to the basin undertake a three-day, two-night loop through the southern section of the basin that we'll call the Maliau Loop. This brilliant route takes in wide swaths of diverse rainforest and four of the basin's waterfalls: **Takob Falls**, **Giluk Falls**, **Maliau Falls** and **Ginseng Falls**. Do not attempt the trek unless you are in excellent shape: adventure-tour operator Sticky Rice Travel (p46), one of a handful of companies operating here, insists that your travel insurance policy covers a helicopter evacuation.

Your tour operator will supply a forest ranger, guide and porters to carry your food.

INDEPENDENT EXPEDITIONS TO THE MALIAU BASIN

It's best to first contact the **Maliau Basin Conservation Area Authority** (☎089-759 214; maliaubasin@gmail.com; 2nd flr, UMNO Building, Jln Dunlop) in Tawau if you want to go there under your own steam. You may need to show up to the office in person, as this is not a tourism body accustomed to dealing with visitors.

To get into the park you need to pay an administration fee (RM50), a vehicle entry fee (RM5 per vehicle), a trekking fee (RM150) and, if you stay overnight, a conservation fee (RM50). If you plan to hike you *must* hire a guide, which costs RM150 per day. Breakfast, lunch and dinner can be taken in the guest camps for RM195. You can also arrange meals while trekking; this requires a porter (RM100, maximum 12kg per porter, additional weight, first 5kg RM40 per porter) and costs RM390 for breakfast/lunch/dinner. If you want to cook for yourself, bring your own supplies and rent their utensils for RM50 per day. Night safaris cost RM160, and night walks RM40 (lasting about an hour).

Ideally, if you're not buying the package tour, we advise prearranging your tour with the office in Tawau, now only 2½ hours away from the basin thanks to the new road.

You'll be in charge of your day pack, camera, leech socks, walking clothes and dry kit for the evening. You should also bring mozzie repellent, swimming outfit, powerful torch, sunscreen, poncho, sleeping sheet, a towel and energy sweets.

A **canopy walkway** stretches near the Basin study centre, and it is pretty astounding to walk its length amid rainforest canopy that has never felt a human cut.

Sleeping

Accommodation varies in standard from the upscale (VIP House/deluxe/standard RM1300/520/390) and regular resthouse rooms (from RM286 to RM325) to dorm beds (RM91) and camping in your own tent (RM39). To be honest, after a day on the trail fighting leeches, they'll all seem like paradise!

There are two ways to get here: with a trusted tour company or on your own. Among those who run treks here, we recommend Sticky Rice Travel (p46), Borneo Adventure (p47) and Borneo Nature Tours (p48), all of which offer four-day, three-night all-inclusive tours of the Maliau for around RM3700, or five-day, four-night options for RM4650 per person for two to three people (this can go as low as RM3696 per person for a group of 10 to 15).

Information

The Maliau Basin is located in the southern part of central Sabah, just north of the logging road that connects Tawau with Keningau. The basin is part of the Yayasan Sabah Forest Management Area, a vast swath of forest in southeastern Sabah under the management of Yayasan Sabah (www.ysnet.org.my), a semigovernmental body tasked with both developing and protecting the natural resources of Sabah.

The MBCA security gate is just off the Tawau–Keningau Rd. From the gate, it's a very rough 25km journey to the Maliau Basin Studies Centre, for researchers, and about 20km to Agathis Camp, the base camp for most visitors to the basin.

Getting There & Away

It's possible to drive yourself to the park, or take a public bus from Tawau or KK. Your tour company will handle all transport if you book through them. It will take around six hours to drive from KK, and 2½ hours from Tawau.

MINIBUS

Minibuses occasionally ply the route bringing loggers to their camps, but this isn't a regular service and cannot be relied upon.

VAN

If you've prearranged with the Maliau Basin Conservation Area Authority in Tawau, that office may get a minivan to take you to the park entrance for RM650. In the park, rangers can arrange vans to take you back to Tawau or Keningau (closer to KK) for a similar price.

SOUTHWESTERN SABAH

The Crocker Range is the backbone of southwestern Sabah, separating coastal lowlands from the wild tracts of jungle in the east. Honey-tinged beaches scallop the shores from KK down to the border, passing the turbid rivers of the Beaufort Division. Offshore you'll find Pulau Tiga, forever etched in the collective consciousness as the genesis site for the eponymous reality show *Survivor,* and Pulau Labuan, centre of the region's oil industry and the transfer point for ferries heading onto Sarawak and Brunei.

The Interior

Sabah's interior constitutes some of the wildest territory in the state, and the best place for accessing this largely unexplored hinterland is via the southwest part of the state.

The landscape is dominated by the Crocker Range, which rises near Tenom in the south and runs north to Mt Kinabalu. The range forms a formidable barrier to the interior of the state and dominates the eastern skyline from Kota Kinabalu down to Sipitang. Once across the Crocker Range, you descend into the green valley of the Sungai Pegalan that runs from Keningau in the south and to Ranau in the north. The heart of the Pegalan Valley is the small town of Tambunan, around which you'll find a few low-key attractions.

Crocker Range National Park

Much of the Crocker Range has been gazetteered as Crocker Range National Park. The main means of accessing this landscape by foot is via the **Salt Trail** (Salt Trails; ☎088-553 500; http://www.sabahparks.org.my/index.php/salt-trail-crp), a series of four treks that trace the path of traditional trade routes across the mountains. At their shortest the trails can be completed in half a day; the longest route, the **Inobong-Terian-Buayan-Kionop-Tikolod trail**, takes three days to finish (if you're fit!). At the time of writing the tourism infrastructure around the Salt Trails was quite minimal, making this an excellent adventure for DIY trekkers who want to get off Sabah's package tourism trail. You'll need to get in touch with Crocker Range National Park to organise guides.

Even if you're not trekking, the Crocker Range and Pegalan Valley make a nice jaunt into rural Sabah for those with rental vehicles. As you make your way over the range between KK and Tambunan, you'll be treated to brilliant views back to the South China Sea and onward to Mt Trus Madi.

Tambunan

Nestled among the green curves of the Crocker hills, Tambunan, a small agricultural service town about 81km from KK, is the first settlement you'll come to in the range. The region was the last stronghold of Mat Salleh, who became a folk hero for rebelling against the British in the late 19th century. Sadly Salleh later blew his reputation by negotiating a truce, which so outraged his own people that he was forced to flee to the Tambunan plain, where he was eventually killed.

Sights

Tambunan Rafflesia Reserve NATURE RESERVE
(☎088-898 500; admission RM5; ⌚8am-3pm) Near the top of the Crocker Range, next to the main highway 20km from Tambunan, is this park devoted to the world's largest flower. Rangers can guide you into the jungle reserve for the day for RM100. Keningau-bound buses will stop here if you ask the driver to let you off, but getting back to Tambunan will require hitching on the highway. A round-trip taxi from Tambunan costs RM120, which includes waiting time.

The rafflesia is a parasitic plant that grows hidden within the stems of jungle vines until it bursts into bloom, at which point it eerily resembles the monster plant from *Little Shop of Horrors*. It emits a stench of rotting flesh mimicking a newly dead animal, to attract carrion flies that help with pollination. The large bulbous flowers can be up to 1m in diameter. The 12 or so species of rafflesia here are found only in Borneo and Sumatra; several species are unique to Sabah, but as they only bloom for a few days, it's hard to predict when you'll be able to see one.

Sleeping

Tambunan Village Resort Centre RESORT $$
(TVRC; ☎087-774 076; http://tvrc.tripod.com; 24 Jln TVRC; r & chalets RM118-248; ❄) Also known as the Borneo Heritage Centre, this rural digs is 2km out of Tambunan, located by a pretty lake. There's boating, hiking, a nice cafe and a choice of basic rooms or self-catering family-size chalet rooms. Staff can help arrange trips up Mt Trus Madi.

If driving from KK, the centre's just south of the Shell station on the main road.

Getting There & Away

Regular minivans ply the roads between Tambunan and KK (RM10, 1½ hours), Ranau (RM15, two hours), Keningau (RM10, one hour) and Tenom (RM20, two hours). KK–Tenom express buses also pass through, though you may have to ask them to stop. The minivan shelter is in the middle of Tambunan town. Minivans to KK pass the entrance to the Rafflesia Reserve; you'll usually be charged for the whole trip to KK.

Mt Trus Madi

About 20km southeast of Tambunan town is the dramatic Mt Trus Madi, Sabah's second-highest peak, rising to 2642mm, and one of the best places in Malaysia to watch the sunrise. Ascents are possible, however, it's more challenging than Mt Kinabalu, and more difficult to arrange. Independent trekkers must be well equipped and bring their own provisions up the mountain. It is possible to go by 4WD (RM500) up to about 1500m, from where it is a five- to seven-hour climb to the top. The trail to the summit is about 4.9km but you'll have to climb three mountains to reach it!

There are two places to stay: **Mirad-Irad Riverside camp** (RM20) at base camp, and **SFD New Rest House** (RM100) halfway up the mountain. Before setting off, you are strongly advised to hire a guide (RM100) or at least get maps and assistance from **Forestry Department** (Jabatan Perhutanan; ☎089-660 811, 087-774 691) in Tambunan. Bring winter clothes, as it gets cold towards the peak, and be prepared for a long, muddy slog.

You can get here on your own, but it's far easier to organise with a tour company. **Tropical Mountain Holidays** (☎013-549 2730, 013-545 7643; www.tropicalmountainholidaysmalaysia.com), based in KK, specialises in Mt Trus Madi ascents. Their two-day, one-night climb up the mountain, which includes transfer from KK, runs US$380 per person, which is close to what you'll pay if you hire guides and your own vehicle to get out here.

Keningau

If you have a bent for the bucolic, you'll probably want to skip Keningau – this busy service town has a touch of urban sprawl about it, and most visitors only pass through to pick up transport, use an ATM or stock up on supplies. As far as attractions go, you might check out **Taipaek-gung**, a colourful Chinese temple in the middle of town, or the large **tamu** (market) held every Thursday.

For a sleepover, try **Hotel Juta** (☎087-337 888; www.sabah.com.my/juta; Lg Milimewa 2; standard/superior r RM175/275; ❄), which towers over the busy town centre. It's convenient to transport, banking and shopping needs, and rooms are nicely appointed in the Western business style. There is a restaurant on the premises. Shabbier options include the nearby **Crown Hotel** (☎087-338 555; Lg Milimewa; standard/superior d from RM40).

There are eight daily express buses to/from KK (RM15, two hours) and four to/from Tenom (RM10, one hour). These buses stop at the Bumiputra Express stop on the main road across from the Shell station. Minivans and share taxis operate from several places in town, including a stop just north of the express bus stop; they all leave when full. There are services to/from KK (RM50, two hours), Ranau (RM30, three hours) and Tenom (RM12, one hour).

Tenom

Tenom was closely involved in uprisings against the British in 1915, led by the famous Murut chief Ontoros Antanom, and there's a **memorial** to the tribe's fallen warriors off the main road. Most people pass through Tenom on their way to the nearby Sabah Agricultural Park.

If you somehow get stuck in town, spend the night at the **Orchid Hotel** (☎087-737 600; Jln Tun Mustapha; s/d RM40/80; ❄). Rooms are clean and well kept and good value for money. There are cheaper hotels in the vicinity, but they're all a bit musty.

Minivans operate from the *padang* (field) in front of the Hotel Sri Perdana. Destinations include Keningau (RM10, one hour) and KK (RM45, two to four hours depending on stops). There are also regular services to Tambunan (RM20, two hours). Taxis congregate at a rank on the west side of the *padang*.

Sabah Agricultural Park

Heaven on earth for horticulturalists, the vast **Sabah Agricultural Park** (Taman Pertanian Sabah; ☎087-737952; www.sabah.net.my/agripark; adult/child RM25/10; ⌚9am-4.30pm Tue-Sun), about 15km northeast of Tenom, is run by the Department of Agriculture and covers about 6 sq km. Originally set up as an orchid centre, the park has expanded to become a major research facility, tourist attraction and offbeat camp site (RM10), building up superb collections of rare plants such as hoyas, and developing new techniques for use in agriculture, agroforestry and domestic cultivation.

Flower gardens and nature paths abound and a minizoo lets you get up close and personal with some farm animals and deer. Exploring by bicycle would be a good idea, but the fleet of rental bikes here has just about rusted to the point of immobility; if they've been replaced by the time you arrive, rentals cost RM3. There is a free 'train' (it's actually more like a bus) that does a 1½-hour loop of the park, leaving from outside the reception hourly from 9.30am to 3.30pm. If you're truly taken with the park, there's a bare bones on-site hostel (dorm beds RM25), which is sometimes taken up by visiting school groups.

Take a minivan from Tenom heading to Lagud Seberang (RM5). Services run throughout the morning, but dry up in the late afternoon. Tell the driver you're going to Taman Pertanian. The park entrance is about 1km off the main road. A taxi from Tenom will cost around RM90.

Sapulot & Batu Punggul

Perhaps even more so than the Maliau Basin, this is as remote as it gets in Sabah. Not far from the Kalimantan border, Batu Punggul is a jungle-topped limestone outcrop riddled with caves, towering nearly 200m above Sungai Sapulot. This is deep in Murut country and the stone formation was one of several sites sacred to these people. Batu Punggul and the adjacent Batu Tinahas are traditionally believed to be longhouses that gradually transformed into stone. The view from the upper reaches of Batu Punggul may be the best in Sabah – in every direction is deep jungle, knifelike limestone outcrops and, if you are lucky, swinging orangutans. It can be difficult and expensive to get here, but this is a beautiful part of Sabah that few tourists visit, and it offers a chance to rub shoulders with the jungle Murut.

It is almost impossible to get out here on your own, as there is virtually no tourism infrastructure and English is almost nonexistent, but even the most independent traveller will likely enjoy booking through Orou Sapulot.

★**Orou Sapulot** CULTURAL TOUR
(☎016-311 0056; www.orousapulot.com; 3-day/2-night per person for a group of 4 RM1122) The two- to three-night adventure encompasses **Romol Eco Village**, a longhouse homestay with the Murut; the **Pungiton Caves**, an extensive cavern system with underground rivers; an **eco-camp** by Pungiton located on the banks of a heavenly river; and finally, a sweat-inducing climb up Batu Punggul, followed by a rapid-shoot downriver all the way to the Kalimantan border.

Set up by Silas Gunting, a descendant of the local Murut, Orou is one of the most innovative eco-tourism projects in the state, and offers one of the most varied, best-value adventures in Sabah. By employing local Murut and encouraging their families to keep their lands for eco-tourism purposes rather than selling them to palm-oil and timber companies, Orou is providing a sustainable income for the communities of Sabah's interior.

The above prices are estimated rates that take in all/some of the activities mentioned above. To share costs, bigger groups are best but if you're a solo visitor, ask when booking if there are other groups to join. In KK, Adventure Alternative Borneo (p46) is Orou Sapulot's preferred booking agency.

Beaufort Division

This shield-shaped peninsula, popping out from Sabah's southwestern coast, is a marshy plain marked with curling rivers and fringed by golden dunes. Tourists with tight travel schedules should consider doing a wildlife river cruise at Klias (p114) or Garama (p114) if they don't have time to reach Sungai Kinabatangan. Yes, the Kinabatangan is better, but packs of proboscis monkeys can still be spotted here and it's only a day trip from KK. You can book trips to Beaufort, Weston and the Klias and Garama rivers in any KK travel agency.

Beaufort

Born as a timber town, Beaufort has reinvented itself with the proliferation of palm-oil plantations. A suitable pit stop for tourists travelling between Sabah and Sarawak, this sleepy township is the gateway to white-water rapids on the **Sungai Padas** and the monkey-filled Klias and Garama areas. The Sungai Padas divides Beaufort into two sections: the aptly named Old Town with its weathered structures, and New Town, a collection of modern shophouses on flood-phobic stilts. During WWII, Beaufort was the site of a major skirmish between the Japanese and Australians.

Sights & Activities

Memorial Stone MEMORIAL

(Jln Tugu) There's a small monument to Private Thomas Leslie Starcevich, an Australian WWII veteran. In 1945, Starcevich single-handedly overwhelmed a Japanese machine-gun position, for which he received the Victoria Cross, the British military's highest decoration. The stone is at the bottom of a small embankment and is marked by brown signs and an arch.

Rafting

White-water rafting enthusiasts can book a river trip with Riverbug (p47), the premier operator in the area. It also offers a combo paintball day!

Meanwhile, Scuba Junkie's affiliated river-rafting outfit, River Junkie (p47), also comes highly recommended by travellers. All trips include transfers by van, and normally require 24 hours' advance notice. Tourists who seek more serene waters can ride the rapids of Sungai Kiulu (bookable through the aforementioned operators), which is located near Mt Kinabalu and calm enough to be popular with families.

Sleeping & Eating

There's really no need to spend the night in Beaufort, but if you must, then try the **River Park Hotel** (087-223 333; Beaufort Jaya; r from RM130-160; P ❄). If you're stopping in town for a bite, make sure you try a pomelo (football-sized citrus fruit) and local *mee Beaufort* (Beaufort noodles) – both are locally famous.

Getting There & Away

BUS

Express buses operate from near the old train station at the south end of Jln Masjid (the ticket booth is opposite the station). There are departures at 9am, 1pm, 2.15pm and 5pm for KK (RM15, 1½ hours). There are departures at 9.10am, 10.30am, 1.45pm and 6.20pm for Sipitang (RM25, 1½ hours). The KK to Lawas express bus passes through Beaufort at around 3pm; the trip from Beaufort to Lawas costs RM30 and takes 1¾ hours.

MINIVAN

Minivans operate from a stop across from the mosque, at the north end of Jln Masjid. There are frequent departures for KK (RM20, two hours), and less-frequent departures for Sipitang (RM30, 1½ hours), Lawas (RM40, 1¾ hours) and Kuala Penyu (RM15, one hour, until around 2.30pm). To Menumbok (for Labuan) there are plenty of minivans until early afternoon (RM15, one hour).

TAXI

Taxis depart from the stand outside the old train station, at the south end of Jln Masjid. Charter rates include KK (RM120), Kuala Penyu (RM100), Sipitang (RM100), Menumbok (RM100) and Lawas (RM120).

Kuala Penyu

Tiny Kuala Penyu, at the northern tip of the peninsula, is the jumping-off point for Pulau Tiga, if you are not accessing 'Survivor Island' via the new boat service from KK. From Beaufort, minivans to Kuala Penyu (RM15) leave throughout the morning, but return services tail off very early in the afternoon, so you may have to negotiate a taxi or local lift back. A minivan to/from Menumbok costs RM90 per vehicle.

Tempurung

Set along the quiet coastal waters of the South China Sea, **Tempurung Seaside Lodge** (088-773 066; www.borneotempurung.com; 2-day, 1-night package per person from RM150, min 2 persons) is a good spot for hermits who seek a pinch of style. The main lodge was originally built as a holiday home, but friends convinced the owners that it would be a crime not to share the lovely property with the world. Rooms are scattered between several bungalows accented with patches of jungle thatch. The packages include fantastic meals. Nightly rates are also available.

Borneo Express (in KK 012-830 7722, in Limbang 085-211 384, in Miri 012-823 7722) runs buses from KK (departing from Wawasan) at 6.45am, 10am and 12.30pm daily. Ask the driver to let you off at the junction with the large Kuala Penyu sign. The bus will turn left (south) to head towards Menumbok; you want to go right (north) in the direction of Kuala Penyu. If you arranged accommodation in advance, the lodge van can pick you up here (it's too far to walk). Buses pass the junction at 9.30am and 3.30pm heading back to KK. If you're driving, take a right at the junction and keep an eye out for the turn-off on the left side of the road just before Kuala Penyu. We suggest calling the lodge for directions. A charter taxi from Beaufort will cost about RM55.

Klias

The tea-brown **Sungai Klias** looks somewhat similar to the mighty Kinabatangan, offering short-stay visitors a chance to spend an evening in the jungle cavorting with saucy primates. There are several companies offering two-hour river cruises. We recommend Borneo Authentic (p47), the first operator to set up shop in the region. Trips include a large buffet dinner and a short night walk to view the swarms of fireflies that light up the evening sky like Christmas lights. Cruises start at dusk (around 5pm), when the sweltering heat starts to burn off and animals emerge for some post-siesta prowling.

There is no accommodation in Klias, although Borneo Authentic can set you up with one of its comfy rooms at the Tempurung Seaside Lodge nearby. Tourists can make their own way to the row of private jetties 20km west of Beaufort; however, most trip-takers usually sign-up for a hassle-free day trip from KK (which ends up being cheaper since you're sharing transport).

Garama

Narrower than the river in Klias, the **Sungai Garama** is another popular spot for river-cruise day trips from KK. Chances of seeing fireflies are slim, but Garama is just as good as Klias (if not better) when it comes to primate life. Gangs of proboscis monkeys and long-tailed macaques scurry around the surrounding floodplain offering, eager tourists plenty of photo fodder.

Like Klias, the tours here start at around 5pm (with KK departures at 2pm), and after a couple of hours along the river, guests chat about the evening's sightings over a buffet dinner before returning to KK. There are several operators offering Garama river tours; we prefer **Only in Borneo** (☎088-260 506; www.oibtours.com; package tour RM190), an offshoot of Traverse Tours. It has a facility along the shores of Sungai Garama and offers an overnight option in prim dorms or double rooms.

It is technically possible to reach Garama with your own vehicle, but the network of unmarked roads can be tricky and frustrating. We recommend leaving early in the morning from KK if you want to get here on your own steam.

Weston

The little village of Weston – a couple of shacks clustered around a gold-domed mosque – is the jumping-off point for a gentle yet jungly patch of **wetlands** that is equal parts serene and overgrown. The area was bombed beyond recognition during WWII, but recent conservation efforts have welcomed groups of curious proboscis monkeys into the tidal marshlands, which are shaded by towering nipa palms and copses of spiderlike mangroves. As the tide rolls in and out, entire swaths of jungle are submerged and revealed. Monkeys, monitor lizards, otters and mud skippers flash through the aquatic undergrowth, and as the sun sets, clouds of flying foxes (ie *big* bats) flap in with the darkness.

Sights

Weston Wetland (☎088-485 103, 013-881 3233, 016-813 4300; www.westonwetlandpark.com) operates a variety of package tours including river-cruise day trips and sleepovers at its swampside longhouse (all-inclusive two-day, one-night package RM250). The dorm facilities are rustic at best, but the quality of the firefly show here is extremely high. Note that the folk at Weston Wetland insist you prebook before visiting.

While you're here, you can ask folk at the lodge to take you to **Che Hwa Schoolhouse**, the oldest wooden school building in Borneo and a fine example of antiquarian Chinese architecture.

Menumbok

The tiny hamlet of Menumbok is where you can catch car ferries to the Serasa Ferry Terminal in Muara, 25km northeast of Bandar Seri Begawan (Brunei), and to Pulau Labuan (adult/car RM30/80, departures every hour from 9.30am to 3.30pm).

On land, a charter taxi from Beaufort costs RM70, minivans from Kuala Penyu cost RM50 per vehicle. There is a direct bus service (RM15) connecting Menumbok to KK.

Pulau Tiga National Park

The name Pulau Tiga actually means 'three islands' – the scrubby islet is part of a small chain created during an eruption of mud volcanoes in the late 1890s. Over 100 years later, in 2001, the island had its 15 minutes of fame when it played host to the smash-hit reality TV series *Survivor,* so is commonly referred to now as as 'Survivor Island'. TV junkies still stop by for a look-see, although the 'Tribal Council' was destroyed in a storm and the debris was cleared after it turned into a home for venomous snakes. Whatever your viewing preferences, it's still a great place for relaxing on the beach, hiking in the forest and taking a cooling dip in burping mud pits at the centre of the island.

Sights & Activities

Pulau Kalampunian Damit is famous for the sea snakes (up to 150 per day) that come ashore to mate, hence the island's nickname, **Snake Island**. Enigmatically, the snakes are never seen on nearby Pulau Tiga. Pulau Tiga Resort runs boat trips to the island (RM50 per person), with a stop en route for snorkelling for RM30 extra. You can also dive off the island for RM100 per dive, or RM200 for a fun dive for those with no scuba experience.

Sleeping & Eating

Sabah Parks CAMPING $

(088-211 881; www.sabahparks.org.my; r from RM75) Sabah Parks runs basic lodging (ie block houses) on the island for less affluent survivalists. It's right next door to Pulau Tiga Resort, about 10m from where 'Tribal Council' was once held (sadly, tiki torches no longer line the way). Facilities are limited and there's no restaurant, though a cooking area is provided. Book through the KK Sabah Parks (p55) office.

Pulau Tiga Resort RESORT $$

(088-240 584; www.pulau-tiga.com; 2-day, 1-night package per person from Kuala Penyu RM305-360, from KK RM455-510;) Built to house the production crew for the first series of *Survivor,* accommodation is available in dorm-style 'longhouse' rooms (three beds in each), while more luxurious private cabins have double beds and air-con. The beach-facing grounds offer amazing views of the sunset, while a map is available should you want to track down the beach where the Pagong Tribe lived (called Pagong-Pagong Beach).

Getting There & Away

From Kuala Penyu the boat ride (RM80 return ticket) takes about 20 minutes. Boats leave at 10am and 3pm. Most visitors to Pulau Tiga come as part of a package, in which case transport is included in the price. You can try showing up in Kuala Penyu and asking if you can board one of the day's boats out to the island (we don't recommend this option as priority is given to resort guests with bookings). For Sabah Parks' lodgings, try to hop a ride with the Pulau Tiga Resort boat – chartering your own craft costs RM600 at least.

Pulau Labuan

087 / POP 86,910

If you've ever wondered what a cross between a duty-free airport mall and a tropical island would look like, check out the federal district of Pulau Labuan. Some call this Sabah's Vegas, and in the sense that Labuan offers both duty-free sin and tacky family fun, we agree. By the way, everything here *is* duty free, because politically, Labuan is governed directly from KL. As such, a lot of the booze you consume and cigarettes you smoke in Sabah and Sarawak are illegally smuggled from Labuan. Thanks to financial deregulation, Labuan is now the home of some major offshore bank accounts, so you may also want to be on the lookout for men in sunglasses with big briefcases, although we suggest not taking pictures of them.

The sultan of Brunei ceded Labuan to the British in 1846 and it remained part of the empire for 115 years. The only interruption came during WWII, when the Japanese held the island for three years. Significantly, it was on Labuan that the Japanese forces in north Borneo surrendered at the end of the war, and the officers responsible for the death marches from Sandakan were tried here.

Bandar Labuan is the main town and the transit point for ferries linking Kota Kinabalu and Brunei.

Sights

Bandar Labuan

Labuan's main settlement is light on character but has a couple of passable attractions.

Labuan Museum MUSEUM

(087-414 135; 364 Jln Dewan; 9am-5pm) FREE This museum on Jln Dewan takes a glossy, if slightly superficial, look at the island's history and culture, from colonial days, through WWII, to the establishment of

Bandar Labuan

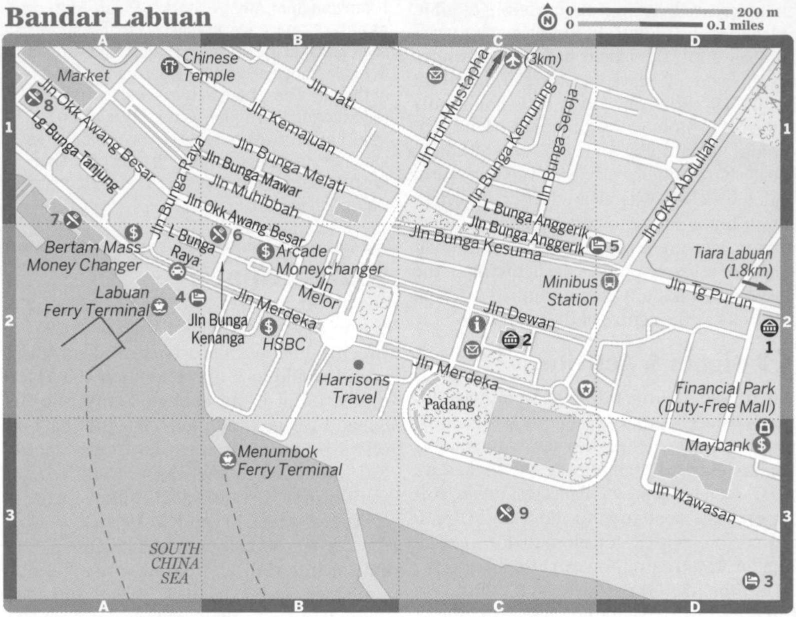

Labuan as an independent federal territory. The most interesting displays are those on the different ethnic groups here, including a diorama of a traditional Chinese tea ceremony (the participants, however, look strangely Western).

Labuan Marine Museum MUSEUM
(☎087-425 927, 087-414 462; Jln Tanjung Purun; ⏲9am-6pm) **FREE** On the coast just east of the centre, the Labuan International Sea Sports Complex houses a decent little museum with a good shell collection and displays of local marine life. Head upstairs to find a 12.8m-long skeleton of an Indian fin whale. The real highlight, however, and a guaranteed hit with the kids, is the 'touch pool' opposite reception. This has to be the only shark-petting zoo we've ever seen (fret not: the sharks are less than a metre long).

Around Pulau Labuan

WWII Memorial (Labuan War Cemetery) CEMETERY
A dignified expanse of lawn with row upon row of headstones dedicated to the nearly 4000 Commonwealth servicemen, mostly Australian and British, who lost their lives in Borneo during WWII. The cemetery is near the golf course, about 2km east of town along Jln OKK Abdullah. A **Peace Park** on the west of the island at Layang Layangan commemorates the place of Japanese surrender and has a Japanese war memorial.

Labuan Bird Park WILDLIFE RESERVE
(☎087-463 544; adult/child/under 5yr RM3/1/free; ⏲10am-5pm, closed Fri) This pretty park offers refuge to a wide range of species in three geodesic domes, and a swath of rainforest – the birds look a little bored, but

healthy. The park is located at the north end of the island on Jln Tanjung Kubong.

Chimney LANDMARK
Believed to be part of an old coal-mining station, this is the only historical monument of its kind in Malaysia, and has good views along the coast. It's at the northeast tip of the island, best accessed by minibus or taxi.

Labuan Marine Park PARK
Pulau Kuraman, Pulau Rusukan Kecil and Pulau Rusukan Besar are uninhabited islands lying southwest of Labuan that are now protected by the federal government. The beaches are pristine, but dynamite fishing has destroyed much of the coral. You can hire boats from the jetty at the Labuan International Sea Sports Complex to explore the marine park. A day's charter costs around RM600 per group of six people.

If you want to dive here, enquire at Borneo Star Dives.

Sleeping

Labuan Homestay Programme HOMESTAY $
(☎013-854 0217, 016-824 6193, 087-422 622; 1/2 days incl full board RM70/150) This excellent service matches visitors with a friendly local in one of three villages around the island: Patau Patau 2, Kampong Sungai Labu and Kampong Bukit Kuda. If you want to be near Bandar Labuan, ask for accommodation at Patau Patau 2 – it's a charming stilt village out on the bay. If you want to enrol in the program, book at least a few days in advance.

★**Tiara Labuan** HOTEL $$
(☎087-414 300; www.tiaralabuan.com; Jln Tanjung Batu; r incl breakfast from RM250;) Pulau Labuan's favourite hotel is a cut above the rest with its cobalt-blue outdoor pool nestled in manicured gardens at Tanjung Batu. There's an excellent Asian-fusion restaurant and open-range kitchen, plus large and very alluring wood-signatured rooms with bed runners, snow-white linen, spotless bathrooms and recessed lighting.

Billion Waterfront Hotel HOTEL $$
(☎087-418 111; leslbn@tm.net.my; 1 Jln Wawasan; r incl breakfast from RM350;) This large business hotel backs onto a lively port, has an open bar, and has large international-style rooms with comfy beds, reading lights, faux-wood floors and modern bathroom. Breakfast is a mix of Western and Malay.

Mariner Hotel HOTEL $$
(☎087-418 822; mhlabuan@streamyx.com; U0468 Jln Tanjung Purun; s/d RM120/140;) Mariner's rooms are spacious, with laminate floors, psychedelic art on the walls, fridges and clean bathrooms. Some rooms smelt a little smoky. Decent breakfast.

Grand Dorsett Labuan HOTEL $$$
(☎087-422 000; www.granddorsett.com/labuan; 462 Jln Merdeka; r from RM405;) One of the most luxurious hotels in town, Dorset is palatial with a columned marble lobby, outdoor pool, pleasant carpeted rooms, fresh walls and bathroom, plus friendly staff. The breakfast buffet, which is packed with fresh fruit and pastry, is tip-top.

Eating

★**The Chillout Cafe** INTERNATIONAL $
(www.thechilloutco.com; unit 2-6, level 2, Labuan Times Sq; mains RM15; 10am-10pm) Cosy, clean, cool and very inviting, the new little sister to its elder sibling on mainland Malaysia is perfect for reading a book while enjoying a cappuccino between tucking into its cakes, pasta dishes, sandwiches, nicely executed Western breakfasts and carefully concocted fruit juices.

Restoran Selera Farizah MALAYSIAN $
(Lg Bunga Tanjung; meals from RM3; 8am-10pm) If you prefer a Muslim *kedai kopi* (coffee shop) you could try this place, which serves roti, curries and *nasi campur* (buffet of curried meats, fish and vegetables, served

DIVING

Labuan is famous for its **wreck diving**, with no fewer than four major shipwrecks off the coast (two from WWII and two from the 1980s). The only dive outfit operating here is **Borneo Star Dives** (☎087-429 278; stardivers2005@yahoo.com; Labuan International Sea Sports Complex, Jln Tanjung Purun; dive packages from RM438), which does island-hopping tours and can take you out to all four sites. Note that only the 'Cement Wreck' is suitable for novice divers; the 'Blue Water Wreck' (in our opinion, the most impressive of the bunch) requires advanced open-water certification, and the 'American' and 'Australian' wrecks are only recommended for those with a wreck diving course under their belt.

GETTING TO BRUNEI: BANDAR LABUAN TO BANDAR SERI BEGAWAN

Getting to the border Ferries depart Bandar Labuan for the Bruneian port of Muara (RM35, 1¼ hours) daily at 9am, 1.30pm, 3.30pm and 4pm.

At the border In Brunei, most visitors are granted a visa on arrival for free, although Australians must pay a fee.

Moving on You'll be dropped at Serasa Ferry Terminal; from here bus 37 or 39 can take you to central Bandar Seri Begawan for B$1 (one hour). A taxi should cost around B$30.

with rice), accompanied by pro wrestling videos.

Choice Restaurant INDIAN $
(☎087-418 086; 104 Jln OKK Awang Besar; dishes RM3-10; ⏰8am-10pm) Forget false modesty, the Choice simply proclaims 'We are the best', and this seems to be corroborated by the popularity of the authentic Indian meals with the authentic Indian residents who turn out for roti, fish-head curry and sambal.

Port View Restaurant SEAFOOD $$
(☎087-422 999; Jln Merdeka; dishes RM15-30; ⏰lunch & dinner) An outpost of the successful Chinese seafood franchise in KK, this waterfront restaurant has air-con indoor seating and outdoor seating that affords a nice view over Labuan's busy harbour, though service can be a little frosty.

Tiara Seafood Restaurant SEAFOOD $$
(seafoodrest@tiaralabuan.com; Tiara Labuan Hotel, Jln Tanjung Batu; mains RM20; ⏰10.30am-2.30pm & 6-10pm) Based at hulking Tiara Labuan Hotel, this glass-accented restaurant has great reports for its fresh seafood. Whether it's scallops, king prawns, salt-and-pepper squid and steamed lobster (frozen) with garlic, or their iced mango sago pudding, there's something for everyone's palate. Efficient service and oblique sea views.

Information

MONEY

Bertam Mass Money Changer (Jln Bunga Raya) Cash and travellers cheques. Near the ferry terminal.

HSBC (☎087-422 610; 189 Jln Merdeka)

TOURIST INFORMATION

Tourist Information Centre (☎087-423 445; www.labuantourism.com.my; cnr Jln Dewan & Jln Berjaya; ⏰8am-5pm Mon-Fri, 9am-3pm Sat) Tourism Malaysia office.

Harrisons Travel (☎087-408 096; www.harrisonstravel.com.my; 1 Jln Merdeka) Handy and reputable travel agency.

Getting There & Away

AIR

Malaysia Airlines (☎1300-883 000; www.malaysiaairlines.com.my) has flights to/from KK (45 minutes) and KL (2½ hours), which are usually booked full of oil prospectors. **AirAsia** (☎087-480 401; www.airasia.com) currently flies to KL only.

BOAT

Kota Kinabalu Passenger ferries (1st/economy class RM48/35, 3¼ hours) depart KK for Labuan from Monday to Saturday at 8am, and 1.30pm (3pm Sundays). In the opposite direction, they depart Labuan for KK from Monday to Saturday at 8am and 1pm, and 10.30am and 3pm on Sundays.

Sarawak There are daily speedboats to Limbang (two hours, RM31) and Lawas (2¼ hours, RM34) in Sarawak's Limbang Division.

Getting Around

MINIBUS

Labuan has a good minibus network based on a six-zone system. Minibuses leave regularly from the parking lot off Jln Tun Mustapha. Their numbers are clearly painted on the front, and fares range from 50 sen for a short trip to RM2.50 for a trip to the top of the island. Services are generally more frequent before sunset.

TAXI

Taxis are plentiful and there's a stand opposite the local ferry terminal. The base rate is RM15 for short journeys, with most destinations costing around RM20.

Sarawak

AREA 124,450 SQ KM

Includes ➜

Why Go?

Sarawak makes access to Borneo's natural wonders and cultural riches a breeze. From Kuching, the island's most sophisticated and dynamic city, pristine rainforests – where you can spot orangutans, proboscis monkeys, crocodiles and the world's largest flower, the Rafflesia – can be visited on day trips, with plenty of time in the evening for a delicious meal and a drink by Kuching's waterfront. More adventurous travellers can take a 'flying coffin' riverboat up the 'Amazon of Borneo', the Batang Rejang, on their way east to hike from longhouse to longhouse in the cool environs of the Kelabit Highlands, or to the spectacular bat caves and extraordinary rock formations of Gunung Mulu National Park. Everywhere you go, you'll encounter the warmth, unforced friendliness and sense of humour that make the people of Malaysia's most culturally diverse state such delightful hosts.

Best Places to Eat

- ➜ Dyak (p133)
- ➜ Top Spot Food Court (p133)
- ➜ Summit Café (p175)
- ➜ Bla Bla Bla (p134)
- ➜ Choon Hui (p132)

Best Places to Stay

- ➜ Batik Boutique Hotel (p131)
- ➜ Dillenia Guesthouse (p174)
- ➜ Threehouse B&B (p130)
- ➜ Nanga Shanti (p144)

When to Go

Kuching

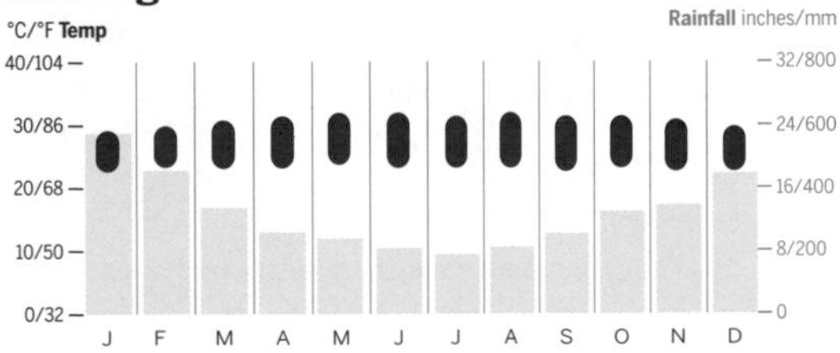

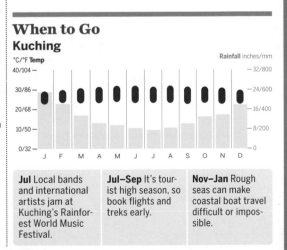

Jul Local bands and international artists jam at Kuching's Rainforest World Music Festival.

Jul–Sep It's tourist high season, so book flights and treks early.

Nov–Jan Rough seas can make coastal boat travel difficult or impossible.

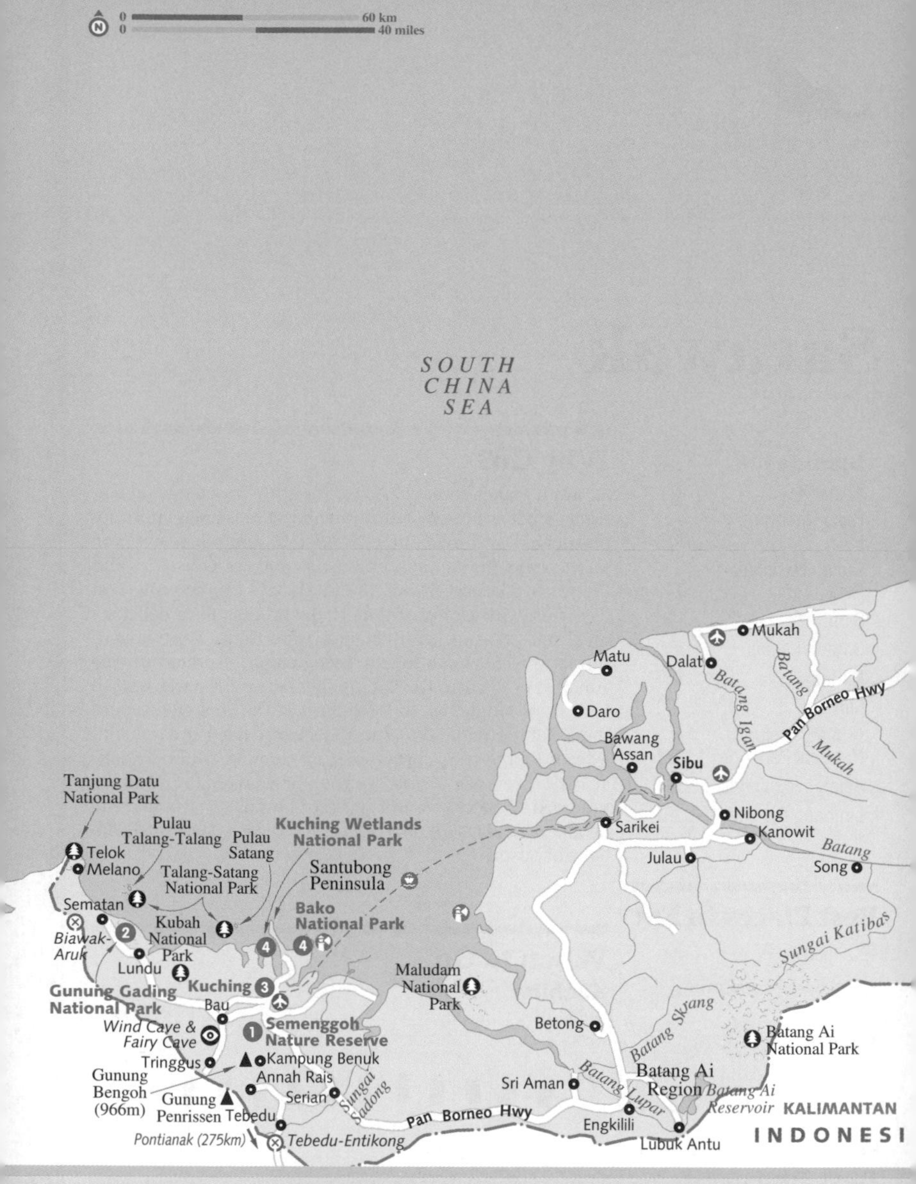

Sarawak Highlights

1 Watching semi-wild orangutans swing through the canopy at **Semenggoh Nature Reserve** (p145).

2 Seeing the elusive Rafflesia, the world's largest flower, at **Gunung Gading National Park** (p152).

3 Strolling the Waterfront Promenade in **Kuching** (p122).

4 Spotting endangered proboscis monkeys in **Bako National Park** (p139) or **Kuching Wetlands National Park** (p145).

5 Watching the jungle glide by as you make your way into

the very heart of Borneo along the **Batang Rejang** (p160), the 'Amazon of Borneo'.

6 Experiencing longhouse life and Kelabit hospitality in the **Kelabit Highlands** (p184).

7 Ascending to the summit of Gunung Mulu, the highest peak in **Gunung Mulu National Park** (p178), Borneo's best nature park, or going spelunking in its caves.

8 Entering a netherworld of stalactites and bats in the caves of **Niah National Park** (p168).

History

After a century of rule by the White Rajahs and four years of Japanese occupation, Sarawak became a British Crown colony in 1946. At Westminster's urging, the territory joined the Malay Peninsula, Sabah and Singapore to form Malaysia in 1963 (Singapore withdrew two years later). At about the same time, neighbouring Indonesia, under the leftist leadership of President Soekarno, laid claim to all of Borneo, including Sarawak, launching a military campaign known as the Konfrontasi (1962–66). Tens of thousands of troops from the UK, Australia and New Zealand were deployed to secure Sarawak's border with Kalimantan.

The appointment of Adenan Satem as chief minister of Sarawak in 2014 marked the end of the 13-year tenure of Abdul Taib Mahmud. Frequently accused of corruption, and with a personal fortune estimated at US$15 billion, Taib is now the Sarawak state governor. Nonetheless, the new chief minister has brought a degree of optimism to the people of Sarawak, who talk hopefully about a new era. Adenan, for his part, has said that he is determined to protect the state's forests from further palm-oil plantations and fight illegal logging and timber corruption.

KUCHING

☎082 / POP 600,000

Borneo's most sophisticated city brings together a kaleidoscope of cultures, crafts and cuisines. The bustling streets – some very modern, others with a colonial vibe – amply reward visitors with a penchant for aimless ambling. Chinese temples decorated with dragons abut shophouses from the time of the White Rajahs, a South Indian mosque is a five-minute walk from stalls selling half-a-dozen Asian cuisines, and a landscaped riverfront park attracts families out for a stroll and a quick bite.

Kuching's other huge asset is its day-trip proximity to a dozen first-rate nature sites.

Sights

The main attraction here is the city itself. Leave plenty of time to wander aimlessly and soak up the relaxed vibe and charming cityscapes of areas such as Jln Carpenter (Old Chinatown), Jln India, Jln Padungan (New Chinatown) and the Waterfront Promenade.

Waterfront Promenade

The south bank of Sungai Sarawak has been turned into a promenade, with paved walkways, grass and trees, and food stalls. It's a fine place for a stroll any time a cool breeze blows off the river, especially at sunset. In the evening, the waterfront is ablaze with colourful fairy lights and full of couples and families eating snacks as *tambang* (small passenger ferries) glide past with their glowing lanterns. The water level is kept constant by a downstream barrage.

Chinese History Museum MUSEUM
(cnr Main Bazaar & Jln Wayang; ⌚9am-4.45pm Mon-Fri, 10am-4pm Sat, Sun & holidays) FREE Housed in the century-old Chinese Court building, the Chinese History Museum provides an excellent introduction to the nine Chinese communities – each with its own dialect, cuisine and temples – who began settling in Sarawak around 1830. Highlights of the evocative exhibits include ceramics, musical instruments, historic photographs and some fearsome dragon- and lion-dance costumes. The entrance is on the river side of the building.

Square Tower HISTORIC BUILDING
Along with Fort Margherita, the Square Tower, built in 1879, once guarded the river against marauders. Over the past century, the structure – still emblazoned with Sarawak's Brooke-era coat-of-arms – has served as a prison, a mess and a dance hall.

Old Court House Complex HISTORIC BUILDING
(btwn Jln Tun Abang Haji Openg & Jln Barrack) The Old Court House was built in the late 1800s to serve as the city's administrative centre. At research time, this collection of airy, colonnaded structures was set to be redeveloped.

Out front, across the street from the Square Tower, stands the **Brooke Memorial**, erected in 1924 to honour Charles Brooke.

Old Chinatown

Lined with evocative, colonial-era shophouses and home to several vibrantly coloured Chinese temples, Jln Carpenter is the heart of Kuching's Old Chinatown

Hong San Si Temple CHINESE TEMPLE
(Say Ong Kong; cnr Jln Wayang & Jln Carpenter; ⌚6am-6pm) FREE Thought to date back to around 1840, this fine Hokkien Chinese temple with intricate rooftop dragons was fully restored in 2004. The new stone carvings,

done by stonemasons brought in from mainland China, are superb.

There is a big celebration here in April, when a long procession of floats, lion and dragon dancers and others wind their way through town following the altar of Kong Teck Choon Ong, the temple's diety.

Hin Ho Bio CHINESE TEMPLE

(36 Jln Carpenter; 6am-5pm) FREE It's easy to miss this temple, tucked away on the roof of the Kuching Hainan Association. Go up the staircase to the top floor and you come to a vivid little Chinese shrine, Hin Ho Bio (Temple of the Queen of Heaven), with rooftop views of Jln Carpenter.

Hiang Thian Siang Temple CHINESE TEMPLE

(Sang Ti Miao Temple; btwn 12 & 14 Jln Carpenter) FREE This temple, rebuilt shortly after the fire of 1884, serves the Teochew congregation as a shrine to Shang Di (the Emperor of Heaven). On the 15th day of the **Hungry Ghosts Festival** (mid-August or early September) a ceremony is held here in which offerings of food, prayer, incense and paper money are made to appease the spirits, blessed by a priest and then burned in a dramatic bonfire.

Sarawak Textile Museum MUSEUM

(Muzium Tekstil Sarawak; Jln Tun Abang Haji Openg; 9am-4.45pm Mon-Fri, 10am-4pm Sat, Sun & holidays) FREE Housed in a 'colonial Baroque'-style building constructed in 1909, this museum displays some superb examples of traditional Sarawakian textiles, including Malay *songket* (gold brocade cloth), as well as the hats, mats, belts, basketwork, beadwork, silverwork, barkwork, bangles and ceremonial headdresses created by the Iban, Bidayuh and Penan and other Dayak groups. Dioramas recreate the sartorial exuberance of Orang Ulu, Malay, Chinese and Indian weddings. Explanatory panels shed light on materials and techniques.

Jalan India Area

Once Kuching's main shopping area for imported textiles, brassware and household goods, pedestrianised Jln India – essentially the western continuation of Jln Carpenter – remains an exuberant commercial thoroughfare. The shops along the eastern section are mostly Chinese-owned; those to the west are run by Indian Muslims with roots in Tamil Nadu. It's *the* place to come in Kuching for cheap textiles.

Indian Mosque MOSQUE

(Indian Mosque Lane; 6am-8.30pm except during prayers) FREE Turn off Jln India (between Nos 37 and 39A) or waterfront Jln Gambier (between Nos 24 and 25A – shops selling spices with a heady aroma) onto tiny **Indian Mosque Lane** (Lg Sempit) and you enter another world. About halfway up, entirely surrounded by houses and shops, stands Kuching's oldest mosque, a modest structure built of *belian* (ironwood) in 1863 by Muslim traders from Tamil Nadu.

Notable for its simplicity, it is an island of peace and cooling shade in the middle of Kuching's commercial hullabaloo. There is usually someone sitting outside the mosque keeping an eye on things. If you would like to go inside, ask permission and he will probably offer to show you around. Women will be given a long cloak and headscarf to wear.

South of Padang Merdeka

The museums in the area just south of Padang Merdeka (Independence Square) contain a first-rate collection of cultural artefacts that no one interested in Borneo's peoples and habitats should miss. At research time, construction was underway on a new five-storey museum, located on the western side of Jln Tun Abang Haji Openg, due to be completed in 2020. The new modern building will bring the archaeology, ethnology, zoology and history collections under one roof, with state-of-the art interactive displays.

★ **Ethnology Museum** MUSEUM

(www.museum.sarawak.gov.my; Jln Tun Abang Haji Openg; 9am-4.45pm Mon-Fri, 10am-4pm Sat, Sun & holidays) FREE At the top of the hill, on the eastern side of Jln Tun Abang Haji Openg, the Ethnology Museum (the Old Building) – guarded by two colonial cannons – spotlights Borneo's incredibly rich indigenous cultures. Upstairs the superb exhibits include a full-sized Iban longhouse, masks and spears; downstairs is an old-fashioned natural-history museum.

At research time, there were plans to renovate the more than 100-year-old building, starting early 2016. During the renovations sections of the museum may be closed.

The museum was established in 1891 by Charles Brooke as a place to exhibit indigenous handicrafts and wildlife specimens, many of them collected by the naturalist Russell Wallace in the 1850s. The rajah's

Kuching

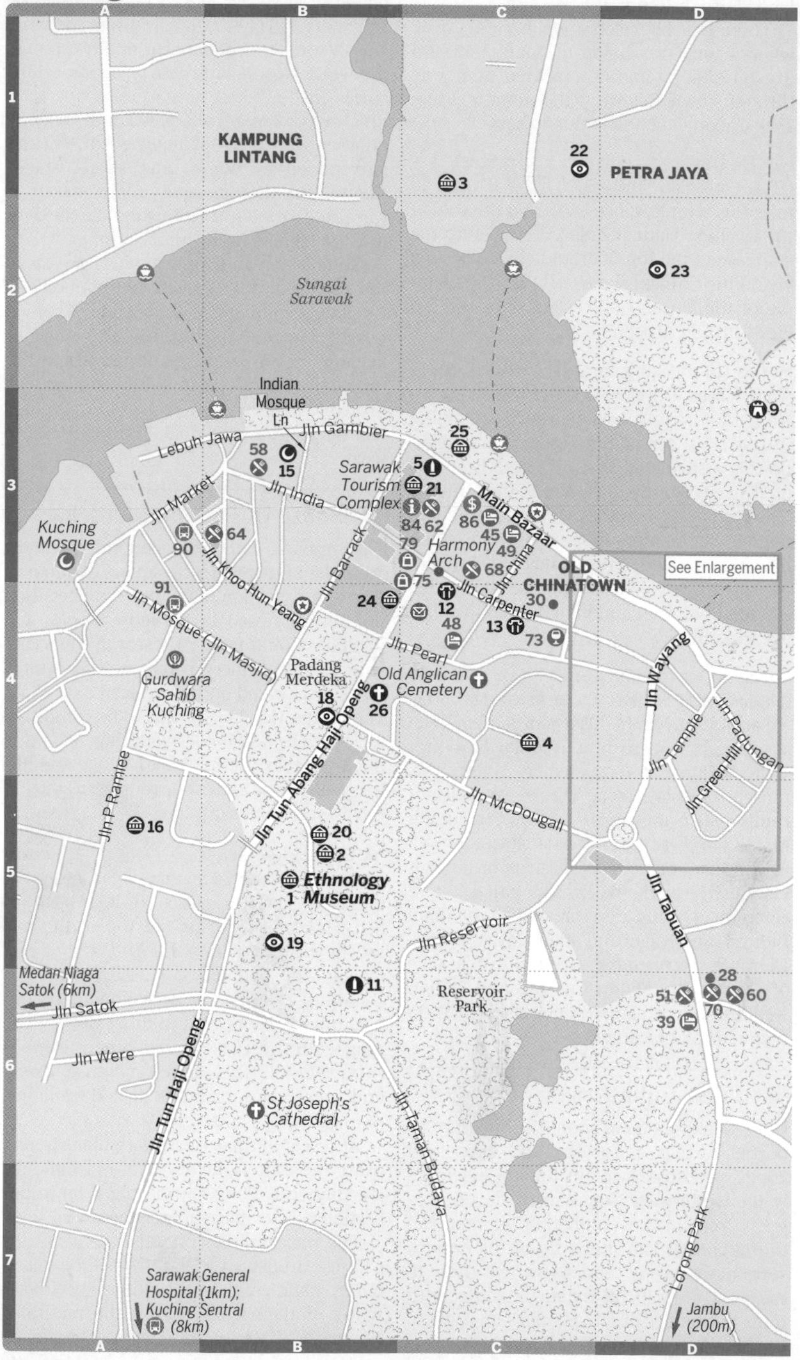
KAMPUNG LINTANG
PETRA JAYA
Sungai Sarawak
Indian Mosque Ln
Jln Gambier
Lebuh Jawa
Jln India
Jln Market
Kuching Mosque
Sarawak Tourism Complex
Main Bazaar
Harmony Arch
Jln China
OLD CHINATOWN
See Enlargement
Jln Carpenter
Jln Khoo Hun Yeang
Jln Mosque (Jln Masjid)
Jln Barrack
Jln Pearl
Gurdwara Sahib Kuching
Padang Merdeka
Old Anglican Cemetery
Jln Wayang
Jln Temple
Jln Padungan
Jln Green Hill
Jln Tun Abang Haji Openg
Jln McDougall
Jln P Ramlee
Ethnology Museum
Jln Tabuan
Jln Reservoir
Reservoir Park
Medan Niaga Satok (6km)
Jln Satok
Jln Were
Jln Tun Haji Openg
St Joseph's Cathedral
Jln Taman Budaya
Lorong Park
Sarawak General Hospital (1km); Kuching Sentral (8km)
Jambu (200m)

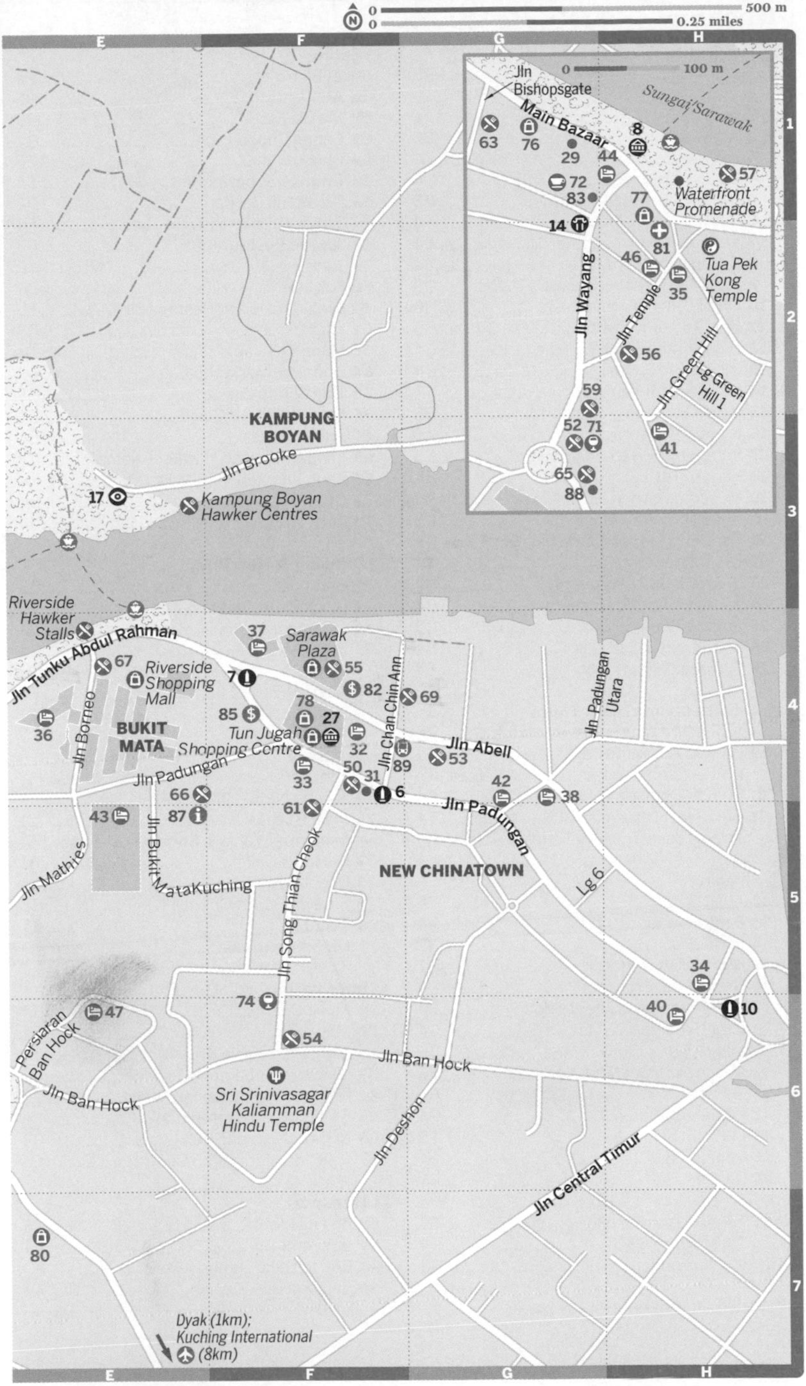
500 m
0.25 miles
100 m
Jln Bishopsgate
Main Bazaar
Sungai Sarawak
Waterfront Promenade
Tua Pek Kong Temple
Jln Wayang
Jln Temple
Jln Green Hill
Lg Green Hill 1
KAMPUNG BOYAN
Jln Brooke
Kampung Boyan Hawker Centres
Riverside Hawker Stalls
Jln Tunku Abdul Rahman
Riverside Shopping Mall
Sarawak Plaza
Tun Jugah Shopping Centre
BUKIT MATA
Jln Borneo
Jln Padungan
Jln Chan Chin Ann
Jln Abell
Jln Padungan Utara
NEW CHINATOWN
Lg 6
Jln Mathies
Jln Bukit Mata Kuching
Jln Song Thian Cheok
Persiaran Ban Hock
Jln Ban Hock
Sri Srinivasagar Kaliamman Hindu Temple
Jln Deshon
Jln Central Timur
Dyak (1km); Kuching International (8km)

Kuching

Top Sights
1 Ethnology Museum ... B5

Sights
2 Art Museum ... B5
3 Astana ... C1
4 Bishop's House ... C4
5 Brooke Memorial ... C3
6 Cat Column ... F4
7 Cat Fountain ... F4
8 Chinese History Museum ... H1
9 Fort Margherita ... D3
10 Great Cat of Kuching ... H6
11 Heroes' Monument ... B6
12 Hiang Thian Siang Temple ... C4
13 Hin Ho Bio ... C4
14 Hong San Si Temple ... G2
15 Indian Mosque ... B3
16 Islamic Museum ... A5
17 Kampung Boyan ... E3
18 Kapok Tree ... B4
19 Museum Garden ... B5
20 Natural History Museum ... B5
21 Old Court House Complex ... C3
22 Orchid Garden ... C1
23 Sarawak State Assembly ... D2
24 Sarawak Textile Museum ... B4
25 Square Tower ... C3
26 St Thomas's Cathedral ... B4
27 Tun Jugah Foundation ... F4

Activities, Courses & Tours
28 Adventure Alternative Borneo ... D6
29 Borneo Adventure ... G1
Borneo Experiences ... (see 46)
30 Bumbu Cooking School ... C4
31 CPH Travel Agencies ... F4
Telang Usan Travel & Tours ... (see 47)

Sleeping
32 Abell Hotel ... F4
33 Batik Boutique Hotel ... F4
34 Beds ... H5
35 Harbour View Hotel ... H2
36 Hilton Kuching Hotel ... E4
37 Hotel Grand Margherita Kuching ... F4
38 Lime Tree Hotel ... G4
39 Lodge 121 ... D6
40 Marco Polo Guesthouse ... H6
41 Nomad B&B ... H3
42 Padungan Hotel ... G4
43 Pullman Kuching ... E5
44 Radioman ... H1
45 Ranee ... C3
46 Singgahsana Lodge ... H2
47 Telang Usan Hotel ... E6
48 Threehouse B&B ... C4
49 Wo Jia Lodge ... C3

Eating
50 21 Bistro ... F4
51 Aroma Café ... D6
52 Bla Bla Bla ... G3
53 Chong Choon Cafe ... G4
54 Choon Hui ... F6
55 Everrise Supermarket ... F4
56 Green Hill Corner ... H2
57 James Brooke Bistro & Cafe ... H1
58 Jubilee Restaurant ... B3
59 Junk ... G2
60 Lok Lok ... D6
61 Lyn's Thandoori Restaurant ... F5
62 Magna Carta ... C3
63 Maria Kek Lapis ... G1
64 Open-Air Market ... B3
65 Ting & Ting ... G3
66 Top Spot Food Court ... E4
67 Tribal Stove ... E4
68 Yang Choon Tai Hawker Centre ... C3
69 Zhun San Yen Vegetarian Food Centre ... G4
70 Zinc ... D6

Drinking & Nightlife
71 Barber ... G3
72 Black Bean Coffee & Tea Company ... G1
73 Drunken Monkey ... C4
Lamin ... (see 47)
74 Monkee Bar ... F6
Ruai ... (see 60)

Shopping
Fabriko ... (see 76)
75 Juliana Native Handwork ... C3
76 Main Bazaar ... G1
Mohamed Yahia & Sons ... (see 55)
77 Nelson's Gallery ... H1
78 Popular Book Co ... F4
79 Sarawak Craft Council ... C3
80 Tanoti ... E7
UD Siburan Jaya ... (see 76)

Information
81 Klinik Chan ... H2
82 Maybank ... F4
Mohamed Yahia & Sons ... (see 55)
83 My Express Laundry Service ... G1
84 National Park Booking Office ... C3
85 Standard Chartered Bank ... F4
86 United Overseas Bank ... C3
87 Visitors Information Centre ... E5

Transport
88 An Hui Motor ... G3
89 Bus Asia ... F4
90 Bus to Bako National Park ... A3
91 Saujana Bus Station ... A4

French aide designed the building, modelling it on Normandy town hall.

The upstairs gallery is decorated with Kayan and Kenyah murals painted by local artists, forming the backdrop to exhibits that include basketry, musical instruments and a Bidayuh door charm for keeping evil spirits at bay, as well as information on native customs such as tattooing and the infamous *palang* penis piercing.

Downstairs in the natural-history gallery the highlight – remembered with horror by generations of Kuching children – is a hairball taken from the stomach of a man-eating crocodile, accompanied by the following explanation: 'human dental plate found attached to the hairball'. And if this isn't enough to put you off taking a dip in a muddy estuary, the 'watch found inside stomach' (the croc's stomach, of course) surely will – unless you'd like your smartphone to feature in some future exhibit.

Museum Garden GARDENS
(Jln Tun Abang Haji Openg; ⌚9am-4.45pm Mon-Fri, 10am-4pm Sat, Sun & holidays) The landscaped Museum Garden stretches south from the hill, leading past flowers and fountains to a white-and-gold column called the **Heroes' Monument**, which commemorates those who died defending Sarawak.

Art Museum MUSEUM
(www.museum.sarawak.gov.my; Jln Tun Abang Haji Openg; ⌚9am-4.45pm Mon-Fri, 10am-4pm Sat, Sun & holidays) FREE This museum features sculpture and paintings using traditional indigenous techniques as well as pieces inspired by Borneo's flora, fauna and landscapes. At research time the museum was closed for renovations but it will reopen with additional exhibits (previously contained in the now permanently closed Dewan Tun Abdul Razak gallery) on Sarawak's fascinating history, from the Brunei sultanate through to the Brooke era, prehistoric archaeology including important finds from the Niah Caves, and Chinese ceramics.

Natural History Museum MUSEUM
(www.museum.sarawak.gov.my; Jln Tun Abang Haji Openg) FREE This building, built in 1908 and adorned with a Wallace butterfly in reference to the naturalist it is named after, is currently being used to store zoological and archaeological specimens (including finds excavated in Niah) and as offices. It is not open to the general public, but researchers and students can apply for access to the collections.

Islamic Museum MUSEUM
(Jln P Ramlee; ⌚9am-4.45pm Mon-Fri, 10am-4pm Sat, Sun & holidays) FREE This museum offers a pretty good introduction to Malay-Muslim culture and its long ties with the Muslim heartland far to the west. Displays range from Bornean-Malay architecture, musical instruments and wood carvings to Arabic calligraphy and astrolabes of the sort that helped Arab mariners travel this far east.

New Chinatown

Built starting in the 1920s, initially with money from the rubber boom, Kuching's liveliest commercial thoroughfare stretches 1.5km along Jln Padungan from Jln Tunku Abdul Rahman to the Great Cat of Kuching. It's lined with Chinese-owned businesses and noodle shops and a growing number of cafes, bars and restaurants. Covered arcades make it a fine place for a rainy-day stroll.

Tun Jugah Foundation MUSEUM
(☎082-239672; www.tunjugahfoundation.org.my; 4th fl, Tun Jugah Tower, 18 Jln Tunku Abdul Rahman; ⌚9am-noon & 1-4.30pm Mon-Fri) FREE The textile gallery and museum of this charitable foundation, which aims to promote and preserve Iban culture, has excellent exhibits on Iban *ikat* and *sungkit* weaving, as well as beadwork. Iban women come here to make traditional textiles using handlooms.

North Bank of the River

To get to Sungai Sarawak's northern bank, take a *tambang* (river ferry; 50 sen) from one of the docks along the Waterfront Promenade.

Kampung Boyan AREA
This sedate, old-time Malay *kampung* (village), filled with joyously colourful houses and a profusion of flowering plants, is a world away from the glitz and bustle of downtown Kuching, to which it's connected by boat. The waterfront area has two roofed hawker centres as well as other Malay-style eateries.

Fort Margherita FORT
(Kampung Boyan; ⌚9am-4.30pm) Built by Charles Brooke in 1879 and named after his wife, Ranee Margaret, this hilltop fortress long protected Kuching against surprise attack by pirates. It did so exclusively as a remarkably successful deterrent: troops stationed here never fired a shot in anger.

To get there from Kampung Boyan, follow the signs up the hill for 500m.

Inspired by an English Renaissance castle, whitewashed Fort Margherita manages to feel both medieval-European and tropical. At research time there were plans to add new exhibits on the Brookes to the almost empty fort.

Astana HISTORIC BUILDING
(Jln Taman Budaya; ⌚closed to public) Built by Charles Brooke in 1869, the Astana (a local word meaning 'palace') – conveniently labelled in giant white letters – and its manicured gardens still serve as the home of the governor of Sarawak. The best views are actually from the south (city centre) bank of the river, so it's not really worth taking a *tambang* across.

Sarawak State Assembly NOTABLE BUILDING
(Dewan Undangan Negeri, north bank of Sungai Sarawak, Petra Jaya) Inaugurated in 2009, the iconic home of Sarawak's State Assembly is an imposing structure whose soaring golden roof is said to resemble either a *payung* (umbrella) or a *terendak* (Melanau sunhat). The best views of the building (not open to the public) are from Jln Bishopsgate and the Waterfront Promenade.

Elsewhere in Kuching

St Thomas's Cathedral CHURCH
(www.stthomascathedralkuching.org; Jln Tun Abang Haji Openg; ⌚8.30am-6pm Mon-Sat, to 7pm Sun) FREE Facing **Padang Merdeka** (Independence Sq), with its huge and ancient **kapok tree**, Kuching's Anglican cathedral (1954) has a mid-20th-century look and, inside, a bright red barrel-vaulted ceiling. Enter from Jln McDougall, named after Kuching's first Anglican bishop, who arrived here in 1848.

At the top of the hill, on the other side of the Parish Centre stands the **Bishop's House**. Kuching's oldest building, it was constructed – in 1849 with admirable solidness – by a German shipwright.

Kuching North City Hall NOTABLE BUILDING
(DBKU; Jln Semariang, Bukit Siol) Situated 8km north of the city centre is the hilltop Kuching North City Hall (known by its Malay abbreviation, DBKU), a landmark prestige project – some say it looks like a UFO – inaugurated in 1993. As well as being a local council building, the Cat Museum is on the ground floor.

To get here, take bus K15 from the Saujana bus station (p139). If you're going to the Santubong Peninsula by car, you can stop here on the way.

Orchid Garden GARDENS
(Jln Astana Lot; ⌚9.30am-6pm Tue-Sun) FREE Sarawak's state flower, the Normah orchid, is just one of the 82 species growing in these peaceful gardens and greenhouse nursery. Other Borneo orchids to look out for are lady's slippers, identifiable by their distinct, insect-trapping pouches.

The easiest way to get here from the city centre is to take a *tambang* across the river to Pengakalan Sapi on the north bank (next to the Sarawak State Assembly building) and walk up the hill.

Medan Niaga Satok MARKET
(Satok Weekend Market; Jln Matang Jaya; ⌚5.30am-7.30pm) Kuching's biggest and liveliest market has now moved to its spacious new digs 9km west of the city centre. It's open every day, but the main event is the larger weekend market, which begins around midday on Saturday, when rural folk, some from area longhouses, arrive with their fruits, vegetables, fish and spices. To get here, take the K7 bus.

The air is heady with the aromas of fresh coriander, ginger, herbs and jungle ferns, which are displayed among piles of bananas, mangoes, custard apples and obscure jungle fruits. If you smell something overpoweringly sickly sweet and pungent, chances are it's a durian. Vendors are friendly and many are happy to tell you about their wares, which are often divided into quantities worth RM1 or RM2.

Activities

Bumbu Cooking School COOKING COURSE
(☎019-879 1050; http://bumbucookingclass.weebly.com; 57 Jln Carpenter; per person RM150; ⌚9am-1pm & 2.30-7pm) Raised in a Bidayuh village, Joseph teaches the secrets of cooking with fresh, organic ingredients from the rainforest. At the market you'll learn how to spot top-quality jungle ferns; back in the kitchen you'll prepare this crunchy delicacy, along with a main dish and a dessert that's served in a *pandan*-leaf basket you weave yourself. Maximum 10 participants.

The small shop that serves as the entrance to the cooking school is like a mini-museum full of pieces Joseph has collected: blow pipes, rattan baskets (one designed to be used as a baby carrier), a rice mill, and ceremonial blankets and masks from Iban and Orang Ulu longhouses.

KUCHING KITTIES

It's just a coincidence that in Bahasa Malaysia, Kuching means 'cat' (spelled '*kucing*'), but the city has milked the homonym for all it's worth, branding Sarawak's capital the 'Cat City' and erecting a number of marvellously kitschy cat statues to beautify the urban landscape.

Cat Fountain (Jln Tunku Abdul Rahman) An ensemble of polychrome cats who pose and preen amid the passing cars.

Cat Column (cnr Jln Padungan & Jln Chan Chin Ann) On the roundabout, the Cat Column features four cats around the bottom and four Rafflesia flowers near the top – the latter are just below the cat-adorned shield of the South Kuching municipality.

Great Cat of Kuching (Jln Padungan) A 2.5m-high white pussycat with blue eyes and wire whiskers is perched at the eastern end of Jln Padungan on a traffic island just outside the Chinese ceremonial gate.

Cat Museum (www.dbku.sarawak.gov.my; Jln Semariang, Bukit Siol; camera/video RM4/5; 9am-5pm) This homage to the city's name, located 8km north of the centre, features hundreds of entertaining, surprising and bizarre *kucing* figurines – some the size of a cow, others tiny – alongside detailed presentations on 'Cats in Malay Society' and 'Cats in Chinese Art'. By the time you reach the exhibits on 'Cats in Stamps' and 'Cats in Film' (in which Bond villain Blofeld's mog features), you may feel it's all getting a little silly. To get here, take bus K15.

Hash House Harriers RUNNING
(Robin Kho 012-887 1420; www.kuchingcityhash.com) Kuching's various Hash House Harriers chapters hold about half-a-dozen one- to two-hour runs, over meadow and dale (and through thick jungle), each week.

Tours

Borneo Adventure TOUR
(082-245 175; www.borneoadventure.com; 55 Main Bazaar) Award-winning company that sets the standard for high-end Borneo tours and is the leader in cooperative projects benefitting Sarawak's indigenous peoples. Known for its excellent guides.

Adventure Alternative Borneo ADVENTURE TOUR
(082-248000, 019-892 9627; www.aaborneo.com; Lot 37, Jln Tabuan) Offers ethical and sustainable trips that combine 'culture, nature and adventure'. Can help you design and coordinate an itinerary for independent travel to remote areas, including the Penan villages of the Upper Baram.

Borneo Experiences TOUR
(082-429239; www.borneoexperiences.com; ground fl, No 1 Jln Temple; 10am-7pm Mon-Sat, may also open Sun) Singgahsana Lodge's (p130) travel agency. Destinations include a remote Bidayuh 'village in the clouds' and an Iban longhouse in the Batang Ai area (two nights RM1370). Also offers cycling tours. Gets excellent reviews.

Borneo à la Carte TOUR
(082-236857; www.borneoalacarte.com) A Kuching-based agency offering innovative, tailor-made trips, mainly for a French-speaking clientele, to indigenous communities other agencies don't cover. Amélie, the owner, is known for having very reasonable prices and sharing receipts equitably with local communities.

One Wayang Tours BICYCLE TOUR
(082-238801; www.paradesaborneo.com; 1 Leboh Wayang) Specialises in bike tours, offering city tours (RM108) and off-road mountain biking (RM188).

Rainforest Kayaking TOUR
(Borneo Trek & Kayak Adventure; 082-240571, 013-804 8338; www.rainforestkayaking.com) Specialises in river trips, which can be combined with a trip to Semenggoh Nature Reserve.

Telang Usan Travel & Tours TOUR
(082-236945; www.telangusan.com; Telang Usan Hotel, Persiaran Ban Hock) A well-regarded, veteran agency based in the Telang Usan Hotel.

Festivals & Events

Chinese New Year NEW YEAR
(late Jan or early Feb) The main festivities are along Jln Padungan.

Rainforest World Music Festival MUSIC
(www.rwmf.net; 1-/3-day pass adult RM340/130, child RM160/60; ⌚Jul or Aug) This three-day gathering, one of the world's great music festivals, is held in the Sarawak Cultural Village. International artists, who usually perform a type of music that is traditional in their country, hold informal workshops in the longhouses in the afternoon, while the main performances are held on the main stage at night. Accommodation gets booked out well in advance.

Kuching Food Fair FOOD
(Kuching City South Council, Jln Padungan; ⌚5-11pm for 1 month Jul-Aug) A huge food extravaganza with hundreds of stalls selling a whole range of meals and snacks – from Mongolian barbecues to Vietnamese spring rolls and deep-fried ice cream. Held in the park in front of the Kuching City South Council (the blue, teepee-shaped building just east of Jln Padungan, on the other side of the roundabout).

Mooncake Festival FAIR
(⌚Sep or early Oct) Musical performances and food stalls selling Chinese food, drink and, of course, mooncakes take over Jln Carpenter.

Sleeping

Kuching's accommodation options range from international-standard suites with high-rise views to windowless, musty cells deep inside converted Chinese shophouses. Many of the guesthouses – a great place to meet other travellers – are on or near Jln Carpenter (Old Chinatown), while the top-end spots are clustered a bit to the east in Kuching's high-rise district, on or near Jln Tunku Abdul Rahman. Cheap Chinese hotels can be found on or just off Jln Padungan and on the *lorong* (alleys) coming off L-shaped Jln Green Hill.

The majority of guesthouse rooms under RM50 have shared bathrooms; prices almost always include a very simple breakfast of the toast-and-jam variety. Rates at some guesthouses rise in July or from June to September.

★Threehouse B&B GUESTHOUSE $
(☎082-423499; www.threehousebnb.com; 51 Jln China; incl breakfast dm RM20, d without bathroom RM60-65; 📶) A spotless, family-friendly guesthouse in a great Old Chinatown location that is warm and welcoming – everything a guesthouse should be. All nine rooms are spaced over three, creaky wooden floors and share a bright-red colour scheme. Amenities include a common room with TV, DVDs and books, a laundry service and a kitchen.

★Singgahsana Lodge GUESTHOUSE $
(☎082-429277; www.singgahsana.com; 1 Jln Temple; dm/d incl breakfast RM31/RM112–132; ❄@📶) Setting the Kuching standard for backpacker digs, this hugely popular guesthouse, decked out with stylish Sarawakian crafts, has an unbeatable location, a great chill-out lobby and a sociable rooftop bar. Dorms have 10 beds and lockers.

Radioman HOSTEL $
(☎082 248816; 1 Jln Wayang; incl breakfast dm RM25, d without bathroom RM70; ❄📶) This centrally located, self-styled 'heritage hostel' occupies a century-old shophouse that was once used for radio repairs. The building still has the original ceilings, floors and fiendishly steep stairs, and it has been thoughtfully designed with nice touches like records on the walls, jungly plants and a courtyard garden.

When the new owners took over, they made use of all the radio equipment that was left behind to decorate the place – look out for lampshades made from pliers and large speakers that have been transformed into tables.

Marco Polo Guesthouse GUESTHOUSE $
(☎082-246679, Samuel Tan 019-888 8505; www.marcopolo.net.tf; 1st fl, 236 Jln Padungan; incl breakfast dm RM27, d without bathrooms RM56-60; ❄📶) A well-run, comfortable place with a breezy verandah and cosy indoor living room. The breakfast of fresh fruit, banana fritters and muffins is a popular bonus. Only some rooms have windows. Owner Sam is happy to give travel advice and sometimes brings guests to the market. Situated about 15 minutes' walk from the waterfront.

Nomad B&B GUESTHOUSE $
(☎082-237831, 016 856 3855; www.borneobnb.com; 1st fl, 3 Jln Green Hill ; incl breakfast dm RM20, with fan & without bathroom s/d RM50/60, d with air-con RM70-75; ❄@📶) There's a buzzing backpacker vibe at this relaxed, Iban-run place – guests often hang out in the lounge area with the friendly management. Breakfast times are flexible to suit late risers and there is a kitchen that guests can use. Of the 17 rooms, 10 have windows (the others make do with exhaust fans). Dorm rooms have eight beds.

Lodge 121 GUESTHOUSE $
(☎ 082-428121; www.lodge121.com; Lot 121, 1st fl, Jln Tabuan; dm/s/d/tr without bathroom, incl breakfast RM30/59/79/99; ❄📶) Polished concrete abounds in this former commercial space that has been transformed into a sleek, low-key guesthouse. The carpeted, 10-bed dorm room, with mattresses on the floor, is in the attic. All rooms share bathrooms that are on the small side.

Beds GUESTHOUSE $
(☎ 082-424229; www.bedsguesthouse.com; 229 Jln Padungan; dm RM20, s/d without bathroom RM40/55; ❄@📶) This guesthouse has attracted a loyal following thanks to comfy couches in the lobby, a kitchen you can cook in and 12 spotless rooms, nine with windows. Dorm rooms have six metal bunks of generous proportions. Located in New Chinatown, about 15 minutes' walk from the Main Bazaar.

Wo Jia Lodge GUESTHOUSE $
(☎ 082-251776; www.wojialodge.com; 17 Main Bazaar; incl breakfast dm/s/d/tr with air-con RM20/47/59/110, s/d with fan RM40/50; ❄@📶) A friendly, central spot to lay your head. The 18 neat rooms (five with windows, the rest with exhaust fans to the hallway) contain beds and nothing else. There is a small kitchen that guests may use. The dorm rooms, downstairs in the basement, are musty and dank, and best avoided.

Housed in an old Chinese shophouse – the lobby still has the original hardwood floors.

★ **Batik Boutique Hotel** BOUTIQUE HOTEL $$
(☎ 082-422845; www.batikboutiquehotel.com; 38 Jln Padungan; d incl breakfast RM280; ❄📶) A superb location, classy design and superfriendly staff make this a top midrange choice. The swirling batik design used on the hotel's facade is continued in the lobby and the 15 spacious rooms, each with a distinct colour theme. Some rooms have balconies overlooking the courtyard.

Lime Tree Hotel HOTEL $$
(☎ 082-414600; www.limetreehotel.com.my; Lot 317, Jln Abell; d incl breakfast RM170-250; ❄@📶) Dashes of lime green – a pillow, a bar of soap, a staff member's tie, the lobby's Cafe Sublime – accent every room of this well-run semi-boutique hotel. The 55 rooms are sleek and minimalist and offer good value; promotional room rates are lower than those quoted here. The rooftop bar has river views and happy hour prices from 5pm to 8pm.

Hotel Grand Margherita Kuching HOTEL $$
(☎ 082-423111; www.grandmargherita.com; Jln Tunku Abdul Rahman; d incl breakfast RM275; ❄@📶🏊) On a fine piece of riverfront real estate, this place will spoil you with a bright, modern lobby, 288 very comfortable rooms and amenities such as a fitness centre, a river-view swimming pool and a spa.

Padungan Hotel HOTEL $$
(☎ 082-257766; www.padunganhotel.com; 115 Jln Padungan; d RM100–115) A comfortable, modern hotel housed in a successfully redesigned commercial building (painted an unmissable orange) that offers good-value rooms in a convenient location.

Telang Usan Hotel HOTEL $$
(☎ 082-415588; www.telangusan.com; Persiaran Ban Hock; d incl breakfast RM130-150) A famously welcoming hotel with gleaming tile hallways and an old-school feel. The rooms are a little old fashioned with aging furniture, but the common areas are decorated with bright Kenyah and Kayan motifs.

The Lamin (p135) is the hotel's longhouse-style bar.

Harbour View Hotel HOTEL $$
(☎ 082-274666, 082-274600; www.harbourview.com.my; Jln Temple; s/d/f RM130/155/200; ❄@📶) If it's modern comforts you're after, this 243-room tower, is one of Kuching's best bargains, offering first-class facilities for reasonable prices. Breakfast is RM20 per person. Try to get a room with a river view.

Pullman Kuching HOTEL $$
(☎ 082-222888; www.pullmankuching.com; 1A Jln Mathies, Bukit Mata; d RM318-360; ❄@📶🏊) The 23-storey-tall Pullman stands on a hill, towering over its neighbours. The vast white lobby is so grandiose in its proportions that the rooms – in subdued tones of aquamarine, brown, white and green – feel small in comparison. The focus is on business travellers. Promotional rates available at less busy times.

Abell Hotel HOTEL $$
(☎ 082-239449; www.abellhotel.com; 22 Jln Tunku Abdul Rahman/Jln Abell; s RM145, d RM205–295; ❄@📶) This nonsmoking hotel offers 80 rooms that are stylish but not luxurious; the cheaper ones look out on an airwell. The name – like that of the street outside – is pronounced like the word 'able'.

★ **Ranee** BOUTIQUE HOTEL $$$
(☎ 082-258833; www.theranee.com; 6 & 7 Main Bazaar; d incl breakfast RM300-585; ❄📶) This

riverfront property, housed in an old shophouse that was completely rebuilt after a fire, has an urban-resort feel. All 24 rooms are different with plenty of design touches (the odd striped wall or globe-like lamp), high ceilings, hardwood floors and huge bathrooms with sleek, indirect lighting.

Hilton Kuching Hotel HOTEL **$$$**
(082-233888; www.hilton.com; cnr Jln Tunku Abdul Rahman & Jln Borneo; d RM405-485, ste RM755-790;) The Hilton has spacious, international-standard rooms in shades of cream, beige and maroon and all the amenities you would expect from this class of hotel. Most rooms have good views of the city; the best look out onto the river and rooftops of Old China Town. Rates vary and may be lower than those quoted here.

Eating

Kuching is the best place in Malaysian Borneo to work your way through the entire range of Sarawak-style cooking. At hawker centres, you can pick and choose from a variety of Chinese and Malay stalls, each specialising in a particular culinary tradition or dish, while Jln Padungan is home to some of the city's best noodle houses. The question of where to find the city's best laksa is a sensitive subject and one sure to spark a heated debate among Kuchingites. The only way to get a definitive answer is to try them all yourself.

★**Choon Hui** MALAYSIAN **$**
(34 Jln Ban Hock; laksa RM5-7; 7-11am Tue-Sun) This old-school *kopitiam* (coffee shop) gets our vote for the most delicious laksa in town, and we're not alone – the place can get crowded, especially at weekends. There is also a stall here selling excellent *popia*, a kind of spring roll made with peanuts, radish and carrot (RM3).

Open-Air Market HAWKER **$**
(Tower Market; Jln Khoo Hun Yeang; mains RM3-6.50; most stalls 6am-4pm, Chinese seafood 3pm-4am) Cheap, tasty dishes to look for include laksa, Chinese-style *mee sapi* (beef noodle soup), red *kolo mee* (noodles with pork and a sweet barbecue sauce), tomato *kueh tiaw* (a fried rice-noodle dish) and shaved ice desserts (ask for 'ABC' at stall 17). The Chinese seafood stalls that open in the afternoon are on the side facing the river.

From early mornings until mid-afternoon there is also a stall selling fish head and duck porridge, if that's your thing.

The market (which isn't strictly speaking open-air) has two sections, separated by a road, on the site of a former fire station; the yellow tower was once used as a fire lookout.

Yang Choon Tai Hawker Centre CHINESE **$**
(23 Jln Carpenter; mains RM3.50-8; 4am-midnight) Six food stalls, run by members of the Teochew Chinese community, serve up an eclectic assortment of native bites, including rice porridge with pork (3am to 9am), *kolo mee* (flash-boiled egg noodles; available from 6am to 2pm), super fish soup (3pm to 10pm) and – the most popular stall – pork satay (from 2pm).

Aroma Café DAYAK **$**
(082-417163; Jln Tabuan; mains RM10-16, buffet per plate RM5-6; 7am-10.30pm Mon-Sat, buffet 10am-2pm) A great place to try local indigenous specialities such as *ayam pansuh* (chicken cooked in bamboo; RM10), fried tapioca leaves (RM6) and *umai* (a Sarawakian version of sushi; RM10). The lunchtime buffet is good value.

Zhun San Yen Vegetarian Food Centre VEGETARIAN **$**
(Lot 165, Jln Chan Chin Ann; mains RM4.30-5.50; 8am-4.30pm Mon-Fri, 9am-4pm Sat;) A meat-free buffet lunch of Chinese-style curries, priced by weight, is served from 11am to 2pm (RM1.90 per 100g). When the buffet is over, you can order from a menu of dishes such as ginger 'chicken' (made with a soy-based meat substitute).

Lok Lok MALAYSIAN **$**
(7D Jln Ban Hock; mains RM5; 6pm-3am) This hugely popular nocturnal eatery specialises in *lok lok*, skewers (eg of fish, prawn, cuttlefish or bean curd; RM1.50 to RM2 each) that are either boiled or deep fried and eaten with sweet, sweet-and-sour, *belacan* (shrimp-paste sauce) or satay sauce. Also serves *rojak* (mixed vegetable dish with a thick shrimp-based sauce) and traditional mains such as curry chicken. Ideal for a late meal.

Chong Choon Cafe HAWKER **$**
(Lot 121, Section 3, Jln Abell; mains RM5-6; 7-11am, closed Tue) You'd never guess it from the picnic tables cooled by a fleet of overhead helicopter fans, but this unassuming, tile-floored cafe serves some of Kuching's best Sarawak laksa.

Jubilee Restaurant INDIAN **$**
(49 Jln India; mains RM5-11; 6.30am-5.30pm) A fixture in the heart of Kuching's Indian

Muslim district since 1974. Halal specialities include *nasi biryani* (rice with chicken, beef or lamb; RM9 to RM11) and *roti canai* (flatbread with egg and/or cheese; RM1 to RM2.50). The cook hails from Madras.

Green Hill Corner MALAYSIAN $
(cnr Jln Temple & Jln Green Hill; meals RM3-6; 7am-10.30pm Mon-Sat, 7am-noon Sun) Look behind the green, Milo-sponsored awnings for the half-a-dozen stalls that crank out porridge, laksa, chicken rice and noodle dishes. Popular with locals.

★Dyak DAYAK $$
(082-234068; Jln Mendu & Jln Simpang Tiga; mains RM25-35; noon-11pm, last order 8.30pm;) This elegant restaurant is the first to treat Dayak home cooking as true cuisine. The chef, classically trained in a Western style, uses traditional recipes, many of them Iban (a few are Kelabit, Kayan or Bidayuh), and fresh, organic jungle produce to create mouth-watering dishes unlike anything you've ever tasted. Situated 2km southeast of Old Chinatown.

The dining room is packed with unusual indigenous artefacts and the menu urges diners to have a walk around to view them. Vegetarian dishes, made without lard, are available upon request; staff are happy to explain the origin of each dish. A meal at the Dyak (the restaurant uses the colonial-era spelling of the word) is not to be missed.

★Top Spot Food Court SEAFOOD $$
(Jln Padungan; fish per kg RM30-70, vegetable dishes RM8-12; noon-11pm) A perennial favourite among local foodies, this neon-lit courtyard and its half-a-dozen humming seafooderies sits, rather improbably, on the roof of a concrete parking garage – look for the giant backlit lobster sign. Grilled white pomfret is a particular delicacy. Ling Loong Seafood and the Bukit Mata Seafood Centre are especially good.

★Tribal Stove DAYAK $$
(082-234873; 10 Jln Borneo; mains RM15-20; 11.30am-10.30pm Mon-Sat;) This laid-back restaurant serving delicious Kelabit food has somehow managed to capture something of the atmosphere of Bario, the Highland 'capital', and transport it to downtown Kuching. Specialities include *labo senutuq* (shredded beef cooked with wild ginger and dried chilli), *ab'eng* (shredded river fish) and pineapple curry. Popular dishes sometimes sell out by early evening. Food is prepared without MSG.

Junk ITALIAN $$
(082-259450; 80 Jln Wayang; mains RM28-68; 6-10.45pm, bar to 2am, closed Tue;) Filled to the brim with antiques, this complex of dining rooms (three) and bars (two) – housed in three 1920s shophouses – is a fashionable spot to see and be seen. Luckily, it's not a case of style over substance: the food here is very good. Pasta and other mains cost RM32 to RM68, pizzas are RM28 to RM48. Portions are generous.

21 Bistro FUSION $$
(64 Jln Padungan; mains RM10-48; 4pm-2am or later Mon-Sat, food to 11pm) This self-consciously classy restaurant-cum-bar serves decent Western, Asian and fusion dishes such as pasta, grilled meats and fish (snapper is a speciality). Even the performance of the live band fails to inject much joy into the uptight crowd.

James Brooke Bistro & Cafe WESTERN $$
(082-412120; Waterfront Promenade opposite Jln Temple; mains RM10-39; 10.30am-10.30pm,

KEK LAPIS – COLOURFUL LAYER CAKES

The people of Kuching – from all communities – love to add a dash of colour to festivities, so it comes as no surprise to see stalls selling *kek lapis* (striped layer cakes) sprouting up around town (especially along Main Bazaar and the Waterfront Promenade) during festivals, including Hari Raya.

Kek lapis is made with wheat flour, egg, prodigious quantities of either butter or margarine, and flavourings such as melon, blueberry or – a local favourite – *pandan* leaves. Since *kek lapis* are prepared one layer at a time and each layer – there can be 30 or more – takes five or six minutes to bake, a single cake can take up to five hours from start to finish.

Over 40 flavours of *kek lapis* are available year-round – to satisfy demand from Peninsular Malaysians – at **Maria Kek Lapis** (012-886 3337; 4 Jln Bishopgate; with butter RM15, with margarine RM20; 8am-5pm). Free tastes are on offer. Cakes stay fresh for one or two weeks at room temperature and up to a month in the fridge.

LAKSA LUCK

Borneo's luckiest visitors start the day with a breakfast of Sarawak laksa, a tangy noodle soup made with coconut milk, lemongrass, sour tamarind and fiery *sambal belacan* (shrimp-paste sauce), with fresh calamansi lime juice squeezed on top. Unbelievably *lazat* ('delicious' in Bahasa Malaysia).

for drinks only to midnight) Gets consistently good reviews both for the cuisine and the lovely river views. Local dishes such as Sarawak laksa (RM12) and its own invention, uniquely flavoursome wild Borneo laksa (RM12), are quite reasonably priced. The beef stroganoff (RM25) has a following.

Jambu MEDITERRANEAN **$$**
(☎082-235292; www.jamburestaurant.com; 32 Jln Crookshank; mains RM28-55; ⏰5.30-10.30pm Tue-Thu & Sun, to 11.30pm Fri & Sat) Once the venue for elegant colonial parties (check out the photos on the way to the bar), this 1920s mansion, with teak floors and soaring ceilings, serves Mediterranean food and tapas. The terrace – with coloured lanterns and a pool table – is a romantic setting. The bar stays open until the last customer leaves. Situated 1.5km south of the centre.

Magna Carta ITALIAN **$$**
(Courthouse, Jln Tun Abang Haji Openg; mains RM10-28; ⏰10.30am-11pm Tue-Sun) For great Brooke-era atmosphere, you can choose between the breezy verandah with garden views, and the interior, whose decor is a mash-up of medieval England and 19th-century Straits Chinese. Good options include pasta, pizza with exquisitely thin crust (RM18), homemade bread and freshly squeezed orange juice.

Lyn's Thandoori Restaurant INDIAN **$$**
(☎019-889 7471; Lot 267, Jln Song Thian Cheok; mains RM16-34; ⏰10am-10pm Mon-Sat, 6-10pm Sun; 📶🌶) This North Indian place, a Kuching fixture since 1994, sports a huge menu featuring tandoori chicken (of course) as well as delicious mutton, fish and veggie options (almost 50 of them, including 22 types of paneer cheese), all made with top-quality ingredients.

★**Bla Bla Bla** FUSION **$$$**
(☎082-233944; 27 Jln Tabuan; mains RM22-90; ⏰6-11.30pm, closed Tue) Innovative and stylish, Bla Bla Bla serves excellent Chinese-inspired fusion dishes that – like the decor, the koi ponds and the Balinese Buddha – range from traditional to far-out. Specialities include *midin* (jungle fern) salad, mango duck (delicious), ostrich and deer, and pandan chicken. The generous portions are designed to be shared.

Zinc MEDITERRANEAN **$$$**
(☎082-243304; 38 Jln Tabuan; mains RM50-140; ⏰6-10.45pm) Well-to-do Kuchingites celebrated the recent opening of Zinc and its selection of European foods: Spanish Iberico ham, French cheeses and high-end wines that aren't available anywhere else in Borneo. Naturally, the finest imported ingredients don't come cheap, but you don't come to Zinc unless you're prepared to splurge. Often has live music; on Thursdays there's a jazz band.

Self-Catering

Ting & Ting SUPERMARKET **$**
(30A Jln Tabuan; ⏰9am-9pm, closed Sun & holidays) A good selection of wine, snack food, chocolate, toiletries and nappies.

Everrise Supermarket SUPERMARKET **$**
(Jln Tunku Abdul Rahman; ⏰9.30am-9.30pm) On the lower floor of the Sarawak Plaza shopping mall.

🍷 Drinking & Nightlife

Bars can be found along Jln Carpenter and Jln Tabuan.

Ruai BAR
(7F Jln Ban Hock; ⏰6pm-2.30am) This Iban-owned bar has a laid-back, welcoming spirit all its own. Decorated with old photos and Orang Ulu art (and, inexplicably, several Mexican sombreros), it serves as an urban *ruai* (the covered verandah of an Iban longhouse) for aficionados of caving, hiking and running. Has a good selection of *tuak* (local rice wine). Starts to pick up after about 9pm.

Barber BAR
(☎016-658 1052; Jln Wayang; ⏰5-11pm, to 1.30am Fri & Sat, closed Tue) The designers of this successfully repurposed barber's salon made use of the original tiled floor, mirrors and even old hairdryers to create a suitably hip hangout for Kuching's in-crowd. Serves a menu of burgers and American-diner-style food (mains RM16 to RM24) and a good selection of desserts (RM16). Beers are three for RM45 on Sunday, Monday and Wednesday.

Monkee Bar BAR

(www.monkeebars.com; Jln Song Thian Cheok; beer RM6.50-12, spirit & mixer RM13; ⌚3pm-2am) At Monkee Bar, 50% of profits go to the Orangutan Project, a wildlife conservation NGO that works at Matang Wildlife Centre (p148). If the idea of 'drinking for conservation' doesn't entice you, the prices might: Monkee Bar has some of the cheapest drinks in town. It's a smokey joint with a young local crowd interspersed with volunteers enjoying downtime from cage-cleaning.

Drunken Monkey BAR

(☎082-242048; 68 Jln Carpenter; ⌚2pm-2am) Despite its youthful name, this bar attracts a mature crowd of locals and tourists. The drinks list includes draught Guinness (RM19 per pint), a range of imported wines and a whole page of whiskys. There's a choice of outdoor seating in a fan-cooled alleyway or air-conditioned indoor tables. Happy hour prices, available until 8pm, offer meagre discounts.

Black Bean Coffee & Tea Company CAFE

(Jln Carpenter; drinks RM3-4.80; ⌚9am-6pm Mon-Sat; 📶) The aroma of freshly ground coffee assaults the senses at this tiny shop, believed by many to purvey Kuching's finest brews. Specialities, roasted daily, include Arabica, Liberica and Robusta coffees grown in Java, Sumatra and, of course, Sarawak. Also serves oolong and green teas from Taiwan. Has just three tables. Decaf not available.

Lamin BAR

(Persiaran Ban Hock; ⌚2-10pm Mon-Thu, noon-11pm Fri & Sat) This rustic, longhouse-style bar also serves a delicious range of homemade alcohol ice creams, including *tuak* and raisin, red wine and mango and Guinness stout (RM13).

Shopping

If it's traditional Borneo arts and crafts you're after, then you've come to the right place – Kuching is the best shopping spot on the island for collectors and cultural enthusiasts. Don't expect many bargains, but don't be afraid to negotiate either – there's plenty to choose from, and the quality varies as much as the price. Dubiously 'aged' items are common, so be sure to spend some time browsing to familiarise yourself with prices and range.

Most of Kuching's shops are closed on Sunday.

Juliana Native Handwork HANDICRAFTS

(☎082-230144; ground fl, Sarawak Textile Museum, Jln Tun Abang Haji Openg; ⌚9am-4.30pm) As well as her own Bidayuh beadwork pieces – most of which have been displayed in an exhibition in Singapore – Juliana sells quality rattan mats made by Penan artists (RM490) and *pua kumba* Iban woven cloths. The intricate, 50cm-long beaded table runners she sells (RM680) take her three months to complete.

Main Bazaar HANDICRAFTS

(Main Bazaar; ⌚some shops closed Sun) The row of old shophouses facing the Waterfront Promenade is chock-full of handicrafts shops, some outfitted like art galleries, others with more of a 'garage sale' appeal, and yet others (especially along the Main Bazaar's western section) stocking little more than kitschy-cute cat souvenirs.

Handmade items worth seeing (if not purchasing) – many from the highlands of Kalimantan – include hand-woven textiles and baskets, masks, drums, brass gongs, statues (up to 2m high), beaded headdresses, swords, spears, painted shields and cannons from Brunei. At many places, staff enjoy explaining the origin and use of each item.

UD Siburan Jaya FOOD

(66 Main Bazaar; ⌚8.30am-9pm Mon-Sat, 9.30am-5pm Sun) Has an excellent selection of Sarawakian specialities such as pepper (black and white), laksa paste, sambal, Bario rice and even *tuak* (rice wine).

Fabriko CLOTHING

(56 Main Bazaar; ⌚9am-5pm Mon-Sat) This fine little boutique has a well-chosen selection of made-in-Sarawak fabrics and clothing in both traditional and modern Orang Ulu–inspired designs, including silk sarongs and men's batik shirts.

Nelson's Gallery ART

(54 Main Bazaar; ⌚9am-5pm) Upstairs, artist Narong Daun patiently creates vibrant jungle-themed batik paintings on silk.

Sarawak Craft Council HANDICRAFTS

(sarawakhandicraft.com.my; Old Courthouse, Jln Tun Abang Haji Openg; ⌚8.30am-4.30pm Mon-Fri) Run by a non-profit government agency, this shop has a pretty good selection of Malay, Bidayuh, Iban and Orang Ulu handicrafts – check out the cowboy hats made entirely of bark and the conical *terendak* (Melanau hats).

Tanoti HANDICRAFTS

(☎082-239277; www.tanoticrafts.com; Tanoti House, 56 Jln Tabuan; ⌚8am-5.30pm, closed public holidays) The group of women at Tanoti are the only people to practise a distinct Sarawakian form of songket weaving, a way of creating embroidered fabrics. Visitors are welcome to visit the workshop and see the weaving, but call first to arrange. There are a small number of pieces for sale in the gallery shop.

The women work to commission, weaving pieces such as *sampin* (a traditional male sarong) and decorative pieces – each one costs about RM10,000 to RM15,000.

Popular Book Co BOOKS
(Level 3, Tun Jugah Shopping Centre, 18 Jln Tunku Abdul Rahman; ⏲10am-9.30pm) A capacious, modern bookshop with a big selection of English titles, including works by local authors and travel guides.

Mohamed Yahia & Sons BOOKS
(☎082-416928; basement, Sarawak Plaza, Jln Tunku Abdul Rahman; ⏲10am-9pm) Specialises in English-language books on Borneo, including the four-volume *Encyclopaedia of Iban Studies*. Also carries Sarawak maps and travel guides.

ℹ Information

Kuching has Indonesian and Bruneian consulates and honorary consuls representing Australia and the UK.

DANGERS & ANNOYANCES

There are occasional incidents of bag snatching by motorbike-mounted thieves. Exercise reasonable caution when walking along deserted stretches of road (eg Jln Reservoir and Jln Tabuan), especially after dark.

In August and September Kuching and the surrounding areas suffer from periods of poor air quality, known as 'the haze'. What looks like a dense fog is actually smoke particles from forest fires, primarily in Indonesia. These are officially attributed to the traditional farming technique of slash and burn but are suspected by some to be caused by the clearing of forests for palm-oil plantations.

In 2015, the air-pollution index in Kuching reached levels deemed 'unhealthy'. Such levels can pose a risk to asthma sufferers, and provoke minor symptoms (stinging eyes, sore throat) in others.

Aside from health concerns, when the haze is bad it affects visibility in such a way as to make sight-seeing and national-park visits feel frustrating, even pointless; attractions do, however, stay open as normal. The haze usually clears after a few days, depending on weather conditions.

EMERGENCY

Police, Ambulance & Fire (☎999)

LAUNDRY

Most hotels have pricey laundry services with per-piece rates, but some guesthouses let you do your washing for just RM5 to RM10 per load, including drying.

My Express Laundry Service (Jln Wayang; 10kg cold/warm/hot RM5/6/7, dryer per 25min RM5; ⏲24hr) A convenient, self-service laundry.

MEDICAL SERVICES

Kuching has some first-rate but affordable medical facilities, so it's no surprise that 'medical tourism', especially from Indonesia, is on the rise. For minor ailments, guesthouses and hotels can refer you to a general practitioner, who may be willing to make a house call.

Klinik Chan (☎082-240307; 98 Main Bazaar; ⏲8am-noon & 2-5pm Mon-Fri, 9am-noon Sat, Sun & holidays) Conveniently central. A consultation for a minor ailment costs from RM35.

Normah Medical Specialist Centre (☎082-440055, emergency 082-311999; www.normah.com.my; 937 Jln Tun Abdul Rahman, Petra Jaya; ⏲emergency 24hr, clinics 8.30am-4.30pm Mon-Fri, to 1pm Sat) Widely considered to be Kuching's best private hospital. Has a 24-hour ambulance. Situated north of the river, about 6km by road from the centre. Served by the bus 1 from Saujana Bus Station (p139), departures on the hour from 7am to 5pm.

Sarawak General Hospital (Hospital Umum Sarawak; ☎082-276666; http://hus.moh.gov.my/v3; Jln Hospital; ⏲24hr) Kuching's large public hospital has modern facilities and remarkably reasonable rates but is often overcrowded. Situated about 2km south of the centre along Jln Tun Abang Haji Openg. To get there, take bus K6, K8 or K18.

Timberland Medical Centre (☎082-234466, emergency 082-234991; www.timberlandmedical.com; Jln Rock, Mile 2½; ⏲emergency 24hr) A private hospital with highly qualified staff. Has a 24-hour ambulance. Situated 5km south of the centre along Jln Tun Abang Haji Openg and then Jln Rock.

MONEY

The majority of Kuching's banks and ATMs are on Jln Tunku Abdul Rahman. If you need to change cash or traveller's cheques, moneychangers are a better bet than banks, which often aren't keen on handling cash or US$100 bills.

Maybank (Jln Tunku Abdul Rahman; ⏲9.15am-4.30pm Mon-Thu, to 4pm Fri) Has an ATM. Situated on the corner near KFC.

Mohamed Yahia & Sons (basement, Sarawak Plaza, Jln Tunku Abdul Rahman; ⏲10am-9pm) No commission, good rates and accepts over 30 currencies (including US$100 bills), as well as traveller's cheques in US dollars, euros,

Australian dollars and pounds sterling. Situated inside the bookshop.

Standard Chartered Bank (Jln Padungan; ⌚9.15am-3.45pm Mon-Fri) Has a 24-hour ATM.

United Overseas Bank (2 Main Bazaar; ⌚9.30am-4.30pm Mon-Fri) Has a 24-hour ATM around the corner on Jln Tun Abang Haji Obeng.

POLICE

Central Police Station (Balai Polis Sentral; ☎082-244444; 2 Jln Khoo Hun Yeang; ⌚24hr) In a blue-and-white building constructed in 1931.

Tourist Police (☎082-250522; Waterfront Promenade; ⌚8am-midnight) Most of the officers speak English. The pavilion is across the street from 96 Main Bazaar.

POST

Main Post Office (Jln Tun Abang Haji Openg; ⌚8am-4.30pm Mon-Fri, 8am-noon Sat) An impressive colonnaded structure built in 1931.

TOURIST INFORMATION

National Park Booking Office (☎082-248088; www.sarawakforestry.com; Jln Tun Abang Haji Openg, Sarawak Tourism Complex; ⌚8am-5pm Mon-Fri, closed public holidays) Sells brochures on each of Sarawak's national parks and can supply the latest newsflash on Rafflesia sightings. Telephone enquiries are not only welcomed but patiently answered. Bookings for accommodation at Bako, Gunung Gading and Kubah National Parks and the Matang Wildlife Centre can be made in person, by phone or via http://ebooking.com.my.

Visa Department (Bahagian Visa; ☎082-245661; www.imi.gov.my; 2nd fl, Bangunan Sultan Iskandar, Kompleks Pejabat Persekutuan, cnr Jln Tun Razak & Jln Simpang Tiga; ⌚8am-5pm Mon-Thu, 8-11.45am & 2.15-5pm Fri) Situated in a 17-storey federal office building about 3km south of the centre (along Jln Tabuan). Served by City Public Link buses K8 or K11, which run every half-hour or so. A taxi from the centre costs RM15.

Visitors Information Centre (☎082-410942, 082-410944; www.sarawaktourism.com; UTC Sarawak, Jln Padungan; ⌚8am-5pm Mon-Fri, closed public holidays) Usually located in the atmospheric old courthouse complex, at research time the Visitors Information Centre was about to move to a temporary new home in the UTC building on Jln Padungan while the Old Court House buildings were redeveloped.

The office has helpful and well-informed staff, lots of brochures and oodles of practical information (eg bus schedules).

ℹ Getting There & Away

As more and more Sarawakians have acquired their own wheels, public bus networks – especially short-haul routes in the Kuching area – have withered. For complicated political reasons, some services have been 'replaced' by unregulated and chaotic minibuses, which have irregular times, lack fixed stops and are basically useless for tourists.

The only way to get to many nature sites in Western Sarawak is to hire a taxi or join a tour. The exceptions are Bako National Park, Semenggoh Nature Reserve, Kubah National Park, Matang Wildlife Centre and, somewhat less conveniently, the Wind Cave and the Fairy Cave.

AIR

Kuching International Airport (www.kuchingairportonline.com), 11km south of the city centre, has direct air links with Singapore, Johor Bahru (the Malaysian city across the causeway from Singapore), Kuala Lumpur (KL), Penang, Kota Kinabalu (KK), Bandar Seri Begawan (BSB) and Pontianak.

MASwings, a subsidiary of Malaysia Airlines, is Malaysian Borneo's very own domestic airline. Flights link its hubs in Miri and Kuching with 14 destinations around Sarawak, including the lowland cities of Sibu, Bintulu, Limbang and Lawas and the upland destinations of Gunung Mulu National Park, Bario and Ba Kelalan.

The airport has three departure halls: 'Domestic Departures' for flights within Sarawak; 'Domestic Departures (Outside Sarawak)' for travel to other parts of Malaysia; and 'International Departures'.

Inside the terminal, there's a **Tourist Information Centre** (arrival level; ⌚8am-5pm Mon-Fri) next to the luggage carousels and customs.

GETTING TO INDONESIA: KUCHING TO PONTIANAK

Getting to the border A number of bus companies ply the route between Kuching Sentral bus terminal (and other cities along the Sarawak coast) and the West Kalimantan city of Pontianak (economy RM60, 1st class RM80, seven/10 hours via the new/old road), passing through the Tebedu-Entikong crossing 80km south of Kuching.

At the border Travellers from 64 countries can get a one-month Indonesian visa on arrival at the road crossing between Tededu (Malaysia) and Entikong (Indonesia), the only official land border between Sarawak and Kalimantan.

Moving on Pontianak is linked to other parts of Indonesia and to Singapore by airlines such as Batavia Air (www.batavia-air.com).

Foreign currency can be exchanged at the **CIMB Bank counter** (arrival level; ⏲7.30am-7.30pm), but rates are poor. Among the ATMs is one in front of McDonald's. For ticketing issues, drop by the **Malaysian Airlines & MASwings office** (departure level; ⏲5am-8pm).

BOAT

Ekspress Bahagia (☎016-889 3013, 016-800 5891, in Kuching 082-412 246, in Sibu 084-319228) runs a daily express ferry from Kuching's Express Wharf, 6km east of the centre, to Sibu. Departures are at 8.30am from Kuching and at 11.30am from Sibu (RM45, five hours). It's a good idea to book a day ahead. A taxi from town to the wharf costs RM35.

BUS

Every half-hour or so from about 6am to 6.30pm, various buses run by City Public Link (eg K9) and STC (eg 3A, 4B, 6 and 2) link central Kuching's Saujana Bus Station (p139) with the Regional Express Bus Terminal. Saujana's ticket windows can point you to the next departure. A taxi from the centre costs RM28 to RM30.

Kuching Sentral

This massive **bus terminal-slash-shopping mall** (cnr Jln Penrissen & Jln Airport) handles most of Kuching's medium-haul routes and all of its long-haul ones. Situated about 10km south of the centre, it's also known as Six-and-a-Half-Mile Bus Station. Amenities include electronic departure boards and cafes offering wi-fi. Book your ticket at a company counter, then pay at counter 2 or 3 (marked 'Cashier/Boarding Pass'). Before boarding, show your tickets to the staff at the check-in desk.

To Central Sarawak

From 6.30am to 10.30pm, a dozen different companies send buses at least hourly along Sarawak's northern coast to Miri (RM80, 14½ hours), with stops at Sibu (RM50, 7½ hours), Bintulu (RM70, 11½ hours), Batu Niah Junction (jumping-off point for Niah National Park) and Lambir Hills National Park. Bus Asia, for instance, has nine departures a day, the first at 7.30am, the last at 10pm; unlike its competitors, the company has a **city centre office** (☎082-411111; cnr Jln Abell & Jln Chan Chin Ann; ⏲6am-10pm) and, from Monday to Saturday, runs shuttle buses out to Kuching Sentral. Luxurious 'VIP buses', eg those run by **Asia Star** (☎082-456999), have just three seats across (28 in total), and some come with on-board toilets, and yet cost a mere RM10 to RM20 more than regular coaches. To get to Brunei, Limbang or Sabah, you have to change buses in Miri.

To Western Sarawak

Buses run to the Semenggoh Wildlife Centre, Bako National Park, Kubah National Park and the Matang Wildlife Sanctuary, all of which stop in town at or near Saujana Bus Station, and to Lundu (including the Wind Cave and Fairy Cave), whose buses use Kuching Sentral.

TAXI

For some destinations, the only transport option – other than taking a tour – is chartering a taxi through your hotel or guesthouse or via a company such as **Kuching City Radio Taxi** (p139). Hiring a red-and-yellow cab for an eight-hour day should cost about RM300 to RM350, with the price depending in part on distance; unofficial taxis may charge less. If you'd like your driver to wait at your destination and then take you back to town, count on paying about RM20 per hour of wait time.

Sample one-way taxi fares from Kuching (prices are 50% higher at night):

DESTINATION	PRICE
Annah Rais Longhouse	from RM90
Bako Bazaar (Bako National Park)	RM55
Express Wharf (ferry to Sibu)	RM35
Fairy Cave	RM70-80 (incl Wind Cave and 3hr wait RM150-200)
Kubah National Park	RM60
Matang Wildlife Centre	RM60
Santubong Peninsula Resorts	RM60
Sarawak Cultural Village	RM60
Semenggoh Nature Reserve	RM60-70 (round-trip incl 1hr wait RM120)
Wind Cave	RM40

Getting Around

Almost all of Kuching's attractions are within easy walking distance of each other, so taxis or buses are only really needed to reach the airport, Kuching Sentral (the long-haul bus terminal), the Express Wharf for the ferry to Sibu and the Cat Museum.

TO/FROM THE AIRPORT

The price of a red-and-yellow taxi into Kuching is fixed at RM30, including luggage; a larger *teksi eksekutiv* (executive taxi), painted blue, costs RM35. Coupons are sold inside the terminal next to the car-rental counters.

BOAT

Bow-steered wooden boats known as *tambang*, powered by an outboard motor, shuttle passengers back and forth across Sungai Sarawak, linking jetties along the Waterfront Promenade with destinations such as Kampung Boyan (for Fort Margherita) and the Astana. The fare for Sarawak's cheapest cruise is 50 sen (more from 10pm to 6am); pay as you disembark. If a *tambang* isn't tied up when you arrive at a dock, just wait and one will usually materialise fairly soon.

BUS

Saujana Bus Station (Jln Masjid & Jln P Ramlee) handles local and short-haul routes. Situated in the city centre on the dead-end street that links Jln Market with the Kuching Mosque. Three companies use the Saujana Bus Station:

City Public Link (☎ 082-239178) Has a proper ticket counter with posted schedules. Line numbers start with K. Urban services run from 6.30am or 7am to about 5.30pm. Buses K3 and K10 go to Kuching Sentral (the long-distance bus station) several times an hour.

Sarawak Transport Company (STC; ☎ 082-233579) The ticket window is in an old shipping container. Buses 2 and 3A go to Kuching Sentral about three times an hour. Bus 2 to Kuching's Sarawak General Hospital and Bau is run in conjunction with **Bau Transport Company**.

BICYCLE

On Jln Carpenter, basic bicycle shops can be found at Nos 83, 88 and 96. **Borneo Experiences** (p129) can rent out bicycles for RM50 per day.

CAR

Not many tourists rent cars in Sarawak. The reasons: road signage is not great; even the best road maps are a useless 1:900,000 scale; and picking up a vehicle in one city and dropping it off in another incurs hefty fees. That said, having your own car can be unbelievably convenient.

Before driving off, make sure the car you've been assigned is in good shape mechanically and has all the requisite safety equipment (eg seatbelts); some companies rent out vehicles that have seen better days.

Half-a-dozen car-rental agencies have desks in the arrivals hall of Kuching airport.

Ami Car Rental (☎ 082-427221, 082-579679; www.amicarrental.com)

Golden System (☎ 016-888 3359; www.gocar.com.my) We've received good reports on this outfit.

Hertz (☎ 082-450740; www.hertz.com) Backed by an international reputation.

Hornbill Tours & Car Rental (☎ 082-457948; hornbill.car.rental@gmail.com; counter 4, Kuching Airport arrivals hall) Rates start at RM80 per day.

MOTORCYCLE

Renting a motorcycle can be a great way to visit Kuching-area sights – provided you know how to ride, your rain gear is up to scratch and you manage to find your way despite the poor signage.

An Hui Motor (☎ 016-886 3328, 082-240508; 29 Jln Tabuan; ⏲ 8am-6pm Mon-Sat, 8am-10.30am Sun) A motorcycle repair shop that charges RM40 per day for a Vespa-like Suzuki RG (110cc) or RGV (120cc) and RM40 for a 125cc scooter (including helmet), plus a deposit of RM100. Insurance covers the bike but not the driver and may be valid only within an 80km radius of Kuching, so check before you head to Sematan, Lundu or Annah Rais.

TAXI

Kuching now has two kinds of taxis: the traditional red-and-yellow kind; and the larger, more comfortable – and pricier – executive taxis (*teksi eksekutiv*), which are painted blue.

Taxis can be hailed on the street, found at taxi ranks (of which the city centre has quite a few, eg at larger hotels) or ordered by phone 24 hours a day from the following:

ABC Radio Call Service (☎ 016-861 1611, 082-611611)

Kuching City Radio Taxi (☎ 082-348898, 082-480000)

T&T Radio Call Taxi (☎ 082-343343, 016-888 2255)

All Kuching taxis – except those on the flat-fare run to/from the airport (RM30) – are required to use meters; overcharging is not common, so taking a taxi is rarely an unpleasant experience. Flagfall is RM10; after the first 3km (or, in traffic, nine minutes of stop-and-go) the price is RM1.20 per km or for each three minutes. There's a RM2 charge to summon a cab by phone. Fares go up by 50% from midnight to 6am.

One-way taxi fares from central Kuching:

- Cat Museum (North Kuching): RM30
- Indonesian consulate: RM25 to RM30
- Kuching Sentral (long-distance bus terminal): RM30
- Visa Department: RM15

WESTERN SARAWAK

Western Sarawak offers a dazzling array of natural sights and indigenous cultures including a number of accessible longhouses, sandy beaches, rainforests and a chance to see their inhabitants – including proboscis monkeys and orangutans – up close.

Bako National Park

Occupying a jagged peninsula jutting into the South China Sea, Sarawak's oldest **national park** (☎ Bako terminal 082-370434;

Around Kuching

www.sarawakforestry.com; RM20; ⌚park office 8am-5pm) is just 37km northeast of downtown Kuching but feels like worlds away. It's one of the best places in Sarawak to see rainforest animals in their native habitats.

The coast of the 27-sq-km peninsula consists of lovely pocket beaches tucked into secret bays interspersed with wind-sculpted cliffs, forested bluffs and stretches of brilliant mangrove swamp. The interior of the park is home to streams, waterfalls and a range of distinct ecosystems, including classic lowland rainforest (mixed dipterocarp forest) and *kerangas* (heath forest). Hiking trails cross the sandstone plateau that forms the peninsula's backbone and connect with some of the main beaches, all of which can be reached by boat from park HQ.

Bako is notable for its incredible biodiversity, which includes almost every vegetation type in Borneo and encompasses everything from terrestrial orchids and pitcher plants to long-tailed macaques and bearded pigs. The stars of the show are the proboscis monkeys – this is one of the best places in Borneo to observe these endemics up close.

Bako is an easy day trip from Kuching, but it would be a shame to rush it – we recommend staying a night or two to really enjoy the wild beauty of the place. Getting to Bako by public transport is easy.

Sights & Activities

Interpretation Centre MUSEUM

(Bako National Park HQ; ⌚7.30am-5pm) Offers an old-fashioned introduction to the park's seven distinct ecosystems and an exposé of the co-dependent relationship between nepenthes (pitcher plants) and ants.

Wildlife Watching

Scientists estimate that Bako is home to 37 species of mammal, including silver-leaf monkeys, palm squirrels and nocturnal creatures such as the mouse deer, civet and colugo (flying lemur); 24 reptile species, among them the common water monitor, which can reach a length of over 1m; and about 190 kinds of bird, some of them migratory.

Jungle creatures are easiest to spot shortly after sunrise and right before sunset, so for the best wildlife-watching you'll have to stay over. Surprisingly, the area around park HQ is a particularly good place to see animals, including reddish-brown proboscis monkeys, whose pot-bellied stomachs are filled with bacteria that help them derive nutrients from almost-indigestible vegetation. You often hear them as they crash through the branches long before seeing a flash of fur – or a male's pendulous nose flopping as he munches on tender young leaves.

Proboscis monkeys, who show little fear of, or interest in, humans, can often be found on branches above the park's visitors cabins, around the mangrove boardwalk between the jetty and park HQ, in the trees along the Teluk Assam beach near park HQ, along the Teluk Paku Trail, where they forage in the trees lining the cliff, and along the Teluk Delima Trail.

The muddy floors of mangrove forests are home to an assortment of peculiar creatures, including hermit crabs, fiddler crabs and mudskippers (fish that spend much of their time skipping around atop the tidal mud under mangrove trees).

The Bornean bearded pigs, striking-looking creatures that hang around near the cafeteria and cabins with their piglets, are easy to spot.

Jungle Walks

Bako's 17 trails are suitable for all levels of fitness and motivation, with routes ranging from short strolls to strenuous all-day treks to the far end of the peninsula. It's easy to find your way around because trails are colour-coded and clearly marked with stripes of paint. Plan your route before starting out and aim to be back at park HQ before dark (by 6pm at the latest). It's possible to hire a boat to one of the far beaches and then hike back, or to hike to one of the beaches and arrange for a boat to meet you there.

Park staff are happy to help you plan your visit, provide updates on trail conditions and tides, help with boat hire and supply you with a B&W map that has details on each of the park's hiking options. A billboard near the Education Centre lists conservative time estimates for each trail. Even if you know your route, let staff know where you'll be going and make a note in the Guest Movement Register Book; sign back in when you return.

Take adequate water, a sun hat and sunscreen, as the *kerangas* (distinctive vegetation zone of Borneo) has precious little shade for long stretches. Sun-sensitive folks might consider lightweight long-sleeved shirts and trousers. Insect repellent is also a good idea.

Lintang Trail HIKING

If you have only one day in Bako, try to get an early start and take the Lintang Trail (5.8km, 3½ to four hours round-trip). It traverses a range of vegetation and climbs the sandstone escarpment up to the *kerangas*, where you'll find some grand views and many pitcher plants (especially along the trail's northeastern segment).

Teluk Pandan Kecil Trail HIKING

One of the most popular trails is the 2.6km path to **Teluk Pandan Kecil**, a gorgeous sandy beach surrounded by spectacular sandstone formations. The trail climbs

CHEEKY MACAQUES

That sign at Bako National Park's campground – 'Naughty monkeys around – watch out!' – is not a joke. The long-tailed macaques that hang about the park HQ are great to watch, but they are mischievous and cunning. Thanks to tourists who insist on offering them food (please don't!), they can become aggressive if they suspect you to be carrying anything edible, making running leaps at anything they think they can carry off. Keep the doors and windows of your room closed, zip your bags and do not leave valuables, food or drink – or anything in a plastic bag (known by macaques as the preferred human repositories for edibles) – unattended, especially on the beaches or on the cabin verandahs.

It's wise to leave the monkeys in peace – the males can be aggressive, and once you've seen a macaque tear open a drink can with his teeth you'll be happy that you didn't mess with them. Rangers advise against looking macaques in the eye (they'll think you're about to attack) or screaming (if they knows you're scared, they'll be more aggressive). Monkeys are not a problem after dark.

through the forest before emerging onto an open plateau covered in scrub. Pitcher plants can be seen on the trail down to the beach. On the way to Teluk Pandan Kecil, it's possible to do a 30-minute detour to a viewpoint overlooking **Teluk Pandan Besar**, an attractive stretch of sand accessible only by boat.

Around the point (to the northwest) of Teluk Pandan Kecil is the famous Bako Sea Stack, an islet that looks like a cobra rearing its head. To get close enough for a photo, though, you'll have to hire a boat (from HQ, RM35 one way or RM70 return for a boat for of up to five people).

Teluk Tajor Trail HIKING

A 3.5km trail leads across scrub, past Tajor waterfall (where you can have a dip) and on to Tajor beach, where it is possible to camp.

Boat Trips BOAT TOUR

(per boat for up to 5 people 1-way/return to Teluk Paku RM18/36, to Teluk Pandan Kecil RM35/70, to Teluk Tajor RM105/210) Catching a boat ride to or from one of the park's beaches is a good way to avoid retracing your steps on a hike. Arrangements can be made at the **Koperasi Warisan Pelancongan Bako Berhad** (Bako boat transfers; ☎011-2513 2711, 011-2509 5070; ⏰7.30am-4pm) counter at park HQ, although boatmen sometimes pass by the more popular beaches looking for tired hikers who might be tempted by a lift back.

Going out on the water is also the best way to view the unique sandstone sea stacks off Bako's coast, and the only way to get close enough to photograph them. Look out for sea snakes, sometimes visible in the water.

Night Walk WILDLIFE WATCHING

(per person RM10; ⏰8pm) The best way to see creatures that are out and about at night – we're talking spiders, fireflies, cicadas, frogs, anemones, owls and the like – is to take a night walk led by a park ranger trained in spotting creatures that city slickers would walk right by. These 1½- to two-hour night walks are not to be missed. Bring a torch.

Swimming

At Bako, it used to be popular to combine rainforest tramping, which quickly gets hot and sweaty, with a refreshing dip in the South China Sea. However, since a large saltwater crocodile was recently spotted on the sand, park staff no longer recommend it. Entering the water is not completely banned, but comes with an 'at your own risk' caveat. Staff recommend that you stay in shallow waters. Forget about taking a dip anywhere near the rivers, which are prime crocodile territory. To keep away the sandflies on the beach, use mozzie repellent.

Teluk Assam Beach BEACH

Some people risk entering the water at the beach near park HQ, but the water can be muddy. In the distance (to the west) you can see the wild east coast of the Santubong Peninsula.

Tours

Park HQ does not have enough permanent staff to accompany individual visitors, so if you'd like to hike with a **licensed guide** (☎Sabariman 019-469 2570; riman1978@gmail.com; Bako Bazaar; per group per hour/day RM35/120), enquire at the boat terminal at Bako Bazaar. The park is very strict about allowing only certified guides (unlicensed guides and the groups they're with are forced to leave).

Sleeping

Bako's accommodation is certainly not luxurious, but although basic its well-run and adequately equipped. There is a RM10 key deposit. Unlocked storage is available at park reception free of charge.

In-park accommodation often fills up, especially from May to September, so if you'd like to stay over book ahead. Some travel agencies reserve blocks of rooms that they release a week ahead if their packages remain unsold, and individual travellers also sometimes cancel, so week-before and last-minute vacancies are common.

Forest Lodge Type 5 CABIN $

(☎park booking office in Kuching 082-248088; ebooking.com.my; r RM100; ❄) 'Type 5' accommodation is in either two-room wooden lodges (three single beds in each) or a newer, concrete terraced block (four single beds in each). All rooms have attached bathrooms and air-con.

Forest Hostel HOSTEL $

(☎park booking office in Kuching 082-248088; ebooking.com.my; dm RM15, q RM40) Built of wood, the old hostel buildings are scuffed and dented but perfectly serviceable. Rooms have four single-storey beds lined up in a row, fridges and wall-mounted fans. Bring your own towel.

Forest Lodge Type 6 CABIN $

(☎park booking office in Kuching 082-248088; ebooking.com.my; d RM50, 2-room cabin RM75)

Each rustic, two-bed room has a wood-plank floor, a private bathroom, a fridge and a fan.

Camping CAMPGROUND $
(per person RM5) To avoid falling prey to raiding monkeys, tents can be set up at park HQ's fenced-in camping zone only after 6pm and must be taken down again early in the morning. You can also pitch your tent at Tajor, 3.5km from park HQ.

Eating

Cooking is not allowed in park accommodation. The nearest food shop is in Bako Bazaar.

Kerangas Café CAFETERIA $
(Canteen; meals RM8–10; 7.30am-10.30pm) The cafeteria, designed to be macaque-proof, serves a varied and tasty selection of fried rice, chicken, fish, cakes, fresh fruit and packaged snacks. Buffet meals are available from 11.30am to 2pm and 6.30pm to 8pm.

Getting There & Away

Getting to the park by public transport is a cinch. First take one of the hourly buses from Kuching to Bako Bazaar, then hop on a motorboat to Teluk Assam jetty, about 400m along a wooden boardwalk from park HQ.

Kuching travel agencies charge about RM300 per person for a tour, including the boat ride.

BOAT

Boat transfers to Bako park HQ from Bako Terminal (at Bako Bazaar) are managed by Koperasi Warisan Pelancongan Bako Berhad, who have a counter at the terminal and at park HQ. The 20-minute journey from the terminal at Bako Bazaar to the park costs RM20 per person. From May to September, transfers are usually every hour from 8am to 4pm (ask at the counter for the day's schedule). The last boat back from Bako is at 4pm.

When the tide is low, boats may not be able to approach the jetty at Teluk Assam, so you may have to wade ashore. Boatmen may insist on an early afternoon return time to beat a late afternoon low tide – but bold outboard jockeys have been known to make the trip back to Bako Bazaar even at the lowest of tides.

From late November to February or March, the sea is often rough and scheduled boat trips may be less frequent.

BUS

Bus 1 (RM3.50) leaves from 6 Jln Khoo Hun Yeang in Kuching, across the street from the food stalls of the Open-Air Market. Departures from Kuching are every hour on the hour from 7am to 5pm, and from Bako Bazaar every hour on the half-hour from 6.30am to (usually) 5.30pm. If you miss the last bus, ask around the village for a minibus or private car (RM55) to Kuching.

In Kuching, bus 1 also picks up passengers at stops along the waterfront, on the river side of the street; motion to the driver to stop. These stops include bus shelters on Jln Gambier across the street from the Brooke Memorial; across the street from 15 Main Bazaar, next to the Chinese Museum; on Jln Tunku Abdul Rahman next to the 7-Eleven in the Riverside Suites; and on Jln Abell in front of Alliance Bank, a block northwest of the Lime Tree Hotel.

TAXI

A cab from Kuching to Bako Bazaar (45 minutes) costs RM55.

Santubong Peninsula

Like Bako National Park 8km to the east, the Santubong Peninsula (also known as Damai) is a 10km-long finger of land jutting out into the South China Sea. With some decent sandy strips, Santubong is the best place in Sarawak for a lazy, pampered beach holiday. The forested interior of the peninsula was declared a national park in 2007.

Sights & Activities

Sarawak Cultural Village MUSEUM
(SCV; 082-846411; www.scv.com.my; Damai Central; adult/child RM90/30; 9am-4.45pm) This living museum is centred on seven traditional dwellings: three longhouses, a Penan hut, a Malay townhouse and a Chinese farmhouse. It may sound contrived but the SCV is held in high esteem by locals for its role in keeping their cultures and traditions alive.

Twice a day (at 11.30am and 4pm) a cultural show presents traditional music and dance. The lively Melanau entry involves whirling women and clacking bamboo poles, while the Orang Ulu dance includes balloons and a blowpipe hunter.

The dwellings are (supposed to be) staffed by members of the ethnic group they represent. Signage, however, is poor, so if you don't ask questions of the 'locals' – who demonstrate crafts – the subtle differences in architecture, cuisine, dress and music between the various groups may not be apparent. At the Penan hut you can try a blowpipe, while the Malay house offers top spinning.

It may be possible to book workshops in handicrafts (eg bead-making), music and dance – contact the SCV in advance. If you're planning to get married, you can choose to tie the knot here with a colourful Iban, Bidayuh, Orang Ulu or Malay ceremony.

Hotels and tour agencies in Kuching offer packages (per person RM 220), but it's easy enough to get out here by shuttle bus. The SCV is located at Damai junction.

Permai Rainforest Resort BEACH
(082-846490; www.permairainforest.com; Damai Beach; adult/child RM5/3; 7am-7pm) The day rate at this bungalow complex is a real bargain. In addition to a safe, fine-sand beach with changing facilities, a variety of leisure and adventure activities are on offer, including a high-ropes course (per person RM60), a perfectly vertical climbing wall (RM48), sea kayaking (RM80 for three hours) and a bird-watching tower (RM45).

Damai Central Beach BEACH
A free beach with places to eat, situated across the parking lot from the Sarawak Cultural Village. Amenities include showers and lockers.

Jungle Walks HIKING
Several trails lead into the jungle interior of the peninsula. One, a challenging route with red trail markings, ascends towering **Gunung Santubong** (810m); the last bit is pretty steep, with steps and rope ladders, so it takes about three hours up and two hours down. The trail can be picked up at Bukit Puteri on the road to Damai Central.

Another trail, an easy-to-moderate circular walk (3km, two hours) with blue markings, passes by a pretty waterfall.

Tours

Coastal areas west and east of the Santubong Peninsula are home to a wide variety of wildlife. Oft-spotted species include endangered Irrawaddy dolphins, dragonflies, proboscis monkeys, estuarine crocodiles and all manner of birds.

Resorts on the peninsula, and guesthouses and tour agencies in Kuching, can make arrangements.

Sleeping

BB Bunkers HOSTEL $
(082-846835; www.bbbunkers.com; Damai Central; dm RM53;) Situated a few metres from Damai Central Beach, this sleek hostel has the peninsula's only dorm beds. The industrial, hangar-like space is subdivided by curtains, creating cosy spaces for one to three beds, either twins or queens. Secure storage is available.

Nanga Shanti HOMESTAY $$
(011-2517 7108; www.nangashanti.weebly.com; Santubong Peninsula; d/tent incl breakfast RM120/170; Apr-Sep) This unique beachside dwelling, located on the wild and undeveloped east side of Santubong Peninsula, is reachable only by boat (RM40 return) or a two-hour hike. Accommodation is in a four-room wooden longhouse or luxury tents. Solar panels provide 24-hour electricity and water comes (filtered) from a mountain stream. Operates as a homestay from April to September.

A 30-minute boat ride from Kampung Buntal, Nanga Shanti feels truly remote. It's run by a French couple who built it themselves using recycled materials where possible; the time and care put into the construction is evident in the details of the design, such as the dining room's *atap* roof and glass bottles used in some of the walls. Activities include walking or kayaking to a nearby beach. Lunch and dinner cost RM10 to RM45. There is a minimum stay of two nights.

Village House GUESTHOUSE $$
(016-860 9389, 082-846166; www.villagehouse.com.my; Lot 634, off Jalan Pantai Puteri, Kampung Santubong; incl breakfast dm/d RM102/278-552;) Tucked away in the quiet Malay village of Santubong, this place has an air of serenity and relaxation. Rooms with belian wood floors and four-poster beds are arranged around a gorgeous pool with frangipani trees at either end. A well-stocked bar and menu of local dishes (mains RM14 to RM60) means there is really no reason to leave.

Nanga Damai Luxury Homestay HOMESTAY $$
(019-887 1017; www.nangadamai.com; Jln Sultan Tengah, Kampung Santubong; d incl breakfast RM120-170; @) A beautiful garden with glimpses of jungle wildlife, friendly family dogs, hospitable owners, an 8m kidney-shaped pool and bright, comfortable rooms (six in total) make it easy to meet the two-night minimum stay. A delicious breakfast on the breezy verandah is included. Not suitable for children under 14. The Kuching-Santubong shuttles pass by here.

Permai Rainforest Resort BUNGALOW $$
(082-846490, 082-846487; www.permairainforest.com; Damai Beach; incl breakfast 6-bed cabin

with fan/air-con RM320/340, treehouse RM310, camping per person not incl breakfast RM15 ; @ wifi) This lushly forested bungalow complex, on a beach-adjacent hillside, hosts macaques and silver-leaf monkeys in addition to paying guests. Accommodation ranges from rustic, simply furnished cabins to air-con wooden bungalows towering 6m off the ground. Offers plenty of outdoor activities. Prices drop from Sunday to Thursday.

Damai Beach Resort RESORT $$$
(082-846999; www.damaibeachresort.com; Teluk Bandung, Kampung Santubong; incl breakfast d from RM487, ste from RM1044; air-con @ wifi pool) This 252-room beach resort has enough activities and amenities to make you feel like you're on a cruise ship (in a good way), including boat excursions, sea kayaking and even an 18-hole **golf course** (www.damaigolf.com) designed by Arnold Palmer. Although in some areas the hotel sometimes falls short of four-star expectations, it's a reasonable option for families looking for a convenient beach location and a decent pool.

Eating

Food Court HAWKER $
(Damai Central; mains RM5-8; 8am-10pm) A convenient food court with 10 stalls selling noodles, fried rice and cold drinks, as well as an excellent *roti canai* stall (RM2.50 to RM4).

Lim Hock Ann Seafood SEAFOOD $$
(Kampung Buntal; mains RM8-20, fish per kg RM46-74; 11am-2pm & 5-10pm, closed Mon lunch) A sprawling, open-air shed on stilts with a wide-plank floor and a tin roof, this classic Chinese-style seafood restaurant is in Kampung Buntal, a fishing village 11km southeast of Damai Central (on the east coast of the base of the peninsula). The fresh, locally landed fish is superb.

Getting There & Away

MINIBUS

Kuching is linked to the Santubong Peninsula (45 minutes) by the slow K15 bus from Saujana Bus Station and minibuses operated by Damai Shuttle.

Damai Shuttle (082-846999; 1-way adult/child RM12/6) Has departures from Kuching's Grand Margherita Hotel to Damai Beach and Sarawak Cultural Village six times a day between 9am and 6.15pm. The last run back to Kuching leaves the Sarawak Cultural Village at 5.15pm.

TAXI

A cab from Kuching to Damai Central costs RM60 (about RM70 from the airport).

Kuching Wetlands National Park

The only way to see the majestic mangroves of 66-sq-km Kuching Wetlands National Park is – as you would expect – by boat. Situated about 15km northwest of Kuching (as the crow flies), the park doesn't have an office, just low-lying islands and saline waterways lined with salt-resistant trees that provide food and shelter to proboscis monkeys, silver-leaf monkeys and fireflies (above the water line); estuarine crocodiles and amphibious fish called mudskippers (at the water line); and countless varieties of fish and prawns (below the water line). Nearby open water is one of the finest places in Sarawak to spot snub-nosed Irrawaddy dolphins.

The morning (about 9am) is the best time to see the dolphins, while late-afternoon cruises are optimal for sighting a flash of reddish-brown fur as proboscis monkeys leap from tree to tree in search of the tenderest, tastiest young leaves. Sunset on the water is magical – and unbelievably romantic, especially if your guide points out an *api-api* tree (a 'firefly tree', surrounded by swirling green points of light). After dark, by holding a torch up at eye level, you can often spot the reflections of animalian eyes, including – if you're lucky – a crocodile.

Tours

CPH Travel Agencies BOAT TOUR
(in Kuching 082-243708; www.cphtravel.com.my; 70 Jln Padungan ; office 8.30am-5pm Mon-Fri, 8.30am-noon Sat) Offers a mangrove and Irrawaddy dolphin-sighting cruise (RM140 per person) at 8.30am and a wildlife cruise (RM165) at 4.30pm. Packages include transfers from and to your hotel. Boats usually set sail from the Sarawak Boat Club.

Semenggoh Nature Reserve

One of the best places in the world to see semi-wild orangutans in their natural rainforest habitat, swinging from trees and scurrying up vines, the **Semenggoh Wildlife Centre** (082-618325; www.sarawakforestry.com; Jln Puncak Borneo; adult RM10; 8-11am &

2-4pm, feeding 9am & 3pm) can be visited on a half-day trip from Kuching or combined with a visit to Annah Rais Longhouse or Kampung Benuk.

Situated within the 6.8-sq-km Semenggoh Nature Reserve, the centre is home to 25 orangutans: 11 of whom were rescued from captivity or orphaned and their 14 Semenggoh-born offspring, some mere babes-in-arms who spend their days hanging onto their mother's shaggy chests. Four of the tree-dwelling creatures are completely wild (that is, they find all their own food), but the rest often swing by (literally) park HQ to dine on bananas, coconuts, eggs and – though they don't know it – medications. There's no guarantee that any orangutans, the world's largest tree-dwelling animal, will show up, but even when there are plenty of fruits in the forest the chances are excellent.

Hour-long feedings, in the rainforest a few hundred metres from park HQ, run from 9am to 10am and from 3pm to 4pm. When the feeding session looks like it's over, rangers sometimes try to shoo away visitors (especially groups, whose guides are in any case eager to get back to Kuching), but orangutans often turn up at park HQ, so don't rush off straightaway if everything seems quiet.

For safety reasons, visitors are asked to stay at least 5m from the orangutans – the animals can be unpredictable – and are advised to keep a tight grip on their backpacks, water bottles and cameras because orangutans have been known to snatch things in search of something yummy. To avoid annoying – or even angering – the orangutans, do not point at them anything that looks like a gun (such as a walking stick or camera tripod); do not scream or make sudden moves; and, when you take pictures, do not use a flash.

Rangers keep an eye out and radio back with news of the approach of Semenggoh's dominant male orangutan Ritchie, who is easily recognised by his cheek flanges. If he decides to stop by, his food must be ready for him when he arrives to avoid provoking his wrath.

Semenggoh Nature Reserve has two trails that pass through primary rainforest: the **Masing Trail** (Main Trail; red trail markings; 30 minutes), which links the HQ with the highway; and the **Brooke's Pool Trail** (yellow and red trail markings), a 2km loop from HQ, but they are not normally open to the public so as to limit the orangutans' contact with humans.

Getting There & Away

Two bus companies provide reliable public transport from Kuching's Saujana Bus Station to the park gate, which is 1.3km down the hill from park HQ (RM3, 45 minutes):

City Public Link (p139) Bus K6 (RM3) departs from Kuching at 7.15am, 10.15am and 1pm, and from Semenggoh at 8.45pm, 11.15am, 2.15pm and 4.15pm.

Sarawak Transport Company (p139) Bus 6 (RM3) has Kuching departures at 6.45am and 12.15pm; buses back to Kuching pass by Semenggoh at 10am and 3.45pm.

A taxi from Kuching costs RM60 to RM70 one-way or RM120 return, including one hour of wait time.

Tours are organised by Kuching guesthouses and tour agencies.

Kampung Benuk

This quiet, flowery **Bidayuh village** (adult RM6), where the loudest sound is often the crowing of a cock, attracted lots of tourists back when the road ended here. These days, it gets relatively few visitors, despite being a pleasant place to spend a few hours.

The traditional, 32-door **longhouse** (Lg 5), with bouncy bamboo common areas, is still home to a few families, though most of the villagers now live in attractive modern houses. In the **barok** (ritual hall), you can see about a dozen head-hunted skulls, bone-white but tinged with green, hanging from the rafters.

Sleeping

Kurakura Homestay HOMESTAY $$

(☎012-892 0051; www.kurakura.asia; Kampung Semadang; per person incl meals for 2 nights RM275; ❄) Run by Norwegian-born Lars and his Bidayuh wife Liza, this super-friendly, sustainable jungle homestay occupies a wooden house built on land that once belonged to Liza's grandfather. Meals are prepared using homegrown vegetables, fruits and herbs, and possible activities include hiking and kayaking. Situated about 30 minutes by boat from Kampung Semadang. Rates include transport to and from Kuching.

Kampung Annah Rais

Although this Bidayuh longhouse village has been on the tourist circuit for decades, it's still a good place to get a sense of what a longhouse is and what longhouse life is like.

The 500 residents of **Annah Rais** (adult/student RM8/4) are as keen as the rest of us to enjoy the comforts of modern life – they do love their mobile phones and 3G internet access – but they've made a conscious decision to preserve their traditional architecture and the social interaction it engenders. They've also decided that welcoming modern tourists is a good way to earn a living without moving to the city, something most young people end up doing.

Sights

Longhouse Veranda HOUSE
(Annah Rais longhouse) Once you've paid your entrance fee you're free to explore Annah Rais' three longhouses (Kupo Saba, Kupo Terekan and, across the river, Kupo Sijo).

The most important feature of a Bidayuh longhouse is the *awah*, a long, covered common verandah with a springy bamboo floor that's used for socialising and celebrations. Along one side, a long row of doors leads to each family's private *bilik* (apartment). Parallel to the *awah* is the *tanju*, an open-air verandah.

Headhouse HOUSE
(Annah Rais longhouse) Whereas the Iban traditionally hung head-hunted heads outside each family's *bilik*, the Bidayuh grouped theirs together in the community's *panggah* or *baruk* (communal meeting hall). The heads are no longer believed to protect the village – these days the people of Annah Rais are almost all Anglican (the Bidayuh of Kalimantan are mainly Catholic) – but about a dozen smoke-blackened human skulls still have pride of place in the headhouse, suspended over an 18th-century Dutch cannon.

Sleeping

Annah Rais is a peaceful, verdant spot to relax. Half-a-dozen families run homestays with shared bathrooms, either in one of the three longhouses or in an adjacent detached house. Standard rates, agreed upon by the community, are RM200 per person for accommodation and delicious Bidayuh board. It is also possible to arrange a package including activities such as hiking, rafting, fishing, (mock) blowgun hunting, soaking in a natural hot spring and a dance performance.

Akam Ganja HOMESTAY $$
(☎010-984 3821; winniejagig@gmail.com; per person incl meals RM200) Akam, a retired forestry official, and his wife Winnie, an English teacher, run a welcoming homestay at their comfortable detached house on the riverbank.

Getting There & Away

Annah Rais is about 40km south of Kuching. A taxi from Kuching costs RM90 one-way.

A variety of Kuching guesthouses and tour agencies offer four-hour tours to Annah Rais (per person from RM100).

Kubah National Park

Mixed dipterocarp forest, among the lushest and most threatened habitats in Borneo, is front and centre at this 22-sq-km **national park** (☎082-845033; www.sarawakforestry.com; admission incl Matang Wildlife Centre RM20; ⏲8am-5pm), which more than lives up to its clunky motto, 'the home of palms and frogs'. Scientists have found here an amazing 98 species of palm, out of 213 species known to live in Sarawak; and they have identified 61 species of frog and toad out of Borneo's more than 190 species. In 2012 researchers identified what they believe to be a new species of frog, adding it to a list that includes the aptly named (but oddly shaped) horned frog and a flying frog that can glide from tree to tree thanks to the webbing between its toes. The forest is also home to a wide variety of orchids.

Kubah's trails offer a good degree of shade, making the park ideal for the sun-averse. And when you're hot and sweaty from walking you can cool off under a crystal-clear waterfall.

Sights & Activities

Rainforest Trails HIKING
When you pay your entry fee, you'll receive a hand-coloured schematic map of the park's five interconnected trails. They're well-marked, so a guide isn't necessary. The park has about half-a-dozen rain shelters – keep an eye out for them so you'll know where to run in case of a downpour.

The **Selang Trail** (40 minutes to 60 minutes; trail-marked in yellow), linking the **Main Trail** (trail-marked in white) with the **Rayu Trail** passes by the **Selang Viewpoint**. Offshore you can see the turtle sanctuary of Pulau Satang.

The concrete-paved **Summit Road** (closed to non-official traffic), also known as the Gunung Serapi Summit Trail, runs along the park's southeastern edge from park HQ right up to the top of Kubah's highest peak, **Gunung Serapi** (911m), which holds aloft a

TV and telecom tower; on foot, it's 3½ hours up and a bit less coming down. As you ascend, notice that the mix of trees and plants (including pitcher plants and ferns) changes with the elevation. The summit is often shrouded in mist but near the top there's a viewing platform. When it's clear, there are stupendous views all the way from Tanjung Datu National Park on the Indonesian border (to the northwest) to Gunung Santubong and Kuching (to the east).

The **Waterfall Trail** (3km or 1½ hours from HQ one-way; trail-marked from the Summit Road in blue) passes by wild durian trees and belian trees, otherwise known as ironwood. This incredibly durable – and valuable, and thus endangered – tropical hardwood was traditionally used in longhouse construction. As you would expect, this trail ends at a waterfall and a natural swimming pool. Some visitors combine the Selang Trail and the Waterfall Trail to create a circuit that takes four to six hours.

The **Rayu Trail** (3.8km or 3½ hours) leads to Matang Wildlife Centre. Walked in the direction of Kubah to Matang the trail is mainly downhill.

Frog Pond WILDLIFE RESERVE

Situated 300m above sea level and about a half-hour's walk from park HQ, this artificial pool provides a breeding ground for numerous frog species. The delicate amphibians are especially active at night, more so when it's raining hard (during the day most prefer to hide in a hole in a tree), though their remarkable chorus begins about an hour before nightfall.

A track recorded at Kubah entitled 'Dusk at the Frog Pond' was recently voted the winner in a competition to find the most beautiful sound in the world.

Palm Garden GARDENS

In this labelled garden, near park HQ on the Main Trail, you'll find examples of the 98 species of palm growing in the park.

Sleeping

Kubah is a lovely spot to kick back and relax. While there's usually space, even on weekends, it's always a good idea to book ahead. The accommodation is often full on public and school holidays.

Forest Hostel HOSTEL $

(082-248088; ebooking.com.my; dm RM15) A comfortable, homely hostel with three small rooms containing four beds. Fan cooled.

Forest Lodge Type 5 CABIN $

(082-248088; ebooking.com.my; 10-bed cabin RM150) These attractive cabins have a living room with couch, chairs and a dining table, and three bedrooms with a total of 10 beds. Fan-cooled.

Forest Lodge Type 4 CABIN $$

(082-248088; ebooking.com.my; 6-bed cabin RM225;) Two-storey, all-wood cabins that come with a balcony, a sitting room, a two-bed room and a four-bed room.

Eating

All accommodation options come with fully equipped kitchens, including a fridge, toaster and hob, but there is nowhere to buy food, so bring all you need.

Getting There & Away

Kubah National Park is 25km northwest of Kuching. A taxi from Kuching costs RM60.

From Kuching's Saujana Bus Station, bus K21 to the Politeknik stops on the main road 400m from park HQ, next to the Kubah Family Park (RM3.50, one hour). Departures from Kuching are at 8am, 11am, 2pm and 5pm, and from the main road (opposite the turn-off for Kubah), at 6.30am, 9.30am, 12.30pm and 3.30pm (be there at 3pm, the bus sometimes leaves early).

Matang Wildlife Centre

Situated at the western edge of Kubah National Park, the **Matang Wildlife Centre** (082-374869; www.sarawakforestry.com; admission incl Kubah National Park RM20; 8am-5pm, animal encloure trail 8.30am-3.30pm) has had remarkable success rehabilitating rainforest animals rescued from captivity, especially orangutans. The highly professional staff do their best to provide their abused charges with natural living conditions on a limited budget, but there's no denying that the centre looks like a low-budget zoo plopped down in the jungle. Because of the centre's unique role, it's home to endangered animals that you're unlikely to see anywhere else in Sarawak.

Sights & Activities

Interpretation Centre MUSEUM

(8am-1pm & 2-5pm Mon-Thu, Fri 8-11.30am & 2-5pm) FREE A good introduction to the wildlife centre and its residents. Most of the display panels provide information on orangutan rehabilitation. Inside the HQ building.

MATANG'S RESCUED ANIMALS

Some of the creatures at the Matang Wildlife Centre were orphaned, some were confiscated and others were surrendered by the public. Unless they're needed as evidence in court, all are released as soon as possible. During a quarantine period staff study the animals' behaviour and assess their suitability for release. Some – especially those that have been kept as pets – lack the necessary skills to survive in the wild. Releasing them would be a death sentence, since they would most likely starve, and having lost their fear of humans, they're liable to wander into a village and get into trouble.

Among the most celebrated residents of Matang is **Aman**, one of the largest male orangutans in the world. Known for his absolutely massive cheek pads, he hit the headlines in 2007 when he became the first of his species to undergo phacoemulsification (cataract surgery). The procedure ended 10 years of blindness, though it did nothing to restore his tongue, removed after he chomped into an electric cable, or his index finger, bitten off by a rival dominant male.

The orangutans that are deemed eligible for rehabilitation (that is, who don't display abnormal behaviours) are taken into the forest by their keepers and trained to forage for foods, build nests and improve their climbing technique. Sometimes they are joined by semi-wild orangutans, some of the 11 former residents at the centre now live nearby in the forest, and come over to join in the nest-building sessions.

Matang is home to three bearcats (binturongs), two of them females, that are too old to be released. This extraordinary tree-dwelling carnivore can tuck away a fertilised egg for months and perhaps years, delaying pregnancy until sufficient fruit is available (the trick is called embryonic diapause).

Other animals that live here include 10 of the happiest captive sun bears in the world. In horrific condition when brought here, they are undergoing a rehabilitation program that's the first of its kind anywhere. The whoops of three gibbons can be heard from the carpark.

Many of the centre's caged animals are fed from 9am to 10am. Orangutan life-skills training sessions are usually from 8am to 11am and 2pm to 4pm.

Trails HIKING
(animal enclosure trail 8.30am-3.30pm) The **Animal Enclosure Trail** takes visitors through the jungle past animals' cages. If they've got time, rangers are happy to guide visitors around. Pitcher plants can be seen on the 15-minute **Special Trail** loop.

The **Rayu Trail**, a 3.8km (three hour) uphill hike to Kubah National Park (p147), is now open. The starting point is near the park accommodation.

Volunteering VOLUNTEERING
(Leo Biddle 013-845 6531; projectorangutan.com; 2 weeks incl food & lodging US$2000) For details on volunteering – nothing glamorous: we're talking hard physical labour – contact Orangutan Project. In keeping with best practice, volunteers have zero direct contact with orangutans because proximity to people (except a handful of trained staff) will set back their rehabilitation by habituating them to humans. Placements are two or four weeks.

Sleeping & Eating

Matang's accommodation options are basic and rustic. Although there is usually no shortage of space, it's best to book in advance so that staff are expecting you and can make sure the room is ready. There is nowhere to buy food in the park, so bring your own. Cooking is forbidden inside the park accommodation, but an electric kettle is available on request and there are barbeque pits outside (but no utensils).

Forest Hostel HOSTEL $
(Kuching booking office 082-248088, Matang Wildlife Centre 082-374869; ebooking.com.my; dm/r RM15/40) The longhouse-style Forest Hostel is fan-cooled and has an attached bathroom. Rooms sleep four in either bunk beds or double beds.

Forest Hut CAMPGROUND
(Kuching Booking Office 082-248088, Matang Wildlife Centre 082-374869; ebooking.com.my; per person RM10) Open-air rain shelters in the jungle. There is no need to bring a tent, just bedding and a mosquito net.

Type 5 Forest Lodge CABIN $$
(☎Kuching booking office 082-242088, Matang Wildlife Centre 082-374869; ebooking.com.my; r/cabin RM100/150; ❄) There are two of these cabins, each with room for eight people (two double beds in each room), attached bathrooms and air-con.

Getting There & Away

Matang is about 33km northwest of Kuching. By the new road, it's 8km from Kubah National Park HQ.

A taxi from Kuching costs RM60 one-way.

Bau & Around

About 26km southwest of Kuching, the one-time gold-mining town of Bau is a good access point to two interesting cave systems and some Bidayuh villages.

Getting There & Away

Bau is 43km southwest of Kuching. The town is linked to Kuching's Saujana Bus Station (RM5, 1½ hours) by bus 2 (every 20 minutes from 6.20am to 6pm).

A taxi from Kuching costs around RM70.

Wind Cave Nature Reserve

Situated 5km southwest of Bau, the **Wind Cave** (Gua Angin; ☎082-765472; adult/child RM5/2; ⏰8.30am-4.30pm) is essentially a network of underground streams. Unlit boardwalks in the form of a figure eight run through the caves, allowing you to wander along the three main passages (total length: 560m) with chittering bats (both fruit- and insect-eating) swooping overhead. In January and February the cave may close if the water level is too high.

Near HQ, 300m from the cave entrance, you can cool off with a refreshing swim in the waters of Sungai Sarawak Kanan.

Flashlights/torches are available for rent (RM3) – if you get a feeble one, ask to exchange it. No food is sold at the reserve itself, though there is a drinks stand.

Getting There & Away

To get from Bau to the Wind Cave turn-off (a 1km walk from the cave), take BTC bus 3A. Departures are at 9am, 11am and 3pm.

A taxi from Kuching costs RM70 one-way, or RM150 to RM200 return including the Fairy Cave and three hours of wait time.

A tour from Kuching to both caves costs about RM150 per person.

> **SEEING MOUNTAINS FROM THE INSIDE**
>
> Many of Sarawak's limestone hills are as filled with holes as a Swiss cheese. Boardwalks let you stroll around inside the Wind Cave, the Fairy Cave and the caverns of Niah National Park and Gunung Mulu National Park, but to get off the beaten track you need an experienced guide – someone just like UK-born James, who runs **Kuching Caving** (☎012-886 2347; www.kuchingcaving.com; per person from RM320). He knows more than almost anyone about the 467 cave entrances that have been found within two hours of Kuching, the longest of which is 11km. For an all-day caving trip, prices start at RM320 per person (minimum four people).

Fairy Cave

About 9km southwest of Bau, the **Fairy Cave** (Gua Pari Pari; adult/child RM5/2; ⏰8.30am-4pm) – almost the size of a football pitch and as high as it is wide – is an extraordinary chamber whose entrance is 30m above the ground in the side of a cliff; access is by staircase. Outside, trees grow out of the sheer rock face at impossible angles. Inside, fanciful rock formations, covered with moss, give the cavern an otherworldly aspect, as do the thickets of ferns straining to suck in every photon they can.

Cliff faces near the Fairy Cave, many rated 6a to 7a according to the UK technical grading system, are popular with members of Kuching's **rock climbing** community. The sheer white cliff 300m back along the access road from the cave has three easy routes and about 15 wall routes with bolts. Nearest the cave is the Tiger Wall; nearby routes include the Orchid Wall and the Batman Wall. For information on guided rock climbing, contact **Outdoor Treks** (☎012-888 6460; www.bikcloud.com; full-day guided climb per person for groups of 1/2/4 RM300/220/180).

Getting There & Away

To get from Bau to the Fairy Cave turn-off (a 1.5km or 30-minute walk from the cave), take BTC bus 3, which departs at 8.40am, 10.30am, 11.40am and 3pm.

From Kuching, a taxi to the Fairy Cave costs RM70 to RM80 one-way, or RM150 to RM200 return including the Wind Cave and three hours of wait time. A tour from Kuching to both caves costs about RM150 per person.

Serikin

Serikin Weekend Market MARKET
(Pasar Serikin; Kampung Serikin; ⌚6am–4pm Sat, 6am–3pm Sun) Vendors from Kalimantan cross the mountains on motorbikes to sell fruit, electronics, handicrafts, rattan furniture and clothes at this sprawling weekend market, which occupies most of the otherwise quiet little border town of Serikin. The lack of a border or customs post here means that there is a free flow of cheap Indonesian produce; Kuchingites often make the drive down in search of a bargain. Serikin is 20km southeast of Bau; a taxi from Kuching is around RM80.

Gunung Bengoh

Inland from Bau, most of the population is Bidayuh. Unlike their distant relations on the eastern side of the Bengoh (Bungo) Range – that is, in the area around Padawan and Annah Rais – the Bau Bidayuh have never lived in longhouses. The area's Bidayuh speak a number of distinct dialects.

Tour agencies in Kuching can arrange treks into the valleys around **Gunung Bengoh** (966m) – including the fabled **Hidden Valley** (aka Lost World) – either from the Bau side or the Padawan side. Kuching's Borneo Experiences (p129), for instance, runs treks to the remote and very traditional Bidayuh longhouse community of **Semban**, where a few old ladies still sport brass ankle bracelets. A three-day, two-night trip, including transport, food and a guide, costs RM780 per person.

Lundu

The pleasant town of Lundu, an overgrown fishing village about 55km west of Kuching, is the gateway to Gunung Gading National Park.

The road north out of town leads not only to Gunung Gading National Park, but also to two beaches that are popular with Kuchingites on weekends and holidays. Romantic, coconut-palm-fringed **Pantai Pandan**, 11km north of Lundu, is one of Sarawak's nicest beaches (despite the sandflies), with a gentle gradient that's perfect for kids. A few beachfront huts sell eats and drinks. Camping is possible. **Pantai Siar**, 8km north of Lundu, is home to several small resorts that appeal mainly to the domestic market.

Sleeping

Lundu Gading Hotel HOTEL $
(☎082-735199; 174 Lundu Bazaar; d RM60; ❄) It may not be the most stylish hotel in Sarawak but Lundu's only hostelry – whose 10 rooms sport blue-tile floors and big windows – provides more than adequate lodgings. Situated diagonally across the street from the RHB Bank.

Pandan Beach Campground CAMPGROUND $
(☎082-735043, 013-820 5888; Pantai Pandan; per tent RM20, cabin fan RM60, air-con RM150) This simple campsite, located next to a beautiful sandy cove, has showers, toilets, and gas cylinders and barbecue areas for cooking. The cabin accommodation is shabby and overpriced.

There is not much food available in the tiny village – just a **food court** (waffles RM2.90; ⌚8am-7pm Mon-Fri, 10am-7pm Sat & Sun) selling instant noodles, packaged snacks and waffles – so bring your own.

★**Retreat** RESORT $$
(☎082-453027; www.sbeu.org.my; Pantai Siar; cabin incl breakfast Sun-Fri from RM158, Sat from RM248; ❄📶🏊) Owned by the Sarawak Bank Employees Union, this is the ideal place to mix chilling on the beach with workers' solidarity. The grassy, family-friendly campus has 38 comfortable rooms, including 21 cabins, and gets enthusiastic reviews from travellers. Day use of the pool costs RM15 for adults and RM5 for children; the beach itself is free. Situated 8km from Lundu.

Eating

Pusat Penjaja Gading Lundu HAWKER $
(Lundu Hawker Centre; Jln Stunggang Malayu Baru; mains RM4-6; ⌚7am-5pm) Above the fruit and vegetable market is a hawker centre with 26 Chinese and Malay food stalls. The Malay buffet at stalls four and five includes delicious fresh crab as well as other local seafood.

Happy Seafood Centre SEAFOOD $$
(☎014-691 8577; Jln Blacksmith; mains RM5-15; ⌚7.30am-9pm Tue-Sun) Lundu's location on the edge of Sungai Stamin and just a few kilometres from the ocean makes for delicious fresh fish from both the river and sea. This informal eatery is a great place to sample it, as well as local jungle vegetables like *midin* (fern). Also serves chicken and pork. Located opposite the bus station.

Getting There & Away

Sarawak Transport Company (p139) runs Bus EP 7, which links Kuching Sentral long-haul bus station with Lundu (RM12, 1½ hours); departures from Kuching are at 7.30am, 10am, 1.30pm and 4pm. Buses from Lundu leave at 7.30am, 10.30am, 1.30pm and 4.30pm

At the Lundu bus station, it's possible to hire a private car to take you to Gunung Gading National Park (RM5 per person) or Sematan.

Gunung Gading National Park

The best place in Sarawak to see the world's largest flower, the renowned Rafflesia, **Gunung Gading National Park** (☎082-735144; www.sarawakforestry.com; adult RM20; ⏰8am-5pm) makes a fine day trip from Kuching. Its old-growth rainforest covers the slopes of four mountains *(gunung)* – Gading, Lundu, Perigi and Sebuloh – traversed by well-marked **walking trails** that are great for day hikes. The park is an excellent spot to experience the incredible biodiversity of lowland mixed dipterocarp forest, so named because it is dominated by a family of trees, the Dipterocarpaceae, whose members are particularly valuable for timber and thus especially vulnerable to clear-cutting.

The star attraction at 41-sq-km Gunung Gading is the *Rafflesia tuan-mudae*, a species that's endemic to Sarawak. Up to 75cm in diameter, they flower pretty much year-round but unpredictably, so to see one you'll need some luck. To find out if a Rafflesia is in bloom – something that happens here only about 25 times a year – and how long it will stay that way (never more than five days), contact the park or call the National Park Booking Office (p137) in Kuching.

Sights & Activities

A variety of well-marked, often steep trails lead through the lush jungle. Park signs give one-way hike times. Except when instructed otherwise by a ranger, keep to the trails to avoid crushing Rafflesia buds underfoot.

Don't count on seeing many animals, as most species found here are nocturnal and wisely prefer the park's upper reaches, safely away from nearby villages.

Since these hikes must be done in one day (camping is permitted only at park HQ), you might want to arrive the day before to facilitate an early morning start. Sign in at park HQ before setting off.

Interpretation Centre MUSEUM
(Gunung Gading National Park HQ; ⏰8am-5pm) FREE The well-presented displays provide detailed information on the Rafflesia, a parasitic plant with buds the size of cabbages and flowers with diameters measuring up to 75cm. The centre also highlights the dangers posed to this critically endangered species, and conservation efforts aimed at protecting it.

Rafflesia Loop Trail WALKING
(per hr for group of up to 10 RM30) This 620m-long plank walk, which begins 50m down the slope from park HQ, goes through a stretch of forest that Rafflesias find especially convivial. If the flower happens to be close to the trail, it is possible to go alone, but since most of the blooms are off the path, finding them requires a ranger or guide.

When the flowers are out, the local freelance (licensed) guide who usually takes groups is likely to already be at the park; if not, the office can give her a call.

Circular Route HIKING
For views of the South China Sea, you can follow a circuit that incorporates the **Viewpoint Trail** (follow the red-and-yellow stripes painted on trees), the **Lintang Trail** (red stripes) and the **Reservoir Trail** (a cement stairway).

Gunung Gading HIKING
Hiking up Gunung Gading (906m) takes seven to eight hours return, but don't expect panoramic views on the way up – the trail is thickly forested, so you'll see mainly the bottom of the rainforest canopy. Only once you reach the summit, where the British army cleared the jungle to make a camp during the Konfrontasi, are you rewarded with views.

At **Batu Berkubu** (10 to 12 hours return; trail marked in red and blue), you can see a communist hideout from the same period.

Waterfalls SWIMMING
Three lovely cascades are easily accessible along the **Main Trail** (marked in red and white). You can take a dip at **Waterfall 1**, **Waterfall 7** (1.5km from park HQ) and the **swimming hole**, fed by a crystal-clear mountain stream, at the beginning of the Rafflesia Loop Trail.

Sleeping & Eating

The busiest times are weekends, school holidays and when a Rafflesia is blooming, but even at quieter times park staff prefer advance bookings.

There is no food available at the park, so bring your own. Another dining option is driving or strolling about 2.5km to Lundu.

Hostel HOSTEL $
(☎Kuching booking office 082-248088, park HQ 082-735144; ebooking.com.my; Gunung Gading National Park HQ; dm/r without bathroom RM15/40) The hostel has four fan rooms, each with four beds (bunks). There is a kitchen with cooking utensils and a barbecue pit for cooking.

Camping CAMPGROUND $
(☎Kuching booking office 082-248088, park HQ 082-735144; www.sarawakforestry.com; Gunung Gading National Park HQ; per person RM5) The campground has a toilet and shower block and barbecue pits.

Forest Lodges CABIN $$
(☎Kuching booking office 082-248088, park HQ 082-735144; ebooking.com.my; Gunung Gading National Park HQ; per r/cabin RM100/150; ❄) Each three-bedroom cabin has one master bedroom with air-con and a double bed, while the other two rooms make do with single beds and a fan. There is a kitchen with cooking utensils and a dining area.

Getting There & Away

Gunung Gading National Park is 85km northwest of Kuching. Four public buses a day link Kuching Sentral long-distance bus station with Lundu, but from there you'll either have to walk north 2.5km to the park, or hire an unofficial taxi (about RM5 per person).

A tour from Kuching costs about RM350 per person including lunch (minimum two people). Groups could consider hiring a taxi for RM250 to RM300 including waiting time.

Sematan

The quiet fishing town of Sematan is Sarawak's westernmost town and the hometown of Sarawak's chief minister Adenan Satem. Most travellers who pass through are on their way to Tanjung Datu National Park, accessible by boat. The nearby Indonesian border – yes, those forested mountains are in Kalimantan – can be crossed at Biawak.

Sights & Activities

A grassy north-south **promenade** lines the waterfront, where a concrete **pier** affords wonderful views of the mouth of the river, its sand banks and the very blue, very clear South China Sea. The deserted beaches of **Teluk Pugu**, a narrow spit of land across the mouth of the Sematan River from Sematan's jetty, can be reached by boat (RM30 return).

At the northern end of the row of stores facing the waterfront, check out the shop called Teck Hunt (the furthest west of the waterfront stores), which hasn't changed in over a century. Built of *belian*, it still has wooden shutters instead of windows.

The sands of shallow **Pantai Sematan**, clean and lined with coconut palms, stretch along the coast northwest of town. It is home to several resorts that fill up with Kuchingites on the weekends.

Sleeping

Sematan Hotel HOTEL $
(☎011-2025 1078; 162 Sematan Bazaar; d RM50; ❄) The four basic rooms have tile floors and rudimentary furnishings. Bathrooms are attached but lack hot water. Situated 150m inland from the waterfront.

Eating

Sam Chai Seafood SEAFOOD $
(☎013-803 4892; Sematan waterfront; mains RM3-6 ; ⏰7am-7pm) A simple seafront *kopitam* serving delicious seafood *mee* (noodles) with fresh prawns (RM6).

Getting There & Away

Sematan is 107km northwest of Kuching, 25km northwest of Lundu and 30km (by sea) from Tanjung Datu National Park.

Buses link Kuching Sentral long-distance bus station with Lundu, and depart Lundu for Sematan (RM4) at 9.30am, 11.30am, 3pm and 5.30pm.

An unofficial taxi from Lundu bus station costs about RM30 one way.

Tanjung Datu National Park

Occupying a remote, rugged peninsula at Sarawak's far northwestern tip, this 14-sq-km **national park** (☎satellite phone for emergencies only 87077673978; www.sarawakforestry.com; adult RM20) features endangered mixed dipterocarp rainforest, jungle trails that hear few footfalls, clear seas, unspoilt coral reefs and near-pristine white-sand beaches on which endangered turtles – the green turtle and olive ridley turtle – occasionally lay their eggs. Few visitors make the effort and brave the expense to travel out here, but those who do often come away absolutely enchanted.

Activities

Park Trails WALKING

The park has four trails, including the **Teluk Melano Trail** from the Malay fishing village of Teluk Melano (a demanding 3.7km), linked to Sematan by boat; and the **Belian Trail** (2km), which goes to the summit of 542m-high **Gunung Melano** (2km, one hour) and affords breathtaking views of the coastlines of Indonesia and Malaysia.

To spot nocturnal animals, you can take a **night walk** on your own or with a ranger.

Snorkelling SNORKELLING

Snorkelling (but not scuba diving) is allowed in certain areas; details are available at park HQ. Bring your own equipment. Please don't touch the easily damaged coral, but bring water shoes just in case (the coral can be sharp).

Sleeping & Eating

For details of homestays in Teluk Melano, a steep, 3½-hour walk from park HQ, contact the National Park Booking Office (p137) in Kuching or ask around at the Sematan jetty.

There is no food at the park, so buy all you need in Sematan before getting the boat. Cooking equipment can be rented for RM11 a day; cooking gas costs RM6.

Guest Rooms CABIN $

(Kuching booking office 082-248088; d without bathroom RM42) These four basic rooms, each with two single beds, share bathrooms and a kitchen.

Shelters HUT $

(Kuching booking office 082-248088; per person RM5) These open-sided huts are as basic as they come, but the location – almost on the beach, looking out at the sea – makes a night here pretty special. The park can provide bedding and mosquito nets (RM16).

Getting There & Away

The only way to get to Tanjung Datu National Park or the nearby village of Teluk Melano, both about 30km northwest of Sematan, is by boat (one to 1½ hours). Weather and waves permitting, locals often (but not necessarily every day) pile into a motorboat and head from Teluk Melano to Sematan early in the morning, returning in the early afternoon (around 2pm or 3pm). If you join them, expect to pay RM30 to RM40 per person one way. Sea conditions are generally good from February or March to October. From October to February, rough seas make Tanjung Datu more or less inaccessible.

Walking from Sematan to Teluk Melano – the only other way to get there – takes a full day.

To hire a motorboat for up to seven people ask at Sematan jetty or contact **Mr Minhat** (013-567 9593) for trips to the park or Teluk Melano (RM450 to RM500 one way).

Talang-Satang National Park

Sarawak's first **marine park** (www.sarawakforestry.com), established in 1999 to protect four species of endangered turtles, consists of the coastline and waters around four islands: the two **Pulau Satang**, known as *besar* (big) and *kecil* (small), which are 16km west of the Santubong Peninsula; and, 45km to the northwest, the two **Pulau Talang-Talang**, also *besar* and *kecil*, situated 8km due north of Pantai Sematan.

Once every four or five years, female turtles (primarily green turtles but occasionally also hawksbill turtles, olive ridley turtles, and leatherback turtles) swim vast distances – sometimes thousands of kilometres – to lay their eggs on the exact same beach where they themselves hatched. Of every 20 turtles that come ashore in Sarawak to lay eggs, 19 do so on a beach in 19.4-sq-km Talang-Satang National Park. But of the 10,000 eggs a female turtle may lay over the course of her life, which can last 100 years, only one in a thousand is likely to survive into adulthood. To increase these odds, park staff patrol the beaches every night during the egg-laying season (mainly June and July, with fewer in August and a handful in April, May and September) and either transfer the eggs to guarded hatcheries or post guards to watch over them in situ.

Snorkelling and diving are permitted but only within certain designated areas, and divers must be accompanied by an approved guide.

Pulau Satang

While the national park's conservation area is managed by Sarawak Forestry, the islands themselves are the property of a family from Telaga Air – their 999-year lease, granted by the last White Rajah, Charles Vyner Brooke, expires in the year 2945. About 100 cousins now share ownership, but day-to-day management has devolved to Abol Hassan Johari, a retired accountant who lives in Telaga Air and is much more interested in conservation and research than in tourists. His family retains customary rights to the turtles' eggs, but these are 'sold' to the state government and the money donated to an orphanage.

The larger of the two islands, 1-sq-km **Pulau Satang Besar**, 14km northwest of Telaga Air, is the only island that is partially open to visitors. Groups are allowed to land but swimming is forbidden within the core protected zone (anywhere within a 2km radius of the islands' highest point).

The island has a fine beach and simple dorm accommodation with generator-powered electricity. Overnight visitors can sometimes watch fragile eggs being moved from the beach to a hatchery and, possibly, witness baby turtles being released into the wild. **CPH Travel** (☎in Kuching 082-243708; www.cphtravel.com.my; Damai Puri Resort & Spa) offers day trips (RM255) and overnight stays (RM695) on the island.

Pulau Talang-Talang

The two Pulau Talang-Talang, accessible from Sematan, are not open to the general public; visitors are only allowed within 2.8km of Pulau Talang Besar, Pulau Talang Kecil, Pulau Satang Kecil or the Ara-Banun Wildlife Sanctuary by special arrangement with Sarawak Forestry. Such permission is normally only granted to bona fide researchers, students, conservation organisations, and people participating in the **Sea Turtle Volunteer Programme** (4 days & 3 nights from RM2624; ⏲ Jun-Sep).

With this programme, paying volunteers can stay on Pulau Talang-Talang Besar and help the staff of the Turtle Conservation Station patrol beaches, transfer eggs to the hatchery and even release hatchlings. For details, contact the National Park Booking Office (p137) in Kuching; booking is through Kuching-based tour agents such as Borneo Adventure (p129).

Getting There & Away

The easiest way to visit Pulau Satang is to book a tour with a Kuching-based agency. Day-trip charters cost RM400 per person and can be arranged through Kuching agencies. Boats usually set out from the coastal villages of Telaga Air, 10km northeast (as the crow flies) from Kubah National Park.

Batang Ai Region

Ask anyone in Kuching where to find old-time **longhouses** – that is, those least impacted by modern life – and the answer is almost always the same: Batang Ai, many of whose settlements can only be reached by boat.

As well as longhouses, Batang Ai is the best place in Sarawak to have a chance of seeing truly wild **orangutans**, or at least their nests. Sightings are not guaranteed, of course, but are not rare either; recent travellers report seeing a group of six of the ginger apes near their camp.

This remote region, about 250km (4½ hours by road) southeast of Kuching, is not really visitable without a guide, but if you're genuinely interested in encountering Iban culture, the money and effort to get out here will be richly rewarded. Trips to the Batang Ai region can be booked in Kuching, either through a tour operator (the four-day, three-night Borneo Adventure, p129, Menyang Tais longhouse to Nanga Sumpa trek, costing RM1590, gets rave reviews) or with a freelance guide.

Sights

Batang Ai National Park NATIONAL PARK
(☎National Park Booking Office in Kuching 082-248088; www.sarawakforestry.com; RM20) Batang Ai National Park's dipterocarp rainforests have the highest density of wild orangutans in central Borneo and are also home to gibbons, langurs and hornbills. Managed with the help of an Iban community cooperative, the park has various forest trails (ranging from an easy 1.8km walk to a strenuous 8.2km hike), but you must go with a guide. The only way to reach the park is by boat from Batang Ai jetty (two hours); there is no food or accommodation available.

The 240-sq-km park is part of a vast contiguous area of protected rainforest that includes the Batang Ai Reservoir (24 sq km) and Sarawak's Lanjak Entimau Wildlife Sanctuary (1688 sq km) as well as protected areas across the border in Kalimantan.

Getting There & Away

A daily shuttle bus goes at 8am from the Hilton Hotel in Kuching to Batang Ai jetty (RM145, four hours). Since nearly all of the longhouses and accommodation are only accessible by boat you will need to arrange to be met at the jetty.

A taxi from Kuching to Batang Ai costs RM400.

CENTRAL SARAWAK

Stretching from Sibu, on the lower Batang Rejang, upriver to Kapit and Belaga and northeastward along the coast to Bintulu and Miri, Sarawak's midsection offers some great river journeys, fine national parks and modern urban conveniences.

Sibu

084 / POP 255,000

Gateway to the Batang Rejang, Sibu has grown rich from trade with Sarawak's interior since the time of James Brooke. These days, although the 'swan city' does not rival Kuching in terms of charm, it's not a bad place to spend a day or two before or after a boat trip to the wild interior.

Situated 60km upriver from the open sea, Sibu is Sarawak's most Chinese city. Two-thirds of locals trace their roots to China, and many of them are descendents of migrants who came from Foochow (Fujian or Fuzhou) province in the early years of the 20th century. The city was twice destroyed by fire, in 1889 and 1928. Much of Sibu's modern-day wealth can be traced to the timber trade, which began in the early 1930s.

Sights

Strolling around the city centre is a good way to get a feel for Sibu's fast-beating commercial pulse. Drop by the tourist office for a brochure covering the **Sibu Heritage Trail**.

Features of architectural interest include the old **shophouses** along Jln Tukang Besi near the Visitor Information Centre and the old **Rex Cinema** (Jln Ramin), where art deco meets shophouse functionality.

Tua Pek Kong Temple TAOIST TEMPLE

(Jln Temple; 6.30am-8pm) FREE A modest wooden structure existed on the site of this colourful riverfront Taoist temple as far back as 1871; it was rebuilt in 1897 but badly damaged by Allied bombs in 1942.

For panoramic views over the town and the muddy Batang Rejang, climb the seven-storey **Kuan Yin Pagoda**, built in 1987; the best time is sunset, when a swirl of swiftlets buzzes around the tower at eye level. Ask for the key at the ground-floor desk.

Anchored outside the temple and visible from the pagoda are 'floating supermarkets', boats used to transport supplies to upriver longhouses.

SWANS

No visitor to Kuching could miss the city's feline theme, but the state capital is not the only Sarawakian city with a mascot. Miri has adopted the seahorse, while Sibu's mascot is the swan, an 'ancient Chinese symbol of good fortune and health, an auspicious omen for a community living in harmony, peace and goodwill'. Keep an eye out for statues as you wander around town.

Sibu Heritage Centre MUSEUM

(Jln Central; 9am-5pm, closed Mon & public holidays) FREE Housed in a gorgeously airy municipal complex built in 1960, this excellent museum explores the captivating history of Sarawak and Sibu. Panels, rich in evocative photographs, take a look at the various Chinese dialect groups and other ethnic groups, Sarawak's communist insurgency (1965–90), Sibu's Christian (including Methodist) traditions, and even local opposition to Sarawak's incorporation into Malaysia in 1963.

Don't miss the photo of a 1940s street dentist – it's painful just to look at.

Rejang Esplanade PARK

(Jln Maju) One of Sibu's 22 community parks – most donated by Chinese clan associations – this pleasant strip of riverfront grass affords views of the wide, muddy river and its motley procession of fishing boats, tugs, timber-laden barges and 'flying coffin' express boats.

Lau King Howe Memorial Museum MUSEUM

(Jln Pulau; 9am-5pm Tue-Sun) One glance at this rather bizarre medical museum's exhibits and you'll be glad saving your life never required the application of early-20th-century drills, saws and stainless-steel clamps – or the use of a ferocious gadget called a 'urological retractor'. Another highlight: an exhibit on the evolution of local nurses' uniforms, which some visitors may find kinky.

Bawang Assan Longhouse Village VILLAGE

An Iban village one hour downstream from Sibu (by road the trip takes just 40 minutes), Bawang Assan has nine 'hybrid' longhouses (longhouses that combine traditional and 21st-century elements). To stay here without

Sibu

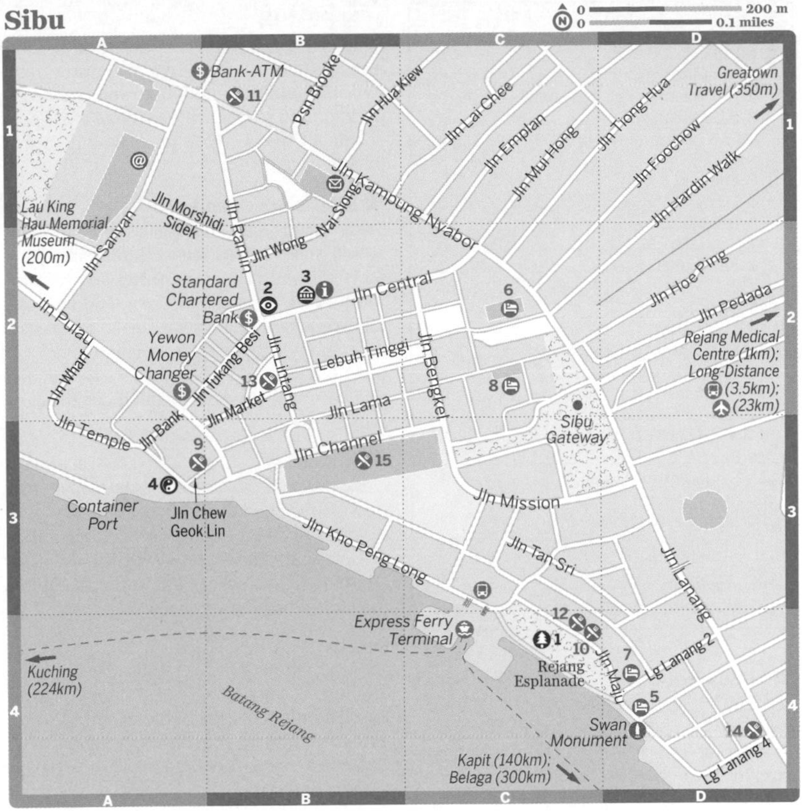

going through a Sibu-based tour company, contact the **Bawang Assan Homestay Programme** (☎014-582 8105; www.ibanlonghouse stay.blogspot.com; per person incl 3 meals RM110); ask for Marcathy Gindau.

Tours

Greatown Travel TOUR
(☎084-211243, 084-219243; www.greatown.com; No 6, 1st fl, Lg Chew Siik Hiong 1A) A well-regarded tour company offering longhouse visits to Bawang Assan and around Sarikei, as well as trips to the 'Melanau heartland' around Mukah. Staff are happy to create an itinerary based on your interests and budget. The office is about 1km northeast of the centre along Jln Pedada.

Great Holiday Travel TOUR
(☎084-348196, 012-890 8035; www.ghtborneo.com; No 23, 1st fl, Pusat Pedada, Jln Pedada; ⌚8am-5pm Mon-Fri, 8am-1pm Sat) Based out near the long-distance bus station, this outfit can organise half-day walking tours of Sibu, visits to Bawang Assan Longhouse (half-day tour RM120, overnight stay RM290) and two-day trips up to the Kapit area, usually with an overnight stay at Rumah Jandok. Reasonably priced.

Festivals

Borneo Cultural Festival PERFORMING ARTS
(⌚Jul) A week-long festival of food, music and dance representing Central Sarawak's Chinese, Iban, Bidayuh, Orang Ulu and Malay-Melanau cultures and traditions.

Sleeping

Sibu has dozens of hotels, so there is no shortage of beds. Some of the ultra-budget places (those charging less than RM35 a room) are of a very low standard and double as brothels.

Sibu

Sights

1 Rejang Esplanade ... C4
2 Rex Cinema ... B2
3 Sibu Heritage Centre ... B2
4 Tua Pek Kong Temple ... A3

Sleeping

5 Li Hua Hotel ... D4
6 Premier Hotel ... C2
7 River Park Hotel ... D4
8 Tanahmas Hotel ... C2

Eating

9 Café Café ... A3
10 Doughnut & Churro Stand ... C4
11 Islamic Nyonya Kafé ... B1
12 Kopitiam ... C4
New Capital Restaurant ... (see 6)
13 Night Market ... B2
14 Payung Café ... D4
15 Sibu Central Market ... B3

Drinking & Nightlife

Queen ... (see 9)

Shopping

Sibu Heritage Handicrafts ... (see 3)

★Li Hua Hotel HOTEL $
(☎084-324000; www.lihua.com.my; cnr Jln Maju & Jln Teo Chong Loh; s/d/ste RM50/65/150; ❄@📶) Sibu's best-value hotel has 68 spotless, tile-floor rooms spread out over nine storeys and staff that are professional and friendly. It's especially convenient if you're arriving or leaving by boat. Light sleepers should avoid the rooms above the karaoke bars on Jln Teo Chong Loh that blare out music late into the night.

River Park Hotel HOTEL $
(fax 084-316688; 51-53 Jln Maju; d RM55-75; ❄📶) A well-run, 30-room hotel in a convenient riverside location. The cheapest rooms don't have windows.

Premier Hotel HOTEL $$
(☎084-323222; www.premierh.com.my; Jln Kampung Nyabor; s/d incl breakfast from RM209/242; ❄📶) This popular, midrange hotel offers 189 nice, spacious rooms in an excellent downtown location.

Tanahmas Hotel HOTEL $$
(☎084-333188; www.tanahmas.com.my; off Jln Kampung Nyabor; d from RM200; ❄@📶🏊) As comfortable as it is central with rooms that are large and bright. Amenities include a small fitness centre and an open-air pool.

Eating

Sibu is famous for Foochow-style Chinese dishes such as the city's signature dish, *kampua mee* (thin noodle strands soaked in pork fat and served with a side of roast pork or mince), and *kompia* (mini sesame bagels filled with pork).

★Sibu Central Market HAWKER $
(Pasar Sentral Sibu; Jln Channel; mains RM3-5; ⏲food stalls 3am-midnight) Malaysia's largest fruit-and-veg market has more than 1000 stalls. Upstairs, Chinese, Malay and Iban-run food stalls serve up local specialities, including porridge (available early in the morning and at night), *kampua mee* and *kompia*. Most of the noodle stalls close around noon.

Night Market MARKET, HAWKER $
(Pasar Malam; Jln Market; ⏲5-11pm or midnight) Chinese stalls (selling pork and rice, steamed buns etc) are at the western end of the lot, while Malay stalls (with superb satay and barbecue chicken) are to the northeast. Also has a few Iban-run places.

Kopitiam CAFE $
(Jln Maju; mains RM3.30-6; ⏲6am-4pm) Several old-time *kopitiam* (coffee shops) can be found along Jln Maju. In the morning, locals gather to dine on Foochow specialities, read Chinese newspapers and chat – a typical Sarawakian scene.

Doughnut & Churro Stand HAWKER $
(27 Jln Maju; doughnuts 40 sen, churros RM1; ⏲6am-7pm) A street stall selling freshly made douhgnuts and churros – perfect to bring on an upriver boat trip.

★Payung Café MALAYSIAN $$
(☎016-890 6061; 20F Jln Lanang; mains RM8-19; ⏲11am-3pm & 6-11pm Mon-Sun) An exquisitely decorated cafe where diners feast on healthy local food (no re-used oil, deep frying or MSG) such as spicy *otak-otak* barbecued fish (RM13), deliciously fresh herb salad (RM8) and generous servings of the volcano-like Mulu icecream.

The walls of the semi-open air, garden-like dining room are adorned with intricate murals painted by the artistic owners, and the place is lit up with coloured lights and paper parasols (*payung* means umbrella in Bahasa Malaysia). The only thing we *didn't* love about this place was the Celine Dion soundtrack.

Café Café FUSION $$
(084-328101; 8 Jln Chew Geok Lin; mains RM18-44, set lunch RM12.90-19.90; noon-4pm & 6-11pm Tue-Sun) Café Café serves decent fusion fare, including Nonya-style chicken, daily specials and inventive desserts such as salted-caramel-apple-crisp cheesecake and Reese's-peanut-butter-chocolate cheesecake (RM10.90). With decor that mixes Balinese, Chinese and Western elements, this is a sophisticated urban dining spot.

Islamic Nyonya Kafé PERANAKAN $$
(141 Jln Kampung Nyabor; mains RM10-30; 8am-11pm Tue-Sun, 4-11pm Sun;) The highlight of the overwhelmingly extensive menu here are the deliciously spicy Nonya dishes, including *kari ayam* (chicken curry) and *kari kambing* (mutton curry).

New Capital Restaurant CHINESE $$
(084-326066; 46 Jln Kampung Nyabor; mains RM10-40; 11am-2pm & 5-9pm) A classy, old-school Chinese restaurant. Foochow specialities include sea-cucumber soup (RM10) and white pomfret (RM70 to RM80 for a portion to share).

Drinking & Nightlife

Queen BAR
(12 Jln Chew Geok Lin; beer from RM10, cocktails RM22-38; 6pm-12.30am Tue-Sun) Decked out like a Victorian sitting room, this dimly lit bar features plush couches and overstuffed wing chairs in black and burgundy velvet. Happy hour prices until 10pm. Sadly, the live music sessions have now been replaced by a karaoke machine.

Shopping

Sibu Heritage Handicrafts HANDICRAFTS
(084-333353; ground fl, Sibu Heritage Centre, Jln Central; 8am-6pm) This great little store is so packed full of Kayan and Iban beads, Penan rattan baskets and Melinau and Kayan handicrafts that it is difficult to move around. Hidden behind the vintage photographs of Queen Elizabeth and her family in the shop window is a chaotic treasure trove. The more time you spend here the more you're likely to unearth.

Information

Terazone IT Centre (Level 4, Wisma Sanyan, 1 Jln Sanyan; per hr RM3; 10am-9.45pm) Internet access.

Main Post Office (084-337700; Jln Kampung Nyabor; 8am-4.30pm Mon-Fri, to 12.30pm Sat) Sibu's main post office.

Rejang Medical Centre (084-323333; www.rejang.com.my; 29 Jln Pedada; emergency 24hr) Has 24-hour emergency services, including an ambulance. Situated about 4km northeast of the city centre.

Sibu General Hospital (084-343333; hsibu.moh.gov.my; Jln Ulu Oya, Km 5½) Situated 8km east of the centre, towards the airport.

Visitors Information Centre (084-340980; www.sarawaktourism.com; Sublot 3a & 3b, Sibu Heritage Centre, Jln Central; 8am-5pm Mon-Fri, closed public holidays) Well worth a stop. Has friendly and informative staff (ask for Jessie), plenty of maps, bus and ferry schedules, and brochures on travel around Sarawak.

Yewon Money Changer (8 Jln Tukang Besi; 9.30am-5pm Mon-Sat, 2-4pm Sun) Changes cash. Look for the gold-on-red sign.

Getting There & Away

AIR

MASwings (084-307888, ext 2; www.maswings.com.my; Sibu Airport, Jln Durin; 6am-8.30pm) Flights to Bintulu (twice daily), Kuching (five daily), Miri (four daily) and Kota Kinabalu (twice daily).

Malaysia Airlines (084-307799; www.malaysiaairlines.com; Sibu airport, Jln Durin) Two flights a day to Kuala Lumpur.

AirAsia (084-307808; www.airasia.com) Flies to Kuching and Kuala Lumpur.

BOAT

All boats leave from the **Express Ferry Terminal** (Terminal Penumpang Sibu; Jln Kho Peng Long;). Make sure you're on board 15 minutes before departure time – boats have been known to depart early.

To Kapit & Belaga

'Flying coffin' express boats head up the Batang Rejang to Kapit (RM25 to RM35, 140km, three hours) hourly from 5.45am to 2.30pm. The 10.45am boat has an upper deck with non-air-con, semi-open seating. Water levels at the Pelagus Rapids permitting, one boat a day, departing at 5.45am, goes all the way to Belaga, 155km upriver from Kapit (RM55, 11 hours).

To Kuching

Unless you fly, the quickest way to get from Sibu to Kuching is by boat. **Ekspress Bahagia** (016-800 5891, in Kuching 082-429242, in Sibu 084-319228; from Sibu 11.30am, from Kuching 8.30am) runs a daily express ferry to/from Kuching's Express Wharf (RM55, five hours), which passes through an Amazonian dystopia of abandoned sawmills and rust-bucket tramp steamers. It's a good idea to book a day ahead.

BUS

Sibu's **long-distance bus station** (Jln Pahlawan) is about 3.5km northeast of the centre along Jln Pedada. A variety of companies send buses to Kuching (RM50 to RM60, seven to eight hours, regular departures between 7am and 4am), Miri (RM50, 6½ hours, roughly hourly from 6am to 3.30am) and Bintulu (RM30, 3¼ hours, roughly hourly from 6am to 3.30am).

Getting Around

TO/FROM THE AIRPORT

Sibu airport is 23km east of the centre; a taxi costs RM35.

From the local bus station, the Panduan Hemat bus to Sibu Jaya passes by the airport junction (RM3, every hour or two from 6am to 6pm), which is five minutes on foot from the terminal.

BUS

To get from the **local bus station**, in front of the Express Ferry Terminal, to the long-distance bus station, take Lanang Bus 21 (RM2, 15 minutes, once or twice an hour 6.30am to 5.15pm).

TAXI

Taxis (☎ 084-313658, 084-315440, 084-320773) can be ordered 24 hours a day. Taking a taxi from the city centre to the long-distance bus station costs RM15.

Batang Rejang

A trip up the tan, churning waters of 640km-long Batang Rejang (Rejang River) – the 'Amazon of Borneo' – is one of Southeast Asia's great river journeys. Express ferries barrel through the currents, eddies and whirlpools, the pilots expertly dodging angular black boulders half-hidden in the roiling waters. Though the area is no longer the jungle-lined wilderness it was in the days before Malaysian independence, it retains a frontier, *ulu-ulu* (upriver, back-of-beyond) vibe, especially in towns and longhouses accessible only by boat.

To get a sense of the extent of logging and palm-oil monoculture, check out Google Earth.

RIDING THE RAPIDS

When the water level in the Batang Rejang is too low for boats to make the trip upriver from Kapit, Belaga-based **Daniel Levoh** (p164) can arrange to collect you in his own small boat at **Punan Bah** longhouse – about halfway between Kapit and Belaga and the last stop before the **Pelagus Rapids**, which larger boats are unable to pass. He can take you to see the longhouse before continuing upriver to Belaga, with lunch on the way (RM500 for up to four people). The trip can also be done in reverse, from Belaga to Kapit.

Getting Around

For the time being, pretty much the only transport arteries into and around the Batang Rejang region are rivers. At research time, a new road from Kapit to Kanowit (already connected to Sarawak's highway network) was nearing completion and a rough logging road already connects Bintulu with Belaga. It seems that easy land access will soon change this part of Borneo.

Boats can navigate the perilous Pelagus Rapids, between Kapit and Belaga, only when the water level is high enough – these days, determined mainly by how much water is released from the Bakun Dam.

Express river boats – nicknamed 'flying coffins' because of their shape, not their safety record – run by half-a-dozen companies head up the broad, muddy Batang Rejang from Sibu with goods and luggage strapped precariously to their roofs. If you opt to ride up top for the view (not that we recommend it...), hang on tight! The passenger cabins tend to be air-conditioned to near-arctic frigidity.

From Sibu, boats to Kapit (140km, 2½ to three hours) leave every hour from 5.45am to 2.30pm; from Kapit, boats heading down to Sibu depart between 6.40am and 3.15pm. Boarding often involves clambering over boats and inching your way along a narrow, rail-less exterior gangway.

If the water level at the Pelagus Rapids (32km upriver from Kapit) is high enough, one 77-seat **express boat** (☎ 013-806 1333) a day goes all the way to Belaga, 155km upriver from Kapit, stopping at various longhouses along the way. Heading upriver, departures are at 5.45am from Sibu (RM85, 11 hours) and 9.30am from Kapit (RM55, 4½ hours). Coming downriver, the boat leaves Belaga at about 7.30am. When the river is too low, the only way to get to Belaga is overland via Bintulu.

Kapit

POP 14,000

The main upriver settlement on the Batang Rejang, Kapit is a bustling trading and transport centre dating back to the days of the White Rajahs. A number of nearby longhouses can be visited by road or river, but

Kapit

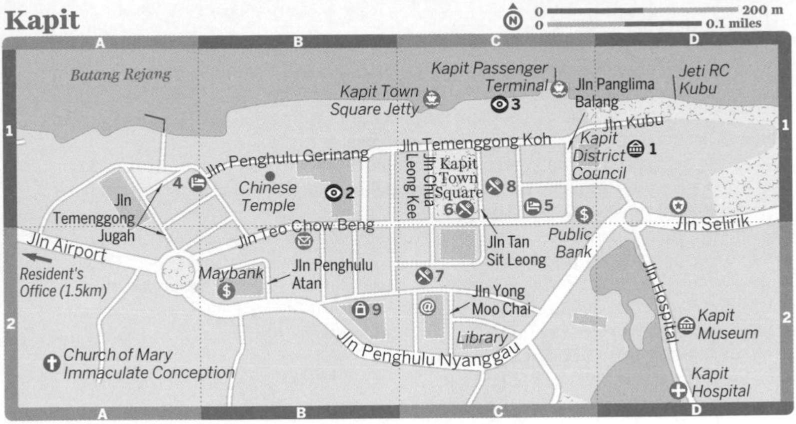

the pickings are thin when it comes to finding a good local guide.

Fans of Redmond O'Hanlon's *Into the Heart of Borneo* may remember Kapit as the starting point of the author's adventures.

Sights

Fort Sylvia MUSEUM

(Jln Kubu; 10am-noon & 2-5pm, closed Mon & public holidays) Built by Charles Brooke in 1880 to take control of the Upper Rejang, this wooden fort – built of *belian* – was renamed in 1925 to honour Ranee Sylvia, Brooke's wife.

The exhibits inside offer a pretty good introduction to the traditional lifestyles of the indigenous groups of the Batang Rejang and include evocative colonial-era photographs. Also on show is the peace jar presented during the historical 1924 peacemaking ceremony between previously warring Iban, Kayan and Kenyah groups.

The museum also devotes space to the story of Domingo 'Mingo' de Rozario, the son of James Brooke's Portuguese Melakan butler and a man described by a contemporary as having 'a burly figure, dark kindly face, utter disregard for personal danger' and the tendency to 'look on life as a huge joke'. Rozario was sent to Kapit and charged with bringing it under the Rajah's control. He became an authority on Upper Rejang enthnography, describing life in the region in a series of colourful letters and reports.

Waterfront PORT

Kapit's waterfront is lined with ferries, barges, longboats and floating docks, all swarming with people. Porters carry impossibly heavy or unwieldy loads – we've seen 15 egg crates stacked in a swaying pile – up the steep steps from the wharfs.

Kapit

Sights
- 1 Fort Sylvia D1
- 2 Pasar Teresang B1
- 3 Waterfront C1

Sleeping
- 4 Hiap Chiong Hotel A1
- 5 New Rejang Inn C1

Eating
- 6 Famous Bakery C1
- Gelanggang Kenyalang .... (see 9)
- 7 Night Market C2
- 8 Soon Kit Café C1

Shopping
- 9 Sula Perengka Kapit B2

Pasar Teresang MARKET

(5.30am-6pm) Some of the goods unloaded at the waterfront end up in this colourful covered market. It's a chatty, noisy hive of grass-roots commerce, with a galaxy of unfamiliar edibles that grow in the jungle, as well as handicrafts. Orang Ulu people sell fried treats and steamed buns.

Tours

Longhouse Tours

Longhouses, many of them quite modern and some accessible by road (river travel is both slower and pricier than going by minibus), can be found along the Batang

LONGHOUSE VISITS

Many of the indigenous people of the Batang Rejang basin, both Iban and members of Orang Ulu groups such as the Kenyah, Kayan and Punan, still live in longhouses. While most aren't as traditional as travellers may envision, visiting one can be a great way to interact with some of Sarawak's indigenous people.

Based on geography, Kapit and Belaga *should* be good bases from which to set out to explore longhouses along the upper Batang Rejang and its tributaries. Unfortunately, travellers may face two types of difficulties.

Firstly, visiting longhouses without an invitation or a guide is becoming more complicated as traditional norms, according to which visitors are always welcome, have given way to more 'modern' (that is, commercial) ideas. But it is not only about commercialism; travellers who turn up unannounced may inadvertently cause offense – for example, by entering a longhouse during a period of mourning. In such cases the headman may ask for payment as a fine.

Secondly, it's very difficult to find a guide in Kapit to take you, and if you do, the guide may demand inflated prices and/or provide services that aren't up to standard. For instance, visitors may be dropped off at a longhouse with nothing to do and no way to communicate with the residents until they're picked up the next day.

If you are flexible and have some time to spend in the area, you may well be lucky enough to be invited by locals to their longhouse. Otherwise, the best option is to make arrangements through one of the tour agencies based in Sibu (p157).

Baleh, which joins the Batang Rejang 9km upstream from Kapit, and the Sungai Sut, a tributary of the Batang Baleh. Longhouses along these rivers tend to be more traditional than their counterparts along the mainline Batang Rejang.

The problem is finding a good guide. Due to the lack of licensed guides in Kapit, and because many of Sarawak's unlicensed guides are competent and knowledgeable, we advise that you talk to other travellers and local hotel owners about which operators are recommended or best avoided. The safest bet is to arrange a tour with an established Sibu-based operator (p157).

Visiting Longhouses on Your Own

A few communities around Kapit are accustomed to independent travellers, charging between RM10 and RM40 for a day visit or RM50 to RM100 per person if you stay overnight, including meals. The headman may also expect a tip, and if you plan to stay overnight, you should also bring a gift. Remember that there may not be much to do at a longhouse, especially if there aren't any English speakers around.

Longhouses you may consider visiting:

Rumah Bundong One of the area's few remaining traditional Iban longhouses. Situated on Sungai Kapit a 45-minute (10km) drive from Kapit.

Rumah Jandok A traditional longhouse on Sungai Yong with quite a few English speakers, situated down the Batang Rejang from Kapit. The longhouse is one hour by road from Kapit and charges RM40 for a visit, plus RM10 for the headman and RM15 for taking photos of the skulls.

To arrange land transport, ask the car and van drivers outside Pasar Teresang (on Jln Teo Chow Beng). Alternatively, you could try joining the locals in the service-taxi minivans that hang out around Kapit Town Sq (at the corner of Jln Teo Chow Beng and Jln Chua Leong Kee) and at Pasar Teresang (on Jln Teo Chow Beng).

To get to longhouses accessible only by river, head to **Jeti RC Kubu** (Jln Kubu), the jetty facing Fort Sylvia, and negotiate for a longboat. These can be expensive – imagine how much fuel the outboard slurps as the boat powers its way upstream.

Festivals & Events

Baleh-Kapit Raft Safari WATER SPORTS

A challenging, two-day race recreating the experience of Iban and Orang Ulu people rafting downstream to bring their jungle produce to Kapit. Often held in April. For details, check with the **Resident's Office** (084-796230; www.kapitro.sarawak.gov.my; 9th fl, Kompleks Kerajaan Negeri Bahagian Kapit, Jln Bleteh; 8am-1pm & 2-5pm Mon-Thu, 8-11.45am & 2.15-5pm Fri) in Kapit or Sibu's Visitors Information Centre (p159).

Sleeping

New Rejang Inn HOTEL $
(☎084-796600, 084-796700; 104 Jln Teo Chow Beng; d RM78; ❄📶) A welcoming and well-run hotel whose 15 spotless, good-sized rooms come with comfortable mattresses, hot water, TV, phone and mini-fridge. The best-value accommodation in town.

Hiap Chiong Hotel HOTEL $
(☎084-796314; 33 Jln Temenggong Jugah; d RM50; 📶) The 15 rooms have outdated furniture but are clean and have tiny flat-screen TVs.

Eating & Drinking

Soon Kit Café CHINESE $
(13 Jln Tan Sit Liong; mains RM5-6; ⌚5am-6pm) An old-time *kopitiam* (coffee shop) with laksa (RM5) in the morning and excellent chicken rice (RM5.50).

Gelanggang Kenyalang HAWKER $
(off Jln Penghulu Nyanggau; mains from RM3.50; ⌚6am-5pm) An indoor food court with Malay and Chinese stalls. A good place for breakfast laksa or *roti canai*.

Night Market MARKET $
(Taman Selera Empurau; mains RM2.50-5; ⌚5-11pm or midnight) Delicious satay and barbecue chicken are the highlight of this night market, which has tables to eat at. Situated a block up the slope from Kapit Town Sq.

Famous Bakery BAKERY $
(22 Jln Teo Chow Beng; pastries RM1-3.50; ⌚5.30am-6pm) Freshly baked Chinese and Western-style pastries, cakes, mini-pizzas and other easy-to-pack day-trip picnic fare.

Shopping

Sula Perengka Kapit HANDICRAFTS
(off Jln Penghulu Nyanggau; ⌚8am-4pm Mon-Sat, 8am-noon Sun) A tiny, Iban-owned handicrafts place (Shop 21) upstairs at the Gelanggang Kenyalang food court.

Information

Kapit Hospital (☎084-796333; Jln Hospital; ⌚24hr) Has three ambulances and half-a-dozen doctors.

King Cyber Sky (Jln Penghulu Gerinang, 1st fl, above Public Cafe; per hr RM3; ⌚10am-11pm)

Getting There & Away

BOAT

Express boats to Sibu (RM25 to RM35, 2½ to three hours, once or twice an hour) depart between 6.40am and 3.15pm from the **Kapit Passenger Terminal** (Jln Panglima Balang; 📶), which has a nice verandah cafe with breezy river views.

Water levels permitting (for details, call **Daniel Levoh,** p164, in Belaga), an express boat heads upriver to Belaga (RM55, 4½ hours) from the **Kapit Town Square jetty** (Kapit Town Sq), two blocks downriver from the Kapit Passenger Terminal, once a day at about 9.30am. Be on board by 9.15am.

One express boat a day heads up the Batang Baleh, going as far as the Iban longhouse of Rumah Penghulu Jampi. It departs from Kapit at about 10am and from Rumah Penghulu Jampi at 12.30pm.

VAN

A small road network around Kapit, unconnected to the outside world, links the town to a number of longhouses. Vans that ply these byways congregate at Kapit Town Sq.

UPPER REJANG TRAVEL PERMITS

Theoretically, a free, two-week permit is required for all travel in the following places:

- Along the Batang Rejang to points upriver from the Pelagus Rapids (32km upstream from Kapit).
- Up the Batang Baleh, which flows into the Batang Rejang 9km upriver from Kapit.

In fact, we've never heard of anyone having their permit checked, and the whole arrangement seems to be a bureaucratic holdover from the time when the government sought to limit foreign activists' access to Orang Ulu communities threatened by logging or the controversial Bakun Dam. Permits are not required, even in theory, if you travel to Belaga overland from Bintulu.

Permits (unneccesary as they are) are issued in Kapit at the Resident's Office, in a nine-storey building 2km west of the centre. To get there, take a van (RM2) from the southeast corner of Pasar Teresang. To get back to town, ask the lobby guards for help catching a ride (offer to pay the driver).

Belaga

POP 2500

By the time you pull into Belaga after the long cruise up the Batang Rejang, you may feel like you've arrived in the very heart of Borneo – in reality, you're only about 100km (as the crow flies) from the coast. There's not much to do here except soak up the frontier vibe, but nearby rivers are home to quite a few Orang Ulu (primarily Kayan and Kenyah) longhouses.

Sights

To get a feel for the pace of local life, wander among the two-storey shophouses of the compact, mostly Chinese **town centre**, or stroll through the manicured **park** – complete with basketball and tennis courts – between Main Bazaar and the river. Along the riverfront, a wooden bridge leads downstream to **Kampung Melayu Belaga**, Belaga's Malay quarter, whose wooden homes are built on stilts. The town's 24-hour electricity is provided by generator – Belaga is not yet connected to the Bakun Dam grid.

Activities

The main reason travellers visit Belaga is to venture up a jungle stream in search of hidden longhouses and secret waterfalls. Possible destinations include the following:

Dong Daah A Kayan longhouse 10 minutes upriver by boat from Belaga.

Lirong Amo A Kayan longhouse half-an-hour's walk from Belaga.

Long Liten A huge, old Kejaman longhouse a ways upriver.

Long Segaham A Kejaman longhouse situated some way upriver.

Sekapan Panjang A traditional, all-wood Sekapan longhouse half-an-hour downstream by boat from Belaga.

Sihan A Penan settlement a two-hour walk from the other bank of the Batang Rejang.

Before you can share shots of *tuak* with the longhouse headman, however, you need to find a guide. A good package should include a boat ride, jungle trekking, a waterfall swim, a night walk and activities such as cooking and fruit harvesting.

Daniel Levoh GUIDE
(☎086-461198, 013-848 6351; daniellevoh@hotmail.com; Jln Teh Ah Kiong) A Kayan former school headmaster, Daniel is friendly and knowledgeable. Possible excursions include walking to Sihan, a Penan settlement across the river, and stopping at a waterfall (this can be done unguided at a cost of RM20 for the boat and a gift for the longhouse; Daniel will call ahead). Can also arrange private transport around Belaga and Bintulu.

Hamdani TOUR
(☎019-886 5770) Former guide Hamdini may be able to help arrange longhouse visits.

Events

Belaga Rainforest Challenge SPORTS
(Jul or Aug of even-numbered yrs) This five-day event combines a 17km jungle run with boat races and traditional music and dance performances.

Sleeping

Belaga's accommodation is of the cheap and shabby variety.

Daniel Levoh's Guesthouse GUESTHOUSE $
(☎013-848 6351, 086-461198; daniellevoh@hotmail.com; Jln Teh Ah Kiong; dm RM20, d without bathroom RM40; wi-fi) The four simple rooms are on the 2nd floor, opening off a large open verandah decorated with a traditional Kayan mural. Owner Daniel Levoh is happy to share stories of longhouse life. Situated two blocks behind Main Bazaar.

Belaga B&B HOTEL $
(☎013-842 9760; freeland205@gmail.com; Main Bazaar; with fan dm/d RM25/15, with air-con d RM35; air-con) Has seven basic rooms, some with air-con, and shared bathroom facilities. Don't let the name fool you: breakfast isn't included. Owned by Hasbee, a former longhouse guide who now runs the eponymous cafe downstairs. He is happy to help arrange longhouse visits.

Eating

There are a few simple cafes serving Chinese and Malay dishes along Main Bazaar.

Night Market HAWKER $
(block behind Main Bazaar; mains RM4.50-12; 3.30-10pm) An outdoor food court with six stalls selling Kayan, Kenyah and Malay food. Look for Robina's stall selling delicious ginger chicken (RM6).

Crystal Cafe MALAYSIAN $
(Jln Temenggong Matu; mains RM3.50-8; 7am-7pm) Owned by an Iban-Kenyah family,

Crystal Cafe is a good bet for a simple meal of mee goreng (RM3.50), laksa Sarawak (RM4.30), *nasi lemak ayam* (chicken with rice boiled in coconut milk; RM5.50) or *nasi ayam penyet* (smashed fried chicken with rice and sambal; RM8).

Information

The town's only ATM is often out of order; bring plenty of cash. The medical clinic has one doctor. Several places to stay have wi-fi.

Getting There & Away

When the express boat is running, it's possible to visit Belaga without backtracking, cruising the Batang Rejang in one direction and taking the logging road to/from Bintulu in the other.

BOAT

If the water levels at the Pelagus Rapids (32km upriver from Kapit) are high enough, you can take an express boat to Kapit (RM55, 4½ hours) departing at about 7.30am. To find out if the boat is running, call tour guide Daniel Levoh. When the river is too low, the only way to get out of Belaga is by 4WD to Bintulu.

LAND

A bone-jarring (and, in the rain, fiendishly slippery) logging road connects Belaga with Bintulu (160km). Part of the way the route follows the 125km-long paved road to the Bakun Dam.

4WD Toyota Land Cruisers link Belaga with Bintulu (RM50 to RM60 per person, RM400 for the whole vehicle, four hours) on most days, with departures from Belaga at about 7.30am and from Bintulu in the early afternoon (between noon and 2pm). In Belaga, vehicles to Bintulu congregate in front of Belaga B&B at about 7am. To arrange a vehicle from Bintulu, call Daniel Levoh.

If you're coming from Miri or Batu Niah Junction or heading up that way (ie northeast), you can arrange to be picked up or dropped off at Simpang Bakun (Bakun Junction), which is on the Inland (old) highway 53km northeast of Bintulu and 159km southwest of Miri.

Upriver from Belaga

About 40km upstream from Belaga, the Batang Rejang divides into several rivers, including the mighty Batang Balui, which wends and winds almost all the way up to the Kalimantan border. Just below this junction, the controversial **Bakun Dam** generates electricity and provides locals with a place to catch fish, which they come down to the dam to sell on Wednesday and Saturday mornings. Belaga-based guides can arrange visits to area longhouses. The 15 longhouses in Sungai Asap are new – built to rehouse the communities displaced by flooding due to the dam – but traditional in style.

The dam is 40km (two hours) by road from Belaga.

Bintulu

☎086 / POP 190,000

Fifty years ago Bintulu was a small fishing village with a population of 5000; now, thanks to its offshore natural gas fields, it is a booming industrial town and Sarawak's most important centre for the production of LNG (liquefied natural gas) and fertiliser.

Most travellers who stop in Bintulu, roughly midway between Sibu and Miri (about 200km from each), plan to visit to Similajau National Park or travel overland to or from Belaga.

Sights

Tua Pek Kong CHINESE TEMPLE

(Main Bazaar; 7am-6pm) FREE This classic Chinese temple adds vibrant colours to the rather drab city centre. The serenity is somewhat marred by the sound of cock-a-doodle-doos drifting over from the paved area around back, where young fighting cocks are kept tethered to avoid strife.

Festivals

Borneo International Kite Festival SPORTS

(www.borneokite.com; Sep) An annual event, usually held over four or five days in September, that brings the world's top kite fliers to Bintulu to compete in the Borneo Sports Kite Championship. Also on the programme are kite-flying demonstrations and workshops.

Sleeping

There are quite a few hotels, some on the dodgy side, on and near Jln Keppel, its southern continuation, Jln Abang Galau, and parallel Jln Masjid.

Kintown Inn HOTEL $

(☎086-333666; 93 Jln Keppel; s/d RM80/86.25;) The carpeted rooms, though small and rather musty, are a reasonable option for those on a budget who aren't put off by a bit of peeling paint.

Riverfront Inn HOTEL $$

(☎086-333111; riverfrontinn@hotmail.com; 256 Taman Sri Dagang; s/d from RM81/104;) A long-standing favourite with business and

Bintulu

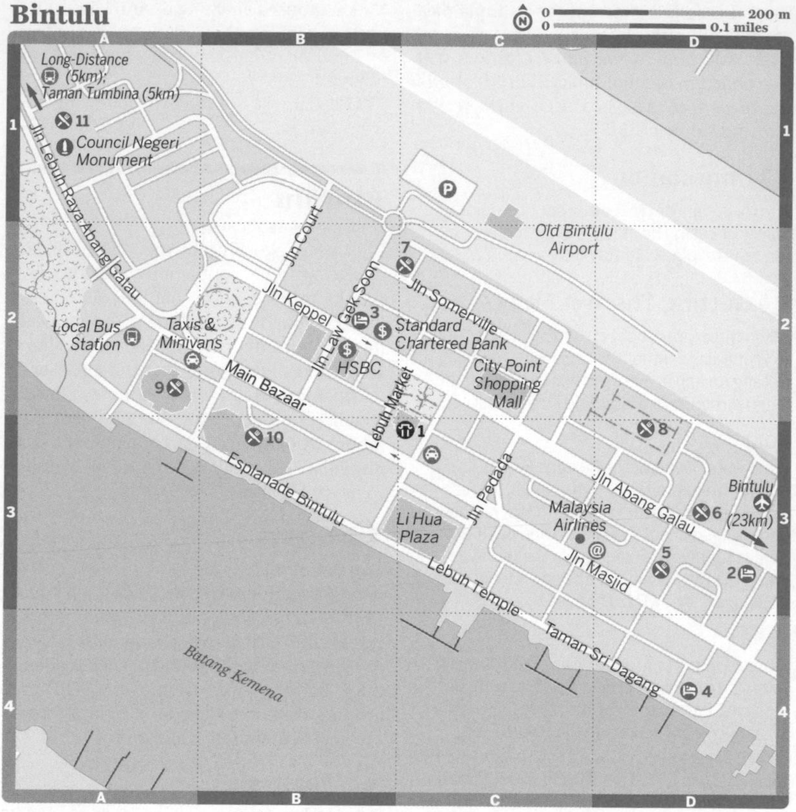

Bintulu

Sights

1 Tua Pek Kong C3

Sleeping

2 Kemena Plaza Hotel D3
3 Kintown Inn B2
4 Riverfront Inn D4

Eating

5 Ban Kee Café D3
6 Chef D3
7 Famous Mama C2
8 Night Market D3
9 Pasar Tamu A2
10 Pasar Utama B3
11 Popular Corner Food Centre A1

leisure visitors alike, the Riverfront is low-key but has a touch of class. Try to get a deluxe room (RM120) overlooking the river – the view is pure Borneo.

Kemena Plaza Hotel HOTEL $$
(☎086-335111; www.kemenahotelgroup.com; 116 Jln Abang Galau; d/ste incl breakfast RM170/290;) Recent renovations have refreshed the hotel's 162 rooms, which are spacious with wooden floors, neutral colours and small bathrooms; rooms on the upper floors overlook the river. The highlight here is a rooftop swimming pool and sun terrace, with spectacular views of the town and river and the ocean beyond them.

Eating & Drinking

Famous Mama MAMAK, HALAL $
(10 Jln Somerville; mains RM5-10;) Famous Mama does Mamak (halal Indian-Malay) cuisine and is a popular place for quick, cheap *nasi kandar* (rice served with side dishes of different curries) and *roti canai*.

Popular Corner Food Centre HAWKER $
(50 BDA Shahida Commercial Centre, Jln Abang Galau; mains RM7-12; 6am-5pm) If you've ever

wanted to try fresh frog porridge (RM12), this is the place to come. Less adventurous diners can chose from one of eight stalls selling dim sum and fresh seafood.

Night Market MALAYSIAN $
(Pasar Malam; off Jln Abang Galau; mains RM2-5; ⌚4-10pm) A good place to pick up snacks, fresh fruit and Malay favourites such as satay and *nasi lemak*.

Pasar Utama HAWKER $
(New Market; Main Bazaar; mains RM3-5; ⌚7am-4pm) Malay and Chinese food stalls fill the upper floor of this blue-coloured fruit and vegetable market. The cone-shaped roofs of Pasar Utama and the next door **Pasar Tamu** (Bintulu Market, Main Bazaar; ⌚7am-6pm) wet market represent *terendak*, the traditional headwear of the Melanau tribe.

Chef BAKERY $
(☎086-312964; 97 Jln Abang Galau; cakes from RM1; ⌚8.30am-9pm) Makes Chinese-inflected baked goods, including sweet and savoury bread rolls, sandwiches, pastries and surprisingly tasty Belgian chocolate cake. Ideal fare for a picnic lunch.

Ban Kee Café SEAFOOD $$
(off Jln Abang Galau; mains RM6-15; ⌚6.30am-11pm) An atmospheric Chinese seafood specialist with seating in a semi-covered outdoor courtyard, selling fresh fish and seafood (per kilogram RM40 to RM80) and breakfast noodles and laksa.

Information

Fi Wee Internet Centre (1st fl, 133 Jln Masjid; per hr RM2; ⌚9am-1am) Popular with gamers.

Getting There & Away

To arrange transport by 4WD Toyota Land Cruiser from Bintulu to Belaga (per person RM50, four hours) on some pretty rough logging roads, call Daniel Levoh (p164). Departures are generally in the early afternoon (between noon and 2pm).

AIR

AirAsia (www.airasia.com) and **Malaysia Airlines** (☎086-331349; www.malaysiaairlines.com) have direct flights to Kuching and Kuala Lumpur. **MASwings** (☎086-331349; www.maswings.com.my; Bintulu airport; ⌚7am-7pm) flies to Kota Kinabalu, Miri, Sibu and Kuching.

BUS

The long-distance bus station is at Medan Jaya, 5km northeast of the centre (aka Bintulu Town); a taxi costs RM20. About a dozen companies have buses approximately hourly to the following destinations:

- Kuching (RM70, 11 hours) via Sibu (RM25, four hours), from 6am to midnight.
- Miri (RM25, four hours) via Niah Junction (RM15, 2¾ hours), from 6am to 9.30pm.

Getting Around

There is no public transport to/from the airport, which is 23km from the centre by road. A taxi costs RM35.

Similajau National Park

An easy 30km northeast of Bintulu, **Similajau National Park** (☎Miri office 085-434184, Park office 086-489003; www.sarawakforestry.com; Kuala Likau; adult/child RM20/7; ⌚park office 8am-1pm & 2-5pm Sat-Thu, 8-11.45am & 2.15-5pm Fri) is a fine little coastal park with golden-sand beaches, good walking trails and simple accommodation. Occupying a narrow, 30km strip along the South China Sea, its 90 sq km encompasses littoral habitats such as mangroves, *kerangas* (heath forest) and mixed dipterocarp forest (classic lowland tropical rainforest). Four species of dolphin, including Irrawaddy dolphins, can sometimes be spotted out at sea, and green turtles occasionally trundle ashore to lay their eggs along Turtle Beach II and Golden Beach. The park is also home to gibbons, long-tailed macaques, mouse deer, barking deer and wild boars.

Bintuluans flock to Similajau (especially the beaches) on weekends and public holidays, but the park is gloriously deserted on weekdays.

Sights & Activities

Similajau Beach BEACH
(Similajau National Park) The casuarina-lined beach at Similajau park HQ, strewn with driftwood but clean, is a great place to chill

BEWARE CROCODILES!

Similajau's waterways are prime crocodile habitat, so do not swim or wade in the rivers or near rivermouths and be careful when walking near riverbanks, especially early or late in the day.

Swimming is forbidden at the two Turtle Beaches and at Golden Beach because of dangerous undertows.

out. It's also a popular spot for taking a dip – if the thought of estuarine crocodiles (those are the big ones) and jellyfish don't deter you, that is. If you do enter the water, make sure you are far away from the rivermouth.

Hiking Trails HIKING

(☎086-489003; Similajau National Park) Similajau's beautiful forest trails are easy to follow and clearly marked, so a guide isn't necessary, though it's possible to hire one (call in advance) for RM30 per hour (RM40 per hour for a **night walk**). Before setting off remember to sign in at park HQ and pick up the simple but useful trail map. Bring plenty of drinking water.

The gently undulating **Main Trail** (Coastal Trail) parallels the coast, starting at the suspension bridge that crosses Sungai Likau and ending at **Golden Beach** (10km, four hours one-way). The trail passes by rocky headlands, small bays and **Turtle Beach I** (6.5km, 2½ hours) and **Turtle Beach II** (7km, three hours). For a view back along the coast towards Bintulu and its natural-gas installations, head to the **View Point** (1.3km from HQ, 40 minutes).

Branching off to the right after crossing the suspension bridge, a 1.7km **Circular Trail** passes through brilliant estuarine mangroves and mixed dipterocarp forest.

Boat Trips BOAT TOUR

(☎086-489003, 019-861 0998; www.sarawakforestry.com; Similajau National Park; boat for up to 5 people to Turtle Beach 1-way/return RM195/245, to Golden Beach 1-way/return RM235/300; ⏲office 8am-5pm) To avoid retracing your steps on a hike, one option is to arrange a ride in the park boat to one of the beaches and walk back. The boat, with space for five passengers, can be hired for one-way or return trips. Sea conditions are often rough later in the day, so it's best to head out before 8am.

Options include a return trip to the rocky island of **Batu Mandi** (RM160), or making a 30-minute stop at the island before continuing on to **Golden Beach** to hike back from there (RM445). It is also possible to arrange a **night river cruise** (RM160) to see the crocs (reserve during office hours).

Sleeping

Similajau's rustic overnight options, just 100m from the beach, sometimes fill up on weekends.

Cabins CABIN $

(☎086-489003, 019-861 0998; www.sarawakforestry.com; Similajau National Park; r RM100, 2-room unit RM150; ❄) Each of the six simple but comfortable cabins has two rooms: one air-conditioned bedroom and a fan-cooled living room, each with a double and single bed (each unit sleeps six).

Hostel HOSTEL $

(☎086-489003, 019-861 0998; www.sarawakforestry.com; Similajau National Park; dm RM15) Each room has four beds (bunks in the case of Hostel 3) and a wall fan. Hostels 1 and 2 have attached bathrooms.

Campground CAMPGROUND $

(☎086-489003, 019-861 0998; www.sarawakforestry.com; Similajau National Park; per person RM5) Camping is only permitted next to park HQ. Showers are provided.

Rest House CABIN $$

(☎086-489003, 019-861 0998; www.sarawakforestry.com; Similajau National Park; 2-room unit RM300; ❄) The park's most luxurious accommodation is a self-contained, air-conditioned 'VIP' cabin with its own living room and verandah.

Eating

Cooking is not allowed in the park cabins or hostel, but there are designated sites for barbecuing.

Cafeteria CAFETERIA $

(mains RM5-13; ⏲7.30am-8.30pm; 🌶) Serves simple rice and noodle dishes and can prepare packed lunches.

Getting There & Away

The HQ of Similajau National Park is about 30km northeast of Bintulu, 9km off the coastal road to Miri.

Count on paying RM55 one way to hire a taxi from Bintulu (there is no public bus).

To get back to Bintulu, you can pre-arrange a pick-up time or ask HQ staff to help you call for a taxi.

Niah National Park

The vast limestone caverns of 31-sq-km **Niah National Park** (☎085-737450, 085-737454; www.sarawakforestry.com; admission RM20; ⏲park office 8am-5pm) are among Borneo's most famous and impressive natural attractions. At the heart of the park is the Great Cave, one of the largest caverns in the world.

Niah's caves have provided groundbreaking insights into human life on Borneo way back when the island was still connected to mainland Southeast Asia. In 1958 archaeologists led by Tom Harrisson discovered the 40,000-year-old skull of an anatomically modern human, the oldest remains of a *Homo sapiens* discovered anywhere in Southeast Asia.

Rock paintings and several small canoe-like coffins ('death ships') indicate that the site was used as a burial ground much more recently. Some of the artefacts found at Niah are kept in Kuching; others (a handful) are in the park's own museum.

Niah's caves accommodate a staggering number of bats and are an important nesting site for swiftlets, some of whose species supply the vital ingredient for bird's-nest soup. Traditionally, the Penan are custodians and collectors of the nests, while the Iban have the rights to the caves' other commodity, bat and bird guano, which is highly valued as fertiliser (no prizes for guessing who got first pick). During the harvesting season (August to March), nest collectors can be seen on towering bamboo structures wedged against the cave roof.

Despite the historical significance of the sight, Niah has not been overly done-up for tourists. It's possible to visit the caves without a guide and during the week you may have the place to yourself. Travellers who have been (or are going) to Gunung Mulu National Park may feel caved-out at the thought of Niah, but for anyone with even a passing interest in human prehistory it is not to be missed.

Sights & Activities

Niah Archaeology Museum MUSEUM
(motor launch per person RM1, 5.30-7.30pm RM1.50; 9am-4.45pm Tue-Fri, 10am-4pm Sat & Sun) Across the river from park HQ, this museum has informative displays on Niah's geology, ecology and prehistoric archaeology, including an original burial canoe that's at least 1200 years old, a reproduction of the Painted Cave, a case featuring swiftlets' nests, and a replica of the 40,000-year-old 'Deep Skull'.

To get to the museum, cross Sungai Niah by motor launch. Torches – essential if you want to go any distance into the caves – can be rented at the museum (RM5).

Great Cave CAVE
A raised boardwalk leads 3.1km (3½ to four hours return) through swampy, old-growth rainforest to the mouth of the Great Cave, a vast cavern approximately 2km long, up to 250m across and up to 60m high. Inside, the trail splits to go around a massive central pillar, but both branches finish at the same point, so it's impossible to get lost if you stick to the boardwalk. The stairs and handrails are usually covered with guano, and can be slippery.

The rock formations are spectacular and ominous by turns, and you may find yourself thinking of Jules Verne's *Journey to the Centre of the Earth*. When the sun hits certain overhead vents, the cave is penetrated by dramatic rays of otherworldly light. When you're halfway through the dark passage known as Gan Kira (Moon Cave), try turning off your torch to enjoy the experience of pure, soupy blackness.

Painted Cave CAVE
After passing through Gan Kira, you emerge into the forest and another section of boardwalk before arriving at the Painted Cave, famed for its ancient drawings, in red hematite, depicting jungle animals, human figures and the souls of the dead being taken to the afterlife by boat. It can be tricky to make out the red hematite figures, as many have faded to little more than indistinct scrawls along a narrow 30m-strip at the back of the cave.

To return, retrace your steps, taking the stairs up to your left to close the loop in the Great Cave.

Bukit Kasut WALKING
This 45-minute trail, part of it a boardwalk through freshwater swamp forest, leads up to the summit of **Bukit Kasut** (205m). In the wet season, it can get muddy and treacherously slippery.

Sleeping & Eating

Bookings for park-run accommodation can be made at park HQ (in person or by phone) or through one of the **National Park Booking Offices** (in Kuching 082-248088, in Miri 085-434184). Lodges and rooms often fill up on Chinese, Malay and public holidays. Cooking is prohibited in park accommodation, but you can, boil water to make instant noodles, except at the hostel.

Batu Niah town, 4km from park HQ (3km if you walk), has a couple of basic hotels.

NIAH'S BATS & SWIFTLETS

The chorus of high-pitched sqwaking you'll hear as you enter the Great Cave is not the sound of bats but of Niah's resident swiftlets; further in, you'll detect the squeaking of bats. At one time, some 470,000 bats and four million swiftlets called Niah home. Current numers are not known, but the walls of the caves are no longer thick with bats and there are fewer bird's nests to harvest.

Several species of swiftlet nest on the cave walls. The most common by far is the glossy swiftlet, whose nest is made of vegetation and is therefore of no use in making soup. For obvious reasons, the species whose nests are edible (those that are made of salivary excretions that are considered by many to be a great delicacy) are far less abundant and can only be seen in the remotest corners of the cavern. Several types of bat also roost in the cave, but not in dense colonies, as at Gunung Mulu National Park.

The best time to see the cave's winged wildlife is at dusk (5.30pm to 6.45pm) during the 'changeover', when the swiftlets stream back to their nests and the bats come swirling out for the night's feeding. If you decide to stick around, let staff at the park HQ's Registration Counter know and make sure you either get back to the boat by 7.30pm or coordinate a later pick-up time with the boatman.

Hostel HOSTEL **$**
(Niah National Park HQ; r RM40, towel rental RM6) Each basic hostel room has space for up to four people.

Rumah Patrick Libau Homestay HOMESTAY **$**
(☎Asan 014-596 2757; Niah National Park; per person incl meals RM70; 📶) The traditional, 100-door Iban longhouse Rumah Patrick Libau, which is home to about 400 people, operates an informal homestay program. Accommodation is basic but the longhouse has wi-fi and 24-hour electricity. To get here, take the signposted turn off the main trail that leads to the caves. Villagers often sit at the junction selling cold drinks and souvenirs.

Campground CAMPGROUND **$**
(Niah National Park HQ; per person RM5) Camping is permitted near park HQ.

Forest Lodges CABIN **$$**
(Niah National Park HQ; with fan q RM100, with air-con d/q RM250/150) The park has six rustic, two-room cabins with attached bathrooms; each room can sleep up to four people. Two additional, more expensive air-con units each have two rooms with twin beds.

ℹ Getting There & Away

Niah National Park is about 115km southwest of Miri and 122km northeast of Bintulu and can be visited as a day trip from either city.

Park HQ is 15km north of Batu Niah Junction, a major transport hub on the inland (old) Miri–Bintulu highway. This makes getting to the park by public transport a tad tricky.

All long-haul buses linking Miri's Pujut Bus Terminal with Bintulu, Sibu and Kuching stop at Batu Niah Junction, but the only way to get from the junction to the park is to hire an unofficial taxi. The price should be RM30 (RM40 for a group of four), but you'll have to nose around the junction to find one. A good place to check: the bench in front of Shen Yang Trading, at the corner of Ngu's Garden Food Court. National park staff (or, after hours, park security personnel) can help arrange a car back to the junction.

From Batu Niah Junction, buses head to Miri (RM12, 1¾ hours) from about 8am to 1am and to Bintulu (RM16, two hours) from about 8am to 10.30pm. Other well-served destinations include Sibu (RM40, five to six hours) and Kuching (RM80, 12 hours). Kiosks representing various companies can be found at both ends of the building directly across the highway from Batu Niah Food Court Centre.

From Miri, a taxi to Niah costs RM150 one way or RM240 return, including waiting time.

It is also worth considering hiring a car or motorbike for the day. See p178 for Miri car and motorcycle hire companies.

Lambir Hills National Park

The 69-sq-km **Lambir Hills National Park** (☎085-471609; www.sarawakforestry.com; Jln Miri-Bintulu; RM20; ⏰8am-5pm, last entry 4pm) shelters dozens of jungle waterfalls, plenty of cool pools where you can take a dip, and a bunch of great walking trails through mixed dipterocarp and *kerangas* forests. A perennial favourite among locals and an important centre of scientific research, Lambir

Hills makes a great day or overnight trip out of the city.

The park encompasses a range of low sandstone hills with an extraordinary variety of plants and animals – perhaps even, as noted in Sarawak Forestry's publications, 'the greatest level of plant biodiversity on the planet'. Studies of a 52-hectare research plot (closed to visitors) have found an amazing 1200 tree species. Fauna include clouded leopards, barking deer, pangolins, tarsiers, five varieties of civet, 10 bat species and 50 other kinds of mammals, though you are unlikely to see many of them around park HQ. Lambir Hills is also home to an unbelievable 237 species of bird, among them eight kinds of hornbill, and 24 species of frog – and more are being found all the time.

Activities

Lambir Hills' interconnected, colour-coded trails branch off four primary routes and lead to 14 destinations – rangers, based in the HQ building, can supply you with a map and are happy to make suggestions. Make sure you get back to park HQ before 5pm – unless you're heading out for a **night walk**, that is, in which case you need to coordinate with park staff. Hiring a guide (optional) costs RM30 per hour for up to five people.

From HQ, the **Main Trail** follows a small river, Sungai Liam, past two attractive waterfalls to the 25m-high **Latak Waterfall** (1km, 15 minutes to 20 minutes one-way), which has a picnic area, changing rooms and a refreshing, sandy pool suitable for **swimming**. It can get pretty crowded on weekends and holidays.

You're likely to enjoy more natural tranquility along the path to **Tengkorong Waterfall**, a somewhat strenuous 6km walk (one way) from park HQ.

There are wonderful views from the top of **Bukit Pantu**, a 3.6km (one way) walk from HQ that is a good option for those on a day trip.

Another more challenging trail, steep in places, goes to the summit of **Bukit Lambir** (465m; 7km one way from HQ), which also affords fine views. Keep an eye out for changes in the vegetation, including wild orchids, as the elevation rises.

Sleeping & Eating

Camping CAMPING $

(☎085-471609; Jln Miri-Bintulu; per person RM5) Camping is permitted near the park HQ.

Cabins CABIN $

(☎085-471609; Jln Miri-Bintulu; 1-/2-bed r with fan RM50/75, with air-con RM100/150) The park's accommodation is in reasonably comfortable, two-room cabins; the old ones are wooden, the four new ones are made of concrete. Fan rooms have two beds, while air-con rooms have three. Individual dorm beds are not available. Cabins are sometimes booked out at weekends and during school holidays.

If you get in before 2pm (check-in time), bags can be left at the camp office.

Canteen CAFETERIA $

(Jln Miri-Bintulu; mains RM4-6; ⏱8am-5pm or later) The park's canteen serves simple rice and noodle dishes. If you are staying in the park and would like to eat an evening meal at the canteen, inform staff in advance. May close early.

Getting There & Away

Park HQ is 32km south of Miri on the inland (old) highway to Bintulu. All the buses that link Miri's Pujut Bus Terminal with Bintulu, Sibu and Kuching pass by here (RM10 from Miri) – just ask the driver to stop. There is a bus stand on the main road by the turn-off for the park, from where you can flag down a bus to Miri for the return journey.

A taxi from Miri costs RM40 one way (RM80 to 120 return, including two hours of wait time).

Miri

☎085 / POP 300,500

Miri, Sarawak's second city, is a thriving oil town that is busy and modern. There's plenty of money sloshing around, so the eating is good, the broad avenues are brightly lit, there's plenty to do when it's raining and the city's friendly guesthouses are a great place to meet other travellers. The population is about 40% Dayak (mainly Iban), 30% Chinese and 18% Malay.

Miri serves as a major transport hub, so if you're travelling to/from Brunei, Sabah, the Kelabit Highlands or the national parks of Gunung Mulu, Niah or Lambir Hills, chances are you'll pass this way.

Sights

Miri is not big on historical sites – it was pretty much destroyed during WWII – but it's not an unattractive city. A walk around the centre is a good way to get a feel for the local vibe. Streets worth a wander include (from north to south) Jln North Yu Seng, Jln South Yu Seng, Jln Maju and Jln High Street.

Miri

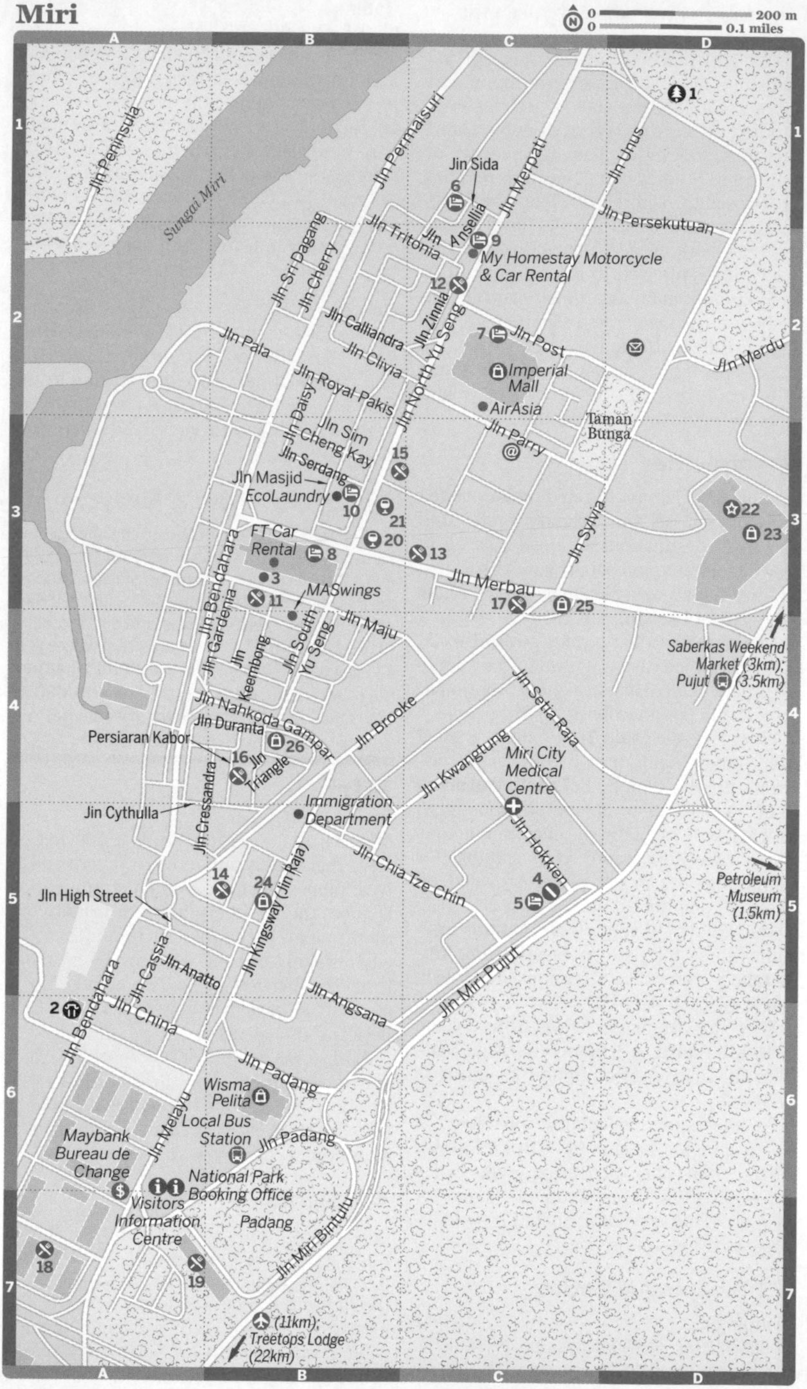
0 200 m
0 0.1 miles
A
B
C
D
1
2
3
4
5
6
7
Jln Peninsula
Sungai Miri
Jln Permaisuri
Jln Sida
Jln Merpati
Jln Unus
Jln Persekutuan
Jln Tritonia
Jln Ansellia
My Homestay Motorcycle & Car Rental
Jln Sri Dagang
Jln Cherry
Jln Calliandra
Jln Zinnia
Jln North Yu Seng
Jln Post
Jln Merdu
Jln Pala
Jln Clivia
Imperial Mall
Jln Royal Pakis
AirAsia
Taman Bunga
Jln Daisy
Jln Sim Cheng Kay
Jln Parry
Jln Serdang
Jln Masjid
EcoLaundry
Jln Sylvia
FT Car Rental
Jln Merbau
Jln Bendahara
Jln Gardenia
MASwings
Jln Maju
Jln Keembong
Jln South Yu Seng
Saberkas Weekend Market (3km); Pujut (3.5km)
Jln Nahkoda Gampar
Jln Duranta
Jln Setia Raja
Jln Brooke
Persiaran Kabor
Jln Triangle
Jln Kwangtung
Miri City Medical Centre
Jln Cressandra
Jln Cythulla
Immigration Department
Jln Hokkien
Jln Chia Tze Chin
Petroleum Museum (1.5km)
Jln Kingsway (Jln Raja)
Jln High Street
Jln Cassia
Jln Anatto
Jln Miri Pujut
Jln Angsana
Jln Bendahara
Jln China
Jln Padang
Wisma Pelita
Jln Melayu
Local Bus Station
Jln Padang
Maybank Bureau de Change
National Park Booking Office
Visitors Information Centre
Padang
Jln Miri Bintulu
(11km); Treetops Lodge (22km)
1
2
3
4
5
6
7
8
9
10
11
12
13
14
15
16
17
18
19
20
21
22
23
24
25
26

Miri

Sights

1 Miri City Fan ... D1
2 Tua Pek Kong Temple ... A6

Activities, Courses & Tours

3 Borneo Tropical Adventure ... B3
4 Coco Dive ... C5
Megalanes East Bowling Alley ... (see 23)

Sleeping

5 Coco House ... C5
6 Dillenia Guesthouse ... C1
7 Imperial Hotel ... C2
8 Mega Hotel ... B3
9 My Homestay ... C2
10 Next Room Guesthouse ... B3

Eating

11 Khan's Islamic Restaurant ... B3
12 Madli's Restaurant ... C2
13 Meng Chai Seafood ... C3
14 Miri Central Market ... B5
15 Muara Restoran ... B3
16 Persiaran Kabor ... B4
17 Rainforest Cafe ... C3
18 Summit Café ... A7
19 Tamu Muhibbah ... A7

Drinking & Nightlife

20 Ming Cafe ... B3
21 Soho Bar & Bistro ... B3

Entertainment

22 Golden Screen Cinema Bintang Megamall ... D3

Shopping

23 Bintang Plaza ... D3
24 Miri Central Superstore ... B5
25 Miri Handicraft Centre ... C3
Popular Book Store ... (see 23)
26 Sin Liang Supermarket ... B4

Miri City Fan PARK

(Jln Kipas; 24hr) An attractive, open, landscaped park with Chinese- and Malay-style gardens and ponds that is a popular spot for walking and jogging. The complex also comprises a library, an indoor stadium and an Olympic-sized public swimming pool (RM1).

Petroleum Museum MUSEUM

(Bukit Tenaga; 9am-4.45pm Tue-Fri, 10am-4pm Sat & Sun) FREE The Petroleum Museum sits atop **Canada Hill**, a low ridge 2km southeast of the town centre that was the site of Malaysia's first oil well, the **Grand Old Lady**, drilled in 1910. Appropriately, the old derrick stands right outside the museum whose interactive exhibits, some designed for kids, are a good, pro-Big Oil introduction to the hugely lucrative industry that has so enriched Miri (and Malaysia's federal government).

The hill itself is a popular exercise spot, and it's worth coming here at sunset for the views across town to the South China Sea.

Saberkas Weekend Market MARKET

(Jln Miri Pujut ; 4-11pm Thu-Sat, 8am-noon Sun) One of the most colourful and friendly markets in Sarawak. Vendors are more than happy to answer questions about their produce, which includes tropical fruits and vegetables, BBQ chicken, satay and handicrafts. Situated about 3km northeast of the centre outside the Saberkas Commercial Centre. A taxi here costs RM15 (there is no bus).

San Ching Tian Temple TAOIST TEMPLE

(Jln Krokop 9; 8am-6pm) FREE This, one of the largest Taoist temples in Southeast Asia, was built in 2000. Set in a peaceful courtyard with soothing wind chimes, the temple's design features intricate dragon reliefs brought from China and majestic figures of the Three Pure Ones. Situated in the suburban neighbourhood of Krokop, 3km northeast of Miri town centre. A taxi here costs RM18.

Tua Pek Kong Temple CHINESE TEMPLE

(Jln Bendahara; 8am-6pm) FREE Miri's oldest Chinese temple – it was founded in 1913 – is a good spot to watch the river traffic float by. During the week-long celebration of Chinese New Year, virtually the whole of this area, including Jln China, is taken over by a lively street fair with plenty of red lanterns and gold foil.

Activities

Although the waters off Miri are better known for drilling than diving, the area – much of it part of the Miri-Sibuti Coral Reef Marine Park – has some excellent 7m- to 30m-deep scuba sites, including old oil platforms teeming with fish and assorted trawler and freighter wrecks. Water visibility is at its best from March to September.

The corals here are in good condition and the water unpolluted, despite the proximity of heavy industry. When visibility is good you might see giant cuttlefish, whale sharks and sting rays.

Coco Dive DIVING
(☎085-417053; www.cocodive.com.my; Lot 2117 Block 9, Jln Miri Pujut; 2 dives RM320, 3 dives RM370) A well-regarded dive company with a fat programme of dive packages and PADI-certification courses. Gets rave reviews for its friendly, professional staff and solid equipment.

Tours

Planet Borneo Tours TOUR
(☎085-414300, 085-415582; www.planetborneotours.com; Lot 273, 1st fl Brighton Centre, Jln Temenggong Datuk Oyong Lawai) Established tour operator with a head office in Miri offering a range of tours and activities in northeastern Sarawak and beyond. Longer itineraries include trekking in the highlands from Ba Kelalan to Bario via Gunung Murud (from RM2567) and a visit to a remote Kenyah longhouse in the upper Baram (four days, RM5880).

Borneo Tropical Adventure TREKKING
(☎085-419337; www.borneotropicaladventures.com; Lot 906, Shop 12, ground fl, Soon Hup Tower, Jln Merbau; ⏲9am-6pm) Veteran Miri-based company offering packages including the Headhunters Trail from Gunung Mulu National Park (five days, from RM1750) as well as longhouse visits and multiday Borneo-wide tours.

Borneo Trekkers TREKKING
(☎012-872 9159; www.borneotrekkers.blogspot.com) Guide Willie Kajan specialises in treks to Mulu along the Headhunters' Trail with the possibility of beginning or ending with a night at a longhouse in Limbang. Can also arrange treks in the Kelabit Highlands.

Festivals

Borneo Jazz MUSIC
(www.jazzborneo.com; Parkcity Everly Hotel, Jln Temenggong Datuk Oyong Lawai; 1-day pass adult/child RM70/30, 2-day pass adult/child RM130/50; ⏲2nd weekend in May) An outdoor jazz festival held over two nights featuring an eclectic ensemble of international talent. Prices quoted here are for door sales; there are hefty discounts for tickets bought online in advance.

Sleeping

Miri has some of Sarawak's best backpackers guesthouses, but if you're on a tight budget, choose your bed carefully – at the cheapie dives catering to oil-rig roustabouts (on and east of Jln South Yu Seng), many of the dreary rooms are windowless and musty, and Miri's brothel business booms at some of the shadier bottom-end digs.

★**Dillenia Guesthouse** GUESTHOUSE $
(☎085-434204; www.sites.google.com/site/dilleniaguesthouse; 1st fl, 846 Jln Sida; dm/s/d/f incl breakfast, without bathroom RM30/50/80/110; ❄@📶) This super-welcoming hostel, with 11 rooms and lots of nice little touches like plants in the bathroom, lives up to its motto, 'a home away from home'. Incredibly helpful Mrs Lee, whose beautiful embroidered quilts adorn the walls, is an artesian well of travel information and tips – and even sells leech socks (RM20).

Coco House GUESTHOUSE $
(☎085-417051; www.cocodive.com.my; Lot 2117, Block 9, Jln Miri Pujut; incl breakfast dm/s/d RM35/55/80; ❄@📶) Coco House has bright, modern dorms with pod-like bunks and private rooms that are small but functional with splashes of colour. The spotless bathrooms have rainwater shower heads and there is a comfy common area with books, boardgames, DVDs and a microwave for heating food. There is talk of putting a barbecue on the roof terrace.

My Homestay GUESTHOUSE $
(☎085-429091; staymyhomestay.blogspot.com; Lot 1091, Jln Merpati; incl breakfast dm RM35, d RM55-120; ❄@📶) A friendly place in a good location with a spacious balcony overlooking the bustling street below. Most rooms, though clean and colourful, are windowless and a little stuffy. Prices are higher at weekends.

Next Room Guesthouse GUESTHOUSE $
(☎085-411422, 085-322090; 1st & 2nd fl, Lot 637, Jln North Yu Seng; incl breakfast dm RM28, d without bathroom RM55-85, d with bathroom RM85-95; ❄@📶) In the heart of Miri's dining and drinking district, this cosy establishment offers 13 rooms, a small kitchen, a DVD lounge and a great rooftop sundeck. Dorm rooms are pretty packed, with eight or 12 beds. Light sleepers be warned: the nightclub across the street pumps out music until 2am.

TreeTops Lodge LODGE $$
(☎019-865 6240; www.treetops-borneo.com; Lot 210, Kampung Siwa Jaya; d with air-con RM129-159, with fan & without bathroom RM99; ❄📶🏊) This

mellow lodge surrounded by tropical fruit trees, run by Mike (a retired British pilot) and his Sarawakian wife Esther, has eight rooms – four of them in a basic wooden longhouse – set in a lovely, calming garden. Located in a small village 15km southwest of Miri along the coastal road to Bintulu; a taxi from Miri costs RM60.

There isn't much to do here besides take a walk to the nearby beach (2km away) or relax; nearby sights are difficult to reach without your own transport, but the lodge has cars available for hire (RM100 per day). A light lunch (RM12) and simple dinner (RM24) are served in a rustic wooden shelter overlooking the gardens. Bring insect repellent.

Imperial Hotel HOTEL **$$**
(085-431133; www.imperialhotel.com.my; Jln Post; incl breakfast d RM260-560, ste RM680-4000;) The city centre's poshest hotel boasts 23 floors, 266 rooms, business and fitness centres, a sauna and a swimming pool.

Mega Hotel HOTEL **$$**
(085-432432; www.megahotel.com.my; Lot 907, Jln Merbau; d RM330-380, ste RM700-4700; @) Don't judge a hotel by its tacky lobby – the 239 rooms here, spread over 16 storeys, are comfortable and spacious, if a bit old-fashioned. Amenities include a fitness centre (7th floor) and a 30m pool with sea views and a jacuzzi (4th floor). Promotional rates offer hefty discounts on prices quoted here.

Eating

★Summit Café DAYAK **$**
(019-885 3920; Lot 1245, Centre Point Commercial Centre, Jln Melayu; meals RM8-15; 7am-4pm Mon-Sat;) If you've never tried Kelabit cuisine, this place will open up whole new worlds for your tastebuds. Queue up and choose from the colourful array of 'jungle food' laid out at the counter, including *dure* (fried jungle leaf), minced tapioca leaves, and *labo senutuk* (wild boar). The best selection is available before 11.30am – once the food runs out it closes.

Owner and chef Sally Bungan Bat uses only Bario salt and homegrown highland rice.

Khan's Islamic Restaurant INDIAN **$**
(012-878 9640; 229 Jln Maju; mains RM6-12; 6.30am-9pm;) This simple canteen is one of Miri's best North Indian eateries, serving up mouth-watering tandoori chicken (RM12), naan bread and mango lassi (RM4) as well as a variety of curries and vegetarian dishes.

Madli's Restaurant MALAYSIAN **$**
(085-426615; www.madli.net; Lot 1088, ground fl, Block 9, Jln Merpati; mains RM6-18.50; 8am-midnight Sun-Thu, 8am-1am Fri & Sat;) A long-running family business that started off as a satay stall in the 1970s; the first of three restaurants was opened in Miri in 1995. As well as lip-smackingly good chicken and lamb satay (RM1 per stick), the menu includes Malaysian dishes like *nasi lemak* and *kampung* (village) fried rice. Serves *roti canai* and Western breakfasts until noon.

Muara Restoran INDONESIAN **$**
(016-882 7370; Jln North Yu Seng; mains RM5-15; 11am-4am) Expat Indonesian oil workers in bright-yellow overalls flock to this tin-roofed shed for *lalapan* (tofu, tempeh, meat, spinach-like greens, raw cucumber and rice, eaten with spicy *sambal belacan*). Good for a late-night meal.

Miri Central Market HAWKER **$**
(Pasar Pusat Miri; Jln Brooke; mains RM2-6; 24hr, most stalls 4am-noon) Of the Chinese food purveyors selling *kari ayam* (chicken curry), porridge and the usual rice and noodle dishes, stall 6 (open 3.30am to 10am) is particularly popular. Stall 20 serves up vegetarian fare.

Persiaran Kabor CHINESE **$**
(Persiaran Kabor btwn Jln Duranta & Jln Cythulla; mains RM3-4.50; 6am-6pm) Come midmorning this atmospheric, covered courtyard, known locally as Old Folks' Street, is full of men of a certain vintage who congregate here to drink coffee, read the paper and play chess (the Chinese Chess Association is located in one of the shop lots). The surrounding coffee shops sell the usual rice and noodle dishes.

Tamu Muhibbah MARKET **$**
(Jln Padang; 2am-6pm or 7pm) Fruit and veggies, some straight from the jungle, are sold at stalls owned by Chinese, Malay, Iban and Orang Ulu people.

Rainforest Cafe CHINESE **$$**
(085-426967; 49 Jln Brooke; mains RM10-30; 10.30am-2pm & 5-11pm) Often packed with families tucking into a banquet of shared dishes, this breezy, open-air eatery specialises in Chinese-style dishes such as 'braised rainforest bean curd', 'crispy roasted chicken' and 'pork leg Philippine style'.

Meng Chai Seafood SEAFOOD $$
(085-413648; 11A Jln Merbau; meals from RM25; 4pm-midnight) Discerning locals crowd this first-rate eatery, housed in two and unassuming adjacent buildings. There is no menu here – make your selection from the fishy candidates lined up on ice, decide how you would like it cooked and order any accompaniments such as rice or *midin* (fern). Seawater tanks hold live clams and prawns. Servings of fish are priced by weight.

Drinking

Ming Cafe BAR
(085-422797; www.mingcafe.com.my; cnr Jln North Yu Seng & Jln Merbau; 10am-2am) This ever-busy corner bar stocks 16 imported bottled beers and has six on tap, including Guinness. The hefty menu also lists Australian and New Zealand wines and has a cocktail list covering several pages. Fresh juices and shakes cost RM5 to RM12. Also serves food ranging from Chinese, Malay and Indian to pizzas and burgers (RM5 to RM30).

Attracts a mixed crowd of local and expat drinkers and diners.

Soho Bar & Bistro BAR
(016-414 8883; Jln North Yu Seng; 4pm-2am, happy hr 4-9pm) A vast, sportsbar-style place with outdoor seating at wooden tables and big screens showing football. Happy-hour offers include Tiger or Heineken beer towers (RM99 for one, RM180 for two). Also serves meals and bar snacks such as chicken wings, nachos and the house speciality 'Soho shrimp cocktail' served in a martini glass.

Shopping

Miri Handicraft Centre HANDICRAFTS
(cnr Jln Brooke & Jln Merbau; 9am-6pm) Thirteen stalls, rented from the city, sell colourful bags, baskets, sarongs, textiles etc made by Iban, Kelabit, Kenyah, Kayan, Lun Bawang, Chinese and Malay artisans. Stall No 7 has some fine Kelabit beadwork from Bario. Some stalls are closed on Sundays.

Popular Book Store BOOKS
(2nd fl, Bintang Plaza, Jln Miri Pujut; 10am-10pm) A mega-bookshop with a large selection of English books, and Lonely Planet titles in English and Chinese.

Bintang Plaza MALL
(Jln Miri Pujut; 10am-10pm) A modern, multi-storey, air-con mall with shops specialising in computers and cameras on the 3rd floor. Rainy-day entertainment comes in the form of **Megalanes East Bowling Alley** (3rd fl, Bintang Plaza; per game RM5.90-7.90, shoes RM3; 9am-11.45pm) and a **cinema** (gsc.com.my; 4th fl, Bintang Plaza; adult RM7.50-11.50, children RM6.50).

Sin Liang Supermarket FOOD & DRINK
(Jln Duranta; 8.30am-9pm) Well stocked with snacks, toiletries and Aussie wines. A good place to pick up supplies for a trek in Mulu or the Kelabit Highlands.

Miri Central Superstore SHOES
(998 Jln Raja; 8am-6pm) Sells rubber 'kampung shoes' (RM7.50), which are perfect for jungle hikes.

Information

For some great tips and an outline of local history, see Miri's unofficial website, www.miriresortcity.com.

ATMs can be found at the airport and all over the city centre.

It's a good idea to stock up on first-aid supplies before heading inland to Gunung Mulu National Park or the Kelabit Highlands.

INTERNET ACCESS

Sky Garden Cyber Cafe (085-418331; 1285 1st fl, 14B Jln Parry; per hr RM3; 9.30am-noon Sun-Thu, 9am-2am Fri & Sat) Plenty of computers, coffee and snacks.

LAUNDRY

EcoLaundry (085-414266; 638 Jln North Yu Seng; per kg RM6; 7am-6pm Mon-Sat, to 5pm Sun) Free pick up and delivery within the town centre.

MEDICAL SERVICES

Colombia Asia Hospital (085-437755; www.columbiaasia.com; Lot 1035-1039 Jln Bulan Sabit; 24hr) A 35-bed private hospital with a 24-hour accident and emergency ward and a 24-hour ambulance. Situated 4km northeast of the city centre.

Miri City Medical Centre (085-426622; 916-920 Jln Hokkien; emergency 24hr) Has an ambulance service, a 24-hour accident and emergency department and various private clinics. Located in the city centre.

POST

Main Post Office (085-433423; Jln Post; 8am-4.30pm Mon-Fri, to 12.30pm Sat)

TOURIST INFORMATION

National Park Booking Office (085-434184; www.sarawakforestry.com; 452 Jln Melayu; 8am-5pm Mon-Fri) Inside the Visitors Information Centre. Has details on

Sarawak's national parks and can book beds and rooms at Niah, Lambir Hills and Similajau (but not Gunung Mulu).

Visitors Information Centre (☎085-434181; www.sarawaktourism.com; 452 Jln Melayu; ⏲8am-5pm Mon-Fri, 9am-3pm Sat, Sun & public holidays) The helpful staff can provide city maps, information on accommodation and a list of licensed guides. Situated in a little park.

VISAS

Immigration Department (Jabatan Imigresen; ☎085-442112; www.imi.gov.my; 2nd fl, Yulan Plaza, cnr Jln Kingsway & Jln Brooke; ⏲7.30am-5.30pm Mon-Thu, 8am-12.15pm & 2.45-5.30pm Fri) For visa extensions.

Getting There & Away

Miri is 212km northeast of Bintulu and 36km southwest of the Brunei border.

AIR

Miri's **airport** (www.miriairport.com; Jln Airport) is 10km south of the town centre.

There is a separate check-in area for MASwings 'Rural Air Service' which includes flights to Bario. If you are flying on a Twin Otter plane you'll be asked weigh to yourself on giant scales while holding your carry-on.

AirAsia (☎600 85 8888; www.airasia.com; Lot 946, Jln Parry; ⏲8.30am-5.30pm Mon-Fri, to 1pm Sat) Flights to Kuching, Kuala Lumpur, Singapore, Kota Kinabalu, Penang and Johor Bahru.

Malaysia Airlines (☎085-414155; www.malaysiaairlines.com; Lot No 10635 Airport Commercial Centre, Jln Airport) Daily flights to Kuala Lumpur. Office at airport.

MASwings (☎085-423500; www.maswings.com.my; ground fl, airport terminal; ⏲6am-9pm) The Malaysia Airlines subsidiary MASwings has flights within Sarawak to Mulu (for Gunung Mulu National Park), Kuching, Bintulu, Sibu, Lawas, Marudi and Limbang, and to Kota Kinabalu in Sabah. It also serves Sarawak's remote, rural communities of Bario, Ba Kelalan, Long Akah, Long Banga, Long Lellang, Mukah and Long Seridan.

BUS & VAN

Long-distance buses use the Pujut Bus Terminal, about 4km northeast of the centre.

About once an hour, buses head to Kuching (RM60 to RM90, 12 to 14 hours, departures from 7.15am to 8.30pm) via the inland (old) Miri–Bintulu highway, with stops at Lambir Hills National Park, Batu Niah Junction (access point for Niah National Park; RM10 to RM12, 1½ hours), Bintulu (RM20 to RM27, 3½ hours) and Sibu (RM40 to RM50, seven to eight hours). This route is highly competitive, so it pays to shop around. Taking a spacious 'VIP bus', with just three seats across, is like flying 1st class. Companies include **Bintang Jaya** (☎Kuching 082-531133, Miri 085-432178; www.bintangjayaexpress.com) and **Miri Transport Company** (MTC; ☎in Kuching 082-531161, in Miri 085-434161; www.mtcmiri.com).

Bintang Jaya also has services northeast to Limbang (RM45, four hours), Lawas (RM75, six hours) and Kota Kinabalu (KK; RM90, 10 hours). Buses leave Miri at 8.30am; departures from KK are at 7.30am. Borneo Express serves the same destinations at 7.45am; departures from KK are also at 7.45am. With both these companies, getting off in Brunei is not allowed.

Getting Around

TO/FROM THE AIRPORT

A taxi from the airport to the city centre (15 minutes, in traffic 25 minutes) costs RM25; a *kupon teksi* (taxi coupon) can be purchased at the taxi

GETTING TO BRUNEI: MIRI TO BANDAR SERI BEGAWAN

Getting to the border The only company that's allowed to take passengers from Miri's Pujut Bus Terminal to destinations inside Brunei is **PHLS Express** (☎in Brunei +673 277 1668, in Miri 085-438301), which sends buses to BSB (RM50) via Kuala Belait (RM38) and Seria (RM38) at 8.15am and 3.45pm. Tickets are sold at the Bintang Jaya counter. Another option for travel between BSB and Miri is a private transfer (which may be shared with other travellers) run by father-and-son team Mr Fu and Ah Pau (RM70 per person, three hours) Call Mr Fu on ☎013-833 2231.

At the border Border formalities are usually quick, and for most nationalities Bruneian visas are free, but the process can slow down buses. If you're eventually headed overland to Sabah, make sure you have enough pages in your passport for 10 new chops (stamps).

Moving on Brunei's Serasa Ferry Terminal, 20km northeast of BSB, is linked by ferry with Pulau Labuan, from where boats go to Kota Kinabalu in Sabah. Several buses a day go from BSB to Sarawak's Limbang Division and destinations in Sabah.

desk just outside the baggage-claim area (next to the car-rental desks). If you're heading from town to the airport, the fare is RM22. There is no public transport from the airport.

BUS

Local bus transport in Miri is handled by three companies: Miri City Bus, Miri Transport Company (MTC) and Miri Belait Transport. The **local bus station** (Jln Padang), next to the Visitors Information Centre, has schedules posted. Fares start at RM1; most lines run from 7am to about 6pm.

Buses 20 and 33A link the local bus station with Pujut Bus Terminal (RM1.60 to RM2.60, hourly until 6.30pm).

CAR

Most of Miri's guesthouses are happy to organise private transport to area destinations such as Lambir Hills National Park (RM85 return) and Niah National Park (RM240 return).

FT Car Rental (☎085-438415; www.ftcarrental.com; 3rd fl, Soon Hup Tower, Jln Maju) Also has a counter at Miri airport.

Golden System Car Rental (☎085-613359, 012-874 1200; www.gocar.com.my; counter 3, ground fl, Miri airport) Prices start at RM100 per day or RM500 per week.

Hertz (☎085-614740; www.hertz.com; arrivals hall, Miri airport; ⏱8am-5pm Mon-Sat) Has a range of vehicles available for hire.

Kong Teck Car Rental (☎085-617767; www.kongteck.com.my; arrivals concourse, Miri airport) Prices start at RM120 per day or RM600 per week.

My Homestay Motorcycle & Car Rental (☎085-429091; staymyhomestay@gmail.com; Jln Merpati) Offers car and motorcycle rentals.

TAXI

Taxi ranks are sprinkled around the city centre. A short cab ride around downtown is RM12, while a ride from the centre to the Pujut Bus Terminal costs RM20. Taxis run by the **Miri Taxi Association** (☎085-432277; ⏱24hr) can be summoned by phone 24 hours a day.

NORTHEASTERN SARAWAK

Gunung Mulu National Park

Also known as the **Gunung Mulu World Heritage Area** (☎085-792300; www.mulupark.com; 5-day pass adult/child RM30/10; ⏱HQ office 8am-5pm), this park is one of the most majestic and thrilling nature destinations anywhere in Southeast Asia. No surprise, then, that Unesco declared it a World Heritage Site in 2005.

Few national parks anywhere in the world pack so many natural marvels into such a small area. Home to caves of mind-boggling proportions, otherworldly geological phenomena such as the Pinnacles, and brilliant old-growth tropical rainforest (the park has 17 different vegetation zones), this is truly one of the world's wonders.

Among the remarkable features in this 529-sq-km park are its two highest peaks, Gunung Mulu (2376m) and Gunung Api (1710m). In between are rugged karst mountains, deep gorges with crystal-clear rivers, and a unique mosaic of habitats supporting fascinating and incredibly diverse wildlife. Mulu's most famous hiking attractions are the **Pinnacles**, a forest of razor-sharp limestone spires, and the so-called **Headhunters' Trail**, which follows an old tribal war path down to Limbang.

Some cave tours (especially the more difficult ones) and treks (especially the longer ones) may be booked out well in advance.

Sights & Activities

When you register, park staff will give you a placemat-sized schematic map of the park on which you can plan out your daily activities. HQ staff are generally very helpful in planning itineraries and are happy to accommodate special needs and interests like family-friendly activities.

The park's excellent website and the brochures available at park HQ have details of the full range of tours and activities available.

Mulu Discovery Centre MUSEUM
(Gunung Mulu National Park HQ; ⏱8am-6pm) FREE Offers a fine introduction to the park as a 'biodiversity hotspot' and to its extraordinary geology. Situated in the HQ building, between the park office and Café Mulu.

Activities Without Guides

Visitors are not allowed to go inside any of the caves without a qualified guide, but you can take a number of **jungle walks** unaccompanied so long as you inform the park office (or, when it's closed, someone across the path in the park security building). The trails are well marked and interconnected, so by using the park's map it's easy to join them up to create your own route.

GUIDES, RESERVATIONS & FEES

For almost all of the caves, walks and treks in **Gunung Mulu National Park** (Gunung Mulu World Heritage Area; ☎085-792300; www.mulupark.com; for five calendar days RM30), visitors must be accompanied by a guide licensed by Sarawak Forestry, generally supplied either by the park or by an adventure-tour agency (such as those based in Kuching, Miri or Limbang). Tours and activities booked directly through the park are cheaper and are often booked up well in advance; agencies charge considerably more but also supply extras, such as meals, and can often offer more flexibility when it comes to advance booking.

If you've got your heart set on **adventure caving**, or on trekking to the **Pinnacles** or up to the summit of **Gunung Mulu**, advance reservations – by phone or email (enquiries@mulupark.com) – are a must. They're doubly important if you're coming in July, August or September, when some routes are booked out several months ahead, and are essential if your travel dates are not flexible. If this is your situation, don't buy your air tickets until your trek or caving dates are confirmed.

That's not to say a last-minute trip to Mulu is impossible. The park may be able to reassign guides to accommodate you, so it's worth getting in touch. And if you are able to spend a week or so hanging out at the park (this usually means staying in a basic guesthouse outside the park's boundaries as in-park accommodation is in very short supply), trekking and caving slots do sometimes open up.

The park's own trekking and caving guides are well trained and speak good English, but there are only about 15 of them. Some travellers hire a freelance guide unattached to a tour agency, usually from a nearby village. Despite being licensed by Sarawak Forestry (they wouldn't be allowed to operate in the park if they weren't), such guides' nature knowledge and English skills vary widely, from excellent to barely sufficient. In addition, they may lack safety training and equipment (such as two-way radios, which the park supplies to all of its own guides) and, perhaps most importantly, are unlikely to have proper insurance, a factor that could be crucial if a helicopter evacuation is necessary.

A caving group must consist of at least four participants (including the guide) so that if someone is injured, one person can stay with them and the other two can head out of the cave together to seek help.

Park prices for caving and treks are on a straight per-person basis (minimum three people).

Paku Valley Loop WALKING

An 8km loop through the forest that passes alongside the Melinau River to the **Paku Waterfall** (3km) where it's possible to swim. The walk takes five to six hours at an easy-going pace.

Botanical Heritage Trail WALKING

This easy 1.5km boardwalk loop has accessible information panels on many of the fascinating plants it passes as it winds through the forest.

Tree Top Tower BIRDWATCHING

FREE Basically a 30m-high bird hide. The best time to spot our feathered friends is early in the morning (5am to 9am) or in the late afternoon and early evening (4pm to 8pm). Reserve a time slot and pick up the key (deposit RM50) at park HQ or, after 4.30pm, from Park Security (across the boardwalk from the park office). Situated about 500m from park HQ.

Guided Forest Walks

Garden of Eden Valley Walk WALKING

(per person RM140; ⏲9.30am-5pm) This memorable day hike takes you through the 2km-long **deer cave** to a seemingly enchanted, enclosed valley. There is a certain amount of walking on bat guano, scrambling over slippery rocks and wading through streams (rubber shoes are best; sandals are not suitable), but emerging into lush green forest surrounded by limestone is a fine reward.

A jungle trail leads up to a **waterfall** and **rock pools** perfect for swimming. Since the only way into – and out of – the garden of Eden is through the deer cave, you need to retrace your step back through the cave to the bat observatory where the walk ends in time to watch the bat exodus at dusk.

The price includes a packed lunch and afternoon tea.

Night Walk WALKING

(per person RM 20; ⌚7pm or 7.30pm, cancelled if raining) This 1½- to two-hour walk wends its way through alluvial forest. Creatures you're likely to see – after the guide points them out – include tree frogs just 1cm long, enormous spiders, vine snakes that are a dead ringer for a vine, and stick insects (phasmids), extraordinary creatures up to 30cm long that look like they've been assembled from pencils and toothpicks.

If you put your torch (bring one!) up to eye level and shine it into the foliage, the eyes of spiders and other creatures will reflect brightly back. Don't wear insect repellent or you risk repelling some of the insects you're trying to see. Mosquitoes are not a problem.

If you order dinner at the Wild Mulu Café before heading out, you can pick it up when you return (make sure you're back before 9.30pm). Eateries outside the park stay open later.

You can take the night walk trail on your own, without a guide after 8pm – make sure you inform either the park office or, when it's closed, someone in the park security pavilion. Between 5pm and 8pm, you can design your own night walk by taking trails the guided group isn't using.

Mulu Canopy Skywalk WALKING

(per person RM42.40; ⌚7am, 8.30am, 10am, 10.30am, 1pm & 2pm) Mulu's 480m-long skywalk, unforgettably anchored to a series of huge trees, has excellent signage and is one of the best in Southeast Asia. Often gets booked out early – for a specific time slot, reserve as soon as you've got your flight.

Climbing up into the rainforest canopy is the only way to see what a tropical rainforest is all about because most of the flora and fauna do their thing high up in the trees, not down on the ground, where less than 2% of the forest's total sunlight is available. Your guide can help point out the nuances of the surrounding forest, including traditional medicine plants that are still gathered and used in the nearby Penan settlement.

Show Caves

Mulu's 'show caves' (the park's name for caves that can be visited without specialised training or equipment) are its most popular attraction and for good reason: they are, quite simply, awesome.

Deer Cave & Lang Cave CAVE

(per person RM30; ⌚2pm & 2.30pm) A 3km walk through the rainforest takes you to these adjacent caverns. The Deer Cave – over 2km in length and 174m high – is the world's largest cave passage open to the public, while the Lang Cave – more understated in its proportions – contains interesting stalactites and stalagmites. Be sure to stay on for the 'bat exodus' at dusk.

The Deer Cave is home to two million to three million bats belonging to 12 species (more than in any other single cave in the world), who cling to the roof in a seething black mass as they gear up for their evening prowl. Every day between 4pm and 6pm (unless it's raining), millions of bats exit the cave in spiralling, twirling clouds that look a bit like swarms of cartoon bees. It's an awe-inspiring sight when viewed from the park's **bat observatory**, a kind of amphitheatre outside the cave. The bats' corkscrew trajectory is designed to foil the dinner plans of bat hawks perched on the surrounding cliffs.

We're not sure who did the calculations or how, but it's said that the Deer Cave's bats devour 30 tonnes of mosquitoes every night. If it's raining, the bats usually stay home because echolocation (the way they find prey) is not very good at homing in on flying insects amid an onslaught of raindrops.

Count on getting back to park HQ at around 7pm; bring a torch for the walk back.

Wind Cave & Clearwater Cave CAVE

(per person incl boat ride RM65; ⌚8.45am & 9.15am) Zipping along a jungle river in a longboat on your way to the caves is not a bad way to start the day. The Wind Cave, named for the cool breezes blowing through it, has several chambers, including the cathedral-like King's Chamber, filled with dreamlike forests of stalagmites and columns. There is a sweaty 200-step climb up to Clearwater Cave and the subterranean river there. The cave itself is vast: more than 200km of passages have been surveyed so far.

After visiting the caves, you can take a dip in the refreshingly cool waters of a sandy swimming spot.

Tours also include a stop at the riverside village of **Batu Bungan**, a Penan settlement set up by the government as part of a campaign to discourage their nomadic lifestyle. Locals sell trinkets and handicrafts.

The Wind Cave and Clearwater Cave tour takes about four hours, leaving time for another cave visit in the afternoon.

Langang Cave CAVE

(per person incl boat RM65; ⌚2pm) Langang Cave can be visited on the park's Fast Lane tour, which passes extraordinary stalactites and stalagmites. Keep an eye out for blue Racer Snakes, and 'moonmilk', a fibrous mineral formation – known to scientists as Lublinite – created when bacteria break down calcite, the main component of limestone. Don't touch it – it's very fragile.

Getting to the cave requires a 20-minute boat ride followed by a 1km walk to the cave entrance. The whole tour lasts three hours.

Adventure Caves

Cave routes that require special equipment and a degree of caving (spelunking) experience are known here as 'adventure caves'. Rosters for the seven half- or full-day options fill up early, so reserve well ahead. Groups are limited to eight participants. Heavy rains can cause caves to flood.

Caving routes are graded beginner, intermediate and advanced; guides determine each visitor's suitability based on their previous caving experience. If you have no background in spelunking, you will be required to do an intermediate route before moving on to an advanced one. Minimum ages are 12 for intermediate and 16 for advanced. Fees include a helmet and a headlamp; bring closed shoes, a first-aid kit and clothes you won't mind getting dirty.

Keep in mind that adventure caving is not for everyone, and halfway into a cave passage is not the best time to discover that you suffer from claustrophobia, fear the dark or simply don't like slithering in the mud with all sorts of unknown creepy crawlies.

Sarawak Chamber CAVING

(per person RM280; ⌚6.30am) This advanced level circuit is very demanding – getting to the entrance of the Good Luck cave involves a three-hour hike and it's an 800m wade through a river channel from there to the chamber. Moving around inside the cave requires some use of fixed ropes. There and back, the whole route takes 10 to 15 hours.

Measuring an incredible 700m long, 400m wide and 70m high, this chamber – discovered in 1981 – has been called the world's largest enclosed space. Don't count on seeing much, though – ordinary lights are no match for the ocean of black emptiness.

Clearwater Connection CAVING

(per person RM200) This 4.8km, four- to eight-hour advanced caving circuit starts at Wind Cave and heads into the wilds of the vast Clearwater Cave system. There's a good bit of scrambling and the route includes a 1.5km river section.

Racer Cave CAVING

(per person RM160) An intermediate caving session with some rope-assisted sections that require a bit of upper-body strength and a fair bit of climbing. It is named after the non-dangerous cave racer snake, which dines mainly on bats. Takes two to four hours.

Trekking & Climbing

Mulu offers some of the best and most accessible **jungle trekking** in Borneo. The forest here is in excellent condition and there are routes for every level of fitness and skill.

Expect rain, leeches, slippery and treacherous conditions, and a very hot workout – carry lots of water. Guides are required for overnights. Book well ahead.

Bring a first-aid kit and a torch.

Pinnacles TREKKING

(per person RM400; ⌚Tue-Thu & Fri-Sun) The Pinnacles are an incredible formation of 45m-high stone spires protruding from the forested flanks of Gunung Api. Getting there involves a boat ride and, in between two overnights at Camp 5 (p183), an unrelentingly steep 2.4km ascent. Coming down is just as taxing, so by the time you stagger back to camp, the cool, clear river may look pretty enticing.

Bring shoes that will give you traction on sharp and slippery rocks, and bedding (many people find that a sleeping bag liner or sarong is sufficient). If you book the tour through the park, you will also need to bring enough food for six meals; it is worth buying supplies in Miri, as the park shop sells only a limited selection of instant noodles and cans. You can buy a packed lunch from the park cafe for the first day, and it may be possible to buy fried rice from staff at Camp 5 (RM10), but don't count on it.

On the way to Camp 5 on day one you can stop off at Wind Cave and Clearwater Cave for a fee of RM30 (if you don't want to see the caves and you are in a group with others who do, you will need to wait for them). From the boat drop-off point it's an 8km hike to Camp 5 along an easy trail (though be prepared for leeches).

Since both nights are spent at Camp 5 you only need to carry a day pack on the Pinnacles climb on day two, but to be sure to bring plenty of water – at least two litres – in two separate containers (one bottle will be left half way up to pick up on the way down), as well as snacks and oral rehydration salts. If it's raining heavily, the guide may deem it necessary to cancel the climb, in which case you will be refunded RM80.

Right from the get-go the trail up to the Pinnacles is steep and rocky. There is plenty of clambering on all fours involved and the rocks are sharp. The final 400m section involves some serious climbing and use of ladders – most of them little more than spaced out metal brackets drilled into the rock, requiring a steady nerve and good balance to avoid falling onto the spikes below. The Pinnacles themselves are only visible from the very top. Factoring in the humidity, the climb is certainly an intense experience, but most people find it rewarding. What's more the trail passes through some gorgeous jungle and there are beautiful views of the valley below – if you dare look up from the track to admire it.

It is possible to continue along the Headhunters' Trail on day three, instead of returning to HQ.

Gunung Mulu Summit TREKKING

(per person RM500, minimum 3 people) The climb to the summit of Gunung Mulu (2376m) – described by one satisfied ascendee as 'gruelling' and, near the top, 'treacherous' – is a classic Borneo adventure. If you're very fit and looking for a challenge, this 24km, three-day, four-night trek may be for you. The climb must be booked at least one month in advance.

Bring proper hiking shoes, a sleeping bag (Camp 4 can get quite chilly, often dropping below 15°C), a sleeping pad (unless you don't mind sleeping on wooden boards), rain gear and enough food for four days. The camps along the way have very basic cooking equipment, including a gas stove. Bring water-purification tablets if you're wary of drinking the rainwater collected at shelters en route.

Near the summit you may spend much of your time inside clouds; a fleece jacket is the best way to ward off the damp and cold. Recent trekkers report having been visited by rats at Camp 3 and by squirrels who were 'keen on noodles' at Camp 4. The steep trail – which is slippery when wet – passes through limestone and sandstone forest. Fauna you might see on the way include gibbons, wild boar and even (possibly) sun bears.

Reaching the summit involves leaving Camp 4 at 3am to arrive at the top in time to see the spectacular sunrise.

Headhunters' Trail TREKKING

The physically undemanding Headhunters' Trail continues on from Camp 5 for 11km in the direction of Limbang and is an overland alternative to flying in or out of Mulu. The park does not offer guided trips along this trail, but several private tour operators do, and it is also (theoretically) possible to do it without a guide.

This backdoor route from Mulu to Limbang takes two days and one night and can be done in either direction, although most people start at the park. After climbing the Pinnacles (p181), it is possible to walk the Headhunters' Trail (unguided) on day three instead of returning back to Park HQ.

From Camp 5, the Headhunters' Trail continues through the forest to Kuala Terikan, from where you'll need to take a boat to Medamit, linked by road with Limbang. If you plan to do this trip without a guide, you must arrange road and river transport ahead of time – Borneo Touch Ecotour (p192) can organise a boat and van in either direction for about RM500. If you are starting in Limbang, remember to contact the park to reserve sleeping space at Camp 5.

The route is named after the Kayan war parties that used to make their way up the Sungai Melinau from the Baram area to the Melinau Gorge, then dragged their canoes overland to the Sungai Terikan to raid the peoples of the Limbang region. New roads mean that the trail is no longer much used, making it more likely to spot wildlife along the way.

Sleeping

Accommodation options range from five-star luxury to extremely basic. Camping is no longer permitted at park HQ, but you can pitch a tent at some of the guesthouses just outside the park (across the bridge from HQ). If you find accommodation within the park is fully booked, don't panic. There is always a bed of some kind available at one of the informal homestays just outside the park gates.

Inside the National Park

Park HQ, a lovely spot set amid semi-wild jungle, has 24-hour electricity and tap water that's safe to drink. All private rooms have attached bathroom. At research time, 12 new longhouse-style rooms were being constructed, which should go some way towards allieviating the accommodation shortage.

Rooms can be cancelled up to 48 hours ahead without penalty, which is why space sometimes opens up late in the game; phone for last-minute availability.

Hostel HOSTEL **$**
(dm incl breakfast RM52) All 20 beds are in a clean, spacious dormitory-style room with ceiling fans.

Garden Bungalows BUNGALOW **$$**
(s/d/tr incl breakfast RM253/294/341; ❄) These eight spacious units, the park's most luxurious accommodation, are light and modern and have their own private verandahs.

Cabins CABIN **$$**
(q incl breakfast RM387 ; ❄) Each of the two cabins has two rooms with four single beds and a huge living room. The minimum number of people per cabin is four (RM387) and the maximum is eight (RM648), with prices for five, six and seven people falling in between.

Longhouse Rooms GUESTHOUSE **$$**
(s/d/tr/q incl breakfast RM209/247/277/313; ❄) There are eight of these, four rooms – which are now starting to look a little dingy – in each of two wooden buildings. Rooms in Longhouse 1 have a double bed and two singles; in Longhouse 2 there are four single beds per room.

Camp 5 HUT **$$**
(per person incl boat ride RM190) A basic wooden 'forest hostel' or large hut divided into four dorms with sleeping platforms and mats, a kitchen (with gas for cooking and boiled water for drinking) and bathrooms with showers. Space is limited to 50 people; reservations are made at the park office. Most people find it's warm enough here without a sleeping bag (a sarong will do).

If you are doing the Pinnacles or Headhunters' Trail you will spend a night at Camp 5, whether you book through the park or a tour operator.

Outside the National Park

Several budget places, unaffiliated with the park, are located just across the bridge from park HQ, along the banks of the Melinau River. Reservations are not necessary, so if you don't mind very basic digs, you can fly up without worrying about room availability.

Mulu River Lodge HOSTEL **$**
(Edward Nyipa Homestay; ☎012-852 7471; dm/d/q incl breakfast RM35/70/140) Has 30 beds, most in a giant, non-bunk dorm room equipped with clean showers and toilets at one end. Electricity flows from 5pm to 11.30pm. One of the few guesthouses outside the park, if not the only one, with a proper septic system. Located a five-minute walk from park HQ, just across the bridge from the entrance.

D'Cave Homestay HOMESTAY **$**
(☎Dina 012-872 9752; beckhamjunior40@yahoo.com; incl breakfast dm RM30, d with/without bathroom RM120/RM80) A friendly, rather ramshackle place with mismatched patterned lino, beds crammed into small rooms and basic, outdoor bathrooms. Owner Dina cooks buffet-style lunches (RM15) and dinners (RM18), has tea and coffee, and has boiled water for water-bottle refills. Situated between the airport and the turning for the park – about a 10-minute walk from each.

Mulu Backpackers GUESTHOUSE **$**
(☎Helen 012-871 2947, Peter 013-846 7250; mulubackpackers@gmail.com; dm incl breakfast RM35) Mulu Backpackers, situated just past the airport, occupies a picturesque spot by the river but is a 15-minute walk from the park. There is a pleasant sheltered outdoor dining area with views of the water and electricity from 6pm to 6am. The 17 beds here are arranged in a large, barn-like space with some randomly positioned partition walls.

AA Homestay HOMESTAY **$**
(☎Albert 017-858 5241, Irene 017-805 3270; marygracealbert@gmail.com; d RM60) The four rooms here, housed in a wooden outbuilding near the family house, have attached bathrooms and mosquito screens. There is electricity from 6pm to about 10.30pm (later on request). Situated about 200m from the park entrance.

Mulu Marriott Resort & Spa RESORT **$$$**
(☎085-792388; www.marriott.com; d/ste incl breakfast from RM640/850; ❄📶🏊) Situated

3km from park HQ, this 101-room, largely wooden complex has been fully refurbished in a way that is both stylish and sympathetic to its jungle surroundings. Rooms come with all the amenities you would expect from a five-star resort and have balconies overlooking the forest or river.

The Balinese-style swimming pool is a real draw here after a sweaty day of caving and hiking. The resort also has its own jetty for river trips that bypass park HQ and go straight to the caves (booked through the hotel for much more than the park tours). A not wholly reliable wi-fi connection is available in the bar area only.

Eating

A handful of tiny shops sell a very limited selection of food items, such as instant noodles. Most food is flown in, which partly explains why prices are significantly higher than on the coast (RM6 for a large bottle of water).

Cooking is not allowed at any park accommodation except Camps 1, 3, 4 and 5.

Café Mulu INTERNATIONAL **$$**
(mains RM12.50-16; ⌚7.30am-8.30pm) This decent cafe serves excellent breakfasts and a varied menu with a few Western items, Indian curries and local dishes including Mulu laksa and *umai* (Sarawak sushi). A beer costs RM12. Staff are happy to prepare packed lunches.

Good Luck Cave'fe Mulu MALAYSIAN **$**
(mains RM8-10; ⌚11.30am-3pm & 5pm-midnight, kitchen closes at 9.15pm) The Good Luck Cave'fe Mulu (geddit?) is located right outside the park gates and stays open later than the park cafe, making it a good dinner option if you come back late from a night walk. Serves the usual noodle and fried-rice dishes. A beer costs RM8.

Information

For sums over RM100, the park accepts Visa and MasterCard. Staff can also do cash withdrawals of RM100 to RM300 (one transaction per day) for a 2% fee, but the machine is temperamental, so try to bring enough cash to cover your expenses (there is no ATM in Mulu).

The shop and cafe area at park HQ has an excruciatingly slow and unreliable wi-fi connection (RM5 per day).

The clinic in the nearby village of Batu Bungan is now staffed by a doctor and has a dispensary.

Getting There & Away

Unless you hike in via the Headhunters' Trail, the only way to get to Mulu is by MASwings plane.

AIR

MASwings (☎085-206900; www.maswings.com.my; ground fl, Mulu airport; ⌚8.30am-5pm) MASwings flies 68-seat ATR 72-500 turboprops to Miri (daily at 10.10am and 2.35pm), Kuching (Monday, Wednesday, Thursday and Saturday at 1.15pm; Tuesday, Friday and Sunday at 3.20pm) and Kota Kinabalu (Monday, Wednesday, Thursday and Saturday at 2.35pm via Miri; Tuesday and Friday at 11.25am; Sunday at 1pm).

Getting Around

Park HQ is a walkable 1.5km from the airport. Vans run by **Melinau Transportation** (☎012-852 6065, 012-871 1372) and other companies meet incoming flights at the airport; transport to park HQ and the adjacent guesthouses costs RM5 per person.

It's possible to hire local longboats for excursions to destinations such as the government-built Penan longhouse village of Long Iman (RM75 per person return, minimum three people), 40 minutes away by river.

Kelabit Highlands

Nestled in Sarawak's northeastern corner, the upland rainforests of the Kelabit (keh-*lah*-bit) Highlands are sandwiched between Gunung Mulu National Park and the Indonesian state of East Kalimantan, and home to the Kelabits, an Orang Ulu group who number only about 6500.

The main activity here, other than enjoying the clean, cool air, is hiking from longhouse to longhouse on mountain trails. Unfortunately, logging roads – ostensibly for 'selective' logging – are encroaching and some of the Highlands' primary forests have already succumbed to the chainsaw.

Bario

POP 1100

The 'capital' of the Highlands, Bario consists of about a dozen 'villages' – each with its own church – spread over a beautiful valley, much of it given over to growing the renowned local rice. Some of the appeal lies in the mountain climate (the valley is 1500m above sea level) and splendid isolation (the only access is by air and torturous 4WD track), but above all it's the unforced hospitality of the Kelabit people that will quickly

DON'T MISS

BARIO'S MYSTERIOUS MEGALITHS

Hidden deep in the jungle around Bario are scores of mysterious megaliths. The Cultured Rainforest Project (www.culturedrainforest.com), led by anthropologist Monica Janowski, involved a recent study of these sites as part of an investigation into how the people of the area interact with the rainforest.

The Kelabits believe in marking the landscape in order to establish rights over it, and these sites are viewed as spiritually significant. The markers include *perupan* (large mounds made from thousands of stones from the river bed), believed to have been built by rich men and women without heirs to bury their possessions and avoid fights breaking out over inheritance.

Pa' Umor Megaliths From Bario it's a 1½-hour walk to Pa' Umor, and another 15 minutes to Arur Bilit Farm, home to **Batu Narit**, an impressive stone carving featuring a human in a spread-eagled position among its designs.

Take the log bridge across the small river to reach **Batu Ipak**. According to legend, this stone formation was created when an angry warrior named Upai Semering pulled out his *parang* (machete) and took a wrathful swing at the rock, cutting it in two.

This circuit should take four or five hours – maybe a tad longer if your guide is a good storyteller.

Pa' Lungan Megaliths The trail from Bario to Pa' Lungan is walkable without a guide. About halfway along you'll see **Batu Arit**, a large stone featuring bird carvings and humanoid figures with heart-shaped faces.

At Pa' Lungan is **Batu Ritung**, a 2m stone table (probably a burial site, although no one is sure). Also near Pa' Lungan is **Perupun**, a huge pile of stones of a type assembled to bury the valuables of the dead who had no descendants to receive their belongings.

If you've got a bit more time, you could consider basing yourself for a day or two in Pa' Lungan, believed by many to produce the very best Bario rice.

win you over. A huge number of travellers find themselves extending their stays in Bario by days, weeks or even years. Do yourself a favour and get stuck here for a while.

Before the Konfrontasi, Bario consisted of only one small longhouse, but in 1963 residents of longhouses near the frontier fled raids by Indonesian troops and settled here for safety.

Except for a few places powered by a small hydroelectric dam and by photovoltaic cells (a large solar farm is planned), Bario has electricity – provided by private generators – only in the evening. It's hard to imagine life in hyper-social Bario without the mobile phone, a technology unknown in these parts until 2009.

Sights & Activities

The area around Bario offers plenty of opportunities for jungle exploration even if you're not a hardcore hiker. The nearby forests are a great place to spot pitcher plants, butterflies and even hornbills – and are an excellent venue for tiger leeches to spot you. Most guesthouses are happy to pack picnic lunches.

Bario Asal Longhouse HOUSE

(admission RM5) This all-wood, 22-door longhouse has the traditional Kelabit layout. On the *dapur* (enclosed front verandah) each family has a hearth, while on the other side of the family units is the *tawa'*, a wide back verandah – essentially an enclosed hall over 100m long – used for weddings, funerals and celebrations and decorated with historic family photos.

A few of the older residents still have earlobes that hang down almost to their shoulders, created by a lifetime of wearing heavy brass earrings. If you'd like a picture, it's good form to chat with them a bit (they may offer you something to drink) and only then to ask if they'd be willing to be photographed. Afterwards you might want to leave a small tip.

Bario Asal has 24-hour electricity (evenings only during dry spells) thanks to a micro-hydro project salvaged from a larger government-funded project that functioned for just 45 minutes after it was switched on in 1999 (it had been designed to operate on a much larger river).

Tom Harrisson Monument MEMORIAL

Shaped like a *sapé* (a traditional stringed instrument), this stainless-steel monument commemorates the March 1945 parachute drop into Bario by British and Australian troops under the command of Major Tom Harrisson. Their goal – achieved with great success – was to enlist the help of locals to fight the Japanese. The statue is across the first bridge heading west from the airport.

After the war, Harrisson stayed on in Borneo and was curator of the Sarawak Museum from 1947 to 1966. During this time, he and his wife Barbara began excavating the Niah caves, leading to the discovery of a 40,000-year-old human skull. For the life story of this colourful and controversial character, see *The Most Offending Soul Alive,* a biography by Judith M Heimann.

Junglebluesdream Art Gallery ART GALLERY

(www.junglebluesdream.weebly.com; Ulung Palang Longhouse; 9am-6pm) Many of artist Stephen Baya's paintings have traditional Kelabit motifs. In April 2013 his colourful illustrations of the Kelabit legend of Tuked Rini were featured at the Museum of Archaeology and Anthropology in Cambridge, England.

Kayaking KAYAKING

(for text messages 019-807 1640; roachas@hotmail.com; per kayak RM60, guide & transport RM200) A typical day trip involves a morning paddle upriver in inflatable kayaks, a barbecue lunch on a sandy river beach and an easy return trip downstream in the afternoon. Transport to the start point close to Pa Umur village is included. Also possible to arrange overnight camping trips in hammocks or tents. Advanced booking preferred.

Prayer Mountain HIKING

From the Bario Asal Longhouse, it's a steep, slippery ascent (two hours) up to the summit of Prayer Mountain, which has a cross that was erected in 1973, thickets of pitcher plants and amazing views of the Bario Valley and of the mixed Penan and Kelabit hamlet of Arur Dalan, with its three defunct wind turbines. Two-thirds of the way up is an extremely rustic church.

Festivals & Events

Bario Food Festival FOOD

(Pesta Nukenen Bario; www.facebook.com/pages/bariofoodfestival; Jul or Aug) Visitors flock to Bario for this three-day culinary festival celebrating traditional Kelabit food cultivation and cooking techniques. Delicacies on offer include plump wiggling grubs known as *kelatang,* river snails *(akep),* wild spinach, asparagus and ginger, and plenty of Bario pineapples.

Sleeping

Bario's various component villages are home to a whopping 19 guesthouses where you can meet English-speaking locals and dine on delicious Kelabit cuisine (accommodation prices almost always include board). Some of the most relaxing establishments are a bit out of town (up to 5km). Air-con is not necessary up in Bario, but hot water – alas, not yet an option – will some day be a nice treat. Almost all rooms have shared bathroom facilities. If you're on a very tight budget, enquire about renting a bed without board.

There is no need to book ahead – available rooms outstrip the space available on flights, and guesthouse owners meet incoming flights at the airport.

BARIO

Libal Paradise GUESTHOUSE $

(019-807 1640; d RM60) Surrounded by a verdant fruit and vegetable garden where you can pick your own pineapples, this sustainably run farm offers accommodation in two neat wooden cabins, each occupying their own idyllic spot in the greenery. Run by Rose and her Canadian husband Stu. From the airport terminal, walk eastward along the road that parallels the runway. Meals cost RM45 per day.

BARIO SALT

Along with pineapples and rice, another of Bario's celebrated local ingredients is salt, produced at the **main tudtu** under an hour's walk from Pa' Umor. Mineral-rich saline water is put in giant vats over a roaring fire until all that's left is high-iodine salt that goes perfectly with local specialities such as deer and wild boar. This traditional production technique is beginning to die out, but in Bario you can still purchase salt made the old way – look for a sausage-shaped 20cm-long leaf (RM17 to RM20).

Junglebluesdream GUESTHOUSE **$**
(☎ 019-884 9892; www.junglebluesdream.weebly.com; Ulung Palang Longhouse, Bario; per person incl meals RM90) Owned by artist and one-time guide Stephen Baya, a Bario native, and his friendly Danish wife Tine, this super-welcoming lodge (and art gallery) has four mural-decorated rooms, good-quality beds and quilts, a library of books on local culture and wildlife and fantastic Kelabit food. Guests can consult Stephen's extraordinary hand-drawn town and trekking maps.

Nancy & Harriss GUESTHOUSE **$**
(Hill View Lodge; ☎ 019-858 5850; nancyharriss@yahoo.com; per person incl meals RM70) This rambling place has seven guest rooms, a lovely verandah, a library-equipped lounge and endearingly tacky floor coverings. Situated 250m along a dirt track south of the main road. Prices include airport transfer.

Bario Asal Longhouse HOMESTAY **$**
(☎ Julian 011-2508 1114; visitbario@gmail.com; per person incl meals RM80; 📶) There are various homestays in this traditional longhouse, including a six-room guesthouse at Sinah Rang Lemulun. Staying at Bario Asal – which is home to 22 families – is a great way to experience longhouse living. Transport from the airport costs RM30.

De Plateau Lodge HOMESTAY **$$**
(☎ 019-855 9458; deplateau@gmail.com; per person incl meals RM100) Situated about 2km east of the centre (bear left at the fork), this two-storey wooden cabin has eight rooms (including six triples) and a homey living room. It is owned by Douglas, a former guide whose son is a big fan of Liverpool FC. Price includes airport pickup.

Ngimat Ayu's House GUESTHOUSE **$$**
(☎ 013-840 6187; engimat_scott@yahoo.com; per person incl meals RM100) This spacious, two-storey family home has five comfortable rooms and paddy-field views. Situated on a slope 200m east of the yellow public library. Rates include transport from and to the airport.

Labang Longhouse Guesthouse GUESTHOUSE **$$**
(☎ 019-815 5453; lucysrb@yahoo.com; per person incl meals RM110) This 15-room, longhouse-style guesthouse, with valley views and a breezy verandah, is full of evocative photographs, each one with a story behind it that owner David will happily share. Prices include airport transport.

RICE & PINEAPPLES

Bario is famous throughout Malaysia for two things: Bario rice, whose grains are smaller and more aromatic than lowland varieties; and sweeter-than-sweet pineapples (RM2.50 in Bario), which are free of the pucker-inducing acidity of their coastal cousins. Outside the Kelabit Highlands, 1kg of Bario rice can cost RM18, and Bario pineapples are usually unavailable at any price.

PA' LUNGAN

Batu Ritung Lodge GUESTHOUSE **$**
(☎ 019-805 2119; baturitunglodge.blogspot.my; Pa' Lungan; per person incl meals RM90) Saupang and Nabu are welcoming hosts at their two-storey wooden lodge built on stilts over a pond, with gorgeous views of the mountains and paddy fields beyond. Plenty of space for larger groups. Meals are cooked using fresh jungle produce.

Mado Homestay HOMESTAY **$**
(☎ 019-854 9700; per person incl meals RM70) This family home is a peaceful spot to relax after a hike. After dinner, host Mado – a guide – likes to sit at the kitchen fire and tell stories of tourists who got lost in the jungle, a warning to anyone thinking of trekking alone.

Eating

Most guesthouses offer full board – almost always tasty local cuisine – but Bario also has several modest eateries. Pasar Bario, the town's yellow-painted commercial centre, is home to two or three **basic cafes** (mains RM6; 7am to about 10pm, closed Sunday morning) selling mainly generic fried noodle and rice dishes, though Kelabit food can sometimes be special-ordered.

Drinking

Finding a beer in Bario can be a bit of a challenge. This is a very evangelical town – you're as likely to hear Christian country music as the sound of the *sapé* (traditional stringed instrument) – so most establishments do not serve alcohol, and some of those that do keep it hidden.

Y2K BAR

(8am-1am) Local men quaff beer (RM4 to RM6) and play pool. Has karaoke in the evening.

Keludai BAR

(mains RM4; noon-1am) An all-wood saloon with beer (RM4), instant noodles, satellite TV and a pool table.

Shopping

Sinah Rang Lemulun HANDICRAFTS

(Bario Asal Longhouse; daily) Sinah sells lovely Kelabit beadwork, all locally made in the longhouse *dapur* (communal verandah). This is a good place to pick up a *kabo'* (RM50 to RM100, depending on the quality of the beads), a beadwork pendant shaped like a little beer barrel that's worn around the neck by Kelabit men.

Y2K FOOD, DRINK

(8am-1am) An old-fashioned, Old West-style general store that sells everything from SIM cards to something called Zam-Zam Hair Oil.

Information

INTERNET ACCESS

Bario Telecentre (www.unimas.my/ebario; Gatuman Bario; per hr RM4 ; 9.30-11.30am & 2-4pm, closed Sat afternoon & Sun) Solar-powered internet access.

MEDICAL SERIVES

Klinik Kesihatan Bario (085-786404, out of hrs emergencies 013-837 1996; Airport Rd intersection; 8am-1pm & 2-5pm Mon-Thu, 8-11.45am & 2.15-5pm Fri, emergency 24hr) Bario's innovative, ecologically sustainable rural health clinic, powered by solar energy, has one doctor, two paramedics, a dispensary (small pharmacy) and a helicopter on standby.

MONEY

At research time there were still no banks, ATMs or credit-card facilities anywhere in the Kelabit Highlands (although there was talk of installing an ATM in Bario), so bring plenty of small-denomination banknotes for accommodation, food and guides, plus some extra in case you get stranded. Commerce is limited to a few basic shops, some of them in Pasar Bario, the yellow commercial centre.

TELEPHONE

The best Malaysian mobile phone company to have up here is Celcom (Maxis works at the airport and in parts of Bario; Digi is useless). The airport has free wi-fi.

USEFUL WEBSITES

The Bario Experience (www.barioexperience.com) Kept up-to-date with the latest info on Bario.

Getting There & Around

AIR

Bario airport (Joanna 013-835 9009;) is linked with Miri twice a day by Twin Otters operated by MASwings (www.maswings.com.my). Weather, especially high winds, sometimes causes delays and cancellations. For flight updates, or if you're having a problem making a flight out of Bario, just ring the friendly staff at the airport.

Twin Otters have strict weight limits, so much so that checked baggage is limited to 10kg, hand luggage to 5kg and passengers themselves are weighed on a giant scale along with their hand-luggage when they check in.

The airport is about a 30-minute walk south of the shophouses, but you're bound to be offered a lift on arrival. As you'll notice, the people of Bario treat the air link to Miri almost like their own private airline and love dropping by the wi-fi-equipped airport terminal to meet flights, hang out with arriving or departing friends, and check emails.

CAR

The overland trip between Bario and Miri, possible only by 4WD (per person RM150), takes 12 hours at the very least and sometimes a lot more, the determining factors being the weather and the condition of the rough logging roads and their old wooden bridges. When things get ugly, vehicles travel in convoys so that when one gets stuck the others can push or winch it out.

In Bario, 4WD vehicles can be hired for RM250 or RM300 a day including a driver and petrol; guesthouses can make arrangements.

BICYCLE

Bike Rental (015-905 671, 013-514 0399; b333solutions_adventures@yahoo.com; per day from RM30) Mountain bikes for hire along with free maps showing suggested cycling routes.

Trekking in the Kelabit Highlands

The temperate highlands up along Sarawak's far eastern border with Indonesia offer some of the best jungle trekking in Borneo, taking in farming villages, rugged peaks and supremely remote Kenyah, Penan and Kelabit settlements. Most trails traverse a variety of primary and secondary forest, as well as an increasing number of logged areas. Treks from Bario range from easy overnight excursions to nearby longhouses to one-week slogs over the border into the wilds of Kalimantan.

While the Highlands are certainly cooler than Borneo's coastal regions, it's still hard work trekking up here and you should be in fairly good shape to consider a multiday trek. Be prepared to encounter leeches – many trails are literally crawling with them. Bring extra mobile-phone and camera batteries as charging may not be possible.

With so many trails in the area, there is ample scope for custom routes and creative planning beyond the most well-known routes.

BARIO TO BA KELALAN

The three- to four-day trek from Bario to Ba Kelalan covers a variety of terrain including paddy fields and primary rainforest – some of it on the Indonesian side of the frontier – and gives a good overview of the Kelabit Highlands.

The first day is an easy walk from Bario to **Pa' Lungan**. If you find a guide to take you from Pa' Lungan, it is possible to do this first day alone. The path follows an open trail for an hour and then continues through the jungle along what used to be the only route between the two villages. With the new logging road connecting Bario with Pa' Lungan, the jungle trail is less used and not as clear as it once was, but armed with directions it's straightforward enough.

From here there are two possible routes to Ba Kelalan. The first involves a night at a jungle shelter at **Long Rebpun** – your guide will find edible jungle mushrooms and ferns to cook for dinner – and on to Ba Kelalan (via Kalimantan) the following day. The alternative route is via the jungle shelter at **Long Pa Diit** and the Kalimantan village

HIRING A GUIDE: THE PRACTICALITIES

With very few exceptions, the only way to explore the Kelabit Highlands is to hire a local guide. Fortunately, this could hardly be easier. Any of the guesthouses in Bario can organise a wide variety of short walks and longer treks led by guides they know and rely on. Some of the best guides for longer treks live in Pa' Lungan, an easy walk from Bario. If you link up with other travellers in Bario or Miri, the cost of a guide can be shared.

Although there's a growing shortage of guides, in general it's no problem to just turn up in Bario and make arrangements after you arrive, especially if you don't mind hanging out for a day or two in Bario. If you're in a hurry, though, or your trip coincides with the prime tourism months of July and August, consider making arrangements with your guesthouse in advance by email or phone.

The going rate for guides is RM120 per day for either a Bario-based day trip or a longer trek. Some itineraries involve either river trips (highly recommended if the water is high enough) or travel by 4WD – naturally, these significantly increase the cost. The going rate for a porter is RM100 a day.

If you are connecting the dots between rural longhouses, expect to pay RM70 to RM80 for a night's sleep plus three meals (you can opt out of lunch and save RM10 or RM15). Gifts are not obligatory, but the people who live in remote longhouses are appreciative if, after you drink tea or coffee with them, you offer RM10 to cover the costs.

If your route requires that you camp in the forest, expect to pay approximately RM120 per night; in addition, you may be asked to supply food, which is provided for both you and your guide when you stay in a longhouse. Equipment for jungle camping (eg a sleeping bag, hammock, mozzie net and bed roll) cannot be purchased in Bario, so it's a good idea to bring your own, though Bario Asal Longhouse may be able to rent it out.

If you're trekking in one direction only (eg Bario to Ba Kelalan), you will need to hire a porter and continue paying the guide and porter's fee while they return home through the jungle (in this scenario, it would take them two days to trek from Ba Kelalan back to Bario). This is so that the guide does not have to spend a night alone in the forest.

Detailed topographical maps of Sarawak exist, but it's nearly impossible to get hold of them. According to one conspiratorial explanation, the government's calculation is that activists will find it harder to fight for native land rights if they lack proper maps.

of **Tanjung Karya** (where it is possible to spend the night at a homestay).

To avoid doubling back, you can trek from Bario to Ba Kelalan and then fly or take a 4WD down to the coast. Remember, though, that you'll have to pay the guide for the two days it will take him to walk back to Bario. It is possible to do the trek in either direction, but finding a guide is much easier in Bario or Pa' Lungan than Ba Kelalan.

BATU LAWI

If you were sitting on the left side of the plane from Miri to Bario, you probably caught a glimpse of the two massive limestone spires known as Batu Lawi, the taller of which soars to 2040m. During WWII they were used as a landmark for parachute drops.

While an ascent of the higher of the two rock formations, known as the 'male peak', is only for expert technical rock climbers, ascending the lower 'female peak' – described by one veteran trekker as 'awe-inspiring' – is possible for fit trekkers without special skills. It's a tough, four- or five-day return trip from Bario. Be prepared to spend the second day passing through areas that have been impacted by logging. Only a handful of guides are experienced enough to tackle Batu Lawi.

GUNUNG MURUD

Sarawak's highest mountain (2423m), part of 598-sq-km **Pulong Tau National Park**, is just begging to be climbed, but very few travellers make the effort to put the trip together. Since 1985, evangelical Christians in the area have made annual pilgrimages up the mountain for prayer meetings.

Gunung Murud is linked by trails with both Ba Kelalan and Bario. From Bario, the more common starting point, a typical return trip takes six or seven days. You can also walk from Bario via Gunung Murud to Ba Kelalan (five days one way), but as you approach Ba Kelalan you'll have to walk along a depressing logging road.

A rough logging road links the base of Gunung Murud with the lowland town of Lawas (five to eight hours by 4WD).

This is an adventure for the fittest of the fit: Planet Borneo Tours (p174) offers a seven-day trek from Ba Kelalan to Bario via Gunung Murud (from RM2567 per person).

> **CROSSING INTO INDONESIA**
>
> Thanks to an agreement between the Indonesian and Malaysian foreign ministries it is possible for Highland residents and tourists to cross from Ba Kelalan into Kalimantan on a trek to Bario (or vice versa), but you must bring your passport (it won't be stamped) and explain your plans. The immigration checkpoint outside Ba Kelalan is not an official border crossing and doesn't issue visas on arrival. If you want to continue your journey into Indonesia, you'll need to get a visa in advance.
>
> Malaysian ringgits are very popular in this remote part of Kalimantan, but US dollars are not.

Ba Kelalan

Known for its rice, organic vegetables and apples, the Lun Bawang town of Ba Kelalan is a popular destination for treks from Bario.

The village is built on a hillside in an attractive valley; when the paddy fields are flooded, the effect of the mirror-like surface reflecting the surrounding mountains is spectacular. This is a deeply religious community; at the head of the large grassy playing field that acts as the town square sits the Borneo Evangelical Mission church, with Sunday services that last most of the day. The church seems incongruously large for such a small town, but at times it is filled to bursting with worshippers who come to Ba Kelalan to climb nearby **Gunung Murud** (2423m), known to some as prayer mountain.

Ba Kelalan is also one of the best places in Sarawak for birdwatching. Twitchers come here to spot ruddy cuckoo doves, oriental bay owls and broadbills, among others.

Sleeping & Eating

Apple Lodge GUESTHOUSE $
(085-435736, 013-286 5656; d RM60-120;)
A long-established guesthouse that was looking a little shabby when we visited, but is nonetheless a welcoming and comfortable place to stay. The owner, Tagal Paran, a former evangelical pastor who is now in his 80s, was the person first responsible for planting apples in Ba Kelalan and establishing the town's annual apple festival.

The walls of the lodge are papered with newspaper articles chronicling the festival's past successes, though sadly it has not been held for several years.

TREKKING WITH THE PENAN

The Penan, an indigenous group that was nomadic – surviving almost exclusively on hunting and gathering – until quite recently, has fared less well than other groups in modern Malaysia. Since independence, the Sarawak state government has often sold off rainforest lands to logging companies and evicted the Penan and other indigenous groups with minimal or no compensation. The **Penan Peace Park** is an unofficial, community-run nature reserve encompassing 18 villages in the remote Upper Baram area with the objective of establishing Penan land rights.

Community-based and sustainably managed, **Borneo Penan Adventure** (www.borneopenanadventure.org) is a pioneering, non-profit tourism initiative that offers intrepid trekkers a rare chance to visit the remote Penan villages of Long Kerong, Long Spigen and Long Sait in the Upper Baram, Penan Peace Park area. The villages are accessible by foot, river or 4WD from the Highland airports of **Long Lellang**, **Long Banga** and **Long Akah** (flights are from Miri with **MASwings**; p192). Itineraries are flexible (the minimum is three nights) and priced accordingly; typical expenses include a guide (RM100 per day), a porter (RM75 per day), boat hire (RM100 to RM250 one-way), hammock hire for jungle camping (RM25 per day) or a homestay (RM65 per person).

Recently returned travellers recommend doing a boat trip and bringing extra food (such as energy bars). There is a community fee of RM50 per person.

Juliasang Homestay HOMESTAY $
(www.homestayborneo.com; incl meals per person RM70) A large family house in the village's grassy main square opposite the church. Electricity from 6pm to 11pm only.

Ponook Santai Café MALAYSIAN $
(mains RM4.50-7; 7pm-midnight) Opposite the airport (on the other side of the runway from the terminal building), this relaxed cafe's speciality is chicken rice. One of the main draws here seems to be the large flat-screen TV, which during our visit was showing Discovery Channel documentaries at full volume.

Getting There & Away

The only way to get from Ba Kelalan to Bario is on foot. A rough, 125km logging road links Ba Kelalan with Lawas (per person RM70 to RM80 by 4WD, seven hours, daily).

It's possible to get from Ba Kelalan to Long Bawan in Kalimantan by motorbike.

MASwings (www.maswings.com.my) flies Twin Otters from Ba Kelalan to Lawas and Miri three times a week.

Limbang Division

Shaped like a crab claw, the Limbang Division slices Brunei in two. Tourism is underdeveloped in these parts, but Bruneians love popping across the border to find shopping bargains, including cheap beer smuggled in from duty-free Pulau Labuan.

The area, snatched from the sultan of Brunei by Charles Brooke in 1890, is still claimed by Brunei.

Limbang

The bustling river port of Limbang (pronounced *lim*-bahng) is something of a backwater, but you may find yourself here before or after taking the Headhunters' Trail to or from Gunung Mulu National Park.

Sights

Limbang's old town stretches inland from riverfront Jln Wong Tsap En (formerly Main Bazaar) and southward along the riverbank.

Limbang Regional Museum MUSEUM
(www.museum.sarawak.gov.my; Jln Kubu; 9am-4.30pm Tue-Fri, 10am-4.30pm Sat & Sun) This small museum features well-presented exhibits on Limbang Division's archaeology, culture and crafts, including Chinese ceramic jars that were a symbol of status and wealth for Orang Ulu communities. It is housed in a Charles Brooke–era fort originally built in 1897 and rebuilt (after a fire) in 1991. Located on the riverbank, about 1km south of the centre.

Limbang Raid Memorial MEMORIAL
(Jln Wong Tsap En) Commemorates four members of the Sarawak Constabulary and five members of the UK's 42 Commando Royal Marines killed during the Limbang Raid of 12 December 1962, which retook the town

from rebels of the pro-Indonesian North Kalimantan National Army. The memorial is 400m south of the centre, on the riverfront across the street from the police station.

Tours

Possible activities around Limbang include canoeing in the Limpaki Wetlands, where proboscis monkeys can sometimes be seen, and a self-spa at the Maritam Mud Spring, 39km outside town.

Borneo Touch Ecotour TREKKING
(013-844 3861; www.walk2mulu.com; 1st fl, 2061 Rickett Commercial Bldg) Run by the dynamic Mr Lim, this local company offers highly recommended treks along the Headhunters' Trail (p182) to or from Gunung Mulu National Park (for three days and two nights, including the Pinnacles: RM1150 per person for a group of two, RM900 per person for a group of three, RM780 per person for a group of four).

Can provide basic lodgings in Limbang (RM30 per person) and arrange for luggage to be sent by air cargo (RM70) so that you don't need to carry it on the trek. Advanced booking recommended.

A half-day trip to the Limpaki Wetlands including transport and two hours' canoeing costs RM60 per person.

Chua Eng Hin HIKING
(019-814 5355; chaulimbang@gmail.com) A well-known local personality with a passion for Limbang District's largely unknown charms. Specialises in climbing tours, but is happy to give advice on other local sights and activities, such as kayaking in the Limpaki Wetlands.

Sleeping

Metro Hotel HOTEL $
(085-211133; Lot 781-782, Jln Bangkita; s/d RM50/60;) Old-school, slightly shabby hotel offering reasonable budget accommodation. Centrally located.

Purnama Hotel HOTEL $$
(085-216700; www.purnamalimbang.com; Jln Buangsiol; s/d incl breakfast RM115/125-175;) Ensconced in Limbang's tallest building (12 storeys), this uninspiring hotel – ornamented with rainbow-hued balconies – has 218 spacious but aesthetically challenged rooms that come with big views and small bathrooms.

Eating

Diyana Cafe INDONESIAN $
(019-486 3342; Jln Wong Tsap Eng; mains RM5-15; 6am-11.30pm Mon-Sun) A buzzing little place with pavement tables and views of the river. Serves up tasty Indonesian fare including *nasi lalapan* (rice, vegetables and tofu served with a spicy sambal sauce).

Chinese Night Market HAWKER $
(Jln Bangkita; mains RM2.50-7; 2-10pm) Ten stalls selling quick, flavoursome bites such as *kolo mee* (RM5) and *wonton mee* (RM5) and fresh juices (RM4) in an attractive covered strip next to the town's football pitch.

Bangunan Tamu Limbang HAWKER $
(Jln Wong Tsap En; mains RM3.50-6; 6.30am-5.30pm) Houses Limbang's wet market, with an upstairs hawker centre where you can try the town's speciality, Limbang *rojak,* a mixed vegetable dish with a thick shrimp-based sauce.

Pusat Penjaja Medan Bangkita MARKET $
(Jln Bangkita; 6am-5pm) Bisaya, Lun Bawang and Iban stallholders sell jungle edibles, sausage-shaped Ba Kelalan salt and a dozen kinds of upland rice. The larger weekly *tamu* (market) takes place all day Thursday and until noon on Friday.

Pasar Malam MARKET $
(Night Market; Jln Wong Tsap En; mains RM3.50-7; 6-11pm) Come evening time the riverfront hawker centre is a good spot for a cheap, tasty meal of the usual Malay fare such as chicken satay, fried rice or noodles.

Information

Limbang has several international ATMs.

Sun City Cybercafe (Jln Bangkita, 1st fl; per hr RM2.50; 8.30am-midnight) A haven for gamers. On the corner of Jln Bangkita and Jln Tarap.

Getting There & Around

AIR

Limbang's small airport is 7km south of the centre. A taxi into town costs RM20. As there are too few taxis to meet flights, your driver may take other passangers in the same car (but still charge you the full rate).

MASwings (085-211086; www.maswings.com.my; Limbang Airport, Jln Rangau; 6.30am-5.50pm) Three flights a day to Miri.

BOAT

Express ferries from Limbang's immigration hall to Pulau Labuan (RM30, two hours, 8am daily) are run by **Royal Limbang** (☎ 013-882 3736). Tickets are sold at the jetty. Departures from Pulau Labuan are at 1.30pm. Bookings can be made by SMS/text message.

BUS

Borneo Express sends a bus to Miri's Pujut Bus Terminal (RM40, four hours) every day at 2.30pm. Tickets are sold at **Hock Chuong Hin Cafe** (Jln Bangkita). **Bintang Jaya** (☎ 016-859 4532) also sends daily buses to Miri (RM40) at 1.45pm, and to Lawas (RM30) and KK (RM50) at 12.30pm. You can buy tickets for Bintang Jaya at the coffee shop two doors up from Hock Chuong Hin Cafe.

A spot in a seven-seater unlicensed van to Miri costs RM50, departing from the tiny old bus station at the eastern end of Jln Wayang, two blocks inland from the river.

The only company that can drop you off inside Brunei is **Jesselton Express** (PHLS; ☎ in Brunei +673-719-3835, +673-717-7755, +673-718-3838, in KK 016-836 0009, in Limbang 016-855 0222, 085-212990), which has daily buses to Bandar Seri Begawan (RM20) at 2.30pm; and to Bangar, Lawas (RM30, two hours) and KK (RM50) at 9.30am. Tickets are sold at **Wan Wan Cafe & Restaurant** (Jln Bangkita). Heading to Limbang, a bus departs from BSB every day at 8am.

TAXI & MINIBUS

Minibuses and red-and-yellow taxis hang out at the **Stesen Teksi** (☎ 085-213781; Jln Wong Tsap En; ⏲ 5am-6pm or later), on the waterfront. If you're heading towards BSB, one-way travel to the Kuala Lurah crossing costs RM60. From there public buses run to BSB until 5.30pm. If you're coming from BSB, taxis wait on the Malaysian side of the Kuala Lurah crossing.

Diving

The waters off northeastern Borneo are as rich in weird and wonderful species as the island's terrestrial habitats. Somewhat wetter and considerably saltier than Borneo's rainforests, these celebrated reefs shelter a mind-boggling variety of corals, fish and marine mammals, offering some of the finest scuba diving in the world.

Borneo's most spectacular reefs fringe a number of tiny islands off the northeast coast. Amid thriving coral, gently waving sea fans and a wealth of sponges, divers often encounter shimmering schools of jacks, bumphead parrotfish and barracudas, and find themselves making the acquaintance of green turtles, dolphins, manta rays and several species of shark. Visibility can reach an incredible 30m to 50m, making the area's famed drop-offs – up to 2000m deep! – a truly breathtaking sight. If you've dreamed of experiencing the extraordinary biodiversity and astonishingly vivid hues of the 'Coral Triangle', Borneo offers some great options for your next underwater adventure.

TOP DIVE SITES

Pulau Sipadan (p33) Legendary for its deep wall dives, Sipadan is a favoured hang-out of turtles, sharks and open-ocean fish.

Layang Layang (p74) A deep-ocean island famed for its pristine coral and 2000m drop-off.

Pulau Mantanani (p74) These isolated, coral-ringed islands are prime habitat for dugongs (sea cows).

Mabul (p99) 'Muck dives' often turn up eels, crabs, squid, octopus and frogfish.

Pulau Derawan & Derawan Archipelago (p265) The area boasts a fantastic assortment of colourful reef fish.

Clockwise from top left
1. Coral reef off Mabul island (p99) **2.** Snorkelling, Semporna Archipelago (p98) **3.** Clown frogfish near Kapalai island (p99) **4.** Diving, Semporna Archipelago (p98)

FOTOTRAV / GETTY IMAGES ©

TIM ROCK / GETTY IMAGES ©

MARK WEBSTER / GETTY IMAGES ©

Culture

Cultural diversity comes naturally to Borneo, where civilisations, languages, religions and culinary traditions have been meeting and mixing for thousands of years. From sophisticated cities with modern urban amenities to remote longhouses on the upland tributaries of mighty rivers, the island's cultural vibrancy never fails to amaze.

Borneo's indigenous peoples, belonging to numerous distinct ethnic groups, but often collectively known as Dayaks, still joke about their headhunting past. Those days are long gone, and today many are working to integrate traditional lifestyles based on sustainability and mutual responsibility with the demands and opportunities of modern life. The best way to experience the traditional lifestyles of indigenous groups is to visit a longhouse.

Many Malays live in picturesque *kampung* (villages) built on stilts over a river or estuary. Halal meals, including a delicious selection of barbecue meat, grilled fish and scrumptious rice and noodle dishes, are available in open-air markets.

Significant Chinese communities are found in many cities and towns. Each dialect group has its own dragon-adorned temples, community festivities and distinct culinary traditions.

1

TOP CULTURAL ATTRACTIONS

Kuching (p122) Borneo's most cosmopolitan city is a laid-back blend of Chinese, Malay, Dayak, Indian and Western culture.

Kelabit Highlands (p184) The area's famously welcoming people are happy to share their traditions and delicious cuisine.

Batang Ai Region (p155) Home to some of Sarawak's most traditional Iban longhouses.

Pegunungan Meratus (Meratus Mountains; p245) Shamans still play an important role in this remote area.

Bandar Seri Begawan (p200) Brunei's traditions live on in the sultanate's water villages and markets.

Clockwise from top left

1. Longhouse (p279), East Kalimantan **2.** Dayak festival, East Kalimantan **3.** Omar Ali Saifuddien Mosque (p200), Bandar Seri Begawan **4.** Tua Pek Kong Temple (p156), Sibu

PETER PTSCHELINZEW / GETTY IMAGES ©

2

BARRY KUSUMA / GETTY IMAGES ©

3

CRAIG PERSHOUSE / GETTY IMAGES ©

Brunei

POP 420,000 / AREA 5765 SQ KM

Includes ➡

Best Places to Eat

- Tamu Selera (p207)
- Pondok Sari Wangi (p208)
- Thiam Hock Restaurant (p209)

Best Places to Stay

- Ulu Ulu Resort (p216)
- Brunei Hotel (p206)
- Sumbiling Eco Village (p215)

Why Go?

Look beneath the surface of this well-ordered and tightly regulated sultanate and you'll see the underlying warmth of Brunei's people and the wildness of its natural environment.

This quiet *darussalam* (Arabic for 'abode of peace') has the largest oilfields in Southeast Asia, and thanks to the money they've generated, Brunei hasn't turned its rainforests into oil palm plantations. Old-growth greenery abounds, especially in verdant Ulu Temburong National Park.

The citizens of the capital, Bandar Seri Begawan (BSB), are mad for food and shopping (booze is banned). Here magnificent mosques contrast with the charmingly haphazard water village, while the nearby mangrove forest is home to proboscis monkeys and crocs.

This tranquil (sometimes somnolent) nation is the realisation of a particular vision: a strict, socially controlled religious state where happiness is found in pious worship and mass consumption. Visit and judge the results for yourself.

When to Go

Bandar Seri Begawan

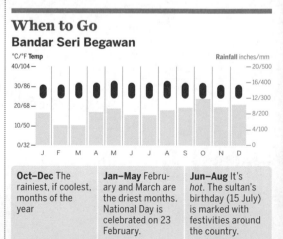

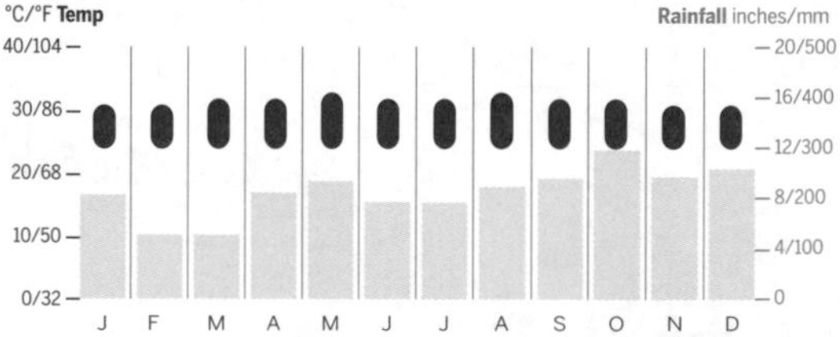

Oct–Dec The rainiest, if coolest, months of the year

Jan–May February and March are the driest months. National Day is celebrated on 23 February.

Jun–Aug It's *hot*. The sultan's birthday (15 July) is marked with festivities around the country.

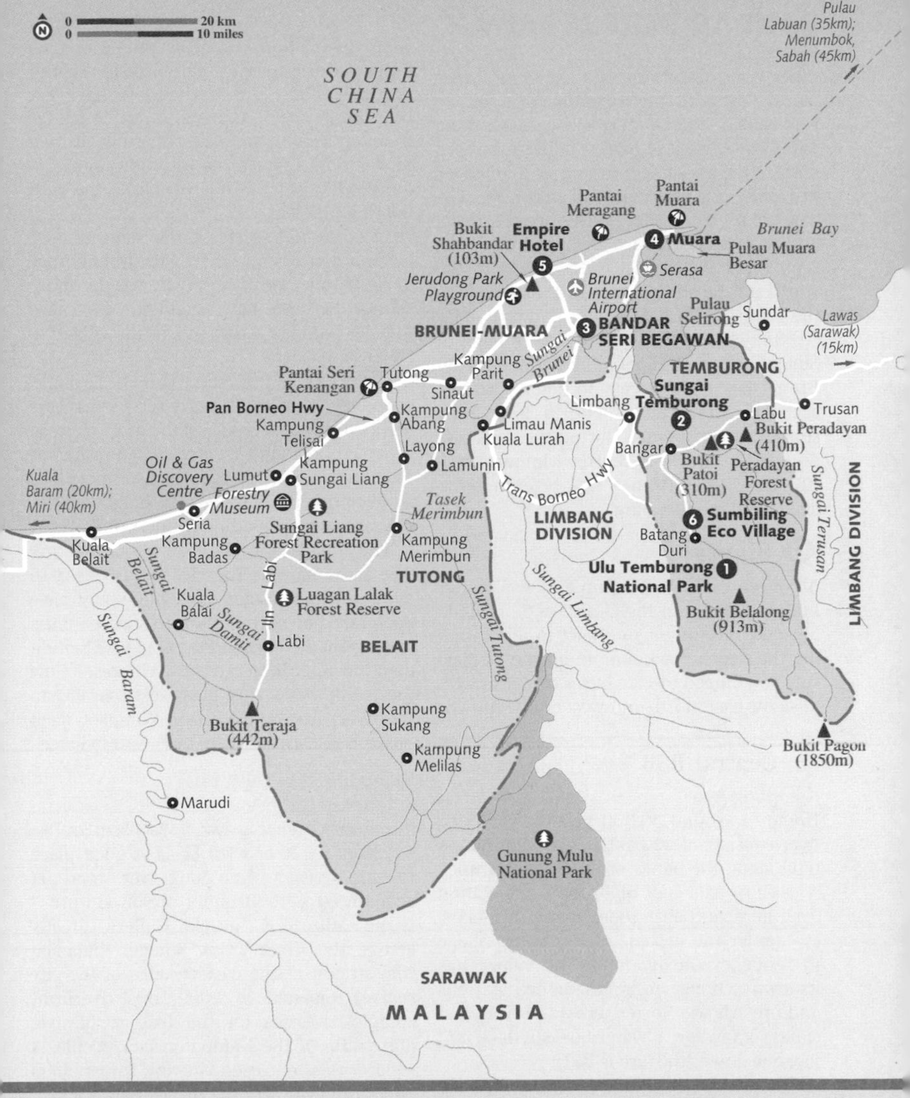

Brunei Highlights

1 Climbing high into the rainforest canopy and swimming in a cool jungle river at **Ulu Temburong National Park** (p216).

2 Tearing along mangrove-lined waterways on a **speedboat** (p214) from BSB to Bangar.

3 Taking a water taxi to the water village of **Kampong Ayer** (p200) and gorging on the culinary delights of **BSB** (p207).

4 Exploring the reefs and wrecks of Brunei's unspoilt **dive sites** (p204).

5 Enjoying the extravagance of the **Empire Hotel & Country Club** (p207) and cooling off in the pool.

6 Relaxing amid rural greenery at **Sumbiling Eco Village** (p215) in Temburong District.

BANDAR SERI BEGAWAN

POP 241,000

Cities built on oil money tend to be flashy places, but with the exception of a palace you usually can't enter, a couple of enormous mosques and one wedding cake of a hotel, Bandar (as the capital is known, or just BSB) is a pretty understated place. Urban life pretty much revolves around malls and restaurants. BSB does have a few museums and the biggest water village in the world, a little slice of vintage that speaks to the Bruneian love of cosiness and nostalgia.

BSB's city centre is on the north bank of Sungai Brunei at a spot – 12km upriver from Brunei Bay – that's easy to defend against seaborne attack and sheltered from both storms and tsunamis. During the Japanese occupation, the city centre – known until 1970 as Brunei Town – was severely damaged by Allied bombing.

Sights

All of central BSB is within easy walking or sailing distance of the Omar Ali Saifuddien Mosque, but unless you don't mind pounding the streets for hours under the tropical sun, you'll need to take buses or taxis to get to sights east, north and west of downtown.

Central BSB

Kampong Ayer WATER VILLAGE

Home to around 30,000 people, Kampong Ayer consists of 42 contiguous stilt villages built along the banks of the Sungai Brunei. A century ago, half of Brunei's population lived here, and even today many Bruneians still prefer the lifestyle of the water village to residency on dry land. The village has its own schools, mosques, police stations and fire brigade. To get across the river, just stand somewhere a water taxi can dock and flag one down (the fare is B$1).

Founded at least 1000 years ago, the village is considered the largest stilt settlement in the world. When Venetian scholar Antonio Pigafetta visited Kampong Ayer in 1521, he dubbed it the 'Venice of the East', which is, as descriptions go, a bit ambitious. The timber houses, painted sun-bleached shades of green, blue, pink and yellow, have not been done-up for tourists, so while it's far from squalid, be prepared for rubbish that, at low tide, carpets the intertidal mud under the banisterless boardwalks, some with missing planks.

In some places smart new houses have been constructed – these sturdy buildings looks better equipped to survive the monsoon storms that have been known to cause flimsier wooden structures in the village to collapse.

If you look to the main roads on the banks opposite the village, you'll see luxury cars lined up on the shoulder of the road; many of these cars belong to water-village residents. That said, Kampong Ayer is also home to a sizable population of the undocumented immigrants who constitute Brunei's underclass.

The villages on the river's **north bank** (the same side as the city centre) used to cover a much larger area, but many have been razed as part of plans to spruce up the waterfront area around the Omar Ali Saifuddien Mosque. To get to these villages, follow the plank walks that lead west (parallel to the river) from the Yayasan Complex, itself built on the site of a one-time water village.

Kampong Ayer Cultural & Tourism Gallery GALLERY

(South Bank, Kampong Ayer; ⌚9am-5pm Sat-Thu, 9-11.30am & 2.30-5pm Fri) FREE A good place to start a visit to Kampong Ayer – and get acquainted with Brunei's pre-oil culture – is the Cultural & Tourism Gallery, directly across the river from Sungai Kianggeh (the stream at the eastern edge of the city centre). Opened in 2009, this riverfront complex focuses on the history, lifestyle and crafts of the Kampong Ayer people. A square, glass-enclosed **viewing tower** offers panoramic views of the scene below.

Omar Ali Saifuddien Mosque MOSQUE

(Jln Stoney; ⌚interior 8.30am-noon, 1.30-3pm & 4.30-5.30pm Sat-Wed, closed Thu & Fri, exterior compound 8am-8.30pm daily except prayer times) FREE Completed in 1958, Masjid Omar Ali Saifuddien – named after the 28th Sultan of Brunei (the late father of the current sultan) – is surrounded by an artificial lagoon that serves as a reflecting pool. This being Brunei, the interior is pretty lavish. The floor and walls are made from the finest Italian

> **FRIDAY OPENING HOURS**
>
> On Fridays all businesses and offices – including restaurants, cafes, museums, shops and even parks – are closed by law between noon and 2pm for Friday prayers.

marble, the chandeliers were crafted in England and the luxurious carpets were flown in from Saudi Arabia. A 3.5-million-piece glass mosaic overlaying real gold leaf covers the main dome.

The mosque's 52m minaret makes it the tallest building in central BSB, and woe betide anyone who tries to outdo it – apparently the nearby Islamic Bank of Brunei building originally exceeded this height and so had the top storey removed by order of the sultan. The ceremonial stone boat sitting in the lagoon is a replica of a 16th-century *mahligai* (royal barge) where Koran-reading competitions were once held.

Come evening, the mosque is basically the happening centre of city life in Bandar; folks come for prayer, then leave to eat or shop, which is sort of Brunei in a nutshell.

Royal Regalia Museum MUSEUM

(Jln Sultan; 9am-5pm Sun-Thu, 9-11.30am & 2.30-5pm Fri, 9.45am-5pm Sat, last entry 4.30pm) FREE When called upon to present a gift to the sultan of Brunei, you must inevitably confront the question: what do you give a man who has everything? At this entertaining museum you'll see how heads of state have solved this conundrum (hint: you'll never go wrong with gold and jewels). Family photos and explanatory texts offer a good overview of the life of the sultan, who is himself depicted in myriad forms (including a hologram) in a series of portraits.

Also on display are the chariot used during the sultan's 1992 silver jubilee procession (the chariot is accompanied by an army of traditionally dressed headless mannequins representing those present on the day) and a second chariot used for the 1968 coronation.

East of Central BSB

Brunei Museum MUSEUM

(Jln Kota Batu; 9am-5pm Sat-Thu, 9-11.30am & 2.30-5pm Fri, last entry 30min before closing; P; 39) FREE Brunei's national museum, with its Islamic-art gallery, has exhibits depicting Brunei's role in Southeast Asian history from the arrival of the Spanish and Portuguese in the 1500s, and a natural-history gallery. It's a decent place to blow an hour of your time. It is 4.5km east of central BSB along the coastal road, at Kota Batu. At research time the museum was closed for ongoing renovations.

The oldest pieces here are ceramics from Iran and Central Asia and blown glass from Egypt and the Levant dating from the 9th and 10th centuries, as well as manuscripts of the Koran, tiny Korans the size of a matchbox and gold jewellery. Don't miss the collection of Brunei's famous ceremonial cannons, known as *bedil*, some with barrels shaped like dragon heads. It was not oil but these bronze-cast weapons that were once the source of the sultanate's wealth and power.

Brunei Darussalam Maritime Museum MUSEUM

(Muzium Maritim; Simpang 482, Jln Kota Batu; 9.30am-4.30pm Sat-Thu, 9am-noon Fri; P; 39) FREE A gleaming building, ship-like in both style and proportion, houses this interesting museum opened in 2015 at Kota Batu, 4.5km east of the city centre (take the 39 bus). On display are some of the more than 13,000 artefacts excavated from a shipwreck discovered by divers in 1997. The ship is believed to have set sail from China sometime in the late 15th or early 16th centuries before being struck by stormy weather as it approached Brunei.

Items exhibited in the well-presented shipwreck gallery include ceramics and glassware from China, Vietnam and Thailand, which would have been brought to Brunei to exchange for local products including spices, rattan, sago and camphor.

RAMADAN RULES

Brunei is an extremely religious, majority-Muslim country that takes Ramadan seriously. Under new laws introduced in 2014 as part of the first phase of the introduction of sharia law, during daylight hours for the month of Ramadan all eating, drinking and smoking in public is illegal. During the day, cafes and restaurants are open for takeaway only (bring food and drinks back to your hotel to consume).

If you're visiting during the holiest month of the Islamic year, it's a good idea to dress conservatively: men and women should cover their shoulders and wear clothes reaching below the knees. Museums close early (at 3pm Saturday to Thursday and noon on Friday) and other businesses may also operate for shorter hours. Mosques are closed to non-Muslim visitors for the whole month.

Bandar Seri Begawan

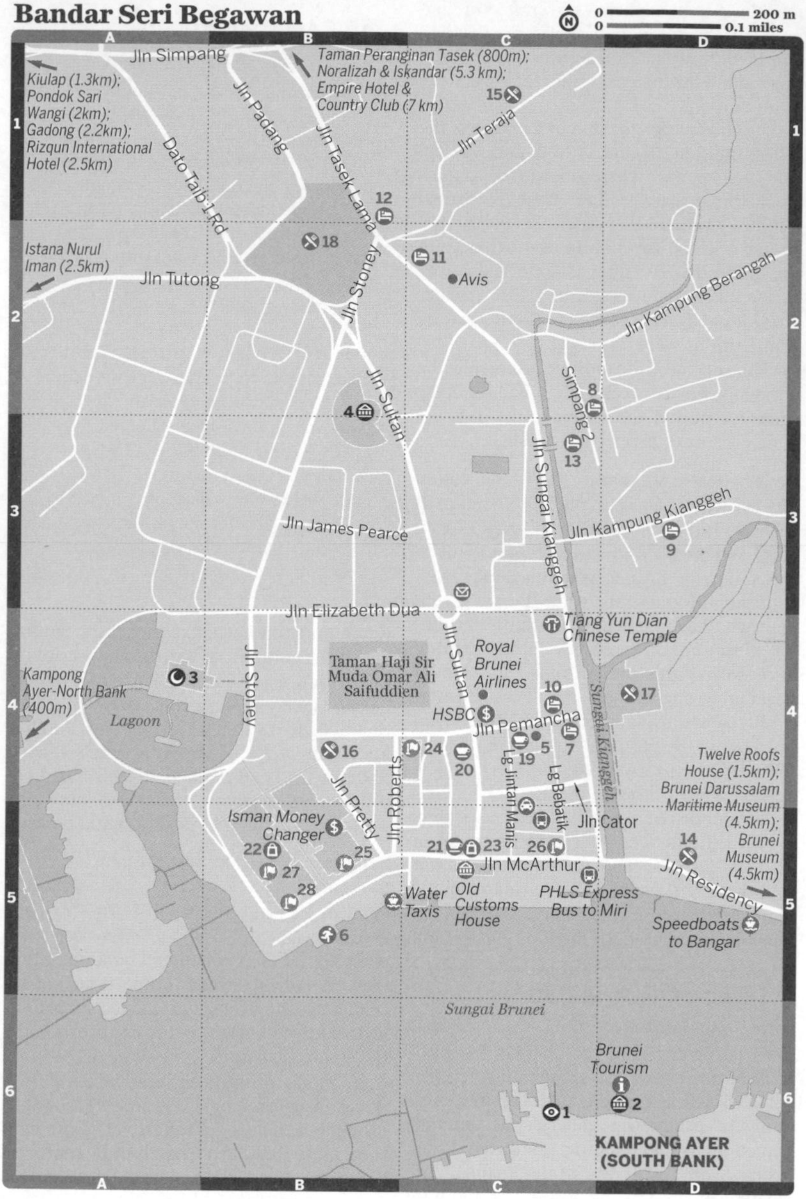

Malay Technology Museum MUSEUM
(Muzium Teknologi Melayu; Jln Kota Batu; ⏲9am-5pm Sun-Thu, 9-11.30am & 2.30-5pm Fri, 9.45am-5pm Sat, last entry 30min before closing) FREE Contrary to its misleading name, this museum focuses not on modern technology but on the traditional lifestyles and practices of Brunei's ethnic groups. The somewhat outdated displays on life in a Malay water village (stilt architecture, boat making, fishing techniques, handicrafts) and a Murut (Lun Bawang) longhouse have a certain charm

Bandar Seri Begawan

Sights
1 Kampong Ayer C6
2 Kampong Ayer Cultural & Tourism Gallery D6
3 Omar Ali Saifuddien Mosque A4
4 Royal Regalia Museum B2

Activities, Courses & Tours
Borneo Guide .... (see 10)
5 Freme Travel Services C4
6 Water-Taxi Cruise B5

Sleeping
7 Brunei Hotel C4
8 Capital Residence Suites C2
9 Jubilee Hotel D3
10 KH Soon Resthouse C4
11 Radisson Hotel C2
12 Terrace Hotel B1
13 Youth Hostel C3

Eating
14 Gerai Makan Jalan Residency D5
15 Lim Ah Siaw C1
16 Seri Damai Restaurant B4
17 Tamu Kianggeh D4
18 Tamu Selera B2

Drinking & Nightlife
19 Another C4
20 De Royalle Café C4
21 Piccolo Café C5

Shopping
22 Hua Ho Department Store B5
23 Paul & Elizabeth Book Services C5

Information
24 Australian High Commission C4
25 British High Commission B5
26 Canadian High Commission C5
27 French Embassy B5
28 German Embassy B5
Paul & Elizabeth Cyber Cafe .... (see 23)

to them. The 39 bus passes along Jln Kota Batu, from where the museum is a five-minute walk down the hill.

Twelve Roofs House MUSEUM
(Bubungan Dua Belas; ☎224 4545; Jln Residency; ⏰9am-4.30pm Mon-Thu, 2.30-4.30pm Fri, Sat 9am-11.30am) FREE The one-time residence of Britain's colonial-era high commissioners, said to be the sultanate's oldest extant building, is now a museum dedicated to the longstanding 'special relationship' between Brunei and the UK. The evocative photos include views of Brunei as it looked a century ago. It's situated 1.5km southeast of the city centre, on a hilltop overlooking the river. When we stopped by in mid-2015 the museum was closed for ongoing extensive structural work (the building had been on the point of collapse).

North & West of Central BSB

Jame'Asr Hassanil Bolkiah Mosque MOSQUE
(Sultan Hassanal Bolkiah Hwy, Kampung Kiarong; ⏰8am-noon, 2-3pm & 5-6pm Mon-Wed & Sat, 10.45am-noon, 2-3pm & 5-6pm Sun, closed Thu & Fri; P) FREE Built in 1992 to celebrate the 25th year of the current sultan's reign, Brunei's largest mosque and its four terrazzo-tiled minarets dominate their surroundings. It's impossible to miss as you head towards Gadong, about 3km from the city centre. The number 1 bus goes here.

It's certainly an impressive building; because the sultan is his dynasty's 29th ruler, the complex is adorned with 29 golden domes. At night the mosque is lit up like a gold flame.

The mosque's interior more than matches its lavish exterior. The sheer volume of it is remarkable, not to mention the myriad woven rugs scattered across the men's prayer hall.

Look out for the sultan's own personal escalator at his private entrance to the mosque.

Istana Nurul Iman PALACE
(Jln Tutong) Istana Nurul Iman (Palace of the Light of Faith), the official residence of the sultan, is one of the largest habitations of any sort in the world – more than four times the size of the Palace of Versailles.

The palace is open to the public during the three-day Hari Raya Aidil Fitri festivities (p204) at the end of Ramadan. The best way to check it out on the other 362 days of the year is to take a water-taxi cruise.

Designed by Filipino architect Leandro Locsin, the palace mixes elements of Malay (the vaulted roofs) and Islamic (the arches and domes) design with the sweep and oversized grandeur of a 200,000-sq-m airport terminal. Nonetheless, it's relatively attractive from a distance or when illuminated in the evening. It is located 3km southwest of the town centre.

Taman Peranginan Tasek PARK
(Tasek Recreational Park; Jln Tasek Lama; ⏲6am-6pm Sun-Thu, 6-11am & 2-6pm Fri; P) If you need a reminder that just beyond BSB's air-conditioned malls lies the Bornean jungle, this city park, with its background chorus of buzzing, chirping and rustling rainforest sounds, should do it. Well-marked paths lead to waterfalls, picnic areas and a hilltop *menara* (tower) offering views of the city and encroaching greenery. There are rougher jungle trails for longer walks (wear proper shoes). The park is 2km north of the city centre.

Muara

Peranginan Pantai Muara BEACH
(Muara Beach Recreational Park; Jln Pantai Muara; ⏲6am-6pm; P) Muara Beach Recreational Park is a popular weekend retreat. It's pretty, but like many beaches in Borneo, it's littered with driftwood and other flotsam that comes in with the tide. Quiet during the week, it has picnic tables and a children's playground. A plaque commemorates the nearby Australian amphibious landings of 10 June 1945.

The beach lies just past Muara town, 27km from central BSB. Take bus 38 to Jln Pelempong, from where it is a 500m walk.

Activities

Diving

Though it's still relatively new, Brunei's burgeoning dive scene has the advantage of having some decent dive operators without the downside of crowds.

There are several interesting wrecks – some dating back to WWII – as well as plenty of undamaged reef here, including patches that are largely unexplored. On most of the shipwrecks and all the coral dive sites there is colourful hard and soft coral, such as large gorgonian fans and wide table corals. Marine life you are likely to see includes cuttlefish, octopus, morays, porcupine fish, giant puffers and sometimes a sea snake or two.

The best time to dive is between March and October; from May to mid-July the conditions are often ideal.

Poni Divers DIVING
(☎223 3655; www.ponidivers.com; Seri Qlap Mall, Unit L3/12, Kiulap; 2 fun dives B$150; ⏲9am-5pm) Brunei's largest dive centre offers a full range of PADI certification courses, recreational dives and various water sports including water skiing and banana boating. Operates from Serasa beach, with a booking office in BSB. Also puts together dive packages including airport transfers and accommodation at the dive centre's homestay.

A typical itinerary for fun dives includes three dives a day (B$180 including lunch) combining shallower reef dives with deeper

INSIDE THE SULTAN'S PALACE

If shaking hands with royalty is your thing, and you happen to be in Brunei for the Hari Raya Aidil Fitri festivities at the end of Ramadan, be sure to call in on the sultan at **Istana Nurul Iman** (p203), his 1788-room primary residence. In keeping with the local tradition of hosting an open house, during which guests are welcomed into the home and plied with a buffet of curries, dried fruit and cake, for three days the sultan receives members of the public at his palace in morning and afternoon sessions. There is no need for an invitation; simply turn up and join the queue (arriving early means a shorter wait). Bruneians will be dressed in their best clothes, some in outfits made especially for the occasion using brightly patterned materials, so wear something modest and reasonably smart.

After piling your plate high with a selection of curries and making multiple trips to the cake table at the free banquet, there is an hour or so of waiting involved. From here on, men and women are segregated. Seats are provided and Hari Raya pop songs played on a loop to keep the crowds entertained. You'll pass through a magnificent banquet hall before being ushered through to shake hands with the sultan (if you are a man) or the queen (if you are a woman), who receive guests in separate rooms. Each visitor is also given a gift.

If your moment with the sultan or queen feels all too fleeting, bear in mind that they will greet some 40,000 people a day during the festivities.

WORTH A TRIP

JERUDONG: PRINCE JEFRI'S PLAYGROUND

For much of the 1990s the sultan's younger brother and Brunei's then Finance Minister, Prince Jefri, was renowned for his extravagance in both his personal and public spending; the legacy of the latter lives on in the neighbourhood of Jerudong, an area so enveloped with Las Vegas–style bling that there is even a roundabout adorned with a giant replica diamond ring.

Amid the rows of mansions lie the **Jerudong Park Polo club** (the sultan himself is a keen polo player) and **Jerudong Park Medical Centre** (p210).

Back in the golden days, a concert hall hosted free shows by the likes of Whitney Houston and Michael Jackson, the latter to celebrate the sultan's 50th birthday in 1996. But in 1997 the party came to a halt when Prince Jefri (dubbed the Playboy Prince) was accused by the Brunei government of embezzling billions of dollars of state funds. After a long dispute involving a series of court cases, Prince Jefri now seems to have been welcomed back into the fold.

Nowhere sums up the legacy of Prince Jefri more than **Jerudong Park Playground** (www.jerudongpark.com.bn; Jerudong; adult/child B$20/10; 4-11pm Wed, 3-11.30pm Fri, 10.30am - 11.30pm Sat & Sun, closed Mon, Tue & Thu;), which reopened in 2014 with brand new rides for children after languishing for years in a poorly maintained state. It's a great place to bring kids, but despite the recent facelift the park continues to feel underused and rather empty. In its 1990s heyday, this B$1 billion attraction was the pride of Brunei, and the only major modern amusement park in Southeast Asia. Bruneians who were teenagers then have fond memories of the rides – all of them free – which included a giant roller coaster. Although the new attractions may be no match for the golden days, the place still evokes a feeling of nostalgia.

The **Empire Hotel & Country Club** (p207), commissioned by Prince Jefri at a cost of US$1.1 billion, is worth a visit if only to gawp at the cavernous, glass atrium and US$500,000 lamp made of gold and Baccarat crystal in the lobby. For B$25 you can use the sea-front swimming pool complex, and the hotel also has eight restaurants including the well-regarded **Pantai** (241 8888; Beachfront, level 1; buffet adult/child B$48/24; 6.30-10pm Fri-Wed). The resort even has its own three-screen **cinema** (261 0001; www.timescineplex.com; adult B$4-8, child B$3-8; 11am-2am).

Jerudong, which lies 20km northwest of BSB, is difficult to explore without private transport, although the 57 bus from the city centre will take you as far as the Empire Hotel.

wreck dives in locations chosen depending on water conditions and diving experience. PADI Open Water courses cost B$570; discounts are offered if booking more than one course.

Oceanic Quest Company DIVING
(277 1190; www.oceanicquest.com; No 6, Simpang 46, Jln Perusahaan, Kampong Serasa) Well-regarded company offering PADI certification courses (B$500) and dives to nearby reefs and wrecks (from B$40 per dive). Oceanic can also arrange airport transfers (B$60 return). Accommodation is available at the dive centre guesthouse in Muara (B$60 per person per night including meals).

Cruises

Water-Taxi Cruise BOATING
(1hr B$30-40) The best way to see BSB's water villages and the sultan's fabled palace, Istana Nurul Iman (p203), is from a water taxi, which can be chartered along the waterfront for about B$30 to B$40 (a bit of negotiating will occur, but at least you know the locals can't claim the petrol is expensive). Finding a boat won't be a problem, as the boatmen will have spotted you before you spot them.

After you admire the palace's backyard, your boatman can take you further upriver into the mangrove to see proboscis monkeys. Head out in the late afternoon if you can; the monkeys are easiest to spot around sunset.

Tours

A number of local agencies offer tours of BSB and trips to nature sites around the sultanate, including Ulu Temburong National Park (p216) and the mangroves of Pulau Selirong (p214), 45 minutes by boat from the city.

Some also offer night safaris where you can spot proboscis monkeys, crocs and fireflies.

★Borneo Guide TOUR
(☎718 7138, 242 6923; www.borneoguide.com; Unit 204, Kiaw Lian Building, Jln Pemancha; ⏰9am-5pm Mon-Thu, 9am-noon & 2-5pm Fri, 9am-1pm Sat & Sun) Excellent service, good prices and a variety of packages around Brunei and Borneo available. A day trip to Ulu Temburong National Park costs B$135 per person from BSB. Also offers overnight trips to Temburong with accommodation at Sumbiling Eco Village (p215; two days and one night from B$185) just outside the park. The office serves as a useful tourism information centre.

Sunshine Borneo Tours TOUR
(☎244 6812; www.bruneiborneo.com; No. 2 Simpang 146, Jln Kiarong; ⏰8am–5pm Mon-Thu & Sat, 8am–noon & 2–5pm Fri) Offers a range of tour packages in Brunei and Borneo, including birdwatching, river cruises, water-village tours and city night tours. Trips to Ulu Temburong National Park start at B$163 for a day trip and from B$330 for two days and one night with accommodation at the Ulu Ulu resort (p216). The office is 3km west of the city centre.

Intrepid Tours TOUR
(☎222 1685, 222 1686; www.bruneibay.net/intrepidtours; Unit G4, ground fl, Bangunan Sungai Akar Central) Offers a range of day tours and multiday packages, including trips to Ulu Temburong National Park (day trips B$100 to B$200 per person) and dawn tours of Pulau Selirong (B$67 to B$110 per person for a four-hour tour); the latter involves zipping across Brunei Bay as the sun rises and guided wildlife-spotting from a boardwalk.

Freme Travel Services TOUR
(☎223 4277; www.freme.com; 4th fl, office 403B, Wisma Jaya, Jln Pemancha) A bit corporate, but has plenty of options, as befits one of Brunei's largest travel agencies. Also has its own lodge close to Ulu Temburong National Park.

Sleeping

Budget options are thin on the ground. Upscale places often offer discounts online.

Youth Hostel HOSTEL $
(Pusat Belia; ☎222 2900, 887 3066; Jln Sungai Kianggeh; dm B$10;) Popular with backpackers, despite the fact that couples can't stay together. The five male and four female sex-segregated dorm rooms with functional furnishings and passable bathrooms are situated at the southern end of the Youth Centre complex, behind the cylindrical staircase. Reception is supposed to be open 7.30am to 4.30pm Monday to Thursday and Saturday, but staffing can be intermittent.

If the office is locked, hang around and someone should (eventually) find you. The hostel may fill up with government guests or school groups, so call ahead to check availability. The adjacent swimming pool costs B$1.

KH Soon Resthouse GUESTHOUSE $
(☎222 2052; http://khsoon-resthouse.tripod.com; 2nd fl, 140 Jln Pemancha; dm B$25, s/d B$40/50, without bathroom B$35/40;) This basic guesthouse, in a converted commercial space with red cement floors, offers budget rates, huge but spartan rooms, and a central location. The reception level rooms that share bathrooms (squat toilets only) are probably a better bet than the ones upstairs, which have private facilities positioned awkwardly behind lower than ceiling-height partitions and dodgy looking electrical wires.

★Brunei Hotel HOTEL $$
(☎224 4828; www.thebruneihotel.com; 95 Jln Pemancha; r/ste incl breakfast B$140-175/240-320; @) A chic, dare we say hip, hotel with clean lines, monochromatic colour schemes, geometric patterns and a general up-to-date style that is pretty unexpected in the sultanate. There's a decent breakfast buffet thrown into the deal served in the downstairs Choices Cafe.

★Capital Residence Suites HOTEL $$
(☎222 0067; www.capitalresidencesuites.com; Simpang 2, Kampong Berangan; d/ste incl breakfast B$80/180-280;) This good value, rather blandly decorated hotel is lifted by friendly, helpful staff and a free shuttle service from 9am to 9pm, which transports guests all around BSB city and to the beaches and attractions beyond. The spacious suites are like small apartments with sofas, a kitchen and washing machine. Standard rooms, though comfortably furnished, are a little cramped.

Terrace Hotel HOTEL $$
(☎224 3555, 224 3554; www.terracebrunei.com; Jln Tasek Lama; d incl breakfast B$85-100;) A classic tourist-class hotel whose 84 rooms are a little dowdy (think 1980s) but clean, and come with marble bathrooms. It also has a great little swimming pool. In a good

LOCAL KNOWLEDGE

AMBUYAT – GUMMY, GLUEY & GLUTINOUS

Remember that kid in kindergarten who used to eat craft glue? Well, *ambuyat*, Brunei's unofficial national dish, comes pretty darn close. It's a gelatinous porridge-like goo made from the ground pith of the sago tree, which is ground to a powder and mixed with water, and eaten with a variety of flavourful sauces.

To eat *ambuyat*, you'll be given a special pair of chopsticks called *chandas* that's attached at the top (don't snap them in two!) to make it easier to twirl up the tenacious mucous. Once you've scooped up a bite-sized quantity, dunk it into the sauce. After your *ambuyat* is sufficiently drenched, place the glob of dripping, quivering, translucent mucilage in your mouth and swallow – don't chew, just let it glide down your throat.

location just 800m north of the waterfront, near the Tamu Selera hawker centre.

Jubilee Hotel HOTEL **$$**
(☎222 8070; www.jubileehotelbrunei.com; Jln Kampung Kianggeh; d/ste incl breakfast from B$95/120; ❄📶) The Jubilee's rooms aren't flash – they may remind you of your old aunt's seldom-used guest bedroom – but are liveable and clean. 'Superior' rooms come with kitchenettes. Prices include transfers to and from the airport, a short city overview tour and one further return trip within the city.

Empire Hotel & Country Club RESORT **$$$**
(☎241 8888; www.theempirehotel.com; Lebuhraya Muara-Tutong, Jerudong; d B$400-600, ste B$1000-16600, villas B$2200-3500; ❄@📶🏊; 🚌57) Pharaonic in its proportions and opulence, this 522-room extravaganza was commissioned by Prince Jefri as lodging for guests of the royal family and quickly transformed into an upscale resort (p205). Even the cheapest rooms have remote-control everything, hand-woven carpets, gold-plated power points and enormous bathrooms with marble floors. Online discounts offer substantial savings on the quoted rates.

Radisson Hotel HOTEL **$$$**
(☎224 4272; www.radisson.com/brunei; Jln Tasek Lama; d/ste B$170/350; ❄@📶🏊) This Radisson chain hotel, on the edge of the town centre, flies the flag for international standards. The sparkling lobby exudes comfort and wealth, as do the business-class rooms. Amenities include a pool, a fitness centre, a spa and two restaurants. Free shuttle service to Gadong and downtown three times daily.

Rizqun International Hotel HOTEL **$$$**
(☎242 3000; www.rizquninternational.com; Abdul Razak Complex; d incl breakfast from B$320; ❄📶🏊) The Rizqun is more sophisticated than you'd expect for something attached to a Gadong shopping mall and has all the usual business-class amenities on hand including a gym and a decent outdoor pool. The opulent lobby is pure Brunei (think marble, wood and stained glass) and the 7th-floor lounge has great views of the Jame'Asr Hassanal Bolkiah Mosque.

Eating

In the city centre, restaurants can be found along the waterfront and on Jln Sultan (south of Jln Pemancha). The big shopping malls, including those out in Gadong, have food courts. Just find a spot that looks busy and chow down.

★**Tamu Selera** HAWKER **$**
(cnr Jln Tasek Lama & Jln Stoney; mains B$2-6; ⏲5pm-midnight) At this old-fashioned hawker centre, set in a shady park, diners eat excellent, cheap Malaysian and Indonesian dishes under colourful tarps and ceiling fans. Options include satay, fried chicken, seafood, rice and noodle dishes, and iced drinks. Situated 1km north of the waterfront.

Pasar Malam Gadong MARKET **$**
(Gadong Night Market; Jln Pasar Gadong; ⏲4-10pm; 🚌1) Thanks to its authentic local snacks and dishes, this is Brunei's most popular night market. Unfortunately, it's geared to car-driving locals who take the food away, so there are almost no places to sit. It's 3km northwest of the city centre, served by bus, but after about 7pm the only way back to town is by taxi (B$15 until 10pm, then B$20).

Noralizah & Iskandar INDIAN **$**
(☎867 5781; 15 ground fl, Kompleks Awang Hj Ibrahim, Jln Berakas; mains B$3-7; ⏲7am-8pm; 🌱) It's all about the roti flatbreads at this busy spot, from flaky roti to deliciously oily paratha, stuffed with ground lamb and onions in a *murtabak*, or bananas and a dusting of sugar

LOCAL KNOWLEDGE

THANIS LIM: FOOD WRITER

Bruneian food writer and chef Thanis Lim lives in BSB and writes about the Brunei food scene for www.thanislim.com.

Describe the local attitude to food In Brunei our social life revolves around food and eating out. A typical night out here is to get together with friends for food or coffee at a restaurant or cafe, or go to a night market. Tamu Selera (p207) is one of my favourites. Go at about 7pm and order *ayam penyet* (Indonesian fried chicken with sambal).

What local foods should visitors try? *Ambuyat*, a kind of starchy, glutinous paste made from sago starch and hot water that is dipped into spicy sauces to give it flavour. *Ambuyat* became popular during the Japanese occupation in the 1940s when there wasn't enough rice to go around. The best place to try it is at Aminah Arif. The *ambuyat* set there comes with other typical local dishes like *belutak*, a sausage made with beef offal and local spices.

And drinks? *Teh tarik* – tea and condensed milk poured into the cup from a height. There used to be speakeasy-type places serving alcohol in Brunei, but they have closed now. Just across the Kuala Lurah border crossing, in Malaysia, there is a food court selling chicken wings and cheap beers that is popular with non-Muslims from Brunei. It's a 30-minute drive from BSB. Make sure you cross back into Brunei before the border closes at 10pm.

Any other tips? Bruneians are very friendly and love receiving visitors, so try to get in touch with locals via social media. Your new friends will probably be happy to show you around.

for a breakfast treat. Dip that deliciousness in one of several bowls of warming curry. The restaurant is located near the airport.

Gerai Makan Jalan Residency HAWKER $
(Jalan Residency Food Stalls; Jln Residency; mains B$2-5; ⌚4pm-midnight) Along the riverbank facing Kampung Ayer, this grouping of food stalls features satay (B$1 for four chicken or three lamb skewers), various kinds of mee goreng and nasi goreng, and soups such as *soto* (noodle soup). Opening hours depend on the whim of the stall holder.

Tamu Kianggeh HAWKER $
(Kianggeh market; Jln Sungai Kianggeh; mains from B$1; ⌚5am-5pm) The food stalls here serve Brunei's cheapest meals, including *nasi katok* (plain rice, a piece of fried or curried chicken and sambal; B$1) and *nasi lemak* (rice cooked in coconut milk and served with chicken, egg and cucumber slices; also B$1). The market feels endearingly chaotic and messy, something of a rarity in the sultanate.

★Pondok Sari Wangi INDONESIAN $$
(☎244 5403; Block A, No 12-13, Abdul Razak Complex, Jln Gadong; mains B$5-18; ⌚10am-10pm; ❄) Located in Gadong, Pondok Sari Wangi is a beloved Bandar institution. The extensive menu includes lots of gloriously rich, decadent, colourful grub like marinated 'smashed chicken', a fried fish with fiery sambal, sweet sauteed local greens and vegetables, mouth-watering satay with a heavily textured peanut sauce and the signature beef ribs, braised to something like perfection.

Seri Damai Restaurant PAKISTANI $$
(☎222 5397; ground fl, 144A Jln Pemancha; mains B$6-18; ⌚9am-10pm; ❄🖉) This friendly, family-run Pakistani restaurant with an all-out green colour scheme (think wedding-style chair covers and plenty of satin) serves up some of the best biryanis, curries, naan breads and lassis in town. There is a good variety of vegetarian as well as meat and seafood dishes available. At B$6 the set menus are good value.

Lim Ah Siaw CHINESE $$
(☎222 3963; Jln Teraja; mains B$8-10; ⌚6:30am-10pm) Though it's only a 10-minute walk from the main road, the jungly setting of the Lim Ah Siaw pork market and restaurant give it an underground feel. And while it might be located away from casual passersby – it must be the least Halal restaurant in Bru-

nei. Crispy braised pork knuckle, pork belly, pork dumplings; this place is Babe's hell.

Popular dishes include *kolo mee* (noodles cooked with pork lard) with pork ribs (B$8 to B$10).

Aminah Arif BRUNEIAN **$$**
(☎223 6198; Unit 2-3, Block B, Rahman Bldg, Simpang 88, Kiulap; mains B$4-28; ⏲7am-10pm; ❄✍) Aminah Arif is synonymous with *ambuyat* (thick, starchy porridge), Brunei's signature dish. If you're up for a generous serving of wiggly white goo, this is a good spot to do so (B$22 for a set meal for two people). Meals can be washed down with iced *kasturi ping* (calamansi lime juice; B$1.50).There are five branches of Aminah Arif in town; this one – located in Kiulap about 3km northwest of the waterfront – is the most central.

Kimchi KOREAN **$$**
(☎222 2233; Unit 19, Block B, Regent Sq, Kiulap; mains B$4.95-30; ⏲11am-10.30pm Sat-Thu, 2-10.30pm Sun; ❄) Korean restaurants are pretty ubiquitous in BSB, and Kimchi, in Regent Sq west of the centre, is the best in town. The titular *kimchi* (fermented cabbage) is delightfully smelly and spicy, rice cakes are drowned in a hot, rich sauce and the chicken wings...well, when are chicken wings a bad idea? The *bulgogi* (grilled marinated beef) is a lovely indulgence.

Thiam Hock Restaurant CHINESE **$$$**
(☎244 1679; 5 Yong Siong Hai Bldg, Gadong; mains from B$10-30; ⏲8.30am-10pm; ❄) This long-standing Chinese restaurant is famous for its curry fish head (some diners may find the blown-up photo of one such head looking back at them from the menu, mouth open and teeth bared, a little off-putting). Less challenging dishes here include delicious butter prawns. Thiam Hock is by the river on the block behind the Mall in Gadong.

Drinking

A double espresso is the most potent drink you're likely to find in Brunei, as the sale and public consumption of alcohol is banned. Locals are fond of the soft drink *air batu campur* (ice mix), usually called ABC, which brings together ice, little green noodles, grass jelly, sago pearls and red beans.

De Royalle Café CAFE
(38 Jln Sultan; ⏲24hr; 📶) With a living-room-style indoor area (complete with leopard-print armchairs) and outdoor pavement tables, this always-open establishment has a supply of perusable English-language newspapers and serves up an international menu (mains B$5.90 to B$15.90) and, of course, freshly brewed coffee. A fine place for a relaxed rendezvous with friends.

Another CAFE
(☎222 3012; G8 ground fl Wisma Jaya, Jln Pemancha; ⏲7.30am-6.30pm Mon-Sat; 📶) Corrugated metal walls, polished concrete floors and a wooden counter lend an industrial feel to this small, urban cafe. Coffee lovers (even the fussy ones) should be more than satisfied by the standard of flat whites served here, and there is a tempting selection of pastries, cakes (chocolate brownies and Dutch apple pie) and sandwiches (B$5 to B$7.50).

Piccolo Café CAFE
(☎224 1558; Lot 11, Jln McArthur; sandwiches RM3.50-6.90; ⏲7.30am-11pm Mon-Wed, 7.30am-1am Thu-Sat, 9.30am-11pm Sun; 📶) This cafe serves up lavender lattes (an original, if not completely delicious, drink) as well as more conventional coffees, teas and smoothies and a range of sandwiches, wraps and desserts, including an extremely tasty sea-salt chocolate tart (B$4.80).

Entertainment

Locals often head to Gadong for a night out, which in Brunei usually amounts to dinner and perhaps a movie (which are censored so that even the kissing scenes are cut). Based on the enthusiasm locals have for Gadong, you might conclude that the area is a seething nightlife zone or at least a fine collection of smart restaurants. Unfortunately, it's neither – just some air-con shopping malls and commercial streets.

Shopping

Shopping is Brunei's national sport. Locals trail through the shopping malls scouting out the best deals while bemoaning the fact that their micro-nation doesn't have as much variety as Singapore.

Arts & Handicrafts Training Centre CRAFTS
(☎224 0676; Jln Residency; ⏲8am-5pm Sat-Thu, 8-11.30am & 2-5pm Fri) Sells silverwork, carved wood items, ornamental brass cannons (from B$500) and ceremonial swords (about B$500), made by the centre's students and graduates, for more than you'd pay in Sarawak or Kalimantan. Not bad for window-shopping, though. Check out the

jong sarat (hand-woven cloth made from gold and silver threads). The centre is on the river 600m east of Sungai Kianggeh.

The Mall SHOPPING CENTRE
(Gadong; ⏲10am-10pm) Sure, this much-touted mall is sleek (the ceiling mural of Royal Brunei planes is an interesting touch), but as air-con malls go it's nothing remarkable: a collection of uninspiring outlets, a useful supermarket, a food court and an eight-screen **cineplex** (☎242 2455; www.themallcineplex.com; 3rd fl, adult B$4-10, child B$3-6; ⏲11am-midnight), the most popular cinema in Brunei!

Paul & Elizabeth Book Services BOOKS
(1st fl, 62 Jln McArthur; ⏲8.30am-8.30pm) Stocks a few books on Brunei, a street map of the entire sultanate and a small range of English-language paperbacks. There's also an internet cafe.

Hua Ho Department Store DEPARTMENT STORE
(Yayasan Complex, Jln McArthur; ⏲10am-10pm) A four-floor department store with a decent supermarket on the basement level.

Information

EMERGENCY

Ambulance (☎991)
Fire Brigade (☎995)
Police (☎993)

INTERNET ACCESS

Paul & Elizabeth Cyber Cafe (1st fl, 62 Jln McArthur; per hr B$1.80; ⏲8.30am-8.30pm) Old-style cybercafe with decent connections but a bad soundtrack.

GETTING TO SABAH: BANDAR SERI BEGAWAN TO KOTA KINABALU

Getting to the border At 8am daily a **Jesselton Express** (☎016-830 0722, 0060 88 751722; www.sipitangexpress.com.my) bus to runs KK (B$45, eight to nine hours) via Limbang, Bangar, Lawas and various towns in Sabah.

At the border Make sure you have your passport ready if you're travelling overland to Sabah, because you'll be stopping at a whopping eight checkpoints. As long as your ID is in order you'll be fine; the trip is tedious rather than dodgy.

Moving on Long-distance buses head to KK and drop you off close to the main stretches of hotels and restaurants.

MEDIA

Borneo Insider's Guide (www.borneoinsidersguide.com) Keep an eye out for the free, glossy magazine published four times a year.

MEDICAL SERVICES

Jerudong Park Medical Centre (☎261 1433; www.jpmc.com.bn; Tutong-Muara Hwy; ⏲24hr) Private medical facility with high standards of care. Located about 27km northwest of BSB centre.

RIPAS Hospital (☎224 2424; www.moh.gov.bn; Jln Putera Al-Muhtadee Billah; ⏲24hr) Brunei's main hospital, with fully equipped, modern facilities. Situated about 2km west of the centre (across the Edinburgh Bridge).

MONEY

Banks and international ATMs are sprinkled around the city centre, especially along Jln McArthur and Jln Sultan. The airport has ATMs.

HSBC (cnr Jln Sultan & Jln Pemancha; ⏲8.45am-4pm Mon-Fri, to 11.30am Sat) Has a 24-hour ATM. You must have an HSBC account to change travellers cheques.

Isman Money Changer (Shop G14, ground fl, Block B, Yayasan Complex, Jln Pretty; ⏲10am-8pm) Changes cash. Just off the central atrium.

POST

Main Post Office (cnr Jln Sultan & Jln Elizabeth Dua; ⏲8am-4.30pm Mon-Thu & Sat, 8-11am & 2-4pm Fri) The Stamp Gallery displays some historic first-day covers and blow-ups of colonial-era stamps.

TOURIST INFORMATION

Brunei Tourism (☎220 0874; www.bruneitourism.travel; Kampong Ayer Cultural & Tourism Gallery; ⏲9am-12.15pm & 1.30-4.30pm Mon-Thu & Sat, 9-11.30am & 2-4.30pm Fri) Free maps, brochures and information about Brunei. The website has oodles of useful information.

Getting There & Away

AIR

Brunei International Airport (☎233 1747; www.civil-aviation.gov.bn) Recent renovations, including new arrival and departure halls, have greatly improved the sultanate's small international airport. The arrival hall has an ATM and a tourist information desk (ground fl, arrival hall, Brunei International Airport; ⏲9am-5pm).

Air Asia (www.airasia.com) Two flights a day to Kuala Lumpur.

Cebu Pacific (www.cebupacificair.com) Flights from BSB to Manila on Monday, Wednesday, Friday, Saturday and Sunday.

Royal Brunei Airlines (☎222 5931; www.flyroyalbrunei.com; RBA Plaza, Jln Sultan; ⏲8am-4pm Mon-Thu & Sat, 8am-noon &

GETTING TO SABAH: BANDAR SERI BEGAWAN TO BANDAR LABUAN

Getting to the border Travelling by sea to Sabah is the easiest option, avoiding the hassles and delays of land borders – traffic at the Kuala Lurah crossing has been known to cause lengthy delays. **PKL Jaya Sendirian** (☎277 1771; www.pkljaya.com; 1st fl, Unit 7, Block A, Muara Centre, Jln Muara) runs daily car ferries from Serasa Ferry Terminal in Muara, about 25km northeast of BSB, to the Malaysian federal territory of Pulau Labuan (1½ hours), leaving Muara at 9am (adult/child/car B$17/10/58) and makes the return journey from Labuan at 4pm (adult/child/car RM38/18/120). Arrive at least an hour before sailing. To get to the ferry terminal by public transport, take the 38 bus to Muara town. From there, it's a short trip on the 33 bus (allow at least an hour for the journey).

At the border Most travellers to Malaysia are granted a 30- or 60-day visa on arrival.

Moving on From Bandar Labuan, twice daily ferries go to Kota Kinabalu (three hours).

2-4pm Fri) Direct flights from BSB to destinations including Bangkok, Kota Kinabalu, Kuala Lumpur, Melbourne and Singapore.

Singapore Airlines (www.singaporeair.com) Five flights a week from BSB to Singapore

TEMBURONG DISTRICT

Although a state-of-the-art bridge is being built that will link Muara and Temburong, for the time being the fastest way to get to Bangar is by speedboat (B$7, 45 minutes, at least hourly from 6am to at least 4.30pm – later on Sundays). The **dock** (Jln Residency) is about 200m east of Sungai Kianggeh.

BUS & VAN

BSB's carbon-monoxide-choked **bus terminal** (Jln Cator) is on the ground floor of a multistorey parking complex two blocks north of the waterfront. It is used by domestic lines, including those to Muara, and Kuala Lurah, but not to Sabah or Sarawak. Schematic signs next to each numbered berth show the route of each line.

There is no longer a public bus service to Tutong, Kuala Belait and Seria. The **PHLS express bus to Miri** stopping in Tutong (B$5), Seria (B$6) and Kuala Belait ($6) leaves BSB waterfront (near Sungai Kianggeh) at 7am and 1pm.

Getting Around

TO/FROM THE AIRPORT

The airport, about 8km north of central BSB, is linked to the city centre, including the bus terminal on Jln Cator, by buses 23, 36 and 38 until about 5.30pm. A cab to/from the airport costs B$25; pay at the taxi counter. Some hotels offer airport pick-up.

BUS

Brunei's limited public bus system, run by a variety of companies, is erratic and rather chaotic, at least to the uninitiated, so getting around by public transport takes effort. Buses (B$1) operate daily from 6.30am to about 6pm; after that, your options are taking a cab or hoofing it. If you're heading out of town and will need to catch a bus back, ask the driver if and when he's coming back and what time the last bus back is.

Finding stops can be a challenge – some are marked by black-and-white-striped uprights or a shelter, others by a yellow triangle painted on the pavement, and yet others by no discernible symbol. Fortunately, numbers are prominently displayed on each 20- or 40-passenger bus.

The bus station lacks an information office or a ticket counter, and while the schematic wall map may make sense to BSB natives, it's hard to decipher for the uninitiated. It may be best to ask about transport options at your hotel before heading to the bus station.

CAR

Brunei has Southeast Asia's cheapest petrol – gasoline is just B$0.53 a litre and diesel goes for only B$0.31. (Since a bottle of water costs B$1, petrol is cheaper than water.) If you're driving a car (eg a rental) with Malaysian plates and are not a Brunei resident, you'll be taken to a special pump to pay more (this is to prevent smuggling).

Hiring a car is a good way to explore Brunei's hinterland. Prices start at about B$85 a day. Surcharges may apply if the car is taken into Sarawak. Most agencies will bring the car to your hotel and pick it up when you've finished, and drivers can also be arranged, though this could add B$100 to the daily cost. The main roads are in good condition, but some back roads require a 4WD.

Avis (☎222 7100; www.avis.com; Raddison Hotel, Jln Tasek Lama 2203; ⏲8am-noon & 1.30-5pm Mon-Thu, 8am-noon & 2-5pm Fri, 8am-noon & 1.30-4pm Sat, 9am-noon & 1.30-3pm Sun) Also has an office at the airport (☎233 3298; airport; ⏲8.30am-5.30pm).

Hertz (☎airport 872 6000; www.hertz.com; airport arrival hall; ⏲8am-5pm) The international car-rental company has a counter at Brunei airport.

GETTING TO SARAWAK: BANDAR SERI BEGAWAN TO MIRI

Getting to the border Twice a day **PHLS Express** (☎277 1668) links BSB with Miri (B$20 from BSB, RM50 from Miri, 3½ hours). Departures from BSB's waterfront are at 7am and 1pm and from Miri's Pujut Bus Terminal at 8.15am and 3.45pm. Tickets are sold on board. Another option for travel between BSB and Miri is a private transfer (which may be shared with other travellers) run by father-and-son team Mr Fu and Ah Pau (B$25 or RM70 per person, three hours). Call Mr Fu on ☎013-833 2231 (Malaysian mobile) or ☎878 2521 (Brunei mobile). Departures from BSB are usually at 1pm or 2pm; departures from Miri are generally at 9am or 10am but may be earlier.

At the border Most travellers to Malaysia are granted a 30- or 60-day visa on arrival.

Moving on The bus will leave you at Miri's Pujut Bus Terminal, a 4km taxi ride from the city centre.

TAXI

Taxis are a convenient way of exploring BSB – if you can find one, that is. There is no centralised taxi dispatcher, and it's difficult or impossible to flag down a cab on the street. Hotels can provide drivers' cell-phone numbers. Most taxis have yellow tops; a few serving the airport are all white.

BSB's only proper **taxi rank** (Jln Cator) is two blocks north of the waterfront at the bus terminal on Jln Cator.

Some taxis use meters, although many drivers will just try to negotiate a fare with you. Fares go up by 50% after 10pm; the charge for an hour of wait time is B$30 to B$35. Sample day-time taxi fares from the city centre include the Brunei Museum (B$25), Gadong (B$15), the airport (B$25), the Serasa Ferry Terminal in Muara (B$40), the Empire Hotel & Country Club (B$35) and the Jerudong Park Playground (B$35). Fares increase after 10pm.

WATER TAXI

If your destination is near the river, water taxis – the same little motorboats that ferry people to and from Kampung Ayer – are a good way of getting there. You can hail a water taxi anywhere on the waterfront a boat can dock, as well as along Venice-esque Sungai Kianggeh. Crossing straight across the river is supposed to cost B$1 per person; diagonal crossings cost more.

TUTONG & BELAIT DISTRICTS

Most travellers merely pass through the districts of Tutong and Belait, west of BSB, en route to Miri in Sarawak, but there are a few worthwhile attractions here. Buses link Kuala Belait, Seria and Tutong with BSB, but if you want to really see the sights, the best way is to take a tour or rent a car.

Tutong

POP 20,000

About halfway between Seria and BSB lies Tutong, the main town in central Brunei. The town itself is neat and unremarkable, but the area is famous in Brunei for two things: pitcher plants and sand. Locals cook a variety of dishes in the insect-catching sacs of the area's six species of pitcher plants, while some of the sand near Tutong is so white that Bruneians take pictures with it, pretending it's snow (have your fun any way you can, Brunei). You can see *pasir putih* (white sand) in patches along the side of the Pan Borneo Hwy.

Sights

Pantai Seri Kenangan BEACH
(Pantai Tutong; Jln Kuala Tutong) Set on a spit of land, with the South China Sea on one side and Sungai Tutong on the other, the casuarina-lined beach is arguably the best in Brunei. Sandflies can be a problem here; if you plan to stay for sunset, be sure to bring repellent. The beach is 2km west of Tutong town, on Jln Kuala Tutong.

Getting There & Away

The PHLS express buses that link BSB with Seria, Kuala Belait and Miri stop here. Departures west to Seria, Kuala Belait and Miri are at 8am and 2pm and east to BSB at 10.45am and 6.15pm (arrive 15 minutes early as times are approximate and the bus doesn't wait).

Jalan Labi

A few kilometres after you enter Belait district (coming from Tutong and BSB), a road branches inland (south) to Labi and beyond, taking you through some prime forest areas. Now fully paved, the road leads to a number of Iban longhouses, which in these parts come complete with mod cons and parking lots.

Sights

Forestry Museum MUSEUM
(Simpang 50, Jln Labi; 8am-12.15pm & 1.30-4.30pm, closed Fri & Sun) FREE The Forestry Museum is located down the Simpang 50 turn-off (on the right as you head towards Labi). It's a small, simple place with seriously thorough information for visitors about the local forest. Exhibits detail the history of logging and conservation in the area with labelled examples of more than 50 types of wood found here, along with taxidermic examples of the resident wildlife – sadly, it's the closest you're likely to come to seeing a clouded leopard in Borneo.

Luagan Lalak Recreation Park PARK
(Jln Labi) If you're craving peace and serenity this is the place to find it: wooden walkways extend across alluvial freshwater swamp with tufts of greenery dotted like islands in mirror-like water. It's a beautiful spot for picnicking, birdwatching or meditating.

Following Jln Labi down from the main highway, the park is 20km before Labi (look for the sign marking this distance). There is no public transport here.

Labi Longhouses HOUSE
Labi is a small Iban settlement about 40km south of the coastal road with four longhouses: Rampayoh, Mendaram Besar, Mendaram Kecil and finally, at the end of the track, Teraja.

If you go without a guide, how much of the longhouse you are able to see will depend on whether there's an English speaker there to show you around. If so, the cost of such a tour might be B$2 per person. Mendaram Besar also has an informal **homestay programme** (Hensona 323 3019; Jln Labi; per person incl food B$55).

These longhouses are a mix of the modern and the traditional: you will see women weaving baskets, though nowadays they may be plastic rather than rattan, and the longhouses have 24-hour electricity. Outside, among the fruit trees and clucking chickens, there is a rustic shelter for a row of gleaming cars.

Seria

POP 34,000

Spread out along the coast between Tutong and Kuala Belait, low-density Seria is home to many of Brunei Shell's major onshore installations.

Sights

Oil & Gas Discovery Centre MUSEUM
(337 7200; www.ogdcbrunei.com; off Jln Tengah; adult/teenager/child B$5/2/1; 8.30am-5pm Mon-Thu & Sat, 9.30am-6pm Sun) Puts an 'edutainment' spin on the oil industry. Likely to appeal to young science buffs and Shell employees. About 700m northwest of Seria town centre.

Billionth Barrel Monument MONUMENT
Commemorates (you guessed it) the billionth barrel of crude oil produced at the Seria field, a landmark reached in 1991. Out to sea, oil rigs producing the sultanate's second billion dot the horizon. Situated on the beach directly in front of Seria town.

Sleeping

Roomz Hotel HOTEL **$$$**
(322 3223; www.roomz.com.bn; s/d incl breakfast B$150/160;) This sophisticated new hotel has slickly decorated rooms with wooden floors, balconies and sea views. The place is easy to find: it's the tallest building in town, situated one block north of the bus station.

Getting There & Away

Frequent purple minibuses go southwest to Kuala Belait (B$1). The PHLS express goes to Miri (B$15) via Kuala Belait at 9am and 2pm, and to BSB (B$6) via Tutong at 9.45am and 5.15pm (arrive 15 minutes early as times are approximate and the bus doesn't wait).

Kuala Belait

POP 35,500

Almost on the Sarawak frontier, coastal Kuala Belait is a modern, sprawling company town – that company being Brunei Shell – of one-storey suburban villas interspersed with grasshopper-like pump jacks, also known as nodding donkeys. Although there's a reasonable beach, most travellers just hustle through on their way to or from Miri.

Look out for the majestic **teapot roundabout** to the east of town, surely one of the region's finest. The four districts of Brunei are represented by four teacups.

Sleeping & Eating

In the town centre, restaurants can be found along Jln McKerron and, two short blocks east, on parallel Jln Pretty, KB's main commercial avenue.

Hotel Sentosa HOTEL $$
(333 1345; www.bruneisentosahotel.com; 92-93 Jln McKerron; d B$108;) Clean, well-run accommodation right in the centre of town. Situated one block south of the bus station.

Information

HSBC Bank (cnr Jln McKerron & Jln Dato Shahbandar) Has an international ATM. Situated diagonally opposite the bus station.

Getting There & Away

Frequent purple minibuses go to Seria (B$1). The PHLS express goes to Miri (B$15) via Kuala Belait at 9.30am and 2.30pm, and to BSB (B$6) via Tutong at 9.15am and 4.45pm (arrive 15 minutes early as times are approximate and the bus doesn't wait).

TEMBURONG DISTRICT

This odd little exclave (part of a country physically separated from the rest of the nation; feel free to take that to the next pub quiz night) is barely larger than Penang, but happens to contain one of the best preserved tracts of primary rainforest in all of Borneo. The main draw is the brilliant Ulu Temburong National Park, accessible only by longboat.

For now, at least, the journey from BSB to Bangar, the district capital, is an exhilarating speedboat ride: you roar down Sungai Brunei, slap through the nipah-lined waterways and then tilt and weave through mangroves into the mouth of Sungai Temburong. At research time, work had already begun on a 30km bridge, which will link the districts of Brunei-Muara and Temburong. Due to be completed in 2018, the bridge will no doubt put an end to the speedboat service.

How the Temburong bridge will effect this wild, remote area is hard to say. Look at Google Earth and the outline of Temburong District is easy to spot: at the Brunei frontier, Malaysia's logging roads – irregular gashes of eroded earth – and trashed hillsides give way to a smooth carpet of trackless, uninhabited virgin rainforest. Not long ago, almost all of Borneo looked like this.

Pulau Selirong

Pulau Selirong Recreational Park MANGROVE FOREST
At the northern tip of Temburong District lies this 25-sq-km mangrove-forested island reachable only by boat (45 minutes from BSB). Intrepid Tours (p206) runs half-day guided trips for around B$80 to B$100 per person depending on group size. Two kilometres of elevated walkways lead through the mangroves, the untamed habitat of proboscis monkeys and flying lemurs – if you're lucky you might spot one gliding down from the trees. Pulau Selirong is also known as Mosquito Island; bring repellent.

At certain times the tide levels are such that it is not possible to travel by boat to the island. Check with tour operators for current water levels.

Bangar & Around

Little Bangar, perched on the banks of Sungai Temburong, is the gateway to, and administrative centre of, Temburong District. It can be visited as a day trip from BSB if you catch an early speedboat, but you'll get more out of the town's easygoing pace if you stay over and explore the area, which has some fine rainforest.

Sights

Bukit Patoi Recreational Park PARK
(Taman Rekreasi Bukit Patoi) Within the protected **Peradayan Forest Reserve**, it is possible to do a 2km (one way) hike to the top of **Bukit Patoi** (310m). The well-marked trail, through pristine jungle, begins at the picnic tables and toilet block at the park entrance, about 15km southeast of Bangar (towards Lawas). To get here from Bangar ask around at the jetty for an unofficial taxi (about B$30 return). Bring plenty of water.

Once you reach the peak, enjoy the views then turn around and come back down; in theory it is possible to continue on to Bukit Peradayan (410m), but the path is poorly maintained.

If you want to explore the Bruneian rainforest without the logistics and expense of a trip further upriver, Peradayan Forest Reserve makes a good alternative that can easily be done as a day-trip from BSB.

Sleeping

Lukat Intan Guesthouse GUESTHOUSE $
(☎864 3766, 522 1078; Bangar; d incl breakfast B$50; P ❄) Run by a friendly couple, Lukat offers spic-and-span rooms and personable service. They're happy to give free rides to Bangar jetty. Call for directions.

Rumah Persinggahan Kerajaan Daerah Temburong GUESTHOUSE $
(☎522 1239; Jln Batang Duri, Bangar; s/d/tr/q B$25/30/40/50, 4-person chalets B$80; ❄ 📶) Set around a grassy, L-shaped courtyard, this government-run guesthouse has friendly, helpful staff and six spacious but slightly fraying rooms with rather more bathtub rust and somewhat cooler hot water than many would deem ideal. Situated about 200m west of the town centre, across the highway from the mosque.

Youth Hostel HOSTEL $
(Pusat Belia; ☎522 1694; Jln Bangar Puni-Ujong, Bangar; dm B$10; ⏲office staffed 7.30am-4.30pm, closed Fri & Sat; ❄) This basic hostel is in a bright-orange building across the road and about 100m downhill from the Bangar ferry terminal. The sex-segregated dorms, each with six beds (bunks), are clean and have air-con. The office is upstairs.

Eating

The fruit and vegetable market, behind the row of shops west of Bangar ferry terminal, has an upstairs **food court** (1st fl, Kompleks Utami Bumiputera; mains B$1-3; ⏲6am or 7am-8pm, closed noon-2pm Fri).

A handful of restaurants serving passable Malay and Chinese food can be found around the market, along and just in from the riverfront.

Information

3 in 1 Services (Shop A1-3, 1st fl, Kompleks Utami Bumiputera; per hr B$1; ⏲8am-5.30pm, closed Sun) Internet access on the 1st floor of the building next to the market (across the pedestrian bridge from the hawker centre).

Bank Islam Brunei Darussalam (⏲8.45am-3.45pm Mon-Thu, 8.45-11am & 2.30-4pm Fri, 8.45-11.15am Sat) The only bank in town's ATM only accepts foreign cards with the cirrus sign (our Visa card didn't work). Non-account holders cannot change money. On the river 150m north of the bridge.

Chop Hock Guan Minimarket (⏲8am-8pm) Exchanges Malaysian ringgits for Brunei dollars. In the first row of shops to the west of Bangar ferry terminal.

Jayamuhibah Shopping Mart Carries some over-the-counter medicines (Temburong District does not have a proper pharmacy). In the second row of shops west of Bangar ferry terminal.

Getting There & Away

BOAT

By far the fastest way to and from BSB is by speedboat (B$7, 45 minutes, hourly from 6am to at least 4.30pm). Bangar's ferry terminal, Terminal Perahu Dan Penumpang, is on the western bank of the river just south of the red bridge.

Boats depart at a scheduled time or when they're full, whichever comes first. When you get to the ticket counters, check which company's boat will be the next to leave and then pay and add your name to the passenger list.

BUS

Buses run by **Jesselton** (☎719 3835, 717 7755, in BSB 718 3838) pick up passengers heading towards Limbang and BSB in the early afternoon; its bus to KK (B$25) and Lawas (B$10) passes through town at about 10am. Buses stop on Jln Labu, just across the bridge on the west side of the river.

TAXI

Bangar doesn't have official taxis, but it's usually not too difficult to hire a car if you ask around under the rain awning in front of the ferry terminal. Drivers may not speak much English. Possible destinations include Limbang in Malaysia (about B$40) and the Peradayan Forest Reserve (Bukit Patoi; about B$30 return).

Taxis do not wait on the Malaysian side of the border, so make sure your transport goes all the way to Limbang

Batang Duri

Batang Duri, 12km south of Bangar, is the jumping-off point for longboat rides to Ulu Temburong National Park. As you head south, the sealed road passes Malay settlements, then Murut (Lun Bawang) hamlets and finally a few partly modern Iban longhouses.

Sleeping

★**Sumbiling Eco Village** CABIN $$
(☎242 6923, 718 7138; www.borneoguide.com/ecovillage; Kampong Sumbiling Lama, Jln Batang Duri; per person incl breakfast & dinner B$85) 🍃 If you're looking for Brunei's version of a jungle

camp with basic amenities and a chilled-out atmosphere that encourages slipping into a state of utterly relaxed Zen, come to Sumbiling. This eco-friendly rustic camp in a beautiful riverside location offers tasty Iban cuisine and accommodation in bamboo huts or tents, which have beds, mosquito nets and fans.

When you're not lounging in a hammock there are plenty of outdoor activities on hand (to be booked in advance) including visits to nearby Ulu Temburong National Park, jungle overnights, inner-tubing on the river, night walks and forest hikes.

Sumbiling is run by Borneo Guide (p206) in cooperation with the local community. It's situated a few minutes downstream from Batang Duri. Price includes transport from Bangar jetty.

Ulu Temburong National Park

It's odd that a small, regulated country such as Brunei should contain a sizable chunk of true untamed wilderness. Therein lies the appeal of Ulu Temburong National Park, located in the heart of a 500-sq-km area of pristine rainforest covering most of southern Temburong. It's so untouched that only about 1 sq km of the park is accessible to tourists, who are only admitted as part of guided tour packages. To protect it, the rest is off-limits to everyone except scientists, who flock here from around the world. Permitted activities include a canopy walk, some short jungle walks, and swimming in the cool mountain waters of Sungai Temburong.

The forests of Ulu Temburong are teeming with life, including as many as 400 kinds of butterfly, but don't count on seeing many vertebrates. The best times to spot birds and animals, in the rainforest and along riverbanks, are around sunrise and sunset, but you're much more likely to hear hornbills and Bornean gibbons than to see them.

Activities

Longboat Trip — BOAT

One of the charms of Ulu Temburong National Park is that the only way to get there is by *temuai* (shallow-draft Iban longboat). The trip upriver from Batang Duri is challenging even for experienced skippers, who need a variety of skills to shoot the rapids in a manner reminiscent of a salmon: submerged boulders and logs have to be dodged, hanging vines must be evaded and the outboard must be taken out of the water at exactly the right moment.

The journey takes between 25 and 45 minutes, depending on current river conditions. When it rains, the water level can quickly rise by up to 2m, but if the river is low you might have to get out and push (wear waterproof shoes).

Aluminium Walkway — CANOPY WALK

The park's main attraction is a delicate aluminium walkway, secured by guy-wires, that brings you level with the jungle canopy, up to 60m above the forest floor. The views of nearby hills and valleys from the walkway are breathtaking, if you can get over the vertigo – the tower, built by Shell using oil-rig scaffolding technology, wobbles in the wind.

In primary rainforests, only limited vegetation can grow on the ground because so little light penetrates, but up in the canopy all manner of life proliferates. Unfortunately there are no explanatory signs here, but a good guide will explain the importance of the canopy ecosystem and point out the huge variety of organisms that can live on a single tree: orchids, bird's-nest ferns and other epiphytes; ants and myriad other insects; amphibians and snakes; and a huge selection of birds.

The trail up to the canopy walk begins near the confluence of Sungai Belalong and Sungai Temburong. It's a short, steep, sweaty walk. If you stay overnight at Ulu Ulu Resort, you can do the canopy walk at sunrise, when birds and animals are most likely to be around.

Rivers & Waterfalls — SWIMMING

Places to take a refreshing dip in the park's pure mountain waters include several rivers and waterfalls – your guide can point out the best spots.

At one small waterfall you can stand in a pool and 2cm- to 4cm-long fish will come up and nibble on your feet, giving you a gentle, ticklish pedicure as they feast on the dry skin between your toes. To get there, head downriver about 500m from the park headquarters. Your guide can help find the creek that you need to follow upstream for a few hundred metres.

Sleeping

★Ulu Ulu Resort — LODGE $$$

(☎ 244 1791; www.uluuluresort.com; Ulu Temburong National Park; per person standard/superior/deluxe B$275/360/395; ❄) The only accommodation inside the park is an upscale riverside lodge, constructed entirely of hardwood, with some rooms built to resemble 1920s Malaysian-style chalets. Standard rooms are dormitory style with shared bathrooms. Prices include transfers from BSB, meals and activities.

Guests at the resort have a 4.30am wake-up call to see the sunrise at the canopy walk, an unforgettable experience.

In Malay, ulu (as in Ulu Temburong) means 'upriver' and ulu ulu means, essentially, 'back of beyond'. The park's wildness and lack of established trails rules out the possibility of unguided walks, so activities are restricted to an easy-going timetable of kayaking and river swimming during the day and a guided night walk.

Getting There & Away

For all intents and purposes, the only way to visit the park is by booking a tour; several BSB-based agencies (p205) organise tour groups and guides.

BRUNEI SURVIVAL GUIDE

Directory A–Z

CURRENCY

Brunei dollar (B$)

EATING PRICE RANGES

$ less than B$6

$$ B$6 to B$16

$$$ more than B$16

EMERGENCY

Ambulance	991
Police	993
Fire	995
Search & Rescue	998
Directory enquiries	113

PUBLIC HOLIDAYS

Brunei shares major public holidays with Malaysia. Holidays specific to Brunei include **Brunei National Day** (23 February), **Royal Brunei Armed Forces Day** (31 May) and the **Sultan of Brunei's Birthday** (15 July).

TOURIST INFORMATION

Brunei Tourism (www.bruneitourism.travel) is a very useful website, containing information on transport, business hours, accommodation, tour agencies and more.

SLEEPING PRICE RANGES

$ less than B$60

$$ B$60 to B$150

$$$ more than B$150

VISAS

Travellers from the US and European Union, Switzerland and Norway are granted a 90-day visa-free stay; travellers from New Zealand, Singapore and Malaysia, among others, receive 30 days; Japanese and Canadians get 14 free days. Australians can apply for the following visas upon arrival: a 72-hour transit (B$5), a 30-day single-entry (B$20) or a multiple-entry (B$30). Israeli travellers are not permitted to enter Brunei.

CULTURAL & LEGAL MATTERS

In May 2014, Brunei began phasing in a new criminal code based on sharia law. Offenses in this first phase are punishable with a fine, imprisonment or both. Subsequent phases will introduce more severe penalties including corporal and capital punishments. As the laws could be applied to non-Muslims, ensure you're on the right side of them.

Drugs & Alcohol

The sale and public consumption of alcohol is forbidden in Brunei. Non-Muslims can import two bottles of wine or spirits and 12 cans of beer, which must be declared at customs, to consume in private. Keep the customs slip in case of inspection. Drug trafficking is punishable by the death penalty.

LGBT Travellers

Homosexual acts are illegal in Brunei and penalties may include prison sentences.

Smoking

Brunei's tough anti-smoking laws ban puffing not only inside shops and malls but also in outdoor markets and around food stalls. There is no duty-free allowance for tobacco and import tax is payable on every cigarette brought into the country.

Women Travellers

Discreet clothing is appropriate here – you certainly don't have to cover your hair, but walking around in a tank top is a bad idea. Loose fitting clothes that cover the shoulders and knees are best, especially when visiting any kind of official or religious building.

Kalimantan

Includes ➡

Best Jungle River Journeys

- Sungai Bungan–Tanjung Lokan by motorised canoe (p230)
- Sungai Ohang–Tanjung Isuy to Mancong by *ces* (p259)
- Sungai Rungan (p237)
- Sungai Sekonyer through Tanjung Puting National Park by *klotok* (p232)
- Danau Sentarum National Park (p229)

Best Places to Stay

- Nunukan Island Resort (p266)
- Wisma Alya (p246)
- Merabu Homestay (p264)
- Hotel Gran Senyiur (p248)
- Betang Sadap (p229)

Why Go?

Skewered by the equator and roasting under a tropical sun, the steamy forests of Kalimantan serve up endless opportunities for epic rainforest exploration. The island has no volcanoes and is protected from tsunamis, which has allowed its ancient forests to grow towering trees that house some of the world's most memorable species. The noble orangutan shares the canopy with acrobatic gibbons, while prehistoric hornbills patrol the air above.

The indigenous people, collectively known as Dayak, have long lived in concert with this rich, challenging landscape. Their longhouses dot the banks of Kalimantan's many waterways, creating a sense of community unmatched elsewhere in a country already well-known for its hospitable people.

Kalimantan's natural resources have made it a prime target for exploitation; just three quarters of Borneo's lowland forests remain, and its once abundant wildlife and rich traditional cultures are rapidly disappearing. Visit this awesome wilderness as soon as you can, while you still can.

When to Go

Pontianak

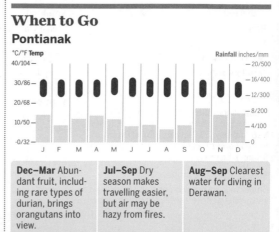

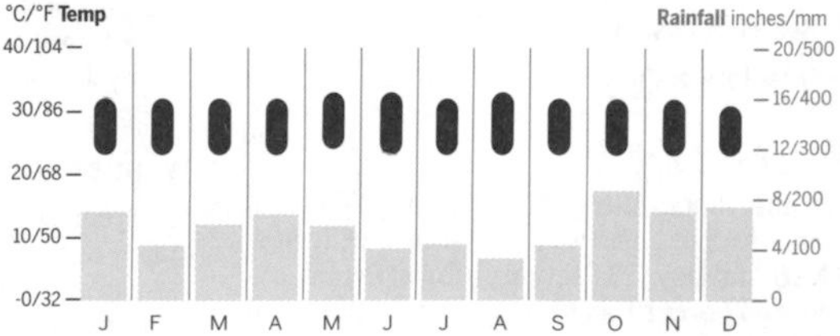

Dec–Mar Abundant fruit, including rare types of durian, brings orangutans into view.

Jul–Sep Dry season makes travelling easier, but air may be hazy from fires.

Aug–Sep Clearest water for diving in Derawan.

History & Culture

Separated from Southeast Asia's mainland 10,000 years ago by rising seas, Kalimantan was originally populated by the Dayak, who still define its public image. The culture of these diverse forest tribes once included headhunting, extensive tattooing, stretched earlobes, blowguns and longhouses – horizontal apartment buildings big enough to house an entire village. That culture has been slowly dismantled by the modern world, so that some elements, such as headhunting (thankfully), no longer exist, while others are slowly disappearing. Tribal identity persists, but many Dayak have either abandoned their traditional folk religion, Kaharingan, or combined it with Christianity (or Islam).

In addition to the Dayak, Kalimantan contains two other large ethnic groups: the Chinese and the Malay. The Chinese are the region's most successful merchants, having traded in Kalimantan since at least 300 BC. They're responsible for the bright red Confucian and Buddhist temples found in many port towns, and for a profusion of Chinese restaurants, some of Kalimantan's best dining. The Malays are predominantly Muslim, a religion that arrived with the Melaka empire in the 15th century. The most obvious signs of their presence are the grand mosques in major cities and towns, along with the call to prayer. Several palaces of Muslim sultanates, some still occupied by royal descendants, can be visited.

Since colonial times, Kalimantan has been a destination for *transmigrasi,* the government-sponsored relocation of people from more densely populated areas of the archipelago. This and an influx of jobseekers from throughout Indonesia has led to some conflict, most notably a year-long struggle between Dayak and Madurese people (from the island of Madura) in 2001, which killed 500 people, and a smaller conflict in 2010 between Dayak and Bugis in Tarakan.

Most of the struggle in Kalimantan, however, has taken place over its bountiful natural resources, and involved foreign powers. Oil, rubber, spices, timber, coal, diamonds and gold have all been pawns on the board, causing many years of intrigue, starting with British and Dutch colonial interests. During World War II oil and other resources made Borneo (the island which is home to Kalimantan) an early target for Japan, leading to a brutal occupation, in which some 21,000 people were murdered in West Kalimantan alone. In 1963 Indonesian President Sukarno led a failed attempt to take over all of Borneo by staging attacks on the Malaysian north.

Today, the struggle for Kalimantan's resources is more insidious. As one watches the endless series of enormous coal barges proceed down rivers lined with tin-roofed shacks, there is the constant sense of an ongoing plunder from which the local people benefit little, as they are outmanoeuvred by a shadowy collection of foreign businesspeople and local government officials overseen from Jakarta. Meanwhile, as palm-oil plantations spread across the landscape, the Bornean jungle recedes, never to return. Numerous conservation groups are struggling to halt the social and environmental damage, and to save some remarkable wildlife. Best to visit soon.

Wildlife

Kalimantan's flora and fauna are among the most diverse in the world. You can find more tree species in a single hectare of its rainforest than in all of the US and Canada combined. There are over 220 species of mammal and over 420 species of bird found on Borneo, many of them endemic to the island. The region is best known for its orangutans, Asia's only great ape and a rare but thrilling sight outside of Kalimantan's many rescue and rehabilitation centres. River cruising commonly reveals proboscis monkeys (unique to Borneo), macaques, gibbons, crocodiles (including gharials), monitor lizards and pythons. Hornbills are commonly seen flying overhead, and are a spiritual symbol for many Dayak. Forests harbour the rare clouded leopard, sun bears, giant moths, tarantulas, and more bizarre species of ants and spiders than you could ever conjure out of your wildest imagination. For divers, the Derawan Archipelago is renowned for its turtles, manta rays and pelagics.

ℹ Getting There & Away

The only entry points to Kalimantan that issue visas on arrival are Balikpapan's Sepinggan Airport, Pontianak's Supadio Airport and the Tebedu–Entikong land crossing between Kuching (Sarawak) and Pontianak. All other entry points require a visa issued in advance.

AIR

Most major cities can be reached from Jakarta or Surabaya. Pontianak connects with Kuching (Malaysia), while Balikpapan has direct flights to

Kalimantan Highlights

1. Completing the landmark **Cross-Borneo Trek** (p223) – if you can.
2. Meeting the orangutans of **Tanjung Puting National Park** (p232).
3. Going native in the **Kapuas Hulu** (p228) region.
4. Taking the slow boat up **Sungai Mahakam** (p255).
5. Living the (inexpensive) high life in **Balikpapan** (p247).
6. Delving into Kalimantan's near and distant past in **Merabu** (p264).
7. Exploring the **Derawan Archipelago** (p265), both under water and above.
8. Settling into village life in lovely **Loksado** (p245).
9. Witnessing the annual spectacle of **Cap Goh Meh** (p226).

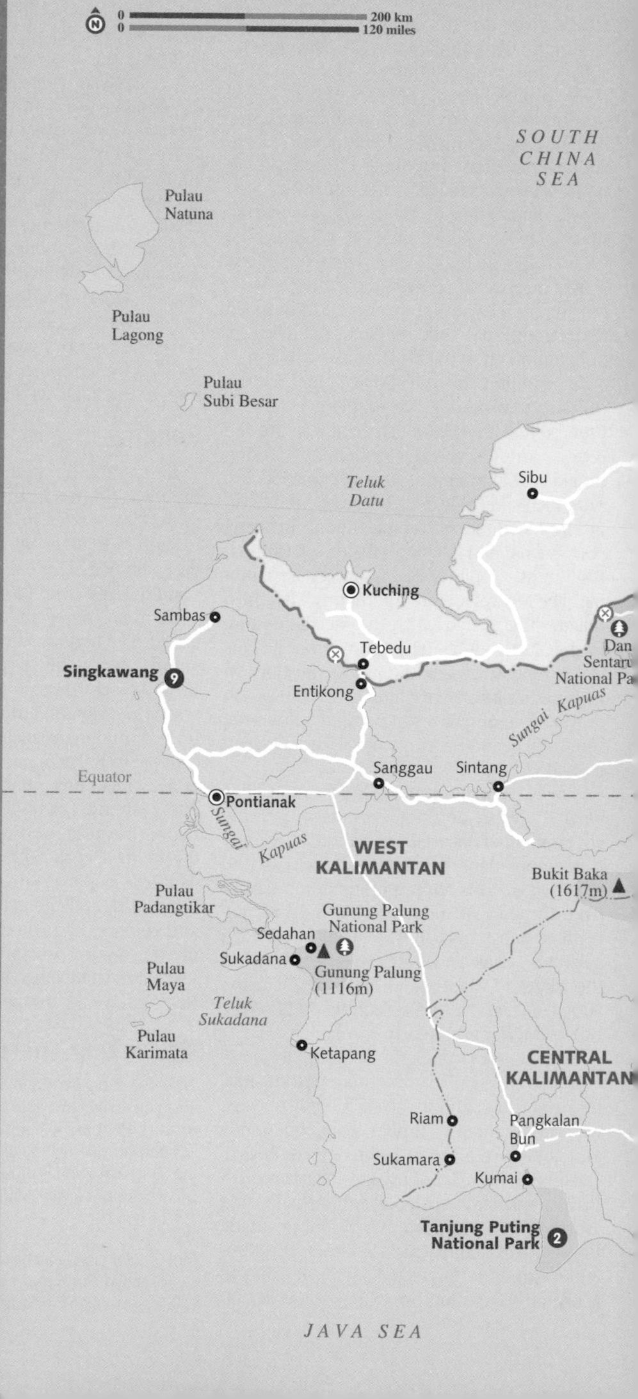

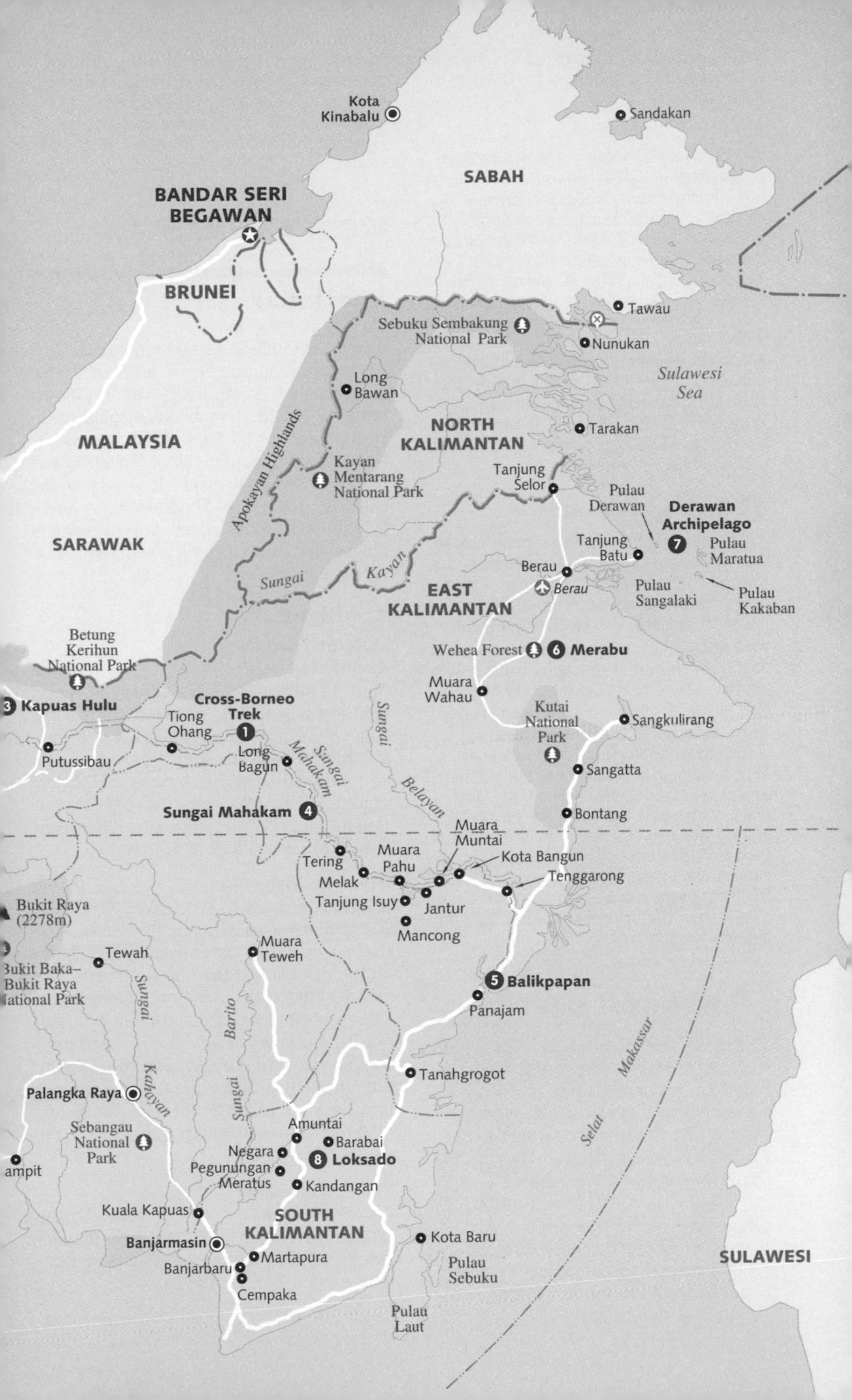

Kota Kinabalu
Sandakan
SABAH
BANDAR SERI BEGAWAN
BRUNEI
Tawau
Sebuku Sembakung National Park
Nunukan
Sulawesi Sea
Long Bawan
Apokayan Highlands
MALAYSIA
NORTH KALIMANTAN
Tarakan
Kayan Mentarang National Park
Tanjung Selor
Pulau Derawan
Derawan Archipelago
7
SARAWAK
Tanjung Batu
Pulau Maratua
Berau
Sungai Kayan
EAST KALIMANTAN
Berau
Pulau Sangalaki
Pulau Kakaban
Betung Kerihun National Park
Wehea Forest
6 Merabu
Muara Wahau
3 Kapuas Hulu
Cross-Borneo Trek
1
Tiong Ohang
Kutai National Park
Sangkulirang
Sungai Belayan
Putussibau
Long Bagun
Sungai Mahakam
Sangatta
Sungai Mahakam 4
Bontang
Muara Muntai
Tering
Muara Pahu
Kota Bangun
Melak
Tenggarong
Tanjung Isuy
Jantur
Mancong
Bukit Raya (2278m)
Tewah
Muara Teweh
Bukit Baka–Bukit Raya National Park
Sungai Barito
5 Balikpapan
Panajam
Sungai Kahayan
Selat Makassar
Tanahgrogot
Palangka Raya
Sebangau National Park
Amuntai
Barabai
Negara
8 Loksado
Pegunungan Meratus
Kandangan
Kuala Kapuas
SOUTH KALIMANTAN
Banjarmasin
Kota Baru
Martapura
Banjarbaru
Pulau Sebuku
Cempaka
SULAWESI
Pulau Laut

Kuala Lumpur, Malaysia and Singapore. There are no direct flights from Europe or the Americas to Kalimantan.

BOAT

Major ferry ports in Kalimantan include Balikpapan, Samarinda, Banjarmasin and Pontianak. Pelni (www.pelni.co.id) and other carriers connect to Jakarta, Semarang and Surabaya on Java, as well as Makassar and Pare Pare on Sulawesi. There is an infrequent ferry between Tawau (Sabah) and Tarakan, with more regular speedboat service from Tawau to Nunukan.

BUS

Air-con buses link Pontianak with Kuching (230,000Rp, nine hours), as well as with other cities along Sarawak's central coast, and even Brunei (650,000Rp, 25 hours). Bus travel between Putussibau and Sarawak requires switching carriers at the border.

Getting Around

Kalimantan is both immense and undeveloped. River travel is as common as road travel, and transport options can form a complex picture. To assess the ever-changing transportation options it is often easiest to visit a local travel agent.

Air Regional flights aboard ATR turboprops are an efficient means of getting from one hub to another, while smaller Cessnas may be your only option for some remote locations.

Road Highways between major cities are improving daily, and range from excellent to pockmarked. Buses are fairly ubiquitous, except in East and North Kalimantan. Most major routes offer air-con for an extra cost. A Kijang (4WD minivan) can often be chartered between cities. Intra-city travel usually involves a minibus known as an *angkot* or *opelet* (or, frustratingly, *taksi* in Banjarmasin) that charges a flat fee per trip. To really go native, take an *ojek* (motorcycle taxi).

TRANSPORT SAFETY

Road washouts, river rapids, dilapidated buses, flash floods, weaving scooters, speeding Kijang, overweight canoes, questionable airlines, and a general lack of both maintenance and safety equipment require an extra dose of diligence when travelling in Kalimantan.

Insist on life jackets on boats. Don't be afraid to remind your driver they aren't filming *Fast & Furious Borneo*. And remember, repeatedly saying *tidak apa apa* (no worries) doesn't make the very real dangers magically disappear.

River A variety of craft ply the rivers, including the *kapal biasa* (large two-storey ferry), the *klotok* (smaller boat with covered passenger cabins), speedboats, and motorised canoes, including the *ces* (the local longtail). Bring your earplugs.

WEST KALIMANTAN

Pontianak

0561 / POP 570,000

Sprawling south of the equator, Pontianak is the concrete cultural mixing bowl and transportation hub of West Kalimantan (known locally as Kalbar, short for Kalimantan Barat. Head inland to visit Dayak longhouses in the **Kapuas Hulu**, south to serene Sukadana and Gunung Palung National Park, or north to the culturally rich city of **Singkawang**. A handful of cultural sights and an improving hotel market make the city itself a perfectly tolerable place to layover.

Sights

Museum Provinsi Kalimantan Barat MUSEUM

(West Kalimantan Provincial Museum; Jl Ahmad Yani; admission 1000Rp; 8am-2.30pm Tue-Thu, 8-11am & 1-2.30pm Fri, 8am-2pm Sat & Sun) A well-maintained collection of artefacts provides an informative English-language overview of local Dayak, Malay and Chinese cultures. Helpful staff offer further insights. Take a red or pink *opelet* south along Jl Yani.

Istana Kadriah MUSEUM

(admission by donation; 7am-noon) For an outing that will show you a bit of town, visit the leaking palace of Pontianak's first sultan on the east bank of the Kapuas. Nearby, the wooden **Mesjid Abdurrahman** stands where a cannonball reportedly landed after the sultan fired it at a *pontianak* (the ghost of a woman who died during childbirth). Explore the surrounding village on stilts for a glimpse into the city's past. Get there by canoe taxi (2000Rp regular, 10,000Rp charter) from the foot of Jl Mahakam.

Vihara Bodhisatva Karaniya Metta BUDDHIST TEMPLE

(Jl Sultan Muhammad) FREE West Kalimantan's oldest Buddhist temple (1673) is a sensory feast.

OFF THE BEATEN TRACK

THE CROSS-BORNEO TREK: A WORLD-CLASS ADVENTURE

Borneo offers one of the world's greatest adventure travel routes. East and West Kalimantan are divided by the Muller mountain range, which also serves as the headwaters for Indonesia's two longest rivers *(sungai)*. Sungai Kapuas snakes 1143km to the west coast near Pontianak, while Sungai Mahakam flows 930km to the east coast, by Samarinda. Thus, by travelling up one, hiking over the Muller Range, and travelling down the other, it is possible to cross the world's third-largest island. Be forewarned, however: this journey holds significant hazards, from deadly rapids to remote and brutal hiking where the smallest misstep could have life-changing consequences. This should not be your first rainforest trek.

Like all good epics, this one comes in a trilogy.

Sungai Mahakam One of Kalimantan's last great river journeys, travelling the Mahakam can easily fill several days in a succession of boats, making side trips into lakes and marshes, spotting wildlife, and visiting small river towns. The trek itself begins (or ends) at Tiong Ohang, up two boat-crushing sets of rapids from Long Bagun.

The Muller Mountains You do this jungle trek for the same reason you climb Mt Everest: because it's there. Noted for its river fording, hordes of leeches, and treacherous slopes, the route requires the knowledge of a professional guiding company. If you walk a taxing eight hours a day, you can make it across in five days, but seven is more comfortable and safer. Plan for 10.

Sungai Kapuas The *hulu* (headwater) region of the Kapuas is home to many of Kalimantan's best and most accessible longhouses. However, public-boat travel below Putussibau is nonexistent, meaning most trekkers fly or bus between Pontianak and Putussibau.

Debate rages as to which direction is preferable. The consensus seems to be that east-to-west is logistically simpler, while west-to-east is physically less brutal. Either way, success is a noteworthy achievement you'll remember for the rest of your life.

Tugu Khatulistiwa MONUMENT
(Equator Monument; Jl Khatulistiwa; ⏲7.30am-4.30pm) If you want to stand on two hemispheres, you can formally do so here – though continental drift has moved the monument 117m south of the actual equator. The gift shop nearby has a colourful collection of T-shirts, sarongs and equator lamps. Cross the river by ferry and take an *opelet* 3km northwest on Jl Khatulistiwa.

Festivals & Events

Gawai Dayak Festival CULTURAL
(⏲May/Jun) The Dayak harvest festival takes place in Pontianak at the end of May, but many villages hold their own sometime between April and June. These generally loud, chaotic and festive week-long affairs have plenty of dancing and food.

Tours

Canopy Indonesia ECOTOUR
(☎0811 574 2228, 0812 5809 2228; info.canopyindonesia@gmail.com) Energetic husband-and-wife team Deny and Venie are passionate about sustainable tourism through community engagement. They reinvest much of the proceeds from their signature Danau Sentarum National Park trips into developing new ecotourism programs throughout West Kalimantan.

Times Tours & Travel CULTURAL TOUR
(☎0819 560 1920; timestravell@yahoo.com; Jl Komyos Sudarso Blok H no 6) Specialising in cultural tours around Pontianak and KalBar since 1995, English-speaking owner Iwan is super-responsive and efficient. Call before visiting.

Sleeping

Green Leaf Inn HOTEL $
(☎0561-769622; Jl Gajah Mada 65; s/d 110,000/216,000Rp; ❄) Large superior rooms have new paint and clean tile floors, while the 'personal' rooms barely have space for a bed. All have cold water and contortionist showers. Breakfast for one is included, but not windows.

Mess Hijas HOTEL $
(☎0561-744068; Jl Hijas 106; s/d 100,000/150,000Rp; ❄) These stalwart budget digs manage to remain relevant and relatively clean. Floors three and four compensate for the hike by offering hot-water showers for

Pontianak

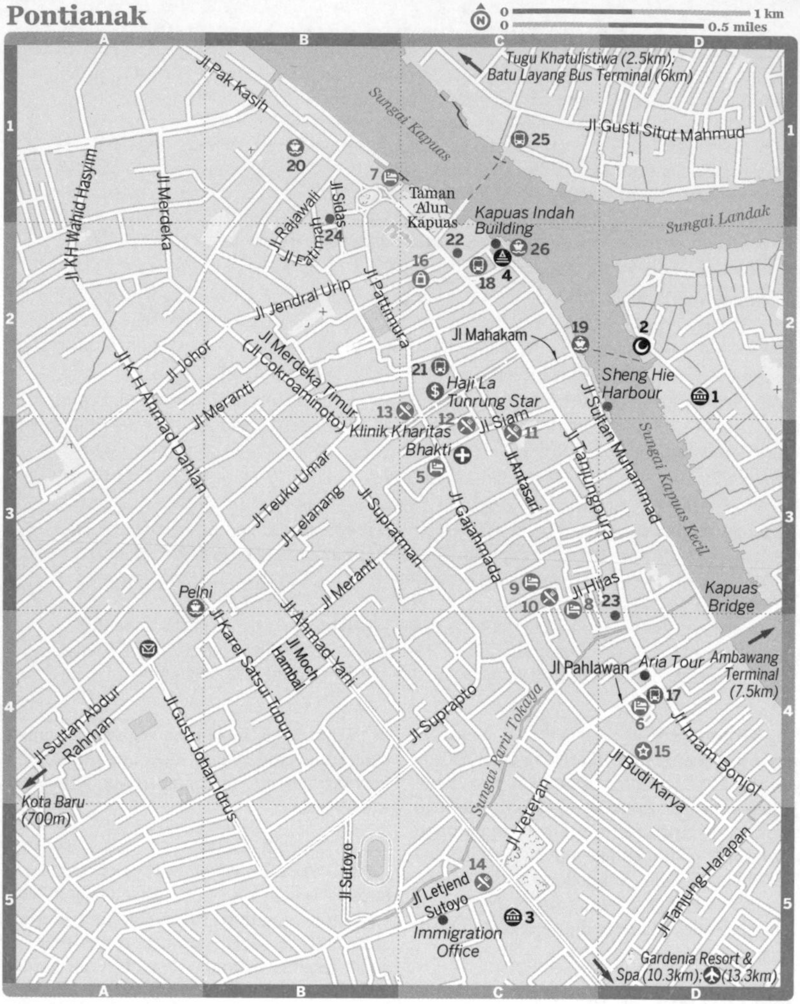

no extra cost. The front gate is locked at midnight, whether you are home or not.

Hosanna Inn HOTEL $

(☎0561-735052; Jl Pahlawan 224/2; s/d incl breakfast 135,000/195,000Rp; ❄📶) The public spaces are pleasantly decorated and the staff are friendly, making this a good option for those taking an early DAMRI bus (next door). However, the cramped and tired budget rooms share impossibly tiny bathrooms. Room 205 has windows and access to a balcony.

Pontianak HOTEL $$

(☎0561-761118; Jl Gajah Mada 21; r incl breakfast 668,000-748,000Rp; ❄📶🏊) This oasis of old-school luxury and sophisticated decor is a steal at regularly discounted rates (listed here). Superiors are spacious, while the executive rooms add a bath and sofa. The RiverX entertainment complex will perk you up at night, and the substantial breakfast buffet will fuel you throughout the day.

Have a drink or two at the wine bar before shopping at the regional handicrafts shop with surprisingly reasonable prices.

Pontianak

Sights

1 Istana Kadriah D2
2 Mesjid Abdurrahman D2
3 Museum Provinsi Kalimantan Barat C5
4 Vihara Bodhisatva Karaniya Metta C2

Sleeping

5 Green Leaf Inn C3
6 Hosanna Inn D4
7 Kartika Hotel B1
8 Mess Hijas C3
9 Pontianak C3

Eating

10 Abang Kepiting C3
11 Ce Pien Chek C3
12 Chai Kue Siam A-Hin C3
13 Mie Tiau Polo C2
14 Rumah Makan Betang C5

Entertainment

15 Café Tisya D4

Shopping

16 Borneo Art Shop C2

Transport

17 ATS D4
18 Bis Sentosa C2
19 Canoe Taxis to Istana Kadriah C2
DAMRI .... (see 6)
20 Dharma Lautan Utama B1
21 Executive Buses to Kuching C2
22 Garuda C2
23 Kalstar D4
24 Lion Air B1
25 Siantan Bus & Ferry Terminal C1
26 Speedboats to Sukadana C2

Gardenia Resort & Spa HOTEL $$
(☎0561-672 6446; www.gardeniaresortandspa.com; Jl Ahmad Yani II; ste 750,000Rp; ❄📶🏊) The closest thing to a resort in Pontianak, the Gardenia is near the airport, making it a great option for those uninterested in the city itself. Spacious private villas connected by boardwalks to the spa and an al fresco restaurant – all built with Balinese notions – provide welcome respite from the chaos of urban Kalimantan.

Kartika Hotel HOTEL $$
(☎0561-734401; Jl Rahadi Usman 2; riverside incl breakfast 477,600Rp; ❄📶) Its location on the river sets this hotel apart. Catch a breeze on the balcony as you plot upstream expeditions like an explorer of yesteryear. If the riverside rooms are full, however, give the place a miss. The open-deck Panorama Restaurant serves cold beer 24 hours.

Eating

At night Jl Gajah Mada becomes crowded with cafe culture, while seafood tents take over the Jl Diponegoro–Agus Salim median.

★ **Chai Kue Siam A-Hin** DUMPLING $
(Jl Siam; 10 dumplings from 20,000Rp; ⏲10am-10pm) Pork or veggies, steamed or fried – whichever you desire, you'll be waiting your turn among the mob of locals jockeying for a table or take away.

Mie Tiau Polo INDONESIAN $
(Jl Pattimura; mains 25,000Rp; ⏲10am-9pm) Not to be confused with Apollo to the left, whose sign proudly states: 'Since 1968. Never moved.' Polo's sign retorts simply: 'Moved from next door.' The dispute is as legendary as the noodles they serve. Draw your own conclusions about which is the best ... or oldest.

Ce Pien Chek VEGETARIAN $
(CPC; ☎0821 5101 8969; Jl Siam 87; mains 15,000Rp; ⏲8.30am-9.30pm; 🌿) Piles of vegetables and fake meat served up with a small, but endearing, touch of self-righteousness.

Rumah Makan Betang DAYAK $
(Jl Letjend Sutoyo 4A; ⏲10am-11pm; 📶) Located behind the replica *betang* (longhouse) this small warung (food stall) cooks up traditional Dayak fare including *babi kecap*, a dish made from sautéed pork and pig fat. Wash it down with a glass of *tuak pulut*, a traditional sweet wine made from sticky rice.

Abang Kepiting SEAFOOD $$
(Jl Hijas; fish per oz 20,000Rp; ⏲5-10pm) Buckets of iced fish out front are begging to be steamed, fried or grilled to your liking. Treat yourself to an experience and dive into a pile of smoked crabs: a full-body, all-evening affair. Come early as the place fills quickly.

Entertainment

Café Tisya LIVE MUSIC
(Jl Budi Karya; ⏲7pm-2am) Have a few Bintang, enjoy some (loud) live music, and meet the locals, from university students to sailors on shore leave.

Shopping

For general souvenirs, visit the craft shops lining Jl Pattimura.

★**Borneo Art Shop** ANTIQUES
(☎0813 7499 6145; Jl Nusa Indah I B24; ⏲9am-5pm) Come here to enter a world of exotic curios from around Borneo including arts, antiques and etcetera. Lots of etcetera.

Information

Aria Tour (☎0561-577868; Jl Tanjungpura 36, near Hotel Garuda) Good for airline tickets and SJS buses to Kuching.

Haji La Tunrung Star (☎0561-743385; Jl Diponegoro 163) Exchange chain dealing in multiple currencies.

Immigration Office (☎0561-765576; Jl Letjend Sutoyo)

Klinik Kharitas Bhakti (☎0561-766975, 0561-734373; Jl Siam 153; ⏲7-12.30am) Emergency open 24 hours.

Main Post Office (☎0561-730641; Jl Sultan Abdur Rahman 49; ⏲7.30am-9.30pm Mon-Sat, 8am-2pm Sun)

Getting There & Away

AIR

Garuda (☎0561-734986; Jl Rahadi Usman 8A)

Kalstar (☎0561-724234, 0561-739090; Jl Tanjungpura 429)

Lion Air (☎0561-721555, 0561-742064; Mahkota Hotel, Jl Sidas)

MASwings (☎0856 5454 5016; Airport)

Sriwijaya Air (Nam Air; ☎0561-706 2400; Airport)

Trigana (☎0561-725513; Airport)

Xpress Air (☎0823 5791 9555, 0561-717 0456; Airport)

BOAT

Ships bound for Java leave from the main harbour on Jl Pak Kasih, north of the Kartika Hotel.

Dharma Lautan Utama (☎0561-765021; Jl Pak Kasih 42F)

Pelni (☎0561-748124; Jl Sultan Abdur Rahman 12)

The **Poly 2 Express** (☎0561-35864; economy 260,000Rp) jet boat to Ketapang leaves from **Sheng Hie Harbour** (Jl Barito) daily. At time of research, the **Bahari Express** (☎0561-760 820) was dry-docked for the foreseeable future.

Speedboats (☎8.30am boat 0857 5484 3414, 9.15am boat 0813 5213 4440) to Sukadana (five hours) leave from behind the Kapuas Indah Building.

There are no scheduled passenger boats upriver to Putussibau. However, if both your time and *bahasa* are abundant, negotiate a ride on a combination houseboat, freighter and general store, that can take several days to a month to make the epic 900km journey. Priceless.

BUS

International Pontianak seems determined to make international bus travel as inconvenient as possible. Malaysia and Brunei arrivals and departures take place at the massively overbuilt Ambawang Terminal, 9km east of the city. The taxi cartel has fixed the rates into town at 150,000Rp and prevents public transport from

WORTH A TRIP

SINGKAWANG, HOME OF KALBAR'S BIGGEST PARTY

Reminiscent of Shanghai 1950, Singkawang's vibrant energy is unique in Kalimantan. The largely Chinese city has some classic shop houses, ancient ceramic kilns, an impressive night market (**Pasar Malam Hongkong**), and nearly 1000 Chinese temples. The city swells beyond its streets during the **Cap Goh Meh** celebration on the 15th day of the lunar new year, when dragons and lions dance among Chinese and Dayak *tatungs* (holy men possessed by spirits who perform acts of self-mutilation and animal sacrifice). A *luar biasa* (extraordinary) spectacle.

The best rooms in town are those at the top of **Villa Bukit Mas** (☎0562 333 5666; Singkawang; s/d 560,000/600,000Rp), a sophisticated hillside hotel with wooden floors, private porches and a refined seclusion. The restaurant has grand open-air seating ringed by plumeria trees, and specialises in shabu-shabu (66,000Rp for two) and cold Bintang beer.

The extensive beaches near Singkawang offer everything from deserted paradise to garish 'resorts' with carnival atmospheres. Catch the public boat (25,000Rp, one hour, departs 8am) from the police station at **Batu Payung** to **Penata Island** for some truly off-the-beaten-path exploration.

DAMRI buses (100,000Rp, three hours) and shared taxis leave for Singkawang regularly from Pontianak's airport and Kota Baru.

TRANSPORT FROM PONTIANAK

Air

DESTINATION	COMPANY	FARE (RP)	DURATION (HR)	FREQUENCY
Balikpapan	Kalstar	1,160,000	2	Mon, Wed, Fri, Sun
Bandung	Kalstar, Xpress	1,000,000	1¼	1 daily
Batam	Lion	717,000	1¼	1 daily
Denpasar	Kalstar	1,161,000	3	Tue, Thu, Sat
Jakarta	Garuda, Lion, Sriwijaya	560,000	1½	18 daily
Ketapang	Kalstar, Trigana	440,000	40min	5 daily
Kuala Lumpur	AirAsia	399,000	2	Sun, Mon, Wed, Fri
Kuching	MASwings, Xpress	850,000	45min	1-2 daily
Palangka Raya	Garuda	1,113,000	1¾	1 daily
Pangkalan Bun	Kalstar, Trigana	854,000	1½	2 daily
Putussibau	Garuda, Kalstar	556,000	1	2 daily
Semarang	Kalstar	1,020,000	2	2 daily
Sintang	Kalstar	700,000	45min	2 daily
Surabaya	Kalstar	923,000	1¼	2 daily
Yogyakarta	Nam, Xpress	1,000,000	1½	1-2 daily

Boat

DESTINATION	COMPANY	FARE (RP)	DURATION (HR)	FREQUENCY
Jakarta	Pelni	288,000	36	weekly
Ketapang (jet boat)	Bahari Express, Poly 2 Express	260,000	8	daily
Natuna Islands	Pelni	184,000	28	weekly
Semarang	Pelni, Dharma Lautan Utama	280,000	40	weekly
Sukadana (long boat)	multiple operators	240,000	5	daily
Surabaya	Pelni	334,000	44	weekly

Bus

DESTINATION	COMPANY	FARE (RP)	DURATION (HR)	FREQUENCY
Brunei	ATS, DAMRI, SJS	650,000	26	daily
Kuching	ATS, Bintang Jaya, Bus Asia, DAMRI, EVA	230,000	9	daily
Pangkalan Bun	DAMRI	350,000	20	daily
Putussibau	Bis Sentosa	200,000-300,000	12	daily
Sambas	DAMRI, local minibus	45,000-90,0000	5	daily
Singkawang	DAMRI, local minibus	35,000-100,000	3	daily
Sintang	ATS, DAMRI	160,000-200,000	6	daily

serving the terminal. Buy international tickets from **ATS** (☎0561-706 8670; Jl Pahlawan 58), **DAMRI** (☎0561-744859, SMS 0812 5420 6001; Jl Pahlawan 226), or one of several companies along Jl Sisingamangaraja.

Domestic On the bright side, improved roads and newer fleets make bus travel within Kalimantan faster and leagues more comfortable than in the past. Regional buses still depart from within the city, with **Bis Sentosa** (☎0856 502 1219; Jl Kopten Marsan B5) serving Putussibau, and DAMRI Pangkalan Bun. Few minibuses depart from Batu Layang terminal these days, instead picking up passengers for Sambas and Singkawang on their way past the Siantan ferry terminal.

CAR

A car with driver costs 450,000Rp per day within the city. Private charters to Singkawang and points north start at 700,000Rp per day.

Getting Around

- Airport taxis cost 110,000Rp to town (17km). Alternately, take a DAMRI bus to the Kota Baru neighbourhood (35,000Rp, every two hours), then an *opelet* (3000Rp) downtown from there.
- *Opelet* (3000Rp) routes converge around Jl Sisingamangaraja.
- Becak (bicycle rickshaws) are available, but are a dying breed.
- Taxis are unmetered and scarce.

Sungai Kapuas

Indonesia's longest river, Sungai Kapuas, begins in the foothills of the Muller range and snakes 1143km west to the sea. Along the way it passes by some of Kalimantan's oldest, friendliest, and most vibrant longhouse communities, the photographer's paradise of Danau Sentarum, and – waaay off in the distance – Bukit Raya, the tallest peak in Kalimantan. Unlike the Mahakam, there is no *kapal biasa* service, making river travel impractical, but improving roads between Pontianak and Putussibau make bus trips manageable.

Sintang

☎0565

Sintang sits at the confluence of Sungai Kapuas and Sungai Melawi, where the sentinel peak of Bukit Kelam looms between you and the **Kapuas Hulu**. A phenomenal weaving **gallery** (☎0565-21098; koperasijmm@ymail.com; ⏱8am-4pm Mon-Fri, to noon Sat) in a replica longhouse and a well-meaning **museum** (Jl Sintang-Putussibau Km14; ⏱8am-3pm Mon-Fri, 9am-3pm Sat-Sun) **FREE** make it a good choice for breaking up your bus journey between Pontianak and Putussibau.

Start here for trips to **Bukit Baka–Bukit Raya National Park** and the seven-day expedition to climb Kalimantan's tallest mountain. Register (mandatory) at the **park office** (☎0565-23521; bukitbakabukitraya.org; Jl Wahidin Sudirohusodo 75) next to the police compound, where they'll explain transport options.

The best lodging near town is the inconveniently located **Bagoes Guesthouse** (☎0565-23733; Jl Dharma Putra 16; r 215,000-389,000Rp), southeast of the five-way intersection *(simpang lima)*.

Getting There & Away

Air Kalstar flies twice daily to Pontianak (700,000Rp, 40 minutes), and Aviastar connects to Ketapang (410,000Rp, Tue and Sat).

Bus Services run daily to/from Pontianak (160,000Rp, 10 hours) from Terminal Sungai Durian, and Putussibau-bound buses pass the Jl Deponegoro/Jl Bhayangkara roundabout. For trips to **Danau Sentarum**, go straight to the park office in Semitau on a minibus from Pasar Inpres (200,000Rp, five hours). Or take a Putussibau-bound bus to Simpang Pala Kota (100,000Rp, 3½ hours) and wait for any vehicle to Semitau.

Getting Around

White *angkot* (5000Rp) connect Terminal Pasar Inpres on the east bank and Terminal Sungai Durian on the west bank, passing most major landmarks.

OFF THE BEATEN TRACK

KALIMANTAN'S FINAL FRONTIER: BETUNG KERIHUN NATIONAL PARK

If you're the type to spend hours poring over satellite images to find the darkest green patches up the furthest reaches of jungle rivers, ripe for exploration, then you've noticed the northeast corner of KalBar. Four major watersheds draining the border with Malaysia are protected as **Betung Kerihun National Park** (☎0567-21935; betungkerihun.dephut.go.id; Jl P Tendean, Putussibau), an expanse of mountains and old-growth forests where trekkers and boaters can spend lifetimes exploring. Facilities are few and river travel expensive; this is raw adventure of a kind increasingly hard to find in Kalimantan.

Putussibau

☎0567

This lively river town is the last stop for airlines and long-distance buses, as well as the last chance for an ATM, before launching into the wilderness.

Sights & Activities

You can't swing a *mandau* (Dayak machete) around Putussibau without hitting a *betang* (the local word for longhouse). Some of these traditional Dayak dwellings house 30 families or more. Stand at one end of the communal front porch, and the other end disappears into converging lines interrupted occasionally by sleeping dogs or playing children. *Betang* range from historic and ornate affairs elevated on ironwood pillars, to almost nondescript row houses resembling company barracks.

Many, but not all, *betang* welcome casual visitors, with overnight stays often possible. Ask permission before entering or taking photographs. Expect to be introduced to the headman or cultural liaison, who will invariably insist you join them for a cup of overly sweet coffee or tea, the modern equivalent of a welcoming ceremony. Homestays, where available, may simply be a mat on the community room floor and a bite of whatever is cooking. You stay here for the experience, not the luxury.

Betang Buana Tengah LONGHOUSE
(homestay 35,000Rp) Built in 1864, this *betang* is home to Tamambaloh Apalin Dayak. Debate over whether it is the oldest longhouse in the region (if not Kalimantan) abruptly ended in 2014, when neighbouring contender Betang Uluk Palin tragically burned to the ground. The floor looms 4.5m above the earth, supported by the original weathered ironwood columns. Take the Badau bus 50km northwest of Putussibau, then an *ojek* 4km southwest on a gravel road.

Betang Sadap LONGHOUSE
(homestay 120,000Rp, meals 20,000Rp) Not the oldest, nor the most picturesque, but perhaps the most welcoming longhouse community. An ecotourism effort spearheaded by Januar, an Iban Matthew Broderick lookalike, will have you angling for prize-winning semah fish or splashing up the cascading rainforest creeks of their community forest. Why pay millions of rupiah for a boat trip to Betung Kerihun when you can have it all here?

Melapi 1 LONGHOUSE
The Taman Dayak longhouses of Melapi 1 to 5 stretch along the Kapuas upriver of Putussibau. As per usual, the sequels don't quite live up to the original. To find Melapi 1, borrow bicycles or a motorbike and head 10km southeast of town on Jl Lintas Timur. Turn left at the church and hail a canoe taxi across the river. A homestay may be negotiable.

OFF THE BEATEN TRACK

DANAU SENTARUM NATIONAL PARK

To avoid accusations of hyperbole, we'll let the numbers describe Danau Sentarum National Park: 4m to 6m of rainfall each year causes water levels to fluctuate by up to 12m – higher than a three-story building. As the water recedes, the lake's 240 fish species are funnelled into narrowing channels, where they must contend with 800km of gill net, 20,000 traps, and 500,000 hooks placed by fishers occupying 20 villages, who haul out as much as 13,000 tons of fish a year. Meanwhile, 237 bird and 143 mammal species inhabit the 1320 sq km of peat swamp, lowland forest and seasonal grasslands so compelling you'll be thankful for packing that extra memory card for your camera.

Enter the park's network of lakes, creeks and channels from Lanjak in the north near Putussibau, or Semitau in the south near Sintang. Be sure to register with the park office at either town (150,000Rp per person per day). Boats run 400,000Rp to 700,000Rp per day, and guides cost 150,000Rp per day. Highlights include staying at **Pelaik** (120,000Rp per room) – the isolated longhouse tucked away in the forest at the end of a hidden lake; fishing at nearby **Meliau** (300,000Rp); watching the sunrise from **Tekenang** hill; and hunting for honey with the villagers at **Semangit**. Arrange a tour through Canopy Indonesia (see p223) in Pontianak, or Kompakh (p230) in Putussibau. Getting here takes some time, so plan to stay a while.

Tours

Kompakh ADVENTURE TOUR
(☎0852 4545 0852; www.kompakh.or.id; Jl Kenanga Komp Ruko Pemda 3D) The folks at this WWF-supported ecotourism initiative know everything about Kapuas Hulu and offer tours ranging from Danau Sentarum National Park to longhouse visits to river cruising to jungle treks, including the Cross-Borneo Trek (p223).

Sleeping

Rindu Kapuas HOTEL $
(☎0567-21010; Jl Merdeka 11; r 165,000-198,000Rp; ❄) Nice rooms, each with air-con and TV, arrayed around the central living area of a large single-level house. From the traditional market, head south toward the river and turn west on Jl Merdeka (which continues under Jl A Yani at the river bridge.)

Aman Sentosa Hotel MOTEL $
(☎0567-21691; Jl Diponegoro 14; r 110,000-352,000Rp; ❄ wi-fi) A variety of clean concrete rooms ring a central parking courtyard. They don't serve breakfast, but do have wi-fi in the lobby and motorbikes for rent (75,000Rp).

Eating & Drinking

Pondok Meranti INDONESIAN $
(☎0567-21454; Jl Yos Sudarso; mains 15,000Rp; ⏰10am-10pm) A big, blue, open warehouse full of polished wooden tables where a limited menu of Indonesian staples, drinks and juice is served. Try the 'extra jos susu' for an afternoon jolt of tachycardia.

Cafe Amanda CAFE
(Alun Park; mains 20,000Rp; ⏰3pm-midnight) This al fresco cafe occupies the riverside park near the bridge, making it a uniquely popular place to hang out.

Information

Rafly Cyber (Jl Yos Sudarso 127; internet access per hour 4000Rp; ⏰7am-10pm)

RS Diponegoro (☎0567-21052; Jl Yos Sudarso 42) Local hospital.

Getting There & Away

Air Kalstar (☎0821 5202 2213; Jl Lintas Selatan 42B) and **Garuda** (☎0567-21870; Jl KS Tubun 7A) offer once daily flights to Pontianak (546,000Rp, one hour). Taxis from the airport (3½km) cost 50,000Rp, an *ojek* 25,000Rp.

Bus Services leave from **Sentosa** (☎0567-22628; Jl Rahadi Usman) and **Perintis** (☎0567-21237; Jl Yos Sudarso 71) offices for Sintang (140,000Rp, nine hours, 6am) and Pontianak (200,000Rp, 12 hours, six daily 10am to 1.30pm). For Badau and Lanjak (120,000Rp, four hours, 10.30am) head to the bus terminal north of the market.

Boat The pier is on Sungai Kapuas east of the bridge.

Getting Around

The only way to get around Putussibau is to hire a motorbike (75,000Rp per day), as *angkot* have gone way.

Tanjung Lokan & Sungai Bungan

Cross-Borneo treks start or end at the village of Tanjung Lokan, a small group of huts located on Sungai Bungan, a rapid-filled tributary of the Kapuas. There is a basic lodge (50,000Rp) and a few guides for hire, but English is hard to come by.

The expense, challenge, and risk of travelling through this section of churning river is not to be underestimated, or underappreciated. Expect to walk around some sections. The cost of the seven-hour downriver trip to Putussibau has been officially set at 1,000,000Rp per seat and up to 4,000,000Rp per per boat. Upstream takes twice as long due to the current, and costs twice as much.

Sukadana

☎0534 / POP 22,000

Sukadana is a most welcome surprise, all the more so because few people seem to know about it. Half the fun is just getting here, commonly via a scenic five-hour speedboat ride from Pontianak through tributaries, estuaries, and the mangrove wonderland near **Batu Ampar**. The region is full of forested hills and attractive islands dotted with isolated fishing villages begging for exploration. Finally you reach wide Melano Bay on the South China Sea and skirt the coastline, passing **Batu Daya**, a vertical wall of rock soaring in the distance as you approach the mountains of **Gunung Palung National Park**.

Sukadana is hidden in a fold of coastline betrayed by its major landmark, the Mahkota Kayong, a completely out of place hotel built over the water. South of town, an attractive beach, surrounded by rolling rainforested hills where gibbons usher in the dawn with melodic duets, helps make this an excellent getaway.

GUNUNG PALUNG: A PARK THAT'S HARD TO LOVE

Gunung Palung's mountain landscape, wildlife diversity and accessibility should make it *the* premier rainforest trekking location in Kalimantan. With a large population of wild orangutans, hundreds of acrobatic gibbons, sun bears, clouded leopards, and old-growth trees so large four people can't reach around them, the park is one of the last great pockets of primary rainforest on the island. Unfortunately, a history of mismanagement coupled with a monopoly on tourism by the park-employee-owned company **Nasalis Tour and Travel** (☎0534-772 2701; www.nasalistour.com; Jl Gajah Mada 34, Ketapang) has long made visiting this unspoiled gem financially challenging. But there may be hope.

Now operating under a new administrator, Gunung Palung has made laudable progress toward both curbing illegal logging, and opening the tourism market to local communities and outside companies. After a nearly four-year struggle, the village of **Sedahan** has regained permission to take visitors to the Swiss Family Robinson camp at **Lubuk Baji** in the foothills behind their home, and Canopy Indonesia (p223) is poised to begin offering the trip as well. Unfortunately, official park zoning makes the primary forests at **Cabang Panti** research camp explicitly off-limits to tourism (though somehow Nasalis still advertises trips there via a Gunung Palung summit trek – for a price.)

Tourism is in its infancy, but USAID-advised ecotourism initiatives in the nearby village of Sedahan, and an increasing focus on the **Karimata Islands**, are putting this undiscovered coastal mountain town solidly on the radar.

Sights

Pulau Datok Beach BEACH

A well-kept town beach, encircled by rainforested hills and looking out on some alluring islands. Dining options come and go as randomly as the Sunda Shelf tides, but you can usually find a few warung serving fresh coconut, assorted juices or satay. During low tide, join a pick-up game of football on the mudflats and meet the locals.

Sedahan Village VILLAGE

(☎Pak Naza, village head 0896 3411 1189, Rachel, an English-speaker 0852 5255 5678) Known for its high-quality rice, this verdant village at the foot of Gunung Palung – 10km northeast of Sukadana – has a unique attitude and aesthetic due to the Balinese *transmigrants*, whose culture blends with the local flavour. A nascent ecotourism initiative, including a community homestay (single 150,000Rp, double 200,000Rp), has opened new opportunities. Local guides can arrange trips to Lubuk Baji in Gunung Palung National Park.

Sleeping & Eating

Sukadana has one very interesting hotel and several budget losmen. For meals, the Mahkota and Anugrah hotels have decent options, and warung can be found near the dock.

Penginapan Family GUESTHOUSE $

(Jl Tanjungpura; r with fan 50,000Rp, s/d with aircon 175,000/190,000Rp; ❄) Among the nicest people you could ever rent a room from, this family is eager to accommodate even when they're not sure what you want. Larger VIP rooms are quieter, set back from the road. Economy rooms are a bit dreary. Bicycle/motorbike/auto rental available (30,000/75,000/300,000Rp).

Mahkota Kayong Hotel HOTEL $$

(☎0534-772 2777; www.mahkotakayonghotel.com; Jl Irama Laut; r/ste 400,000/800,000Rp; ❄📶) Built on piles over the water, this grand anomaly dwarfs anything in town. It is usually empty outside of occasional government conventions, which seems to make some staff forget why they are here. Sea-facing rooms get blazingly hot until the sun sets with predictably stunning displays.

It's worth visiting at low-tide to watch the bizarre skin-breathing mudskippers scurry beneath the building.

Shopping

Gallery Dekranasda HANDICRAFTS

(☎0858 2001 6977; Jl Tanjungpura; 9am-noon & 2-4pm) Locally sourced handicrafts and wares, some made with unexpected refinement. And T-shirts. Find it 500m east from the durian monument.

Getting There & Around

There is no public transport within town. Most commerce is found between the dock and the durian monument. For the beach and points around, rent a bike from Penginapan Family or you could try hitching.

Speedboats (☎ Bersoul 0812 5613 3570, Synergy 0823 5737 0151; 175,000Rp; ⏰ departs 9am) to Pontianak depart Sukadana harbour twice each morning; the trip takes five hours. Sukadana can also be reached by Ketapang via bus (25,000Rp, 1½ hours, up to four daily) or **taxi** (☎ Eki, no English 0853 4524 3869); Ketapang has an airport that connects to Pontianak and Pangkalan Bun (for Tanjung Puting).

CENTRAL KALIMANTAN

Tanjung Puting National Park

Tanjung Puting is the most popular tourist destination in Kalimantan, and for good reasons. A near guarantee you'll see free-roaming orangutans, combined with a storybook journey up a winding jungle river, accessed by direct flights to Surabaya and Jakarta, give this adventure world-class appeal.

Tanjung Puting was initially set aside as a wildlife preserve by the Dutch in 1939. It gained park status and its international reputation largely thanks to Dr Biruté Galdikas, one of Leakey's Angels – the trio of female primatologists, including Dian Fossey and Jane Goodall, trained by Louis Leakey. Working from Camp Leakey since 1971, Galdikas has made such seminal discoveries as the great ape's eight-year birth cycle, which makes the species highly vulnerable to extinction. Her controversial hands-on approach to orangutan care may have lost her some supporters in the academic and conservation communities, but there is no denying the impact she has had on our understanding and appreciation of these amazing creatures and the threats they face.

The park is best seen from a *klotok,* a two-storey romantic liveaboard boat that travels up Sungai Sekonyer to Camp Leakey. During the day you lounge on deck surveying the jungle with binoculars in one hand and a drink in the other as the boat chugs along its narrowing channel. Watch for the quick flash of the colorful kingfisher, and scan the shallows for the toothy false gharail as your cook serves up fantastic meals. In the evening, you can spot proboscis monkeys bedding down in the treetops with the river at their backs for protection. These curious golden-haired, round-bellied, bulbous-nosed primates are found only on Borneo and are sometimes called *monyet belanda* (Dutch monkey – for some reason...) At night, you tie up on the river, set mattresses and mosquito nets on deck, and enjoy the finest sleep, while the hum of the rainforest purifies your ears.

Klotok call at several stations where rangers stack piles of bananas and buckets of milk to feed the resident population of ex-captive and semiwild orangutans. There are no fences or cages, but you'll be kept at a distance by ropes: a boundary ignored by the animals themselves who often wander nonchalantly through the shutter-snapping crowd on their way to lunch. While some orangutans appear deceptively tame, do not attempt to touch or feed them, and do not get between a mother and child. Orangutans are several times more powerful than you, and may bite if provoked.

Visitation has increased rapidly in recent years. There are now over 60 *klotok* running nearly nonstop during the busy dry season (June through September), with no plans by the park to limit the impact. Toilets flush directly into the creek, a questionable practice anywhere, but even more concerning given the high traffic. Some *klotok* are now outfitted with freshwater tanks, which they fill in town for showers and dish washing – a wise addition.

Despite the visitor numbers, the trip is still a fine introduction to the rainforest, and one of the most memorable experiences you'll have on the island. The park's 200 varieties of wild orchid bloom mainly from January to March, although the abundance of March fruit may lure orangutans away from feeding platforms. At any time, bring rain protection and insect repellent.

Sights & Activities

Sungai Sekonyer is opposite the port town of Kumai, where you meet your *klotok*. It is largely muddy due to upstream mining operations, although it eventually forks into a naturally tea-coloured tributary, typical of peat swamp waterways. The upriver journey contains several noteworthy stops; you won't necessarily see everything, nor in this order.

Tanjung Harapan is an orangutan feeding station with decaying interpretation centre; feedings at 3pm daily.

Sekonyer Village is a small village that arose around Tanjung Harapan, but has since been relocated across the river. There's a small souvenir shop and lodgings.

ORANGUTANS 101

Four great ape species belong to the Hominidae family: orangutans, chimpanzees, gorillas and humans. Although our auburn-haired cousins branched off from the family tree long ago, spend any time observing these *orang hutan* (Bahasa Indonesia for forest person, a name likely bestowed by the Dutch) and you'll notice similarities between us that are as striking as the differences.

The bond between a mother and her young is among the strongest in the animal kingdom. For the first two years infants are entirely dependant and carried everywhere. For up to seven years mothers continue to teach them how to thrive in the rainforest, including how to climb through the canopy and build a nest at night, the medicinal qualities of plants, what foods are poisonous, which critters they should avoid, and how to locate reliable feeding trees.

The territorial males are entirely absent from child rearing, living mostly solitary lives punctuated by sometimes violent battles for alpha status. Once a young male secures a territory, he rapidly undergoes physical changes, growing impressive cheek pads and throat pouches. He advertises his dominion by issuing booming long calls that echo through the forest for kilometres. The call both induces stress in younger males – suppressing their sexual development – and attracts females ready for breeding. It is one of dozens of vocalisations orangutans use to interact with each other and their surroundings.

Both species of orangutan, Sumatran and Bornean, are endangered. Much of their habitat is being converted to oil palm plantations. Mothers are frequently shot, their infants sold as pets. If these animals are lucky enough to be rescued, rehabilitation is long and difficult, and finding suitable places to release them is becoming nearly impossible. Currently, all of the orangutan rescue and rehabilitation centres in Indonesia are operating at or above capacity.

For more information on orangutan conservation efforts and volunteer opportunities in Kalimantan, check out the following:

Friends of the National Parks Foundation (www.fnpf.org) Funds forest restoration at Pasalat.

Orangutan Foundation International (www.orangutan.org) Founded by Biruté Galdikas; runs the park's feeding stations.

Orangutan Foundation UK (www.orangutan.org.uk) UK organisation focused on saving orangutan habitats.

Orangutan Land Trust (www.forests4orangutans.org) Influences policy and supports a wide range of organisations dedicated to the long-term survival of orangutans.

Pasalat is a reforestation camp where Pak Ledan single-handedly plants 180 saplings a month and maintains the medicinal plant garden. Be careful on the 800m forest boardwalk badly in need of donations for repairs.

Pondok Tanggui is a feeding station; feedings at 9am daily.

Pondok Ambung is popular for spotting tarantulas and glowing mushrooms on night hikes.

Camp Leakey Feedings here occur at 2pm daily at station with visitor information.

The ideal journey length is three days and two nights, giving you ample time to see everything. If you only have one day, you should take a speedboat from Kumai. A *klotok* can reach Camp Leakey in 4½ hours, making a return trip possible in one day if you leave at 6am, but this is not recommended.

During the dry season, an overnight trek from Pondok Tanggui to Pasalat (1,500,000Rp all inclusive, 22km) is a unique chance to see nocturnal wildlife. Talk to Pak Bana at Flora Homestay (p234) in Sekonyer village.

Tours

You have the choice of hiring both a *klotok* and a guide yourself, or having a tour operator do it for you. The former is moderately cheaper, the latter leagues easier. Beware: some companies advertise under multiple websites (which never list who's behind them), and others are just resellers who double the price.

Organised Tours

★Jenie Subaru ADVENTURE TOUR
(☎0857 6422 0991; jeniesubaru@gmail.com) It is a shame the passionate and charismatic Jenie does few trips these days, instead (admirably) devoting much of his time to training the next batch of local guides in sustainable tourism. Proceeds from his trips go toward buying land along the park's border to protect orangutan habitat.

Orangutan House Boat Tours ADVENTURE TOUR
(☎0857 5134 9756; www.orangutanhouseboattour.com) Local resident Fardi may be young, but he's hard-working and passionate about both his homeland and orangutans.

Borneo Orangutan Adventure Tour ADVENTURE TOUR
(☎0852 4930 9250; www.orangutantravel.com) Run by the excellent Ahmad Yani, the first official guide in the area.

Orangutan Green Tours ADVENTURE TOUR
(Harry Yacht Service; ☎0812 508 6105; www.orangutangreentours.com) Excellent at logistics for large groups, long-time guiding pioneer Herry Roustaman is also your point of contact if you're coming to Kumai aboard a yacht.

DIY Tours

Guides are now mandated for all visitors to Tanjung Puting. Fortunately, with nearly 90 guides registered with the park, they are relatively easy to come by. Unfortunately, they are not all created equal. To acquire a licence, a guide must speak basic English, undergo survival training and demonstrate basic wildlife knowledge. For some that is as far as it goes. If you are arranging a trip yourself on the ground, take the time to meet as many guides as you can (they'll find you) before choosing one.

The cost of hiring a *klotok* varies with its size. They range from small (two to four passengers, 450,000Rp to 550,000Rp per day) to large (eight to 10 passengers, 650,000Rp to 1,000,000Rp per day), including captain, mate and fuel. Cooks are an additional 100,000Rp per day, with food on top of that. When you factor in a guide (150,000Rp to 250,000Rp per day), permits (150,000Rp per person per day) and boat parking fees (100,000Rp per boat per day) the total cost for a three-day, two-night guided trip for two people easily tops 4,000,000Rp, even if you painstakingly haggle every step of the way.

Considering these prices, the hassle, transport to and from the airport, and all the other moving parts, the additional cost you may pay going through a reasonably priced company suddenly feels more affordable.

Sleeping

If you're looking to stay outside the park (typically before or after your cruise), try Kumai or Pangkalan Bun; the latter offers the only upscale accommodation in the area.

★Flora Homestay HOMESTAY $$
(☎0812 516 4727; r 500,000Rp, set meals 75,000Rp) Located directly on the river at the end of Sekonyer village, these rough-hewn wood cabins provide everything you need for a truly immersive Borneo experience. Pak Bana is eager to please, even offering to boil up water if you require a hot shower. Tours to a feeding station, canoe trips and jungle trekking are all available.

Rimba Lodge HOTEL $$$
(☎0361-747 4205; www.rimbaecolodge.com; s incl breakfast US$100-140, d incl breakfast US$110-150; ❄) Toeing a delicate line between resort and forest hut, Rimba achieves success in design and comfort, but falls short in maintenance and staff attentiveness. Although it is located near Sekonyer, access to the village is via a sketchy balance-beam path hidden behind the maintenance shed. The recent addition of solar panels lends more credence to the eco-claims.

Getting There & Around

- Tanjung Puting is typically reached via a flight to nearby Pangkalan Bun, then taxi to Kumai (150,000Rp, 20 minutes).
- Independent travellers must register at Pangkalan Bun police station upon arrival. Bring photocopies of your passport and visa (airport taxi drivers know the steps). This can also be organised by your guide.
- Speedboats from Kumai cost 700,000Rp per day, and take about two hours to reach Camp Leakey, but this is pure transport, not wildlife-spotting.
- For the cheapest route to Sekonyer village, take a ferry from Kumai across the bay (5000Rp), then an *ojek* (25,000Rp, 30 minutes) to the village.
- Canoes are a quiet alternative for exploring the river's shallow tributaries, and can be rented at Sekonyer village store for 50,000Rp per day.

Kumai

☎0532 / POP 25,000

The port of departure for Tanjung Puting National Park, Kumai is also known for its bird's-nest business, which fills the town with screeching warehouses. A handful of guesthouses and warungs line the main street, Jl HM Idris. Backpackers sometimes meet here to share the price of a *klotok*. There is an ATM downriver near the port, and the national park dock is upriver on the edge of town.

Sleeping & Eating

Permata Hijau GUESTHOUSE $

(☎0532-61325; Jl HM Idris, near Bank BNI; r with fan/air-con 100,000/175,000Rp; ❄) These budget rooms are clean, though you might find the electrical wiring a touch shocking. Located in the middle of the busy dockside nightlife, where food stalls and high jinks abound.

Mentari Hotel HOTEL $

(Jl Gerliya 98; r with cold mandi/hot shower 150,000/200,000Rp; ❄) Basic concrete boxes, although they do have windows and air-con. It's 600m away from the river.

Majid Hotel HOTEL $$

(☎0532-61740; Jl HM Idris; r incl breakfast 250,000Rp) The first place in town built with Western tourists in mind has all the right amenities. Owner Majid also has several *klotok* and can help solo travellers find shared boats. Upriver near the park dock.

★**Acil Laila** INDONESIAN $

(Jl Gerilya 5; mains 15,000Rp; ⏲7.30am-10pm) Don't let the oodles of offal waiting to be skewered throw you off: this place does a mean grilled chicken and a divine *nasi bakar* (seasoned rice wrapped in a banana leaf and charred to perfection).

Getting There & Away

- Get to Kumai from Pangkalan Bun via the morning minibus (20,000Rp, 20 minutes), an *ojek* (50,000Rp), or Kijang (100,000Rp).
- Taxis from Pangkalan Bun airport to Kumai cost 150,000Rp, maximum three people.
- **Pelni** (☎0532-24420; Jl HM Idris; ⏲on days when boats arrive 8-11am & 2-4pm) and **Dharma Lautan Utama** (☎0532-61520; Jl Bahari 561) runs ferries connecting Kumai with Semarang (200,000Rp, 28 hours) once or twice weekly, and Surabaya (220,000Rp, 26 hours) almost daily.
- **Anggun Jaya Travel** (☎0532-61096, 0812 5366 2967; Jl Gerilya) sells boat, plane and **Yessoe Travel** (p237) bus tickets.

Pangkalan Bun

☎0532 / POP 200,000

Pangkalan Bun is largely a transit city, but with a few hidden surprises. Unlike many Kalimantan towns, the residents here have embraced the river instead of turning their backs on it, making a stroll up the boardwalk a colourful and engaging experience. If you want something better than backpacker digs before or after visiting Tanjung Puting, you'll only find it here.

Sights & Activities

Wander downriver along the Sungai Arut boardwalk to experience life before concrete and asphalt. Brightly painted *ces* (long-tail canoes) are parked between equally festive floating outhouses and fish farms. In the afternoon, children swim or fly kites while women pound spices. If you tire from walking, wave to almost any boat to take you back (negotiable, roughly 50,000Rp per hour)

Istana Kuning PALACE

(Yellow Palace; donations accepted; ⏲8am-1pm Mon-Fri, to 11am Sat, closed Sun) The mostly empty hilltop palace overlooking Pangkalan Bun

FLIGHTS FROM PANGKALAN BUN

DESTINATION	COMPANY	FARE (RP)	DURATION	FREQUENCY
Banjarmasin	Kalstar, Trigana	520,000	1½hr	1-2 daily
Jakarta	Kalstar, Trigana	700,000	1¼hr	2 daily
Ketapang	Kalstar, Trigana	400,000	40min	2 daily
Pontianak	Kalstar, Trigana	700,000	2hr	2 daily
Sampit	Kalstar	400,000	30min	1 daily
Semarang	Kalstar, Trigana	500,000	45min	2 daily
Surabaya	Kalstar, Trigana	600,000	1hr	2 daily

Pangkalan Bun

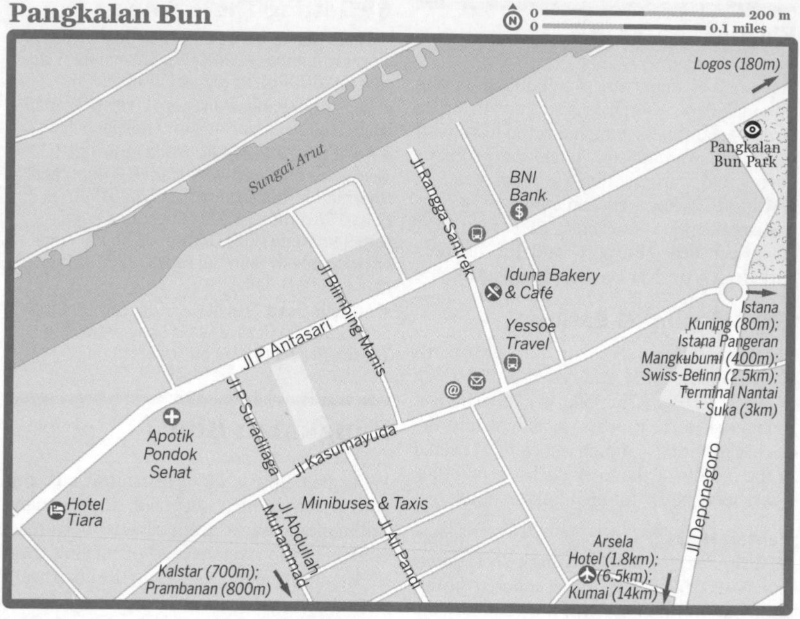

Park celebrates three architectural traditions of the sultans' assorted wives: Chinese, Dayak and Malay. Built in 1806 (and rebuilt in 1990 after a deranged woman burned it to the ground) it is not yellow, but was traditionally draped in yellow fabric.

Nearby, rambling **Istana Pangeran Mangkubumi** (⊘ open by luck, or by appointment), built to house the sultan's seven daughters, fights against gravity among well-kept gardens.

🛏 Sleeping & Eating

Hotel Tiara
HOTEL $

(☑ 0532-22717; Jl P Antasari 16; r fan/air-con 120,000/170,000Rp; ✸) With its high-ceilinged, well-maintained, convenient and cheap rooms, Hotel Tiara is a great backpacker stay. A new addition next door promises to provide even more options.

★ Yayorin Homestay
HOMESTAY $$

(Yayasan Orangutan Indonesia; ☑ 0532-29057; info@yayorin.com; Jl Bhayangkara Km1; r incl breakfast 300,000Rp) 🍃 Woven rattan walls. Solar-powered lights. Verdant woodland setting. These peaceful cottages are a fundraising effort by Yayorin, a local NGO working to preserve Kalimantan's forests through education and community engagement.

About 7km south of town; take Jl HM Rafi'i at the paratrooper roundabout.

Arsela Hotel
BOUTIQUE HOTEL $$

(☑ 0532-28808; www.arselahotel.com; Jl Iskandar 15; r superior/deluxe incl breakfast 435,000/495,000Rp; ✸ 🛜) This architecturally compelling building with attached cafe sat empty for years before being lovingly brought back to life as a comfortable boutique hotel with lots of class. Set back from the road, the upstairs rooms have wood accents, rattan furniture, and a luxurious rain shower in the well-trimmed bathroom.

Swiss-Belinn
HOTEL $$

(☑ 0532-27888; www.swiss-belhotel.com; Jl Ahmad Yani Km2; r incl breakfast 750,000-1,200,000Rp; ✸ 🛜) Lacking originality or charm, this chain hotel sits on the far edge of town, hoping its impressive breakfast buffet (95,000Rp for nonguests, 6am to 9am) and polished service will compensate for the fraying edges and dearth of character. The Royal Suite (2,700,000Rp) does get you a bathtub for a long soak after your rainforest adventure.

Iduna Bakery & Café
BAKERY $

(☑ 0532-21031; Jl Rangga Santrek 42; snacks/mains 20,000/30,000Rp; ⊘ 9am-9pm; ✸) Choose from a variety of fresh pastries next door, before sliding into a contemporary, air-conditioned space with stuffed chairs and cool lighting. Good luck explaining the concept of an Americano.

Prambanan SEAFOOD $
(☎0532-2126; Jl Hasanudin; mains 40,000Rp; ⏲7am-9pm) Average chicken. Above average fish. Next to Hotel Andika, this semi-al-fresco restaurant is renowned among locals and expats. The low-key, friendly vibe epitomises Pangkalan Bun.

Information

Many businesses close late in the afternoon and reopen after dark.

Apotik Pondok Sehat (☎0532-21167; Jl P Antasari 86) Well-stocked pharmacy with doctors' offices.

BNI Bank (Jl P Antasari) Buys crisp US$100 notes only.

Pahala Net (Jl Kasumayuda; per hour 4000Rp; ⏲8.30am-9pm; ❄) Quick internet connection.

Post Office (Jl Kasumayuda 29)

Getting There & Away

AIR

Kalstar (☎0532-21266; Jl Hassanudin 39)

Trigana (☎0532-27115; Jl Iskandar 3; ⏲8am-4.30pm & 6.30-9.30pm)

BUS

DAMRI's (☎0812 5186 3651; Nantai Suka Terminal) service to Pontianak (350,000Rp, 13 hours, daily at 7am) and all **Logos** (☎0532-24954; Jl Pangeran Antasari) buses depart from **Terminal Nantai Suka** (Jl Jend A Yani), while **Yessoe Travel** (☎0532-21276; Jl Kawitan 68) services depart from its own office. Destinations aboard Logos and Yessoe include Sampit (85,000Rp, six hours), Palangka Raya (125,000Rp, 12 hours), and Banjarmasin (175,000Rp to 290,000Rp, 16 hours).

Getting Around

Taxis to/from the airport (8km) cost 70,000Rp. Taxis to Kumai start at 100,000Rp.

Opelet around town cost 10,000Rp.

Minibuses to Kumai (20,000Rp, 20 minutes) leave across from Hotel Abadi.

Palangka Raya

☎0536 / POP 220,000

Originally envisioned by President Sukarno as a new capital city for Indonesia – and even for a pan-Asian state – Palangka Raya was built beginning in 1957. It shows in the refreshingly ordered streets and wide boulevards. While Sukarno's dream died, the city has a few surpriscs in store, including Kalimantan's only high-end jungle river cruise, two luxury hotels, some trendy cafes and a spot of nightlife. The market and old town are east, while government buildings and sprawl are west.

Sights

Museum Balanga MUSEUM
(Jl Cilik Riwut Km2.5; admission 15,000Rp; ⏲7.30am-3pm Mon-Fri, 8am-2pm Sat & Sun) An excellent, if small, museum introducing just enough Dayak ritual, custom and livelihood to inspire you to head into the forest in search of the real thing.

Old Town AREA
This network of boardwalks connecting wooden shops and houses lines the riverbank downstream of the planned city. The atmosphere here is more relaxed, and the smiles bigger.

Pasar Malam MARKET
The food stalls around Jl Halmahera and Jl Jawa run all day, but the the maze of shops here comes alive at night.

Borneo Orangutan Survival Foundation WILDLIFE RESERVE
(☎0536-330 8416; www.orangutan.or.id; Jl Cilik Riwut Km28; admission by donation; ⏲9am-3pm Sat & Sun) The centre is typically closed to visitors, in order to increase the rehabilitation success of its some 600 orangutans. The tiny visitor's centre opens on the weekends; you can see a few caged animals through its large windows. It is 2km from the main road. Follow signs for the arboretum.

Tours

★**Wow Borneo** BOAT TOUR
(☎0536-322 2099; www.wowborneo.com; Jl Barito 11; ⏲9am-5pm Mon-Fri, to 3pm Sat) Take everything you think you know about river travel in Kalimantan and throw it in the water. Wow Borneo's river cruises up the Sungai Rungan prove that exploring the jungle and its inhabitants doesn't have to be an exercise in stoic suffering. Built on the hulls of traditional wooden boats, their fleet of four cruisers offers amenities such as air-conditioned en-suite cabins and rattan sofas on the split-level decks.

Palangka Raya

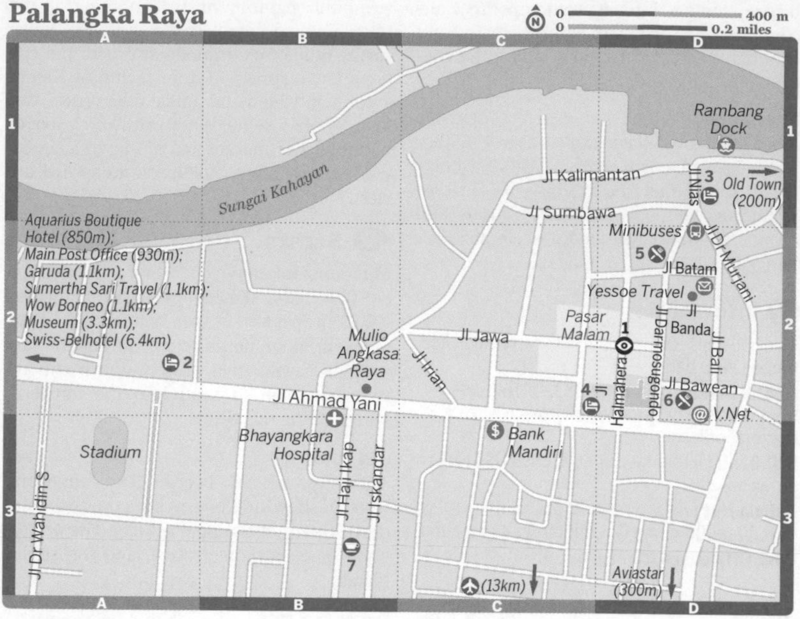

Palangka Raya

Sights
1 Pasar Malam.......D2

Sleeping
2 Hotel Dian Wisata.......A2
3 Hotel Mahkota.......D1
4 Hotel Sakura.......C2

Eating
5 Al Mu'Minun.......D2
6 Family.......D2

Drinking & Nightlife
7 Coffee Garage.......B3

Blue Betang ADVENTURE TOUR
(☎0813 4965 5021; blubetang_eventorganizer@yahoo.co.id; 9916 Jl Beliang 29) Honest and earnest guide Dodi specialises in hands-on, immersive, affordable, go-anywhere travel deep into Dayak country. Also provides day trips in the immediate vicinity of Palangka Raya.

Sleeping

Hotel Mahkota HOTEL $
(☎0536-322 1672; Jl Nias 5; r fan/air-con 100,000/190,000-375,000Rp; ❄📶) Popular with students and families, this hotel offers a range of ageing basic, clean rooms in a good location for exploring the market, river and old town. Hot-water showers start with the VIP rooms (275,000Rp). Wi-fi in lobby only.

Hotel Dian Wisata HOTEL $
(☎0536-322 1241; Jl Ahmad Yani 68; r with fan/air-con incl breakfast 150,000/230,000Rp; ❄) The odd design of this hotel, with its central well-lit atrium and colourful stairwell leading down to subterranean rooms, separates it from the boring concrete boxes that define its competition.

Hotel Sakura HOTEL $$
(☎0536-322 1680; Jl Ahmad Yani 87; r incl breakfast 300,000-400,000Rp; ❄) This hotel's courtyard, populated with concrete critters, offers a welcome respite from the city. Some of the rooms have two-person tubs; the best overlook the courtyard.

Aquarius Boutique Hotel HOTEL $$
(☎0536-324 2121; www.aquariusboutiquehotels.com; Jl Imam Bonjol 5; d incl breakfast 685,000-950,000Rp; ❄📶🏊) A rooftop pool with a view. A 2nd-floor restaurant with a waterfall. A three-storey lounge, dance club, and karaoke complex. This hotel has all the trimmings, if a lack of upkeep. All room classes

are the same size, but have increasingly plush details. Avoid floors five and six due to noise.

★Swiss-Belhotel Danum HOTEL $$$
(☎0536-323 2777; www.swiss-belhotel.com; Jl Tjilik Km5; r with breakfast from 850,000Rp; ❄📶🏊) This luxury property with resort intentions raises the local bar. The vast marble lobby drops to the restaurant (which serves an excellent buffet breakfast) before opening into the courtyard with its winding pool and palm trees. The place is trimmed with fractal Dayak motifs, and the rooms are well-thought out with attention to style and comfort.

Options range from entry-level standards to the 8,400,000Rp presidential suite with a whirlpool bathtub for two. The fitness centre is extensive with modern machines and free weights. Walk-in promo rates are often lower than even the internet discounts.

Eating & Drinking

At night, seafood and nasi goreng (fried rice) stalls sprout along Jl Yos Sudarso near the *bundaran besar* (large roundabout) – the place to see and be seen.

Al Mu'Minun INDONESIAN $
(☎0536-322 8659; Jl Darmosugondo 5; mains 20,000Rp; ⏲7am-8pm) Meaty chunks of fish are grilled up at this local favourite.

Family CHINESE $
(☎0536-322 9560; Jl Bawean 16; mains 25,000Rp; ⏲8am-10pm; ❄) The best Chinese food in the city, with a standard menu. Known for its *ikan jelawat* (90,000Rp), a river fish cooked many ways. Serves beer.

★Coffee Garage CAFE
(Jl Haji Ikap 22; coffee 10,000Rp; ⏲5.30pm-midnight; 📶) A rare find, this trendy cafe comes alive at night serving all manner of coffee drinks in a colourfully painted house, garage included. It offers free wi-fi, basic food (spaghetti, desserts), outdoor seating and live music.

☆ Entertainment

For nightlife in Palangka Raya, the entertainment complex at the Aquarius Boutique Hotel is the only game in town. It includes **Blu Music Hall** (Jl Imam Bonjol 5; ⏲8pm-1am), a small but atmospheric blues bar, the adjacent **Vino Club** (Jl Imam Bonjol 5; ⏲10pm-3am), a cosy DJ club which doubles as the city's major performance venue, and **Luna Karaoke** (Jl Imam Bonjol 5; ⏲2pm-3am), which provides more traditional local entertainment. This is where the city's style-conscious young professionals come to hang out, representing a new wave of urban life.

Shopping

A collection of Dayak carvings and woven rattan crafts can be found in several shops along Jl Batam.

MEGA RICE DISASTER

On the drive between Palangka Raya and Banjarmasin you might notice a conspicuous lack of two things: forests and rice fields. The former is alarming since this was once a densely treed home to orangutans. The latter is tragic because the promise of rice destroyed the forest, leading to one of Indonesia's largest environmental disasters.

In the 1990s, President Suharto decided to boost Indonesia's food production by converting one million hectares of 'unproductive' peat forest into verdant rice fields. After the trees were cleared and 4600km of canals dug to drain the swamps, 60,000 transmigrants were relocated from Java to discover one small but important detail Suharto overlooked: nothing grows on the acidic soils of drained peat.

As peat dries it collapses and oxidises, releasing sulphuric acid into the water and carbon dioxide into the atmosphere. Further, when it rains, compacted peat floods. Catastrophically. When it stops raining, dried peat burns. Unstoppably. During the powerful El Nino drought of 1997, mega fires released over a billion tons of carbon dioxide into the environment.

Today, the area remains a wasteland. Some transmigrant communities have turned to illegal logging to try and make a living. Oil palm companies eye the land for planting. Local NGOs try to block the drainage channels in a noble attempt to right the horrific wrong. Meanwhile, Indonesia continues to import over one million metric tonnes of rice every year.

Information

Bank Mandiri (Jl Ahmad Yani; ⏲8am-3pm Mon-Fri) Currency exchange.

Bhayangkara Hospital (☎0536-322 1520; Jl Ahmad Yani 22)

Mulio Angkasa Raya (☎0536-322 1031; Jl Ahmad Yani 55) Offers booking for flights, car rental and Kijang. Not many staff speak English, though.

Sumertha Sari Travel (☎0536-322 1033; Jalan Tjilik Riwut Km0.5) Kijang transport and charter.

Post Office (Jl Batam) Branch office. Main office is located on Jl Imam Bonjol.

V.Net (Jl Ahmad Yani 99; per hour 4000Rp; ⏲8.30am-2am) Internet access.

Yessoe Travel (☎0852 4679 8939, 0536-322 1436; Jl Banda 7) All things bus.

Getting There & Away

AIR

For smaller regional destinations, try Susi Air and Aviastar. Airlines no longer sell tickets at the airport.

Aviastar (☎0536-323 8848; Jl PM Noor 5)

Garuda (☎0536-322 3573; Jl Kinibalu 1, PALMA mall)

Lion Air (Airport)

Susi Air (Jl Adonis Samad Gang Damai 9) South of town, in a residential area.

BUS & KIJANG

All long-haul buses deposit passengers at the new terminal 10km south of town, which annoyingly has no public transport options to the city. If you're coming from Banjarmasin, have them drop you at the Bangkirai four-way intersection 1.5km east of the terminal, and wait for an *angkot* heading north. Otherwise, an *ojek* will cost 50,000Rp. **Yessoe Travel** offers departing passengers free transport to the terminal from their office on Jl Batam, near the market.

Sumertha Sari Travel Kijang serve the same destinations, with higher costs and more exhaust fumes per passenger.

Getting Around

- Yellow minibuses (*angkot* or 'taxis', 5000Rp) ply major thoroughfares, converging at Jl Darmosugondo near the market.
- Airport service (13km, 20 minutes) costs 80,000Rp.
- Hire a boat at **Rambang dock** (Dermaga Rambang) to tour around, or head further upriver.

SOUTH KALIMANTAN

Banjarmasin

☎0511 / POP 625,000

Banjarmasin capitalises on its waterways and river life. But, as more locals board up their back porches to bathe without fear of prying eyes and snapping cameras, and as the government buys up waterfront property for parks and mixed commerce, the riverfront dynamic is slowly changing, perhaps for

TRANSPORT FROM PALANGKA RAYA

Air

DESTINATION	COMPANY	FARE (RP)	DURATION (HR)	FREQUENCY
Balikpapan	Garuda	670,000	1¼	daily
Jakarta	Garuda, Lion	680,000	1¾	4 daily
Ketapang	Aviastar	666,000	1¼	Mon, Fri
Muara Tewah	Susi Air	500,000	1	Wed, Fri, Sun
Pangkalan Bun	Susi Air	495,000	1	Wed, Fri, Sun
Pontianak	Garuda	910,000	1¼	daily
Surabaya	Citilink, Lion	520,000	1¼	3 daily

Bus

DESTINATION	FARE (RP)	DURATION (HR)	FREQUENCY
Banjarmasin	80,000	6	3am & 8am daily
Pangkalan Bun	100,000-200,000	10	7am & 4pm daily
Sampit	60,000-100,000	5	7am & 4pm daily

WORTH A TRIP

SEBANGAU NATIONAL PARK: MEET PEAT

Spared the destruction of the Mega Rice Disaster (p239), this area of peat swamp forest was gazetted as Sebangau National Park in 2004. Although it has seen its share of degradation, Sebangau is still home to over 5000 wild orangutans, and the forest itself is a fascinating draw.

Peat forms over thousands of years as organic material accumulates in seasonally flooded regions. The semidecayed material can extend as deep as 20m below the surface, and contains more carbon than the forest growing above. Due to habitat loss, nearly half of the mammals and one-third of the bird species found in peat swamps are endangered or threatened.

Travelling through a peat forest ranges from delightfully challenging to extremely adventurous. During the dry season, the uneven spongy trail will occasionally give way as your foot plunges into a pocket of wet peat. During the rainy season, you may spend significant stretches submerged to your knees or chest as you hunt for hornbills, red leaf and proboscis monkeys, and sun bears. Travelling by boat between ranger posts and dry hills makes for an extraordinary adventure through the true wilds of Borneo.

The closest access from Palangka Raya is **Sungai Koran** on the north edge of the park. Take a regular *angkot* (10,000Rp, 40 minutes) south to **Dermaga Kereng Bangkirai** and talk to the rangers at the national park post. If nobody is around, try calling Pak Ian (☎0852 2191 9160). Expenses include 150,000Rp per day for park entrance, 150,000Rp per day for a guide, and 250,000Rp per day for boat rental plus fuel. If you wish to stay overnight at any of the ranger posts (recommended), you'll also need a cook (90,000Rp) and food. The west edge of the park is less degraded and is accessible via a two-hour drive to **Baun Bango**, where you can check in with the park rangers and arrange a boat to the outpost on **Punggualas Lake**.

the best. The rest of the city is a sprawling beast, with the chaotic commerce of downtown turning eerily quiet at night, save for the night market holding out against the megamalls sprouting up in the suburbs.

Sights

Mesjid Raya Sabilal Muhtadin MOSQUE
(Jl Sudirman) FREE This large flat-domed mosque looks like something off a *Star Wars* set. During Ramadan, the famous **Pasar Wadai** (Cake Fair) runs along the adjacent riverfront.

Masjid Sultan Suriansyah MOSQUE
FREE Though it marks the first Islamic place of worship in Borneo, the beautiful angular wooden building was reconstructed in 1746, leaving the oldest physical mosque accolade to Banua Lawas from the Tabalong Regency (1625). Take a Kuin *angkot* to the end of the line.

Soetji Nurani Temple BUDDHIST TEMPLE
(Jl Niaga Timur 45) FREE Step into this 1898 temple, and the hobbit-sized candles and incense coils that smoulder for days will transport you 3000km north to China.

Tours

See Banjarmasin in a single journey: arrange a predawn boat near Jembatan Merdeka (Merdeka Bridge) to the floating markets. It takes an hour or so to navigate the canals lined with ramshackle homes, where the day is just beginning with a bath and tooth-brushing in the murky trash-strewn water. It feels a touch invasive until the waves and beaming smiles betray an unflappable Indonesian pride.

There are two markets: **Kuin** is closer, but by all accounts **Lok Baintan** is more traditional. At the markets, women paddle canoes brimming with exotic produce in search of a buyer among the tourist boats bristling with selfie-sticks. If it all sounds a bit bizarre, that's because it is, but it's also profoundly educational, and astoundingly beautiful.

Trips can be combined with a stop at **Kembang Island** (tours from 100,000Rp), where macaques walk the boardwalk, or at Masjid Sultan Suriansyah, site of the first (but not oldest) mosque in Kalimantan.

You'll need a guide (who will secure a boat as well) to explain what you're seeing on the floating markets tour (such as the significance of how women tie their sarongs). Tours

Central Banjarmasin

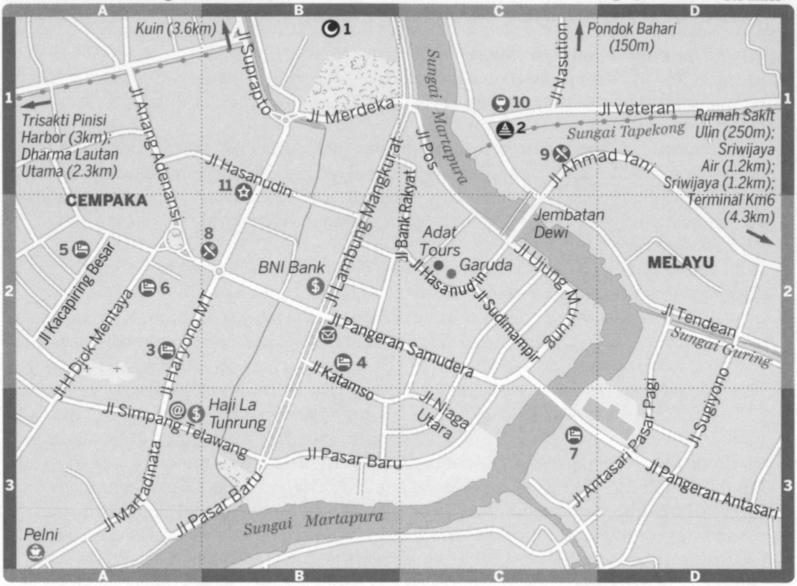

Central Banjarmasin

Sights
1 Mesjid Raya Sabilal Muhtadin............. B1
2 Soetji Nurani Temple........................... C1

Sleeping
3 Hotel Biuti A2
4 Hotel Perdana B2
5 Hotel SAS...A2
6 NASA Hotel...A2
7 Swiss-Belhotel Borneo.........................C3

Eating
8 Cendrawasih Sarahai...........................B2
9 Said Abdullah C1

Drinking & Nightlife
10 People's Place C1

Entertainment
11 Dynasty B1

including a guide cost about 200,000Rp, and run from 5.30am to 9.30am.

Some Banjarmasin guides tour up into the Meratus Mountains, too, though we recommend supporting local guides in places such as Loksado.

Sarkani Gambi GUIDE
(☎0813 5187 7858; kani286@yahoo.com) Friendly and informative Sarkani runs tours for large foreign groups as well as customised trips for individuals.

Mulyadi Yasin GUIDE
(☎0813 5193 6200; yadi_yasin@yahoo.co.id) Professional and responsive.

Muhammad Yusuf GUIDE
(☎0813 4732 5958; yusuf_guidekalimantan@yahoo.co.id) The energetic head of the thriving South Kalimantan Guiding Association can also help you find other guides in a pinch.

Sleeping

A few questionable sub-100,000Rp options exist near Jl Hasanudin.

★**Hotel SAS** HOTEL $
(☎0511-335 3054; Jl Kacapiring Besar 2; r incl breakfast 190,000-279,000Rp; ❄) A delightful find off a quiet side street, this hotel is built around an imposing Banjar home with towering roof and central stair. The *mandiangin* rooms are newly renovated to good effect – avoid the others. Head down Jl Cempaka and turn left at the old woman selling bananas.

Hotel Biuti HOTEL $
(☎0511-335 4493; Jl Haryono MT 21; r incl breakfast 210,000-300,000Rp; ❄📶) Biuti has some of the more beautiful and colourful rooms in its class, with decorative wood walls, comfortable artistic public spaces and clean bathrooms. Even the fake lobby trees work (sort of). Cheaper rooms are in the older wing. Upgrade and be happy.

Hotel Perdana HOTEL $
(☎0511-335 3276; hotelperdana@plasa.com; Jl Katamso 8; r 120,000-300,000Rp; ❄) This rambling Escher-esque complex has a variety of musty multicoloured rooms popular with backpackers. Out front is a cacophony of commerce by day, and a reasonably entertaining night market after dark. English-speaking Linda can point you in whichever direction you need pointing, or find guides. Beware of mosquitoes.

NASA Hotel HOTEL $$
(☎0511-336 6868; Jl H Djok Mentaya 8; r incl breakfast 490,000-560,000Rp; ❄📶) Aimed at modern business travellers, the spotless superior rooms don't have any windows, but do have modern art and safety deposit boxes. The staff are efficient – sometimes to a fault. Live music in the lounge and the attached karaoke complex may appeal to some.

Swiss-Belhotel Borneo HOTEL $$
(☎0511-327 1111; www.swiss-belhotel.com; Jl Pangeran Antasari 86A; r incl breakfast 600,000-700,000Rp, ste incl breakfast 1,300,0000Rp; ❄📶) This traditional boutique-style hotel with warm wooden accents is undergoing a tasteful renovation. The deluxe is a significant upgrade in style for not much money. Rooms come with a free trip to the Kuin floating market (no guide) for one guest, additional guests are 100,000Rp. Boat leaves at 5am.

Eating & Drinking

Seek out the local speciality *soto Banjar,* a delicious soup found across the city. The Kawasan Wisata Kuliner (tourist food region), riverside between the Merdeka and Dewi bridges, has many good, but not great, options.

★**People's Place** PUB $
(☎0511-327 7007; Jl Veteran 3, Summer B&B rooftop; beer 30,000Rp, snacks 20,000Rp; ⏲11am-11pm; 📶) With 270 degrees of floor-to-ceiling windows and an open-air porch overlooking the river and mosque, this is *the* best hang-out in town. An eclectic Anglophilic atmosphere and live acoustic music draws a crowd. The lychee beer is embarrassingly refreshing.

Pondok Bahari INDONESIAN $
(☎0511-325 3688; Jl Simpang Pierre Tendean 108; mains from 20,000Rp; ⏲24hr) Pull up some floor space near the fountain and sink your teeth into some *ketupat,* sticky rice cooked in woven banana-leaf packets. Locals recommend the *rowon daging* soup, a Banjar take on an east Java favourite. Patient staff bring reinforcements to help you translate the menu.

Cendrawasih Sarahai SEAFOOD $
(Jl Pangeran Samudera; mains 20,000Rp; ⏲9am-10pm) Delve deeper into Banjar cuisine at this renowned spot (not to be confused with the mediocre other Cendrawasih, established next door to the right by a competitive relative.) Pick fish, seafood or chicken grilled to order. Please avoid (and politely shame them for) the endangered turtle eggs.

Said Abdullah INDONESIAN $
(Jl Ahmad Yani Km1; mains 25,000Rp; ⏲10am-11.30pm) Locals say the *nasi kuning* (saffron rice) at this unassuming place is Banjarmasin's best. You can restock your supply of propolis and Tahitian Noni elixir while you're here.

☆ Entertainment

Dynasty KARAOKE
(Hotel Aria Barito, Jl Haryono MT; admission male/female 50,000/25,000Rp) This entertainment complex with disco, bar, and karaoke tries… and, at times, succeeds.

Information

Adat Tours (☎0821 4888 8801; Jl Hasanudin 27) Flight bookings, some tours, little English.

BNI Bank (Bank Negara Indonesia; Jl Lambung Mangkurat)

Haji La Tunrung (☎0511-336 5559; Jl Haryono MT 24) Exchange chain dealing in multiple currencies.

Internet (Jl Haryono MT 24; per hour 3000Rp; ⏲3pm-late)

Main Post Office (Jl Lambung Mangkurat)

Rumah Sakit Ulin (☎0511-252180; Jl Ahmad Yani 42) Medical centre.

Getting There & Away

AIR

Garuda (☎0511-336 6747; Jl Hasanudin 31)

Kalstar (☎0511-327 2470; Jl Ahmad Yani Km6 553)

Lion Air (☎ 0511-747 7480; Jl Ahmad Yani Km6, Efa Hotel lobby; ⏰ 9.30am-7.30pm)

Sriwijaya Air (☎ 0511-327 2377; Jl Ahmad Yani Km3.5; ⏰ 9am-5pm)

BOAT

Ocean ferries depart from Trisakti Pinisi Harbour (3km west on Jl Soetoyo). Pelni services Semarang (420,000Rp, 24 hours, weekly), while Dharma Lautan Utama services Surabaya (260,000Rp, 22 hours, five services a week). For boats to the interior, take a bus to Muara Tewah and start your journey there.

Dharma Lautan Utama (☎ 0511-441 0555; www.dluonline.co.id; Jl Yos Sudarso 4C, next to Hotel Queen)

Pelni (☎ 0511-335 3077; Jl Martadinata 10)

BUS

All buses leave from the Kilo Enam terminal at Jl Ahmad Yani Km6, southeast of downtown, accessible by *angkot*.

Getting Around

Angkot (5000Rp) routes are labelled by their destination, and fan out from terminals at Jl Pangeran Samudera circle, in the city core, and Antasari Centre, to the east. Becak and *ojeks* for hire gather around market areas. Taxis to/from Syamsuddin Noor Airport (26km) cost 120,000Rp.

Kandangan

☎ 0517 / POP 45,000

A local transport hub, Kandagan is also a fairly attractive town worth exploring. Tidy and well planned, it has decent budget hotels, a bustling market and numerous restaurants. It is also the gateway to the mountain oasis of Loksado and the buffalo herds of Nagara. Reserve ahead as rooms are few.

Sleeping & Eating

The Kandagan bus terminal doubles as a food court, and is lined with warungs to keep you well fed for days.

★ Wisma Duta HOTEL $
(☎ 0571-21073; Jl Permuda 9; r fan/air-con with breakfast 130,000/250,000Rp; ❄📶) This converted country home is a rare and welcome find. Rattan walls are a nice touch, even when adorned with assorted glass armaments. Head down the alley northeast from the bus terminal and turn left.

Hotel Mutia HOTEL $
(☎ 0517-21270; Jl Soeprapto; r incl breakfast 200,000-330,000Rp; ❄📶) Basic box rooms, convenient to the bus station and market.

TRANSPORT FROM BANJARMASIN

Air

DESTINATION	COMPANY	PRICE (RP)	DURATION (HR)	FREQUENCY
Balikpapan	Lion, Sriwijaya	400,000	1	daily
Jakarta	Citilink, Garuda, Lion	600,000	1¾	daily
Makassar	Sriwijaya	680,000	1¼	Mon, Wed, Fri, Sun
Pangkalan Bun	Kalstar, Trigana	700,000	1	1-2 daily
Surabaya	Citilink, Garuda	450,000	1	daily
Yogyakarta	Garuda, Lion	660,000	1¼	daily

Bus

DESTINATION	PRICE (RP)	DURATION (HR)	FREQUENCY
Balikpapan	155,000-185,000	12	4 daily 2-5pm
Kandangan	50,000	4	several daily 9am-6pm
Muara Tewah	110,000	12	2 daily
Negara	60,000	5	several daily 9am-6pm
Palangka Raya	70,000-85,000	5	5 daily 5-11am
Pangkalan Bun	180,000-235,000	12	5 daily 5-11am
Samarinda	180,000-215,000	15	4 daily 2-5pm

Medina HOTEL $$
(☎0517-21219; Jl M Johansyah 26; r incl breakfast 350,000Rp) The newest concrete box in town is clean, if uninspired. Hot showers. Just up the block from the bus terminal.

Getting There & Around

Minibuses run frequently to/from Banjarmasin's Km6 terminal (50,000Rp, four hours) until midafternoon. Buses for Balikpapan and Samarinda (125,000Rp to 165,000Rp) pass the Kandangan terminal regularly. *Ojek* are abundant, while becak are slowly dwindling.

Pick-up trucks for Loksado (30,000Rp, 1½ hours, 9am) leave from **Muara Bilui**, a nondescript stop on a residential street 800m east of the bus terminal.

Negara

Northwest of Kandangan, the riverside town of Negara is the gateway to a vast wetland ranch, where water buffalo swim from their elevated corrals at sunrise in search of grazing areas and are herded back at dusk by cowboys in canoes – an intriguing sight if you're there in late afternoon. Rent a boat at the dock near the mosque to see the swimming herds (200,000Rp).

The trip to Negara is memorable, too, along an elevated road through seasonally flooded wetlands lined with communities on stilts. To get here from Kandagan take a public minibus (15,000Rp, one hour) or taxi (150,000Rp return). Annoyingly there is no hotel in town.

Loksado

Nestled at the end of the road in the foothills of the **Meratus Mountains**, Loksado is as close to an earthly Elysium as you'll find in Kalimantan. The main village sits inside a large bend in the clear chattering stream which acts as a moat protecting it from the onslaught of the modern world. Numerous trails – some paved – connect remote villages with even more remote settlements, making the area ideal for adventurers with a habit of wandering to the end of things. A mountain bike would be the perfect tool for exploration, but alas, nobody rents them in town (yet). Base here for treks to mountain peaks, waterfalls, or remote Dayak villages. Or do none of the above and just enjoy carefree mountain-town life Kalimantan style.

Activities

Muara Tanuhi Hot Springs HOT SPRING
(admission 5000Rp) These developed hot springs, located in an undermaintained resort 7km west of Loksado, make a relaxing end to a long trek. Stay across the street at Pondok Bamboo (100,000Rp) and enjoy all-night access to the pools.

Mountain Hikes
Hiking trails in the Meratus combine forest, villages, rivers, suspension bridges and *balai adat* (community house) visits. One-day walks from Loksado reach a seemingly endless number of waterfalls, and range from moderate to billy-goating up the side of impossible slopes. A long history of shifting cultivation means it is a good five-hour walk to primary forest, but there's still plenty of picture-worthy scenery closer to town. For all but the closest destinations, a local guide is highly recommended. A popular multiday trek includes summiting **Gunung Besar** (aka Halau Halau, 1901m, three to four days) the tallest mountain in the Meratus range and one of the few Kalimantan peaks with a view.

Be prepared for your particular route, read up on jungle trekking (see boxed text, p261), and don't be afraid to rein in your guide if the pace or terrain is beyond your skill level.

Bamboo Rafting
Being poled downriver on a narrow hand-tied bamboo raft ranges from relaxing to spirited, depending on water levels. Three hours (300,000Rp) might test your attention span, but the 90-minute option is just about right.

Guides

Although guides from Banjarmasin range into this area, nothing beats the perspective of a local. English speakers are smart for more involved trips, but day treks can be a world of fun with a dictionary, sign language, and an enthusiastic villager.

Pak Amat GUIDE
(☎0813 4876 6573) An English-speaking, personable Dayak and long-standing Loksado resident, with complete knowledge of the area.

Samuil Noil GUIDE
(☎0812 5127 3802) Unassuming and with a great attitude, Loksado native Noil will happily put his gardening on hold to show you the land he is so passionate about. Speaks English.

WORTH A TRIP

BANJARBARU

Three curious stops accessible from the Banjarbaru roundabout (20,000Rp, 38km southeast of Banjarmasin) can be seen in a half-day return from Banjarmasin or on your way to or from Kandangan.

Cempaka Diamond Fields (Desa Pumpung; ⏲Sat-Thu) Wooden sluices filter muck from pits where men stand chest deep blasting away at the sediment with water cannons. Mining at its most basic, cheapest, picturesque, and – for the bold – participatory. At the Banjarbaru roundabout take a green passenger truck southbound to Desa Pumpung (6000Rp, 15 minutes, 7km), then walk 700m south from the main road.

Museum Lambung Mangkurat (☎051 1477 2453; Jl Ahmad Yani 36; admission 5000Rp; ⏲8am-4pm Sun-Thu, 8.30-11am Fri, 8.30am-3.30pm Sat) An above-average museum of local arts and history with approximate English translations providing nuggets of information about pivotal events – like the Banjar people sinking a Dutch warship in 1860, armed with only canoes and knives. Also, learn the architectural differences between a scholar's and a married princess' house. Head 1km west of the Banjarbaru roundabout.

Penggosokkan Intan (Diamond Polishing and Information Center; ⏲9am-4pm Sat-Thu) Lots of shops polish diamonds, but this is the official place for tourists to watch; 700m north of the Banjarbaru roundabout.

Shady GUIDE
(☎0821 5306 0515; www.borneo-discoverytours.com) A young and enthusiastic English-speaking guide from Kandangan with extensive trekking experience and a great sense of humour.

Sleeping & Eating

Sleeping options are expanding, with two new losmen opening near the tourist info centre, and a bona fide resort downriver. Avoid the sad concrete Wisma Loksado hotel on the eroding island.

A smattering of warung along the river provide basic Indonesian fare, with the best one found across the street from Mount Martuas Resort.

★ **Wisma Alya** GUESTHOUSE $
(☎0821 5330 8276; r 150,000Rp) This two-storey backpackers haven, with just five bare wooden rooms, hangs over the rushing Sungai Amandit, making the upstairs porch the best hang-out in town. Don't let them slough you off to the *cabang* (branch lodge) down river; it's set back from the road and removed from the village.

New competition nearby puts you in a good negotiating position, but the husband and wife team are so helpful for finding guides and other services, you may feel guilty about haggling.

Mangkuraksa Malaris HOMESTAY $
(☎0856 5129 8492; floor space 150,000Rp) At tiny Loklahong village, 2km downriver from Loksado, you can sleep with the locals in a breezy bamboo-walled hut next to the *balai adat*. You'll only get a chunk of floor in the living room, but you'll also meet some phenomenal folks, and have one of Kalimantan's premier swimming holes at the end of your block.

Mount Martuas Resort HOTEL $$
(☎0812 5150 4866; r/villa 400,000/1,500,000Rp; ❄) Loksado's official entrant into the near-luxury class. Located 800m downriver from town, it's not in the thick of village life, but you will have your own private bend of the river here. The well-crafted, rough-wood rooms come with fans and open-air stone bathrooms. Add 50,000Rp to upgrade to hot water.

The two villas are set back from the river, and offer air-con and a large kitchen/living area. Dine at the open-air restaurant, or at the tasty warung across the street.

Getting There & Around

Pick-up trucks leave for Loksado from **Muara Bilui** in Kandangan (30,000Rp, 1½ hours, 9am). They leave Loksado for Kandangan at 7am. Enquire at Wisma Alya for an *ojek* to trailheads.

EAST KALIMANTAN

Balikpapan

0542 / POP 560,000

As Kalimantan's only cosmopolitan city, Balikpapan is almost worthy of being considered a destination unto itself. A long history of oil money and foreign workers has had a tremendous impact, bringing Western aesthetics to this Eastern port town. The city is clean and vibrant, with several enormous shopping areas and some decent beaches. High-end hotels with reasonable rates abound, and the nightlife surprises. The city sprawls in all directions, but most of the action takes place in the centre off Jl Sudirman, which comes alive at night. Overall the city makes a fine weekend break, and a great place to begin or end more adventurous travels. See how many sun bear motifs you can spot.

Sights

Most sights of note lie outside of Balikpapan's borders (see boxed text, p251).

Kemala Beach BEACH
(Jl Sudirman) A clean, white-sand beach with adjacent cafes and restaurants, and a laid-back vibe. If you need a break from the jungle (urban or natural) this is your best local option. Although it gets hot at midday, you probably won't want to swim in the polluted waters.

Masjid Agung At-Taqwa MOSQUE
(Jl Sudirman) FREE An impressive sight, this mosque is adorned with a complex sheath of Islamic geometrical patterns, and is lit up in multicoloured splendour at night.

Tours

Rusdiansyah GUIDE
(0812 5331 2333; www.borneokalimantan.com) Now chair of the East Borneo Guiding Association, Pak Rusdy has been guiding throughout the island for 20 years and knows the land well.

Indra GUIDE
(081 2585 9800; indrahadi91@yahoo.com) The first choice for Japanese tourists; his English is serviceable, too.

Sleeping

The budget digs here are generally dismal and depressing, and we can't recommend them. Splurge. Ask about discounts everywhere.

★ **Wisma Kemala Bhayangkari** HOTEL $$
(0812 5490 2392, 0542-421260; Jl Sudirman 6; r250,000-385,000Rp;) Recently re-established as public lodging after a period as the residence of the police chief (who moved into a new mansion next door), this place is a steal for its clean and simple rooms on the beach. Don't come expecting luxury (there is no hot water), but the VIP rooms up front are spacious and freshly painted. On *angkot* route 3.

Access Kemala Beach and its cafes just off the back lawn.

Ibis Hotel HOTEL $$
(0542-820821; www.ibishotels.com; Jl Suparjan 2; r 350,000Rp;) Balikpapan's great steal. The cosy, design-conscious rooms are stylish and sophisticated, with bursts of bright colour and funky space-station bathrooms. Best of all, guests are welcome to use the considerable amenities of the adjoining five-star Novotel. Basically, you're staying at the Novotel for a third of the price. Breakfast 60,000Rp.

Hotel Pacific HOTEL $$
(0542-750888; Jl Ahmad Yani 33; d incl breakfast 400,000-500,000Rp;) An excellent, classic Asian hotel with very accommodating staff and a convenient location for food options. The wooden floor and dark trim are dated, but manage to be warming rather than foreboding. Spotless bathrooms all come with bathtubs.

Hotel Gajah Mada HOTEL $$
(0542-734634; Jl Sudirman 328; s 229,000-418,000Rp, d 270,000-467,000Rp;) These clean, bare rooms are located on prime real estate next to Balikpapan Plaza. Cheaper rooms have fans only, but the ocean breeze down the shotgun hallway keeps things cool. A large back deck overlooks the ocean, with a filthy beach next door.

Aiqo Hotel HOTEL $$
(0542-750288; Jl Pranoto 9; s 248,000Rp, d 268,000-328,000Rp;) A clean midmarket option with tiny soak-everything-when-you-shower bathrooms. The 30,000Rp surcharge for a superior room adds nothing but an in-room coffee maker. Wi-fi in the lobby only.

Balikpapan

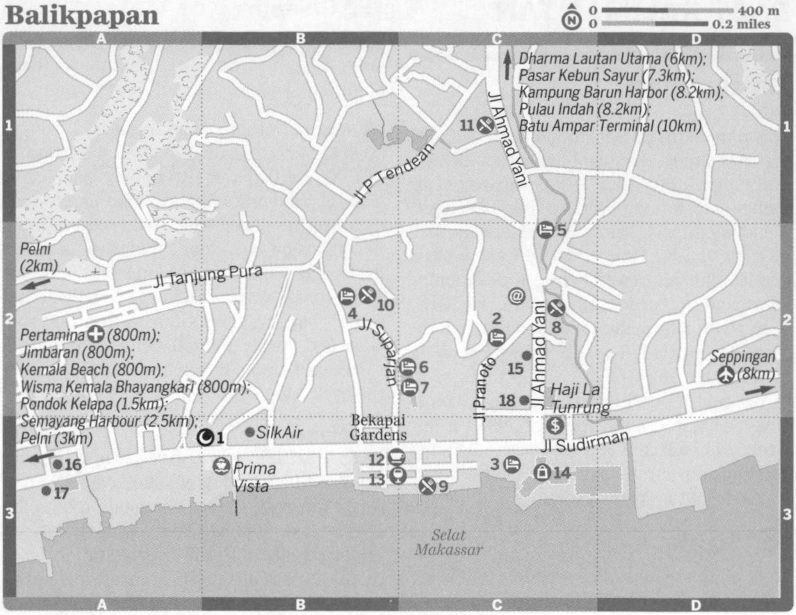

Balikpapan

Sights
1 Masjid Agung At-Taqwa ... B3

Sleeping
2 Aiqo Hotel ... C2
3 Hotel Gajah Mada ... C3
4 Hotel Gran Senyiur ... B2
5 Hotel Pacific ... C2
6 Ibis Hotel ... C2
7 Novotel Balikpapan ... C2

Eating
8 Bondy ... C2
9 Ocean's Resto ... C3
10 Sky Bar/Sky Grill ... B2
11 Soto Queen ... C1

Drinking & Nightlife
12 Book Cafe ... B3
13 Ruko Bandar ... B3

Shopping
14 Balikpapan Plaza ... C3

Information
15 Aero Travel ... C2
16 Kantorimigrasi Kelas ... A3
17 New Sedayu Wisata ... A3
18 Totogasono Sekawan ... C2

★ Hotel Gran Senyiur HOTEL **$$$**
(0542-820211; gran.senyiurhotels.com; Jl ARS Muhammad 7; r incl breakfast from 860,000Rp;) Unique in Kalimantan, this old-world Asian luxury hotel proves to the younger generic business hotels that experience and wisdom count ... a lot. Fine woodwork warms spaces throughout, and rooms are priced well for their elevated class. From the lobby lounge to the world-class Sky Bar, which adds a modern note to the roof, everything is upscale without being ostentatious.

Deluxe rooms are really just superior rooms with a useless kitchen space. For those in a suite mood, the opulent 'governor's room' has Victorian furniture, while the 'executive' gets you the exact same layout and killer view, with a slight downgrade in furniture.

Le Grandeur Balikpapan HOTEL **$$$**
(0542-420155; Jl Sudirman; r with breakfast from 870,000Rp;) A venerable luxury hotel, oozing sophistication. The 4th-floor business-class rooms have been renovated to great effect, while open-air waterfront dining

and live jazz make for a classy stay. Unfortunately, an abundance of trash tarnishes the beachfront location. On Jl Sudirman about 2km east of Plaza Balikpapan.

Novotel Balikpapan HOTEL **$$$**
(☎0542-820820; www.novotel.com/asia; Jl Suparjan 2; r incl breakfast 985,000-1,160,000Rp; ❄📶🏊) A family-friendly hotel, with an ubermodern interior and all amenities, including a patisserie, cafe, gym and 2nd-floor rooftop pool with a swim-up bar (50,000Rp to nonguests). However, the stained superior rooms with laminate furniture don't quite live up to the price.

The fitness centre has multiple modern machines and free weights. Parents are liberated by the free kids club.

Eating

★Soto Queen INDONESIAN **$**
(Warung Kuin Abduh, SQ; Jl Ahmad Yani; soto Banjar 15,000Rp; ⏲2-11pm) We're not sure if they serve anything besides *soto Banjar* (chicken soup seasoned with a delicate blend of spices including cinnamon)... we've never felt the need to ask. You'll likely have to wait for a seat.

Jimbaran BALINESE **$**
(Dapur Bali; Jl Sudirman, Kemala Beach; mains 25,000Rp; ⏲10am-11pm) Billowing white curtains beckon you to this open-air Balinese restaurant at the end of Kemala Beach. Locals swear by the *ayam taliwang*, a fried-grilled chicken from Lombok, and the *ayam betutu*, a spicy recipe that will transport you to Bali. Live music Saturday and Monday.

Bondy INTERNATIONAL **$**
(☎0542-424285; Jl Ahmad Yani 1; mains 35,000Rp; ⏲10am-10pm) Dine among sculpted trees and thriving flowers in a tranquil courtyard in the middle of the city. Popular with locals and expats, mostly for their extensive homemade ice cream menu. A banana split is 30,000Rp; steaks start at 90,000Rp.

★Ocean's Resto SEAFOOD, INTERNATIONAL **$$**
(☎0542-739439; Ruko Bandar; mains 40,000Rp; ⏲9am-11pm; 📶) An entire reef's worth of fish, steaks aplenty, plus burgers, pizza, and 14 types of fried rice all served above the surf. Ocean's anchors a row of cafes along the waterfront, and is (deservedly) the most popular. The tiny open-air 2nd-floor curry house is a good place for appetisers.

Pondok Kelapa SEAFOOD **$$**
(☎0542-733956; Jl Yos Sudarso 72; mains 35,000Rp; ⏲11am-10pm) Strategically located on the tip of Balikpapan bay, come here for epic sunset dining; watch the oil tankers pass while dining on gigantic *udang gala* (river prawns).

Sky Bar / Sky Grill SEAFOOD **$$**
(Jl ARS Muhammad, Grand Senyiur Hotel; mains 55,000Rp; ⏲3-11pm) The Grand Senyiur Hotel has an awesome rooftop, combining glass-walled al fresco dining and a sophisticated piano bar with panoramic city views.

Open House INTERNATIONAL **$$$**
(☎0542-744823; Jl Puncak Markoni Atas 88; mains from 160,000Rp; ⏲11am-11pm) Balikpapan's most romantic place to blow your last rupiah on a date is defined by architecturally dizzying spaces atop a prominent hill. Reserve your *puncak* (summit) table for two at the top of the spiral staircase. The above-average food blends Mediterranean, international and Indian menus; bring your own wine. A blanket 20% discount on weekdays drops to 15% on weekends.

Drinking & Nightlife

Balikpapan's expat community has fuelled a more relaxed attitude toward alcohol and nightlife than is found in other parts of Kalimantan. Most hotels serve spirits, and package liquor is available (for a price) at the Swiss-Belhotel. To get the pulse of the local scene, head to the **Ruko Bandar** (Jl Sudirman, waterfront) complex.

Book Cafe COFFEE
(☎0542-739168; Ruko Bandar; snacks 15,000Rp; ⏲10am-midnight; ❄📶) Monopoly anyone? A chill nonalcoholic hang-out in the Ruko Bandar complex, Book Cafe has games aplenty and, yes, books in English and Bahasa Indonesia to buy, borrow or trade. For a truly humbling experience, get trounced by a local student in a game of Scrabble... in English.

Shopping

Shopping is concentrated around **Balikpapan Plaza** (cnr Jls Sudirman & Ahmad Yani) which has a Hypermart (for groceries).

Pasar Kebun Sayur SOUVENIRS
(⏲9am-6pm) An eclectic market for local handicrafts, gemstones and souvenirs. North of the city centre on yellow *angkot* 5.

Information

Aero Travel (☎0542-443350; Jl Ahmad Yani 19) Airline tickets.

Haji La Tunrung (☎0542-731975; Jl Ahmad Yani 6A; ⌚7.30am-9pm) Exchange chain dealing in multiple currencies.

Kantorimigrasi Kelas (☎0542-421175; Jl Sudirman 23) Immigration office.

New Sedayu Wisata (NSW; ☎0542-420601; Jl Sudirman 2B) Best source for all things ferry.

Pertamina Hospital (☎0542-421212; Jl Sudirman 1)

Rebel Net Internet (off Jl Ahmad Yani; per hour 5000Rp)

Totogasono Sekawan (☎0542-421539; tour@totogasono.com; Jl Ahmad Yani 40) Efficient English-speaking agent for airline bookings. Has contracts with **Pak Rusdy** (p247) for trips up the Mahakam and beyond.

Getting There & Away

AIR

Citilink (☎0542-764362; Airport)

Garuda (☎0542-766844; Airport)

Kalstar (☎0542-737473; Jl Marsaiswahyudi 12)

Lion Air (☎0542-703 3761; Airport)

SilkAir (☎0542-730800; Jl Jend Sudirman 37, BRI Tower 6th fl)

Sriwijaya (☎0542-749777; Airport)

Susi Air (☎0542-761196; Airport)

TRANSPORT FROM BALIKPAPAN

Air

DESTINATION	COMPANY	FARE (RP)	DURATION	FREQUENCY
Banjarmasin	Garuda, Lion	465,000	50min	4 daily
Berau	Garuda, Sriwijaya, Wings	470,000	50min	7 daily
Denpasar	Citilink	770,000	1½hr	Mon, Fri, Sun
Jakarta	Cililink, Garuda, Lion, Sriwijaya	810,000	2hr	many daily
Kuala Lumpur	Air Asia	550,000	2½hr	Mon, Wed, Fri, Sun
Makassar	Citilink, Garuda, Lion, Sriwijaya	480,000	1¼hr	7 daily
Melak	Kalstar	760,000	30min	2 daily
Pontianak	Kalstar	1,200,000	2hr	1 daily
Samarinda	Kalstar, Susi	350,000	20min	3 daily
Singapore	Silk	3,500,000	2¼hr	Mon, Wed, Fri, Sat
Surabaya	Citilink, Garuda, Lion, Sriwijaya	620,000	1½hr	many daily
Tarakan	Garuda, Lion, Sriwijaya	500,000	1hr	many daily
Yogyakarta	Citilink, Garuda, Lion	720,000	1¾hr	6 daily

Boat

DESTINATION	COMPANY	PRICE (RP)	DURATION (HR)	FREQUENCY
Makassar	Dharma Lautan Utama, Prima Visat, Pelni	215,000	24	5-6 weekly
Pare Pare	Prima Vista, Pelni	295,000	18	almost daily
Surabaya	Dharma Lautan Utama, Prima Vista, Pelni	400,000	40	almost daily
Tarakan-Nunukan	Pelni	273,000	12	3 weekly

WORTH A TRIP

AROUND BALIKPAPAN

A potpourri of sights around Balikpapan make for fine day trips. Some are accessible by public transit while others will require a vehicle. A guide can help.

KWPLH Balikpapan (☎0542-710 8304; www.beruangmadu.org; Jl Soekarno-Hatta Km23; ⌚9am-5pm, feedings 9am & 3pm) This informative sun bear conservation centre is surprisingly straight to the point about the heart-breaking plight of all of Kalimantan's animals. Seven resident bears hide in their 1.3-hectare walled enclosure until feeding time, when you can observe them near the clinic. Take *angkot* 8 to the large gate at Km23 (7000Rp), then walk or hitch 1.7km south.

Samboja Lestari (☎0542-702 3600; www.orangutan.or.id; Jl Balikpapan-Handil Km44; adult incl meal morning/afternoon 550,000/800,000Rp, child incl meal morning/afternoon 275,000/475,000Rp) A Borneo Orangutan Survival Foundation (p237) project, Samboja Lestari houses around 200 orangutans and 50 sun bears. Half day tours (9am to 1pm and 2pm to 8pm, reserve ahead) show off the centre's residents and accomplishments; or stay overnight at the stunning lodge.

Sungai Wain (☎Agus 0812 580 6329; agusdin_wain@yahoo.co.id; mandatory guides 100,000Rp) In the mid-'90s, 82 orangutans were released in this protected forest, but fires and illegal logging have taken their toll. Get a 6am start to maximise wildlife viewing. Take *angkot* 8 to Km15 (6000Rp), and an *ojek* 6km west.

BOAT

Semayang Harbour, at the entrance to the gulf, is the main cargo and passenger port.

Dharma Lautan Utama (☎0542-442222; Jl Soekarno-Hatta Km0.5)

Pelni (☎0542-422110; Jl Yos Sudarso, near Pelabuhan Semayang)

Prima Vista (☎0542-428888; Jl Sudirman 138)

BUS

Buses to Samarinda (30,000Rp, three hours, departing every 15 minutes, 5.30am-8pm) and minibuses to points north leave from Batu Ampar Terminal on *angkot* route 3 (light blue). Your best company for Banjarmasin (150,000Rp to 205,000Rp, 15 hours, eight daily, noon-8pm) is **Pulau Indah** (☎0542-420289; Jl Soekarno-Hatta Km 2.5).

Getting Around

- Taxis to the city centre from the airport cost 70,000Rp. Alternately, walk 150m to the road, and hail a green-and-white *angkot* 7 heading west (5000Rp).
- City *angkot* run regular routes converging at Balikpapan Plaza, and charge 5000Rp a ride.

Samarinda

☎0541 / POP 840,000

Samarinda! The very name oozes exoticism. And happily you will find some of that here in this sprawling riverfront city, including the enormous mosque of the new Islamic Center, which stands like a sentinel at the gates of the mighty Sungai Mahakam (Mahakam River), a most impressive sight. But as with many fairy tales, there is a dark side to this story. Over half of Samarinda's land has been opened for coal mining, resulting in numerous health and environmental effects, and causing hotels to advertise their 'flood-free event halls.' Meanwhile, a proliferation of monster malls has been gutting downtown, leaving some streets eerily vacant; take a taxi after dark.

Sights

Islamic Center MOSQUE
(Masjid Baitul Muttaqien; Jl Slamet Riyadi; mosque/tower free/10,000Rp; ⌚8am-6pm) The western skyline of Samarinda is dominated by this must-see complex containing an ornate and colourful mosque with adjacent observation tower. The latter is the highest point in the city, offering panoramic views up and down a great bend in the Mahakam. The muezzin's sunset call is a captivating moment.

Masjid Shirathal Mustaqiem MOSQUE
(Samarinda Seberang) FREE Built in 1881 to tame a neighbourhood notorious for gambling and drinking, the mosque's four main pillars were reportedly set by a mysterious elderly woman while nobody was looking. The yellow ironwood minaret is a distinct Kalimantan-Muslim take on the pagoda. Take

Samarinda

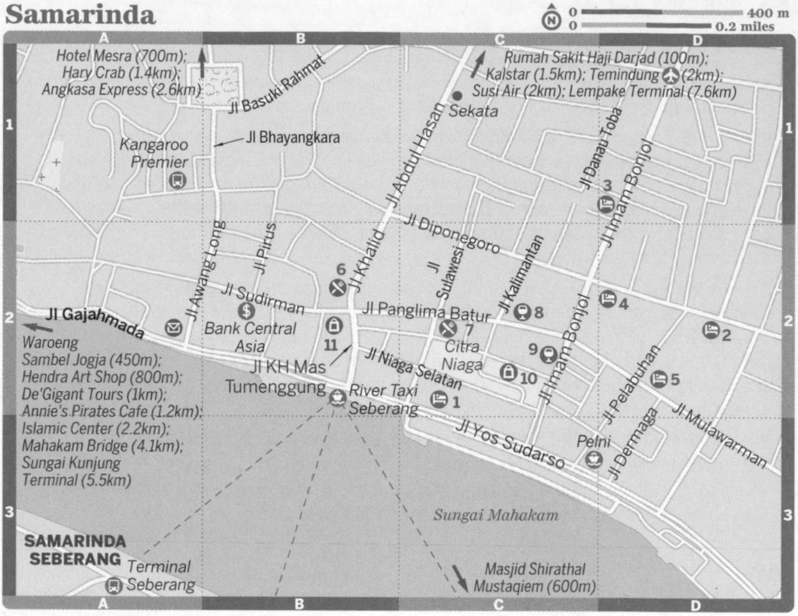

Samarinda

Sleeping
1 Akasia 8 Guesthouse C2
2 Aston Samarinda D2
3 Horison D1
4 Kost Samarinda D2
5 Swiss-Belhotel D2

Eating
6 Hero Supermarket B2
7 Sari Pacific Restaurant C2

Drinking & Nightlife
8 Dejavu Kitchen Bar & KTV C2
9 Maximum C2

Shopping
10 Citra Niaga C2
11 Pasar Pagi B2

a boat (25,000Rp, five minutes) direct to the mosque in Samarinda Seberang.

Tours

Abdullah GUIDE
(☎0813 4727 2817, 0821 5772 0171; doe1L@yahoo.com) Friendly, resourceful and realistic. Abdullah speaks excellent English, and understands backpackers. Also a Dayak antiques agent.

Rustam GUIDE
(☎0812 585 4915; rustam_kalimantan@yahoo.co.id) Rustam universally gets good reviews.

Suryadi GUIDE
(☎0816 459 8263) Even after guiding for almost 30 years, wise Pak Suryadi is probably still in better shape than you are. Speaks German as well as English.

De'Gigant Tours ADVENTURE TOUR
(☎0812 584 6578; www.borneotourgigant.com; Jl Martadinata Raudah 21) De'Gigant (also X-Treme Borneo and Kalimantan Tours) specialises in trips in East Kalimantan and has safely shepherded dozens of clients through the renowned Cross-Borneo Trek. However, readers report inconsistent guide quality.

Sleeping

Top-end hotels can be good value, but suffer from inattention. The almost-finished Ibis/Mercure megacomplex will likely reset the hospitality bar.

★Kost Samarinda HOTEL $
(Samarinda Guesthouse; ☎0541-734337; www.kostsamarinda.com; s/d 125,000/200,000Rp; ❄📶) The excessively accommodating owners understand what backpackers need: a clean, cheap, friendly, no-frills place strategically located in the middle of the action. Rooms share a large cold-water *mandi* (Indonesian bath, consisting of a large water tank from which water is ladled over the body) and speedy wi-fi. The icing: motorbikes for rent (50,000Rp).

Akasia 8 Guesthouse GUESTHOUSE $
(☎0541-701 9590; Jl Yos Sudarso 34; s/d with breakfast 145,000/180,000Rp) The overly small *mandi* at this clean and bare dockside losmen will torment your inner claustrophobe; spring for the en suite option to buy some wiggle room.

Hotel Mesra HOTEL $$
(☎0541-732772; www.hotelmesrasamarinda.com; Jl Pahlawan 1; s incl breakfast 425,000Rp, d incl breakfast 525,000-925,000Rp; ❄📶🏊) This polished resort, owned by the Mesra Coal conglomerate, is located on a private hilltop downtown. Some rooms have balconies overlooking the manicured grounds, which include two pools open to the public (50,000Rp), gardens, tennis courts, a spa and minigolf. It's worth coming just for the breakfast (125,000Rp) – assuming you don't mind dining under the watchful eye of an enormous *garuda* (mythical bird.)

Rooms here vary greatly, even in the same building, so inspect a few before committing.

Aston Samarinda HOTEL $$
(☎0541-732600; www.astonsamarinda.com; Jl P Hidayatullah; r/ste with breakfast 700,000/830,000Rp; ❄📶🏊) This attractive, well-designed hotel is the place to come for spotless luxury. The colonnaded pool with its two-storey waterfall may be ostentatious, but the rooms have just the right amount of style and comfort. Some superiors have grand views of the river, while others have no windows but extra space. Fine dining and an in-house spa round out the scene nicely.

Horison HOTEL $$
(☎0541-727 2900; www.myhorison.com; Jl Imam Bonjol 9; r incl breakfast 685,000Rp; ❄📶🏊) This chain hotel adds a touch of class to the otherwise standard business hotel market. The fresh rooms all have work desks, flat-screen TVs and bone-chilling central air-con. The top-floor indoor pool has expansive views, while the bottom-floor lobby has batik demonstrations.

WORTH A TRIP

PAMPANG DAYAK CEREMONIES

Every Sunday at 2pm, the Kenyah Dayak village of Pampang (relocated here from the highlands in the 1970s), puts on a show (5000Rp) of traditional dances aimed squarely at camera-toting tourists. Enjoy it for what it is: an engaging, staged performance that allows a long-marginalised group to benefit economically from their rich heritage. It is also one of the last places to see women with traditional long earlobes (photos 25,000Rp). Take a public minibus (15,000Rp) from Lempake Terminal to the intersection 25km north of Samarinda.

Swiss-Belhotel HOTEL $$
(☎0541-200888; www.swiss-belhotel.com; Jl Mulawarman 6; r incl breakfast 500,000-954,000Rp; ❄📶🏊) The rooms at this business hotel are all the same size. An upgrade in price gets you touches such as a river view and face towel. The executive rooms were being nicely renovated when we visited, while the rest have touches of style, as well as touches of bathroom mould and mildly stained bed sheets.

✕ Eating

Samarinda's food scene is a bit spread out, though there are some great options you won't regret walking for.

Annie's Pirates Cafe INDONESIAN $
(☎0541-739009; Jl Martadinata 7; mains 30,000Rp, coffee drinks 25,000Rp; ⏲3-11pm) While piracy off the shores of Samarinda has declined in recent years, Annie's business is still booming. This creatively themed resto maximises its rooftop river-breeze dining with an extensive menu, including a hogshead of rum (flavoured) drinks. Yarr.

Hero Supermarket SUPERMARKET $
(Mesra Indah Mall; ⏲10am-9pm) Good place to stock up on snacks before heading upriver.

★Waroeng Sambel Jogja INDONESIAN $$
(☎0541-743913; Jl Gaja Madah 1; mains from 25,000Rp) Serving eight very different varieties of sambal (salsa) designed to knock your socks off, this large complex near the riverfront is packed on the weekends. Their house speciality, the onion-y sambel bawang Jogja,

was a bit salty for our liking, but the sambel tempe lit us up right.

Hary Crab SEAFOOD **$$**
(Jl Pahlawan 41; crab 75,000Rp; 6-10pm) A unique local institution, these streetside outdoor benches are generally packed with people who believe dinner should be a fully immersive affair. Wear your bib.

Sari Pacific Restaurant INTERNATIONAL **$$**
(Jl Panglima Batur; mains from 35,000Rp; 9am-10pm) Features a selection of New Zealand steaks (120,000Rp) as well as burgers, chicken and fish – all in frustratingly small portions. The house favourite, Ikan Patin bakar (grilled fish), is pure greasy deliciousness. Bonus: fried ice cream!

Drinking & Nightlife

Dejavu Kitchen Bar & KTV BAR
(0541-747880; Jl Panglima Batur 9; 10pm-2am) This complex contains a booming nightclub (admission 75,000Rp) with lots of security, while a separate classy dinner restaurant is frequented by a hip and dressy crowd. The menu includes international cuisine plus a spectrum of cocktails at premium prices.

Maximum CLUB
(Jl Niaga Timur 21; 8pm-late) In Plaza 21, this ear-splitter is one of the more popular dance clubs in the city. Go after midnight. Taxis available around the corner.

Shopping

★**Hendra Art Shop** ANTIQUES
(0541-734949; hendra.art@gmail.com; Jl Martadinata; 9am-5pm) The two storeys of curios, antiques, and other Borneo exotica found in this shop can't be beat. Haggling, and an eye for authenticity, are required. Shipping is available, but that 6m carved longhouse ladder will cost you.

Citra Niaga MARKET
This daily market contains several souvenir shops offering batik sarongs and Dayak carvings. Food stalls serve *amplang* (famous crunchy fishy puffs) and standard Indonesian fare (mains 25,000Rp).

TRANSPORT FROM SAMARINDA

Air

Several airlines have planned additional routes when (if) the new airport 23km north of town is ever completed.

DESTINATION	COMPANY	FARE (RP)	DURATION	FREQUENCY
Balikpapan	Kalstar, Susi	300,000	20min	4 daily
Berau	Kalstar	830,000	45min	2 daily
Melak	Susi	500,000	40min	Mon, Wed, Fri, Sat
Tanjung Selor	Kalstar	1,140,000	1hr	1 daily

Bus

DESTINATION	TERMINAL	FARE (RP)	DURATION (HR)	FREQUENCY
Balikpapan	Sungai Kunjang	35,000	2	every 10min, 6am-8pm
Banjarmasin	Samarinda Seberang	175,000-235,000	16	8 daily 9am-5pm
Berau	Lempake	200,000	17	call 0812 5417 3997
Bontang	Lempake	35,000	3	every 25min, 7am-7pm
Kota Bangun	Sungai Kunjang	35,000	3½	6 daily, 7am-3pm
Melak	Sungai Kunjang	110,000	9	3 daily
Sangatta	Lampake	42,000	4	every 25min, 6am-5pm
Tenggarong	roadside across bridge	25,000	1	regular when full

Pasar Pagi MARKET
(Morning Market; Jl Sudirman) A wonderfully chaotic morning market.

Information

Angkasa Express (☎0541-200280; Plaza Lembuswana D3; ⏰8am-9pm Mon-Fri, to 1pm Sat) Air tickets.

Bank Central Asia (BCA; Jl Sudirman; ⏰8am-3pm Mon-Fri) Foreign exchange.

Main Post Office (cnr Jls Gajah Mada & Awang Long)

Rumah Sakit Haji Darjad (☎0541-732698; Jl Dahlia 4) Large hospital off Jl Basuki Rahmat.

Sekata (☎0541-742098; Jl Abdul Hasan 59) Airline tickets and car transport. English spoken.

Getting There & Away

AIR

Kalstar (☎0541-743780; Jl Gatot Subroto 80)
Susi Air (Airport)

BOAT

Mahakam ferries *(kapal biasa)* leave at 7am from Sungai Kunjang terminal, 6km upriver on green *angkot* A (5000Rp). At time of research, **Pelni** (☎0541-741402; Jl Yos Sudarso 76) ferries were no longer serving Samarinda, but the office will sell tickets for Balikpapan departures.

BUS

Samarinda has three main bus terminals:

Sungai Kunjang terminal (6km west on green *angkot* A) serves Mahakam river destinations as well as points south.

Lempake terminal (8km north on red *angkot* B) serves all points north, including an irregular daily bus to Berau. *Taksi gelap* (unlicensed taxis) for Berau troll the terminal, effectively killing the public bus market.

Terminal Seberang (cross the river via water taxi) serves Banjarmasin.

Minibuses for Tenggarong leave from the east side of the Mahakam Bridge. Cross it on *angkot* G and head south 500m where buses gather opposite the PLTD electric station.

Kangaroo Premier (☎0812 555 1199; www.kangaroo.id; Jl WR Supratman 7A) sends minibuses to Balikpapan airport every 10 minutes.

Getting Around

Angkot (5000Rp) converge at Pasar Pagi market. Taxis from Tumindung Airport (3km) cost 60,000Rp. Alternatively, walk 200m to Jl Gatot Subroto, turn left and catch *angkot* B south into town.

Cross-Mahakam ferries to Samarinda Seberang (5000Rp) leave from the end of Jl Tumenggung.

Sungai Mahakam

The second-largest river in Indonesia, the mighty Mahakam is a microcosm of Kalimantan. As you float upriver in search of the 'Heart of Borneo', you'll pass countless barges hauling it downriver to sell to the highest bidder. You'll see centuries-old villages just around the bend from coal mines and logging camps, and impossibly tall trees looming next to oil palm plantations. You'll pass imposing government offices with flash SUVs parked out front on your way to haggle over the price of a hand-carved *mandau* (machete) with a man who's barely keeping his family fed. This is Kalimantan in all of its conflicting, powerful, confusing and compelling beauty. And, there is no better way to see it than a trip up the Mahakam: a journey you'll remember for a lifetime.

Activities

Travelling up this major artery of Kalimantan is a journey in the fullest sense of the word. As you head away from the industrial centre of Samarinda you slip deeper into the interior, and into Borneo's past. You won't be alone (there is a daily public boat, after all) but you won't see many other foreigners – if any.

Opportunities for exploration abound, from towns and longhouses, to huge lakes, wetlands and side creeks. Wildlife is abundant, but elusive. Your odds of meeting river otters, pythons, macaques, proboscis monkeys, monitor lizards or hornbills increase exponentially with your distance from the main corridor. Jump off the boat at any random village and wait for the next one, even if it means staying overnight – especially if. The Mahakam is one of those places where you shouldn't worry too much about the details. Homestays materialise, 'my brother's boat' appears, closed stores open. Hospitality is the *lingua franca,* and the people are universally welcoming.

Heading up the main river gets you into the interior, but taking any tributary will open up a whole new world of adventures and experiences.

Stages of Travel

The Mahakam stretches from Samarinda to the highlands through several distinct regions:

Lower Mahakam: Samarinda to Kota Bangun Many travellers opt to cover this fairly developed stretch by land. Otherwise, it is an eight-hour journey from Samarinda by *kapal biasa,* which depart Samarinda every morning at 7am. Notable stops include the former Kutai sultanate in Tenggarong city.

The Lake District: Kota Bangun to Melak This diverse section of rivers, lakes and marshes is full of wildlife and dotted with villages, each completely unique in its own way. Base out of Muara Muntai for day trips to Lake Jempang, or take creative side passages upriver to Muara Pahu.

Middle Mahakam: Melak to Long Bagun The upper reach of the *kapal biasa* begins to feel like the wild Kalimantan you've dreamed about.

Upper Mahakam: Long Bagun to Tiong Ohang The most exhilarating and dangerous part of the river includes two major sets of rapids that claim multiple lives each year.

Note that *kapal biasa* reach Long Bagun when water levels permit. Otherwise they stop in Tering or Long Iram, at which point speed boats will surround your boat looking for passengers for Long Bagun.

Guides

As you head further upriver, Bahasa skills become more essential as English is almost nonexistent. You can get by with rudimentary phrases, but your travel options will be limited and your understanding of the area restricted to surface observations.

Most guides prefer package trips with preset costs, and tend not to deviate from their scripted route. However, some may agree to a more flexible itinerary for a daily fee, with you covering their food, lodging and transport as well. Independent guiding fees range from 150,000Rp to 350,000Rp per day depending on experience, skill and demand. The best guides will look out for their client's financial interests, negotiating on your behalf and making savings which may defray their fee.

Take the time to find a suitable guide in Samarinda (p252) or Balikpapan (p247), where they are relatively plentiful. An interview is essential to confirm language skills and identify personality [in]compatibilities that can make or break a long trip together.

Tenggarong

☎0541 / POP 75,000

Once the capital of the mighty Kutai sultanate, Tenggarong has been attempting to recreate its past glory, with mixed results. Flush with mining profits, the government has invested heavily in infrastructure – good. However, development largely focused on turning Kumala Island into a gaudy tourist attraction, which now lies abandoned and bankrupt, plagued by a corruption scandal – bad. Far worse, in 2011 the 10-year-old bridge across the Mahakam, dubbed 'Indonesia's Golden Gate', suddenly collapsed into the river, killing 36 people. Most travellers come for the lively annual Erau Festival, otherwise the informative museum is your primary draw.

Sights

Mulawarman Museum MUSEUM

(Jl Diponegoro; admission 5000Rp; 9am-4pm, closed Mon & Fri) The former sultan's palace, built by the Dutch in 1937, is now a decent museum chronicling the culture, natural history and industry of Indonesia's oldest kingdom – as evidenced by 5th-century Sanskrit engravings (originals in Jakarta). The ornate Yuan and Ming Dynasty ceramics are compelling, while the wedding headwear from around Indonesia is entertaining. (Ladies, get married in West Sumatra. Gentlemen, South Kalimantan.) The architecturally incongruous building is itself an attraction, with strong parallel lines reminiscent of Frank Lloyd Wright's work.

Don't miss the exquisitely decorative wooden palace out back, which stands empty outside of the Erau Festival, when the current sultan takes up residence.

Festivals & Events

Erau International Folk & Art Festival CULTURAL

(EIFAF; www.facebook.com/EIFAF) Originally held in celebration of a sultan's coronation, the Erau (from the Kutai word *eroh*, meaning joyful, boisterous crowd) became a biannual, then annual, gathering to celebrate Dayak culture and custom. It's usually in August, occasionally in June. Book lodging in advance.

The event has recently joined with the International Folk & Art Festival to expand the menu of twirling dancers in traditional costume to include 17 countries from Bulgaria to South Korea to Venezuela.

THE LAST IRRAWADDY DOLPHINS

Once common along the Mahakam, the population of the Critically Endangered freshwater Irrawaddy dolphin *(pesut)* has declined precipitously in recent years. Today, there are less than 90 left, and they must dodge gill nets and ship rotors in an increasingly murky river polluted with coal mine and oil palm plantation run-off. The playful, round-faced survivors can often be seen in the Pela/Lake Semayang area.

Sleeping & Eating

Hotel Karya Tapin HOTEL $
(☎0541-661258; Jl Maduningrat 29; r incl breakfast 245,000Rp; ❄) Spotless lavender-striped rooms at this small hotel include high ceilings, TVs, showers and homely touches. Head west on Jl Kartini along the south bank of the creek beside the Keraton to Jl Maduningrat. Hot water is extra (when it's working). Hot water rooms are 50,000Rp extra, even if it's not working.

Grand Elty Singgasana Hotel HOTEL $$
(☎0541-664703; Jl Pahlawan 1; r incl breakfast 694,000-814,000Rp; ❄📶🏊) Located on a beautiful hillside south of town, the stately wood-trimmed rooms are marred by peeling paint, broken walkways, and staff who seem surprised to discover someone is actually staying here. The pool (35,000Rp for nonguests) has a phenomenal view. Transport into town is 100,000Rp a trip.

Etam Fried Chicken INDONESIAN $
(☎0541-665701; Jl Muchsin Timbau; mains 20,000Rp; ⌚11am-10pm) The local recommendation for tasty fried (and more) chicken; 2km south of the museum.

Getting There & Away

Boat The *kapal biasa* dock (Pelabuhan Mangkurawang) is 2.5km north of town, with *angkot* (5000Rp) service to the centre. Boats pass heading downriver to Samarinda around 7am daily (25,000Rp, two hours) and for Kota Bangun at 9am daily (50,000Rp, six hours).

Bus Timbau bus terminal is 4km south of the museum area, with *angkot* service to the centre (5000Rp). Buses depart hourly from 9am to 4pm for Samarinda (25,000Rp) but you'll need to hail passing Kota Bangun–bound buses (30,000Rp) or Kijang (150,000Rp) on the street.

Kota Bangun

This small town is where many Mahakam journeys begin. From here, take the *kapal biasa* direct to Muara Muntai on the river, or hire a *ces* to get there via the northern scenic route through Lakes Semayang and Melintang. You'll twist and turn through narrow channels, cross endless marshes, and pass through forests of silver-barked trees, pausing for the odd monkey or some of the last Irrawaddy dolphins.

Sleeping & Eating

Warung Etam and Warung Maskur, next to the dock, serve excellent grilled chicken and chicken soup respectively. Pak Maskur speaks passable English and can help in a pinch.

Penginapan Etam GUESTHOUSE $
(Jl HM Aini H 19; r fan/air-con 60,000/120,000Rp; ❄) If you enjoyed visiting grandmother's house, you'll enjoy staying at this friendly upstairs guesthouse. Enjoy the foot-massaging floors in the clean shared *mandi*. It's 140m upriver of the *kapal biasa* dock.

Penginapan Mukjizat GUESTHOUSE $
(☎0541-666 3586; Jl A Yani 5; s/d 50,000/100,000Rp) The chill rear balcony above the river is a plus. Its proximity to the megaphonic mosque, not so much. It's 200m downriver from the *kapal biasa* dock.

Getting There & Around

Kapal biasa pass in the afternoon heading upriver, and in the predawn morning heading down. Buses to Samarinda (35,000Rp, four hours) leave at least three times daily between 7am and 2pm. Regular *ces* service runs to Muara Pela (30,000Rp), Semayang (50,000Rp) and Melintang (65,000Rp) three times daily starting at 11am. Charter a private *ces* for **dolphin watching at Pela** (☎Pak Darwis 0852 5065 0961; 2hrs 200,000Rp), or for the back-channel journey to Muara Muntai (1,000,000Rp per day).

Muara Muntai

Considering the price of ironwood these days, the streets of Muara Muntai might as well be paved with gold. This riverside town's nearly 20km network of richly weathered boardwalks clack loudly with passing motorbikes, adding to the rich Mahakam soundscape. The sound of money has also caught the attention of unscrupulous traders who offer to replace the boardwalks at cost, then sell the 'reclaimed' lumber to builders in Bali, circumventing restrictions on the trade of new ironwood. Base yourself here for day trips to Lakes Jempang or Melintang.

Sleeping

Penginapan Sri Muntai GUESTHOUSE $
(☎0853 4963 0030; s/d 50,000/100,000Rp) Bright-green Sri Muntai wins the award for best front porch: a breezy hang-out above the street. Wide hallways and clean rooms are also a nice touch.

Penginapan Adi Guna GUESTHOUSE $
(☎0823 5241 8233; r 50,000Rp) Basic fan-cooled rooms and large, shared *mandi*.

Getting There & Away

- *Kapal biasa* pass in the afternoon heading upriver, and around midnight heading down.
- A *ces* to/from Kota Bangun (the nearest bus) runs 200,000Rp for the two-hour journey.
- Charter a *ces* (400,000Rp to 700,000Rp) to Lake Jempang country, to visit villages and longhouses, with the impeccably cheerful **Udin Ban** (☎0813 3241 2089).

Lake Jempang

Located south of the Mahakam, seasonally flooded Jempang is the largest of the three major wetlands in the lake region. This birdwatcher's paradise is home to over 57 waterbird, 12 birds of prey and six kingfisher species. The fishing village of Jantur occupies the main outlet (sometimes inlet) on the east end, while the Dayak villages of Tanjung Isuy and Mancong are hidden on the southwest end. During high water, *ces* can cut back to the main river at Muara Pahu from the west edge of the lake.

JANTUR

During the wet season, Jantur appears to be floating in the middle of Lake Jempang. It is built entirely on stilts in the marshy wetlands which disappear under 6m of water in the rainy season. During the dry season, floating mats of water hyacinth can choke the channel through town, creating a transportation nightmare.

Gardening here may be difficult, but the residents do have fish – plenty of fish – producing more *ikan kering* (dried fish) than any other village in the regency. The boardwalks and rooftops are typically covered with thousands of splayed fish, some protected under the watchful eye of meter-tall pet storks.

If you can manage a homestay, you'll find Jantur is a pleasant village filled with friendly people. At the very least, stroll the boardwalk and say hello to the groups of laughing Banjarese women squatting by the river processing the morning's catch.

TANJUNG ISUY

Tranquil Tanjung Isuy is the first Dayak village most people visit on their Mahakam journey. A fire took out the waterfront in 2015, giving the new mosque skyline supremacy. The historical longhouse, Louu Taman Jamrud, still stands as a sort of museum/craft shop/losmen.

Sights

Lamin Batu Bura HISTORIC BUILDING
Few *lamin* (the local word for longhouse) around here are occupied outside of community ceremonies these days, but this Benuaq Dayak house is bucking the trend. While the men are off in the fields, women sit on the split bamboo floor weaving naturally died

BOAT TRAVEL ON THE SUNGAI MAHAKAM

Distances, costs and duration are based on a Samarinda start point. Be aware that travel times fluctuate significantly based on water levels and the number of stops. Consult locally for current conditions.

DESTINATION	DISTANCE (KM)	FARE (RP)	DURATION (HR)
Tenggarong	35	50,000	2
Kota Bangun	153	75,000	8
Muara Muntai	195	100,000	11
Muara Pahu	256	130,000	15
Melak	303	150,000	19
Tering	381	200,000	25
Long Bagung (if possible)	539	380,000	37

fibres of the doyo leaf into beautiful decorative cloth called *ulap doyo*. Walk 1.5km south of Tanjung Isuy, staying left at the fork.

Sleeping

Louu Taman Jamrud LONGHOUSE $
(Jl Indonesia Australia; r 110,000Rp) Vacated in the 1970s and refurbished as a tourist hostel by the provincial government, this stately longhouse is guarded by an impressive array of carved totems (some of which may be NSFW.) Travellers can commission a Dayak dance for 600,000Rp to 1,000,000Rp, depending on how many performers you require.

Losmen Wisata LONGHOUSE $
(Jl Indonesia Australia; r 110,000Rp) Long, but not culturally significant, this lodge's common areas have wall-to-wall windows giving you a superior view of the lake; views that formerly were enjoyed by Louu Taman Jamrud next door.

Getting There & Away

- Charter a *ces* in Muara Muntai to get here via Jantur, or in Muara Pahu to get here via the Sungai Baroh (Baroh River), if the water level permits.
- Tanjung Isuy is 25 minutes by Kijang or *ojek* from Mancong.
- A truck leaves in the morning for the intersection with the main road between Samarinda and Melak, where you can hop on a bus.

MANCONG

For optimum jungle drama Mancong is best reached by boat on the Ohong creek from Lake Jempang. You'll meander past monitor lizards, sapphire-hued kingfishers, bulb-nosed proboscis monkeys, banded kraits and marauding macaques. They'll see you, but whether or not you see them... The journey beneath towering banyan trees is as much a part of the experience as your arrival.

Sights

Mancong Longhouse HISTORIC BUILDING
This exquisitely restored 1930s longhouse is flanked by intricately carved totems. Those with chickens represent a healing ceremony. The souvenir shop across the parking lot can rustle up blankets and mosquito nets if you absolutely must sleep in the otherwise vacant building (75,000Rp).

FLOATING HOMESTAY

Floating houses and shops are a defining feature of the Sungai Mahakam. Where basic buildings are constructed on logs pulled from the river, people live lives as recognisable as they are different. Children jump into the river to bathe before putting on class uniforms. Their school bus is a canoe. Satellite dishes sit on roofs made from cast-off lumber. Homestays are basic, and involve sleeping on a mat and using the river outhouse, like everyone else. But, sitting at river level with a cup of coffee, watching river traffic at sunset, is an inimitable and unforgettable experience. **Murni** (☎ no English 0813 5042 8447; Melak; r incl dinner & breakfast per person 50,000Rp) offers a homestay in his floating house directly across from the Melak harbour with free transport in his *ces*. Additional sightseeing trips are negotiable.

Getting There & Away

To visit Mancong from Tanjung Isuy, charter a *ces* (500,000Rp return, three hours each way) or take an *ojek* (100,000Rp, 10km, 25 minutes).

Muara Pahu

Lining one side of a big curve in the Mahakam, this town is the upriver exit point from Lake Jempang when the water is high enough. You can stroll the boardwalk, or sit and watch the tugboats haul coal downriver while waiting for the evening *kapal biasa*.

Sleeping

Pension Anna GUESTHOUSE $
(s/d 50,000/100,000Rp) Four rooms in a small signless home, 90m upstream of the Sungai Baroh bridge.

Getting There & Around

Although dolphins are increasingly rare here, you can still charter a *ces* (700,000Rp per day) to explore the primate and bird life of Sungai Baroh, which leads to Lake Jempang and Tanjung Isuy. **Pak Aco** (☎ 0813 4652 3132) knows how to slow down for wildlife. *Kapal biasa* pass after 8pm heading both up and down river.

Melak

Melak could be anywhere in Indonesia. **Sendawar**, the regency seat next door, is trying to out-develop itself, with each new government building more massive than the last. It is all very disorienting, and somewhat alarming considering this is likely a preview of what's to come upriver.

That being said, however, centuries of culture can't be erased with a few years of coal money. Start your wandering with the still-occupied longhouse at **Eheng** (30km southwest of Melak) or the **Kersik Luway** (8am-4pm) FREE orchid preserve.

Sleeping & Eating

Despite (or perhaps because of) the development around Melak, the lodging options here are limited and uninspired. Instead, consider spending the night in a floating homestay (p259), or see about negotiating sparse accommodation at Eheng longhouse.

Basic food stalls can be found along Jl Pierre Tendean. Head downriver from the dock and turn right at the next major road.

Hotel Flamboyan HOTEL $
(0545-41033; Jl A Yani; r fan/air-con 115,000/165,000Rp;) Offers private *mandi* with Western toilets. Clean, but definitely not flamboyant.

Hotel Monita HOTEL $$
(0545-41798; Jl Dr Sutomo 76; r incl breakfast 240,000-360,000Rp;) The best option in town, but about 2km uphill from the *kapal biasa* dock. It's often full with mining clients, so book ahead.

Rumah Makan Jawah Indah SEAFOOD, INDONESIAN $
(Jl A Yani; mains 25,000-35,000Rp; 24hr;) Ready to cook any Javanese food you desire at any hour you require. Across from the dock.

Information

88 Net (Jl Pierre Tendean 58; per hr 5000Rp) Internet access. Head downriver 150m from the dock, and turn right on Jl Pierre Tendean; it's next to hotel Anugerah.

Getting There & Away

Air Kalstar flies to Balikpapan twice daily (720,000Rp, 30 minutes), while Susi Air services Samarinda (544,000Rp, Mon and Wed) and Data Dawai (390,000Rp, Mon and Wed).

Boat *Kapal biasa* leave for Samarinda daily at 8pm or 10pm and pass heading upriver at 1am. Charter a *ces* for 500,000Rp to 800,000Rp per day depending on your negotiating skills.

Bus Two buses for Samarinda depart in the morning (100,000Rp, nine hours).

Kijang Run to Samarinda (200,000Rp, eight hours), Balikpapan (275,000Rp, 12 hours), and Tering (150,000Rp, one hour).

DON'T MISS

THE WAY TO BORNEO'S HEART

From Long Bagun you embark upon the most thrilling ride on the Mahakam: the longboat to **Tiong Ohang** (800,000Rp, four hours). This serpentine adventure takes you through some spectacular gorges with scenic waterfalls and ancient volcanic peaks. At some undefined point, the uncanny realisation strikes... you've entered the heart of Borneo.

Be warned, however. Two major sets of rapids bar the way. Riam Udang is dangerous at high water, while Riam Panjang gets nasty at low water. In 2015 yet another boat broke apart in the tumultuous waters killing five passengers including one foreign backpacker and her guide. Insist on, and wear, a life jacket *(baju pelampung)*.

A nearly completed dirt road from **Long Bagun** to **Long Apari** (three hours upriver from Tiong Ohang) will likely be paved in a few years, changing the mystique of this journey entirely.

Tering

A planned community deep in gold-mining country, Tering is sometimes the last stop for *kapal biasa*, depending on the water level. It is really two settlements straddling the river: **Tering Baru**, a Malay village where the *kapal biasa* docks, and **Tering Lama**, a Bahau Dayak village on the northern bank, where a magnificent wooden church with intricate painted pillars has a bell tower supported by totem poles.

Kapal biasa arrive at 9am. Even during low water, they sometimes continue to Long Iram, an hour further upriver. Downriver *kapal biasa* leave around noon. A speedboat to Long Bagun is 300,000Rp for the four-hour journey. Kijang depart from the dock for Samarinda (300,000Rp) and Melak (150,000Rp).

Long Bagun

The misty mountain village of Long Bagun is the end of the *kapal biasa* route at high water and is a fine terminus for your Mahakam adventure. Somewhere in the village, a local entrepreneur is bent over a grinder, polishing a semi-precious stone into a pendant... a Chinese shopkeeper is sweating over a forge, melting gold from nearby mines to sell in Samarinda... a group of women is tying intricate beadwork for their children's next traditional dance performance... and you can see it all, or simply sit beside the river with a cup of coffee and just be.

Sleeping

★Penginapan Polewali GUESTHOUSE $
(☎081 350 538 997; r 100,000Rp) This mountain lodge with traditional furnishings is a breath of fresh air after the concrete boxes downriver. In fact, it is the best hotel on the upper Mahakam. Rooms are small, and bathrooms shared, but a nice breeze on the porch keeps you outside. Find it at the upriver edge of town, across from the longhouse.

Getting There & Away

Boats now pause at Ujoh Bilang, 3km downriver from Long Bagun, where you'll be required to register with the tourism office on the dock.

Speedboats heading up- and downriver troll for passengers along the waterfront in the morning. We've heard of at least one intrepid Huck Finn building a bamboo raft and floating back to Samarinda.

Tiong Ohang

Divided by the Mahakam, Tiong Ohang is united by its creaking suspension bridge which offers scenic views of the surrounding hills. This is the last stop before starting, or ending, the second stage of the Cross-Borneo Trek (p223) in the Muller Mountains. This is where local guides and porters are assembled, but these services are best arranged in advance by a tour company. The trailhead is two hours upriver by *ces* (1,000,000Rp).

Sleeping

Putra Apari GUESTHOUSE $
(r 60,000Rp) The only accommodation in town. Rooms have no fan and share *mandi,* but there is a nice porch with a cross-breeze, overlooking main street.

The Muller Mountains

The second stage of the Cross-Borneo Trek (p223), the journey across the Muller Mountains, is a very different experience from what precedes it. This is neither a cultural tour nor a wildlife-spotting expedition. In fact, views of any kind are scarce. This is a purpose-driven rainforest trek, and a difficult one.

Most people do the crossing in seven or more long, wet days. The trek follows a narrow path – if that – through a green maze

MULLER TREK SAFETY REQUIREMENTS

- Choose a professional local tour company. Do not even think of organising this yourself.
- Ensure that someone in your party has a complete first-aid kit and knows how to use it. Pack epinephrine, and know why.
- Wear proper shoes. The trail will be extremely greasy at times. Your feet will be constantly wet. The locals wear rubber sneakers with cleats. A sturdy pair of trail runners is a good option. Leather will quickly disintegrate. Take care of your feet.
- Wear proper leech protection. Tucking your trousers into two pairs of tight-knit socks is fairly effective. Some people swear by spandex, which can also help with chafing.
- Be firm about setting the pace at which you walk. Local guides and porters are not always aware of the difference between their skill level and your own. It is also in their interest to get across and back as soon as possible. Be sure to spread walking hours evenly among the days of the journey.
- Do not trek at night. Locals have no problem with this, but it greatly magnifies the risk, particularly if it is raining.
- Bring 10 days' worth of food. If there is a problem midway, you'll need enough to last until someone walks to the nearest village and returns with help.

with uncertain footing and nearly constant creek crossings, some chest high. Campsites are a tarp. Cooking is done over an open fire. There will be blood – from leeches if nothing else. They are harmless, but their bites easily become infected in the damp environment.

All things considered, the experience hasn't changed much since George Muller first crossed his namesake range in 1825. While that first trek ended with the locals cutting off Muller's head (likely at the behest of the Sultan of Kutai), the primary risk today is breaking a leg or merely twisting an ankle so far from outside help. To that end, heed all the precautions, and choose an experienced tour company or guide, which has considered the concept of risk management.

The Muller Trek is a horizontal Everest. You tackle it for the same reasons you climb. And when you succeed, it is both a lifetime memory and a noteworthy achievement.

Kutai National Park

Kutai National Park has seen its share of troubles. All but abandoned in the late '90s as a conservation failure ransacked by logging and fires, new studies are showing all is not lost. The wild orangutan population has recovered to as many as 2000 individuals, and pockets of forest are still relatively intact. Research is happening at the north end of the park, while Prevab station near Sangatta offers Kalimantan's best chance to see truly wild orangutans.

There are plans to restore the unfortunately abandoned Kakap Camp at Prevab, but until then, you can stay in the bare musty rooms of the ranger station. From there, several kilometres of trail fan out through decent secondary forest, where large buttressed trees still provide plenty of hiding spots for orangutans. The rangers are experts at moving slowly and listening for the telltale rustle of the canopy that betrays a critter's location. Bring mosquito repellent.

Call the lead ranger, Pak Supiani (☎0813 4634 8803), before visiting so he can organise your permit and a boat. To get here, take a bus from Samarinda to Sangatta (42,000Rp, four hours) and a taxi to Kabo Jaya, where a park boat will ferry you to the ranger station (300,000Rp return, 15 minutes). Park permits are 150,000Rp per day (225,000Rp during holidays). Guides (required) cost 120,000Rp per two-hour trek.

Berau

☎0554 / POP 63,000

Once the inspiration for Joseph Conrad's first novel, *Almayer's Folly,* Berau now only inspires you to move on to your ultimate destination. Fortunately, you have two great choices: the Derawan Archipelago to the east, or the karst wonderland of Merabu to the south. Choose wisely, as neither option is cheap nor easy to get to – but both are immensely rewarding.

Sights

Museum Batiwakkal MUSEUM

(Gunung Tabur Keraton; admission by donation; 8am-2pm Mon-Sat) Located at the site of Berau's original Keraton, this 1981 building houses an eclectic collection of sultan-obilia starting from the 17th century.

Keraton Sambaliung MUSEUM

(Sambaliung; 9am-1pm Mon-Sat) FREE This 215 year-old Keraton was built after descendants of brothers from other mothers (same father: the 9th sultan) got tired of alternating rule at Gunung Tabor and split the sultanate. The colossal crocodile of questionable taxidermy is an impressive, if somewhat random, addition.

Sleeping & Eating

Rooms in Tanjung Redeb (the main district of Berau) often fill with mine workers. Book in advance.

Hotel Mitra HOTEL $

(☎0812 5315 0715; Jl Gajah Mada 531A; r incl breakfast 220,000-240,000Rp;) Immaculate with friendly staff, Mitra feels less like a hotel and more like a giant homestay. As a long-standing favourite with local NGOs, Mitra has a staff well-used to dealing with foreigners. All rooms have air-con and cold water only.

Room 505 in the corner has the best natural light. Bikes are available for a quick jaunt around town, and motorbikes rent for 75,000Rp a day.

★ **Rumah Kedaung** GUESTHOUSE $$

(☎0821 5326 6291; rumahkedaung@yahoo.com; Jl Kedaung, Borneo IV, Sei Bedungun; r incl breakfast 320,000Rp;) Located between the airport and Tanjung Redeb, this guesthouse sits on top of a small treed hill. The common areas are decked out with Dayak art, and the rough wood duplex bungalows have a creaky charm.

Berau

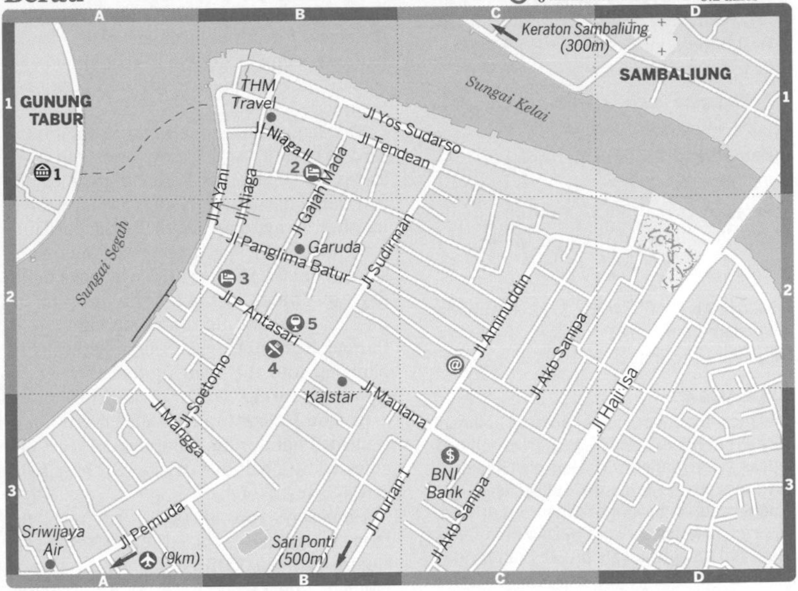

Berau

Sights
1 Museum Batiwakkal A1

Sleeping
2 Hotel Mitra B1
3 Hotel Palmy B2

Eating
4 De Bunda Cafe B2

Drinking & Nightlife
5 Club BP B2

The cafe serves up solid local fare – a plus since there is not much nearby. Wi-fi is spotty.

Hotel Palmy HOTEL $$
(☎0554-202 0333; palmyhotel@yahoo.com; Jl Pangeran Antasari 26; r incl breakfast 500,000Rp; ❄📶) The newest and sharpest offering catering to jet-setting business managers. The top two floors have the best, indeed only, views. Expect to be upcharged by any taxi picking you up here.

★ **De Bunda Cafe** BAKERY $
(☎0554-21305; Jl Pangeran Antasari 5; mains 15,000-30,000Rp; ⏱7am-8pm; 📶) Owner, Ibu Ayu, is well travelled and understands your needs. She speaks English and vegetarian, and is happy to make omelettes and other off-menu dishes by request. Worth the walk.

Sari Ponti Restaurant CHINESE $
(☎0554-26688; Jl Durian II 36; mains 40,000Rp; ⏱8am-9pm) A reliable Chinese mainstay with an extensive menu. A genuine bird's-nest drink will set you back 150,000Rp – it's good for curing pretty much everything, including cancer…apparently.

Drinking & Nightlife

Club BP CLUB
(Jl Antasari, Hotel Berau Plaza; 7pm-2am) The most popular nightclub in the city.

Information

BNI Bank (Jl Maulana) Foreign exchange.

Mailbox Warnet (Jl Aminuddin; per hour 5000Rp; ⏱9am-late) Internet access.

THM Travel (☎0554-21238; Jl Niaga I) Some English-speaking staff.

Getting There & Away

AIR

Garuda (☎0554-202 0285; Jl Panglima Batur 396, Hotel Derawan Indah; ⏱8am-4.30pm Mon-Fri, 9am-3pm Sat & Sun; ❄)

Kalstar (☎0554-21007; Jl Maulana 45)

FLIGHTS FROM BERAU

Destinations serviced from Berau include the following:

Balikpapan Garuda, Sriwijaya, Wings; 450,000Rp; one hour; seven daily

Samarinda Kalstar, 674,000Rp, 45 minutes, two daily

Tarakan Kalstar, 540,000Rp, 25 minutes, one daily

Sriwijaya Air (☎0554-202 8777; Jl Pemuda 50; ⊙8am-5pm)

Wings Air (Airport)

BUS & KIJANG

Until recently, buses in this corner of Kalimantan were all but nonexistent. Transport is handled by *taksi gelap* (dark taxis), a cartel of Kijang operators, many of whom are unlicensed, inexperienced, or downright dangerous drivers. However, new bus services by DAMRI to Tanjung Selor, and a single private **bus to Samarinda** (☎0812 5417 3997; 200,000Rp; 17 hours) are signs of slow improvement.

Kijang gather in the morning across from the former bus terminal and demand a minimum of three passengers; you can buy multiple seats to leave faster. Destinations include Tanjung Batu (100,000Rp, 2½ hours), Tanjung Selor (120,000Rp, three hours), Samarinda (300,000Rp, 14 hours), and Balikpapan (400,000Rp, over 20 hours).

Getting Around

- Taxis to the airport (9km) cost 80,000Rp.
- *Angkot* cost 5000Rp to 10,000Rp, depending on distance.
- River crossings by canoe cost 5000Rp, or canoes can be chartered for 30,000Rp per hour.

Merabu

Isolated between a small river and a fortress of karst pinnacles, the Dayak Lebo villagers of Merabu never worried much about politics or the outside world. So they were understandably shocked the day they found bulldozers clearing nearby forests for an oil palm plantation, and confused to learn their gardens were soon to become a coal mine.

Rather than be bought off, however, they waged a long (and occasionally ugly) battle for their homeland. Finally, in 2014, they became the first village in Berau District to gain official recognition of their village forest, an important step towards securing the rights of indigenous communities. As part of their new forest management plan, Merabu has also opened its doors to ecotourism – an activity they are particularly well-positioned to provide.

The jagged limestone forest in their backyard is one of the least-explored and least-accessible regions in Kalimantan, meaning its wildlife has largely been spared from over hunting. Orangutan dwell in the lowlands while clouded leopard prowl the mountainsides. From the village you can arrange multiday expeditions to **Lake Tebo**, deep in the interior, or spend an afternoon climbing to **Puncak Ketepu** to whet your appetite before plunging into the vivid turquoise waters of **Nyadeng spring**. The drawcard site, however, is **Goa Beloyot**, a cliff-side cavern full of stencilled handprints thousands of years old, accessed by a half-day trek worthy of Indiana Jones (bring a torch).

Homestays run 200,000Rp per night per room, with meals provided at 25,000Rp a pop. Guides cost 100,000Rp a trip while a boat to Nyadeng and Ketepu is 175,000Rp. Additionally, there is a required 200,000Rp donation to the village, and you have the option to adopt a tree in the community forest for 1,500,000Rp for three years. The expenses add up, but remember this is one way the visionaries in the community demonstrate to their neighbours that the forest has value as it is.

It takes a bit of work to get here, but once you do, you may never want leave.

Getting There & Away

Before visiting, contact the village head, Franly Oley (☎0878 1030 3330, franlyoley@gmail.com), who speaks passable English. Your best transport option is to come from Berau to the north. Charter a Kijang (1,800,000Rp) for the four-hour dirt-road journey through Lesan village. Driver Pak Asri (☎0853 4135 9088) is familiar with the route.

From Muara Wahau, to the south, the route is a little more tricky. You'll want a 4WD or a motorbike for the sketchy road. Head 55km north to the Merapun gate (Garpu Dayak Merapun), then turn east into the oil palm plantation. At the first major fork (15km), head left to Merapun to hire a boat to Merabu (price negotiable, 1½ hours) or turn right to continue 40km over land (impassable when wet) to the Lesan road where you'll make a hard right. Just under 4km beyond, you'll arrive at the river. Merabu is opposite.

Once you arrive at the end of the road, shout across the river for a *ketinting* (canoe ferry; 25,000Rp).

Derawan Archipelago

Completely different from the rest of Kalimantan, the classic tropical islands of the Derawan Archipelago are where you go to trade jungle trekking and orangutans for beach combing and manta rays. Of the 31 named islands found here, the four most accessible to visitors are the crowded weekend getaway of Derawan, the peaceful paradise of Maratua atoll, and the wildernesses of Sangalaki and Kakaban. The scuba diving and snorkelling rank among the best in Indonesia, offering an assortment of reef and pelagic species including barracuda, sharks, mantas and turtles, all the way down. Travel between the islands is expensive, so plan your trip carefully and find friends with which to share costs. There are no ATMs on the islands. Seas are rough in January and February, limiting diving and increasing travel risks.

Getting There & Around

Most trips to the islands leave from the coastal town of Tanjung Batu, accessible from Berau by road (500,000Rp charter, 100,000Rp regular seat, 2½ hours). From there, a regular morning boat takes passengers to Pulau Derawan (100,000Rp per person, 30 minutes); otherwise your must charter a speedboat (300,000Rp, seats four).

A charter to Maratua is 1,300,000Rp for the 1½-hour journey from Tanjung Batu, or 1,100,000Rp for the one-hour trip from Derawan. Prices are sometimes negotiable.

A full-day snorkelling trip in the area runs between 1,500,000Rp to 2,000,000Rp depending on how far you go. It is four hours of spine-compressing travel from Derawan to the popular snorkelling areas around Kakaban and Sangalaki, return.

The cheapest, and slowest, way to get between islands is by *klotok*, a local open fishing boat with a noisy little engine. You can arrange this in any village, but be aware of the time involved, as you may be bobbing around in the sun for hours. Having said that, it is a fun way to get between nearby islands, such as Maratua and Nabucco.

On Friday, take a direct speed boat from Tarakan to Pulau Derawan (250,000Rp, 2pm, three hours), and return Sunday.

The new airport on Maratua is sure to change the travel dynamic considerably, but routes were still unconfirmed at time of research.

Do not attempt any passages if seas are rough. Insist on life jackets, and carry a compass or GPS – basic equipment your boat will undoubtedly lack.

Pulau Derawan

The tiny, funky backpacker's magnet of Derawan is the best known of the islands, and the closest to the mainland. It is also increasingly crowded and dirty. Along the waterfront newer guesthouses clamber over the old, reaching out into the ocean like a sprawling octopus. However, despite the near constant presence of tourists, the locals still maintain a friendly attitude and kids are eager to steal high-fives. You'll compete for solitude with local tourists on banana boats during weekends and holidays. For more idyllic surroundings, consider Maratua instead.

Sleeping & Eating

New guesthouses appear and just as quickly succumb to the ravages of the ocean. Evaluate your options before committing.

★**Miranda Homestay** HOMESTAY $
(☎0813 4662 3550; r 200,000Rp) Tucked back toward shore with not much of a view, these two spotless rooms are still great value. Pak Marudi's spacious and relaxing *klotok* is at your disposal for slow coffee-filled snorkelling excursions (700,000Rp per day), or transport to Tanjung Batu (100,000Rp per person).

Sari Cottages GUESTHOUSE $$
(☎0813 4653 8448; r 350,000Rp; ❄) Centrally located Sari has 22 freshly painted rooms, strung along two parallel piers connected by a footbridge. The large, private back porches all have (as yet) unobstructed views, and the restaurant has the best location in town. Turn off the street at the sign for 'Pinades,' and keep walking the plank.

Mirroliz Pelangi Guesthouse GUESTHOUSE $$
(☎0813 4780 7078; r with fan/air-con 275,000/380,000Rp; ❄) With its brightly painted rooms and creative lighting, the festive Pelangi may be showing signs of age, but it still retains a chill hang-out vibe. Watch the sunset from the open-air, over-water restaurant as turtles ply the shallows beneath. The further you go out to sea, the more expensive the stay. On the west edge of town.

Derawan Dive Lodge LODGE $$$
(☎0431-824445; www.derawandivelodge.com; s/d incl breakfast US$80/95) A small enclave of 10 comfortable, individually designed rooms, with a cosy outdoor cafe and private beach, at the west end of the island. If you want to combine a dive holiday with some island life, this is your top choice on Derawan.

DERAWAN DIVING HIGHLIGHTS

Pulau Sangalaki Famous for its manta rays, which are present throughout the year. Turtles also abound.

Pulau Kakaban Big pelagic fish and a cave dive offshore; a rare lake full of nonstinging jellyfish inland.

Pulau Maratua Known for 'the channel' frequented by big pelagic fish, eagle rays and huge schools of barracuda. Occasional thresher sharks.

Pulau Derawan Small creatures draw photographers: ghostpipe fish, frogfish, harlequin shrimp, jawfish, and blue-ringed octopus.

Rumah Makan Nur INDONESIAN **$**
(☎0853 4689 7827; mains 30,000Rp) Nur's serves up tasty Indonesian favourites with creative twists such as shrimp and coconut aubergine with rice. The large juice menu is welcome on a hot day – as are the set prices.

Pulau Maratua

For those with time on their hands, Maratua is a slice of heaven. This enormous U-shaped atoll is almost completely untouched by tourism. Four tiny fishing villages are evenly spaced along the narrow strip of land, three of which are connected by a paved 15km path. Central to the island, near the northern end of the road, the large village of Tanjung Harapan offers several homestays, bicycle rental, and access to the island's only upscale lodging options. Bohe Silian, at the southern end of both road and island, also has a few homestays, pleasant sea views and Sembat cave – the coolest swimming hole on the island.

Hire a scooter for a day (150,000Rp) and explore to your heart's content, passing over bridges between islets, chasing green parakeets and swimming in the lagoon. Local guides (150,000Rp per day) can direct you to the island's hidden caves and private beaches. Add a special someone and a visit here could easily stretch into days…

However, the new airport and tourism port are likely to rapidly change the character of the place forever – so go now.

Diving (single dive €43) can be arranged through Nabucco Island Resort, 30 minutes across the lagoon.

Sleeping

★**Maratua Guesthouse** GUESTHOUSE
(www.maratuaguesthouse.com; d & tw cabins US$59) Nestled in a limestone forest between the island's cleanest beach and an inland tidal pond, this complex boasts a commanding view of the Celebes Sea from its open-air restaurant out front, and shady private cabins out back. The rooms all come with a mosquito net, fan, and front porch from which to watch the resident kingfishers and parakeets.

Nabucco & Nunukan Island Resorts

These two small islets in the mouth of the Maratua atoll are owned by Extra Divers, a German dive resort operator providing a refinement and attention to detail rarely experienced in Kalimantan. The owner works closely with scientists and the local leadership to continually improve the resorts' environmental and social sustainability. When we visited, the finishing touches were being put on a third even more luxurious resort, connected to Nunukan by a 1km boardwalk.

Sleeping

★**Nabucco Island Resort** RESORT **$$$**
(☎0812 540 6636; www.extradivers-worldwide.com; r per person incl full board s/d €131/99; ❄📶) The sign above the dock at Nabucco says 'Welcome to Paradise': a fair sentiment. At the edge of the Maratua lagoon, this compact island dive resort packs plenty into a tiny manicured space. Surrounding a central common area, each varnished duplex bungalow shares an ocean-view porch with access to mangroves, a white-sand beach, or a slice of house reef.

Nunukan Island Resort RESORT **$$$**
(☎0812 340 3451; www.extradivers-worldwide.com; r per person incl full board s/d €131/99) From the long jetty welcoming you across the 4km house reef, to the common areas hovering over razor-sharp limestone, there is nothing typical – and everything exotic – about this island resort. The luxurious beachfront bungalows have spacious porches with sofa beds begging you to soak in the serenity. Inside, you'll find four-poster beds and inventive showers with one-way windows to the sea.

NORTH KALIMANTAN TRANSIT OPTIONS

Navigating through the province can be confusing. Consult the table below for transit options for moving from north to south.

FROM	TO	VIA	FARE	DURATION	FREQUENCY
Tawau (Sabah)	Nunukan	speedboat	RM75	1½hr	frequent
Tawau (Sabah)	Tarakan	plane (MASwings)	1,600,000Rp	40min	Mon, Wed, Thu, Sat, Sun
Tawau (Sabah)	Tarakan	ferry	RM130	4hr	10am Mon, Wed, Fri
Nunukan	Tarakan	speedboat	240,000Rp	2½hr	5 daily from 7am-1.30pm
Tarakan	Long Bawan	plane (Susi Air)	460,000Rp	1hr	Mon, Fri, Sat, Sun
Tarakan	Derawan	speedboat	250,000Rp	3hr	2pm Fri only
Tarakan	Tanjung Selor	speedboat	120,000Rp	1hr	frequent 7am-2.30pm
Tanjung Selor	Long Pujungan	longboat	800,000Rp	2 days	weekly
Tanjung Selor	Berau (Tanjung Redeb)	Kijang	120,000Rp	3hr	when full
Tanjung Selor	Berau (Tanjung Redeb)	bus (DAMRI)	50,000Rp	3hr	9am Mon, Wed, Fri

Pulau Kakaban & Pulau Sangalaki

These two undeveloped islands 40 minutes southwest of Maratua and an hour southeast of Derawan are popular day-trip destinations. Pulau Sangalaki has decent diving but is known primarily for its consistent manta ray spotting. For a close encounter of the eerie kind, visit the inland lake of Pulau Kakaban and swim through an ethereal swarm of millions of stingless jellyfish, some as tiny as your fingertip. If tides permit, snorkel through Kakaban's tidal cave tunnel to a hidden outcrop of protected pristine coral.

NORTH KALIMANTAN

☎0551

Due to its isolation, North Kalimantan contains some of the most pristine forests on Borneo, making it one of the last and best frontiers for hardcore jungle trekking. The 1.36 million hectare **Kayan Mentarang National Park** represents a significant chunk of the heart of Borneo, and contains a dizzying diversity of life, with new species still being discovered. When it comes to travelling here, the rewards are returned in direct proportion with the level of difficulty.

The two best places to access the park are via **Long Bawan** to the north, and **Long Punjungan** to the south. Many of the ecotourism initiatives developed by WWF (www.borneoecotourism.com) have been left fallow, but the information they provide is a great orientation to the area.

In Long Bawan, contact English-speaking Alex Balang (☎0852 4705 7469, alexbalang@hotmail.com) to get the lay of the land and to arrange treks further afield.

To the south, the path is even more untrodden, and Bahasa Indonesia is essential. Start your journey at **Tanjung Selor**, where sizeable longboats powered by multiple outboard engines load wares for the long haul upstream to **Long Punjungan**. Pak Muming at Hotel Asoy (☎0812 540 4256) and Pak Heri (☎0822 5053 8995) both regularly make the trip.

North Kalimantan is also a common, though convoluted, transit option for those travelling to or from Malaysian Borneo. Take note: there is no visa on arrival service at the borders on Nunukan or Tarakan, but the Indonesian consulate in Tawau, Sabah, is among the most efficient we have worked with.

Understand Borneo

Borneo Today

Nothing rankles with Borneans more than corrupt politicians who line their pockets at the expense of the public purse, the island's dwindling rainforests and indigenous land rights. Accounts of back-room deals with logging companies and palm-oil conglomerates provoke rage and despair in the people of Sabah, Sarawak and Kalimantan. Such tensions have yet to surface in Brunei, where the population calmly accepts both the sultan's supremacy and his oil-revenue-funded generosity.

Best on Film

Three Came Home (1950) A tale of survival in a Japanese prisoner-of-war camp in WWII Borneo. Based on a book by Agnes Newton Keith.

David Attenborough's Conquest of the Skies (2015) Borneo plays a starring role in this remarkable three-part documentary series, including fascinating scenes in Gomantong Cave.

Best in Print

Stranger in the Forest (Eric Hansen; 1988) Recounts the tale of the author's journey across Borneo on foot in the company of indigenous guides.

The Casuarina Tree (Somerset Maugham; 1926) A compilation of short stories including some set in British Borneo.

Into the Heart of Borneo (Redmond O'Hanlon; 1984) The funny and detailed account of O'Hanlon's trip upriver in Sarawak in the company of the poet James Fenton.

Politics & Economics

In Kalimantan the policy of *transmigrasi,* the government-sponsored relocation of people from more densely populated areas of the country to Indonesian Borneo, has led to tensions between immigrants and the indigenous populations, but it is the struggle for resources that is the more prevalent issue affecting the island today. While Kalimantan's riches are plundered by foreign businesses in cahoots with the government, the local population enjoys little of the spoils.

Sabahans are well aware that while their state was Malaysia's second-richest in the 1970s, it is now the country's poorest. A major reason, they claim, is that all but a tiny percentage of Sabah's (and Sarawak's) oil revenue flows into federal coffers. The movement 'Sarawak for Sarawakians', a slogan that adorned car bumper stickers and T-shirts across the state following a rally of the same name in July 2015, was an expression of dissatisfaction with the current system and a demand for a more equitable return of state profits from the federal government; it was never intended to be a secessionist movement.

In August 2015, yellow-shirted supporters of Bersih 2.0 (www.bersih.org), a civil-rights organisation campaigning for electoral reform, held rallies in Kuching in Sarawak, Kota Kinabalu in Sabah and Kuala Lumpur in Peninsular Malaysia – the fourth such rally to be held since 2011. The protest was prompted by a corruption scandal embroiling Malaysian prime minister Najib Razak and the 1Malaysia fund (1MDB), as well as by state oppression of media outlets opposed to the government, including the blocking of news website the Sarawak Report (www.sarawakreport.org) and the issuing of an arrest warrant for the London-based founder and editor Clare Rewcastle-Brown.

Malaysian Multiculturalism

Following the race riots of 1969, the Malaysian government implemented a policy of 'affirmative action' (ie positive discrimination) to give the majority Malays a more equitable share of the economic pie. The result was a range of subsidies and preferences designed to benefit a category of people called *bumiputra* ('sons of the soil') that encompasses Malays and, in Sabah and Sarawak, indigenous groups (Dayaks) – that is, virtually everyone except the Chinese. As a result of these policies, ethnic Chinese have found themselves facing quotas and discrimination in housing, higher education and public-sector jobs.

Relations between the dozens of ethnic groups in Sarawak and Sabah tend to be more relaxed and open than in Peninsular Malaysia, but the states are not quite the multicultural paradise portrayed in Tourism Malaysia's 'Malaysia – Truly Asia!' campaign. Malays form the majority in a country based on *ketuanan Melayu* (Malay supremacy), but they are a minority in Sabah and Sarawak; ethnic Chinese wonder about their place in a society that often treats them as outsiders generations after their ancestors put down roots; and members of indigenous groups juggle tribal identity and religious affiliation (the majority are Christian) in a Muslim-majority society.

Brunei: An Islamic Monarchy

The implementation of the first step of a three-phase process introducing sharia law in Brunei made global headlines in 2014, but more than a year later the new penal code has made minimal impact on life in the quiet, law-abiding sultanate. The new penal code applies to both Muslims and non-Muslims and will include corporal punishments for crimes such as theft and adultery. Legislation was also tightened up concerning Friday prayers – which Muslims are required by law to attend – and Ramadan (during which eating, drinking and smoking in public during daylight hours is prohibited for both Muslims and non-Muslims).

Since Brunei's economy is almost entirely reliant on oil, the crucial question facing the sultanate in the 21st century is what will happen when this resource runs out? At the current pace of extraction, it is estimated Brunei has two decades of oil left. Back-up plans for economic diversification remain thin on the ground, although the construction of a 30km bridge linking Brunei-Maura with Temburong, due to be completed in 2018, may prove a boost to tourism. For now, at least, Bruneians seem happy to enjoy the benefits of living in an oil-rich sultanate, while accepting and observing the laws of an increasingly controlling and religiously conservative government.

COMBINED POPULATION: **19.9 MILLION**

AREA: **743,000 SQ KM**

GDP PER CAPITA: **BRUNEI US$73,200, INDONESIA US$10,600, MALAYSIA US$24,700**

UNEMPLOYMENT: **BRUNEI 2.7%, INDONESIA 6.1%, MALAYSIA 2.9%**

if Borneo were 100 people

29 would be Dayak
19 would be Banjarese
14 would be Malay
12 would be Javanese
7 would be Chinese
19 would be other

belief systems

(% of population)

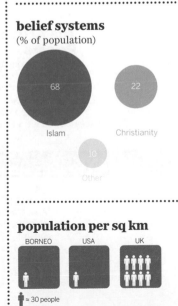

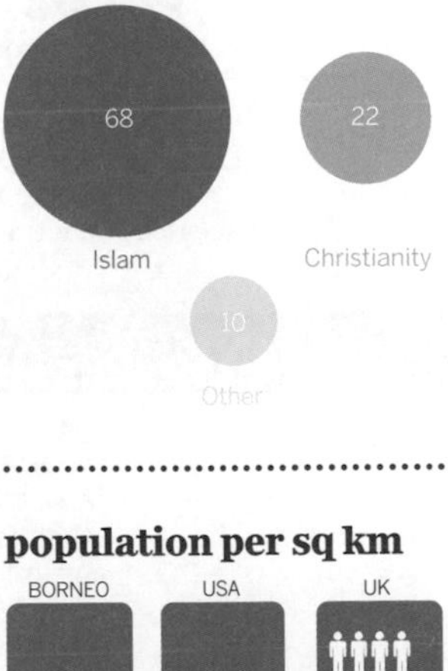

population per sq km

History

Considering Borneo's relatively remote location, it comes as no surprise that the island has rarely served as a major commercial or cultural crossroads. But neither has it been isolated from Asia's trade routes and religious currents. India and China have influenced and inspired Borneo's peoples for some 2000 years, and since the 15th century the island has been a meeting point of Islam and Christianity. For several centuries Borneo was buffeted by the epic rivalries between Dayak tribes and among the European powers.

Archaeological finds in western Borneo include glass beads made in the Roman Empire.

Borneo Becomes an Island

Borneo was connected to mainland Southeast Asia – as part of a land mass known as Sundaland – from 2.5 million years ago until some 10,000 years ago, when global deglaciation turned it back into an island. Archaeological evidence suggests that human beings arrived in Sarawak – overland – at least 40,000 years ago. More migrants arrived about 3000 years ago, probably from southern China, mixing with earlier inhabitants to form some of Borneo's indigenous groups.

Traders from India and China began stopping by Borneo – as a sideshow to their bilateral commerce – around the 1st century AD, introducing Hinduism and Buddhism. From about AD 500, Chinese traders started settling along Borneo's coasts. It is believed that the influence of the Sumatra-based kingdom of Srivijaya (7th to 13th centuries) extended to Borneo. During this time, Brunei emerged as a centre for trade with China; some historians believe that the first Muslims to visit Borneo came from China in the 10th century.

The Arrival of Islam & the European Powers

Islam was brought to present-day Peninsular Malaysia, including Melaka, by traders from South India in the early 15th century. Over time, diplomacy, often cemented by marriage, oriented Borneo's coastal sultanates towards Melaka and Islam.

In the late 15th century, Europeans began to seek a direct role in the rich Asian trade. In 1511 Portugal conquered Melaka in its bid to control

TIMELINE

2.5 million BC

Borneo is attached to mainland Southeast Asia, affording plants, insects, animals and eventually people easy migration routes.

8000 BC

Rising sea levels at the end of the last ice age submerge much of the Sundaland continental plate, transforming Borneo into the world's third-largest island.

1st century AD

Chinese and Indian traders detour to Borneo. By AD 500, Chinese are settling in coastal present-day West Kalimantan.

the lucrative spice trade. As a result, Muslim merchants moved much of their custom to Borneo's sultanates, and Brunei succeeded Melaka as the regional Islamic trading centre.

The British and Dutch began sparring over Borneo in the 17th century, extending a regional rivalry that began in Java and spread to the Malay Peninsula. The Anglo-Dutch Treaty of 1824 carved the region into spheres of commercial, political and linguistic influence that would turn into national boundaries in the 20th century. The Dutch got what became Indonesia, while Britain got the Malay Peninsula and Singapore. At the time, neither seemed much interested in Borneo.

The Venetian explorer Antonio Pigafetta, who sailed with Ferdinand Magellan on his last voyage, visited Brunei in 1521 and dubbed Kampong Ayer water village the 'Venice of the East'.

Brunei: Empire in Decline

Under Sultan Bolkiah in the 16th century, Brunei was Borneo's most powerful kingdom, its influence extending from Kuching all the way to the island of Luzon, now in the Philippines. In subsequent centuries, however, facing internal strife, rebellions and piracy, Brunei's rulers repeatedly turned to foreigners, including the Spanish, for help. In exchange for assistance in suppressing an uprising in 1701, Brunei ceded Sabah to the Sultan of Sulu (an archipelago between Borneo and Mindanao). That cession is the basis for ongoing Philippine claims to Sabah.

Brunei's decline in the late 18th century led Sarawak to assert its independence, emboldened by a flourishing trade in antimony (*sarawak* in old Malay). In 1839 Brunei's sultan dispatched his uncle Rajah Muda Hashim, but he failed to quell the separatists. Seeing a chance to be rid of Bruneian rule, the rebels looked south for Dutch aid.

Sarawak's White Rajahs

In a case of impeccable timing, James Brooke, the independently wealthy, India-born son of a British magistrate, moored his armed schooner at Kuching. Rajah Muda offered to make the Englishman the rajah of Sungai Sarawak if he helped suppress the worsening revolt. Brooke, confident London would support any move to counter Dutch influence, accepted the deal. Backed by superior firepower, he quashed the rebellion and held a reluctant Rajah Muda to his word. In 1841 Sarawak became Brooke's personal fiefdom. The White Rajahs would rule Sarawak for the next 100 years.

Unlike British colonial administrators, Brooke and his successors included tribal leaders in their ruling council and respected local customs (except headhunting). They battled pirates (a policy that boosted trade), were disinclined towards European immigration, and discouraged European companies from destroying native jungle to create rubber plantations. They also invited Chinese, many from Fujian and Guandong, to work in Sarawak as miners, farmers and traders. Despite a bloody rebellion by Hakka immigrants in 1857, Chinese came to dominate Sarawak's economy.

While maritime kingdoms and seafaring Europeans were vying for control of coastal Borneo, indigenous groups were developing their own societies deep in the rainforest. Little is known about their history due to the lack of written records.

600s–1200s

Sumatra's Hindu-Buddhist Srivijaya kingdom dominates Southeast Asia's sea trade. Under Srivijaya, ethnic Malays immigrate to Borneo.

1445

Islam becomes the state religion of Melaka, Srivijaya's successor as Southeast Asia's trading power. Merchants spread a predominantly tolerant, mild form of Sunni Islam that accommodates existing traditions.

1511

Portugal conquers Melaka in a bid to control the spice trade. Brunei succeeds Melaka as Southeast Asia's leading Islamic kingdom and trading centre.

1610

The Dutch build a diamond-trading post in Sambas, West Kalimantan, beginning more than 300 years of Dutch interest in Kalimantan and its natural resources.

When James Brooke died in 1868, he was succeeded by his nephew, Charles Johnson, who changed his surname to Brooke. During his long reign, which lasted until his death in 1917, Charles Brooke extended the borders of his kingdom (at the expense of the sultan of Brunei), developed Sarawak's economy and slashed government debt.

In 1917 Charles Vyner Brooke, son of Charles Brooke, ascended to the throne of Sarawak. A veteran of government service, he professionalised Sarawak's administration, preparing it for a modern form of rule.

In Borneo's interior, tribal wars are believed to have been frequent for centuries, with long-standing rivalries pitting some groups, such as the Kenyah and Iban, against each other.

Brunei's Continuing Decline

In 1865, 15 years after Brunei and the United States signed a Treaty of Peace, Friendship, Commerce and Navigation, Brunei's ailing sultan leased Sabah to – of all people – the American consul in Brunei, Claude Lee Moses. His rights eventually passed to an Englishman, Alfred Dent, who also received Sulu's blessing. In 1881, with London's support, Dent formed the British North Borneo Company (later called the North Borneo Chartered Company) to administer the territory. Once again, Britain managed to bag a slice of Borneo on the cheap.

In 1888 the prospect of further territorial losses led the Sultanate of Brunei, tiny and in danger of becoming even tinier, to become a British protectorate. But British 'protection' did not prevent Brunei from losing Limbang to Sarawak in 1890, absurdly chopping the sultanate into two discontiguous parts (Brunei still claims the Limbang area). Ironically, Brunei's colonial status in the 19th century paved the way for its transformation into Borneo's only independent country a century later.

The Dutch in Kalimantan

The presence of the British along Borneo's northern coast spurred the Dutch to beef up their presence in Kalimantan. Dutch commercial exploitation of the archipelago, begun in the very late 1500s, reached its peak at the end of the 19th century with thriving rubber, pepper, copra, tin, coal and coffee exports, plus oil drilling in East Kalimantan. This assertiveness sparked disputes with indigenous groups, culminating in 1859 in a four-year war between the Dutch and the Banjarmasin sultanate; resistance continued until 1905.

World War II

Imperial Japan, in need of Borneo's natural resources to power its war machine, seized Sarawak's Miri oilfields on 16 December 1941; other targets in the poorly defended region quickly fell. The retreating British sabotaged oil rigs and other key petroleum installations, but the Japanese soon had the oil flowing again.

1824

The Anglo-Dutch Treaty divides the region into spheres of influence. The Dutch are granted Kalimantan, but are preoccupied with Sumatra and Java.

1841

After helping the sultan of Brunei's emissary suppress an uprising, Englishman James Brooke becomes the first White Rajah of Sarawak.

1881

The British North Borneo Company is established in Sandakan to administer Sabah. It is the state's governing authority until Sabah (and Sarawak) become Crown colonies after WWII.

1888

Once Southeast Asia's pre-eminent Islamic trading centre, Brunei (or what's left of it) slumps into British arms as a protectorate.

As elsewhere in Asia, the Japanese occupation of Borneo unleashed local nationalist sentiments, but at the same time Japanese forces acquired a reputation for brutality. At Mandor (about 90km north of Pontianak in West Kalimantan), 21,037 people – sultans, intellectuals and common people, all accused of plotting against Japanese rule – were murdered. In Sabah, the infamous labour camp at Sandakan's Agricultural Experimental Station housed Allied captives from across Southeast Asia. Of the 2434 Australian and British POWs incarcerated there, only six survived the war.

In 1944 a primarily British and Australian force parachuted into Bario in the Kelabit Highlands and allied with indigenous Kelabits against the Japanese. In 1945, Australian troops landed in East Kalimantan, fighting bloody battles in Tarakan and Balikpapan. But Japanese forces in Borneo surrendered only after the atomic bombings of Hiroshima and Nagasaki.

As part of the resistance to Japan's occupation, Australian commandos encouraged a headhunting revival, offering 'ten bob a nob' for Japanese heads. Many of the skulls now displayed in Dayak longhouses are thought to be Japanese.

Colonisation & Decolonisation

After the war, which left many of Borneo's cities in ruins (mainly from Allied bombing), the North Borneo Chartered Company ceded authority over what is now Sabah to the British Crown. In Sarawak, the White Rajah returned briefly under Australian military administration but, overwhelmed by the cost of rebuilding, transferred sovereignty to the British government.

Local opposition to Sarawak's transformation from an independent kingdom into a Crown colony was widespread. Those demanding continued rule by the White Rajahs encompassed not only Anthony Brooke, Charles Vyner Brooke's nephew and heir apparent, but also many indigenous Sarawakians. The White Rajahs may have been of British stock, but after three generations in Borneo, many Sarawakians did not consider them outsiders, but rather an integral part of Sarawak's cultural and ethnic patchwork.

Allied bombing raids against Japanese targets in 1945 left Sandakan in ruins, so authorities moved Sabah's capital to Jesselton, now Kota Kinabalu.

In 1949, after a four-year war, the Dutch – facing tremendous international pressure, including an American threat to cut off postwar reconstruction aid – withdrew from the Dutch East Indies. Indonesia, including Kalimantan, which had remained on the sidelines during the conflict, gained independence.

Later that year, Sarawak's second colonial governor, Duncan Stewart, was stabbed to death in Sibu. Secret British documents uncovered in 2012 indicate that the assassins, hanged in Kuching in 1950, were not partisans of Anthony Brooke, as long suspected, but rather were seeking an Indonesian takeover of Sarawak. Anthony Brooke, who spent his life as a self-appointed ambassador of peace, died in New Zealand in 2011 at the age of 98.

1929

Commercial quantities of oil are discovered in Brunei, 30 years after the sultanate's first oil well is drilled.

1941–45

Imperial Japan occupies Borneo. Early resistance by local Chinese is brutally repressed. Nascent nationalists greet the Japanese as liberators, but the occupiers' cruelty turns opinion.

1946

As British colonial rule is about to end in India, the third White Rajah and the North Borneo Chartered Company cede rule of Sarawak and Sabah to Westminster.

1963

Sarawak and Sabah join Malaya and Singapore to create Malaysia. Their role: to maintain a non-Chinese majority. Indonesia claims all of Borneo and declares *konfrontasi* against Malaysia.

Malaysian Independence

When the Federation of Malaya, consisting of the states of Peninsular Malaysia, was granted independence in 1957, Sarawak, British North Borneo (Sabah) and Brunei remained under British rule.

In 1962 the British proposed incorporating their Bornean territories into Malaya. At the last minute, Brunei pulled out of the deal, as the sultan (and, one suspects, Shell Oil) didn't want to see the revenue from its vast oil reserves channelled to the peninsula. In September 1963 Malaysia – made up of the Malay Peninsula, Singapore, Sabah and Sarawak – achieved *merdeka* (independence). Singapore withdrew in 1965.

Konfrontasi & Transmigrasi

In the early 1960s, Indonesia's increasingly radicalised, left-leaning President Soekarno laid claim to all of Borneo. His response to the incorporation of northern Borneo into Malaysia was an undeclared war dubbed the *konfrontasi* (literally, 'confrontation'; 1962–66), to which Indonesians were rallied with the bellicose slogan *ganyang Malaysia* (smash Malaysia). Soviet-equipped Indonesian armed forces crossed into Sabah and Sarawak from Kalimantan. At the height of the conflict, 50,000 troops from Britain, Australia and New Zealand patrolled Sabah and Sarawak's borders with Indonesia. In all, hundreds of soldiers and civilians on both sides were killed. When Soekarno's successor, President Soeharto (ruled 1967–98), came to power, he quickly quieted tensions.

The name 'Borneo', introduced by the Spaniards, is a mispronunciation of 'Brunei' (or, according to another theory, of *buah nyiur*, Malay for coconut). In both Bahasa Malaysia and Bahasa Indonesia the entire island is called Kalimantan.

Soeharto also expanded the *transmigrasi* (transmigration) policies initiated by the Dutch in the 1930s, which moved millions of people from densely populated islands such as Java, Bali and Madura to more remote areas, including Kalimantan. From 1996 to 2001, hundreds of Madurese migrants were killed in attacks by Dayaks, joined at times by local Malays and Chinese. The conflict made international headlines because of the many reported cases of headhunting. In 2010, tensions flared again in a riot at Tarakan in which four people died. Long-term, the most insidious effect of *transmigrasi* has been to marginalise Kalimantan's indigenous communities.

Bruneian Independence

Brunei achieved self-government, except in matters of defence and foreign affairs, in 1971. In 1984 Sultan Haji Hassanal Bolkiah reluctantly led his country to complete independence from Britain. A graduate of the Royal Military Academy Sandhurst, he continues to maintain very close political and military ties with the UK and rules under a system of Melayu Islam Beraja (MIB; Malay Islamic Monarchy). This 'national philosophy' of Brunei emphasises Malay language, culture and customs, Islamic laws and values, and the supreme rule of the sultan.

1967

Brunei sultan Omar Ali Saifuddien abdicates in favour of his eldest son, Hassanal Bolkiah, who remains in power to this day.

1984

Brunei achieves full independence, but continues close ties with Great Britain. The last British military base in eastern Asia, home to a Gurkha battalion, is at Seria.

2000

Abu Sayyaf Islamic separatists from the southern Philippines kidnap 21 people on Sabah's resort island of Sipadan. Libya pays a ransom to free them.

2014

The first phase of a three-phase introduction of sharia law is implemented in Brunei. The new code includes brutal corporal punishments for crimes such as adultery and theft.

Peoples & Cultures

Borneo's indigenous peoples, known collectively as Dayaks, belong to more than 50 different ethnic groups that speak about 140 languages and dialects. Some live on the coast, others along the remote upland tributaries of great rivers. A few generations ago, some tribes still practised headhunting; today, many Dayaks are well-integrated into 21st-century economic life, and it's not unusual to meet university professors, lawyers, government officials and airline pilots who grew up in longhouses.

Among the ancestors of today's Dayaks were migrants from southern China who came to Borneo about 3000 years ago, bringing with them elements of the Dongson culture, including irrigated rice cultivation, buffalo-sacrifice rituals and ikat (fabric patterned by tie-dying the yarn before weaving). These newcomers mixed with native groups – people like the cave dwellers of Niah – and eventually developed into more than 200 distinct tribes.

Who's a Dayak?

Not all of Borneo's indigenous tribes refer to themselves as Dayaks, but the term usefully groups together peoples who have a great deal in common – and not just from an outsider's point of view.

Traceable back to about 1840, the term 'Dayak' (or 'Dyak') gained currency thanks to its use by colonial authorities. It appears to be derived from the last two syllables of 'Bidayuh', itself an exonym (a name originally used by outsiders). As a result, while contemporary Iban in Sarawak think of, and refer to, themselves as Iban (although this term is also an exonym), when they talk about Dayaks they are likely to be referring to the Bidayuh. However, shared cultural practices, values and political, economic and environmental interests – and several generations of Christian faith and inter-group marriages – make it beneficial for different groups to work together. The only term that embraces everyone is 'Dayak'.

Stranger in the Forest tells the extraordinary tale of Eric Hansen's solo trek across Borneo and his encounters with various Dayak groups, including the Penan.

None of Sabah's indigenous ethnicities are particularly keen on using the term 'Dayak', preferring instead to see themselves as Kadazan, Dusun, Rungus, Murut etc. Not so in Kalimantan, where native groups have rallied around the Dayak banner and the term has become a focus for political unity across tribal lines.

For the purposes of affirmative action (positive discrimination) in Malaysia, Dayaks, like Malays, are considered *bumiputra* ('sons of the soil'; ie people considered indigenous under Malaysian law).

Sabah

More than 30 indigenous groups make Sabah a medley of traditions and cultures. The state's largest ethnic group, known as the Kadazan–Dusun, make up 18% of the population. Mainly Roman Catholic, the Kadazan and the Dusun share a common language and have similar customs, though the former originally lived mainly in the state's western coastal areas and river deltas, while the latter inhabited the interior highlands.

Indigenous non-Malays, mainly Iban and Kelabit, account for less than 10% of Brunei's population.

The Murut (3.2% of the population) traditionally lived in the southwestern hills bordering Kalimantan and Brunei, growing hill-rice and hunting with spears and blowpipes. Soldiers for Brunei's sultans, they were the last group in Sabah to abandon headhunting.

THE PENAN

The least integrated – and most economically disadvantaged – aboriginal group in Sarawak and Brunei is the Penan, traditionally nomadic hunter-gatherers known for never taking more than they require from the jungle – and for never having engaged in headhunting. Their distinct culture and lifestyle separates the Penan from other Dayak groups.

Christian missionaries and the Sarawak government have long pressured the Penan to settle in longhouses, and today many live sedentary lives in northern Sarawak's Baram, Belaga and Limbang districts; only a few hundred are believed to remain true nomads. Settled Penan may plant rice, but they continue to rely on the jungle for medicine and food, including sago from palm trees and game that they hunt with blowpipes.

With their lands and way of life under severe threat from timber concessions and dams, the Penan have long engaged in civil-disobedience campaigns that have included blocking logging roads. While many sympathisers – such as the celebrated Bruno Manser (www.brunomanser.ch), an environmental activist who disappeared near Bario in 2000 – seek to protect the Penan's unique way of life, Malaysian authorities argue that they should be assimilated into mainstream society, living in settled communities with modern medical facilities and schools.

As of 2015, the campaign for Penan land rights focused on the proposed Penan Peace Park (www.penanpeacepark.org), an area of 1630 sq km around the Gunung Murud Kecil mountain range in the Upper Baram in Sarawak, close to the border with Kalimantan. Local Penan groups hope that the area – estimated to be over 50% primary rainforest – can be designated their land, protecting not only the jungle, but also Penan culture.

Sarawak

Dayak culture and lifestyles are probably easiest to observe and experience in Sarawak, where Dayaks make up about 48% of the population.

Up the Notched-Log Ladder is Sydwell Mouw Flynn's memoir of her parents' missionary work among Sarawak's Dayaks from 1933 to 1950, and her return to the land where she was raised half a century later.

About 29% of Sarawakians are Iban, descended from groups that migrated from West Kalimantan's Sungai Kapuas starting five to eight centuries ago. Previously known as Sea Dayaks for their exploits as pirates, the Iban are traditionally rice growers and longhouse dwellers. A reluctance to renounce headhunting enhanced their ferocious reputation.

The Bidayuh (8% of the population), once known as Land Dayaks, live mainly in the hills south and southwest of Kuching, near the Kalimantan border. Their ancestors are thought to have migrated from the Sungkong area of what is now West Kalimantan many centuries ago. As with many Dayak groups, identities and traditions are very local, and adjacent villages sometimes speak dialects so distinct that people find it easier to communicate in English or Malay. Few Bidayuh still live in longhouses.

Upland groups such as the Kelabit, Kayan and Kenyah – that is, almost everyone except the Bidayuh, the Iban and the coastal-dwelling Melanau – are often grouped together under the term Orang Ulu (upriver peoples). The Kenyah and Kayan are known for their elaborately decorated longhouses and the *kalong* motif, with its sinuous, intertwined creepers and vines.

The Borneo Project's 2014 documentary *Damming Our Future*, about a proposed dam in Sarawak, can be viewed online at www.borneoproject.org (under 'Our Work').

Kalimantan

In Indonesian Borneo, the terms Dayak and Dayakism imply pan-Dayak political and ethnic solidarity.

In Central Kalimantan, the largest indigenous group is the Ngaju Dayak, who live along major rivers and do more fishing than hunting. The Ot Danum Dayaks, who live further upriver, grow fruit, collect natural rubber and make dugout canoes that they sell to downriver tribes.

Along East Kalimantan's Sungai Mahakam, the Kutai are the main indigenous group in the lower reaches, hosting the annual Erau Festival at their capital Tenggarong.

The Kayan and the closely related Kenyah are found in the Apo Kayan Highlands, as well as in Sarawak and Brunei. They are known for building the most elaborately decorated longhouses and for having a strict social hierarchy.

The unique Punan cave dwellers live between the headwaters of the Mahakam and Kapuas rivers, spanning East and West Kalimantan. Today, most have given up troglodytic living.

West Kalimantan is home to a large population of Bidayuh, most of whom are Catholic (in Sarawak, quite a few of the Bidayuh are Anglican). Many identify strongly with the locality they're from – for instance, Bidayuh from Terebung refer to themselves as 'Dayak Terebung'.

Some Dayak societies, such as the Iban and Bidayuh, are remarkably egalitarian, while others, such as the Kayan, used to have a strict social hierarchy – now somewhat blurred – with classes of nobles *(maren)*, aristocrats *(hipuy)*, commoners *(panyin)* and slaves *(dipen)*.

The Longhouse

One of the most distinctive features of Dayak life is the longhouse (*rumah batang* or *rumah panjai*), which is essentially an entire village under one seemingly interminable roof. Longhouses take a variety of shapes and styles, but all are raised above the damp jungle floor on hardwood stilts and most are built on or near river banks. For reasons of geography, traditional Dayak societies did not develop a government structure beyond that of the longhouse.

The focus of longhouse life is the covered common verandah, known as a *ruai* to the Iban and an *awah* to the Bidayuh; the Kelabits have two, a *tawa'* for celebrations and a *dapur* for cooking (other groups use other terms). Residents use these communal spaces to socialise, engage in economic activities, cook and eat meals, and hold communal celebrations. It is also the place where, come nightfall, groups would traditionally gather round and tell stories.

One wall of the verandah, which can be up to 250m long, is pierced by doors to individual family *bilik* (apartments), where there's space for sleeping and storage. If you ask about the size of a longhouse, you will usually be told how many doors, ie family units, it has. Traditional Iban courtship, known as *ngayap,* involved surreptitious night-time liaisons in the young woman's room.

Like the rest of us, Dayaks love their mod cons, so these days longhouses fuse age-old practices with modern conveniences – the resulting mash-up frequently mixes traditional materials (bamboo slat floors) with highly functional features such as corrugated iron, linoleum, satellite

GAWAI DAYAK

In Sarawak and Brunei, the main pan-Dayak event of the year is Gawai Dayak (literally, 'Dayak Festival'), usually referred to as Gawai. Coinciding with the rice harvest of some groups, it brings Dayak singles and families who live in the city back to their ancestral longhouses for round after round of socialising, eating, singing, dancing and the consumption of *tuak* (rice wine). As one ebullient host once scolded, proffering *tuak* in bamboo cups, 'too much talking, no drinking, cannot!'

Many Dayak groups also hold community events such as dance performances, sports competitions and beauty contests, to which revellers (especially women) wear brightly coloured traditional costumes, including headdresses, bangles and beads.

Ceremonies marking the rice harvest are age-old, but Gawai as a festival celebrated simultaneously by once-rival tribes all across Sarawak was introduced by the state government and only dates from the late 1950s. The festival officially begins on the night of 31 May and lasts for two days (1 and 2 June are public holidays in Sarawak), but in some areas (eg around Bau), family-friendly village-level events take place on other dates between mid-May and the end of June.

Gawai festivities in longhouses and villages are invitation-only, but thanks to Dayak traditions of hospitality, Western visitors are often welcome to join in the fun.

dishes and, out the front, a car park. The new longhouses built by the government for resettled Dayak villages usually follow the old floor plan, but use unremarkable modern construction techniques.

The Iban traditionally kept headhunted skulls outside the head-taker's family apartment, on the longhouse verandah *(ruai)*, while the Bidayuh exhibited theirs in a communal headhouse *(baruk* or *panggah)*.

Most young Dayaks move away from the longhouse for greener pastures, seeking higher education and good jobs in the cities. But almost all keep close ties to their home longhouse, returning for major family and community celebrations. Some families that choose to remain in the longhouse community build a private house nearby, in part to escape the fire hazard inherent in living in a flammable structure with so many other people.

Visiting a Longhouse

According to longstanding Dayak tradition, anyone who shows up at a longhouse must be welcomed and given accommodation. Since almost all longhouses were, until quite recently, a considerable jungle trek or longboat ride from the nearest human settlement, this custom made a great deal of sense.

Generations of jungle travellers knew the routine: upon arrival they would present themselves to the headman (known as a *ketua kaum* in Malay, *tuai rumah* in Iban and *maren uma* in Kayan), who would arrange for very basic sleeping quarters. But in the last decade or two, as transport has become easier and tourist numbers have soared, this tradition has come under strain, and these days turning up at a longhouse unannounced may be an unwelcome imposition on longhouse residents – in short, bad manners.

The upshot is that in many areas of Borneo, the days when anyone could turn up unexpectedly at a longhouse and stay the night are largely over. And even if you make your own way to a longhouse that's happy to have you, you are likely to face significant communication and cultural barriers. Interacting spontaneously with locals isn't always easy, as the elders usually don't speak English, and the younger people are often out working the fields or have moved to the city to pursue careers.

Finding a Guide

Unless you are lucky enough to be invited by a local, hiring a guide who can coordinate your visit with longhouse residents and make introductions will help you avoid language and cultural barriers.

When considering a tour operator or freelance guide, it's best to keep an open mind about the itinerary, but do not hesitate to be upfront about preferences and concerns. Do you require a certain level of sleeping comfort? Do you have any dietary restrictions? How important is it that you be able to communicate with your hosts in English? Will you be disappointed if you see a satellite dish dangling off the side of the longhouse's cellphone tower? Do you want to be the only traveller around, or would you prefer to share the experience with others? Finding the right guide – and, through them, the right longhouse – can mean the difference between spending a sleepless night with other sweaty, bored tourists, or having a spirited evening (double entendre intended) swapping smiles, stories and shots of *tuak* with the longhouse residents.

Sarawak has plenty of tour operators and guides eager to take you (and your money) on Borneo's ultimate cultural adventure. From Kuching, it's easy to arrange day trips and overnights to Annah Rais Longhouse, for example. For something off the beaten track, Kuching-based tour agencies and guides can take you to the remote Sri Aman Division, to rivers such as the Batang Skrang, Batang Lemanak and Batang Ai. The upper Batang Rejang has lots of longhouses, but it has become harder to visit them due to a lack of licensed guides (and reputable unlicensed guides) in Kapit – although it is still possible to arrange trips through Sibu-based agencies to longhouses there and in Belaga. Hikers interested in walking from longhouse to longhouse in the Kelabit Highlands should head to Bario and plan their adventure from there.

There are a number of reliable tour agencies available. The Sarawak Tourism Board (www.sarawaktourism.com) has an online listing of about 100 licensed 'travel service providers'. Some of the best guides work for tour operators, which saves them from having to go through the rigmarole of getting their own STB license. While many freelance guides are friendly and knowledgeable, unfortunately some are not – ask your fellow travellers for recommendations. In any case, it can be hard to hold an unlicensed guide accountable if something goes wrong.

At the Sarawak Cultural Village near Kuching, you can visit four Dayak longhouses – including the only remaining Melanau longhouse – constructed using traditional materials and techniques. No tin roofs or satellite dishes!

What to Expect

When you arrive at a longhouse, don't be surprised to find that it wouldn't make a very good film set for a period drama about headhunters. Borneo's indigenous communities are living in the 21st century and many of their dwellings reflect it. Remember, though, that a longhouse, more than being a building, is a way of life embodying a communal lifestyle and a very real sense of mutual reliance and responsibility. It is this spirit, rather than the physical building, that makes a visit special.

Every longhouse is led by a headman. Depending on the tribe, he (or in a handful of cases, she) may be appointed by his predecessor or elected; either way, heredity often plays a key role in selection. In many areas, longhouses are known by the name of the headman, so if you know the name of your destination you'll already know the name of the chief.

Depending on the various goings-on at the longhouse you're visiting, you may or may not spend time with the headman, although he will usually 'show face' as it is impolite for him not to do so. Your guide will usually be the one showing you where to sleep, which is likely to be on the longhouse verandah, in a resident's living room, or in a specially built hut next door to the longhouse.

Do your best to engage with the inhabitants of any community you are allowed to enter, rather than just wandering around snapping photographs. A good guide can act as a translator when you strike up conversations, and he or she will keep you abreast of any cultural norms – like when and where to take off your shoes – so you won't have to worry too much about saying or doing the wrong thing.

Eat, Drink & Be Merry

If you are travelling with your own guide, he or she will be in charge of organising your meals – whether it's a separately prepared repast or a feast with some of the longhouse residents.

The Iban, in particular, like to honour their guests by offering meat on special occasions. Vegetarians and vegans should be clear about their dietary restrictions, as vegetable dishes are often served in a chicken sauce. Meals

GIFTS

Gift giving has become rather controversial over the last few years, with locals, tourists and tour operators offering a wide variety of advice on the subject. Longhouse communities do not traditionally require gifts from guests; in fact, some say that the tradition of gift giving actually began when travellers started visiting.

To avoid any awkward cultural miscommunications, your best bet is to ask your guide. Longhouses set far off the beaten track may appreciate bulk bags of rice or sugar, while communities that are a bit more in touch with the modern world might appreciate items such as pens or other such supplies. Some travellers bring something edible that can be shared over glasses of *tuak*. Any way you do it, gifts are never a must, nor are they expected.

Many tourists prefer contributing to the longhouse economy by hiring locals for a longboat trip or buying one of the craft items offered for sale. If you are visiting independently, it's polite to bring a small gift for the family of the person who invited you.

will be plentiful no matter what, though it is not considered rude or disrespectful to bring your own food, too. Two important things to remember when eating with longhouse residents: don't put your feet near the food (which is always served in a 'family-style' communal fashion); and don't step over anyone's plate if you need to excuse yourself from the eating area.

After dinner, when the generators start clicking off, it may be time to hunker down with the evening's bottle of bootleg spirits: *tuak*. The ceremonial shot glass will be passed from person to person amid chit-chat and belly laughter. Drink the shot when it's your turn (you won't really have a choice) and pass the glass along. *Tuak* may taste mild, but some types are pretty potent, and you can expect a stunning hangover the next day. When you reach your limit, simply press the rim of the glass with your finger like you're pushing an eject button. If you don't want to drink, you can claim a medical condition – just make sure you don't get caught sneaking a sip later on. Smiles, big hand gestures and jokes go a long way, even in your native language (and it'll all be second nature when you're nicely lubricated).

The White Rajahs of Sarawak allowed the Dayaks to live according to their age-old traditions and beliefs except in one area – headhunting – which they made great efforts to suppress.

Dayak ceremonies feature a variety of traditional dances. Accepting an invitation to join the dance and making a fool of yourself are sure crowd-pleasers.

Indigenous Spiritual & Cultural Practices

Traditional Dayak animism, which varies from tribe to tribe, focuses on the spirits associated with virtually all places and things. In Kalimantan it is known collectively as Kaharingan.

Carvings, totems, tattoos and other objects (including, in earlier times, headhunted skulls) are used to keep bad spirits at bay, attract good spirits and soothe spirits that may be upset. Totems at entrances to villages and longhouses are markers for spirits. The hornbill is considered a powerful spirit, and is honoured in dance and ceremony, its feathers treasured. Black is widely considered a godly colour, so it features in traditional outfits. In some tribes, women have special roles – for instance, a female priest, called a *bobohizan*, presides over many key Kadazan-Dusun traditional rituals in Sabah.

Ancestor worship plays a large part in Kaharingan. After death, Dayaks join their ancestors in the spirit world. For some groups, spirits may reside in a particular mountain or other natural shrine. Burial customs include elaborately carved mausoleums, memorial monoliths and interment in ceramic jars.

Many Dayaks take their Christian faith very seriously, so much so that some communities have banned alcohol – including *tuak* (rice wine) – entirely.

Most Dayaks now belong to mainstream Protestant groups (such as the Anglican Church), evangelical denominations (especially the Borneo Evangelical Church, also known as the SIB) and the Roman Catholic Church. Some evangelicals insist on purging all vestiges of previous beliefs, but in most instances Christianity overlays older cultural practices. Very few Dayaks still follow traditional religious practices.

Festivities such as Gawai Dayak, the harvest festival in Sarawak, are usually considered to be an expression of Dayak culture rather than of pre-Christian religious beliefs.

Tribal Body Art

The most striking fashion feature of many older Dayak women (and, in some groups such as the Kelabit, men) is their elongated, pierced earlobes, stretched over the years by the weight of heavy gold or brass rings. Young people rarely follow this custom, and older Dayaks sometimes trim their ear lobes as a sign of having converted to Christianity.

Iban Tattoos

Iban tattoos are closely linked to the concept of *bejalai,* which can be loosely defined as a journey, or a voyage of discovery. With each life skill

MUSIC OF THE RAINFOREST

A *sape* (pronounced sah-pey) is an Orang Ulu lute, shaped like a boat and often hand-carved with the traditional motifs of the Kayan and Kenyah people of the longhouses of the Upper Baram in Central Borneo. One of Sarawak's most celebrated *sape* players is Kenyah musician Matthew Ngau Jau, who is a regular at the Rainforest World Music Festival (www.rwmf.net), an annual event held in the Sarawak Cultural Village near Kuching at which Borneo's best musicians jam alongside bands from all over the world.

mastered, an Iban warrior-to-be would traditionally add a tattoo to their body, creating a biographical constellation of swirling designs.

At around the age of 10 or 11, a young Iban would get their first tattoo, a *bungai terung* (eggplant flower) drawn on each shoulder. The design, created using soot mixed with fermented sugarcane juice and hand-tapped bamboo or bone needles, commemorated the beginning of one's journey as a man (women were known to get them as well). The squiggly centre of the flower symbolised new life and represented the intestines of a tadpole, visible through their translucent skin. The plant's petals were a reminder that patience is a virtue, and that only a patient man can truly learn life's lessons.

Further attainments – for instance, mastering boatbuilding, hunting, shamanism and even traditional dancing – brought more ink, including the popular crab design, which symbolised strength and evoked the strong legs and hard shell of the crafty sideways walkers. Traditionally, the Iban believed that when drawn with magical ink, the design could act like the shell of a crab, protecting bearers from the blade of a machete.

The bravest travellers received the coveted throat tattoo as they evolved into a *bujang berani* (brave bachelor). The design – a fish body that morphs into a double-headed dragon – wanders up from the soft spot at the centre of the clavicle, known as the 'life point' to the Iban.

Through all this, elaborate rules had to be followed. For instance, only men who had taken a head were permitted to tattoo the top of their hands. Also, every animal inked facing inward must have something to eat – dragons were always depicted with a small lizard near their mouths – because if the creature was left hungry it would feed on the bearer's soul.

When the warriors returned to their village, the tattoos were a bit like passport stamps, tracing borders crossed and frontiers explored. A large collection of blueish-black 'merit badges' greatly increased one's desirability as a bachelor and, it was believed, enabled a soul to shine brightly in the afterlife.

These days, after decades of decline, tattooing is making something of a comeback. In urban areas, some young Iban get tattoos to commemorate achievements such as travelling abroad or completing their military service or a university degree. Sometimes the tattoos are eclectic, combining designs from tribes that once warred with each other with modern motifs.

Body Piercing

The *palang*, a long-standing Dayak tradition, is a horizontal rod of metal or bone that pierces the penis, mimicking the natural genitalia of the Sumatran rhino. As times change, this type of procedure is becoming less common, but many villages still have an appointed piercer, who uses the traditional method: a bamboo vice in a cold river. The real macho men opt for some seriously extreme adornments, from multiple *palang* to deliberate scarification of the penis.

The impetus behind these self-inflicted 'works of art' is actually to enhance a woman's pleasure rather than personal adornment. Among some communities these radical procedures were once just as important as lopping off heads.

Land of the Headhunters

Headhunting *(ngayau)* has long been relegated to the realm of tourist brochures, T-shirts and Dayaks' self-deprecating witticisms, but for over 500 years it was an important element of Borneo's indigenous culture.

Dayak slash-and-burn (swidden) agriculture is sometimes blamed for deforestation and forest fires, but in fact indigenous farmers are responsible for only a very small fraction of the island's habitat loss.

Many of the rites, rituals and beliefs surrounding this gruesome tradition remain shrouded in mystery, but one aspect was unchanging: the act of taking heads was always treated with the utmost seriousness. Warriors would go out on two types of expeditions: *kayo bala,* a group raid involving several warriors; and *kayo anak,* performed by a *bujang berani* (lone brave). The takers of heads often bore no personal animosity to their victims.

In the upper regions of the Batang Rejang, the *kayo anak* was a common method of wooing a prospective bride. The most valuable heads were those belonging to women and children because only the savviest and stealthiest warrior could ambush a child or woman as they bathed or picked berries. Such heads were usually hidden away from marauders near the longhouse hearth.

After a successful hunt, the warrior would wander the jungle, wrestling with the taken spirit rather than letting down his guard for a nap. In the morning, he would return to his longhouse where the head would be smoked and strung up for the others to see and honour. Heads were worshipped and revered, and food offerings were not uncommon. A longhouse with many heads was feared and respected by the neighbouring clans.

The tradition began its gradual decline in 1841 when James Brooke, at the behest of Brunei's sultan, started quashing the hunt for heads, in part to attract foreign traders, who had understandably tended to keep their distance from Borneo's shores. A nasty skirmish involving a knife-wielding pirate and a Chinese merchant's cranium gave Brooke the opportunity to show the Dayaks that he meant business – he promptly executed the criminal.

Headhunting, to the extent that it continued, flew under the government's radar until WWII, when British commandos found the practice useful for the war effort – so long as the victims were Japanese. Many of the heads that now adorn longhouses date from this period.

These days, sensationalised accounts of inter-ethnic conflict in Indonesian Borneo often describe the violence as latter-day headhunting. If press descriptions are to be believed, the last '*tête* offensive' (so to speak) took place in Kalimantan in the early years of the 21st century, when migrants from the island of Madura who settled, or were resettled by the Indonesian government, in Dayak and Malay areas, were the victims.

As Borneo's indigenous people embraced Christianity and rejected traditional animistic superstitions, many longhouses dismantled their dangling skulls. Though if you ask around, you'll quickly learn that the heads haven't actually been tossed away – that would just be bad luck!

Native Land Rights

When a tract of forest is cut down for timber or to make way for a dam or palm-oil plantation, animals are not the only ones who lose their homes – Borneo's forest-dwelling indigenous peoples are also displaced.

The Penan have been especially hard hit by logging and forced relocations. In Sarawak, the government under former chief minister Abdul Taib Mahmud tried to quash Penan and other minority group protests and often responded to any sign of civil disobedience with arrests. The appointment of Adenan Satem as chief minister in 2014 has brought some hope to these groups; Adenan has shown a willingness to listen to native land rights proposals and has said he is determined to protect the state's forests from further logging.

In Kalimantan, migrants from other parts of Indonesia have encroached upon the Dayaks' traditional lands, producing a sometimes violent backlash.

The Cuisines of Borneo

Eating in Borneo is never boring. Located right near Southeast Asia's historical trade, immigration and colonisation routes, the island's cuisines include Malay food, dishes from various provinces of southern China, and even food from southern India, as well as delicious indigenous (Dayak) fare based on ingredients that grow wild in the rainforest.

Throughout Borneo, *nasi* (rice) and *mee* (noodles) are the staples, and one or the other makes an appearance at almost every meal, including breakfast. Rice is eaten steamed, as *nasi goreng* (fried with other ingredients) or boiled as *bubur* (sweet or savoury porridge that is very popular for breakfast). Glutinous varieties are steamed and moulded into tubes or cubes and often wrapped with leaves. Noodles, in a variety of widths and thicknesses, can be made from wheat (with or without egg), rice or mung beans, and are served boiled in soup (*soto* or *sup*) – a Chinese favourite for breakfast – or fried *(mee goreng)* with other ingredients.

In some parts of Borneo, people get their carbs not from rice or noodles, but from starch extracted from the pith of the sago tree. In Brunei it is served in an unbelievably gooey form known as *ambuyat.*

Dayak Cuisines

Borneo's indigenous peoples are remarkably diverse, expressing themselves with a rich variety of languages, traditions and artistic forms. But when it comes to cooking, they all turn to pretty much the same uniquely Bornean selection of leaves, flowers, fruits, roots, vines, ferns, fish and meats that the rainforest shares with all who know its edible secrets.

Each indigenous tribe has its own ideas about the best way to combine, season and prepare the natural bounty of the forest. Some dishes are tangy, others bitter or surprisingly spicy, and yet others characterised by peaty, jungly flavours unknown in other Asian culinary traditions. Many dishes are cooked and/or served in leaves (such as *daun isip,* used by the Kelabits) that add delicate flavours in addition to serving as eco-friendly packaging and plates. Parcels of glutinous rice wrapped in a leaf – sometimes with meat, too – is a typical 'packed lunch' to bring with you when hiking from longhouse to longhouse in the highlands.

Some ingredients, such as ferns, are so perishable they have to be eaten within a day of being picked, so exporting them – even to Peninsular Malaysia – is virtually impossible. As a result, the only way to experience

BAMBOO CHICKEN

In many parts of Borneo, a perennial Dayak favourite is bamboo chicken (*asam siok* in Bidayuh, *pansoh manok* in Iban). To make it, rice, marinated chicken and spices such as lemon grass, garlic, ginger and chillies are stuffed into a length of bamboo, which is then sealed with turmeric leaves. The resulting cylinder is then cooked near (but not too near) an open fire, thereby infusing the dish with the delicate aromas of bamboo and turmeric, sealing in the spices, and ensuring that the meat emerges deliciously tender. An easy and delicious meal to cook at a jungle campfire and eat beneath the stars.

the mouth-watering, eye-opening and tongue-tickling world of Dayak cuisine is to come to Borneo.

But even on the island, sampling Dayak cuisine – naturally organic and MSG-free – is rarely as easy as walking up to a hawker centre. There are a handful of restaurants in cities such as Kuching and Miri – of special note is Dyak (p133), a pioneering gourmet establishment in Kuching – but otherwise the only way to savour indigenous dishes is to dine at a longhouse or be invited to dinner in a family home.

Rice

A dozen or more varieties of Borneo-grown rice can be found in the markets, often in clear plastic sacks that let you see the colour, size and shape of the grains. Dayak groups traditionally grow rice using swidden (slash-and-burn) techniques.

Hill paddy, grown by upland villagers mainly for their own use, is generally unpolished and unprocessed. Red rice is generically known as *beras merah* (in Iban and Bahasa Malaysia), but other varieties of Bornean rice are white, light brown, dark brown and even reddish orange. Bario rice (from the cool Kelabit Highlands), Borneo's most prestigious rice variety, is famous for its small grains and delicate taste and aroma.

Sarawak is famous all over Malaysia for its intricate and colourful *kek lapis* (striped layer cakes), available in Kuching along the Main Bazaar.

Glutinous rice (*pulut* in Iban and Bidayuh) is sometimes combined with coconut milk *(santan)*, vegetable oil and a bit of salt and cooked in a length of bamboo lined with a banana leaf to produce *lemang*.

Other Ingredients

Other ingredients you're likely to encounter in Dayak cooking (some are also used by Borneo's Malays and Chinese):

Bamboo shoots (*puluh* in Kelabit) Made from very young bamboo and often grown in people's gardens; in the Kelabit Highlands, *puluh* are sliced thin, boiled and then stir-fried with salt, pepper and small local fish.

Bitter beans *(petai)* Bright green beans that grow in long pods; they appear in dishes such as *petai gulai kechala* (stir-fried with wild ginger flowers, onions and anchovies).

Cassava leaves (*pucuk ubi* in Iban) Young leaves are often stir-fried (eg with chicken, or with anchovies, garlic and onions) and eaten with rice.

Chicken (*ayam* in Bahasa Malaysia) The tastiest kind comes from the *kampung* (villages), rather than from large-scale commercial producers.

Chilli paste (*bua' ladah* in Kelabit) Extremely hot, this condiment is made with chilli peppers, ginger, onion, garlic and salt.

Daun bungkang A leaf that grows on a fruit tree and, like bay leaves, is used to add flavour.

Doray (in Kelabit) A dark green goop that tastes a bit like spinach, made by boiling a leaf that grows along river banks with salt; said to be rich in vitamins and especially healthy for children, who often eat it with rice or porridge.

Eggplant (*terung* in Iban and Bahasa Malaysia) Bornean eggplants, which are the size of a peach, are often planted together with the hill rice and harvested before the rice stalks mature.

SARAWAK LAKSA

Tangy, chewy, spicy, crunchy and thoroughly lip-smacking, *Sarawak laksa* brings a hot, tangy broth – made with a paste of chilli, garlic, shallots, peanuts, galangal (a relative of ginger), candlenuts and lemon grass – together with *bee hoon* (vermicelli noodles) and an array of tasty toppings with toothsome textures: bean sprouts, omelette strips, chicken slices, shrimp and chopped cilantro (coriander). Diners squeeze calamansi lime on top and decide how much fiery *sambal belacan* they can handle.

Fish (*ikan* in Bahasa Malaysia) Small fish grow in paddy fields, larger fish are caught in streams and rivers and, along the coast, in the sea.

Ginger flower (*bungai kechala* or *tepus*; *busak luduh* in Kelabit) Grows wild along river banks, has a lemony flavour and tastes a bit like artichoke heart; often chopped into very fine slivers, boiled and then fast-sautéed with onions.

Hot chilli (*cili*) Hot peppers used by all the various tribes.

Lemon grass (*sorai* in Bidayuh) The Bornean variety, which grows in the jungle, is more herbal and less sharp than the Thai variety.

Midin ferns These wild fiddlehead ferns (their curled-up tips resemble the scroll of a violin or cello) were once eaten mainly by the rural poor, who collected the young fronds in forest clearings. Recently, though, they have been rediscovered by foodies and are hugely popular among Dayak, Malay and Chinese cooks.

Paku ferns A type of fiddlehead fern that grows wild in moist parts of the forest.

Pumpkin (*bua' tecak* in Kelabit) Orange on the outside and, when cooked, soft and creamy inside. Can be stir-fried, steamed or puréed to make cream-of-pumpkin soup.

Salt In upland Borneo, mineral-rich saline spring water is boiled in huge vats to produce high-iodine salt; it's sold in markets in leaf-wrapped 'sausages'.

Tempoyak Preserved durian; the Bidayuh recipe (there are also Malay versions) calls for mixing deseeded durian pulp with coarse sugar, leaving it to ferment for a day or two, and then draining off the juices.

Tumeric leaves (*umiet* in Bidayuh) Used to wrap fish for steaming so that the flavour infuses the fish, or to seal the bamboo tube used to make bamboo chicken; contains minute quantities of cyanide, which the Dayaks remove by shredding the leaves and washing them before pounding them into a pulp.

Venison (*payo* in Kelabit) Deer are still hunted in the forest in places such as the Kelabit Highlands; after the animal is killed, the meat is immediately smoked (to preserve it) and then brought back to the village, where it is pounded (to soften it), boiled and finally stir-fried, often with lemon grass, ginger and onion. Before refrigeration, smoked meat was hung above the family hearth, where it would remain edible for months.

People either adore, or are utterly disgusted by, Southeast Asia's most notorious fruit, the flamboyantly odoriferous durian. Hotels and airlines often post drawings of the spiky fruit slashed by a horizontal red bar to remind durian lovers to indulge elsewhere.

Tuak

When members of Borneo's indigenous groups get together for a celebration or to entertain visitors, festivities are traditionally lubricated with *tuak* (rice wine). Almost always home-brewed, it comes in two main versions: *tuak laki* (gentlemen's *tuak*), which packs an alcoholic punch of 18% or more; and *tuak induk* (ladies' *tuak*), which is sweeter and has somewhat less alcohol. *Tuak* (known as *burak* to the Kelabits), made from glutinous rice, sugar, yeast and water, is fermented for somewhere between two weeks and two or three months (the longer the better). Some versions are infused with fruits or wild herbs.

Each Dayak group has traditions associated with *tuak*. Before drinking a bamboo cup of the potent liquid, bottoms-up style, the Bidayuh say 'tra-tra-tra-tra-ooooh-ah', with a rising tone on the 'ooooh' and a falling tone on the 'ah', while the Orang Ulu say something that sounds like 'ooh-weh-weh-weh-weeeeeeh aah-ah-ah'. To make the merry-making merrier, the Iban, at their festivities, send around a *sadong*, whose role is to *sadong* (pour) shots of *tuak* and cajole everyone to imbibe. The catch is that every time he asks someone to drink, they have the right to demand that he do so as well, with predictably mirthful results.

Other wines you may encounter at Dayak festivals include sugarcane wine (*tuak tobuh* in Bidayuh), which tastes a bit like port. To make it, sugarcane juice is boiled (to increase the concentration) and then fermented with a kind of bark the Bidayuh call *kohong*. Palm sap wine (*tuak tumbang* in Bidayuh, *ijok* in Iban), yellow in colour, is slightly fizzy, with a fruity flavour.

Malay Cuisine

Thanks to the spice trade, Malay cooking has absorbed ingredients and cooking methods from a variety of culinary traditions, including those of India, China and mainland Southeast Asia. Malay dishes are often made with hot chillies, ginger, galangal, lemon grass, garlic, shallots, turmeric leaves and, to add a rich, creamy texture, coconut milk.

Malay food is always halal – that is, it follows Muslim dietary rules: no pork or porcine derivatives, no products from animals that were hunted, and no alcohol.

Some of the Malay dishes and condiments widely available in Borneo:

Belacan Fermented shrimp paste.

Bubur Rice porridge; often eaten for breakfast.

Ikan bilis Tiny dried anchovies.

Kangkung belacan Water spinach quick-fried in a wok with *belacan*.

Kari ayam Chicken curry; one of many Malay *kari* (curry) dishes.

Mee goreng Malay-style fried noodles; usually made with wheat-and-egg noodles.

Mee sapi Noodles with beef, either served in a hearty broth or with a light gravy.

Nasi campur Rice served with a selection of side dishes, sometimes buffet-style (pricing is by weight); known as *nasi padang* in Indonesia.

Nasi goreng Malay-style fried rice is distinguished from Chinese fried rice by the frequent presence of *belacan* (shrimp paste) and by the absence of pork.

Nasi lemak White rice cooked in coconut milk and served with side dishes such as salted fish or egg; Malaysia's unofficial national dish, it's popular for breakfast.

Pulut Glutinous rice.

Rendang Spicy beef or chicken stew made with coconut milk.

Roti canai Grill-fried Indian-style bread, often with a savoury or sweet filling; popular for breakfast.

Sambal Any of a wide variety of spicy condiments or sauces made with hot chillies.

Sambal belacan Ubiquitous condiment made with *belacan*, hot chillies, *limau kasturi* (calamansi lime), sugar and sometimes other ingredients.

Satay Skewers of *ayam* (chicken), *kambing* (goat, also used for lamb and mutton) and occasionally *ikan* (fish), *cumi* (squid) or *udang* (shrimp) grilled over an open fire and served with peanut sauce.

Soto ayam Chicken soup made with rice vermicelli.

Chinese Cuisines

The ancestors of Borneo's ethnic Chinese population migrated from a variety of provinces in southern China (Kuching's Chinese History Museum spotlights nine different dialect groups). Their distinct culinary traditions – Hokkien, Teochow, Foochow, Hakka etc – are alive and well to this day, especially in the cities and larger towns of Sarawak and Sabah and in Singkawang (West Kalimantan), where many of the foodstalls and restaurants are run by Chinese.

Marriages between Malays and Straits Chinese resulted in a delicious fusion cuisine, known as Nonya or Peranakan, that mixes Chinese recipes and Malay spices. It can be a bit hard to find in Borneo, but is well worth trying if you get a chance.

Near the coast, keep an eye out for Chinese fish and seafood restaurants that display the day's catch either alive, swimming in tanks or laid out neatly on ice. Diners point to the creature they'd like to eat and specify the mode of preparation; the charge is by weight.

The flavours in Chinese cuisine tend to be muted compared to Malay cooking, and it has fewer complex spice combinations – the taste of the primary ingredients is usually foremost. Another defining aspect of Chinese food is its heavy reliance on pork and lard, both assiduously avoided by the Malays, though these days some Chinese eateries have stopped using pork in order to receive halal certification.

Chinese food stalls often serve up the following dishes:

Bee hoon Rice vermicelli (very thin rice noodles).

Bubur Rice porridge (congee), often garnished with minced chicken or pork; popular for breakfast.

Chicken rice White rice cooked with chicken stock and served with slices of non-deboned chicken breast, sambal and cucumber slices.

Fish ball soup Fish balls and stuffed tofu in a broth that's often made from pig bones; usually made with *tang hoon* (mung bean noodles).

Kam pua mee Foochow-style thin noodles soaked in pork fat and served with a side of roast pork; Sibu's signature dish.

Kolo mee Wheat noodles tossed in a mixture of oil and light soy sauce and garnished with barbecued pork and vegetables; a speciality of the Kuching area.

Kueh chap Tasty soup made with various spare piggy parts.

Kueh teow Wide, flat rice noodles, served stir-fried or in soup.

Lok-lok Deep-fried or boiled skewers of fish, bean curd etc that are eaten with sweet, sweet-and-sour or satay sauce, or with *belacan*.

Lui char Traditional Hakka soup, bitter in taste, made of finely chopped herbs and vegetables; served with rice and roasted peanuts.

Mee goreng When this Bahasa Malaysia term appears on a Chinese food stall, it's referring to Chinese-style fried noodles.

Mee sua Wheat vermicelli; served by the Foochows with chicken and mushrooms in a large bowl of broth laced with Chinese wine.

For a cooling dessert, try ABC *(ais batu campur)*, also known as *ais kacang*, a hillock of shaved ice garnished with red beans, palm seeds, grass jelly, sweet corn and luridly coloured syrups.

Vegetarian Cuisine

The Chinese and Indians have venerable vegetarian traditions, and all of Borneo's gastronomies include plenty of dishes made with vegetables such as *daun ubi* (cassava leaves), *cangkok manis* (a dark green leafy vegetable often fried with eggs), *sayur manis* (often called 'Sabah veg') and *kangkong* (water spinach or convolvulus). Soy beans (*dao* or *tau*) are widely available, often in the form of *tauhu* (bean curd) or tempe (fermented whole beans). Chinese establishments may be able to whip up *cap cai* (mixed vegetables), and you can always order a soup without meat, fish or seafood. At Malay places, the rice part of *nasi lemak* and *nasi campur* is vegetarian, though some of the side dishes they're served with are not.

That's the good news. The bad news is that unless you specify otherwise, Malay-style stir-fried vegetables are often made with *belacan* (fermented shrimp paste), and Chinese stalls usually make their soup stock with animal bones, and slip into all sorts of dishes small quantities of pork (minced or ground) or lard. These ingredients may also make an unnoticed appearance in Dayak dishes.

If you're vegetarian, say: *'Saya hanya makan sayuran'* (I only eat vegetables). If you're a vegan, you may want to take it a step further: *'Saya tidak makan yang di perbuat dari sayur, telur, ikan atau daging'* (I don't eat dairy products, eggs, fish or meat).

SENSATIONAL SAMBAL

These fiery relishes – considered the calling card of any Malay cook – vary in strength and flavour and can be made with fresh or dried chilli and a range of additional ingredients such as dried fish or fruit. Sambal is served as a dip to accompany all kinds of dishes, from *ikan bakar* (barbecued fish) to simple noodle soups. The most common variation is *sambal belacan*, made from fresh or dried chillies pounded with dried *belacan* (fermented shrimp paste) – Sarawak laksa is served with a ramekin of the stuff to add further fire to the broth. *Sambal belacan* packs a pungent punch that takes some getting used to, but it's a flavour that soon has many hooked.

Natural World

Borneo is one of the most biologically diverse places on the planet. It is also one of the most critically imperilled. Its ancient forests and towering mountains house a breathtaking assortment of life, ranging from charismatic megafauna such as the rhinoceros and orangutan, to bizarre bugs such as a half-metre stick insect. These live among 15,000 species of plants, including carnivorous pitcher plants, and the world's largest flower.

This abundance of life has also made Borneo a prime target for exploitation. In an alarmingly short span of time, much of the island's old-growth forest has been logged and replaced with oil-palm plantations. Vast swathes of land are being ground up by strip mines, while grand plans for hydropower dams threaten to drown countless more hectares.

Fortunately, several large tracts of the interior of Kalimantan, as well as some areas of Sarawak, Sabah and Brunei included in the 'Heart of Borneo' initiative, are still relatively untouched and have gained protection thanks to the hard work of NGOs and local advocates. But these largely mountainous areas are difficult habitats to call home and many of Borneo's amazing species may not be able to survive there.

For an excellent, colourful introduction to Borneo's environment, track down a copy of *Wild Borneo* by Nick Garbutt.

The Land

At roughly 743,330 sq km, Borneo is the third-largest island in the world (after Greenland and New Guinea). It is about one-third larger than France and almost exactly the same size as Chile.

Bisected by the equator, Borneo is remarkably flat, with over half of the landscape less than 150m above sea level. Lowland areas tend to be swampy, with serpentine rivers and poor drainage. Malaysia's longest river is the Batang Rejang (563km) in Sarawak, while Indonesia's three longest rivers are in Kalimantan: Sungai Kapuas (1143km), Sungai Mahakam (980km) and Sungai Barito (890km).

Mountains dominate much of the centre of the island, running on a diagonal axis from Mt Kinabalu in the northeast down to Bukit Raya, the tallest peak in Kalimantan (Indonesian Borneo), to the southwest. Borneo sits on the eastern edge of the Sunda Shelf, a relatively stable chunk of earth. Unlike many islands in Indonesia and the Philippines, there are no truly active volcanoes – although Mt Bombalai on the edge of the tectonic plate in present-day Sabah may have produced lava flows within the last 12,000 years. Earthquakes are relatively rare, but a magnitude-5.9 quake

COLONIALISM & CONSERVATION

Borders established in the 19th century ended up having a profound impact on the fate of Borneo's rainforests in the 21st century. Vast areas of forested land pried away from the sultan of Brunei by the White Rajahs and the British North Borneo Company ended up being clear-cut in the decades after Malaysian independence, whereas the majority of the territory that the sultan managed to retain is now pristine and protected wilderness. Dutch Borneo, now Indonesia's Kalimantan, was late to the deforestation game, but is now rapidly converting what remains of Borneo's rich ecological diversity into plantations and strip mines.

on Mt Kinabalu in 2015, which killed 18 people, rekindled concerns that the fault lines may be growing more active.

Extensive deposits of limestone in northern and eastern Borneo show where ancient coral reefs were buried under thousands of metres of sediment, then lifted to form ranges of hills and mountains. In some areas water has dissolved the limestone to form impressive caves. Sarawak's Gunung Mulu National Park is one of the world's premier limestone landscapes, boasting towering rock pinnacles and the world's second-largest cave chamber. Niah National Park is also famous for its huge caves, while the caverns and pinnacles of East Kalimantan are still relatively unexplored.

Borneo's most celebrated peak is 4096m Mt Kinabalu in Sabah, the highest mountain between the Himalayas and New Guinea and arguably the epicentre of Borneo's fabulous biodiversity. This colossal dome of granite forced through the earth's crust as molten rock 10 to 15 million years ago, and continues to rise about 5mm a year. Despite its location just north of the equator, Mt Kinabalu was high enough to be exquisitely sculpted by glaciers during the ice ages.

At the time of the last glacial maximum, Borneo's rainforests were connected to the Asia mainland by a vast tropical grassland that allowed for the migration of animals and humans onto the island. This land bridge is now submerged under the South China and Java Seas, where the average depth of around 40m creates unpredictable tides but protects much of the island's coast from tsunamis.

Borneo's two Unesco World Heritage sites, Gunung Mulu National Park in Sarawak and Kinabalu National Park in Sabah, may soon be joined by the Sangkulirang–Mangkalihat Karts in East Kalimantan and Betung Kerihun National Park in West Kalimantan. Both are on the tentative inclusion list.

Habitats

Coral Reef

Borneo's east coast is included in the Coral Triangle, a fantastically rich portion of the South China Sea that's home to 75% of the world's coral species and over 3000 types of marine fish. Reefs are in the best shape in the northeast, where the water is clear and free of sediment. The islands of Sipadan in Sabah and the Derawan Archipelago in East Kalimantan have the greatest concentrations of reefs. Other protected areas include Tun Sakaran Marine Park in Sabah and Talang-Satang National Park in Sarawak.

Most of Borneo receives more than 200mm of rain a month, with some areas totalling over 4m of rain each year.

Kerangas (Heath Forest)

Sandy soils that are highly acidic and drain quickly support a specialised habitat known as *kerangas,* an Iban word meaning 'land that cannot grow rice'. This forest type is composed of small, densely packed trees that seldom exceed 20m in height. Due to difficult growing conditions, plants of the *kerangas* have developed extraordinary ways to protect their leaves from the blazing sun and acquire needed minerals. Some, for example, obtain nitrogen and other nutrients by providing a home for ant colonies that, like tiny pizza-delivery people, bring food to the plant. Others take a more primal approach, such as the pitcher plants (Nepenthes), which lure ants into their slippery-sided, enzyme-filled cups – and then digest them.

Borneo's remaining *kerangas* is increasingly restricted to protected coastal areas such as Sarawak's Bako National Park and remote mountaintops like those in Sabah's Maliau Basin Conservation Area.

Lowland Dipterocarp Forest

California has its redwoods, but Borneo has its dipterocarps. Occupying the lowlands, but found up to as high as 900m, the towering trees belonging to the dipterocarp family include more than 150 species, some of which can reach a height of 60m. Collectively, they define Borneo's most important ecosystem: the lowland dipterocarp forest, which has more species of flora than any other rainforest habitat in the world. A single hectare may contain more tree species than all of the US and Canada combined.

The rainforests of Borneo are exposed to twice as much sunlight as temperate forests, but just 2% penetrates all the way to the forest floor. That is why so much jungle biodiversity is up in the canopy.

Most trees in lowland dipterocarp forests synchronise their flowering and fruiting in one of the world's most impressive ecological phenomena, known as masting. Seemingly triggered by El Niño weather patterns, a mast event produces so much fruit that seed predators – gorge themselves though they may – are unable to devour them all, leaving plenty left to germinate. In recent years, however, this pattern seems to have been less predictable, possibly as a result of deforestation, which has weakened the chemical signals trees use to communicate with each other. Dipterocarps also produce some of the most valuable tropical hardwood, making them a prime target for deforestation.

Seven distinct forest types are found uniquely compacted together in Gunung Palung National Park in West Kalimantan, making it an excellent ecology laboratory.

Montane Forest

On mountains above 900m, dipterocarp forest gives way to a magical world of stunted oaks and myrtle and laurel trees. Montane forests are damp, drippy places due to their proximity to the clouds, but poor soils and more extreme temperatures stunt the growth of its resident trees. The canopy of a montane forest might not reach much above 10m. The landscape is full of ferns, rhododendrons, lichens and thick moss, as well as a stunning cornucopia of orchids and a diversity of pitcher plants.

Due to the difficulty of accessing them, montane forests are some of the most well protected on the island. Although gibbons, orangutans and other large mammals may occasionally be seen here, it is believed that these animals are unable to survive and reproduce in this challenging landscape without the lowland forests surrounding them.

Mangrove

Flourishing in a tidal world where land meets sea, mangroves have developed extraordinary ways to deal with an ever-changing mix of salt and fresh water, all the while anchored happily in suffocating mud. These remarkable trees protect coastlines against flood, erosion and even tsunamis.

Uncounted marine organisms and nearly every commercially important seafood species find sanctuary and nursery sites among mangrove roots. The forests' more endearing species include the proboscis monkey and the mudskipper, a fish that spends much of its time on almost-dry land, skipping along the muddy shore in search of food. Mangroves were once ubiquitous around the entire island, especially in river deltas, but have been systematically cut for firewood, coastal development and aquaculture.

Peat Forest

Peat forests form in flatlands where dead plant matter, too waterlogged to decompose, accumulates in the form of peat several meters deep. The amount of carbon stored in peat can be many times greater than the carbon found in the forest growing above it, making their protection doubly vital. When peat land is deforested and drained – for instance, to establish oil-palm plantations – the below-ground peat oxidises and releases vast quantities of carbon dioxide into the atmosphere.

In addition, dry peat is frightfully combustible and can burn unchecked, underground, for months, releasing yet more carbon, popping up in unexpected locations (eg inside protected areas) and carpeting much of Southeast Asia with haze. The smoke from Borneo's nearly annual peat fire fiascos have grounded aircraft, caused widespread respiratory ailments and seriously ticked off neighbouring Singapore.

Borneo has about 15,000 species of flowering plant. All of North America – from the Panama Canal to the Arctic – only has about 20,000.

Plants

The stats on Borneo's flora are astonishing. The island has as many species of flowering plants as the entire continent of Africa, which is 40 times larger. In Lambir Hills National Park scientists found a dizzying 1200 species of tree in a single 52-hectare research plot, and the island is home to more than 1000 species of fern. Of Borneo's 2000 species of orchid, over 1000 live on Mt Kinabalu.

Many of Borneo's plants struggle to survive in thin, nutrient-poor soils. Some trees hold themselves upright with wide, flaring buttresses that compensate for shallow root systems.

Strangler figs start life as tiny seeds that are defecated by birds in the rainforest canopy, where they sprout and then send spindly roots downward in search of the forest floor. Eventually some figs grow large enough to embrace their host tree in a death grip. Once the host tree dies and rots away, the giant fig stands upright on a fantastic hollow latticework of its own interlaced air roots. Orangutans, wild pigs and birds are only some of the creatures that feed on the fruit of the strangler fig.

Wildlife

With close to 420 bird species, over 220 mammal species – including 13 primates – 166 species of snakes and around 100 amphibian species, you are sure to spot something remarkable in Borneo's rainforests. Add to that roughly 3000 arthropods, including 1000 species of ants, and the diversity of life is beyond astounding, it is incomprehensible.

You won't necessarily find these creatures dripping off the trees, however. Borneo's forests are much less creepy and crawly than you probably imagine and even trained researchers might never spot such shy creatures as the Western tarsier, clouded leopard or sun bear. Most rainforest residents are masters of disguise, wisely keep their distance from humans, and are therefore nearly impossible to see...but more than likely, they'll see you.

'The orangutan's future is dependent on the forests. As more are cleared and converted to agricultural plantations orangutan populations will continue to decline'. Ashley Leiman, OBE, Director of Orangutan Foundation (UK).

Orangutan

Borneo's biggest celebrity is an awesome sight to behold, especially if you are lucky enough to cross paths with a wild orangutan ponderously swinging

POWER FLOWER

One of the wonders of the botanical world, the rafflesia flower is astonishing not only because of its world-record size – up to 1m in diameter – but also because of its extraordinary and mysterious life.

Rafflesias are parasites that lack roots, stems or leaves. In fact, they consist of just two parts: tiny filaments that burrow into the host vine – a member of the grape family called *Tetrastigma* – to extract nutrients; and the flower itself, which often erupts directly from the forest floor, bursting forth from a cabbage-sized bud that takes nine to 12 months to mature, if they aren't devoured by small mammals.

Scientists have yet to figure out the rafflesia's sex life. The red flowers are either male or female, but it is not clear how they manage to effect pollination since two flowers rarely bloom anywhere near each other at the same time. Pollination is carried out by carrion flies, which are attracted by the flowers' revolting rotten-meat odour, and the resulting fruit seeds are distributed by small rodents such as tree shrews and squirrels. How the plants manage to attach themselves to their host vines, and why they grow only on *Tetrastigmas*, remains a mystery.

There are approximately 17 species of rafflesia (estimates vary) and all are threatened to some degree, mainly by loss of habitat but also by bud poaching for medicinal use.

Borneo is one of the best places in the world to see rafflesia, which bloom irregularly, year-round, but only for three to five days before turning into a ring of black slime. It takes a fair bit of luck to see one. For the low-down on when and where, ask at your guesthouse or hotel, or contact one of the following:

- In Sarawak, the park headquarters of Gunung Gading National Park or contact the National Parks and Wildlife Booking Office in Kuching.
- In Sabah, Tambunan Rafflesia Reserve. You can also look for signs around Poring Hot Springs.

AN EPIDEMIC OF ENDEMICS

Borneo's plants and animals are as unique as they are diverse, with many found nowhere else on earth. This phenomenon, known as endemism, occurs in isolated regions where species evolve without mixing with outside populations. The different habitats found in Borneo, which range from lowland swamps to high montane forests, also allows for a high degree of specialisation. It is difficult to know the actual numbers in a place this diverse (especially as new species are constantly being found), but Borneo is home to at least 44 mammal, 37 bird, 19 fish and over 5000 plant species found only on this island, making them very susceptible to extinction.

through the trees of a forest. Endemic to Borneo and Sumatra, the orangutan is Asia's only great ape and all populations are threatened by habitat loss and hunting. Around 78% live outside of protected parks and reserves – that is, in forests that could be logged or turned into oil-palm plantations at any time. Scientists estimate that before human encroachment, the world's orangutan population was roughly 100 times what it is today.

Wild orangutans are now difficult to find except in places such as Sabah's Danum Valley Conservation Area, Sarawak's Batang Ai region and Kalimantan's Kutai National Park. Semi-wild animals can be seen at the Semenggoh Nature Reserve in Sarawak, Kalimantan's Tanjung Puting National Park and the Sepilok Orangutan Rehabilitation Centre in Sabah.

Proboscis Monkey

Borneo's most peculiar primate, named for the male's pendulous nose, lives mainly along the island's waterways, including in mangrove forests. They are strictly herbivorous, which is why both sexes need prodigious quantities of cellulose-digesting bacteria – stored in their distinctive pot bellies – to turn their food into usable energy. Scientists are still not quite certain why the males have developed such a protuberant proboscis, but in addition to attracting a mate (right, ladies?), evidence suggests the nose swells when the animal is stressed, creating a resonance chamber to amplify warning calls.

The endangered proboscis monkeys are only found on Borneo, and can be spotted in Sabah at the Labuk Bay Proboscis Monkey Sanctuary, and in Sarawak at Bako National Park. In Tanjung Puting National Park in South Kalimantan, they famously swim across the river behind passing boats that have hopefully scared off the hungry crocodiles.

Gibbon

Gibbons swing by their powerful hook-like hands, a mode of travel called brachiation. It is not fail-safe, however: most gibbons have bone fractures from falling.

These operatic, acrobatic lesser apes are Borneo's adorable daredevils. Winging effortlessly from branch to branch, gibbons move with such speed (up to 56km/h) and agility that it seems as if they are redirecting gravity, shooting around trees like a comet around the sun.

Unfortunately for primate lovers, the endangered gibbons are much easier to hear than see, staging melodic morning duets high in the canopy to stake their territorial claim. You can find gibbons throughout Borneo, including in Brunei's Ulu Temburong National Park and West Kalimantan's Gunung Palung National Park.

Elephant

Less than 1500 Borneo pygmy elephants (a subspecies of the Asian elephant) are estimated to live in northeastern Borneo, and the numbers are decreasing. These petite pachyderms can live up to 60 years in the wild, but their long birth intervals (four to six years) make them susceptible to population decline. The largest population is found in Sabah, where they regularly come into conflict with owners of the sprawling oil-palm plantations that have replaced their lowland habitat.

New genetic evidence puts to rest the theory that humans introduced the creatures to the island in the mid-1700s. It turns out this genetically distinct species has been here for at least 18,000 years.

Rhinoceros

Little is known about the elusive, critically endangered and possibly extinct-in-Borneo Sumatran rhinoceros. In 2015 the Malaysian government admitted the rhino was likely gone from Sabah after maintaining there were still at least 10 in 2013.

It is the world's smallest rhinoceros in both stature and number. Its global population is estimated to be less than 100, with the only viable population residing in Sumatra. A camera trap in 2013 did record at least one animal in Kalimantan, while the World Wide Fund for Nature (WWF) has recorded wallows and other signs near Putussibau as recently as 2015.

Rhinos have long been the victims of exploitation, hunted for over 1000 years for their horns, which natives traded to Chinese merchants who sold them for traditional Chinese medicine. Now conservationists are desperately trying to bring them back from the brink through breeding programs, which have had little success.

There is no record of any human entering Sabah's Maliau Basin until the 1980s.

Bearded Pig

Bearded pigs are encountered in nearly every type of forested area on the island. These rotund animals can weigh up to 150kg and will travel in large herds, migrating incredible distances in search of fruit, nuts and seeds.

Although they are an extremely popular game animal (except, of course, among Muslims), they are one creature that hunters truly fear. Aside from the tame pigs that live in and around the headquarters of Bako National Park, be wary of these unpredictable animals and their sharp tusks – they are capable of goring a human in the flash of a whisker.

Mouse Deer

Few Bornean mammals are more surprising than the lesser mouse deer, the world's smallest hoofed animal. It is the size of a rabbit (it weighs just 2kg), but looks like a tiny deer. Males defend themselves and their mates using protruding canines instead of antlers. They are also a delicacy among forest people, and numbers are dwindling.

BORNEO'S FLYING CIRCUS

Perhaps the most impressive of Borneo's animals are those that have given up on the whole walking-along-the-ground thing, and instead have taken giant evolutionary leaps to soar between canopy trees. Borneo is home to the world's largest collection of animals that glide – 33 species at last count – including squirrels, lizards, geckos, frogs and...snakes.

Interestingly, these creatures have evolved several different and creative ways to cheat gravity and direct their free falls for more convenient landings. For the giant red flying squirrel (the world's largest flying squirrel, reaching about 1.2m in length nose-to-tail) and flying lemurs, it is a flap of skin stretched between their arms, legs and tail. The flying dragon lizard flails its rib cage, while some frogs and geckos prefer four independent wing flaps stretched between their toes. Paradise tree snakes don't have flaps of any kind, but instead shape their bodies into an air foil and manoeuvre different sections to direct their flight.

Scientists differ about why there are so many gliders in these forests, while the Amazon has none. Prevailing theories suggest taller trees make crawling down then back up too much of a resource drain, while others suggest a lack of liana and vine bridges between the trees pressured creatures to find another path. Whatever the reason, one thing is certain: catching one of these creatures in flight is one of Borneo's most rare and astonishing sights.

Birds

A fantastic assortment of birds belonging to at least 420 species, 37 of them endemic, fill the forests of Borneo with flashes of feather and ethereal calls.

The most famous of Borneo's birds are its eight species of hornbill, some of which have an oversized 'helmet' or 'horn' perched on their beak. The 105cm-long rhinoceros hornbill, with its orange-red casque and loud whooping calls, serves as Sarawak's state emblem. When the 125cm-long helmeted hornbill swoops across the sky, you might think you're seeing a pterodactyl, with the distinctive whooshing sound of its wings almost as primal as the maniacal laughter of its call. Hornbills have a curious nesting habit: the females barricade themselves inside a tree hollow with the eggs, while the male feeds her from the outside through a small hole. Hornbills are revered and hunted by Borneo's indigenous peoples and are highly threatened by habitat loss.

Bird Watching Websites

www.borneobirdclub.blogspot.com

www.borneobirdimages.com

www.borneobirdfestival.com

www.borneobirds.com

Environmental Issues

Borneo is a land in ecological crisis. If used sustainably its vast forests could provide valuable resources for countless generations. When the forest is logged and fragmented, however, the entire ecosystem falls apart. Soils become degraded, peat dries out and catches fire, rivers silt up, plants and animals disappear and indigenous human communities lose their sources of sustenance, both physical and spiritual.

Despite the best efforts of local and international environmental groups, the governments that rule Borneo (except that of Brunei) tend to view rainforests as an impediment to 'progress', or as political spoils, with a handful of well-connected people deriving profits from logging concessions and plantation permits granted without public oversight.

The 3rd edition of *Phillipps' Field Guide to the Birds of Borneo: Sabah, Sarawak, Brunei, and Kalimantan* (2014) is the Borneo birdwatcher's bible.

Deforestation

Borneo's forests are being destroyed twice as fast as the rest of the world's rainforests. In 1973 about 75% of the island still had its original forest cover. By 2005 the figure was just 53%. By 2009 over 80% of the forests of Sabah and Sarawak had been impacted by logging, with Kalimantan not faring much better. The impacts of this destruction are immeasurable, both on a local and global scale.

Only a tiny fraction of Borneo's land is protected by law, and even less is subject to laws that are systematically enforced. Bowing to international pressures, the governments of Indonesia and Malaysia make sweeping declarations about ending logging, but continue business as usual. Companies independently make grandiose pledges to end their deforestation, then turn around and hire local smallholders to clear and plant the land for them.

In Kalimantan, which suffers from an almost-complete lack of enforcement, local officials sell off timber permits in federally protected lands. Kutai National Park in East Kalimantan has been so completely devastated by a combination of logging and fires it has long been considered a complete conservation failure. Malaysian Borneo is used as a sales conduit for illegal timber logged in Kalimantan.

With this land clearing comes a whole assortment of issues. Floods and landslides wash away valuable topsoil and envelope cities, rivers become sluggish and fetid and haze from land-clearing fires blankets Singapore and Peninsular Malaysia every dry season, increasing international tensions.

Despite a ban on export, Indonesian companies still openly sell Borneo ironwood online for as much as US$3000 a cubic metre.

Oil-Palm Plantations

Alongside logging, the greatest single threat to Borneo's biodiversity comes from expanding oil-palm plantations. Palm oil is in almost everything: shampoo, cosmetics, cookies, chips, candy bars, detergent, bread, margarine and biofuel, to name a few. It hides under a variety of names, including vegetable oil, palmate, sodium lauryl sulfate, vegetable fat and stearic acid, among others. However, what is completely obvious is the thousands of square kilometres of primary and secondary forest in Sabah, Sarawak and Kalimantan that have been destroyed to produce 85% of the world's palm oil.

Originally brought from Africa in 1848, oil palms produce more edible oil per hectare (about 5000kg, or 6000L of crude oil) than any other crop, especially in Borneo's ideal growing conditions. The oil is extracted from the orange-coloured fruit, which grows in bunches just below the fronds and is used primarily for cooking, although it can also be refined into biodiesel, an alternative to fossil fuels.

For all the crops' benefits, unbridled, irresponsible and unsustainable expansion of monoculture plantations has had huge environmental consequences. In Kalimantan the area given over to oil palms has increased by 300% since 2000, while in Sabah around 20% of the land – about 14,000 sq km – is now carpeted with oil palms. To see what this means, just look out the window of any airplane flying over Borneo or check out Google Earth, where deceptively green swathes of the island resolve into neatly gridded rows of trees as you zoom closer in.

Oil-palm plantations may appear green – after all, they are covered with living plants – but from an ecological point of view they are almost dead zones. Even forest land that has been clear-cut can recover much of its biodiversity if allowed to grow back as secondary forest, but oil-palm plantations convert land into permanent monoculture (leases are usually for 99 years), reducing the number of plant species by 80% and resident mammal, reptile and bird species by 80% to 90%.

Oil palms require large quantities of herbicides and pesticides that can seep into rivers, polluting settlements downstream. Drainage canals lower water tables, drying out nearby peat forests, making them more susceptible to burning. Plantations fragment or destroy the natural habitats that are especially important to large mammals.

Further, local populations that depend on the forest for their livelihood have seen their land suddenly sold off and converted with little or no warning. Those villages that do have legal claims to the land are often bought off with token amounts of cash and promises of jobs, only to later find their water sources polluted and the forest resources they took for granted no longer available.

The Roundtable on Sustainable Palm Oil tries to look at the issue from all sides while seeking to develop and implement global standards to mitigate palm oil's impacts. However, in a comedy of errors, even companies that try to do the right thing are sometimes penalised by government regulations that dictate that land permitted for palm oil must be planted as such and can not be set aside as conservation easements.

Watch Borneo's forests disappear in near-real-time at www.globalforestwatch.org.

If all of the remaining land in Borneo currently designated as 'production forest' were to be logged, only 11% of the island would remain forested.

PALM OIL: BIOFUELLING FOREST DESTRUCTION

Replacing fossil fuels with renewable biofuels made from palm oil sounds like a great way to reduce carbon emissions and thus mitigate global warming. Unfortunately, it is not that simple. Palm oil production comes with significant ecological damage and carbon loss when forests are converted to oil-palm plantations.

Beyond the destruction of habitat and displacement of indigenous people, there is quite a bit of carbon lost when you convert a forest to an oil-palm plantation. In the best of circumstances, it would take a hectare of oil palm 60 years of biofuel production to offset the carbon lost while producing it. In the worst case it would be 220 years, with the actual number likely somewhere in between. The equation is especially unbalanced when the plantation replaces a peat-swamp forest, which releases colossal quantities of greenhouse gases as it dries out – even more so when it burns.

Everything from mining chemicals to human waste pours into Kalimantan's rivers. In a single generation, the water at Samarinda has gone from drinkable to not batheable.

A series of public-awareness campaigns has begun to get the attention of the world's bigger consumers of palm oil. In 2010 Nestlé committed to 100% sustainable palm oil after an intensive Greeenpeace campaign. Hershey's, Kellogg's and General Mills have followed suit, though all still need work to be true leaders in the field, according to the Rainforest Action Network's Snackfood 20 Scorecard (www.ran.org/sf20scorecard).

Hydroelectric Dams

Hydroelectric dams are touted as sources of environmentally friendly, carbon-free energy, but these huge projects often cause serious environmental and cultural damage. Projects are often planned without public access to feasibility studies, without public feedback and without proper environmental-impact assessments.

Sarawak's controversial Bakun Dam submerged an area of pristine rainforest about the size of Singapore (695 sq km) and displaced 9000 indigenous people who were forced to purchase the homes where they were relocated. The dam was justified by Malaysia's growing power need, yet cables to connect Borneo to the mainland have proven to be too expensive, and efforts to sell the power locally have been mired in fears of corruption. Further, failure to effectively remove enough biomass behind the dam combined with run-off from upstream plantations has made the water polluted with high levels of nitrogen and aluminium.

Meanwhile, plans stutter along for the Baram Dam, one of 12 more proposed dams in Sarawak, which will displace 20,000 people from longhouse communities. The government of Sarawak put the plan on hold again after enraged locals successfully maintained a blockade of the construction site for over a year.

In Kalimantan a 2013 threat by China to invest $17 billion in dams has fortunately not moved forward. However, Indonesia stated in 2015 that it planned to begin construction of four dams on the island, but little concrete information has been released to the public.

Wildlife Trade

Although theoretically illegal, the hugely lucrative trade in wild animals continues. Baby orangutans are captured for sale as pets, while clouded leopards are killed for their teeth, bones and pelts. Pangolin (scaly anteaters) are smuggled off the island by the boatload and sun bears are butchered so body parts such as gall bladders can be used in traditional Chinese medicine, despite absolutely no evidence to support their efficacy.

Since Malaysia, Indonesia and Brunei signed the Heart of Borneo Declaration in 2007 which protects 220,000 sq km of forest land, well over 600 new species have been discovered in the area it covers, including a 57cm-long stick insect, the world's longest.

Protecting Borneo's Natural World: What You Can Do

Every time a traveller visits a nature site, hires a trekking guide, pays a boatman for transport to a remote longhouse, or supports a local ecotourism initiative, they are casting a vote – by putting cash in local pockets – for the economic value of sustainability and habitat conservation. Wherever you go, tread lightly, buy locally, support responsible tourism and give respectful, constructive feedback to local operators.

Be an informed traveller and visit the following websites to learn more about the campaigns to save Borneo's forests.

Borneo Futures (www.borneofutures.org) Brings solid, science-based solutions to the discussions about Borneo's fate.

WWF (www.panda.org) With its Malaysian affiliate, WWF Malaysia (www.wwf.org.my), it's fighting for change on an international scale.

Orangutan Land Trust (www.forests4orangutans.org) Supports a wide variety of projects throughout Borneo that protect orangutans and their habitat.

Mongabay (www.mongabay.com) One of the world's leading providers of rainforest conservation and science news.

Survival Guide

Responsible Travel

Cultural Etiquette

Borneo is a melting pot of different nationalities and faiths, and in the interior, an exotic ethnic quilt of indigenous tribes. While it's not possible to mention every social indiscretion you might innocently make, following are a few helpful tips to bear in mind.

Brunei

Brunei is rigorous in enforcing its Islamic code of ethics, particularly since a three-phase sharia penal code was partly introduced in 2014. The laws mainly apply to Muslims, however non-Muslims can also be charged for certain offenses including drinking alcohol in public, adultery and homosexual acts committed with a Muslim. The application of rules regarding Friday prayers and fasting during Ramadan have also been toughened up; during Ramadan, all eating, drinking or smoking in public is prohibited during daylight hours (and carries the penalty of a B$4000 fine or a year in prison).

Sabah & Sarawak

More tolerant than Brunei, but still in many parts adherent to the Muslim faith, try and avoid no-nos such as pointing with your feet or eating with your left (toileting) hand. Malaysians pride themselves on being calm and not letting their emotions inflame, and as such you should endeavour to do the same, remaining patient even in difficult and trying situations. A common gesture seen in Malaysia is the touch of hand to heart to signify gratitude.

If visiting a longhouse or tribal village ensure you show deference to the elder. Muslim women may choose not to shake your hand; don't be offended. During Ramadan, Muslims continue to work on very little food and fluid (for a whole month); out of consideration, if you're climbing or traipsing through jungle, try not to drink in front of your guide.

Kalimantan

Kalimantan is heavily Muslim, so whether you are male or female, avoid wearing skimpy clothes in places of worship (covering arms and legs), and remove shoes when entering someone's house. If visiting tribal villages, refrain from giving money or sweets to kids – not to mention their dental health, it will encourage them to expect the same from future visitors.

Wildlife

Turtle Encounters

Green and hawksbill turtles will be a prominent feature of any underwater adventure in Borneo. You'll also be given the chance in numerous places to see turtles rising at night from the sea and digging nests to deposit their eggs on beaches or to see the hatchlings – a magical privilege. Below is a list of questions worth asking the travel outfit or turtle sanctuary to ensure your turtle-watching experience is of benefit to (or at least has a minimal impact on) these magnificent creatures.

- Do they give the mother space and privacy and discourage people from crowding around her? Groups should be kept small so as not to disrupt the progress of the female laying eggs.
- Do they actively discourage the handling of baby hatchlings? Newly hatched turtles should make their own way to the ocean and should not be picked up (which exhausts and disorientates them).
- Do they use only turtle-safe red LED-flashlights? Rangers and visitors should refrain from shining torches on the turtles, as bright lights can disorientate them.
- How much of your money will go directly back into developing conservation for the animals?

Orangutan & Monkey Encounters

It's very hard to resist a cuddly orangutan extending its hand to you, but we strongly recommend keeping a safe distance; given our close genetic similarities (we share 97% of the same DNA) the closer you get to them the more likely they are to contract a cold or virus from you. At Camp Leakey in Kalimantan, the rehabilitated apes roam free and have been habituated to humans to the extent that close and uninvited contact with tourists is a regular occurrence. Bear in mind that Kusasi, the long-reigning, fully pouched monarch, has severely injured staff in the past, and held tourists captive, with staff resorting to beating him to release the unfortunates. Male orangutans are *much* stronger than us and cannot be blamed for their actions if we get too close.

Feeding wild monkeys, be it macaques or proboscis, should be avoided; your responsibility to their habitat is to leave it and them as unmolested by your presence as possible. Macaques, if they feel threatened, can be very aggressive; avoid prolonged eye contact with the large males.

Diving

Diving in Borneo brings you into contact with some of the world's finest coral reefs, however it also places these rare havens of marine biodiversity under a great deal of pressure. Ensuring you observe a few commonsense rules makes a big difference:

➡ Avoid touching living marine organisms, standing on coral or dragging equipment such as fins across a reef. Coral grows extremely slowly; accidentally knocking a branch off can destroy decades of growth.

➡ Never feed fish or allow your dive operator to dispose of surplus food in the water, as fish soon become dependent on these handouts and neglect their role of cleaning algae from the coral, thus causing harm to the reef.

➡ If you've enjoyed your time in the deep, put something back by joining a clean-up operation with outfits such as Scuba Junkie (www.scuba-junkie.com) in Mabul.

➡ Never collect shells or coral.

➡ Give sea turtles some space, and don't try to chase or touch them.

Volunteering

Voluntourism has become a booming business in Borneo, with travel companies coopting the idea as a branch of their for-profit enterprises. Although you give your time for free, you will be expected to pay for food and lodging, and you may also be asked to pay a placement fee; try to find out exactly how much of your placement fee is going into Borneo, and how much is going towards company profit and administrative costs. Fees paid to local agencies tend to be much lower than those charged by international agencies.

When looking for a placement, it is essential to investigate what your chosen organisation does and, more importantly, how it goes about it. To avoid the bulk of your placement fees going into the pockets of third-party agencies, it's important to do your research on the hundreds of organisations that now offer work, and to find a suitable one that supports your skills. If the focus is not primarily on your skills, and how these can be applied to help local people, this should ring alarm bells.

For any organisation working with children, child protection is a serious concern; organisations that do not conduct background checks on applicants should be regarded with extreme caution. A three-month commitment to programs with children is recommended by childsafe tourism experts.

Following is a list of organisations offering opportunities to volunteer with wildlife in Borneo, but Lonely Planet does not endorse any organisations that we do not work with directly, so it is essential that you do your own thorough research before agreeing to volunteer with any organisation.

➡ Pay-to-volunteer programs are available in Sabah at the Sepilok Orangutan Rehabilitation Centre (see www.travellersworldwide.com), and in Sarawak at the Matang Wildlife Centre (www.orangutanproject.com) and through Talang-Satang National Park's Sea Turtle Volunteer Programme (contact the national park booking office in Kuching).

➡ The Mescot Initiative (www.mescot.org), run by Kopel Ltd, protects the forest habitat and wildlife of the Lower Kinabatangan in Sabah; contact them to get involved with their inspiring conservation program.

➡ In Kalimantan, the Great Projects (www.thegreatprojects.com/indonesia) offers one-month opportunities to help at IAR and Samboja orangutan rehabilitation centres.

Directory A–Z

Accommodation

Accommodation in Borneo runs the gamut from international-standard hotels to upland Dayak longhouses, which themselves range from mod-con central to wood-and-palm structures deep in the jungle. In smaller towns, on outlying islands and in the hinterlands, your options may be limited to very simple lodgings. Sabah and Sarawak have the best range of accommodation, particularly in the upper brackets, while Kalimantan has fewer top-end hotels and resorts. Brunei boasts one of the world's most opulent hotels, but has limited budget options.

On the ceilings of some hotel rooms, arrows point towards Mecca so Muslim guests know which direction to face when praying.

International-Standard Hotels

➡ All of Borneo's major cities have hotels with the full range of mod cons and amenities, but standards vary, from top-notch in Kuching, Kota Kinabalu (KK), Bandar Seri Begawan (BSB) and Balikpapan to close-but-no-cigar in places such as Miri and Sibu.

➡ Many of the island's top hotels are now run by international chains and are well acquitted to the needs of business travellers.

➡ Booking online is the way to go at most of these places, and you'll often find offers well below rack rates – in Malaysia, excellent rooms can be found for less than US$100 per night and sometimes much less, and in Kalimantan luxury comes even cheaper.

➡ In Malaysia and Brunei, most room prices include the 10% service charge. If you're unsure if your rate is all-inclusive, ask if the quote is 'plus-plus' – a 'yes' means that the service charge and taxes have *not* been factored in.

Local Hotels

➡ The island's small hotels – in Malaysia often run by people of Chinese ancestry – have long been the mainstay of the domestic hospitality market. The more salubrious ones are a decent option for budget travellers (some that we don't mention double as brothels). Starting at about US$20 for a double room in Sarawak and Sabah, they're generally fairly spartan.

➡ Showers and toilets are usually en suite, but may be down the hall for cheaper rooms.

➡ Some places ask you to leave a deposit for the TV remote.

Resorts

➡ Some places that style themselves as 'resorts' have plenty of seaside (or jungle) activities and impeccable service, but others cater mainly to the domestic business-conference market.

➡ For a relaxing, resort-style holiday in Sabah, you can choose among several excellent seaside resorts in and near KK, or head to an offshore island such as Pulau Mantanani, Pulau Manukan, Pulau Tiga or Layang Layang, or the islands of the Semporna Archipelago.

➡ Sarawak's best-known resort area is the Santubong Peninsula.

➡ Brunei will blow you away with the over-the-top Empire Hotel & Country Club, or you can relax at the jungle lodge in Ulu Temburong National Park.

➡ Kalimantan has a few resorts, limited mostly to private islands in the Derawan Archipelago, and a handful of large hotels with resort notions in the bigger cities.

BOOK YOUR STAY ONLINE

For more accommodation reviews by Lonely Planet authors, check out lonelyplanet.com/borneo/hotels. You'll find independent reviews, as well as recommendations on the best places to stay. Best of all, you can book online.

Guesthouses & Backpacker Accommodation

➡ Malaysian Borneo's main tourist cities offer laid-back accommodation designed for visitors on a budget. Ideal for meeting fellow travellers, these places generally offer a choice of dorm beds or small private rooms (usually with shared bathrooms), and also have a common area for lounging, an internet terminal or two, a basic kitchen and, if you're lucky, a washing machine and a rooftop garden for hanging out in the evening. Some rent bicycles and conduct tours of local sights; for many it's a point of pride to provide up-to-the-minute travel information (eg regarding transport).

➡ Dorm beds start at about US$9 per night, while private rooms go for US$16 and up. If you want your own room, cheap hotels often offer better value.

➡ Because many guesthouses (especially in Kuching) are situated in converted commercial buildings and old shophouses, not all rooms come with windows.

➡ Kalimantan does not yet have a hostel scene, so backpackers looking for cheap digs usually bed down in an inexpensive hotel or losmen.

Longhouses

Until the last decade or two, passers-by were always welcome to stay overnight at longhouses, the age-old dwellings of many (but not all) of the indigenous peoples of Borneo. But this is changing, especially in Malaysia. For more information, see p280.

Homestays

➡ Sabah and Kalimantan have plenty of welcoming homestays offering good value and a local vibe.

➡ Brunei's homestays tend to cater to tour groups and domestic tourists with their own cars.

➡ Some of Sarawak's homestays are superb (eg in the Kelabit Highlands), while others have rundown facilities, hosts who speak no English, and nothing to do.

ACCOMMODATION PRICE RANGES

The following price ranges refer to a double room with private bathroom, except in some budget places.

	Sabah & Sarawak	Brunei	Kalimantan
$	less than RM100	less than B$60	less than 250,000Rp
$$	RM100–400	B$60–150	250,000–800,000Rp
$$$	more than RM400	more than B$150	more than 800,000Rp

Camping

➡ In many national parks, camping is permitted only near park headquarters.

➡ If you pitch your tent in the vicinity of a longhouse, residents may get the impression you're spurning their hospitality. Some travellers set up their tent on the longhouse's covered verandah.

➡ A two-season tent with mosquito netting is ideal, and a summer-weight sleeping bag or just a bag liner will usually suffice unless you intend to hike at altitude.

Children

➡ Malaysian Borneo and Brunei are great for family travel, especially if the kids like monkeys, flowers, bugs, vibrantly variegated temples, food and fauna. Babies will attract a lot of adoring attention.

➡ Destinations with facilities and activities for children include Kota Kinabalu (KK), Sandakan and Sepilok in Sabah, and Kuching, the Santubong Peninsula, Bako National Park, Semenggoh Nature Reserve and Gunung Mulu National Park in Sarawak.

➡ In Malaysia, children receive discounts for both attractions and public transport. Cots are not widely available in cheaper accommodation. Some top-end places allow two children under 12 to stay with their parents at no extra charge.

➡ In Kalimantan, only Balikpapan has hotels that specially cater to children.

➡ Baby food, formula and nappies (diapers) are widely available, but stock up on such items before heading to remote destinations or islands.

➡ Lonely Planet's *Travel with Children* is packed with useful information.

Customs Regulations

➡ Tourists to Malaysia and Indonesia can bring up to 1L of liquor and 200 cigarettes duty free.

➡ Non-Muslim visitors to Brunei, provided you're 18 or older, are allowed to import 12 cans of beer and two bottles of wine or spirits for personal consumption. There is no longer an allowance for cigarettes, which are taxed at a rate of B$5 per pack of 20 (B$0.25 each).

➡ For travellers coming from Malaysia, Singapore's duty-free liquor allowance is zero. Travellers to Singapore, whatever your port of embarkation, must declare all cigarettes they are carrying.

Electricity

Kalimantan (Indonesia) uses European-style plugs with two round prongs. Sarawak and Sabah (Malaysia) and Brunei use UK-style plugs with three large rectangular pins.

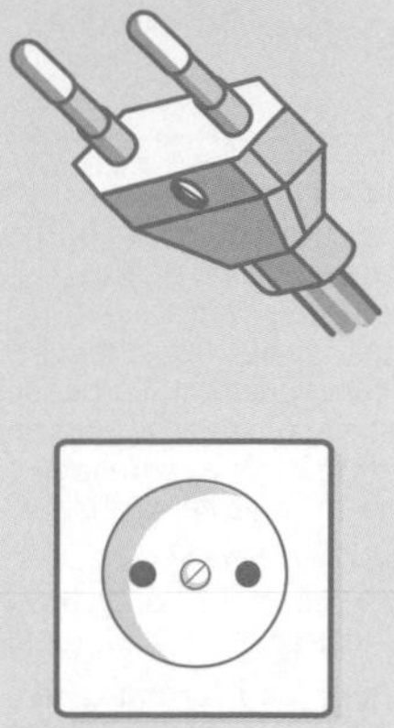

220V/230V/50Hz

240V/50Hz

Embassies & Consulates

Sabah

Australian Consulate (☎088-267151, in KL 03-2146 5555; www.malaysia.embassy.gov.au; Suite 10.1, Level 10, Wisma Great Eastern, 65 Jln Gaya, Kota Kinabalu) Honorary consul; report emergencies to the High Commission in Kuala Lumpur (KL).

Indonesian Consulate (☎088-218 600; Lg Kemajuan, Karamunsing; ⌚9am-5pm Mon-Fri)

UK Consulate (☎088-251775, 24hr in KL 03-2170 2200; www.ukinmalaysia.fco.gov.uk) Honorary consul; contact the High Commission in KL for emergency travel documents. Consul can visit UK citizens who are in hospital or prison.

Sarawak

Australian Consulate (☎082-313388, in KL 03-2146 5555; www.malaysia.embassy.gov.au; E39 Level 2, Taman Sri Sarawak Mall, Jln Tunku Abdul Rahman, Kuching) Honorary consul; report emergencies to the embassy in KL.

Indonesian Consulate (☎082-460734; www.kemlu.go.id; Jln Stutong, Kuching; ⌚visa applications 9am-noon Mon-Fri, visa collections 3-5pm Mon-Fri, closed Malaysian & Indonesian holidays) To get here from Saujana Bus Station (RM2), take City Public Link bus K8 (every 30 to 45 minutes) to 'Jln Song/Friendship Park' or Sarawak Transport Company's buses 8G1, 8G2 or 8G3. A taxi from the centre costs RM25 one way.

Brunei

All embassies and high commissions are in BSB or its suburbs unless otherwise noted.

Australian High Commission (☎222 9435; www.bruneidarussalam.embassy.gov.au; 6th fl, Dar Takaful IBB Utama, Jln Pemancha)

British High Commission (☎222 2231; www.ukinbrunei.fco.gov.uk; Unit 2.01, 2nd fl, Block D, Yayasan Complex, Jln Pretty)

Canadian High Commission (☎222 0043; www.brunei.gc.ca; 5th fl, Jalan McArthur Bldg, 1 Jln McArthur)

Dutch Consulate (☎337 7285/2579; fax 337 4018; Brunei Shell Petroleum, Jln Utara, Panaga, Seria) Honorary consul.

French Embassy (☎222 0960; www.ambafrance-bn.org; 51-55, 3rd fl, Kompleks Jalan Sultan, Jln Sultan)

German Embassy (☎222 5547; www.bandar-seri-begawan.diplo.de; Unit 2.01, 2nd fl, Block A, Yayasan Complex, Jln Pretty)

Indonesian Embassy (☎233 0180; www.kemlu.go.id/bandarseribegawan; Lot 4498, Simpang 528, Jln Muara, Kampung Sungai Hanching)

Malaysian Embassy (☎238 1095/1096/1097; www.kln.gov.my/web/brn_begawan; No 61, Simpang 336, Jln Kebangsaan)

New Zealand Consulate (☎222 5880/2422; www.mfat.govt.nz; c/o Deloitte & Touche, 5th fl, Wisma Hajjah Fatimah, 22-23 Jln Sultan) Honorary consul.

Philippine Embassy (☎224 1465/6; www.philippine-embassybrunei.com; Simpang 336-17, Diplomatic Enclave, Jln Kebangsaan)

Singapore High Commission (☎226 2741; www.mfa.gov.sg/brunei; No 8, Simpang 74, Jln Subok)

US Embassy (☎238 4616; http://brunei.usembassy.gov; Simpang 336-52-16-9, Jln Duta) About 5km northeast of downtown BSB.

Kalimantan

Malaysian Consulate (☎0561-736 061; www.kln.gov.my/web/idn_pontianak; Jln Perdana No 001, Pontianak)

Food

- A splendid array of delicious cuisines are cooked up by Borneo's many ethnic groups.
- During the month of Ramadan, Muslims are forbidden by Sharia law to eat or drink from dawn to sunset. See The Cuisines of Borneo (p285) for more information.

EATING PRICE RANGES

The following price ranges are for a typical meal including starter and soft drink.

	Sabah & Sarawak	Brunei	Kalimantan
$	less than RM15	less than B$6	less than 50,000Rp
$$	RM15–60	B$6–16	50,000–200,000Rp
$$$	more than RM60	more than B$16	more than 200,000Rp

Insurance

- We do not recommend travelling without travel insurance. Before you buy a policy, check the fine print to see if it excludes 'risky' activities such as scuba diving, mountain climbing or caving. If you'd like to do overnight trekking or visit remote areas such as Sabah's Maliau Basin Conservation Area, make sure your plan covers emergency helicopter evacuation.
- Worldwide travel insurance is available at www.lonelyplanet.com/travel-insurance. You can buy, extend and claim online anytime – even if you're already on the road.

Internet Access

- Wi-fi is available at virtually all top-end hotels and at backpackers' guesthouses, at least in the lobby. Midrange places, including Malaysia's Chinese hotels, are a mixed bag, though more and more offer wi-fi.
- Internet cafes (that double as video-game parlours) can still be found in cities and large towns, but they're becoming thin on the ground as smartphones proliferate. Access usually costs US$1 per hour or less.
- Western-style coffee shops and an increasing number of other eateries are wired for wi-fi.
- Areas without internet access of any sort include many of Borneo's offshore islands and huge swaths of the interior.

Legal Matters

- In Malaysia, certain drug crimes carry a 'mandatory death sentence', and when entering Brunei you'll see signs reading 'Warning: Death for drug traffickers under Brunei law'. Indonesia also has harsh penalties for the smuggling or possession of drugs.
- Gambling and the possession of pornography are punishable by severe penalties.
- It is illegal to work without a proper working visa.
- The sale and public consumption of alcohol is forbidden in Brunei.
- Under Indonesian law, you must carry identification at all times.

LGBT Travellers

- Malaysia is a socially conservative society and 'out' behaviour is looked upon disapprovingly; we strongly suggest discretion. Homosexual acts between males are illegal and penalties include corporal punishment and long prison sentences. Homosexual acts between women can also include imprisonment.
- In May 2014 the Sultan of Brunei pushed ahead plans to increase sharia law, progressing from fines for failing to attend Friday prayers to eventually the severing of limbs for theft and robbery, and death by stoning for sodomy and adultery.
- Homosexuality is not illegal in Indonesia, but 'out' behaviour is a very bad idea.

Maps

Small-scale road maps of Borneo, some available from Amazon, are published by several companies:

World Express Mapping Sdn Bhd (www.wems.com.my) Based in Johor Bahru, Peninsular Malaysia. Publishes serviceable 1:900,000-scale maps of Sabah and Sarawak (sold in most bookshops in Malaysian Borneo) that include insets of major cities.

Periplus (www.periplus.com) Publishes 1:1,000,000-scale maps of Sabah and Sarawak that include city and town maps.

Globetrotter (www.newholland-publishers.com) Has a 1:1,300,000-scale map covering both Sabah and Sarawak.

Nelles Verlag (www.nelles-verlag.de) Based in Munich. Produces a 1:500,000-scale map of the entire island entitled *Indonesia: Kalimantan, East Malaysia & Brunei*.

Reise Know-How (www.reise-know-how.de) Publishes a 1:200,000-scale map of the entire island (1st edition 2011).

➡ Getting hold of accurate, up-to-date topographical maps of Borneo is nearly impossible. Brunei doesn't officially release any of its maps to non-Bruneians, and accurate maps of Kalimantan are simply impossible to get.

➡ The most user-friendly map of Brunei is the tourist office's free *Official Map of Brunei Darussalam*.

➡ Google Earth (www.google.com/earth) is a very useful resource, providing a fairly clear overview of river and road networks, particularly along the northern coast. For those planning a trek into the sticks, it offers the best way to check the extent of remaining jungle cover.

➡ OpenStreetMap (www.openstreetmap.org) is also very useful.

➡ The coverage of Borneo by Google Maps (www.maps.google.com) is poor.

Money

Tipping is not practised much in Borneo.

Sabah & Sarawak

➡ Malaysia's currency is the ringgit (RM, for Ringgit Malaysia, or MYR), which is divided into 100 sen. Banknote denominations are RM1, RM5, RM10, RM50 and RM100.

➡ The amount of Malaysian currency you are allowed to bring into or take out of the country is limited to RM1000, a legacy of the 1997 Asian financial crisis. As a result, outside of Malaysia the exchange rates for ringgit are often poor.

➡ ATMs are widely available in cities, towns and big-city airports, but not in rural areas. Some ATMs do not take international cards. Many banks are able to do cash advances at the counter.

➡ Credit cards can be used at upscale hotels and restaurants, though some places may only take cards with embedded SIM chips.

➡ Banknotes in US, Australian and Singapore dollars and pounds sterling are the easiest to exchange. Moneychangers, some of which also take other currencies, can be found in cities and large towns, and even smaller towns often have a shop that will change foreign currency. Some banks may not handle exchange transactions at all.

Brunei

➡ The Brunei dollar (B$) is available in denominations of B$1, B$5, B$10, B$50, B$100, B$500 and B$1000 and, believe it or not, B$10,000. Thanks to the 1967 Currency Interchangeability Agreement between Brunei and Singapore, the two countries' dollars are worth exactly the same and can be used freely in both countries. Singaporean banknotes (with the possible exception of S$2, which has no Bruneian counterpart) are universally accepted in Brunei, and Brunei banknotes can be used almost everywhere in Singapore. To celebrate the pact's 40th anniversary, a commemorative B$20/S$20 note was issued in 2007.

➡ For currency exchange, moneychangers are generally a better bet than banks, though some places in BSB have a pretty hefty spread between their buy and sell rates.

➡ ATMs are widely available, though not all take international credit/debit cards.

➡ Major credit cards are widely accepted.

Kalimantan

➡ Indonesia's currency is the rupiah (Rp). Banknotes come in denominations of 1000Rp, 2000Rp, 5000Rp, 10,000Rp, 20,000Rp, 50,000Rp and 100,000Rp (sounds like a lot, but it's worth just US$7). Coins you may see include 50Rp, 100Rp, 200Rp, 500Rp and 1000Rp; newer ones are lightweight aluminium, older ones are either bronze-coloured or bi-metal.

➡ ATMs can be found in most urban areas (even in tiny towns), but are not available in the Upper Mahakam and the Derawan Archipelago.

➡ All major cities have exchange bureaux and/or banks that handle foreign currency.

➡ In general, credit cards are accepted at midrange and top-end hotels, as well as at the most fancy restaurants.

Opening Hours

➡ Opening hours for eateries vary widely. Many proper restaurants open from around 11.30am to 10pm or so. *Kopitiam* and *kedai kopi* (Borneo's ubiquitous 'coffee shops'; ie no-frills restaurants) that cater to the breakfast crowd open very early – well before dawn – but may close in the mid-afternoon or even before lunch.

➡ Bars usually open around dinner time and close at 2am.

➡ Bank hours are generally 10am to 3pm or 4pm on weekdays and 9.30am to 11.30am on Saturday.

➡ Shop hours are variable, although small shops are generally open Monday to Saturday from 9am to 6pm. Major department stores, shopping malls, Chinese emporiums and some large stores are open from around 10am until 9pm or 10pm seven days a week.

➡ Government offices are usually open Monday to Friday from 8am to 4.15pm, and on Saturday from 8am to 12.45pm. Most close for lunch from 12.45pm to 2pm; in Sarawak, the

Friday lunch break is from 12.15pm to 2.45pm to accommodate Muslim prayers at the mosque. In Brunei, Friday prayers are obligatory for Muslims and no business transactions can be conducted between 12pm and 2pm on Fridays (all restaurants, parks, malls etc are closed to remove all possible distractions). Therefore, everything is closed by law between 12pm and 2pm on Fridays.

➡ During Ramadan, business and office hours are often shortened and Muslim-owned restaurants may close during daylight hours. In Brunei, many offices end the day at 2pm from Monday to Thursday and at 11.30am on Friday and Saturday.

Public Holidays

The dates of Muslim, Buddhist and Hindu holidays, as well as some Christian festivals, follow lunar or lunisolar calendars and so vary relative to the Gregorian (Western) calendar. Muslim holidays fall 11 or 12 days earlier each year; their final dates are determined by the sighting of the moon and therefore may vary slightly relative to the dates below. The dates we give for some other religious holidays are also approximate. Many religious celebrations begin the night before the dates that appear in this section.

For details on public and religious holidays (as well as cultural events), see the events calendars posted by Sabah Tourism (www.sabahtourism.com), Sarawak Ministry of Tourism (www.mot.sarawak.gov.my) and Brunei Tourism (www.tourismbrunei.com).

Sabah & Sarawak

New Year's Day 1 January

Lunar New Year 28 January 2017, 16 February 2018, 5 February 2019

Federal Territory Day (Pulau Labuan only) 1 February

Good Friday 14 April 2017, 30 March 2018, 19 April 2019

Labour Day 1 May

Wesak Day (Buddha's Birthday) 10 May 2017, 29 May 2018, 19 May 2019

Harvest Festival (Sabah only) 30 and 31 May

Gawai Dayak (Sarawak only) evening of 31 May to 2 June

Birthday of Yang di-Pertuan Agong 1st Saturday in June

Hari Raya Puasa (Eid al-Fitr) End of Ramadan; 25 June 2017, 14 June 2018, 4 June 2019

Independence Day 31 August

Hari Raya Aidiladha (Eid al-Adha) 12 September 2016, 2 September 2017, 22 August 2018

Sarawak Head of State's Birthday (Sarawak only) 8 September

Malaysia Day 16th September

Awal Muharram (Muslim New Year) 2 October 2016, 22 September 2017, 12 September 2018

Sabah Head of State's Birthday (Sabah only) 1st Saturday in October

Malaysia Day 23 October

Deepavali (not in Sarawak or Pulau Labuan) 29 October 2016, 19 October 2017, 7 November 2018

Maulidur Rasul (Prophet's Birthday) 12 December 2016, 1 December 2017, 21 November 2018

Christmas Day 25 December

Brunei

New Year's Day 1 January

Lunar New Year 28 January 2017, 16 February 2018, 5 February 2019

Brunei National Day 23 February

Israk Mikraj (Prophet's Ascension) 24 April 2017, 13 April 2018, 3 April 2019

First Day of Ramadan 27 May 2017, 16 May 2018, 6 May 2019

Royal Brunei Armed Forces Day 31 May

Gawai Dayak (Ibans only) Evening of 31 May to 2 June

PRACTICALITIES

Media Almost all of Malaysia's print media are owned or controlled by pro-government factions so they're not the place to look for explosive exposés.

Newspapers There are two English-language newspapers published in Borneo: *Borneo Post* (RM1; www.theborneopost.com), based in Kuching, is the main English-language daily in Sabah and Sarawak; and *New Sarawak Tribune* (RM1; http://tribune.my). Also available in Malaysian Borneo is the Kuala Lumpur–based *New Straits Times* (RM1.80; www.nst.com.my). In Brunei, the *Borneo Bulletin* (B$0.80; www.borneobulletin.com.bn) steers clear of hard-hitting investigative reporting.

Smoking Brunei's tough anti-smoking laws ban puffing not only inside shops and malls, but also in outdoor markets and around food stalls. At the time of writing, a new tobacco bill was being drafted in Malaysia to raise the age for purchasing tobacco products, from 18 to 21.

TV Top-end hotels usually have satellite-TV relays of CNN, BBC, Star and other English-language stations.

Weights and Measures The metric system is used across Borneo.

Nuzul Quraan (Koran Revelation Day) 12 June 2017

Hari Raya Aidil Fitri End of Ramadan; three-day holiday begins 25 June 2017, 14 June 2018, 4 June 2019

Sultan of Brunei's Birthday 15 July

Hari Raya Aidil Adha 11 September 2016, 1 September 2017, 21 August 2018

Islamic New Year 2 October 2016, 21 September 2017

Maulidur Rasul (Prophet's Birthday) 12 December 2016, 1 December 2017, 21 November 2018

Christmas Day 25 December

Kalimantan

Tahun Baru Masehi (New Year's Day) 1 January

Tahun Baru Imlek (Lunar New Year) 28 January 2017, 16 February 2018, 5 February 2019

Hari Raya Nyepi (Balinese Day of Silence) 28 March 2017, 17 March 2018, 7 March 2019

Wafat Yesus Kristus (Good Friday) 14 April 2017, 30 March 2018, 19 April 2019

Isra' Mi'raj Nabi Muhammed (Prophet's Ascension) 24 April 2017, 13 Apr 2018, 3 April 2019

Waisak (Buddha's Birthday) 10 May 2017, 22 May 2018, 12 May 2019

Kenaikan Yesus Kristus (Ascension of Jesus Christ) 25 May 2017, 10 May 2018, 30 May 2019

Idul Fitri End of Ramadan; 26 June 2017, 14 June 2018, 4 June 2019

Hari Proklamasi Kemerdekaan (Independence Day) 17 August

Idul Adha 12 September 2016, 2 September 2017, 22 August 2018

Tahun Baru Hijriyah (Islamic New Year) 2 October 2016, 21 September 2017, 11 September 2018

Maulid Nabi Muhammed (Prophet's Birthday) 12 December 2016, 1 December 2017, 21 November 2018

Hari Natal (Christmas Day) 25 December

Safe Travel

➡ The Australian government (www.smartraveller.gov.au) warns travellers of a 'high threat of kidnapping by terrorists and criminals' in 'the islands, dive sites and coastal areas of eastern Sabah', including Sipadan, Mataking and Pandanan. Concern about the area is ongoing as of 2015. The 6pm curfew endures – for travellers to be off the beach and in their resorts – following an incident in 2014 when a police officer was killed and another kidnapped on Mabul.

➡ Borneo is generally very safe for travellers of both sexes, but in villages and logging camps things can get dodgy when alcohol enters the picture.

➡ Saltwater crocodiles are a very real danger in waterways, especially in muddy estuaries. Exercise caution when swimming in rivers, and never swim near river mouths.

➡ In Kalimantan, transport standards on land, water and air are dodgy, with roads and bridges frequently washed out; many drivers, particularly scooters, are a menace to themselves and other road users.

➡ The Indonesian part of the island isn't anywhere near as dangerous as many Malaysians think, but keep your wits about you, especially in the cities.

GOVERNMENT TRAVEL ADVICE

The following government websites offer travel advisories and information on current hot spots:

Australian Department of Foreign Affairs (www.smartraveller.gov.au)

British Foreign Office (www.fco.gov.uk)

Canadian Department of Foreign Affairs (www.dfait-maeci.gc.ca)

US State Department (www.travel.state.gov)

Telephone

Cheap prepaid SIM cards make it easy and remarkably inexpensive to keep in touch, both with local contacts, and family and friends around the world. If you bring your own gadget, make sure it can handle 900/1800MHz and is not locked. In Borneo, the cheapest Nokia mobile phones start at about US$40.

Sabah & Sarawak

MOBILE PHONES

Sabah and Sarawak have three networks on which various companies buy air time: Celcom (www.celcom.com.my); DiGi (www.digi.com.my); and Hotlink (www.hotlink.com.my).

Celcom generally has the best coverage, making it possible to phone home from places such as Bario (in the Kelabit Highlands) and the slopes of Mt Kinabalu. A prepaid SIM card, available at shops and kiosks in all but the tiniest villages (as well as at Miri airport and on the Departure level of Kuching airport), costs just RM8.50, the equivalent of a minute or two of international roaming charges. It takes about 10 minutes to activate; you'll have to show your passport. Recharge cardlets come in denominations ranging from RM5 to RM50. Calls cost just pennies per minute whether they're local or to landline phones around the world (calling mobile phones usually costs a bit more).

The best way to pay for 3G internet access, available mainly in the cities, is per day (Celcom charges RM5 for 500MB) or per week (RM18 for 1GB). Without a plan, you'll be charged a whopping RM10 per MB!

PHONE CODES

- Malaysia's country code is ☎60. When calling Malaysia from overseas, dial the international access code followed by ☎60, then the area code or mobile-phone access code (minus the initial zero) and the local number (six to eight digits).
- Within Malaysia, the access code for making international calls is ☎00.

Brunei

MOBILE PHONES

Bruneian prepaid SIM cards cost B$30 (including B$5 of credit) and must be registered within a week of activation (after that the number will be blocked). The cheapest and easiest way to buy one is to go to the office of DST Communications (www.dst-group.com) in central BSB; bring your passport. Various shops also sell DST 'Easi' SIM cards, but they often charge a premium and neglect to handle registration. Local calls cost B$0.05 to B$0.30 a minute, depending on the time of day. For international calls, using the access code ☎095 ('IDD 095') is cheaper than ☎00; calls to Australia, the UK and the USA cost B$0.30 to B$0.50 a minute.

The sultanate's other mobile-phone service provider, B-Mobile (www.bmobile.com.bn) sells SIM-card starter packs for B$30.

If you have a Malaysian SIM card, it will not work in Brunei unless you pay astronomical roaming charges – or climb to the top of Ulu Temburong National Park's canopy walk for line-of-sight microwave reception.

PHONE CODES

- Brunei's country code is ☎673. There are no area codes.
- Within Brunei, the access code for making international calls is ☎00.

Kalimantan

MOBILE PHONES

Prepaid SIM cards can be bought anywhere for about 15,000Rp and can be activated on the spot by the shop owner. Telkomsel (www.telkomsel.com) SIM cards have the best coverage and faster data speeds in the cities. In more remote areas, Indosat (www.indosat.com) may have better coverage.

Calls, SMS and data all deduct from your 'pulsa', which can be topped up anywhere phone cards are sold. Many Indonesians carry two phones, and will commonly reply to you on a different number if it will use less pulsa. All major companies offer cheap international calling using special codes. For Telkomsel dial ☎01017 plus the number, for Indosat dial ☎01016 plus the number.

3G Internet, available in most major towns, has killed off the internet cafe. Purchasing a prepaid packet (around 100,000Rp for 3GB for one month) is cheaper than using your pulsa directly.

PHONE CODES

- Indonesia's country code is ☎62. When calling Indonesia from overseas, dial the international access code followed by ☎62, then the area code (minus the first zero) and local number.
- Within Indonesia, the access code for making international calls is ☎001.

Time

- Sabah, Sarawak and Brunei are all eight hours ahead of Greenwich Mean Time (GMT/UTC+8). They do not observe daylight-saving time.
- Kalimantan is divided into two time zones: Indonesian Western Standard Time (UTC+7), which is observed in West and Central Kalimantan; and Indonesian Central Standard Time (UTC+8), which is observed in East, North and South Kalimantan.

Toilets

- You'll find a lot of squat-style toilets in Borneo, particularly in public bathrooms.
- Western-style seated toilets are the norm in hotels and guesthouses. You may be expected to flush using water from a plastic bucket.
- Toilet paper is often unavailable in public toilets, so keep a stash handy. In urban areas you can usually discard used toilet paper into the bowl without causing clogging, but if there is a wastepaper basket – as there often is in rural toilets – it's meant to be used.

Tourist Information

The best sources of information are often guesthouse owners, guides, tour agencies and, of course, fellow travellers.

Sabah & Sarawak

- The two state tourism authorities, the Sabah Tourism Board (www.sabahtourism.com) and Sarawak Tourism Board (www.sarawaktourism.com), have excellent websites with details on festivals, all major sights plus admission times, and events.

- Tourist information offices in larger cities generally have helpful staff and entire walls filled with up-to-date information.
- Sabah's national parks are run by Sabah Parks (www.sabahparks.org), which has an information office in KK.
- Sarawak's national parks are run by Sarawak Forestry (www.sarawakforestry.com), which has an especially informative website, publishes useful park brochures (RM1.50), and runs very helpful offices in Kuching and Miri. Staff even answer the phone! Accommodation at certain national parks can be booked at its offices, through its website or via http://ebooking.com.my.

Brunei

- Brunei Tourism (www.tourismbrunei.com) has a very useful – though not necessarily up-to-the-minute – website.
- KH Soon Resthouse in BSB can supply information on land transport to Miri (Sarawak) and Sabah.

Kalimantan

- The newly revamped Ministry of Tourism website (www.indonesia.travel) has an eclectic collection of travel tidbits.

Travellers with Disabilities

- Borneo has a long way to go in this regard. Most buildings, tourist destinations and public transport in Borneo are not wheelchair accessible, however Sepilok in Sabah is wheelchair-friendly.
- Navigating Malaysian Borneo's city centres in a wheelchair can be tricky due to high kerbs and footpaths of varying heights.
- Most tour companies offering trips to the interior do not accommodate people with physical disabilities.

Visas

Make sure your passport is valid for at least six months beyond your date of entry and, if you'll be travelling overland through Brunei, that you have enough pages for lots of entry stamps (no fewer than 10 if you travel by road from Sabah to Sarawak!).

SABAH & SARAWAK PASSPORT STAMPS

Under the terms of Sabah and Sarawak's entry into Malaysia, both states retain a certain degree of state-level control of their borders. Malaysian citizens from Peninsular Malaysia (West Malaysia) cannot work legally in Malaysian Borneo (East Malaysia) without special permits, and tourists travelling within Malaysia must go through passport control and have their passports stamped whenever they:

- Arrive in Sabah or Sarawak from Peninsular Malaysia or the federal district of Pulau Labuan;
- Exit Sabah or Sarawak on their way to Peninsular Malaysia or Pulau Labuan;
- Travel between Sabah and Sarawak.

Note: When you enter Sabah or Sarawak from another part of Malaysia, your new visa stamp will be valid only for the remainder of the period left on your original Malaysian visa.

Sabah & Sarawak

- Visas valid for three months are issued upon arrival to citizens of the US, Canada, Western Europe (except Greece, Monaco and Portugal, whose nationals get one month), Japan, South Korea and most Commonwealth countries.
- One-month visas are issued on arrival to citizens of Singapore, most countries in Latin America and most countries in the former Soviet Union.
- Israeli passport holders are issued Malaysian visas only in exceptional circumstances.
- For complete information on visa types, who needs them and how to get them, see the website of Malaysia's Ministry of Foreign Affairs (www.kln.gov.my) – under 'Quick Info' (at the bottom of the page), click 'Visa Information'.

VISA EXTENSIONS

- Malaysian visas can be extended in the Sarawak towns of Kuching, Bintulu, Kapit, Lawas, Limbang, Miri and Sibu; and in the Sabah towns of KK, Keningau, Kudat, Lahad Datu, Sandakan, Semporna, Sipitang, Tawau and Tenom.
- In general, Malaysian visas can be extended for 60 days. Bring your departure ticket and be ready to explain why you would like to stay longer and where you'll be staying; a photo is not required. Approval is usually given on the same day.
- Extensions take effect on the day they're issued, so the best time to extend a visa is right before the old one expires. If your visa still has a month of validity left, that time will not be added to the period covered by the extension.
- Some travellers report they've been able to extend their Malaysian visas by going through Malaysian

border control at the Brunei border and then, without officially entering Brunei, turning around and re-entering Malaysia. Others do visa runs by crossing from Sarawak into Indonesia at Tebedu–Entikong.

➡ Overstaying your visa by a few days is not usually a big deal, especially if you're a genuine tourist and have no prior offences. However, at the discretion of immigration officers, any violation of Malaysia's visa rules can result in your being turned over to the Immigration Department's enforcement section and, if you're in Sarawak, taken to Serian, 60km southeast of Kuching, for questioning.

Brunei

➡ When it comes to getting into Brunei, Americans and travellers from the European Union, Switzerland and Norway get a free 90-day visa on arrival, while visitors from New Zealand, Singapore, Malaysia and a few other countries score 30 days at the border. Canadians and Japanese get 14 days. Israelis are not permitted to enter the country.

➡ Australians don't need to apply for a visa in advance, but do have to pay B$5 (payable only in Brunei or Singapore dollars) for a three-day transit visa (you need to show a ticket out), B$20 for a single-entry visa valid for two weeks, or B$30 for a multiple-entry visa valid for a month (this is the one to get if you'll be going overland between Sarawak and Sabah).

➡ People of most other nationalities must obtain a visa (single/multiple entry B$20/30) in advance from a Brunei Darussalam diplomatic mission – unless, that is, they'll just be transiting through Brunei (defined as arriving from one country and continuing on to a different country), in which case a 72-hour visa is available upon arrival.

➡ For more information, see the website of the Immigration Department (www.immigration.gov.bn/visiting.htm).

Kalimantan

➡ Tourists from 34 countries – including Australia, Canada, the EU, India, Japan, New Zealand, South Africa and the US – can receive a 30-day Indonesian visa on arrival (VOA) at three entry points to Kalimantan: the Tebedu–Entikong land crossing, between Kuching (Sarawak) and Pontianak (West Kalimantan); Balikpapan (Sepinggan Airport); and Pontianak (Supadio Airport).

➡ The cost is US$35, payable in US dollars (at the Tebedu–Entikong crossing, at least, ringgit and rupiah may not be accepted). Once in the country, a VOA can be extended by another 30 days for US$35.

➡ If you arrive in Kalimantan – by land, sea or air – from outside Indonesia at any other entry point, or if your passport is not from one of the designated VOA countries, you must obtain a visa in advance. You might also want to apply for a visa ahead of time if you know you'll be staying in Kalimantan for longer than 30 days.

➡ In Sabah, Indonesia has consulates in KK and Tawau, and in Sarawak there's a consulate in Kuching. A 60-day visa costs RM170; bring a photo, your ticket out of Indonesia, and a credit card or cash to show that you've got funds. Visas are generally issued the same day.

➡ For a full list of the countries whose nationals score a VOA and details on the entry points at which they are issued, see www.embassyofindonesia.org/consular/voa.htm.

Volunteering

Lonely Planet does not endorse any organisations that we do not work with directly. See Responsible Travel (p300) for more information.

Women Travellers

➡ Borneo is a relatively easy and pleasant place for women travellers. Things are considerably more laid-back and liberal in Borneo, including Kalimantan, than, say, in northeastern Peninsular Malaysia or Java. Brunei is more conservative than Sabah or Sarawak.

➡ Although many local women (especially ethnic Chinese) wear shorts and tank tops in the cities, it's a good idea to dress fairly conservatively in Muslim areas and to cover up when visiting a mosque (robes and headscarves are sometimes provided).

➡ As with anywhere else, use common sense and caution. Do not get lulled into a false sense of security just because everyone seems so easygoing. Take great care walking alone anywhere at night.

Transport

GETTING THERE & AWAY

Entering Borneo

Most travellers arrive in Borneo by air, often from Singapore, Kuala Lumpur (KL) or Jakarta. Kalimantan has ferry links to Java and Sulawesi, and there are also ferries between Sabah and the southern Philippines. The main requirements for entry are a passport that's valid for travel for at least six months, proof of an onward ticket and adequate funds for your stay, although you will rarely be asked to prove this.

Flights and tours can be booked online at lonelyplanet.com/bookings.

Air

Airports & Airlines

There are a number of major airports in Borneo, including Kota Kinabalu International Airport (Sabah) and Kuching International Airport (Sarawak) in Malaysian Borneo; Brunei International Airport in Brunei; and Sultan Aji Muhammad Sulaiman Airport (Balikpapan) and Syamsudin Noor Airport (Banjarmasin) in Indonesian Borneo.

SABAH

Air Asia (www.airasia.com) Kota Kinabalu (KK) to Peninsular Malaysia (KL, Johor Bahru and Penang), Singapore, Jakarta, Clark (Philippines), Taipei, Shenzhen and Hong Kong; Sandakan to KL; Tawau to KL; and Pulau Labuan to KL.

Malaysia Airlines (www.malaysiaairlines.com) KK to KL, Hong Kong, Tapei, Osaka and Perth.

Silk Air (www.silkair.com) KK to Singapore.

SARAWAK

Air Asia (www.airasia.com) Kuching to Singapore, KL, Johor Bahru and Penang; Miri to Singapore, KL and Johor Bahru; Sibu to KL and Johor Bahru; Bintulu to KL.

Malaysia Airlines (www.malaysiaairlines.com.my) Kuching to KL and Singapore.

Silk Air (www.silkair.com) Kuching to Singapore.

BRUNEI

Air Asia (www.airasia.com) Bandar Seri Begawan (BSB) to KL.

Cebu Pacific Air (www.cebupacificair.com) BSB to Manila.

Royal Brunei Airlines (www.flyroyalbrunei.com) BSB to London, Dubai, Hong Kong, Shanghai, Bangkok, Manila, Melbourne, Singapore, Surabaya, Jakarta and KL. Offers reasonably priced long-haul flights with a stopover in BSB. Flights are alcohol free.

Singapore Airlines (www.singaporeair.com) BSB to Singapore.

KALIMANTAN

Flying to and around Kalimantan is much safer than a few years ago.

Air Asia (www.airasia.com) Balikpapan to KL.

Citilink (www.citilink.co.id) Balikpapan to Denpasar,

CLIMATE CHANGE & TRAVEL

Every form of transport that relies on carbon-based fuel generates CO_2, the main cause of human-induced climate change. Modern travel is dependent on aeroplanes, which might use less fuel per kilometre per person than most cars but travel much greater distances. The altitude at which aircraft emit gases (including CO_2) and particles also contributes to their climate change impact. Many websites offer 'carbon calculators' that allow people to estimate the carbon emissions generated by their journey and, for those who wish to do so, to offset the impact of the greenhouse gases emitted with contributions to portfolios of climate-friendly initiatives throughout the world. Lonely Planet offsets the carbon footprint of all staff and author travel.

Jakarta, Makassar, Surabaya and Yogyakarta.

Garuda (www.garuda-indonesia.com) Balikpapan to Jakarta, Jogjakarta, Makassar and Surabaya; Banjarmasin to Jakarta, Jogjakarta, Surabaya; Pontianak to Jakarta.

Kalstar (www.kalstaronline.com) Pontianak to Bandung, Denpasar, Semarang and Surabaya.

Lion Air (www.lionair.co.id) Balikpapan to Jakarta, Makassar, Semarang and Yogyakarta; Banjarmasin to Jakarta and Jogjakarta; Pontianak to Batam and Jakarta.

MASwings (www.maswings.com.my) Tarakan to Tewau; Pontianak to Kuching.

Silk Air (www.silkair.com) Balikpapan to Singapore.

Sriwijaya Air (www.sriwijayaair.co.id) Expanding airline with routes to Malaysia, Singapore and Timor-Leste.

Sea

Sabah

Ferries link Sandakan with Zamboanga, on the Philippine island of Mindanao, twice a week.

Kalimantan

Ferries run by Pelni (www.pelni.co.id), Dharma Lautan (www.dluonline.co.id) and **Prima Vista** (☎0542-428888; Jl Sudirman 138) connect Balikpapan, Samarinda, Banjarmasin and Pontianak with Java (Jakarta, Semarang and Surabaya) and Sulawesi (Makassar, Pare Pare and others).

GETTING AROUND

Air

Airlines in Borneo

Borneo is well catered for by very reasonable flights. Air travel is the only practical way to reach some destinations, such as Sarawak's Kelabit Highlands and Gunung Mulu National Park.

Tickets for most flights can be purchased online.

SABAH & SARAWAK

Air Asia (www.airasia.com) Kuching to Sibu, Bintulu, Miri and KK; KK to Tawau, Sandakan, Miri and Kuching.

Malaysia Airlines (www.malaysiaairlines.com) Kuching to KK, Sibu and Bintulu; KK to Tawau, Labuan and Bintulu.

MASwings (www.maswings.com.my) Serves two dozen destinations in Sabah (including Sandakan, Lahad Datu and Tawau), Sarawak (including Lawas, Limbang, Bario, Miri, Gunung Mulu National Park, Bintulu and Sibu) and Brunei, plus handles Kuching to Pontianak. Has hubs in KK, Kuching and Miri. Member of Star Alliance. ATRs and Twin Otters board from the tail, so the most accessible seats are at the back of the plane.

BRUNEI

MASwings (www.maswings.com.my) BSB to KK and Kuching.

KALIMANTAN

Kalimantan has a comprehensive network of air links.

Kalstar (www.kalstaronline.com) Intra-Kalimantan connections.

Trigana Air (www.trigana-air.com) Operates primarily in West, Central and South Kalimantan.

Bicycle

Road and all-terrain cycling have recently taken off around Kuching, while organised mountain-bike treks are increasingly popular in Sabah. If riding independently, take extreme caution with traffic, remember to bring a helmet, a reflective vest, high-power lights and a wealth of inner tubes and spare parts.

Boat

Rivers still play a major transport role, and in some trackless areas – such as Sarawak's Batang Rejang and parts of Kalimantan – they're the only ride in town.

On wider rivers, 'flying coffins' – long, narrow express boats with about 70 seats – are the norm. Way upstream, the only craft that can make headway against the rapids are motorised wooden longboats.

Rates for water travel are often quite high, the crucial factor being the cost of petrol. Chartering a boat costs much more than taking a water taxi.

Sabah

Nature sites accessible by boat include Tunku Abdul Rahman National Park, the Semporna Archipelago and Pulau Tiga National Park.

In the west, sea ferries link Menumbok with Muara in Brunei; KK with Pulau Labuan; and Pulau Labuan with Muara. In Sabah's southeast corner, speedboats link Tawau with Tarakan and Nunukan in Kalimantan.

Sarawak

Sarawak's Batang Rejang is sometimes called the 'Amazon of Borneo' and a journey upriver is still very romantic, despite the lack of intact forest en route.

Along the coast, speedboats link Limbang with Pulau Labuan. In western Sarawak, motorboats are the only way to get to Bako, Tanjung Datu and Talang-Satang National Parks.

Brunei

Speedboats link BSB with Bangar (in Brunei's Temburong District), and car ferries go from the Serasa Ferry Terminal in Muara, 25km northeast of BSB, to Pulau Labuan and the Sabah port of Menumbok. The only way to get to Ulu Temburong National Park is by longboat.

Kalimantan

The ferry from Tawau (Sabah) to Tarakan (North Kalimantan) runs three times per week. Otherwise take the regular speedboat services from Tawau to Tarakan via

Border Crossings

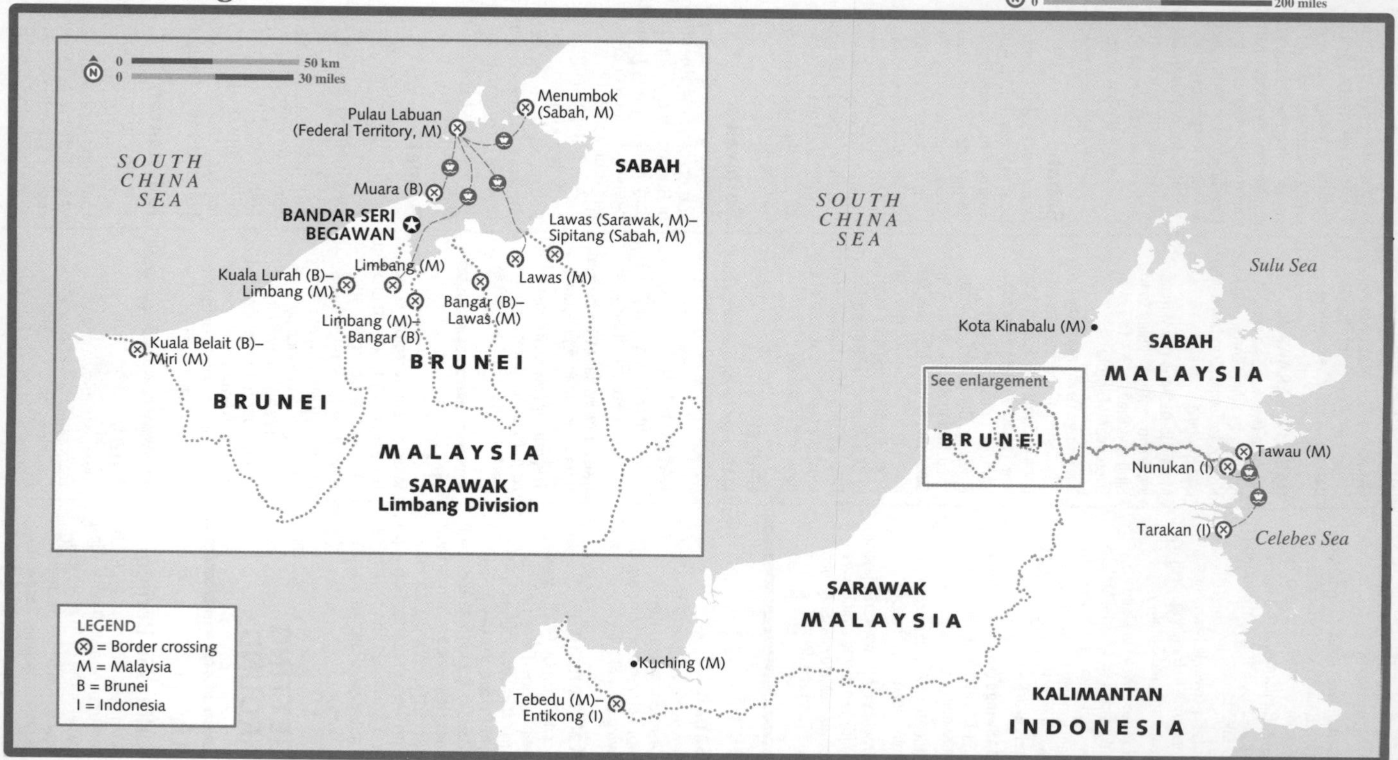
0 400 km
0 200 miles
0 50 km
0 30 miles
SOUTH CHINA SEA
Pulau Labuan (Federal Territory, M)
Menumbok (Sabah, M)
SABAH
Muara (B)
BANDAR SERI BEGAWAN
Lawas (Sarawak, M)–Sipitang (Sabah, M)
Limbang (M)
Kuala Lurah (B)–Limbang (M)
Lawas (M)
Bangar (B)–Lawas (M)
Limbang (M)–Bangar (B)
Kuala Belait (B)–Miri (M)
BRUNEI
BRUNEI
MALAYSIA
SARAWAK
Limbang Division
SOUTH CHINA SEA
Sulu Sea
Kota Kinabalu (M)
SABAH
MALAYSIA
See enlargement
BRUNEI
Tawau (M)
Nunukan (I)
Tarakan (I)
Celebes Sea
SARAWAK
MALAYSIA
Kuching (M)
Tebedu (M)–Entikong (I)
KALIMANTAN
INDONESIA
LEGEND
⊗ = Border crossing
M = Malaysia
B = Brunei
I = Indonesia

Nunukan. A visa-on-arrival is available if you're entering Sabah, but not if you're travelling in the other direction, ie into Kalimantan.

To get around Kalimantan, the only scheduled public boats are found on the Sungai Mahakam (Mahakam River), which go as far as Long Bagun if the water is high enough, otherwise they stop at Tering. For other rivers, it's necessary to charter, or else wait for a local boat to fill up.

Bus, Van & Taxi

Malaysian Borneo's coastal cities are connected by a network of cheap, comfortable buses.

Intercity buses generally depart from a long-distance bus terminal on the outskirts of town, linked to the city centre by bus and taxi. For many destinations, departures are most frequent in the mornings, but on some routes (eg Miri to Kuching) there are also afternoon and overnight buses.

Sabah

An arc of excellent paved roads extends from KK southeast to Tawau, passing Mt Kinabalu, Sepilok, Sandakan, Lahad Datu and Semporna (gateway to Sipadan) along the way. Large buses ply this route on a daily basis, as do minivans, share taxis and jeeps. Getting from KK to any towns north, all the way to Kudat, and southwest to the Brunei border, is easy. The same applies if going from Sandakan to any towns south to Tawau, but take your journey before 5pm.

The southern road connecting Tawau to Sapulot is now paved, with a bus journey from KK to Tawau taking only six hours. Getting to very remote villages by public transport is tougher – in these situations you need to hope share taxis and jeeps have enough passengers. These vehicles typically leave very early in the morning.

Sarawak

Frequent buses run by a clutch of companies ply the Pan Borneo Hwy from Kuching to Miri, stopping along the way in Sibu and Bintulu, near Niah National Park, and at Lambir Hills National Park. From Miri, several buses a day head via Brunei to Sabah.

Long-haul buses link Sarawak's coastal cities, including Kuching, with Pontianak (West Kalimantan) via the Tebedu–Entikong border crossing.

Bus service from Kuching to destinations in Western Sarawak is very limited or non-existent, except to Lundu, Kubah National Park, Matang Wildlife Centre, Bako Bazaar (near Bako National Park) and Semenggoh Nature Reserve. For some destinations, the only transport options are hiring a car or taxi or joining a tour group.

Brunei

Only one company, known as Jesselton Express (for services heading from BSB towards KK) and PHLS (for services from BSB towards Miri), is allowed to pick up and drop off passengers inside the sultanate. Two buses a day go from BSB southwest to Miri (via Seria and Kuala Belait) and northeast to KK (via Limbang, Lawas and various destinations in Sabah).

Kalimantan

Buses and Kijang (4WD minivans that ply intercity routes) are a mixed affair, ranging from comfy to purgatorial. The same can also be said of Kalimantan's highways and minor roads, which vary from silk-smooth asphalt to a muddy, potholed pumpkin soup during the wet season, when you may have to disembark and push. VIP-style buses with air-con operate between Balikpapan and Samarinda, and from Samarinda to Banjarmasin and Bontang. The rest of the country involves patchy roads, inhumanly quick drivers and, often, overcrowding on woefully smoky, dilapidated buses. Bring with you patience, an inflatable neck cushion, an iPod and anything else to ease the journey.

The only official land crossing between Kalimantan and Malaysian Borneo serviced by long-haul buses is at Tebedu–Entikong, in western Sarawak between Kuching and Pontianak. Long-haul buses link Pontianak with Kuching, the cities of Sarawak's central coast and Brunei.

Car & Motorcycle

Driving is on the left in all three countries that share Borneo. The (generally) nicely paved Pan Borneo Hwy runs all along Borneo's northern coast, from Sematan in Sarawak's far west via Brunei (and its many border crossings) to Tawau in the southeast corner of Sabah. Kalimantan's road network is limited, with lots of sections yet to be paved and frequent washouts and flash floods; however, it is now possible to travel around Kalimantan from Pontianak to Berau on mostly paved road, with plans to connect through to Tawau.

Road signage is often haphazard, with many junctions – including T-junctions – lacking any indication of where to go.

Car Rental

Driving a rental car gives you maximum flexibility, but can involve major hassles – in Borneo, these are likely to include poor or non-existent road signage, a dearth of proper road maps, dilapidated vehicles, and small rental companies that may try to foist repair charges onto you. In Kalimantan you may have trouble asking for directions unless you speak Bahasa Indonesia. On the brighter side, in Malaysia petrol costs only about US$0.60 per litre (US$2.30 per US gallon).

Car-hire companies have desks in the arrivals halls of larger airports; in city centres, hotels and guesthouses can help find an agency. We've heard reports that small local companies sometimes try to rent out 10-year-old cars with bald tyres and leaky boots (trunks). Before you sign anything or hand over any cash, check over your vehicle very carefully (eg for seatbelts in back), especially if it's an older Malaysian-made model such as a tiny Perodua Kancil or Proton Wira.

In Sabah and Sarawak, prices for a very used 660cc Kancil start at an absolute minimum of RM90/500 per day/week at the cheapest outfits; a Perodua Viva or Proton Saga will cost a bit more. Renting a Hyundai Matrix through an international company such as Hertz (www.hertz.com) costs about double that, but your vehicle is likely to be newer, safer and better maintained. As always, verify the insurance excess/deductible, the default of which may be RM2000 or more; reducing this to RM500 can cost as little as RM15 a day.

In Brunei, prices start at about B$80 a day. In Kalimantan – where available – at about 1,500,000Rp per day.

With some Malaysian companies you can visit Brunei for no extra charge, while others charge a fee of RM50 or RM100. Renting a car in one city and returning it in another can be expensive – count on paying RM500 extra to pick up a vehicle in Miri and drop it off in Kuching. Some insurance plans are only valid in a limited geographical area.

A valid overseas licence is needed to rent a car. An International Driving Permit (a translation of your licence and its provisions) is usually not required by local car-hire companies, but it's recommended that you bring one. Minimum age limits (generally 23, sometimes 21) often apply, and some companies won't rent to anyone over 60 or 65.

Taxi Hire

For travel to places within a 50km or 70km radius of where you're staying, hiring a taxi on a per-trip, half-day or per-day basis is often a good option, especially for three or four people. For day trips from public-transport-challenged Kuching, for instance, count on paying about RM250 for an eight-hour excursion. When you factor in fuel, this often works out only slightly more expensive than renting. Bonuses: you bear no liability in case the car is damaged, and you've got the driver to take care of navigation and mechanical problems – and to find places to eat.

In Kalimantan, taxis are scarce, but can usually be found at major airports. More common are illegal taxis (called taksi gelap), which ask a per-seat fee for set routes between major towns. In East Kalimantan these are so prevalent they have killed off the public bus market.

Hitching

Hitching is possible in most parts of Borneo, but as hitching is never entirely safe, we don't recommend it. If you do choose to hitch it will be safer travelling in pairs and letting someone know where you are planning to go, and when you expect to arrive.

Some drivers will expect a small 'tip' or assistance with petrol costs for driving you. At the very least, if you stop for food, you should offer to pay for their meal.

Local Transport

Bicycle

Within cities, bicycles have become a rare sight as increased prosperity has brought the creature comforts of gas guzzling to Malaysia and Brunei. However, some guesthouses rent or lend bicycles to their guests. Out in the country, locals still use bicycles to get around small *kampung* (villages), and if you can get hold of a bicycle – rental options are rare – this can be a very pleasant way to soak up the atmosphere.

Boat

Small motorboats and motorised longboats are often used for short trips across rivers and bays. Examples include traversing Kuching's Sungai Sarawak (Sarawak River) and transport from central BSB (Brunei) to the water village of Kampung Ayer.

Taxi

Taxis are common in Borneo's larger cities; meters, drivers who use them and fixed rates are not, except in Kuching. Luckily, you'll find that most drivers in Borneo are quite honest. Just be sure to set the price before starting out and only pay upon arrival.

Tours

One way to get the most out of a national park visit, jungle trek or longhouse sojourn is to go with a guide who knows the territory (and, in the case of longhouses, the headman). Indeed, it's the only way to see some things – for instance, the summits of Gunung Mulu and Mt Kinabalu, the longhouses of Sarawak's Batang Ai region and the Kelabit Highlands, and Ulu Temburong National Park in Brunei.

Borneo has a wealth of excellent guides and tour agencies. Most guesthouses and hotels have relationships with at least one local tour operator, and some run their own in-house travel agencies.

For more information see Outdoor Adventures, p26.

Train

Borneo's only railway line, run by the Sabah State Railway (www.sabah.gov.my/railway), runs two trains a day from Tanjung Aru, 4km southwest of central KK, south to Beaufort and Tenom, a distance of 134km. Inaugurated in 1896, this scenic line underwent a major renovation in 2011.

Health

Travellers to Borneo tend to worry about contracting infectious diseases, but infections are not nearly as common in Borneo as you might think and rarely cause serious illness. Malaria does exist, but is usually limited to isolated upland areas.

The information we provide should be used only as a general guide and should not replace the advice of a doctor trained in travel medicine.

BEFORE YOU GO

If you take any regular medication, bring double your needs in case of loss or theft, and carry these supplies separately. You may be able to buy some medications over the counter in Borneo without a prescription, but it can be difficult to find some newer drugs, particularly the latest antidepressants, blood-pressure medications and contraceptive pills.

Insurance

Even if you're fit and healthy, we don't recommend travelling without health insurance. Extra cover may be required for adventure activities such as rock climbing, caving or scuba diving. If you're uninsured, emergency evacuation can be expensive; bills of over US$100,000 are not uncommon. Travel insurance is available online from lonelyplanet.com/travel-insurance.

Recommended Vaccinations

Most vaccines don't produce immunity until at least two weeks after they're given, so visit a doctor four to eight weeks before departure. Ask for an International Certificate of Vaccination (known as the 'yellow booklet'), which will list all the vaccinations you've received.

Proof of vaccination against yellow fever will be required only if you have visited a country in the yellow-fever zone (parts of Africa and South America) within six days prior to entering Malaysia, Brunei or Indonesia. If you're coming from Africa or South America, check to see if you require proof of vaccination.

Medical Checklist

- Antibiotics – consider bringing if you're travelling well off the beaten track; see your doctor and carry the prescription with you
- Antifungal cream or powder – for fungal skin infections and thrush
- Antihistamine – for allergies such as hay fever, to ease the itch from insect bites or stings, and to prevent motion sickness
- Antiseptic (such as povidone-iodine or betadine) – for cuts and grazes
- Antispasmodic (eg Buscopan) – for stomach cramps
- Aspirin or paracetamol (acetaminophen in the USA) – for pain or fever
- Adhesive bandages and other wound dressings
- Calamine lotion, sting relief spray or aloe vera – to ease irritation from sunburn and insect bites or stings
- Cold and flu tablets, throat lozenges, nasal decongestant

RECOMMENDED VACCINATIONS

The World Health Organization recommends the following vaccinations for travellers to Borneo:

- Hepatitis A
- Hepatitis B
- Typhoid
- Polio
- Adult diphtheria & tetanus
- Measles, mumps & rubella
- Varicella

Recommended for longer-term travellers (more than one month) or those at special risk:

- Japanese B Encephalitis
- Meningitis
- Rabies
- Tuberculosis

- Contraceptives
- DEET-based insect repellent
- Ibuprofen or another anti-inflammatory
- Iodine tablets (unless you are pregnant or have a thyroid problem) – to purify water
- Loperamide or diphenoxylate – 'blockers' for diarrhoea
- Multivitamins – for long trips, when dietary vitamin intake may be inadequate
- Permethrin – to impregnate clothing and mosquito nets
- Prochlorperazine or metaclopramide – for nausea and vomiting
- Rehydration mixture – to prevent dehydration, which may occur, for example, during bouts of diarrhoea
- Scissors, tweezers and a thermometer (note that mercury thermometers are prohibited by airlines)
- Sterile kit – in case you need injections in a country with medical-hygiene problems; discuss with your doctor
- Sunscreen, lip balm and eye drops

Websites

Centers for Disease Control & Prevention (USA) (www.cdc.gov) Excellent general information.

World Health Organization (www.who.int/ith) Publishes a superb book – *International Travel and Health* (downloadable) – and is the best source of information on disease distribution.

Further Reading

Lonely Planet's *Travel with Children* includes advice on travel health for young children.

Other good travel health references include the 5th (2012) edition of *Travellers' Health* by Dr Richard Dawood (Oxford University Press) and the 17th (2012) edition of *Travelling Well* by Dr Deborah Mills (available from www.travellingwell.com.au)

IN BORNEO

Availability & Cost of Health Care

There are good medical facilities – charging reasonable rates – in Borneo's larger cities. This is especially true in Sabah, Sarawak and Brunei, where even upland towns such as Bario and Belaga are now served by full-time doctors. As you head into the hinterlands, however, especially in Kalimantan, you'll find few, if any, medical facilities.

In Sabah, Sarawak and Brunei you will have no problem communicating with doctors in English, and almost all nurses know at least some English. Pharmacists also tend to speak reasonable English – this can be important, as many medications are marketed under a variety of names in different parts of the world.

Infectious Diseases

Dengue Fever

This mosquito-borne disease is present in Borneo. As there's no vaccine available, it can only be prevented by avoiding mosquito bites. The mosquito that carries dengue fever bites during day and night, so use insect-avoidance measures at all times. Symptoms include high fever, severe headache and body ache. Some people develop a rash and experience diarrhoea. There's no specific treatment, just rest and paracetamol – don't take aspirin, as it increases the likelihood of haemorrhaging. Some forms of dengue fever can be dangerous, so see a doctor to be diagnosed and monitored. In Malaysia (collectively) the spread of Dengue rose between 2013 and 2014 by 34%, with a reported 14 cases in Sarawak.

Leptospirosis

Leptospirosis is a bacterial disease that's most commonly contracted after river rafting, canyoning or caving, sometimes as a result of contact with rat urine or faeces. Early symptoms are similar to the flu, and include headache and fever. It can vary from a very mild to fatal disease. Diagnosis is through blood tests and it is easily treated with Doxycycline.

Malaria

Malaria is not common, but is present, in Borneo, particularly in parts of Kalimantan. Brunei is malaria-free; in Sabah and Sarawak, the disease is absent from coastal areas and only occasionally found in or around remote lumber camps. One reason for the relative rarity of malaria is the relatively low mosquito population in much of Borneo – thanks in part to the island's millions of cave-dwelling, insectivorous bats. Get up-to-date information on infected areas before your trip and as soon as you arrive in the country.

In areas with minimal to no risk of malaria, the potential side effects from antimalarial tablets may outweigh the risk of getting the disease. For some rural and upland areas, however, the risk of contracting the disease outweighs any tablet side effects. Remember that malaria can be fatal. Before you travel, seek medical advice on the right medication and dosage for you.

Malaria is caused by a parasite transmitted through the bite of an infected mosquito. The most important symptom is fever, but general symptoms such as headache, diarrhoea, cough or chills may also occur. Diagnosis can be made only by taking a blood sample.

Two strategies should be combined to prevent malaria: mosquito avoidance and antimalarial medications.

Most people who catch malaria are taking inadequate or no medication. Travellers in malarial areas are advised to prevent mosquito bites by taking these steps:

- Use a DEET-containing insect repellent on exposed skin. Wash this off at night (if you're sleeping under a mosquito net treated with permethrin). Natural repellents such as citronella can be effective, but must be applied more frequently than products containing DEET.
- Choose accommodation with screens and fans (if not air-con).
- Sleep under a mosquito net impregnated with permethrin.
- Wear long sleeves and trousers in light colours.
- Impregnate clothing with permethrin (in high-risk areas).
- Use mosquito coils.

Rabies

Rabies is present in Kalimantan, but much less common in Sabah, Sarawak and Brunei. This fatal disease is spread by the bite or lick of an infected animal, most commonly a dog or monkey. Seek medical advice *immediately* after any animal bite.

Having pre-travel vaccination means the post-bite treatment is greatly simplified. If you are not pre-vaccinated, you will need to receive rabies immunoglobulin as soon as possible.

Environmental Hazards

Diving

Divers and surfers should seek specialised advice before they travel, and ensure their medical kit contains treatment for coral cuts and tropical ear infections. Divers should ensure their insurance covers them for decompression illness – specialised dive insurance is available through DAN Asia-Pacific (www.danasiapacific.org). Have a dive medical before you leave your home country.

Heat

Borneo is hot and humid throughout the year. Most people take at least two weeks to adapt to the climate. Swelling of the feet and ankles is common, as are muscle cramps caused by excessive sweating. Prevent these by avoiding dehydration and too much activity in the heat. Take it easy when you first arrive. Don't eat salt tablets (they aggravate the gut), but drinking rehydration solution or eating salty food helps. Treat cramps by stopping activity, resting, rehydrating with double-strength rehydration solution and gently stretching.

Dehydration is the main contributor to heat exhaustion. Symptoms include feeling weak, headache, irritability, nausea or vomiting, sweaty skin, a fast, weak pulse and a slightly increased body temperature. Treatment involves getting the sufferer out of the heat and/or sun, fanning them and applying cool wet cloths to the skin, laying the victim flat with their legs raised and rehydrating with water containing a quarter of a teaspoon of salt per litre. Recovery is usually rapid, although it's common to feel weak for some days afterwards.

Heatstroke is a serious medical emergency. Symptoms come on suddenly and include weakness, nausea, a hot, dry body with a body temperature of over 41°C, dizziness, confusion, loss of coordination, fits, and eventual collapse and loss of consciousness. Seek medical help and commence cooling by getting the sufferer out of the heat, removing their clothes, fanning them and applying cool, wet cloths or ice packs to their body, especially to the groin and armpits.

Prickly heat is a common skin rash in the tropics, caused by sweat being trapped under the skin. The result is an itchy rash of tiny lumps. If you develop prickly heat, treat it by moving out of the heat and into an air-conditioned area for a few hours and by having cool showers. Creams and ointments clog the skin, so they should be avoided. Locally bought prickly-heat powder can be helpful for relief.

Insect Bites & Stings

Ticks are contracted walking in the bush and are commonly found behind the ears, on the belly and in armpits. If you have had a tick bite and experience symptoms such as a rash at the site of the bite or elsewhere, a fever, or muscle aches, you should see a doctor.

Leeches are found in humid rainforest areas. They do not transmit any disease, but their bites are often intensely itchy for weeks and can easily become infected. Apply iodine-based antiseptic to leech bites to help prevent infection.

Bee and wasp stings mainly cause problems for people who are allergic to them. Anyone with a serious bee or wasp allergy should carry an injection of adrenalin (eg an EpiPen) for emergency treatment. For others, pain is the main problem – apply ice to the sting and take painkillers.

Most jellyfish in Southeast Asian waters are not dangerous, just irritating. First aid for

HEALTH ADVISORIES

Australia (www.smartraveller.gov.au)

Canada (www.travelhealth.gc.ca)

New Zealand (www.safetravel.govt.nz)

United Kingdom (www.dh.gov.uk)

United States (www.cdc.gov/travel)

jellyfish stings involves pouring vinegar onto the affected area to neutralise the poison. Don't rub sand or water onto the stings. Take painkillers, and if you feel ill in any way after being stung seek medical advice. Take local advice if there are dangerous jellyfish around and keep out of the water.

Skin Problems

Fungal rashes are common in humid climates. There are two common fungal rashes that affect travellers. The first occurs in moist areas that get less air such as the groin, armpits and between the toes. It starts as a red patch that slowly spreads and is usually itchy. Treatment involves keeping the skin dry, avoiding chafing and using an antifungal cream such as Clotrimazole or Lamisil. Tinea versicolour is also common – this fungus causes small, light-coloured patches, most commonly on the back, chest and shoulders. Consult a doctor.

Cuts and scratches become easily infected in humid climates. Take meticulous care of wounds – immediately washing them in clean water and applying antiseptic – to prevent complications such as abscesses. If you develop signs of infection (increasing pain and redness), see a doctor. Divers and surfers should be particularly careful with coral cuts as they can become easily infected.

Traveller's Diarrhoea

Traveller's diarrhoea is by far the most common problem affecting travellers – between 30% to 50% of people will suffer from it within two weeks of starting their trip. In over 80% of cases, it's caused by a bacteria, and therefore responds promptly to treatment with antibiotics. Treatment will depend on your situation – how sick you are, how quickly you need to get better, where you are etc. Traveller's diarrhoea is defined as the passage of more than three watery bowel movements within 24 hours, plus at least one other symptom such as fever, cramps, nausea, vomiting or feeling generally unwell. Treatment consists of staying well hydrated; rehydration solutions such as Gastrolyte are the best for this.

Always seek reliable medical care if you have blood in your diarrhoea.

Loperamide is just a 'stopper' and doesn't get to the cause of the problem (it can be helpful, for example, if you have to go on a long bus ride). Don't take it if you have a fever, or blood in your stools.

Ways to avoid traveller's diarrhoea include eating only freshly cooked food and avoiding shellfish and food that has been sitting around in buffets. Peel all fruit, cook vegetables, and soak salads in iodine water for at least 20 minutes. Eat in busy restaurants with a high turnover of customers.

TAP WATER

- Never drink tap water unless you've verified that it's safe (many parts of Sabah, Sarawak and Brunei have modern treatment plants).
- Bottled water is generally safe – check the seal is intact at purchase.
- Avoid ice in eateries that look dubious, especially in Kalimantan.
- Avoid fruit juices if they're not freshly squeezed or you suspect they have been watered down.
- Boiling water is the most efficient way to purify it.
- The best chemical purifier is iodine (not to be used if you are pregnant or have thyroid problems).
- Water filters should also filter out viruses. Ensure your filter has a chemical barrier such as iodine and a small pore size (less than 4 microns).

Travelling with Children

Borneo is a great place to travel with children. However, there are specific health issues you need to consider.

All of your children's routine vaccinations should be up to date, as many of the common childhood diseases that have been eliminated in the West are still present in parts of Borneo. A travel-health clinic can advise you on specific vaccines, but think seriously about rabies vaccination if you're visiting rural areas or travelling for more than a month, as children are more vulnerable to severe animal bites.

Children are more prone to getting serious forms of mosquito-borne diseases such as malaria, Japanese B encephalitis and dengue fever. In particular, malaria is very serious in children and can rapidly lead to death – think seriously before taking your child into a malaria risk area. Permethrin-impregnated clothing is safe to use, and insect repellents should contain between 10% and 20% DEET.

Diarrhoea can cause rapid dehydration and you should pay particular attention to keeping your child well hydrated. The best antibiotic for children with diarrhoea is Azithromycin.

Women's Health

In urban areas, supplies of sanitary products are readily available, however tampons can be difficult to come by in some areas (Chinese-owned supermarkets are often a good bet). Birth-control options may be limited, so bring adequate supplies.

Language

Malay, or Bahasa Malaysia, is the official language of Malaysian Borneo (Sabah and Sarawak) and Brunei; it's the native language of people of Malay descent there. Bahasa Indonesia is the official language of Kalimantan and the mother tongue of most people of non-Chinese descent living there. The two languages are very similar, and if you can speak a little of either you'll be able to use it across the island. We've avoided duplication in this language guide by providing translations in both languages – indicated by (I) and (M) – only where the differences are significant enough to cause confusion.

Each of Borneo's indigenous groups has its own language, but their members all speak Bahasa Malaysia or Bahasa Indonesia. Various dialects of Chinese are spoken by those of Chinese ancestry in Borneo, although Mandarin is fairly widely spoken and understood.

You'll find it easy to get by with only English in Borneo, particularly in Sabah, Sarawak and Brunei. English is the most common second language for Borneo's ethnic groups and is often used by people of different backgrounds, like ethnic Chinese and ethnic Malays, to communicate with one another.

In both Bahasa Malaysia and Bahasa Indonesia, most letters are pronounced more or less the same as their English counterparts, except for the letter c which is always pronounced as the 'ch' in 'chair'. Nearly all syllables carry equal emphasis, but a good approximation is to lightly stress the second-last syllable. The main exception to the rule is the unstressed e in words such as besar (big), which sounds like the 'a' in 'ago'.

Pronouns, particularly 'you', are rarely used in both Bahasa Malaysia and Bahasa Indonesia. Anda (in Bahasa Indonesia) and kamu (in Malay) are the egalitarian forms designed to overcome the plethora of terms relating to a person's age and gender that are used for the second person.

WANT MORE?

For in-depth language information and handy phrases, check out Lonely Planet's *Indonesian Phrasebook* and *Malay Phrasebook*. You'll find them at **shop.lonelyplanet.com**, or you can buy Lonely Planet's iPhone phrasebooks at the Apple App Store.

BASICS

Hello.	*Salam./Helo.* (I/M)
Goodbye.	*Selamat tinggal/jalan.* (by person leaving/staying)
How are you?	*Apa kabar?*
I'm fine.	*Kabar baik.*
Excuse me.	*Maaf.*
Sorry.	*Maaf.*
Yes.	*Ya.*
No.	*Tidak.*
Please.	*Silakan.*
Thank you.	*Terima kasih.*
You're welcome.	*Kembali.* (I) *Sama-sama.* (M)

My name is ...
Nama saya ...

What's your name?
Siapa nama anda/kamu? (I/M)

Do you speak English?
Anda bisa Bahasa Inggris? (I)
Adakah anda berbahasa Inggeris? (M)

I (don't) understand.
Saya (tidak) mengerti. (I)
Saya (tidak) faham. (M)

KEY PATTERNS

To get by in Bahasa Indonesia and Malay, mix and match these simple patterns with words of your choice:

When's (the next bus)?
Jam berapa (bis yang berikutnya)?

Where's (the station)?
Di mana (stasiun)?

How much is it (per night)?
Berapa (satu malam)?

I'm looking for (a hotel).
Saya cari (hotel).

Do you have (a local map)?
Ada (peta daerah)?

Is there a (lift)?
Ada (lift)?

Can I (enter)?
Boleh saya (masuk)?

Do I need (a visa)?
Saya harus pakai (visa)?

I have (a reservation).
Saya (sudah punya booking).

I need (assistance).
Saya perlu (dibantu).

I'd like (the menu).
Saya minta (daftar makanan).

I'd like (to hire a car).
Saya mau (sewa mobil).

Could you (help me)?
Bisa Anda (bantu) saya?

ACCOMMODATION

Do you have any rooms available?
Ada kamar/bilik kosongkah? (I/M)

How much is it per day/person?
Berapa harga satu malam/orang?

Is breakfast included?
Makan pagi termasukkah?

campsite	*tempat kemah* (I) *tempat perkhemahan* (M)
guesthouse	*rumah yang disewakan* (I) *rumah tetamu* (M)
hotel	*hotel*
youth hostel	*losmen pemuda* (I) *asrama belia* (M)

single room	*kamar untuk seorang* (I) *bilik untuk seorang* (M)
room with a double bed	*tempat tidur besar satu kamar* (I) *bilik untuk dua orang* (M)
room with two beds	*kamar dengan dua tempat tidur* (I) *bilik yang ada dua katil* (M)

air-con	*AC* (pronounced 'a-se') (I) *pendingin udara* (M)
bathroom	*kamar mandi* (I) *bilik air* (M)
mosquito coil	*obat nyamuk*
window	*jendela/tingkap* (I/M)

DIRECTIONS

Where is ...?
Di mana ...?

What's the address?
Apa alamatnya?

Could you write it down, please?
Anda bisa tolong tuliskan? (I)
Tolong tuliskan alamat itu? (M)

Can you show me (on the map)?
Bisa tunjukkan kepada saya (di peta)? (I)
Tolong tunjukkan (di peta)? (M)

at the corner	*di sudut/simpang* (I/M)
at the traffic lights	*di lampu lalu-lintas* (I) *di tempat lampu isyarat* (M)
behind	*di belakang*
far (from)	*jauh (dari)*
in front of	*di depan*
near (to)	*dekat (dengan)*
opposite	*di seberang* (I) *berhadapan dengan* (M)
Turn left/right.	*Belok kiri/kanan.*
Go straight ahead.	*Jalan terus.*

EATING & DRINKING

A table for (two), please.
Meja untuk (dua) orang.

What's in that dish?
Hidangan itu isinya apa? (I)
Ada apa dalam masakan itu? (M)

Bring the bill/check, please.
Tolong bawa kuitansi/bil. (I/M)

I don't eat ...	*Saya tidak mau makan ...* (I) *Saya tak suka makan ...* (M)
chicken	*ayam*
fish	*ikan*
(red) meat	*daging (merah)*
nuts	*biji-bijian/kacang* (I/M)

Key Words

bottle	*botol*
breakfast	*sarapan pagi*
cold	*dingin/sejuk* (I/M)
cup	*cangkir/cawan* (I/M)
dinner	*makan malam*
food	*makanan*
fork	*garpu/garfu* (I/M)
glass	*gelas*
hot	*panas*
knife	*pisau*
lunch	*makan siang* (I) *tengahari* (M)
market	*pasar*
menu	*daftar makanan* (I) *menu* (M)
plate	*piring/pinggan* (I/M)
restaurant	*restoran*
spicy	*pedas*
spoon	*sendok/sedu* (I/M)
vegetarian	*makanan tanpa daging* (I) *sayuran saja* (M)
with	*dengan*
without	*tanpa*

Meat & Fish

beef	*daging sapi/lembu* (I/M)
chicken	*ayam*
crab	*kepiting/ketam* (I/M)
fish	*ikan*
lamb	*daging anak domba* (I) *anak biri-biri* (M)
mussels	*remis/kepah* (I/M)
pork	*babi*
shrimp	*udang*

QUESTION WORDS

How?	*Bagaimana?*
What?	*Apa?*
When?	*Kapan?* (I) *Bila?* (M)
Where?	*Di mana?*
Who?	*Siapa?*
Why?	*Mengapa?*

Fruit & Vegetables

apple	*apel/epal* (I/M)
banana	*pisang*
carrot	*wortel/lobak* (I/M)
cucumber	*ketimun/timun* (I/M)
jackfruit	*nangka*
mango	*mangga*
orange	*jeruk manis/oren* (I/M)
peanut	*kacang*
starfruit	*belimbing*
tomato	*tomat/tomato* (I/M)
watermelon	*semangka/tembikai* (I/M)

Other

bread	*roti*
cheese	*keju*
egg	*telur*
ice	*es/ais* (I/M)
rice	*nasi*
salt	*garam*
sugar	*gula*

Drinks

beer	*bir*
bottled water	*air botol*
citrus juice	*air jeruk/limau* (I/M)
coffee	*kopi*
milk	*susu*
tea	*teh*
water	*air*
wine	*anggur/wain* (I/M)

EMERGENCIES

Help!	*Tolong!*
Stop!	*Berhenti!*
I'm lost.	*Saya sesat.*
Go away!	*Pergi!*

There's been an accident.
Ada kecelakaan/kemalangan. (I/M)

Call the doctor/police!
Panggil doktor/polis!

I'm ill.
Saya sakit.

It hurts here.
Sakitnya di sini. (I)
Sini sakit. (M)

I'm allergic to (nuts).
Saya alergi terhadap (biji-bijian). (I)
Saya alergik kepada (kacang). (M)

SHOPPING & SERVICES

I'd like to buy ...
Saya mau/nak beli ... (I/M)

I'm just looking.
Saya lihat-lihat saja. (I)
Saya nak tengok saja. (M)

May I look at it?
Boleh saya lihat? (I)
Boleh saya tengok barang itu? (M)

How much is it?
Berapa harganya?

It's too expensive.
Itu terlalu mahal. (I)
Mahalnya. (M)

Can you lower the price?
Boleh kurang?

There's a mistake in the bill.
Ada kesalahan dalam kuitansi ini. (I)
Bil ini salah. (M)

ATM	*ATM* (pronounced 'a-te-em')
credit card	*kartu/kad kredit* (I/M)
internet cafe	*warnet* (I) *cyber cafe* (M)
post office	*kantor/pejabat pos* (I/M)
public phone	*telpon umum/awam* (I/M)
tourist office	*kantor pariwisata* (I) *pejabat pelancong* (M)

TIME & DATES

What time is it?
Jam berapa sekarang? (I)
Pukul berapa? (M)

It's (seven) o'clock.
Jam/Pukul (tujuh). (I/M)

It's half past (one).
Setengah (dua). (I)
(lit: half two)
Pukul (satu) setengah. (M)

in the morning	*pagi*
in the afternoon	*siang/tengahari* (I/M)
in the evening	*malam/petang* (I/M)

yesterday	*kemarin/semalam* (I/M)
today	*hari ini*
tomorrow	*besok/esok* (I/M)

Monday	*hari Senin/Isnin* (I/M)
Tuesday	*hari Selasa*
Wednesday	*hari Rabu*
Thursday	*hari Kamis*
Friday	*hari Jumat/Jumaat* (I/M)
Saturday	*hari Sabtu*
Sunday	*hari Minggu*

January	*Januari*
February	*Februari*
March	*Maret/Mac* (I/M)
April	*April*
May	*Mei*
June	*Juni/Jun* (I/M)
July	*Juli/Julai* (I/M)
August	*Agustus/Ogos* (I/M)
September	*September*
October	*Oktober*
November	*November*
December	*Desember*

TRANSPORT

Public Transport

What time does the ... leave?	*Jam/Pukul berapa ... berangkat?* (I/M)
boat	*kapal*
bus	*bis/bas* (I/M)
plane	*pesawat* (I) *kapal terbang* (M)
train	*kereta api*

I want to go to ...
Saya mau/nak ke ... (I/M)

SIGNS

Buka	Open
Dilarang	Prohibited
Kamar Kecil (I)	Toilets
Keluar	Exit
Lelaki (M)	Men
Masuk	Entrance
Perempuan (M)	Women
Pria (I)	Men
Tandas (M)	Toilets
Tutup	Closed
Wanita (I)	Women

Does it stop at ... ?
Berhenti di ...?

How long will it be delayed?
Berapa lama keterlambatannya? (I)
Berapa lambatnya? (M)

I'd like to get off at ...
Saya mau/nak turun di ... (I/M)

Please put the meter on.
Tolong pakai argo/meter. (I/M)

Please stop here.
Tolong berhenti di sini.

I'd like a ... ticket. (I/M)	*Saya mau/nak tiket ...*
1st-class	*kelas satu* (I) *kelas pertama* (M)
2nd-class	*kelas dua* (I) *kelas kedual* (M)
one-way	*sekali jalan* (I) *sehala* (M)
return	*pulang pergi* (I) *pergi balik* (M)

the first	*pertama*
the last	*terakhir*
the next	*berikutnya*

bus station	*terminal bis* (I) *stesen bas* (M)
bus stop	*halte bis* (I) *perhentian bas* (M)
cancelled	*dibatalkan*
delayed	*terlambat/lambat* (I/M)
platform	*peron/landasan* (I/M)
ticket office	*loket/pejabat tiket* (I/M)
timetable	*jadwal/jadual waktu* (I/M)

Driving & Cycling

I'd like to hire a ...	*Saya mau sewa ...* (I) *Saya nak menyewa ...* (M)
bicycle	*sepeda/basikal* (I/M)
car	*mobil/kereta* (I/M)
jeep	*jip*
motorbike	*sepeda motor* (I) *motosikal* (M)

diesel	*solar/disel* (I/M)
helmet	*helem* (I) *topi keledar* (M)

NUMBERS

1	*satu*
2	*dua*
3	*tiga*
4	*empat*
5	*lima*
6	*enam*
7	*tujuh*
8	*delapan* (I) *lapan* (M)
9	*sembilan*
10	*sepuluh*
20	*dua puluh*
30	*tiga puluh*
40	*empat puluh*
50	*lima puluh*
60	*enam puluh*
70	*tujuh puluh*
80	*delapan puluh* (I) *lapan puluh* (M)
90	*sembilan puluh*
100	*seratus*
1000	*seribu*

petrol	*bensin/petrol* (I/M)
pump	*pompa/pam* (I/M)

Is this the road to ...?
Ini jalan ke ...?

Where's a service station?
Di mana pompa bensin? (I)
Stesen minyak di mana? (M)

(How long) Can I park here?
(Berapa lama) Saya boleh parkir di sini? (I)
(Beberapa lama) Boleh saya letak kereta di sini? (M)

I need a mechanic.
Saya perlu montir. (I)
Kami memerlukan mekanik. (M)

The car has broken down at ...
Mobil mogok di ... (I)
Kereta saya telah rosak di ... (M)

I have a flat tyre.
Ban saya kempes. (I)
Tayarnya kempis. (M)

I've run out of petrol/gas.
Saya kehabisan bensin. (I)
Minyak sudah habis. (M)

GLOSSARY

m) indicates masculine gender, (f) feminine gender and (pl) plural

ai – small river
air – water
angkot – short for angkutan kota (city transport); small minibuses covering city routes in Kalimantan

Bahasa Indonesia – official language of Indonesia
Bahasa Malaysia – official language of Malaysia
bandar – seaport; town
bandung – floating general store (Kalimantan)
batang – stem; tree trunk; the main branch of a river
batik – technique of imprinting cloth with dye to produce multi-coloured patterns
batu – stone; rock; milepost
becak – bicycle rickshaw (Kalimantan)
belian – ironwood
BSB – Bandar Seri Begawan; capital of Brunei
bukit – hill
bumiputra – literally, 'sons of the soil'; people considered indigenous under Malaysian law

ces – motorised canoe

Dayak – indigenous peoples of Borneo; term used mostly in Kalimantan and Sarawak
dipterocarp – family of commercially valuable rainforest trees
dusun – small town; orchard; fruit grove

gua – cave
gunung – mountain

ikat – fabric patterned by tie-dying the yarn before weaving
istana – palace
jalan – road (abbreviated as 'Jln' or 'Jl')
kampung – village; also spelt *kampong*
kapal biasa – river boats with second-storey accommodation (Kalimantan)
karst – characteristic scenery of a limestone region, including features such as underground streams and caverns
kedai kopi – eatery, often with several food stalls; literally, 'coffee shop' (Bahasa Malaysia)
kerangas – heath forest; in Iban, means 'land that cannot grow rice'
keraton – palace
Kijang – taxi (Kalimantan); Indonesian brand name of a Toyota minibus or pick-up
klotok – houseboat (Kalimantan)
Konfrontasi – literally, 'confrontation'; catchphrase of the early 1960s when Soekarno embarked on a confrontational campaign against Western imperialism aimed at Malaysia
kopitiam – eatery, often with several food stalls; literally, 'coffee shop' (Chinese term)
kota – fort; city
kuala – river mouth; place where a tributary joins a larger river

laut – sea
lebuh – street
lorong – narrow street; alley (abbreviated 'Lg')
losmen – budget guesthouse

macaque – any of several small species of monkey
mandi – bathe; Southeast Asian wash basin
masjid – mosque
Melayu Islam Beraja – Malay Islamic Monarchy, known as MIB; Brunei's national ideology
merdeka – independence
muara – river mouth
negara – country
negeri – state

ojek – motorcycle taxi (Kalimantan)
opelet – minibus (Kalimantan)
Orang Ulu – literally, 'upriver people'

padang – grassy area; field; also the city square
pantai – beach
parang – long jungle knife
pasar – market
pasar malam – night market
pegunungan – mountain (Kalimantan)
pelabuhan – port
pondok – hut or shelter
pulau – island

rajah – prince; ruler
ranee – princess or rajah's wife
rattan – stems from climbing palms used for wickerwork and canes
rimba – jungle
rumah – house
rumah batang – longhouse (Kalimantan)
rumah panjai – longhouse; also spelt *rumah panjang*

sarong – all-purpose cloth, often sewn into a tube, and worn by women, men and children; also spelt *sarung*
seberang – opposite side of road; far bank of a river
selat – strait
simpang – crossing; junction
songket – traditional Malay hand-woven fabric with gold threads
sungai – river

tambang – river ferry; fare
tamu – market
tanjung – headland
teksi – taxi

teluk – bay; sometimes spelt *telok*

temenggong – Malay administrator

temuai – shallow-draft Iban longboat

transmigrasi – transmigration; Indonesian government policy to move people from densely populated islands such as Java, Bali and Madura to more remote areas, including Kalimantan

tuak – rice wine

tunku – prince

ulu – upriver

UMNO – United Malays National Organisation; Malaysia's largest political party

warung – small eating stalls

White Rajahs – dynasty that founded and ruled the Kingdom of Sarawak from 1841 to 1946

wisma – office block or shopping centre

WWF – World Wide Fund for Nature

Behind the Scenes

SEND US YOUR FEEDBACK

We love to hear from travellers – your comments keep us on our toes and help make our books better. Our well-travelled team reads every word on what you loved or loathed about this book. Although we cannot reply individually to your submissions, we always guarantee that your feedback goes straight to the appropriate authors, in time for the next edition. Each person who sends us information is thanked in the next edition – the most useful submissions are rewarded with a selection of digital PDF chapters.

Visit **lonelyplanet.com/contact** to submit your updates and suggestions or to ask for help. Our award-winning website also features inspirational travel stories, news and discussions.

Note: We may edit, reproduce and incorporate your comments in Lonely Planet products such as guidebooks, websites and digital products, so let us know if you don't want your comments reproduced or your name acknowledged. For a copy of our privacy policy visit lonelyplanet.com/privacy.

OUR READERS

Many thanks to the travellers who used the last edition and wrote to us with helpful hints, useful advice and interesting anecdotes:

A Aisling Kelly, Amar Bakir **B** Barbara Wolfke, Brodie Lea **C** Connie Early **D** Daniel Jespersen **E** Erhard Trittibach **K** Kevin Sarkin **M** Maarten Verboven, Megan Mooney **P** Pieter Heesterbeek **R** Robin Hedges **S** Sarah Richardson, Shira Salingre, Steve Athey **V** Valerio Magliola **W** Wolfgang Schweitzer

AUTHOR THANKS

Isabel Albiston

Thanks to everyone who helped out along the way, especially Mrs Lee, Stephen Baya and Tine Hjetting, Mado in Pa Lungan, Dina Bailey, Chongteah Lim, Leslie Chiang, Anthony Chieng, Polycarp Teo Sebum and Louise, Jacqueline Fong and Jo-Lynn Liao. Cheers also to Stefan Arestis and Sebastien Chaneac for making me laugh and to my friends and family for their love and support. Lastly, huge thanks to Sarah and Simon.

Loren Bell

Terima kasih banyak dua kali to every person I met while on the road – from local guides, to the villagers who kept refilling my glass with *tuak*, to the taxi driver who brought his extended family on our excursion. You are too numerous to name, but it's the people of Kalimantan that make this place amazing. And a special thank you to Kari – for your love, support and patience, even when I might not have deserved it.

Richard Waters

Sincere thanks to Eljer for his patience and skill, Daniken for keeping my dinner warm, Diana without whose help much of this trip would have been so much harder, Arwen, Walter and staff, Kurt (easily the best wildlife guide in 15 years' travel writing), Mr Reward and brother James Bond, tireless Bobby who braved the mudslides and aftershocks to take me to Mt K, Charlie and Jess for all their fabulous help, Brodie, Emma and Sadie for their lovely co, Jan for his hospitality and Ellen for her reef, Tom, Fanny and finally Carmalita, Mr Robin and May at Sabah Tourism for their fantastic support.

ACKNOWLEDGMENTS

Climate map data adapted from Peel MC, Finlayson BL & McMahon TA (2007) 'Updated World Map of the Köppen-Geiger Climate Classification', *Hydrology and Earth System Sciences*, 11, 163344.

Cover photograph: A young orangutan in Tanjung Puting National Park, Central Kalimantan, Nigel Parvitt/AWL.

THIS BOOK

This 4th edition of Lonely Planet's *Borneo* guidebook was researched and written by Isabel Albiston, Loren Bell and Richard Waters. The 3rd edition was written by Daniel Robinson, Paul Styles and Adam Karlin. This guidebook was produced by the following:

Destination Editor Sarah Reid

Product Editors Grace Dobell, Elizabeth Jones

Senior Cartographer Julie Sheridan

Book Designer Wibowo Rusli

Assisting Editors Andrew Bain, Katie Connolly, Saralinda Turner

Cover Researcher Naomi Parker

Thanks to Shahara Ahmed, Brendan Dempsey, Jenna Myers, Darren O'Connell, Kirsten Rawlings, Alison Ridgway, Kathryn Rowan, Angela Tinson

Index

Map Pages **000**
Photo Pages **000**

Map Legend

Sights

- Beach
- Bird Sanctuary
- Buddhist
- Castle/Palace
- Christian
- Confucian
- Hindu
- Islamic
- Jain
- Jewish
- Monument
- Museum/Gallery/Historic Building
- Ruin
- Shinto
- Sikh
- Taoist
- Winery/Vineyard
- Zoo/Wildlife Sanctuary
- Other Sight

Activities, Courses & Tours

- Bodysurfing
- Diving
- Canoeing/Kayaking
- Course/Tour
- Sento Hot Baths/Onsen
- Skiing
- Snorkelling
- Surfing
- Swimming/Pool
- Walking
- Windsurfing
- Other Activity

Sleeping

- Sleeping
- Camping

Eating

- Eating

Drinking & Nightlife

- Drinking & Nightlife
- Cafe

Entertainment

- Entertainment

Shopping

- Shopping

Information

- Bank
- Embassy/Consulate
- Hospital/Medical
- Internet
- Police
- Post Office
- Telephone
- Toilet
- Tourist Information
- Other Information

Geographic

- Beach
- Gate
- Hut/Shelter
- Lighthouse
- Lookout
- Mountain/Volcano
- Oasis
- Park
- Pass
- Picnic Area
- Waterfall

Population

- Capital (National)
- Capital (State/Province)
- City/Large Town
- Town/Village

Transport

- Airport
- Border crossing
- Bus
- Cable car/Funicular
- Cycling
- Ferry
- Metro/MRT/MTR station
- Monorail
- Parking
- Petrol station
- Skytrain/Subway station
- Taxi
- Train station/Railway
- Tram
- Underground station
- Other Transport

Note: Not all symbols displayed above appear on the maps in this book

Routes

- Tollway
- Freeway
- Primary
- Secondary
- Tertiary
- Lane
- Unsealed road
- Road under construction
- Plaza/Mall
- Steps
- Tunnel
- Pedestrian overpass
- Walking Tour
- Walking Tour detour
- Path/Walking Trail

Boundaries

- International
- State/Province
- Disputed
- Regional/Suburb
- Marine Park
- Cliff
- Wall

Hydrography

- River, Creek
- Intermittent River
- Canal
- Water
- Dry/Salt/Intermittent Lake
- Reef

Areas

- Airport/Runway
- Beach/Desert
- Cemetery (Christian)
- Cemetery (Other)
- Glacier
- Mudflat
- Park/Forest
- Sight (Building)
- Sportsground
- Swamp/Mangrove

OUR STORY

A beat-up old car, a few dollars in the pocket and a sense of adventure. In 1972 that's all Tony and Maureen Wheeler needed for the trip of a lifetime – across Europe and Asia overland to Australia. It took several months, and at the end – broke but inspired – they sat at their kitchen table writing and stapling together their first travel guide, *Across Asia on the Cheap*. Within a week they'd sold 1500 copies. Lonely Planet was born.

Today, Lonely Planet has offices in Dublin, Franklin, London, Melbourne, Oakland, Beijing and Delhi, with more than 600 staff and writers. We share Tony's belief that 'a great guidebook should do three things: inform, educate and amuse'.

OUR WRITERS

Isabel Albiston

Plan Your Trip, Sarawak, Brunei, Borneo Today, History, Peoples & Cultures, The Cuisines of Borneo Since her first trip to Malaysia six years ago, Isabel has grown to love clambering up slippery trails on sweaty jungle hikes. After three months exploring Borneo's forests and longhouses, feasting on Sarawak laksa, downing shots of *tuak*, dancing at the Rainforest World Music Festival and dropping in on the sultan at his palace in Brunei, the temptation to stay nearly won out. Isabel is a journalist who has written for a number of newspapers and magazines including the UK's *Daily Telegraph*.

Read more about Isabel at:
http://auth.lonelyplanet.com/profiles/isabelalbiston

Loren Bell

Kalimantan, Natural World Loren fell in love with Kalimantan during his three years managing a remote rainforest research station, and has returned every year since. For this book he stoically slept in hotels (on real beds!) and ate in actual restaurants before darting back to the jungle in search of more remote Dayak villages and the forest *pondok* where he feels most at ease. He also writes about Indonesia's environment for www.mongabay.com, and consults for NGOs working to protect Kalimantan's forests.

Richard Waters

Sabah, Survival Guide Richard is an award-winning journalist and writes about travel for *The Daily Telegraph, The Independent* and *Sunday Times, Sunday Times Travel Magazine, Elle* and *National Geographic Traveller*. He lives with his family in the Cotswolds, UK, and when he's not travelling, loves surfing and diving. Exploring Sabah was an absolute joy, his favourite moments being watching sharks in Sipadan, and seeing the sun rise over the jungle in the Danum Valley. He also writes a family wellbeing, adventure blog called Soul Tonic for Sanlam Bank. Check it out on: www.sanlam.co.uk/Media/Blogs/Soul-Tonic.aspx

Published by Lonely Planet Publications Pty Ltd
ABN 36 005 607 983
4th edition – Aug 2016
ISBN 978 1 74321 394 0

10 9 8 7 6 5 4 3 2 1
Printed in China